STUDYING ENGLISH LITERATURE AND LANGUAGE

Studying English Literature and Language is unique in offering both an introduction and a companion for students taking English Literature and Language degrees. Combining the functions of study guide, critical dictionary and text anthology, this is a freshly recast version of the highly acclaimed *The English Studies Book*.

This third edition features:

♦ fresh sections on the essential skills and study strategies needed to complete a degree in English – from close reading, research and referencing to full guidelines and tips on essay writing, participating in seminars, presentation and revision
♦ an authoritative guide to the life skills, further study options and career pathways open to graduates of the subject
♦ updated introductions to the major theoretical positions and approaches taken by scholars in the field, from earlier twentieth-century practical criticism to the latest global and ecological perspectives
♦ extensive entries on key terms such as 'author', 'genre', 'narrative' and 'translation' widely current in debates across language, literature and culture
♦ coverage of both local and global varieties of the English language in a range of media and discourses, including news, advertising, text messaging, rap, pop and street art
♦ an expansive anthology representing genres and discourses from early elegy and novel to contemporary performance and flash fiction, including writers as diverse as Aphra Behn, Emily Dickinson, J.M. Coetzee, Angela Carter, Russell Hoban, Adrienne Rich and Arundhati Roy
♦ a comprehensive, regularly updated companion website supplying further information and activities, sample analyses and a wealth of stimulating and reliable links to further online resources.

Studying English Literature and Language is a wide-ranging and invaluable reference for anyone interested in the study of English language, literature and culture.

Rob Pope is Professor of English at Oxford Brookes University and a National Teaching Fellow.

Praise for the Third Edition

'This splendid book is at once primer and provocation. . . . Rarely does a companion for English Studies manage to connect the investigation of language and literature so closely to a student's imaginative and practical needs.'

Jerome McGann, *University of Virginia, USA*

'Rob Pope provides a pathway between the claims and counterclaims that have been made about subject English. He shows that the differences between scholars within the field are a source of its vitality and its capacity to renew itself. This book provides an invaluable resource for students in undergraduate and teacher education programs. It is also a useful reminder to English teachers at secondary and tertiary levels of the richness, complexity and importance of their work.'

Brenton Doecke, *Deakin University, Australia*

'Rob Pope's *Studying English* is an impressively wide-ranging textbook that effortlessly covers such topics as the historical, social, and cultural dimensions of the English language, the principles of close reading, the intricacies of literary theory, and much, much more, while along the way it makes its readers familiar with the taking of notes, with preparing a bibliography, even with the pitfalls of job interviews and writing applications. All of this is wonderfully supported by a choice of excerpts and texts that is equally generous and varied, ranging from the canonical to real life conversations and beer commercials.

Studying English is critical, creative, and enjoyable – the conditions, as Pope himself notes, for genuine learning – but it is also, and perhaps even more importantly, as interactive as a textbook could possibly be.

Rob Pope casts a very wide net and his – and our – reward is an amazing catch.'

Hans Bertens, *The University of Utrecht, The Netherlands*

Praise for the Second Edition

'Innovative, imaginative, resourceful and full of surprises, the second edition of *The English Studies Book* continues to be an outstanding introduction to all aspects of the study of English literature, language and culture.'

Robert Eaglestone, *Royal Holloway, University of London, UK*

'This is without question the very best text available for the new "gateway" (introductory) courses to the English major.'

David Stacey, *Humboldt State University, USA*

STUDYING ENGLISH LITERATURE AND LANGUAGE

An Introduction and Companion

Third edition

Rob Pope

Routledge
Taylor & Francis Group

LONDON AND NEW YORK

First published 1998
This third edition published 2012
by Routledge
2 Park Square, Milton Park, Abingdon, Oxon, OX14 4RN

Simultaneously published in the USA and Canada
by Routledge
711 Third Avenue, New York, NY 10017

Routledge is an imprint of the Taylor & Francis Group, an informa business

British Library Cataloguing in Publication Data
A catalogue record for this book is available from the British Library

Library of Congress Cataloging in Publication Data
Pope, Rob.
 [English studies book]
 Studying English literature and language : an introduction and companion / Rob Pope. —
3rd ed.
      p. cm.
  1. English philology—Handbooks, manuals, etc. 2. English philology—Outlines, syllabi,
  etc. I. Title.
  PE31.P67 2012
  420—dc23   2011031910

ISBN: 978–0–415–49877–7 (hbk)
ISBN: 978–0–415–49876–0 (pbk)

Typeset in Bell Gothic and Sabon
by Keystroke, Station Road, Codsall, Wolverhampton

Gladly would we learn, and gladly teach

(after Chaucer's Clerk of Oxford)

For all the students and colleagues with whom I have really *done* English

CONTENTS

LIST OF FIGURES AND TABLES

FIGURES

TABLES

PREFACE AND ACKNOWLEDGEMENTS

Prefaces tend to be written last but read (if at all) first. So from the writer's point of view they are really more of a *postface*, looking back to where the book came from even while looking forward to what, for the reader, is coming up. This is a routine paradox of the writing–reading process. *Acknowledgements*, meanwhile, have that word 'knowledge' nestled snugly at their heart. And that too is suggestive. Much of what we know comes to us through other people, living or dead, directly or indirectly. (There is a list of formal acknowledgements for quotations at the end of the preface, and the bibliography should be read as an extension of this.) But when people influence us personally, the effect is often more subtle and pervasive as well as pragmatic. Acknowledgement then becomes a pleasure as well as an obligation.

Below, then, are some beginning lists of people who have directly influenced (encouraged, supported, inspired) the present book over its three editions, and some of them have influenced me from before, right back to my own student days. For all their prodigious differences, there are two things these people have in common. One – to recall the book's dedication – is that each and every one of these people would 'gladly learn' and 'gladly teach'. They enjoy studying and they enjoy English (though not all of them are from a department of that name) and they believe that others can and should do too. This is a keynote sounding throughout the book. The other common element is more personal. It is that these are all people with whom I have had to square things in my head while writing. They are, so to speak, the first addressees that the book has sought to engage and if possible convince. It is their faces and attitudes – grins or grimaces, approving nods or raised eyebrows – that have regularly come to mind whenever I have broached certain topics. If I could square it with them, at least in imagination, it might be alright. If I couldn't, then it needed revising or rejecting and replacing. This is doubtless a circle I have not been able to square all the time; and that's my problem not theirs.

First of all, then, there are the fellow teachers and learners, writers and readers. They are here hailed (and organised alphabetically) by first rather than last name; for that is how they come to mind: Alan Jenkins, Alcuin Blamires, Andrea Macrae, Archie Burnett, Ben Knights, Brian Turner, Caroline Jackson-Houlston, Catherine Stewart-Beer, Claire Woods, Colin Evans, Colin Pedley, Dan Lea, David Homer, David Pepper, David Stacey, Derek Pearsall, Douglas Gray, Elaine Hunter, Elizabeth Salter, Eric White, Graeme Harper, Gyorgy Szonyi, Hilary Jenkins, Jane Spiro, Joan Swann, John Dolan, John McRae, Mario Petrucci, Nathalie Blondel, Nigel Messenger, Norman Schwenk, Paul O'Flinn, Richard Francis, Robert Eaglestone, Robyn Bolam, Ron Carter, Sally-ann Thomas, Sarah Goodgame, Sean Matthews, Simon Kövesi, Stewart Young, Susan Bassnett, Terry Hawkes, Thierry Jutel, Yoskiaki Shirai.

Institutions are important too. Though nominally impersonal, they are far from 'faceless'; in fact, for me, they are populated by many of the people already referred to. The important thing about institutions is that they have the power (resource, structure, capacity) to sustain and develop the growth of subjects and whole communities far beyond the influence of particular people. And yet, like individuals, institutions are very various and constantly changing. They also need nurturing. The ones below range from universities and colleges (some are university colleges) to national and international associations. All in one way or another, at one time or another, have provided essential sites and contexts for the development of the materials and methods in the following pages. Along with their commitment to language and literature, all these institutions have one thing in common. They are firmly in the public domain. So their mission, actual as well as stated, has been to ensure that knowledge in general, and here knowledge of English in particular, remain common wealth not private property, accessed on the basis of merit not money. (This did not seem to need saying for the first two editions. It does now, in the UK at least, and may elsewhere.)

The name of the university/college here stands as shorthand for the Department or Faculty of English ... or Literature or Languages or Communication or Education ... within it. (You know which you are.): Aix-en-Provence, Anglia Ruskin, Blackpool and the Fylde, Cardiff, East Anglia, Goldsmiths, Hertfordshire, Humboldt State, Iasi, IST Athens, Lampeter, Loughborough, Missouri Western State, Moscow State, Nottingham, Open University, Otago, Oxford Brookes, Ruskin, Sheffield, South Australia, Szeged, Warwick, Yokohama City, York. And thanks, too, to the following national and international associations – usually graced with a 'The': Australian Association for the Teaching of English; British Council; English Association; Conference on College Composition and Communication (US); English Subject Centre; European Society for the Study of English; German Association of University Teachers of English; Higher Education Academy; New Writing and Great Writers; National Association for the Teaching of English; National Association of Writers in Education; Poetics and Linguistics Association.

Finally, mention must be made of some communities especially close to home. ('Home' in the sense of *habitus*, the essential places and spaces for study, including study habits, is a core concept in the present book.) One of these 'homes' is Oxford Brookes University (formerly Oxford Polytechnic) where much of my teaching and research has been based. In particular I would like to thank all those students and colleagues with whom I have really *done* English, on: Skills and Strategies for English; Language, Literature, Discourse I, II and III; Advanced Textual Analysis (latterly Style in Action); Language through Literature; Changing Stories; Comedy, Creativity and Critique; Experiment in Writing; and the MAs in English Literature, Language and Culture and in Creative Writing, especially the Core courses and my option in Changing Literature. Another crucial group is Routledge, the publishers with whom I have worked closely on these three editions and several other books besides. In particular, I would like to thank (again): Moira Taylor, Jody Ball and Beth Humphries on the first edition; Louisa Semlyen, Christy Kirkpatrick and Julie Tschinkel on the second; and Nadia Seemungal, Isabelle Cheng and Cathy Hurren on this one. There are also all the expert readers, many of them anonymous, who have previewed the various editions for Routledge and often made invaluable suggestions. Thank you too. The book has always been a hydra-headed monster, and the website has just added a few more heads. Taming it – but not too much – has been tricky, and making it presentable a mammoth task. Not all publishers have the patience, resource and imagination. These people have.

Finally – on a line all of our own – there is my actual home. Thanks to all at '47'!

Rob Pope, Bristol

FURTHER ACKNOWLEDGEMENTS

The publishers would like to thank the following for permission to reprint their material:

PATIENCE AGBABI, "'Two Loves I Have' from BLOODSHOT MONOCHROME by Patience Agbabi, first published in Great Britain by Canongate Books Ltd, 14 High Street, Edinburgh, EH1 1TE. Reprinted with permission.

PATIENCE AGBABI, "Prologue: Give me a word. . ." from TRANSFORMATRIX by Patience Agbabi, first published in Great Britain by Canongate Books Ltd, 14 High Street, Edinburgh, EH1 1TE. Reprinted with permission.

ANON / TRADITIONAL SEMINOLE, 'Song for Bringing a Child into the World' and 'Song for the Dying' (Native American Chants), from Frances Denmore, Seminole Music, Smithsonian Institution, Washington D.C., Bureau of Ethnology Bulletin no. 161, 1956.

CHINUA ACHEBE extract from Things Fall Apart, Everyman's Library, 1958, reprinted by permission of Pearson Education.

MARGARET ATWOOD, "Happy Endings", reprinted from MURDER IN THE DARK by Margaret Atwood with permission from Virago, an imprint of Little, Brown Group, Ltd.

"Happy Endings" from Good Bones and Simple Murders by Margaret Atwood © 1983, 1992, 1994 by O.W. Toad, Ltd. Published by McClelland & Stewart Ltd. Used with permission of the publisher.

DONALD BARTHELME, 'The Death of Edward Lear' taken from SIXTY STORIES by Donald Barthelme. © 1981, 1982 Donald Barthelme All rights reserved. Reprinted with permission of the Wylie Agency (UK) Ltd.

HARRY BECK, 1931 Map of the London Underground, reproduced by permission of London's Transport Museum.

SAMUEL BECKETT, from Not I, play extract from Collected Shorter Plays. Copyright 1973 by Samuel Beckett, reprinted by permission of Grove/Atlantic Inc. Excerpt from Not I, copyright ©1973 by Samuel Beckett.

SAMUEL BECKETT, from Not I, play extract from Collected Shorter Plays. Copyright © 1973 by Samuel Beckett. Reprinted with permission of Faber and Faber Ltd.

ROBYN BOLAM, 'Gruoch' published under the name of Marion Lomax, Raiding the Borders, Bloodaxe Books, 1996. Reprinted with permission of Bloodaxe Books.

BILL BRYSON, from Notes from a Small Island by Bill Bryson, published by Black Swan. Reprinted by permission of The Random House Group Ltd. Also reprinted with permission from Harper Collins Publishers US. www.harpercollins.com. Copyright © 1995 by Bill Bryson.

ANGELA CARTER, 'The Werewolf', complete short story (two pages), in her *The Bloody Chamber* (1979). Copyright © Angela Carter. Reproduced by permission of the author c/o Rogers, Coleridge & White, Ltd., 20 Powis Mews, London W11 1JN.

CLARINS "Clarins the Skin Problem Solver" advert published in Cosmopolitan February 1985.

"FOE by J. M. COETZEE, copyright © 1986 by J. M. Coetzee. Used by permission of Viking Penguin, a division of the Penguin Group (USA) Inc." Also reprinted by permission of David Higham Associates Ltd.

PHILIP DICK, excerpt from DO ANDROIDS DREAM OF ELECTRIC SHEEP? By Philip K. Dick. Copyright ©1968 by Philip K. Dick, used with permission of The Wylie Agency LLC. Also reprinted by permission of Victor Gollancz, an imprint of the Orion Publishing Group, London.

RODDY DOYLE, 'Gorillas in Vietnam', from Paddy Clarke Ha! Ha! Ha! By Roddy Doyle, published by Secker and Warburg. Reprinted by permission of The Random House Group Ltd.

The Wylie Agency for permission to reprint DAVE EGGERS, 'What the Water Feels Like to the Fishes', *Short short stories*, London: Penguin, pp. 5–6.

U.A. FANTHORPE, 'Knowing About Sonnets', from Voices Off, published by Peterloo Poets 1984. Reproduced by permission of R V Bailey. Copyright © R V Bailey.

THE FLOBOTS, "Handlebars"

Copyright 2008 Sony/ATV Music Publishing LLC, Flobots Music Publishing.

All rights administered by Sony/ATV Music Publishing LLC

All rights reserved.

Used by permission.

BRIAN FRIEL, extract from Translations, Faber and Faber, 1981. Reprinted with permission of Faber and Faber, Limited.

ATHOL FUGARD, SELECTED PLAYS by Fugard, Circa 1987 from Boesman and Lena By permission of Oxford University Press.

PHILIP GROSS 'Severn Song' from 'The Water Table', Tarset, Northumberland: Bloodaxe Books, 2009, p. 64. Reprinted with permission of Bloodaxe Books.

HEINEKEN: transcript extract from Lowe Howard-Spink's 'Windermere' commercial 'Heineken refreshes the poets other beers can't reach'. Reprinted with kind permission of Lowe Worldwide.

RUSSELL HOBAN, a continuous prose passage, 'The Lissener and the Other Voyce Owl of the Worl . . . My storys done' (pp.82–3, 480 words) from his *Riddley Walker*, Picador/ Macmillan (1982); first published by Jonathan Cape 1980. Reprinted with permission of David Higham Associates.

GEOFF HOLDSWORTH, for his re-write of Defoe: 'I call him Tuesday afternoon'. By kind permission of the author.

ALAN HOLLINGHURST, extract from The Swimming Pool Library, first published by Chatto and Windus Ltd., 1988. © Alan Hollinghurst 1988. Reprinted with permission of Antony Harwood Ltd.

JEREMY JACOBSON, extract from 'The Postmodern Lecture', from Poetry as a Foreign Language: Poems connected with English as Foreign or Second Language, ed. Martin Bates, White Adder Press, 1999, reprinted by permission of the White Adder Press and the author.

KATHLEEN JAMIE, extract from'Pathologies – A startling tour of our bodies' in *The New Nature Writing*, ed. Jason Cowley, London: Granta, 2008, p. 44–5. Copyright © Kathleen Jamie by kind permission of the author c/o Rogers, Coleridge & White Ltd., 20 Powis Mews, London W11 1JN.

LLOYD JONES, extract from his *Mister Pip*, by Lloyd Jones. "Copyright © 2006 by Lloyd Jones. Reproduced with permission of John Murray (Publishers) Limited."

From MISTER PIP by Lloyd Jones, Copyright © 2006 by Lloyd Jones. Used by permission of The Dial Press/ Dell Publishing, a division of Random House, Inc.

JAMES KELMAN, How Late it was, how late, London: Secker & Warburg, 1994: 52–3. Reprinted with kind permission of Rogers Coleridge and White Ltd.

RUDYARD KIPLING, 'The Story of Muhammad Din', short story from Plain Tales from the Hills, 1988. Reprinted by permission of A P Watt Ltd, on behalf of The National Trust for Places of Historical Interest or Natural Beauty.

URSULA LE GUIN, extract from The Left Hand of Darkness, Virago Press, 1969. Reprinted with permission of Little, Brown Book Group.

"The Question of Sex", from THE LEFT HAND OF DARKNESS by Ursula K. Le Guin, copyright © 1969 by Ursula K. Le Guin. Used by permission of Ace Books, an imprint of the Berkley Publishing Group, a division of Penguin Group (USA) Inc.

TOM LEONARD, 'This is thi six a clock news', © Tom Leonard from *Outside the narrative: poems 1965–2009* Etruscan/WordPower 2009.

BILLY MARSHALL-STONEKING, 'Passage', from Singing the Snake, 1990 (Angus & Robertson). Re-published in The New Oxford Book of Australian Verse, 2nd edition, 1991, Oxford University Press, Australia. Reprinted with permission of the author. Visit Billy Marshall Stoneking's website at http://www.wheresthedrama.com

IAN McEWAN, 'Only love and then oblivion', First published in *The Guardian*, 15 September 2001. Copyright © 2001, Ian McEwan. Reproduced by permission of the author c/o Rogers, Coleridge and White Ltd., 20 Powis Mews, London W11 1JN.

MARTIN MCDONAGH, Excerpt from 'Act 1, Scene 2' THE PILLOWMAN, by Martin McDonagh, pp. 31–35. Copyright © 2003 by Martin McDonagh. Reprinted by permission of Faber and Faber Inc. an affiliate of Farrar, Straus and Giroux, LLC; and with permission of Faber and Faber, Limited.

ANDY McNAB, from *Spoken from the Front: Real Voices from the Battlefields of Afghanistan*, edited by Andy McNab. Excerpt by Colour Sergeant Simon Panter, pp. 231–3, and excerpt from Captain Nick Barton, pp. 309–10. Published by Bantam Press. Reprinted by permission of the Random House Group Ltd.

TONI MORRISON, prose extract from Beloved: A Novel. Reprinted by permission of International Creative Management Inc. Copyright © 1987 by Toni Morrison.

GRACE NICHOLS, 'Tropical Death', from The Fat Black Woman's Poems, Virago, 1984, reprinted by permission of Virago, a division of Little, Brown Book Group.

ALICE OSWALD, *Dart*, Faber & Faber 2002, pp. 28–30. Reprinted with permission of Faber and Faber Limited and with permission of United Agents.

πo, '7 Daiz', first printed in The Fitzroy Poem, 1989, Collective Effort Press, P.O. Box 2430V, GPO Melbourne, Victoria 3001, Australia. Reprinted by permission of the author.

LYNN PETERS, 'Why Dorothy Wordsworth is not as famous as her brother', from The Virago Book of Wicked Verse, Virago, 1992. Copyright © Lynn Peters. Reprinted with permission of the author.

MARIO PETRUCCI, 'The Complete Letter Guide', 'Mutations', 'Reflections', 'Trench', reprinted by permission of the author.

TERRY PRATCHETT and NEIL GAIMAN, prose extract from Good Omens, Corgi. Copyright Terry Pratchett and Neil Gaiman. Reprinted by permission of Carole Blake of Blake Friedmann.

CARYL PHILLIPS, extract from *Crossing the River*, London: Vintage (2007); first published by Bloomsbury Publishing (1993). Reprinted with permission of A P Watt, Ltd, Literary Agents, and the Genert Company, Inc.

QUEEN, "BOHEMIAN RHAPSODY" Words and Music by Freddie Mercury © 1975, Reproduced by Permission of Queen Music Ltd, London W8 5SW.

JEAN RHYS, prose extract from Wide Sargasso Sea. First published by Andre Deutsch, 1966. Copyright 1966 Jean Rhys. Reprinted by permission of Penguin UK and W.W. Norton & Co. Inc. Credit line: "From WIDE SARGASSO SEA by Jean Rhys. Copyright © 1966 by Jean Rhys. Used by permission of W. W. Norton & Company, Inc."

ADRIENNE RICH, "Dialogue". Copyright © 2002 by Adrienne Rich. Copyright © 1973 by W. W. Norton & Company Inc, from THE FACT OF A DOORFRAME: SELECTED POEMS 1950-2001 by Adrienne Rich. Used by permission of the author and W.W. Norton & Company Inc.

ARUNDHATI ROY, prose extract from 'Algebra of Infinite Justice' "By Arundhati Roy, copyright © Arundhati Roy, 2002." First published in *The Guardian*, 29 September 2001. Reprinted with permission of David Godwin Associates.

WILLY RUSSELL, play extract from *Educating Rita*, Methuen, 1988. Reprinted with permission of A&C Black.

MAY SARTON, prose extract from AS WE ARE NOW. Copyright © 1973 by May Sarton. Reprinted by permission of W.W. Norton & Company Inc.

As We Are Now by May Sarton (Copyright © May Sarton, 1973). Also reprinted with permission of AM Heath.

DENNIS SCOTT, 'Uncle Time' from collection Uncle Time. Copyright © 1973. Reprinted by permission of the University of Pittsburg Press.

W.G. SEBALD, 489 words from AUSTERLITZ, by W.G. Sebald, translated by Anthea Bell, (Hamish Hamilton, 2001). Copyright © the Estate of W.G. Sebald 2001. Translation copyright © Anthea Bell, 2001.

W.G. SEBALD, extract from AUSTERLITZ, translated by Anthea Bell, translation copyright © 2001 by Anthea Bell. Used by permission of Random House, Inc.

WILL SELF, extract from *Dorian*, first published by Viking 2002. Copyright © 2002 Will Self. Reprinted with permission of Penguin Books. Excerpt from Dorian © 2002 by Will Self. Used by permission of Grove/Atlantic, Inc.

JO SHAPCOTT, 'Rosa gallica' (p. 59); 'Rosa hemisphaerica' (p. 60), from 'Tender Taxes', London: Faber & Faber, 2001. Reprinted with kind permission of the author and Faber and Faber, Limited.

SUSUMU TAKIGUCHI, three versions of a haiku by Basho, in *The Twaddle of an Oxonian – Haiku Poems and Essays*, Ami-Net International Press, 1997, reprinted by permission of the author.

AMY TAN, From THE JOY LUCK CLUB by Amy Tan, copyright © 1989 by Amy Tan. Used by permission of G. P. Putnam's Sons, a division of Penguin Group (USA) Inc. AMY TAN, Copyright © 1989 by Amy Tan. First appeared in THE JOY LUCK CLUB. Reprinted by permission of the author and the Sandra Dijkstra Literary Agency.

DYLAN THOMAS, from Under Milk Wood: A Play for Voices, first published by Dent. reprinted by permission of David Higham Associates Ltd.

DYLAN THOMAS, from Under Milk Wood: A Play for Voices. "By Dylan Thomas, from UNDER MILK WOOD, copyright ©1952 by Dylan Thomas. Reprinted by permission of New Directions Publishing Corp."

AMOS TUTUOLA, prose extract from The Palm-Wine Drinkard, Faber and Faber, 1987, pp. 18–19. Reprinted with permission of Faber and Faber Ltd.

"AMOS TUTUOLA. Excerpt from The Palm-Wine Drinkard by Amos Tutuola, copyright © 1953 by George Braziller. Used by permission of Grove/Atlantic, Inc."

DISCLAIMER

WHAT THE BOOK IS ABOUT
AND HOW TO USE IT

This book provides an introduction to the theory and practice of contemporary English Studies with emphasis on Literature and Language. It combines the functions of study guide, critical dictionary and text anthology, and is designed to support learning and teaching across a wide range of courses. Most undergraduate English courses now have a considerable variety of emphases – literary, linguistic and more broadly cultural. This book aims to recognise and support all, or at least most, of them in a flexible yet coherent way. The choice of the label 'English Studies' is calculating not casual. It signals an extremely capacious subject matter (English) and puts equal emphasis on the educational process of understanding it (Studies). Indeed, the book, like the contemporary subject, is in many senses *inter*disciplinary. So any talk of 'the subject' (definite article and singular) can be misleading if it obscures the fact that English (sometimes controversially dubbed 'englishes') is a fundamentally plural and constantly changing series of subjects (Studies). 'It' often turns out to be 'they'.

This is a handbook in that it is designed for flexible handling and for freedom of movement. Don't aim to read it straight through from cover to cover. But do expect to move from one part to another, and from this text in one hand to another text in front of you, or on the associated website (of which more shortly). Most sections are just a few pages long. They can be used on their own as focuses for a single session, or in interrelated clusters over several sessions. Cross-referencing is copious and provides constant reminders of connected issues and larger frameworks. The book is also a kind of 'companion' in that it is designed to be of continuing and cumulative use across a wide range of courses right through from introductory to advanced levels. It can be used as a coursebook in its own right or for self-directed study.

Who the book is for: 'You', it is imagined, are primarily a student. You are somewhere between first and final years of a degree or similar programme (perhaps nearer the beginning when you first pick this up). Your programme probably involves a fair amount of English Literature (including Literature in English) and at least some work in English Language. There may also be some dimensions of Communication and Composition or Cultural and Media Studies to what you do. You may be spending most or all of your time in a department called 'English'. However, you may also be studying English as part of a joint, combined, major-minor or modular programme. In any event, it is imagined that you are interested in exploring the rich variety of subjects called 'English' both in themselves and in relation to other subjects that interest you, inside and outside formal education.

But you may also be a teacher or lecturer of English, or perhaps a trainee teacher. An important, albeit secondary, function of this book is to contribute to debate about the present shape and future directions of the subject. It is framed so as to prompt discussion and provide a practical aid to course (re-)design, while also supporting teaching and learning on existing programmes. In any case, whether nominally teachers or learners, we are all in a fundamental sense *students* of English. The past, present and future of our subject is everybody's business and a shared concern. Indeed, it is as much the diversity as the unity of English Studies that exercises us here: variations over time, place and social space as much as any supposedly homogeneous object or project.

The book is organised in six distinct yet interconnected parts (seven including the Prelude):

Prelude: Changing 'English' Now
1   *Introduction to English Studies*
2   *Critical and Creative Strategies for Analysis and Interpretation*
3   *Theoretical Positions, Practical Approaches*
4   *Key Terms, Core Topics*
5   *Anthology*
6   *Taking it all Further – English and the Rest of Your Life*

Each part is supplemented by yet further information, activities and texts in the corresponding parts of the associated website: @ 1, @ 2, etc. It is recommended that you read the Prelude and the Introduction (Part One) early on to get some initial bearings. Thereafter move around the rest of the book in whatever order and patterns meet you needs.

HOW TO MOVE AROUND

For ease of use the book is variously signposted and cross-referenced. In addition to the extensive *Contents* pages at the beginning there are *Preview* pages that preface each of the six parts. There is also a comprehensive *Index* at the end where you can find page references for all the main terms, topics and authors. 'Hot' terms featured within the body of the text are of two kinds.

- UPPER CASE refers to major approaches and theories featured in Part Three (e.g. NEW CRITICISM, PSYCHOLOGY, POSTCOLONIALISM), also LANGUAGE, LITERATURE and CULTURE where that is useful.
- **Bold** signals key terms and core topics featured in Part Four (e.g. **canon, discourse, intertextuality**).
- The website icon in the margin refers to that section of the book's website (e.g. @ 1.2).

So go straight to them there or check the Contents and Index pages.

Here is a brief summary of each of the six parts of the book. Fuller summaries can be found in the Previews to each part in the body of the book, and further information and examples can be found on the corresponding parts of the website: @ 1, @ 2, etc.

Part One: *Introduction to English Studies* provides a fundamental grounding in the subject at an advanced level. It begins by surveying the many things that English has been, is currently and yet may be. The opening question '*Which Englishes?*' (1.1) draws attention to the fact that 'English' is the name for a wide variety of languages, literatures and cultures. These are traced historically, geographically, socially and by medium, and range from Anglo-Saxon poetry to the Anglo-Indian novel, with many kinds of British, American and other texts, literary and otherwise, besides. A preliminary conclusion is that English is 'one and many', and this sets the scene for the sheer plurality of the subject at large and the deep particularity of any specific instance.

'Doing English' (1.2) provides guidance on the many and various ways in which English is actually studied in higher education: through lectures, seminars, notes, reading, research, use of the library and web, essay-writing, portfolios, oral presentations and formal exams. These are framed as *ten essential actions* and in each case there is theoretical consideration of the 'whys and wherefores' as well as practical checklists of 'dos and don'ts'. Genuine learning, it is suggested, must be both critical and creative and be enjoyable to be effective. So there is a realistic recognition of the gloriously 'chaotic' as well as 'orderly' dimensions of a subject that should be a source of great pleasure and power. This is a skills guide with attitude.

The Introduction concludes with a provisional mapping of the *Fields of Study* of English in terms of Language, Literature, Culture, Communication and Media (1.3). It features some sample readings and is designed to help you get your bearings on the particular course you are doing. The emphasis throughout is on grasping your own English as the most immediately important one amongst many – and one which develops through vigorous contact with all the others. (A history of English as a subject in universities and colleges between the late nineteenth and early twenty-first centuries can be found @ 1. This ranges from Rhetoric and Composition to Critical Theory and Creative Writing, and also includes further frameworks for study now.)

Part Two: *Critical and Creative Strategies for Analysis and Interpretation* builds on the skills and insights established in Part One. It shows how a variety of readings can be turned into a variety of writings, and emphasises the creative as well as critical dimensions of interpretation. *Initial analysis* (2.1) supplies some memorable questions and suggestions that can be put to any text. The method is demonstrated in action with poetry and carried through with applications to prose fiction, play-script and critical essay. This leads to frameworks for *Full interpretation* (2.2), which show how close reading can be informed by wider reading and lead to a fully contextual, cultural-historical understanding. The method is modelled with the same texts (now fully annotated), and the 'interpretations' range from critical essay to creative performance.

Longer projects (2.3) shows how to go about fashioning a sustained, independent piece of work such as an extended essay, dissertation or portfolio. This is the kind of project that tends to be done later on in a programme. Here it is illustrated with sample topics and materials drawn from the clusters of texts in the Anthology (Part Five). These are then extended into examples of the most common kinds of project including a review of kinds of critical–creative writing. This part concludes with an overview of textual activities and learning strategies. This effectively draws together the essential study skills and critical and creative strategies of the first two parts of the book and projects them forward to the last, on 'Taking it all Further: English and the Rest of Your Life' (Part Six).

Part Three: *Theoretical Positions, Practical Approaches* offers a 'hands-on' introduction to all the major theories and approaches that inform contemporary English Studies. The emphasis throughout is upon theory that works and on getting you to work (and play) with theory for yourself. This part of the book spans everything from the relatively un- or under-theorised practices of PRACTICAL CRITICISM and (old) NEW CRITICISM to the hyper-theorised (some would say over-theorised) models of POSTSTRUCTURALISM and POSTMODERNISM. Meanwhile, at the core of this section we explore a range of psychological and political approaches that continue to inform and transform critical agendas: PSYCHOLOGICAL, MARXIST and NEW HISTORICIST, FEMINIST and GENDERED, POSTCOLONIAL and MULTICULTURAL. The final section on ECOLOGY, ETHICS and AESTHETICS draws attention to points of convergence in contemporary debates on humanity, nature, science and responsibility. It thereby tentatively sketches the grounds for a kind of NEW ECLECTICISM – though in effect the gathering and applying of whatever works (eclectically and pragmatically) is fundamental to the present theoretical–practical project as a whole. Each section includes simple yet comprehensive advice on *'How to practise'* the theory or approach in question. There are worked examples, further activities and cues for discussion. The overall aim is to encourage reflective critical practice and a habit of actively engaged theorising – not vague gestures to 'Theory' in the abstract or the parroting of '-isms'. The result is as likely to be idiosyncratic synthesis as exclusive allegiance.

Part Four: *Key Terms, Core Topics* is especially concerned with the 'study' aspects of English. It provides an overview of ways of reading and writing about texts (including 'alternative' modes of adaptation, imitation, parody and intervention). It also provides guidance on traditional modes such as the essay, and pays particular attention to the impact of computers in research and writing. There is a method and checklist for close reading of texts of all kinds. This part of the book is therefore expressly addressed to teachers and lecturers as well as to students. While supporting a considered review of current courses and programmes, it also aims to prompt debate about the shape and nature of future, potential courses and programmes. Either way, the emphasis is on English as something we *do* (*know-how*, skills, techniques, strategies, interaction) as much as on what English *is* (*know-what*, knowledges, a body of set texts, a hierarchy of textual and social relations).

Part Five: *Anthology* provides examples of the main kinds of text encountered on English Studies courses today. These are organised in open clusters to encourage critical comparison and supplementing with other materials (further examples are offered on the web), and specific texts are featured in activities and discussion in the rest of the book. Historical and cross-cultural in range, the emphasis is on the sheer variety of English and the versatility of people using it at full stretch. The first three sections offer a capaciously plural and overlapping view of the traditional literary genres: *Poetries*, from ballads and sonnets to pop song and performance pieces; *Proses*, including news reports and street texts as well as passages from novels and complete short stories; and *Voices*, featuring dramatic scripts alongside transcripts of conversation and representations of speech in verse and prose fiction. *Crossings*, the final section, draws together still more heterogeneous and richly relatable materials. Here the clusters are organised thematically under such headings as 'Mapping journeys', 'Translations / Transformations' and 'Versions of ageing', and there are competing visions of everything from epitaphs to daffodils. Together, all these materials model the processes of sense-making and project-building. The overall aim of the Anthology is to encourage an open and lively sense of interrelation and to support an ongoing commitment to critical enquiry and creative experiment. Ideally, eventually, this means not just refining and extending the present anthology but replacing it with one put together according to your own criteria. It promotes 'anthologising' as itself a critical and creative activity.

Part Six: *Taking it All Further: English and the Rest of Your Life* This is the last part of the book but its concerns are in play throughout, and you – the onus is firmly on 'you' – are invited to look at it regularly. 'Taking it all further . . .' moves in as many directions and dimensions as you care to see or dare to imagine at the time. 'The rest of your life' is, literally and metaphorically, everything else that is not strictly 'English' but in some way relates to it – if only because it's also part of your life. Most immediately, in plainly instrumental terms, this part is all about completing a course, getting a job, carrying on studying, getting on with life. Through personal reviews and checklists, questions and suggestions, it shows how to transform the essential skills and subject-based knowledges acquired 'doing English' into whatever will help get you *into work* or *further study*. It surveys the kinds of job and career pathways open to people who have done English at undergraduate level, and the postgraduate opportunities for vocational and academic study beyond, including the MA, PhD and teaching qualifications. To these ends, it provides detailed advice on putting together applications and doing interviews.

More generally, and just as vitally, there is a theoretical and reflective dimension to this last part too. The 'all', at least in principle, really is 'all'. We are here concerned with English Studies in relation to life as whole and living as an ongoing and at least potentially integrated process. The emphasis is upon *studying–working–playing* as a dynamically interrelated complex, and upon living *as* learning. Embracing a model of 'lifelong learning' and resisting the rhetoric of 'work–life balance', this final part is a reminder to celebrate the richness and flexibility of *English again, afresh, otherwise*. There is a handy clock/compass displaying 'English *and* or *as* other subjects', which extends to work and play beyond formal education. And there is an insistence on the radically 're-creative' (not just recreational) powers and pleasures involved in continuing to do English at full stretch, with others as well as for yourself. *Afterwords* is a parting gesture designed to carry way beyond the covers of the present book. It opens with some seriously playful rewrites of earlier parts . . . and continues however you choose, beginning with some empty pages at the end.

There are some *Appendices* just before the end. These supply a quick guide to grammatical terms (supplemented by a full glossary of linguistic terms on the web); an alphabet of speech sounds; a chronology of English language, literature and culture; and some historical maps of English in Britain, the United States, and the world at large. Thus, at the end as at the beginning, we are engaging with a subject that certainly appears to be 'one' but also turns out to be 'many'. The *Bibliography* includes full references for everything in the Further Reading sections, while the *Index*, as already mentioned, is a comprehensive guide to the terms, topics, texts and authors referred to. These and the Contents pages are likely to be the bits of the book you turn to first. However, once in, the cross-referencing should enable you to move around freely. Indeed, all six parts of the book complement one another and can be dipped into at any point, while the website is designed to supplement each of them and to offer further links beyond. So, if the book soon looks well-thumbed and dog-eared and the website is a space you keep returning to for more, then the whole thing is evidently working as it was meant to do. Or rather, to put the onus back where it belongs, you will be working at and playing with English for yourself – but not on your own. Seriously, enjoy!

PRELUDE
Changing 'English' now

English Studies is continuing to experience fundamental changes, and this prelude offers a preliminary overview of the main ones. It is called 'Prelude' (rather than 'Prologue') because it is seriously playful and invites lively response rather than dutiful nod. So, right from the start, picking up from the above heading, it is important to stress that such 'changing' is complex and fascinating, as is 'English' (with and without inverted commas), and so is whatever and whenever we mean by 'now'. Each of these terms will be reviewed in turn, and the phrase gradually unpacked and re-packed till the remarkably rich and various nature of its contents, plural, becomes clear. References to relevant items elsewhere in the book will be thrown in too, to encourage moving around not just settling down. The essential thing, theoretically and practically, is to put the seemingly simple and straightforward object – here the phrase 'Changing "English" Now' – under critical and creative pressure: to subject it to attentive analysis, and to tease out a range of readings leading to some alternative rewritings. The key axes on which everything turns, here as throughout the book are *critical–creative*, *reading–writing* and *theory–practice*. We return to these in the 'Forewords' at the end of this prelude, and they should still be going be round, in and on your own terms, in the 'Afterwords' (currently blank) at the close of the book. First, however, the pressing matter of *CHANGING 'ENGLISH' NOW*.

CHANGING is a particularly slippery and versatile word, and refers to a correspondingly elusive and volatile concept. (Technical terms can be checked in the 'Quick Reference' in Appendix A.) Grammatically, 'chan*ging*' (like the other *-ing* forms) is a progressive participle, and can therefore function as any or all of the three main word-types: as a verb ('She is changing the room' – she is doing that); as an adjective ('a changing room' – the kind of room it is); and as a noun ('Changing can be done in there' – that's the thing for there). In short, 'changing' can be thought of as a process (verb), an attribute (adjective) and a thing (noun). Which 'changing' is which obviously makes a huge difference. 'Changing English', for instance, can be meant and taken in two quite distinct ways, depending whether the 'changing' is understood as a verb or as an adjective. Grasped verbally, 'Changing English' implies an *action*, a process of doing, for example, what people and technologies *do* to and with English. To be precise, the phrase then has the structure 'changing' (progressive verb, transitive) + 'English' (object). Grasped adjectivally, however, the 'changing' in 'Changing English' has a quite different sense. It then refers to a quality or attribute of English, something that English just has or does itself. The phrase-structure would then be analysed as 'changing' (adjective) + 'English'.

Clearly, the implications of all of this are of more than *purely grammatical* (merely 'academic', narrowly logical) interest. Rather, they are of *massively linguistic* (fully educational, broadly philosophical) significance. In fact, they involve the whole, vexed and complex, frustrating and fascinating matter of *CHANGE*. Change as what someone or something does and/or change as something that just happens? In this case it's the question of how far English changes because of what people and human technologies do with and to it, and how far English just seems to change on its own, by its own laws, for non-human or at least impersonal reasons. These issues are picked up in 1.3, Language (esp. *Language change – a transitive or intransitive process*). Here it's time to concentrate on the second term in the phrase, adding the inverted commas for good measure.

CHANGING *'ENGLISH'* The inverted commas round 'English' are a reminder that we are here concerned as much with a subject called 'English' as with the various languages, literatures and cultures that go by that name. Indeed, typically, by the very act of doing 'English Studies' we are inevitably concerned with all of these: 'English' as designated subject areas (discipline, time-table slot) and English as objects of study (the words and worlds we thereby engage with). In fact, routinely yet quite remarkably, this is precisely what has been going on so far. The above – and ongoing – comments are observations *on* English *in* English. This is what is generally called a *meta-language* (language about language), and the metalinguistic dimension is one that naturally and necessarily keeps on opening out whenever we actually – and actively – practise 'English Studies'. In fact, the latter might be dubbed 'Meta-English' or 'English-on-English', if the words didn't sound so odd and outlandish.

Meanwhile, this whole matter of 'Changing "English"' – grasping subject-through-object, English-through-English in the one movement – is also an instance of what social scientists call 'participant-observation'. That is, you and I in our various roles as writer and/or reader (we are usually a combination) are actively engaging with and participating in all these observations *through* English. 'Simply reading' is never simple; it involves complex thinking and imagining, a kind of 'rewriting' in the head (see Part Four, Writing and reading, response and rewriting). And there is no such thing as 'simply taking notes'; this invariably turns into 'making notes' (see 1.2.3). In short, doing English is a participant-observer activity. So 'Changing English' might itself be changed to, say, 'English-on-English Participation-Observation' with 'The Return of the Critical–Creative Reader–Writer' thrown in for good measure. This sounds even more odd-ball but may still be suggestive. It also, of course, depends on the particular occasion in play. And that brings us to . . .

CHANGING 'ENGLISH' *NOW* The 'Now' – like the 'New' with which it is sometimes wrongly confused – is obviously constantly changing. It is – we are – ceaselessly, cumulatively being updated from moment to moment to moment: 'Now . . . Now . . . Now . . .'. It's the same word but has constantly changing points of reference. It all depends on context – place and person as well as time. For that reason, linguistically, 'now' is what is called a 'context-sensitive' word, otherwise known as a 'shifter' or 'deictic' (remember the 'Quick Reference' in Appendix A). Many common words are context-sensitive: 'here' and 'I' and 'we' and 'you' and 'this' (which often go with 'now' because they depend on a sense of immediate presence, 'nowness'); just as 'there' and 'he' and 'she' and 'they' and 'that' often go with 'then', because of a sense of being further back in time as well as further away in distance. Such is the complex and shifting interplay of person–place–time that may be invoked by the use of even a single, common and apparently simple word such as 'Now' or 'Then'. Again and again, what it actually means in practice turns out to be many and various and remarkably complex. (The whole matter of English being 'one *and* many' in time, place, person and medium is the theme of 1.1.)

'Now' has both an immediately personal appeal and a deep cultural resonance. (*Both/and* rather than *either/or* is a note that sounds throughout the book.) Most immediately, you and I can both jot or tap down the words 'I am writing this here now'. The broad *sense* will be the same: there is a common claim by someone-who-writes to be some such thing there and then (notice the act is already beginning to slip away in person, time and place – 'someone', 'that', 'there', 'then'). But the precise *references* in each case will be completely different: you not me;

then not my now; here but not your there – not to mention what we were, are, will be writing or typing with and how (pen, pencil, laptop, mobile, etc.), let alone how we might continue. Significantly, all this latter, highly specific, 'referential' information is precisely what goes into what, appropriately enough, are called *references* in formal academic writing (see 1.2.6, *Taking responsibility: referencing and plagiarism*). Typically, these must include name of author, date and place of publication, along with title. They do this precisely so as to identify the particular 'I's and 'here's and 'now's in play (reduced to moment of publication), along with the particular substance of the writing, the title. Together, the whole 'reference' thereby serves as a kind of institutionalised 'signature' to the work. And indeed, exactly the same range of essential information goes onto the signed claim and disclaimer attached when formally submitting a piece of work for assessment: 'I hereby certify that this is all my own work and that all sources are fully acknowledged and referenced' (or some such); along with name, date, course, title of piece, and probably student number too. In all these ways an 'I-am-writing-here-now' becomes, say, a 'She-was-writing-there-then' plus a 'They-were-publishing-somewhere-else-later'. The result for the present book, interestingly but as is conventional, is the one reference you will *not* find in its bibliography: Pope, R. (2012) *Studying English Literature and Language*, London and New York, Routledge, 3rd edn. Your own next essay or project – or article or book – will do the same.

Claims to 'Nowness' have another, more general theoretical claim on our attention too. For in fact any claim to Modernity and Contemporaneity – especially if 'Now' is narrowed to 'New' – is no sooner said than superseded. 'Now = New' is instantly out-of-date. This would be true of the present claim to speak of 'Changing English Now' if it were taken reductively, in terms this prelude seeks to evade or replace. 'Nowness' does *not* equal 'Newness', and that makes all the difference. Again, we need to come to terms with our terms. English 'modern' comes via French from Latin *modo*, meaning 'now', while the 'con-temporary' is whatever goes along 'with-the-time'. So all 'nows', once written or spoken, are inevitably destined to be 'after the event'. 'Now . . . Now . . . Now' promptly becomes 'Post . . . Post . . . Post . . .'. The tricky yet in some ways inevitable matter of writing 'After the Post-' is picked up at length in Part Three, when dealing with the three major posts- in Postmodernism, Poststructuralism and Postcolonialism (3.6–8). All that need be said here is that all these posts- should be read as meaning 'after' in two senses, senses that are complementary not contradictory: both 'after and a continuation of' and 'after and a break with'. (Another case of both/and, in fact.) Indeed, truly 'timely' tasks always involve looking both between and beyond the pressing possibilities of an ever-shifting present – not just 'before' and 'after' in a narrowly chronological sense.

Such, then, is the ongoing *project* that is 'Changing "English" Now'. Neither a single subject nor a simple object, most immediately *it is* what *we do*. And ultimately the emphasis must be on an open plurality of essentially imaginable, even if practically unfinishable projects. English*es* will then continue to become whatever we find them to be and make of them for ourselves. The following brief surveys, each with a task attached, are designed to help provide some terms of reference to help plot – but not fix – a changing project. They offer maps not territories, and sketch some observable trajectories without specifying absolute objectives. Paths are to be made as well as followed.

CROSSING BORDERS, ESTABLISHING BOUNDARIES

The overall trend is still clearly towards a multicultural and cross-disciplinary construction of the subject. This is manifest in attention to previously marginal or excluded genres such as life-writing (auto/biography), travel writing, and utopian and science fiction; and above all in an increasingly broader and deeper engagement with postcolonial and women's writing, literatures in English (plural) and, latterly, gay writing. Within British Studies, Irish and Scottish writing continue to have particular appeals, as do Hispanic and Native American writing in American Studies. Often such interests are pushed back historically; so it is now becoming more common to study, say, seventeenth-century women writers or eighteenth- and nineteenth-century slave narratives, and not only modern and contemporary instances. Sometimes study is supported by visual, audio-visual and other documentary material; and film increasingly features as an object and process in its own right, not just as illustration or enhancement of a verbal text.

There are counter-trends, however. Some practitioners of English insist upon a distinctly 'literary' emphasis, and upon a return to or consolidation of narrower, often national 'canons' and critical traditions. The concentration on literature meaning basically printed poems, novels and plays also remains constitutive for many. Partly this is a result of the independent development of Cultural, Communication, and Film and Media Studies, and a corresponding attempt to define English more exclusively, less inclusively. Partly this is a national or regional response to the perceived threat (rather than promise) of globalisation. To some extent, all this is a continuation of the 'canon' debates and 'culture wars' of the 1980s and 1990s. But it goes further and deeper in that it is not only the selection of texts but the framing of the curriculum and the methods and aims of study that are at stake.

♦   *The challenge, then, is how far the borders of the subject need to be further crossed, extended and re-drawn – or even re-trenched; also whether we need an entirely new 'map' or metaphor – 'net', 'web', 'field', 'journey', 'trajectory', etc.* (See Part One.)

TEXTS IN CONTEXTS: LITERATURE IN HISTORY

It is becoming increasingly common to see texts continuously with their contexts, and to grasp literature *in* history, not just above or to one side of it. Conversely, it is becoming increasingly uncommon to see literature as *only* 'the words on the page', the 'text in itself'. However, context (literally 'with-text') has to be conceived in flexible and plural ways. For contexts include not only the writer's personal circumstances and the historical events and current world-views that helped shape and inform the initial moment of composition, but also all the subsequent moments and modes of re-production and reception. Crucially, and for each of us with great immediacy, this includes the moments in which we read and study the text now – in our own times and to some extent on our own terms. Moreover, con-texts ('with texts') include all the other texts around – also 'then' and 'now' – from the sources and influences drawn upon, through the genres in which the text is placed, to any other text with which it subsequently becomes accidentally associated or deliberately linked. Context is thus continuous with intertextuality.

All this leaves us with problems as well as possibilities. Where does 'text' stop (or start) and 'context' begin (or end)? And, 'intertextually' speaking, how do we handle the fact that one text leads to another and another and another . . . ? Meanwhile, if literature is *in and among* history and *a part of* it, how can we also see literature as in some sense *apart from* history and *alongside* or even *beyond* it? For clearly there are important distinctions as well as connections to be made between words and the (rest of the) world, between all that *is* text and all that is *not*. So we need to grasp both, simultaneously or by turns – that is, if we are to have a relatively determinate *object* of study together with a relatively dynamic sense of the *subject* of study.

♦   *The task, then, is to combine 'close' reading with 'far' reading: looking at and through the text so as to see literature as both a part of and apart from history. Practically, it means identifying and drawing together a range of contextual (including intertextual) materials while still in some way keeping an eye trained on the specific words of the text in hand – and while recognising that there are more texts and hands than one.* (See 1.2.3–4, 2.2–3, and 'Text, context, intertextuality' in Part Four.)

SEEING THROUGH THEORY

For a few people the moment of 'Theory' – i.e. highly abstract, stand-alone Theory with a capital T – has passed. For a few others it never arrived. But for most people in and around the subject the choice of texts and range of approaches have been profoundly influenced by the theorising of the past twenty or thirty years. In fact, it would be difficult to find a current syllabus at universities and colleges that did not in some way, perhaps centrally, engage critically with such issues as: the category Literature and the nature of 'literary' language; the concept of the author ('dead', alive or otherwise); reading as an opaque and contentious activity; shifting relations between text and context, and between one text and another (intertextuality) – all with a wide range of emphases and orientations with respect to gender, ethnicity, class, nationality and region. Such issues may or may not be explicitly framed in terms of various *-isms* and *posts-* (Formalism, New Historicism, Feminism, Poststructuralism, Postcolonialism, Postmodernism, etc.). Indeed, such 'frames' may be fitted earlier, later, or never. But even the closest kind of 'close reading' is likely to be done with at least half an eye to the structures of meaning and identities in play within and around the text – including those of the readers present.

In some respects, then, expectations and agendas have been transformed. Some would claim that theoretical battles have been won or lost and that, for better and worse, new orthodoxies have been instituted. Others, however, would insist that basically nothing has changed and proceed to celebrate or lament this state of affairs accordingly. For if radical theory has 'won', how come much classroom practice – let alone society at large – has not changed? But if it has 'lost' and it's basically 'business as usual', what *is* that business, and what business has it in the modern world and culture at large – whether or not one recognises that world as postmodern or postcolonial or multicultural? In such a context, periodic calls to 'Post-theory' (the latest but assuredly not the last *Post-*) must be greeted circumspectly and with caution. If *Post*-theory means 'after' in the sense of past and gone (with the strong implication of 'done and dusted'), this is a delusion or an evasion. Far too much has been fundamentally transformed for these processes simply to be ignored or suppressed. But if *Post*-theory means 'after and a continuation of' – in the sense of building on or out from or even against – this is very much to the good. History cannot be undone, but it is perpetually re-made. And in any case, for most people the aim has always been pragmatic: the encouragement and enabling of theoris*ing* as an ongoing process of reflective practice; not so much theory as a finished product, and still less the institution of an additional or alternative canon of theorists.

♦   *The task, then, is to 'see through theory' in at least three senses: (1) to see through and expose the more esoteric ideas and exotic jargon of Theory in so far as these merely institute a new orthodoxy and underwrite a new professional elite; (2) to see through the lenses offered by theories in so far as these enable us to have perspectives and visions, including re-visions, we would otherwise be denied and be unaware of; (3) to see through and carry through the project of reflective practice in and on our own terms as well as those supplied by others.* (See Part Three, esp. 3.9.)

ENGLISH LITERATURE AND CREATIVE WRITING

'Creative Writing' courses are currently burgeoning at a prodigious rate in UK Higher Education. Once the preserve of a few specialist and well-known programmes or of extra-mural courses at further education colleges, they are now a regular and increasingly central feature of degree programmes, from first year undergraduate through to PhD. This has been the situation in the USA and, to a lesser extent, Australia for some time. In both these cases Creative Writing tends to run alongside, occasionally in harness with, more or less generalised courses in Rhetoric and Composition and, latterly, specialised courses in professional writing (including Journalism and Technical Writing). In the UK, as in the USA earlier, many of the courses in Creative Writing are growing from within Departments of English; occasionally they arise in the context of creative and performing arts. Rarely, as yet, do they stand alone. But whatever the institutional configuration there are tensions, both productive and disturbing, with 'English Literature' as traditionally conceived. For the latter is still basically reckoned to be *writing about writing by other people* (many of them classic, often dead, novelists, poets and playwrights); typically this takes the form of essays and analyses. Creative Writing, meanwhile, tends to concentrate on *one's own writing and writing by other members of the group*; typically, this takes the form of poems, stories and scripts prepared alone, shared in workshop, and presented as a portfolio.

At root, then, there is a potential conflict – but equally obviously a potential complementarity – between the study of Literature and the practice of Creative Writing. Where the one emphasises past product, the other emphasises present process. The one is primarily critical and concerned with analysis; the other is primarily creative and concerned with synthesis (the crucial term here is 'primarily' – not 'exclusively'). There ought, one would have thought, to be a ready synergy of these two approaches to writing. And sometimes there is, notably in the shared areas of re-writing and re-reading (including adaptation, imitation and parody) and through 'interpretation' in the fullest sense (including reading and performance as well as analysis and critique). But still, as yet – and still in many departments in the USA and Australia – there is a common resistance to the kinds of fruitful interchange between analysis and practice, history and performance, more commonly found in areas such as music, theatre studies and the visual arts. Partly to blame are the persistent myths and misperceptions that attach to courses in 'Creative Writing' and 'Eng. Lit.' respectively. Students of the former, it is casually assumed, do little more than 'express themselves' and pick up a few technical tricks on the side. Students of Literature, meanwhile, supposedly just sit around in cosy groups swapping clever remarks about Jane Austen and reciting bits of Shakespeare – with sherry as an Oxbridge extra. The realities of the situation are, of course, far different; and both areas commonly require a great deal of preparation and participation.

Another, perhaps less illusory, obstacle is the fact that English Literature now involves a fair amount of literary theory whereas, traditionally at least, practitioners of creative writing have tended to be resistant to and sceptical about theorising the practice of writing. If anything, they prefer to talk of method and technique and working practices. The same theory/practice divisions are often experienced in music, art and performance. Again, however, as with the reflective use of contemporary technology, it is clear that many of the most significant issues in contemporary theory are most immediately grasped in the actual practice of writing but can only be extended through concerted reflection, a reading of theory and a knowledge of literary history. Again, such issues include: the nature of authorship, the dynamic relation between reading and writing, intertextuality, influence, genre, and subject position or point of view, etc. A sense of literary history and of literature in history may not be cultivated if the course in creative writing concentrates mainly on contemporary writing. Conversely, a purely academic 'hands-off' approach to classic texts may increase a kind of dutiful reverence but preclude deep understanding and appreciation and lose the dynamic sense of literature in the making.

♦ *The task, then, is to develop practices of reading and writing that operate in a variety of dimensions and develop in a variety of directions, simultaneously or by turns: critical and creative, theoretical and practical, historical and contemporary. For only in this way can texts be fully grasped as ongoing processes as well as achieved products, and words be used for experiment and exploration as well as analysis and argument. In short, for serious play. (See 'Writing and reading, response and rewriting' in Part Four and @ 4 'Creative writing, creativity, re-creation'.)*

ENGLISH LANGUAGE TEACHING

This itself spells a challenge for those who do not recognise all the acronyms in this area. For others it is part of a very familiar story. But the primary reference will be obvious to most people. English as a Foreign Language (EFL) or as a Second Language (ESL) or for Special Purposes (ESP) or for Academic Purposes (EAP) all come under the general rubric 'ELT' ('English Language Teaching'). Moreover, all tend at some point to be tied up with international examining and accreditation bodies such as the International English Language Testing System (IELTS) and the Test of English as a Foreign Language (TOEFL). Such a profusion of acronyms and explanations will doubtless appear irrelevant to some and impertinent to others. The point, however, is that for many people learning or teaching 'English' at schools, colleges and universities, the primary reference *is* English as a Foreign or Second Language, etc. Moreover, there is currently no sign that the global educational demand for English in business, technology, science and culture at large is slackening. If anything, intensified by the widespread use of English in computing and communications, it is increasing.

As a result, quite a few students currently studying English at university, whether Language or Literature, are likely at some point to find themselves teaching English in some such area, whether at home or abroad, temporarily or as a career. What's more, there are very many university departments of English the world over that specialise in advanced linguistic, literary and cultural studies, even though for many of the students and lecturers English is not a first language. For all these reasons, the matters highlighted here are of relevance to all – not just some – students and teachers of English, whether 'native' or 'non-native' speakers, and whether using English as a first or second (or third) language.

♦ *The tasks are therefore manifold and will resonate in different ways with different readers. They can be expressed in a number of interrelated and perhaps contentious propositions:*
(i) *There can be no learning of Language in a full sense without some grasp of Culture in general and Literature in particular (this last often representing language and culture at full stretch). Conversely, there can be no learning of Literature in a full sense without some grasp of Culture in general and Language in particular (the resources of which literature draws upon).*
(ii) *Every 'English' in education is in a sense for a 'Special Purpose', just as all Englishes are potentially relevant in grasping just what is so 'special' about each of them. (This applies to 'English Literature' no less than to 'English for Academic Purposes'.) The challenge is to be clear about what those purposes are, and where there is no narrowly instrumental communicative or vocational purpose to identify a broadly cultural and educational one.*
   (See 1.1 and 1.3 for English language at large; 6.3–4 on English for further study and teaching; and @ 1.4.3 for 'English as a foreign or second language'.)

TECHNOLOGISING THE SUBJECT: ACTUAL AND VIRTUAL COMMUNITIES

Technology has always been implicitly central to an understanding of what 'English' is or can be. After all, without manuscript and pens and without paper and print technologies (the first two communications revolutions) there would be no texts and nothing to read, and virtually no historical dimension to the subject at all. Indeed, the very concept of 'literature' is inextricably tied up with the materials and methods of reading and writing (i.e. with literacy in general). During the twentieth century, however, as is widely recognised but not always fully grasped, humanity experienced at least three further communications revolutions: one in the audio-visual and telecommunications media of telephone, radio, film, television, and audio- and video-recording; another in electronic computing technologies and digital information processing; and the last combining the multi-media potential of the first three with the computing capacity of the fourth. Hence the present proliferation of multi-media interfaces ranging from CD and DVD (moderately interactive but relatively closed) to the World Wide Web/Internet (highly interactive and relatively open). The full consequences and implications of such changes have yet to be registered. However, it is now commonly acknowledged that film and TV adaptations of Shakespeare, in particular, and of older 'classic' novelists such as Defoe, Austen, Dickens, Melville and Forster, often serve as the first points of contact and kindling interest with current generations of viewer/reader; and this process extends to works by contemporary writers such as Ishiguro, Winterson, Tan and Ondaatje. The effect of current technological transformations is felt particularly acutely in a subject called 'English' because that – by dint of historical accident, past and present empires, and, latterly, a virtual monopoly by Microsoft© – is precisely the language in which an increasing amount of global communications takes place – from net marketing to tweets and WikiLeaks. The implications include, but also exceed, 'computer literacy' and 'keyboard skills' in a narrow sense.

There are, for example, profound implications for a practical grasp of central issues in cultural theory. 'The Web' is intertextuality *and* commodification in action; it enables the rapid retrieval and assembling of a whole host of contexts – though often at a price, in terms of reliability as well as money. Similarly, the now routine yet still remarkable capacity to copy, cut and paste documents with ease from multiple sources has for some time demonstrated the instability and mutability of texts and therefore the uncertain identity (though hardly the 'death') of authors. But it also prompts the question of what precisely, in the language of assessment, is 'independent' – let alone 'original' – work. Both plagiarism and intellectual property are particularly fuzzy areas in cyber-space. It can sometimes be difficult to catch people on the web, though search and checking systems are improving all the time (see 1.2.6). There are profound consequences for what and how we study, too. For one thing, manuscript and print archives or corpora of texts that were once the exclusive preserve of specialist scholars are being increasingly opened up for study on line. For another, illustration and graphic design or music and sound can once more be recognised as intrinsic, not optional, aspects of textuality. This applies to everything from an all-round grasp of Blake as engraver, publisher and poet, and an appreciation of Dickens in the context of the illustrations and adverts that accompanied his serialised stories, to the study of Renaissance lyric and contemporary pop song as words and music, poetry and performance. Meanwhile, on-line and CD text corpora offer instances of naturally occurring conversation for authentic language learning; this tends to support the development of more accurate and authoritative models of spoken grammar and conversational interaction.

The overall tensions within English Studies may be illustrated by a couple of caricatures. The traditional image of 'University English' (reinforced by the photos in most prospectuses) shows a tutor with a small group of students all intently talking about the text in hand. This is a venerable and valuable model: an ideal of open and informed dialogue in an *actual academic community.* (It's 'Socratic', too, except for the presence of both sexes and the absence of slaves!) Face-to-face and mind-with-mind, it is one of the main reasons that people actually come to university to study the subject rather than do it on their own or at home. For many (myself included) it is the most enduring and enjoyable aspect of teaching and learning the subject at any level. *When it works.* (That is, when the teacher and just one or two students do not dominate the discussion; when everyone has had time and energy to prepare properly; when texts are available and affordable; and when the small group has not grown from 'large' to 'unmanageable'!) But there is another, more contemporary model, and it too has its appealing or appalling aspects. This is a *virtual academic community*: one in which on-line tutors provide or point to verbal and audio-visual resources and monitor the work of students they 'meet' electronically. Students, meanwhile, work 'at a distance' but perhaps in collaboration with fellow students, producing a range of work that is individually customised but may be collaboratively framed and perhaps multi-media in mode. (All this happens, of course, when the electronic networks really work and don't 'crash'; when every student has ready access to a computer and telephone line, on site and/or at home; and when people need and perhaps enjoy the security of relatively anonymous, autonomous contact in their own time and on their own terms.)

Obviously both the above academic communities, actual and virtual, 'face-to-face' and 'distance', are exaggerations. And the obvious answer is to combine the best of both worlds, avoiding their respective pitfalls. (See @ Prelude for a project that attempts to do this.) But we must also bear in mind that there are many societies and education systems (or under-resourced parts of otherwise affluent systems) that can afford neither intensive personal contact nor extensive technological support. The issue then is not so much *how* as *which* and *for whom* – or even *whether*. For the simple fact is that high technology requires high capital investment, and this can be way beyond the range of countries oppressed by international debt and still struggling to raise basic literacy levels. As a result, the much-vaunted 'global village' of the electronic media still manages to miss many actual 'villages' (i.e. communities) altogether; and you need access to a high-powered machine and to have plenty of air-time to really fly on the 'information superhighway'. It is in the shadow as well as the light of this state of affairs that our sense of the current problems and possibilities of a whole host of communities, actual and virtual, must be framed.

♦ ***The immediate task*** *is to choose and combine techniques and technologies that are felt to be appropriate for the texts and tasks in hand, while keeping actual as well as virtual communities firmly in mind.* ***The ultimate task*** *is to develop a 'global village' that is genuinely 'local' as well as 'global' and doesn't cost the earth, economically and ecologically, to be a full member of. (See 1.2.5 for practical guidance and @ Prelude for an extended project combining actual/virtual interfaces and local/global communities. 1.3.3 maps the configuration 'Culture, communication and media' theoretically; @ 1.4.11 does it in terms of disciplinary history; and Appendix C does it in terms of history at large. 5.2.6 features 'Media messages and street texts' and further discussion and materials can be found @ 4 Multimodal, cyber and hypertexts and @ 5.2.6 Image/Texts.)*

FOREWORDS! SOME PROPOSITIONS AND PROVOCATIONS

The final movement in this prelude is a variety of gestures forwards – into the rest of the book and into the still-to-be-made futures of English. It also picks up notes sounded earlier in this prelude. Below are three blocks of propositions about what might be called 'Studies English'.

(What, who? Everyone who studies English. You and me, for example.) These propositions are also offered by way of provocation. They seek to 'give voice to' and 'call for' certain changes that are either already happening or, I suggest, could and should be (the root sense of Latin *pro-vocare* covers both these meanings). Also, of course, in the routine modern English, these observations are meant to *provoke*. They invite dis/agreement, debate, lively response, refinement and, indeed, replacement with propositions and provocations of your own. In that sense they require you to be a reader-writer, participant-observer, creative critic. And that brings us to the first 'forewords!' to be proposed.

(i) **Axes, fields, and other shapes of things to come.** Here are some paired terms that represent the *axes* on which the present book turns. Each axis is to be read in terms of *both/and* not *either/or*. The two ends of an axis are connected not just separated by everything between, just as the two polarities of a magnet are simply the same field flowing between. English should be conceived as turning on such axes, operating through the interplay of such **fields** (also see 1.3):

English<<<<<>>>>>englishes   reading<<<<<>>>>>writing
theory<<<<<>>>>>practice   critical<<<<<>>>>>creative
actual<<<<<>>>>>virtual   local<<<<<>>>>>global
£££——————$$$???——————-???

Such two-term linear models (dyads) are simple and striking, but still only a beginning. Other terms and shapes are possible, imaginable. Triads and triangles, quartets and squares, for instance, and cones and clusters, stacks and scatters . . . (see 1.2.3–5 and 3.1 for variously 'orderly' and 'chaotic' working/playing models).

(ii) **Ten Statements in Search of a Subject** *or* **A Declaration of Interdependence.** (Respond to the following statements – this declaration – as you see fit.)

1   In reading texts we rewrite them – in our heads if not on the page.
2   Interpretation *of* texts always involves interaction *with* texts.
3   Interaction *with* texts necessarily entails intervention *in* texts.
4   Translation fully grasped is a form of transformation, never mere transference. All writing and reading is a form of 'translation' – from one set of wor(l)ds to another.
5   One text leads to another and another and another – so we had better grasp texts intertextually (in the spaces between) and transversally (in their movements across).
6   Our own words are always implicated in those of others – so we had better grasp our selves interpersonally through dialogue: voicing dissent as well as assent, and thereby joining in the ongoing 'conversations' we variously call Culture, History, Life.
7   Because textual *changes* always involve social *exchanges* you can't have the one without the other – and one another. Perhaps we should therefore think in terms of *ex/changes*.
8   *Responding* fully and being *responsive* are responsible acts. Perhaps we should therefore also talk about the *responsibility* of 'response-ability', of actively *answering* as well as being *answerable*.
9   *Creating* involves re-combining as well as replacing. *Criticising* can be a constructive as well as destructive activity. *De*-construction, therefore, is best realised through *re*-construction; just as thoroughgoing *critique* comes out as radical *re-creation* – taking apart to put together differently. 'Creative' or 'critical', these are the differences that make a difference.
10   THEREFORE '*interpretation*' can be done through acts of 'creative' *performance* (as in dance, music and drama, and all kinds of adaptation) as well as through 'critical' commentary and

'ENGLISH' – A PRELIMINARY INTERROGATION' (BASED ON THE
OXFORD ENGLISH DICTIONARY, 1989)

ENGLISH

B. *substantive*
1.a. **The English language.**
First in the adverbial phrase,
on (now in) *English.* Also in
phrase **the King's, the
Queen's English,**
apparently suggested by
phrases like 'to deface the
king's coin'. In ninth century,
and probably much earlier,
Englisc was the name applied
to all the Angle and Saxon
dialects spoken in Britain.
The name English for the
language is thus older than
the name England for the
country. In its most
comprehensive use, it
includes all the dialects
**descended from the language
of the early Teutonic
conquerors of Britain;** but it
is sometimes popularly
restricted to the language
since the close of the
**'Anglo-Saxon' or fully
inflected stage,** sometimes
to the language and dialects
of **England proper as
distinguished** from those
of **Scotland, Ireland, US,
etc.;** and sometimes to the
literary or standard form
of the language as distinct
from **illiterate** or
ungrammatical speech,
etc.

ungrammatical speech But how far does speech have different structures and functions from the
literary form? And can or should a single model of 'grammar' be superimposed on all language
use?

Another **etc.** which leaves a lot unsaid. What of the vast and increasingly pervasive networks
of the modern media: TV, film, radio, audio, video, computer interfaces, the World-Wide-Web
. . . ? And where will 'English' as language(s) or literature(s) or culture(s) figure in our as yet
unheard, unseen and unlived futures?

The English language or englishes? One or many – historically, geographically, socially and by medium?

the King's, the Queen's English? Or anyone's and everyone's, regardless of rank, sex, age, education, region and nation? Yours and mine, for instance?

The name English . . . the name England . . . So the people(s), language(s) and country need to be carefully distinguished. We/they/it should not be collapsed and simply identified with one another.

descended from the language of the early Teutonic conquerors of Britain. So the origins of English are to be traced beyond Britain – as are subsequent developments. 'It' is always coming from or going to somewhere else. And what of the earlier and later *non*-Teutonic languages and cultures which also conquered or settled Britain: Celtic, Roman, French, Gujarati, Hindi . . . ?

Is **Anglo-Saxon** (i.e. English before the mid-eleventh century) a crucial or incidental part of English Studies? Do we acknowledge or ignore the **fully inflected** stage of the language, the primarily oral poetry, and the peculiar blends of heroic paganism and Christianity?

England proper, as distinguished from . . . Scotland, Ireland . . . Or perhaps we should be 'improper' and recognise British (not English) Studies, and the multicultural diversity of the Dis/United or Devolved Kingdom, including Scottish, Irish and Welsh cultures in and on their own terms?

as distinguished from . . . US. Where do 'English Studies' end and 'American Studies' begin? And is/are the the United States any more 'united' than the United Kingdom? What of black, white, Native American, Hispanic, Chinese, Jewish . . . cultures? Or is the whole of the world in some respects already 'American'?

What if you are part of this **etc.**? One of the first-, second-, or third-language English speakers in Australia, New Zealand, Africa, India, Singapore, Hong Kong . . . ? What if you are still only represented by ' . . . .'?!

But how **standard** *are* the **literary** forms of various kinds of poem, novel and play? Does standard mean 'of approved quality' (as in 'keeping up standards') or simply 'average, usual' (the 'standard' as opposed to the 'deluxe' model)? Is everything else merely '*non*-standard', including most speech and all less privileged regional and social varieties?

Does **illiterate** mean technically 'without literacy', 'unable to read and write', or is it generally stigmatised as 'uneducated', even 'ignorant'? Either way, what of oral and visual cultures in pre- and post-literate phases of English, and the positive revaluation of communicative practices other than writing and print? What other kinds of technological 'literacy'/competency are also in play – and demand – now?

analysis (in the full-blown 'essay', for example). For we are all in various ways or at different moments performers *and* commentators, adopters *and* adapters, critics *and* creators. We are all working and playing in and around notionally the same community, actual and virtual, local and global; we are all, for example, doing 'English' of one kind or another. Though each of us does so distinctly, in our own times and on our own terms. And all of us belong to or long for different communities – or our present community recast and perhaps connected up better. To and through other people doing English, for example . . .

Note. There is a paradox – both a problem and a possibility – about these statements. This is therefore a declaration you should be careful about signing up to – or not signing up to. The puzzle is this: *If you agree completely and wouldn't change a single word, they are wrong! But if you disagree with them completely and would change the lot, they are right!!* It's a real puzzle. How you address it in practice, while actually studying English, will say a lot about how you see yourself and other people as well as the subject. It's a puzzle that cannot be solved and a paradox that cannot be resolved in theory alone. But in theory<<<<<>>>>> practice it may be.

(iii) *'Studies English'? You do.* So with a mix of critical and historical as well as theoretical and practical considerations in play, you are invited to turn to the dictionary definition of 'English' presented and interrogated on pages 16–17. It's from the biggest, most authoritative and informative dictionary of English that exists. And yet, as the attached questions suggest, even that cannot – and in principle could never – have the last word; for there are always others and its users always have the next. (Further activities on the *OED* can be found on pages 30–31 and @ Prologue.)

INTRODUCTION TO ENGLISH STUDIES

PART ONE

PREVIEW

This introduces the sheer richness and variety as well as the complexity and contentiousness involved in studying English nowadays. Following through from issues raised in the Prelude, it is shown that *English* can refer to many interrelated things: languages, literatures, peoples and cultures. Ranging from Anglo-Saxon to Afro-Caribbean – with many words and worlds between, around and beyond – the focus oscillates between *English* (upper case and singular) as a nominally unified, intricately interrelated 'whole' . . . and *englishes* (a lower-case plural some find quite appealing and others quite appalling) as an openly variable and heterogeneous assemblage of projects full of 'holes'. Whether one welcomes or resists the 'w/hole' idea is itself the main issue at stake. *Which 'Englishes'?* (1.1) (upper case *and* plural) is an attempt to pose the question in ways which anyone can address. And the preliminary answer – 'one *and* many' – is offered in a spirit of committed inclusivity not mere compromise. (That is, it's not mean and I really mean it.)

Studying English, with the focus shifting to the 'study' aspects, is the main concern of the rest of the Introduction. *'Doing English'* (1.2) emphasises the fact that the subject is something we actively do (make, construct) as well as perceptively discover (find, respond to). (Passivity in a weak sense hardly comes into it; though being 'response-able' does.) The *Ten essential actions* therefore involve taking *and* making notes, close *and* wide reading, reading *and* researching *and* writing, doing presentations *and* other projects, and so on. These are far more than mechanical and merely generic 'study skills'. They are English-in-action, theory-in-practice, the subject in the making: what you yourself do with others, not just what is done for or to you.

At the same time, 'English' already exists as an educational subject, and it is made up of a number of recognisable *Fields of study* (1.3). There are basically three: *Language*, *Literature* and *Culture* (including communication and media). They constantly overlap but they also exert their own peculiar pressures. The precise configuration varies from institution to institution and person to person. The last section, therefore, is about keeping on course *and* making your own way. (A corresponding cultural history of English in education can be found on the web @ 1.4.)

1.1   WHICH 'ENGLISHES'?

> The point about 'English' as the name of a subject is that it is an adjective being made to serve
> as a noun. So 'English' is always pointing towards an absence – the noun. *Is the subject English*
> *literature, language, society, culture, people?*
>
>   Colin Evans, *English People* (1993: 184) (my emphasis)

We open with an overview of the many things that go to make up contemporary English Studies.
To do this, we make some preliminary sightings (and sitings) of the vast range of subjects that
'English' has been, is and yet may be. In principle these include all the various persons and
peoples, times and places, words and worlds – real and imaginary – that may be embraced by
that term 'English'. As the above quotation reminds us, this means repeatedly filling and refilling
that tantalising absence after the adjective 'English ——'. But with what? What is, are or can
be the subject(s) of 'English' – Language? Literature? Culture? People? If all of these in varying
measures, then in what proportions and who is doing the measuring?

Should we, for instance, speak of the medium of our subject as 'the English Language'
(definite article, upper case and singular) 'varieties of English' (plural features of a single entity)
or, more provocatively, 'englishes' (flatly lower case and plural)? When speaking of one of our
main objects of study, should it be 'English Literature' or 'literatures in English'? (There's a big
difference.) And in either case we need to be sure whether we're talking about canonical and/or
non-canonical texts – conventionally recognised 'classics of Eng. Lit.' or something else. Yet
again, in a still more challenging vein, perhaps we had better say our subject is 'writings,
speeches, performances, films and other media partly in some variety of english'?

It's the same with the 'cultural' dimensions of our subject. Should 'English' be conceived
primarily as the cultural heritage, even the property of a specific people located in or identified
with just one part of the British Isles (i.e. England)? Or should 'English' be recognised as a
global resource, cutting across many cultures and charged with expressing (or appropriating
or negotiating) many different kinds of personal, social and historical experience, and many
kinds of ethnic, regional, gender and class identity? Alternatively, in another sphere, do we hail
'English' as a conduit for high **art** and 'elite' culture, or as a site where popular, 'mass media'
and other versions of culture can be played out? Finally (or perhaps first) do we see English
Studies as a dimension of Cultural or Communication Studies? Do we align it with Humanities
or Arts or Education or even Social Sciences? Or do we see it as a pervasively multidisciplinary
resource, as in 'English/Writing across the Curriculum' programmes?

Clearly, then, the very act of naming and 'placing' the subject is itself part of the challenge.
Simply to say what we are studying turns out to be a remarkably complex business. Sometimes
it is a matter of deciding between a plural and a singular, an upper or a lower case ('English'
or 'englishes', say, or 'English Studies *are* . . . ' as opposed to 'English Studies *is* . . . '). More
often it is a matter of deciding precisely which other words we shall attach to 'English' and
thereby get an extra handle on whatever it is we think we are picking up. At any rate English
Studies is the catch-all term favoured here. It leaves the matter of precisely which English we
are dealing with (Language/s? Literature/s? Culture/s?) tantalisingly open. It also allows us to
recognise a variety of intellectual and educational trajectories, some converging and some
diverging, while not insisting upon identical points of departure or arrival.

At this point we also need to ask how far our ultimate subjects are the people(s) responsible
for using (or for being) 'English'. In that case the English we are concerned with is likely to be
bound up with a whole range of other subjects: History, Politics, Economics, Sociology,
Anthropology and Psychology, for instance. For how can we really understand how and why
certain forms of language, literature and culture have come into and gone out of existence unless

we also try to grasp who used and made them, when and where and why? At the very least, we must get to know something about English people, past and present, actual and imagined. And this in turn will oblige us to enquire what it means or has meant for specific groups at specific moments to be 'English' or 'English-speaking' (again there's a big difference), as well as what can be called 'English-spoken-to' (i.e., addressed, and perhaps instructed, commanded or labelled, through some form of English). All this is especially necessary in that competing versions and visions of 'England' and 'Englishness' have been highly influential in the formulation of numerous social and historical agendas: political, commercial, educational, technological and scientific. By extension, we must also pay attention to competing versions and visions of 'Britain', 'Briton', 'British', as well as, say, 'America(n)', 'Australia(n)', 'Africa(n)', 'India(n)', 'Asia(n)'. Indeed, the teaching and learning of English (and American, etc.) have often served as sites for the airing (or stifling) of precisely such issues. At any rate it will be clear that *what* we mean by English cannot finally be separated from *who* we mean by English.

The sheer complexity and potential contentiousness of everything connected with 'England', 'English' and 'Englishness' can be confirmed by a few pithy observations and questions. (These follow directly from those offered in *'English' – a preliminary interrogation* in the Prelude and are still going strong in 'English again, afresh, otherwise' (6.2). The chronology and maps in Appendices C and D supply general historical and geographical contexts.)

England is not Britain. England is only one part of the British Isles

The latter at present include Scotland, Northern Ireland, Eire (the Republic of Ireland), Wales, the Isle of Man, the Hebrides and some of the Channel Islands. This casual mistaking of part for whole is widespread. It is readily understandable amongst non-natives but perhaps more remarkable amongst natives. (Predictably, the latter tend to have been born and bred in England rather than Scotland, Wales or Ireland.)

A United – or disunited – Kingdom?

Britain has constantly been subject to the redrawing of national and regional boundaries. It is easy to forget that the United Kingdom is a comparatively recent and very variable geopolitical entity: it was only formally constituted in 1801. Indeed, through the Middle Ages and right up to the twentieth century the internal history of the British Isles has been characterised by internecine wars, exploitation, 'plantations', clearances and migrations, as well as by education policies which had the effect of eradicating or marginalising other native (i.e. non-English) languages and cultures. All these were the subsequently naturalised and normalised effects of colonisation *within* the British Isles: the consolidation of England and English in Wales, Scotland and Ireland. Henry VIII formally annexed Wales by a series of Acts (1536–43) (there had been 'plantations' of English settlers in Ireland and Wales since the twelfth century). Meanwhile, in Scotland the 'Union of Crowns' (1603) was one attempt to concentrate the monarchy in a single figure (James VI of Scotland / James I of England). However, the Revolution of 1649 cut off its head (in the person of Charles I) and set up a Commonwealth and Protectorate under Cromwell instead. Following the Restoration of the monarchy (1660), it was not until 1801 that the United Kingdom (including Ireland) came into being even as a constitutional entity. But clearances, enclosures, migration and uneven regional development continued; hence, in the nineteenth and early twentieth centuries, the 'industrial North', the 'rural South' and London as Cobbett's 'Great Wen'. Mutual suspicion and regional/national stereotyping also persist, as witnessed by the perennial joke formula 'Have you heard the one about the Irishman, the Scotsman, the Welshman and the Englishman . . . ?' In some respects, then, none of these 'unions' guaranteed a genuine Union of Peoples. As recently as 1921 the British Isles saw the creation of Eire (Southern Ireland) as a sovereign republic. And even today, in view of their patchy economic development and distinctive political histories, it is still far from certain that Northern Ireland, Scotland and Wales (all of which have their own regional or national assemblies – Scotland has its own Parliament) will always remain parts of the United Kingdom. Finally, notice that the phrase the United *Kingdom* marks the place as residually *male* and *royal*. There is still no 'United *Queen*dom' – nor yet any sign of a 'British *Republic*'. All this is particularly remarkable given the recent preponderance of long-lived *female* monarchs (Victoria and Elizabeth II) and the recurrently shaky position of the British monarchy as a whole.

Britain in or out of Europe?

England, Scotland, Ireland and Wales have all had very specific and to some extent separate historical relations with various parts of continental Europe. Shifting permutations of alliance with France, Spain and Germany have been common – sometimes *against* England. Ireland and Scotland, in particular, have often maintained continental ties and traditions (especially with France and Spain) even when England has broken them in times of war and intense economic competition. Wales, meanwhile, has close linguistic and cultural links with Brittany as well as with Ireland. In recent times, uncertainties about Britain's relations with the rest of Europe have been acutely obvious. Successive post-war governments have prevaricated about membership of the Common Market, the European Community, the European Parliament and, latterly, the European Monetary Union (with its single currency). Until recently the following formulas were etched into the language. Should Britain 'go in' or 'stay out'? When 'in', what terms should this be 'on' – purely commercial or also social, legal and political? How far could Britain 'go it alone'? What of some supposed 'special relationship' with the USA? And where, if anywhere, does all this leave that vestige of empire, the British Commonwealth? More generally, what are the pros and cons of Britain joining some future 'United States of Europe'? Would this really amount to a 'loss of sovereignty'? Such questions rumble on even – especially – while Britain is *within* the European Union, but *without* its currency, the Euro. Whatever the short-term answers to these questions, it is clear that in the longer term precisely what we mean by 'Britain' and 'Britons', as well as 'England' and 'English', is closely tied up with what we mean by 'Europe' and 'European' (now, again, including the problems and potentials of Eastern Europe). Significantly, for those who see England and Britain from outside Europe (from Japan or Africa or America, for instance), this has long been the perception. They usually speak of 'going to Europe', and casually assume that this includes Britain. In any case, even the much vaunted (or lamented) status of Britons as an 'island race' no longer holds. The road and rail tunnel has linked Britain directly to mainland Europe since 1994. Technically, the British *Isles* no longer are!

Britain and or as its empire? America and or as its sphere of influence?

When a country becomes as globally extensive and influential as Britain has been and as America is, it becomes difficult to decide where it begins and ends. How far is the empire to be identified with the 'motherland' or the colonies? Does the sphere of influence have one or many centres? For, obviously, in the course of military, commercial and cultural expansion, other centres continually spring up and are recognised. Gradually these new centres compete with the old centre and eventually they may displace it. The margins thereby become independent centres in their own rights, while the orginal centre may itself become marginal or dependent. America's colonial and POSTCOLONIAL relation to Britain is symptomatic in this respect. America was once a dependent colony but is now a superpower which dwarfs the mother country. This process of ceaseless de- and re-location, de- and recentring, does much to explain the elusiveness of 'English' when we try to grasp it in a fully historical and global context. If so many English-speaking cultures turn out to be 'elsewhere', then we need to radically rethink our notions of 'here' and 'there', 'inside' and 'outside', as well as centres and margins. Acts of international terrorism and war as well as the pervasive fact of global communication forcibly remind us if we are inclined to forget.

English as a national and international resource – local and global

As a result both of earlier British imperial expansion and later American spheres of influence, it is impossible to pin down either the English language or English-speaking peoples within a single set of national boundaries. English is a massively international resource. It pervades and often dominates areas of global life ranging from technology, science and education to commerce, advertising and pop. Around a third of the world's population (i.e. two billion people) is routinely exposed to some version of English. English is spoken in far more countries than any other language. English is the international language of air traffic control, tele-communications and Microsoft. By the same token, as a system of social exchange and cultural capital, English is the exclusive property of neither Britons nor Americans. (Nor, incidentally, do all British and American citizens speak English as a 'mother tongue' or first language.) One thing, at any rate, is clear. The vast majority of literature, film and performance in English is currently produced by and for people who have *no* direct experience of or association with England. It is *not* made in England: such labels as 'made in America' or 'made in Asia' or 'made in Jamaica' would need to be affixed to most work produced in English now. Indeed, to be even more discriminating, for the work of routinely migrant figures such as Derek Walcott, we would need a label like 'made somewhere between St Lucia, Trinidad, New England, New York, Africa and India'! Of course such labels are crude. Like passports, they tell us little more than places of birth and residence, countries of departure and destination, nominal citizenship. Notwithstanding, they still remind us that texts and utterances in English can be identified with distinct national and regional cultures, even as they transgress, transcend or transform the boundaries of those cultures. English language(s) and literature(s) are at once both national and international, local and global, bounded and boundless. We must therefore ask the next question with persistence, resource and sensitivity. It is perhaps *the* question, and is therefore given a section of its own.

ONE ENGLISH LANGUAGE, LITERATURE, CULTURE – OR MANY?

This question can be put in four dimensions: historically, geographically, socially and in terms of medium. All these dimensions both converge and diverge, and are simply distinguished for convenience. (Illustrations can be found in Part Five.)

Historically one or many?

English, like other languages, changes over time. Gradually it changes into 'other' Englishes. For instance, Britain has long been – and continues to be – home to many other languages, literatures and cultures than English alone. All have contributed to the constitution of the changing thing we call, for convenience, English.

A Germanic base   Germanic languages form the fundamental substratum of English, which is based on the various Scandinavian languages and dialects introduced by successive waves of Norse invaders and settlers from the sixth to tenth centuries. At that time the language was much more highly inflected and had much freer word-order than modern English. It probably sounded more like modern Norwegian or Dutch, and had some distinctive letter forms based on the older Runic alphabet. Much of the poetry was oral, had a distinctive **verse-form** based on alliteration and stress (not rhyme and syllable length) and explored a combination of pagan heroic and Christian themes. Society at the time was primarily based on *cynn* (kin, blood ties) and life organised around the village or small town. For a sharp sense of the many linguistic, literary and cultural differences between this form of 'English' and one with which you are more familiar, see 'Wulf and Eadwacer' (5.1.1).

Early Celtic survivals   Vestiges of Celtic culture in English often have to do with nature, especially the landscape. They include the words 'brock' for badger, 'dunn' for grey, 'torr' and 'crag' for outcrops and high rocks, as well as such names of rivers as Avon (Celtic for 'water'), Exe, Thames, Usk, and names of regions such as Cumberland and Cornwall (both of which feature the names of Celtic tribes); so does *Ireland* (the 'Iershe') and, most prominently, the name *Brit*ain itself (from the 'Britto/Brettas'). Meanwhile, Welsh along with Irish and Scots Gaelic persist to the present day as languages in their own right, latterly sustained by national revival movements and bilingual educational programmes. (Cornish, another Celtic language, disappeared in the eighteenth century.) In conjunction with English, the result has been a wide range of regional/national **varieties** of Anglo-Irish, Anglo-Welsh and Scots which are distinctive in **accent** and **dialect**. The associated cultures have their own highly developed and distinctive traditions in writing, performance and the arts, and in the church and education. Some of these features can be found in the work by Burns (5.4.5), Leonard (5.1.4), Kelman (5.3.2), Doyle (5.3.2) and Thomas (5.3.3). Always, however, precisely because they are *in* English (and not in a Celtic language as such), these vestiges of Celtic culture are highly mediated and radically transformed as well as 'translated' (see, for example, Friel 5.4.3 and Bolam 5.1.4).

Latinate traces of colonisation, Christianity and classical learning   Latin is evident at a variety of levels corresponding to different historical moments. Elements of *Imperial Roman Latin* were already present in the languages of the Norse invaders and settlers. Many had to do with building and settlement ('tigle'/tile, 'weall'/wall, 'straet'/street); with trade ('pund'/pound, 'ceapian'/to buy (hence cheap), 'mangian'/to trade (hence fishmonger); and domestic utensils ('disc'/dish, 'cetel'/kettle, 'candel'/candle). In Britain the early Germanic tribes also met some Roman place-names more or less intact (e.g., the elements -caster/-cester/chester, all derived from Latin *castra* meaning 'camp', as in Lancaster, Leicester, Manchester and Chester). A second, later phase of *Christian, ecclesiastical and educational Latin* began to make its mark in the fourth century with the first Romano-Christian missions, and these were reinforced by the Benedictine revival of the ninth and tenth centuries. The words 'school', 'epistle', 'grammar', 'bishop', 'calendar', 'creed', 'choir', 'cleric', 'demon', 'hymn' and 'paradise' all came into English from Latin at this time. For the third phase of Latin influence we must look to late medieval and especially Renaissance borrowings. These were often of a specifically *classical, learned* nature, chiefly to do with literature and the law. Characteristic examples are 'allegory', 'contradiction', 'encyclopedia', 'equator', 'prosecute', 'suppress', 'testimony', 'imaginary', 'monosyllable' and 'transcribe'. From the sixteenth century these words were supplemented by specialist words from the recently rediscovered classical *Greek* (e.g., 'absurdity', 'autograph', 'critic', 'presbyter(ian)'/elder). This phase of borrowing, along with the literary and artistic imitations of Roman and Greek models which accompanied it, is generally called *neo*-classical. Translations of the Bible in particular contributed to the naturalising of many Latin and Greek forms as English during this period. Individual writers, and even whole discourses, can to some extent be distinguished in so far as their language is more or less Latinate. Milton's poetry is quite heavily Latinate, for instance (see 5.1.3); whereas the poetry of Clare is not (see 5.3.4). Certain specialist varieties of the language such as those of medicine, the law, science and technology are often characterised by a preponderance of Latin- and Greek-derived elements. So are the generalised varieties of administration and bureaucracy.

English becomes partly French.   French influences within English can be identified with two phases: Norman colonisation and Parisian Court French. First there was the Norman French phase associated with the Norman Conquest and its aftermath (1066–twelfth century). The borrowings at this time signalled the superimposition of a new kind of feudal organisation on the existing social structures of Anglo-Saxon England. The result was the adoption of Anglo-Norman words such as 'master' and 'mistress', 'castle', 'garrison', 'judgement', 'mansion' and 'bailiff'. Also observable during this period is the widespread tendency to differentiate natural objects and cultural practices along lines laid down by the language at its various social levels. Thus, famously, we find the Anglo-Saxon words for 'pig', 'sheep' and 'calf' used to refer to the live or 'raw' animals, while their Anglo-Norman counterparts were used to refer to the dead, prepared or 'cooked' meats: respectively, bacon/pork, mutton and veal (cf. Modern French *porc, mouton* and *veau*). In this way a social hierarchy was woven into the very fabric of the language. There is the low-status Anglo-Saxon of the colonis*ed* who tend the animals, as distinct from high-status Anglo-Norman of the colonis*ers* who tend to eat the animals! Such socio-linguistic stratification reminds us that a perceived **difference** *between* cultures is often embodied as a perceived difference *within* a culture once those cultures blend. Similar processes can be observed in the later phase of French influence. Court French (also called 'Paris' or 'Ile de France' French) was influential throughout Europe from the twelfth to nineteenth centuries, most notably in the arts, fashion, and food and drink. Thus it is to this period, especially the later Middle Ages, that we can attribute the introduction of a whole range of French words which have come to dominate, even designate, these areas. And they did this by displacing or replacing their Anglo-Saxon equivalents. Of immediate relevance to us is the fact that all the following 'key' terms are French (not Old English: OE) in origin:

> 'LANGUAGE' (cf. OE 'tongue'); 'LITERATURE' (cf. OE '(ge)writ'); 'CULTURE' (cf. OE 'game(n)', 'play'); 'poet' and **author** (cf. OE 'scop/shaper' and 'maker'); 'music' (cf. OE 'glee'); 'conversation' (cf. OE 'speech'), 'story' (cf. OE 'tale'); also 'rhyme' and 'romance'. (These last two have no Old English equivalents and signal the distinctive contribution of French literary forms as such.)

Chaucer, for instance, was famed as a remarkable 'translateur' of things French (as well as Italian) and wrote several romances. Moreover, all his poetry is in rhyme modelled substantially on French and Italian forms, not in the alliterative stressed measure favoured by his Anglo-Saxon predecessors and some of his more northerly contemporaries.

But French had a much wider and deeper effect on the language and, by implication, the culture as a whole. Witness the French origins of words connected with *food and cooking*:

appetite, dinner, supper, taste, fry, spice, sugar, cuisine; and *the home*: basin, plate, cellar, chair, chamber, chimney, closet, pantry, parlour, towel. Also notable are the French origins of such routine terms in all the major word-classes: *adjectives*: blue, brown, real, royal, sure and special; *nouns*: city, country, power, poverty and person; *verbs*: advise, allow, obey, please, prefer, refuse and receive. All these lists could be massively extended; for the vocabulary of English more than doubled in size and was throughly transformed between its Old and Middle English phases (i.e. the tenth to the fifteenth centuries).

Anglo-Saxon, French and Latin together provide the main MULTICULTURAL foundation of the English language. A handy way of distinguishing the various strains within English is in terms of three levels of style. Words derived from Anglo-Saxon tend to be more basic and direct and are often monosyllabic; French-derived words tend to be a little more refined and polite or formal; Latin-derived words tend to be more learned and technical and are often polysyllabic.

THREE LEVELS OF 'ENGLISH' STYLE

from *Anglo-Saxon* (basic)	from *French* (refined)	from *Latin* (learned)
holy	sacred	consecrated
ask	question	interrogate
rise	mount	ascend
fire	flame	conflagration
kingly	royal	regal

English continued to change in many ways from the seventeenth century onwards. However, for subsequent developments we must increasingly look beyond, and not just within, the British Isles. This will allow us to see that the *internal* multiculturalism of English (both embracing and being embraced by aspects of French and Latin, as well as Celtic cultures) is supplemented by an *external* multiculturalism involving languages, peoples and ways of life beyond Europe altogether.

Geographically one or many?

English varies from place to place, sometimes beyond recognition. Currently, for instance, there are many highly distinctive national varieties of English, even to the point of competing **standards**: Caribbean, Indian, African, Australian and Singaporean, as well as British and American. Regional **varieties** are also myriad. These range over minor or pronounced differences in **accent**: within Britain alone, the words 'This is the news' may be delivered so diversely in Glasgow, Belfast, Cardiff, Liverpool and London as to confound many native speakers (e.g., Leonard 5.1.4). Often they extend to marked differences in **dialect**, affecting vocabulary and grammar as well as pronunciation. Cumberland in England, Kingston in Jamaica, Brooklyn in the USA, for instance, can all boast huge differences in word choice, inflection, combination and order, especially when the conversation runs to talk about such basics as food, sex, work, play and death. For examples, see Nichols (5.4.5, Guyana); Tutuola and Achebe (5.3.2 and 5.4.5, Nigeria, Yoruba and Igbo); πο (5.1.5, Greek Australian); Chan Wei Meng (5.1.4, Singapore); Fugard (5.3.3, S. Africa). Meanwhile some differences amount to virtually different languages. This is the case with restricted-use pidgins and full-blown creoles. In the latter we witness new languages in the making from the fusion of old ones, only one of which may be some form of English.

ENGLISH AND EMPIRES FROM THE SIXTEENTH TO THE TWENTY-FIRST CENTURY

The following samples of English vocabulary demonstrate the complex material and cultural **differences** characterising various moments of colonisation from the seventeenth century to the present. These are just a few of the many verbal traces of past empires which survive in the living language:

- from *Spanish* and *Portuguese*: apricot, armada, banana, cannibal, cocoa, guitar, maize, mulatto, negro, potato, tobacco, yam;
- from *Italian*: balcony, carnival, opera, sonnet, stanza, violin;
- from *Dutch*: cruise, easel, landscape, yacht;
- from *Arabic, Persian and Turkish*: caravan, coffee, harem, sheikh, yoghurt;
- from *North America*: names of states – Virginia (after Elizabeth I, the 'Virgin Queen'); Pennsylvania (after William Penn plus Latin 'woodland'); N. and S. Carolina (after Charles II); Georgia (after George III); California (Spanish 'earthly paradise'); Texas (Spanish for 'allies'); Oklahoma (Choctaw for 'red people'); Kansas (Sioux for 'land of the south wind people'); N. and S. Dakotas (Sioux for 'friends'); also powwow, chipmunk, toboggan, skunk, totem, wigwam;
- from *Africa: South* – Hottentot, voodoo; apartheid, trek, kraal (from Dutch/Boer); *Central* – bongo, bwana, marimba, safari; *North* – assassin, emir, sherbet, zero;
- from *the Caribbean*: barbecue, cannibal, canoe, potato, yucca;
- from *India*: bungalow, chutney, curry, catamaran, guru, jungle, pyjama, pundit;
- from *Australia*: boomerang, dingo, kangaroo, koala, wombat (a third of Australian place-names are from 'Aboriginal' languages);
- from *New Zealand*: haka, hongi, kiwi, pakeha (white) (many place-names are Maori);
- from *Japan*: sushi, tsunami, Pokémon, manga.

Socially one or many?

English varies from group to group and situation to situation, sometimes so as to be hardly recognisable as the same language. We all use different kinds of words, or similar words differently, in different situations: when we speak informally with family or friends as opposed to when we speak more or less formally with someone in authority (the police, doctors, teachers, etc.). The words 'I love you' whispered in private in bed and the words 'I solemnly swear to tell the truth, the whole truth and nothing but the truth' sworn in public in a court of law are clearly worlds apart. So is 'high' in 'high temperature', 'high school', 'high opinion of . . .', 'high time that . . .', 'high on speed', etc. – or 'love' when used of everything from chocolates to people, and pets to God. (You can go through the same operations with most words, drawing on a dictionary and word association. Most words touch on many worlds.) Notice, too, the myriad worlds involved in the languages (i.e. specialist terminologies) of, say, knitting and nuclear physics, skate-boarding and stylistics, computing and greetings cards, instruction manuals and product labels, personal ads and sports commentary, accounting and acupuncture. These are all ostensibly parts of the same language, but each has its own highly distinctive choices and combinations, forms and functions.

Moreover, no single person or group ever uses the whole language (in this respect 'the whole language' is an illusory construct). Instead, each of us draws on different parts in so far as we deal with certain topics (common or specialist) or belong to certain social groups (defined by education, occupation, class, gender, ethnicity and region, etc.). Current English has over a million words, and rising. And yet the active vocabulary of even a highly educated person is scarcely more than 30,000 words (70,000 if we add recognised but not used words: i.e passive vocabulary). In this sense, paradoxically, 'the whole language' is everybody's and yet nobody's. We all routinely switch from one social variety to another. But still nobody uses more than a tiny fraction of the varieties available. And in any case these are always changing over time and space, being ceaselessly replaced or regenerated. (Do *you* know the technical terms and specialist practices of, say, thatching, basket weaving *and* racing pigeons *as well as* those of maxillo-facial surgery, glue-sniffing, econometrics and 'cyberpunk' . . . ? I'm sure I don't!)

One 'code', many media?

People speak differently from how they write. If for no other reason, this is because sounds in the air and marks on paper or screens have substantially distinct properties and potentialities. The basic linguistic 'code' may be common but it is realised in materially different MEDIA. In this respect the medium *is* the message. Moreover, within **speech** there are clearly crucial distinctions between casual conversation and formal 'speech-making', between scripted and unscripted delivery, between monologue and dialogue. A chat over coffee is different from a class presentation; a 'word in the ear' is different from a sermon; a collectively workshopped improvisation is different from a film shooting-script.

Writing, too, takes place in many materials and on many occasions: inscriptions cut into marble or wood or bone; letters dyed or painted on cloth; ink scratched into manuscript or pressed into smudgy newsprint or high gloss paper; shopping lists scribbled on scraps of envelopes with children's crayons; ball-penned postcard messages partly obscured by the stamp; carefully redrafted letters or essays; chalk on blackboards and marker pens on overhead transparencies; meticulously typed and corrected c.v.s or forms for job applications; hastily typed e-mail messages; the embossed lettering on plastic credit-cards; computer-assisted letter-designs which form and re-form on TV and PC screens; letters blazing forth from neon lights or stored away in paper archives or electronic circuits, buried in the ground or circulating in hyperspace. And so on to the last syllable of recordable language.

But even that is not the end. All of these words may be accompanied by, shot through – even transformed into – still and moving **images**, as well as music and sounds in general. Clearly, 'the word' leads a hectic and versatile life. It gets around in a prodigious variety of media: on the lips, in the ear and eye, in the air, on the street, on the page, on the screen, in the mind, in the memory (human or machine) – in fact in every conceivable material from fire and sand to brain cells and electronic circuitry. In short, rolling all the above together, English is a prodigiously and increasingly multimedia resource. Of course, the same can be said of other 'world' languages: Spanish, French, German, Russian and Japanese, for instance. But it needs to be said loud and clear with a language as globally, socially and technologically ubiquitous as English. Subject to such diverse pressures and carrier of so many meanings in such diverse materials and contexts, we may well wonder whether we all really are 'speaking the same language' – let alone writing and viewing it.

SUMMARY: ONE *AND* MANY

And yet, for all their differences, the many 'Englishes' referred to above *are* related. All the historical, geographical, social and media varieties are interconnected. They have what Wittgenstein would call 'family resemblances'. They *share* their differences. For one thing, most moderately competent readers of English can to some extent understand most of the varieties of English represented in Part Five. And with only a little assistance, in the way of notes and guidance, they can grasp them quite fully. This can happen because, despite differences in vocabulary and spelling and grammar, there are enough consistent and commonly recognisable items and structures for us to say 'Yes, this is *some* kind of English!' Even English-speakers who could not read would still recognise and to some extent understand many of these samples if they were read out loud. Many Middle English and Afro-Caribbean varieties are actually more not less comprehensible when heard rather than read. Many of these texts were built for oral delivery, and differences of spelling can be deceptive.

For all these reasons it is perhaps best to see English language/s, literature/s, culture/s as one *and* many. Theoretically, we can express this dynamic in a number of ways. Bakhtin would speak of English, as he also spoke of Russian, as a shifting site defined by the interplay of centrifugal and centripetal forces. These forces simultaneously thrust outwards and inwards, but never with equal force. The system is always 'off balance'. He would also point to the fact that the internal heteroglossia of a language (its inherent 'varied-tonguedness') is deeply implicated in, and cannot finally be distinguished from, its relations to the external polyglossia (the surrounding 'many-tonguedness'). Languages thus exist and shift through the dialogic interplay of 'internal' and 'external' forces. They are braced against and even within other languages.

Chomsky would talk of the 'generative' qualities of language, the fact that an infinite array of permutations can be generated by a finite number of principles. POSTSTRUCTURALISTS would push that idea further and in different directions. They would insist that 'English', like any other system or structure, is a product of its *inter*relations, the relations *between* its elements, and cannot be located in any item or part as such. Derrida, for instance, would insist that the structure of English is 'open', incomplete, always already in process. Consequently, we must speak of it as having not one 'origin', 'centre' or 'aim', but potentially many and different. Indeed, Derrida would add that, strictly, we have to 'defer' the notion of 'English as a whole', and had better conceive of it as a series of 'holes'. Its infinite **differences** lead to playful plurality not solemn sameness. POSTMODERNISTS would maintain something similar but in another dimension. They point particularly to the contemporary sphere and the sheer multiplicity of media as well as the global heterogeneity of cultures now involved in any communicative activity. English as a 'world language' and, in its American form, a 'world culture' is especially amenable to such global dispersals and localised reconfigurations. In a full-blown postmodernist view, 'English' is a compound of language/literature/culture/media (the terms merge or are no longer relevant); is everywhere hybrid and nowhere 'pure'; and is consequently constantly reforming under the pressure of other languages/literatures/ cultures/media.

But whatever model we use or theorist we invoke, the main thing is to attempt to grasp English as a process as well as a series of products. It is a system which is interrelated and bound together over time and space and peoples by certain principles of coherence. But at the same time it is a system which is open, always in the making – never closed and never finally made. One *and* many.

'ENGLISH' IS WHAT SOMEONE SAYS IT IS . . .

In a practical and pressing sense, it is the designers and teachers of your courses who will have already framed the main terms of reference within which you will address 'English'. And every department of English, even every person within that department, will frame the subject with slightly or very different emphases. Nonetheless, ultimately and most importantly, it is still only you who can decide 'which English' is most interesting and important to you. With this in mind, work over the passages, maps and diagrams in the activities that follow.

ACTIVITIES, READING

(a)   *The 'Oxford English Dictionary' (OED) revisited*
Return to the extract from the *OED* featured at the end of the Prelude: 'English' – a preliminary interrogation (pp. 16–17). Go on to read the following account of the development of the dictionary then discuss each of the points highlighted on that double-page spread.

The *OED*, initially called the *New English Dictionary on Historical Principles*, was conceived as a monument of late nineteenth- and early twentieth-century scholarship. First conceived in 1857, it was executed by teams of editors and legions of contributors between 1878 and 1928 (when it was first published). By 1989 it had grown to twenty volumes with supplements integrated, and contained entries on over half a million words illustrated by two and a half million quotations. The *OED* thus constitutes one of the most impressive and informative dictionaries on earth.

However, like all texts, dictionaries are a product of their historical moment. The *OED* is no exception. It emphasises **writing** (chiefly from 'literary' sources) not speech, and older not contemporary forms. It also assumes or asserts the primacy of narrowly native 'English from England' (rather than from the British Isles in general), let alone from America, Australasia, India and Africa. In short, the *OED* is a supreme monument to empire too. Consequently, notwithstanding the thorough revisions of the 1989 edition, it has been estimated that there are at least as many 'English' words which do not appear in the *OED* as ones that do (i.e. a further half-million). The *OED* therefore has to be supplemented by extra entries and alternative definitions from other inter/national and specialist dictionaries: of American, Australian, Anglo-Indian and Afro-Caribbean Englishes; of Anglo-Saxon and Middle English; of dialects and 'slang'; of technology and science; of occupations and hobbies; of linguistics and literature, of cultural theory, communications and computing, and so on. All in all, then, the *OED* offers an extremely powerful but also extremely partial version of English. (For further confirmation, see the very different entries on 'English' in Webster's *New American Dictionary* (1828; third edition 1961) and Ramson's *Australian National Dictionary* (1988).)

Go on to look at the full entries of 'English' and the introduction in the current edition of the *OED*. This is available on the web as well as in book form in any higher education institution. For further activities on the *OED* see @ 1.

That initial interrogation of the entry on 'English' in the *OED* (pp. 16–17) may have been surprising in various ways. It certainly tends to disturb those who casually appeal to 'the dictionary' and 'dictionary definitions' as absolute authorities without caring to specify which one. But it would not altogether surprise the initial editors of the *OED* themselves. Here are some of *their* observations from the 'General Explanations' (1933, pp. xxi–xxii). Use these as focuses for further discussion:

(i)   The vocabulary of a widely-diffused and highly cultivated living language is not a fixed quantity circumscribed by definite limits [. . .] And there is absolutely no defining line in any direction: the circle of the English language has a well-defined centre but no discernible circumference.

(ii)   The Language presents yet another undefined frontier when it is viewed in relation to time. The living vocabulary is no more permanent in its constitution than definite in its extent. It is not today what it was a century ago, still less what it will be a century hence.

(iii) No one man's English is all English.

(For some suggestive updates and rewrites of these passages from the *OED*, see @ 1.)

(b)   *Putting yourself on the map(s)*
Turn to the maps of Britain, the USA and the world in Appendix D. Use one or all three, as appropriate.

◆   Mark where you are now, where you have lived, and where you were born.
◆   Where in the world, as far as you know, did your family and ancestors come from or go to? Mark those places too.
◆   Identify those English-speaking cultures that are most familiar to you and those that are more or less remote.
◆   Mark the countries associated with the following writers, all featured in the Anthology in Part Five, using the notes supplied there:

On the map of the world: Achebe 5.4.5; Atwood 5.2.1; Kipling 5.2.1; Behn 5.2.2; Coetzee 5.2.2; Doyle 5.3.2; Bryson 5.4.2; Tutuola 5.3.2; Jones 5.3.1; Nichols 5.4.5; Rich 5.3.4; Dickinson 5.3.4; Morrison 5.4.5; Phillips 5.4.2; Tan 5.2.1; Eggers 5.2.1; Byron 5.1.3; Barton and Panter 5.2.5; Fugard 5.3.3; Rilke 5.4.3; Rhys 5.2.3; Marchall-Stoneking 5.4.2; πo 5.1.5; Wei Meng 5.1.4; Roy 5.2.5.
On the map of Britain: Chaucer 5.1.1; Austen 5.3.2; Byron 5.1.3; Leonard 5.1.4; McDonagh 5.3.3; Thomas 5.3.3; Kelman 5.3.2; Doyle 5.3.2; Jamie 5.4.2; Phillips 5.4.2; Wordsworth 5.4.1; Wilde 5.2.3.

Compare your answers with those of friends and colleagues. Gather them all together and superimpose a group map on the ones supplied. How much of the English-speaking world have you collectively 'covered'? Conversely, what for you remains as yet relatively unknown?

READING: Lively and informative surveys of English which combine global and historical perspectives with attention to language, literature and culture are: Crystal 2004; Bragg 2005; Graddol, Leith and Swann 1996; McCrum, Cran and MacNeil 1992; Bailey 1992. A concise companion is Maybin and Swann 2010, and Crystal 2003 is an invaluable encyclopedia. Burnley 2000 provides a documentary history, Carter and McRae 2012 a literary history (British), and Jenkins 2009 a resource book for World Englishes. This builds on classic work such as Kachru 1992 and Pennycook 1994 and runs interestingly alongside Kachru, Kachru and Nelson 2009. The dual focus on English as 'one and many' is maintained in McArthur 1998; while the emphasis on 'varieties' is carried through in Trudgill and Hannah 1994 (internationally) and Fennell 2001 (historically). Many of these books include maps and diagrams (to go with those below in Appendix D), and Gikandi 1996 offers mappings of Englishness. Also see 'Mapping Journeys' 5.4.2.

1.2   'DOING ENGLISH' – TEN ESSENTIAL ACTIONS

> Criticism begins with the recognition of textual power and ends in the attempt to exercise it.
>
> Robert Scholes, *Textual Power* (1985)

This part of the book is designed to help develop skills and attitudes that are essential when studying English at an advanced level. Studying nowadays means more than just 'reading English', in the scholarly yet potentially passive sense of that archaic phrase. Certainly there is a lot of reading to be done, closely and widely, of literary, critical, theoretical and other texts. But 'doing English' is more dynamic and capacious. It extends to writing and speaking, embraces creative as well as critical activity, and in general draws attention to active engagement and personal responsibility – working and playing with others as well as on your own.

The emphasis is therefore on English as a series of *actions*. For convenience, though obviously somewhat arbitrarily, these are identified as *ten*. They are *essential* in that they underpin just about everything you will do. They introduce the study practices that inform the 'Activities' sections in the rest of the book and are extended in the Critical and Creative Strategies in Part Two. They also look forward to what you may 'do' with English after your present programme of study – in work, further study and the rest of life (see Part Six). Together, all these parts of the book can be used to complement whatever 'skills' course you may be taking or handbook you are using.

Each action is cued by a quotation that gestures to its broader and deeper significance and may be returned to for general discussion. The action in question is then introduced in terms of its main principles and aims; key terms are defined; checklists are provided, and the action is clinched with a practical list of things 'to do immediately'. Cumulatively, all these actions build towards the tenth and final one – 'Seriously enjoy studying English' – which in effect embraces all the others. This is an open invitation to keep reinforcing and refining all the actions over the course of your studies – not just because they will help you get higher grades (which they will) but because they are deeply pleasurable as well as extremely empowering. 'English', it is insisted, is however you find it and whatever you make of it. For yourself yet with others. It's as simple – and complex – as that. Seriously, enjoy . . .

1.2.1   Getting your bearings and getting organised

> Whoever looks into themselves, as into vast space, carries galaxies within themselves, and also knows how irregular all galaxies are: they lead into the chaos and labyrinth of existence.
>
> Friedrich Nietzsche, *The Gay Science* (1882, no. 322)

This is the crucial first step into fresh territory. It may well feel risky – scary and exhilarating. So the best thing is to take stock of where you are at the moment with your English studies and try to see what to do next. Here are three sets of questions to help you gauge *what* you have done in English so far, *how* and *why*. Respond with as much detail as possible. Expect plenty of gaps and whole areas as yet unexplored, but also notice the distinct islands of knowledge you already have. Also notice that, as with 'English' in general (see 1.1), there is no single exhaustive list or fixed map, and no one could possibly cover everything anyway. So each person must do their own list and sketch their own map. It is worth taking some time and trouble over this.

What have you done in English so far, and what particularly interests you? Circle some, list others, and add comments on points of interest.

- *English Literature and/or Language* – including Irish, Scottish, Welsh, American, Canadian, Australian, African, Indian, New Zealand . . . (see maps in Appendix D)
- *Texts and authors*: list them all, including those you have read but not studied
- *Genres, kinds of text*: poetry; plays; novels; short stories; auto/biography; news; advertising; conversation; speeches; . . . (what specific kinds of poem, play, etc. ?)
- *Periods and movements*: Medieval; Renaissance; 17th century; 18th century; Romantic; 19th century; Victorian; Modern – early or late 20th Century; Contemporary (21st century), etc. . . . (for an overview, see Appendix C)
- *Critical approaches and theories*: You will have practised some but may not have named or known them as such (the Contents of Part Three offer a representative list)
- Anything else relevant outside 'English': perhaps drama and performance, other languages and literatures, media, art, music, history, etc. (see 6.2 for 'English *and* or *as* other subjects')

This gives a good sense of what you *have* done in the foreground, against a background of what you have *not* done or may yet do *differently*.

How have you done English so far, and how do you feel about the following? Try ranking each on a scale 1 (very confident) to 5 (very unsure).

- working on your own
- doing a presentation to a group
- planning and writing essays
- doing creative writing
- searching (rather than just browsing) the web
- discussing in groups
- doing group project work
- doing close analyses of texts
- using libraries
- taking exams

No one is equally good at everything, and being confident doesn't always mean you are good at it. But you can gradually edge everything closer to 1. (There is an overview of a full array of *textual activities* and learning *strategies* in 2.4.)

Why are you studying English? Here are ten of the reasons most commonly given. Add another in your own words and try ranking them in order of personal importance from 1 (high) to 11 (low).

- because you've always enjoyed reading
- because you enjoy writing / want to be a writer
- because English was one of your best subjects at school
- because a particular teacher influenced / inspired you
- because you are passionate about a particular author or kind of literature
- because you want a broad education and English seems to offer it
- because of the influence / example / pressure of family or friends
- because you are very interested in the language (its history / how it is used)
- because you want to get a job using English (teaching / advertising / journalism . . .)
- because you want a qualification and English is good for many kinds of job.

The order you have come up with gives a current snapshot. It may in fact tell you more about your past reasons and present awareness. But the future is where you are going and what you make it – with 'English' somewhere in the picture. If possible, go on to discuss the above responses with other students in the same situation. You may be surprised to learn how common certain hopes and fears are, and be both cheered and chastened by what you know that other people don't – and vice versa.

Expectations are another important area of common concern. What, broadly, are the differences between studying English at school and at university? The following two lists outline *What (not) to expect doing advanced English*. Again they are best weighed on your own and then discussed with other students and with tutors.

EXPECT TO . . .

- have a lot of apparently 'free' time that you will need to learn how to manage so as to use productively (this is the biggest challenge for most students straight from school)
- work independently and resourcefully, within broad guidelines and to strict deadlines
- read a lot of texts, both 'primary' and 'secondary' – about the equivalent of a novel and/or play a week plus supporting reading and preparation
- develop analytical, critical and research skills that can be deployed flexibly with many texts – not just applied mechanically to one
- approach texts strategically, with a view to understanding what is distinctive and significant about each and with an eye for significant detail
- build up an understanding of how texts can be compared and contrasted with one another and how they relate to different historical and cultural contexts
- explore different critical approaches and emphases and recognise that your own position is complex and evolving
- encounter unfamiliar terms and difficult ideas that need getting used to and grappling with, and sometimes adapting – not simply adopting
- experiment with different ways of reading, writing about, rewriting and presenting your materials – being creative as well as critical
- find the study of English hard and demanding but enjoyable and rewarding.

DON'T EXPECT TO . . .

- be constantly told what to do or repeatedly reminded when assignments are due
- study a single text in minute detail over many weeks, till you know it inside out but not much else
- be spoon-fed with detailed blow-by-blow, page-by-page accounts that you can just regurgitate
- get by with descriptions of character, plot summaries and a few features of style (these are important but only a beginning)
- discover a single 'message' or 'meaning' in a text, and arrive at the 'right' or 'wrong' answer to a critical question (there are usually many and various, and it is up to you to make as well as find them)
- understand everything at a first reading and without further effort, enquiry and discussion (re-reading, like re-drafting, is essential)
- get away with superficial preparation, rushed assignments and generally shoddy work
- have an easy – or boring – ride!

Having a sense of where you are up to personally and what is generally expected of you is important. Equally important is turning that awareness into action: what are you going to *do* with it? This is where getting your bearings turns into getting organised. To put it more pointedly, it's about *getting your act together*. What follows is therefore a very particular kind of 'hit list'. If you don't get into it yourself, everything you have *not* done will come back and not just haunt but *hit* you. Probably sooner rather than later.

To do immediately . . .

- *Get a diary and use it.* Put in your time-table, deadlines, schedules, big socialising events you need to work around. Look at the weeks ahead and plan roughly what you need to do when:

there will usually be two or three courses on the go, and therefore pieces of work at various stages. Make a list every day of what you need to do. You never complete your list but it gives the day some structure and purpose.

♦ *Get a folder for each course and use them.* Throw things in as you go and keep them together. You can sort them out from time to time when you need.

♦ *Get a library card and check out the catalogue.* Go on a library tour and get to know the sections where books you most need are; ready reference section and journals. Wander and browse, too. A combination of concerted and random search is best: what you deliberately look for and what you accidentally come across.

♦ *Get a few essential reference books of your own:* a good dictionary and thesaurus; a Companion to English Literature and/or Language; a dictionary of critical terms; a big anthology or two (see Action 4, 1.2.4, for suggestions).

♦ *Set up a convenient place to work regularly.* This is where you can put your things out and, if possible, return to them and just carry on. Keep your files, reference books, disks, and so forth there. Treat it – and demand it be treated by others – as your work-space and 'home-base'. Even if it is just a tray, it's yours!

♦ *Get an e-mail account and Internet connection and use them to inform your work.* Most institutions supply them and much of the day-to-day communication on programmes takes place by e-mail. This account usually includes access to the library catalogue, specialist study facilities, reference sources, on-line journal collections and perhaps a course-related VLE (Virtual Learning Environment) – along with general web access. (NB. The latter is an invaluable work-tool but also has infinite capacity for distraction and casual social use. Be strict with yourself about when you are using it for what.)

♦ *Set up a computer file for each course and always back up.* Print out before turning off if it's precious and irreplaceable. Most people don't delete things till the memory is full or the machine slows down. Tidying up files occasionally is very therapeutic.

READING: Durant and Fabb 1990: 1–17; Green 2009: 23–67; Cottrell 2010.

1.2.2   Turning up, taking part – lectures and seminars

> For the smallest social unit is not the single person but two people. In life too we develop one another.
>
> Bertolt Brecht, *A Short Organum for the Theatre* (1948)

Tune in to lectures, *take part* in seminars, and (it almost goes without saying) *turn up* to both. That is what you have to do if you want to know and have a say in what is going on. For the plain fact is that students and teachers are involved in hundreds and hundreds of hours of lectures and seminars over the course of a programme. They are the main points of formal contact. It is therefore well worth thinking about what each can be and do and how they can work off one another. Some initial definitions will help. So will some reflection on the dynamic relation between **monologue** (one-way communication) and **dialogue** (two- and many-way communication). Both lectures and seminars involve both, but of different kinds at different moments, and it is important to see the connections as well as the distinctions.

LECTURE This is the usual *monologic* (one-way) form of larger group teaching and learning. The classical *lectio* was initially a 'reading' and the *lector* someone who read out a text word by word from a *lectern* (like a priest) so that it could be copied out by students or their scribes (*amanuenses*). This was the typical way of multiplying copies of texts in pre-print culture, and is still used when books are in short supply. (For just such an archaic way of spreading knowledge, by written summary and word of mouth, see *Mister Pip* in 5.3.1.) There is usually no need for such verbatim dictation in modern teaching situations. Still, however, the lecture is predominantly a monologue based on a written script, and the habit lingers on in the academic practice of 'reading a paper'. That is, it involves a single person who addresses many people in a very specific form of face-to-face encounter, sometimes in a specially designed *lecture theatre*. Again the term is significant. The classic lecture theatre is designed like an amphitheatre with banks of fixed seating radiating out from the stage. So, as in a conventional theatre, the lecturer can in principle see everyone's face and everyone can see the lecturer's; but unless they turn around most people in the audience can only see backs or sides of heads. Modern lecture theatres are also increasingly fitted with screens, sound-systems and data projectors, so there is a comparison with cinema too. But the situation and space are still fundamentally built for monologue: speaker, sound, images on the one side; audience and spectators on the other. This physical lay out and its communicative dynamics are significant.

The lecture is obviously an educational **genre** and **discourse** that expresses a particular array of social relations involving authority and power, especially who has the right to speak and control topic. The traditional role of the person attending a lecture is to look and listen, and to respond by taking a few judicious notes – not to chip in or speak out as in conversation. If there are to be questions and comments, these are usually reserved for a special section at the end. In other words, the basic role of students in lectures is to be quietly attentive and active, and to be prepared (in every sense) to voice a response or ask a question should one be invited. This is what is meant by actively *tuning in* to lectures. It is very different from either soaking everything up and pouring it straight onto paper or lolling around and waiting to be entertained. In short, it is a specific kind of work and requires the cultivation of specific skills. (These are treated at length in the next action on 'Taking and making notes'. For a poetic and witty response to an academic lecture that is evidently a remorseless monologue – despite the potential playfulness of its topic – see Jacobson's 'The Post-modern Lecture', 5.3.1.)

SEMINAR This is the usual *dialogic* (two- and many-way) form of smaller group teaching and learning. The word derives from Latin *semen*, 'seed' and means a 'seed-bed' or 'sowing place', and this is still a good guide to what can go on. The aim is to nurture growth and cultivate variety: 'let a thousand flowers bloom' and produce some useful crops too. Typically the seminar is a discussion led by a lecturer/tutor, who may well have set the text and agenda too. But students may also lead with presentations or activities, help develop the agenda and provide a framework for discussion (see Action, 1.2.8). In fact the whole session may be based on tasks prepared earlier and activities undertaken in the session. Seminars usually take place in rooms where chairs and tables can be moved around: set in large circles or open squares for full group discussion ('boardroom style'); or broken down into clusters of three or four for small group discussion ('café style'). Either way, everyone can usually see everyone else's face and address them more or less directly. This is precisely what makes it *dia*logic, two- *and* many-way (the Greek prefix *dia-* means 'across', as in 'diameter' and 'diaspora' – not just 'two'). This means student–student as well as student–lecturer exchanges.

LECTURES AND *SEMINARS* (together) are usually organised so as to work and play off one another. Often they will treat the same texts and follow up similar issues in different ways: the lecture offers an exposition by one person (monologue) and the seminar invites a discussion by many (dialogue). This is a handy initial way of seeing the difference and, in effect, dividing the labour. However, it is also useful to go back to first principles and weigh what may be involved if we see lectures and seminars *together* as opportunities for various *kinds* of monologue and dialogue: to see them on a continuum and review the possibilities accordingly.

Lectures nowadays take many forms, including bouts of dialogue. They may be supported by Power-point and audio-visual, perhaps web-based, media, with copies available on the intranet; though overhead transparencies, paper hand-outs, white boards and marker-pens or even blackboards and chalk still prove serviceable and each have their own capacities. Whatever the materials used, and even (perhaps especially) with the appeal of the multi-media, the crucial issue is still the kind of interpersonal dynamic in play: how far the communication is monologic (one-way) or dialogic (two- or many-way). Lectures may therefore be interspersed with pauses for discussion with the person next to you or brief activities that feed back into the topic; and even formal lectures commonly close with question-and-answer sessions anyway. All this obviously makes lectures much less of a 'reading out' and more of a 'taking part' – in short *dialogic*.

Seminars nowadays are also often varied in form, and they may include (but should not be dominated by) bouts of monologue. At the core, still, is the essential mix of texts and talk, questions and responses, and sometimes open discussion. This may be supported or prompted by activities (readings, writings, presentations, performances) prepared beforehand or undertaken in the session itself. Sometimes (to use the most common terms) the session may involve the *whole class*; at other times it means breaking into *sub-groups* of three, four or more, or working in *pairs*; and occasionally doing things *individually*. Invariably, however, everyone comes back together to *pool* their various findings and makings in some way. So even if there is an individual or group *presentation* to the rest of the seminar, this is usually done with a view to stimulating a response and is followed by a question-and-answer session (see 1.2.8).

'Tutorials' and 'Office hours' These are the most usual forms of one-to-one, face-to-face communication between student and teacher; though sometimes the terms are used to cover one teacher and several learners and are partly interchangeable with 'seminar'. Tutorials are minimal and primary kinds of dialogue; the word comes from Latin *tutus*, meaning 'safe' or 'secure', and so ideally designates such a 'safe space' for tuition. Sometimes tutorials are scheduled in relation to a particular piece of work; sometimes they are framed as regular and more or less open *office hours*. Tutorials and office hours are rare and precious opportunities for 'live', flexible and highly nuanced exchanges *about* 'English' *in* English. For everything more than a quick query or point of information, they are far better than e-mail and, at best, are the person-to-person life-blood of the subject. They may be enriched and extended but can never be replaced by the kinds of Virtual Learning Environments treated later, in Action 5. (For a dramatic and amusing representation of an encounter between a mature student and her English tutor, see Willy Russell's *Educating Rita*, 5.3.1.)

To do immediately – and then keep on doing for all your lectures and seminars

for Lectures

◆ *Before – Read the text and think about the topic for yourself.* Get together a few ideas of your own. That way you will know what is being talked about, can be selective, and won't have to take everything at face value.

◆ *During – Set yourself to tune in and actively listen for that hour or so.* Don't let your mind wander or anyone else distract you. Take notes selectively and don't try to write everything down verbatim. Put most of your effort into understanding what is said and registering that in a few well-chosen words and phrases, whether as lists, clusters or other shapes. If there is a printed hand-out, supplement it with your comments.

◆ *After – Immediately after*, try to gather your thoughts and impressions on your own for a few minutes or through talking with others who were there. (Dashing straight off to do something else dissipates most of the immediate value.) *Later on*, return to your notes to (i) check they are clear and still make sense; (ii) add extra thoughts and comments that have occurred to you since. Pop them in the relevant folder or type them up in the relevant computer file the same day.

for Seminars

♦ *Before – Check the topic, read the text and at least some of the recommended reading.* This is even more important for seminars than lectures so that you can take part. Otherwise you risk being embarrassed and may take the easy (but lazy) way out and not turn up at all.

♦ *During – Promise yourself to do three things:* (i) *speak at least once* so as to voice your own view of the text or topic, preferably early on to get yourself going; (ii) *support someone else* in developing what they have to say; (iii) *listen attentively* to what everyone has to say, paying particular attention to those who seem prepared and committed.

♦ *After – Immediately after*, go along with those who want to carry on the discussion. *Later on*, think over and write up any notes you took and materials you looked at. Seminar notes should be few and brief, so will need unpacking and filling out.

Also see: Taking and making notes (Action 3); Giving a presentation (Action 8); and in Part Four: **Speech, conversation and dialogue;** also @ 4 **Addresser, address, addressee.**

READING: Stott, Young and Bryan 2001; Green 2009: 68–111; Knights and Thurgar-Dawson 2008: 75–96.

1.2.3   Taking and making notes

> Dialogue, active response, is always a matter of another's language in one's own words.
>
> Mikhail Bakhtin, *The Dialogic Imagination* (1981)

A great deal of what you will write while doing English is 'notes' – in lectures and seminars, from books and articles and the web, on paper or cards or on screen, on coloured post-its or in the margins of your own books. Clearly, then, it is well worth reflecting on the kinds of thing this may involve. It will help to begin with a handy distinction between *taking* and *making* notes:

♦ *Taking notes* is about recording other people's words exactly as you *find* them – *transferring* their words to your page or screen so as to be able to retrieve them.

♦ *Making notes* is about registering the sense you *make* of other people's words – *transforming* them into your own terms so as to help develop your own ideas.

Obviously the two processes are closely connected. We may *take* notes from a book or website and then *make* notes with a view to turning them into an essay or presentation. Indeed, we often do this so quickly that, in the heat of the moment, we become unaware which are other people's words and which are our own. This is especially so afterwards when returning cold to what we have written. The thing about taking and making notes when studying is that you *must* be aware of the difference and *must* mark it clearly. Otherwise, whether accidentally or not, you run the risk of presenting someone else's words as your own and may be found guilty of plagiarism – which can lead to failing a whole course. Detailed guidance on full referencing and avoiding plagiarism is supplied in Action 6 (1.2.6). Here it is sufficient to underscore a simple procedure for observing the one and avoiding the other: *Note what you take in 'quotation marks' and take a note of where it came from.*

A simple and effective way of doing this on paper is to have a fold or imaginary line down the middle of the page. Everything to the left is 'someone else's words' and ideas; everything to the right is your own words and ideas in response; and the reference goes across the middle. Another way is to use different coloured pens when hand-writing or different fonts when word-processing. But whatever system you use, the distinction needs to be clearly and consistently made till it becomes virtually automatic when writing and visually obvious when reading.

But there are more positive reasons for maintaining the distinction – and exploring the connection – between taking notes and making notes than just avoiding cheating. Deploying notes in these ways gives visible shape to the kind of critical and creative dialogue we are routinely engaged in when turning a reading into a writing. *Taking* what we find, we can clearly see how we *make* it into something else. The following diagram (organised visually as a kind of sliding 'z') will help confirm both the distinction and connection between the two processes:

TAKE notes to	Record	Retrieve	Revise
		. . . Reflect	
		Explicate	
		Criticise	
	Sketch		
	Design		
MAKE notes to	Explore	Experiment	Create . . .

Because notes have so many functions they can assume a wide variety of forms. Again these exist on a sliding scale, and in reality they constantly flow back and forth. But at the extremes it is helpful to think of notes that are *informative* (and more or less 'orderly') and *imaginative* (and more or less 'chaotic').

- *Informative notes* tend to be 'orderly', stacked across and down the page in lists. They are at the 'taking notes' end of things and are readily retrievable.
- *Imaginative notes* tend to be chaotic – in clusters and all over the place. They are at the 'making notes' end of things and are openly experimental.

Examples of both kinds of notes can be found in the actions that follow; for they correspond to various kinds of reading (Action 4) as well as various kinds of writing. (There are also some examples @ 1.2.3.) The important thing with your own note-taking and -making is to ask yourself when you are doing the one rather than the other – or, more dynamically, when you had better move from one to another. For English depends upon imagination as well as information. If you spend all your time taking notes from other writers you will have no time to make anything of them yourself. Conversely, if you try to make it all up from your own head, without finding out things and what others have already thought and said, then whatever you write is likely to be thin in texture and limited in outlook as well as insight. The following tips – if acted on – will help you take and make the best of all worlds, through other people's words as well as your own.

To do immediately . . .
- *Start **taking** notes and **making** notes from books and lectures so that the two are clearly distinguished.* Try the folded-paper, line-down-the-middle method. Put 'other people's words' (in quotation marks) and their ideas to the left and your own comments and ideas to the right, and put a full reference across the middle. *See* the shape of the dialogue.

- *Next time you are doing some notes, decide whether you need to be doing* **informative** *('orderly') notes or* **imaginative** *('chaotic') notes.* That is, ask yourself whether you are taking notes to record and retrieve information, making notes to explore and experiment, or a mixture. Change the form – the look and feel – of your notes accordingly.
- *Use various levels and layers of notes to* **analyse a short text.** For example, take a copy of the text and fill the margins with notes attached to individual words, phrases and structures (see the examples in 2.1). Corresponding things can be done with computers using different windows and multiple versions.

Also see: Actions 4–9, where many different kinds of note are illustrated, and @ 1.2.3 for further examples and discussion. Action 6 treats the scholarly use of foot- and end-notes. For critical-analytical notes around a short text, see 2.1; for illustration of primarily informative annotation, here footnotes, see 2.2; and for some of the many shapes of exploratory as well as expository notes, see 2.3.

READING: Carroll *et al.* 2010; Crook in Stott, Snaith and Rylance 2001: 76–94; Young 2008: 88–105; Childs 2008: 89–94; Green 2009: 109–10, 178–81.

1.2.4   Close reading – wide reading

> Reading means approaching something that is just coming into being.
>
> Italo Calvino, *If on a Winter's Night a Traveller* (1979)

Reading closely and reading widely might seem to be contradictory activities but in fact they are wholly complementary. You have to do both to be a 'good' (informed, insightful) reader. Wide reading is essential so that you can relate the particular text in hand to other texts in mind and to its context. A sonnet or a science fiction novel is strange indeed till you have read a few; then you recognise that they tend to assume particular forms and are conventionally concerned with, respectively, formalised love from a male point of view and technologised humanity at some point in the future. Exceptions and variants then stand out. Close reading is essential so that you can grasp the specific poem, novel, play, essay or whatever in and on its own terms, as specific choices and combinations of 'words on the page'. With a particular sonnet you may then be struck by divergence from or variation within the conventional fourteen-line structure, the fact that some are not concerned with love at all but with God or nature or the nature of writing, and that many are written by women (see 5.1.2 for examples). Similarly, with a particular work of science fiction, you may become aware that it is only marginally concerned with machines and that it is set at some indeterminate point in time (see 5.2.4 for examples).

The crucial thing, then, is to keep moving between close and wide reading, and to do so more or less consciously, as the need arises. It's like deciding to look through different lenses for different purposes: microscope for fine detail, telescope for scanning from a distance; or like shifting and switching between close-ups and wide-angle shots in film. A particularly suggestive analogy is the kind of computerised mapping now available on the web. You can zoom in or out from global to local views and back again; the choice of scale and focus depends on what you are interested in and where you want to go. (See 'Mapping journeys' (5.4.2) for some very different perspectives on the London Underground.) In any event, strategically and tactically, the trick is to know when and where to gradually shift or suddenly switch from one perspective to another – and then back again or to yet another. Fully grasped, reading creatively as well as critically, it's never simply a matter of 'close' *or* 'wide' reading but of many and various and moving readings. We concentrate on close reading first because that, quite rightly, is where most people start: text in hand or words on the screen. This is also, historically and pedagogically, where much of the subject has been grounded. Close attention to 'words on the page' and verbal 'devices' and rhetorical 'effects' is the enduring legacy both of Practical and New Critical and of Formalist approaches (see 3.2–3), and these still inform some of the best practices of close reading in class. (The suspension dots are a reminder that this naturally leads on to other ways of writing as well as reading.)

CLOSE READING . . .

Here is a close reading strategy that can be adapted for any text you meet. It consists of four opening moves and six core questions, and is explained at greater length in **Initial analysis: how to approach a text** (2.1). There it is fleshed out theoretically and demonstrated in action with examples of poetry, prose fiction, drama and literary criticism; here it is stripped down to essentials and offers a point of ready reference when confronted by a piece of text and the need to analyse it closely. This is, however, a recipe for close – not closed – readings.

Opening moves

1   Say what you first *notice* about the text – something that for you stands out.
2   Now look for a *pattern* – something that repeats or is similar.
3   Then look for a *contrast* – something that varies or is different.
4   Gauge the initial *feeling* – how, overall, it makes you feel, think, respond.

Core questions

◆   WHAT, basically, is it *about*? Try to say this in a phrase or two to begin with, and then a full sentence.
◆   WHAT *kind* of text is it? Think of how you would categorise it (poetry, novel, play . . . of what kind), and perhaps some other texts it reminds you of.
◆   WHO is *addressing* WHOM – 'inside' and 'outside' the text, directly or indirectly? Consider a range between 'internal' narrator and characters and 'external' author and reader.
◆   WHERE and WHEN is the text located in *place* and *time*? Again distinguish between the 'internal' times and places represented within the text and (as far as you know or can guess) the 'external' times and places of when and where it was written or produced.
◆   HOW precisely is it *done*? Consider this at every level of language from the most localised features of sound or punctuation, through the kinds of word used, and phrasing and sentences, to pervasive matters of speech, narrative and imagery, and how the text hangs together – or falls apart – as a whole. (For a detailed list, see 2.2.1.)
◆   WHY do you think it was *written* – and why do you *respond* as you do? This is to begin engaging with more complex and contentious matters of motivation, function and value. And finally, or if you wish, from the first . . .
◆   WHAT IF the text were *changed* – in some way *similar yet different*? Perhaps written from a different point of view? Written in a style (colloquial, formal, technical) with which you are more familiar? Updated or done in the manner, and with the matter, of another author or period? Adapted for another genre or medium (e.g. poetry as prose; novel as play or film, or any of them as song, feature article, TV news report, text-message, Twitter, etc.).

This may appear a lot to do, and certainly close reading is very demanding. But it should be observed that the strategy is open to improvisation and easy to remember. It all basically comes down to four opening moves and half a dozen questions:

Notice, Pattern, Contrast, Feeling!
What? Who? When? Where? How? Why? and *What if?*

(Turn to 2.1 for some very various applications of this method to a poem, piece of prose, play script and critical essay.)

. . . WIDE READING

What follow are a couple of frameworks for connecting close reading to kinds of wide reading. Both feature Emily Brontë's *Wuthering Heights* (see 2.2.3); but the principles apply to any author and text. The first framework is relatively simple but robust and serviceable. Graphically, it takes the form of a triangle and relates close reading of the words on the page (text in itself) to other texts (intertextually) and to its locations in time and place (contexts). The double arrows are a reminder to keep moving from text to context and from the text in hand to others in mind (in the library, on the web).

Close reading Textually
(the text in itself)
e.g. Emily Brontë's, *Wuthering Heights*
editions: Penguin (1995); Norton (2003)

Wide reading Intertextually
(the text and other texts)
e.g. Emily Brontë's *Poems* (1850)
Kate Bush's song and video, 'Wuthering Heights' (1978)
films: dir. Wyler (1939); dir. Kosminsky (1992)

Wide reading Contextually
(the text in time, place and culture)
e.g. Charlotte Brontë's Preface & Biographical
Notice 1850.
Terry Eagleton, *Myths of Power: A Marxist
Study of the Brontës* (1975)
Elaine Showalter, *A Literature of Their Own* (1977)

Figure 1.1   A Text–Context–Intertext triangle

This model shows how close reading of the *text* in itself (here *Wuthering Heights*) may be widened by taking on board related *intertexts* (say, Emily Brontë's *Poems* or Kate Bush's song, or one of the films) and be widened another way by reading about aspects of the novel's *context* (here represented by Charlotte's 'Preface' and 'Biographical Notice' of her sisters, a couple of classic Marxist and Feminist studies featuring the novel and novelist). This model of reading is most suitable when conducting a tightly 'text-centred' study, often with a set text or essay question.

The second model for relating close to wide reading is much more open, plural and dynamic (see Figure 1.2). It includes many points of reference (only some of which are directly to do with Emily Brontë or *Wuthering Heights*) and it is especially useful when opening up lines of enquiry and framing a longer, more 'independent' project. This approach is *open* in that it is not bounded and can in principle be infinitely extended; *plural* in that each of its aspects is not defined by a single point but a number of layers or levels; and has distinct *patterns* depending upon which configuration is preferred. In short, it could lead to and enable not just 'wide' but also *deep* and *moving* and *timely readings*. What's more, these 'readings' naturally lead on to writings

. . . yet others   yet others . . .

other songs and videos by Kate Bush;   other texts that might be selected, ' set'
films directed by Wyler, featuring Olivier   and centred, e.g. Brontë's *Jane Eyre*;
                                                                  Dickens's *Bleak House*; Byron's *Manfred*

INTERTEXT(S)   TEXT(S)
e.g. Kate Bush song and video   *Wuthering Heights*, written 1831–46, published
films, graphic novels . . .   variously before and after death: 1846, 1850

other individual readers (she, he)   other individual writers (e.g. Charlotte, Anne;
and communities of readers, academic, popular (them)   Byron, Dickens) and communities of writer/artist
                                                 (Romantic, Victorian, 19th–c.)

<<< READER(S)   WRITER(S) >>>
you, me (insert names and dates)   Emily Brontë

. . . future CONTEXT(S) 'here & now'   <<< moments between >>>   CONTEXT(S) 'there & then' earlier contexts . . .
e.g. immediate course, class, essay question,   Yorkshire (scene), London (publication),
culture and technology: web, film, music . . .   Germany (writing)

Figure 1.2 Openly plural patterns
(Wide and deep and moving and timely readings 3, 4, 5, . . . n)

and speakings and other kinds of reproduction: from student essay and presentation to hypothetical or actual adaptations, continuations and translations of all kinds. This is an overtly active and creative aspect of 'reading' already picked up in the approach to close reading through 'What if . . . ?'. It is here reinforced by the express recognition of *Reader(s)* (singular and plural) as potentially primary agents in – not merely passive recipients of – the reading process. In fact, as signalled at the outset of this section, it is precisely the capacity of the individual reader to decide on the precise scale, pace and purpose of reading that proves decisive in this whole activity. For it is you (I, we, he, she, they) who decide whether the reading will be 'close' or 'wide' in the first place, and when, where, how and why it will move from one to the other along the way.

Crucially, therefore, there is no pre-given centre in the above 'Openly Plural Patterns' approach to reading. It deals, so to speak, with 'fluid' rather than 'set' texts, and the centre of textual–contextual–intertextual attention is something you have to arrive at or create for yourself. For example, you could explore a 'triangle' (triangulate), an area of issues defined primarily by Reader (you) – Intertext (Kate Bush) – Context ('Here and now'). This would produce a broadly Contemporary/Popular/Cultural/Media studies construction of its object as both subject and project. Alternatively you could explore another triangle defined by Writer (Emily B) – Context (there and then) – Other writers (Charlotte and Anne); this would produce a Literary Historical/(Auto)Biographical/Heritage construction of its object–subject–project. (Constructions of English on variously linguistic, literary and cultural lines are picked up in 1.3.)

Finally, it is important to note that, in terms of substance, much of the above information on and around Emily Brontë's *Wuthering Heights* draws on a small yet reliable and readily available body of materials. Basically these comprise a good edition of the text, some standard reference books and anthologies, and a couple of authoritative sites on the web. These are what, in the next section (Action 5), are called a 'home base': the basic sources and resources around which visits to the library and the web are organised. For those are the actual and virtual spaces where close readings become wide and are enriched accordingly (see 'Poetry +', Prose fiction +', etc.; 2.2). Before pressing further, however, it is important to clinch the business of the present action.

To do immediately . . .

- *Learn and get used to using the 'Close reading' formulae*: the suggestions **Notice, Pattern, Contrast, Feeling!** and the questions **What, Who, When, Where, How, Why and What if?** See how these are used with the pages of poetry, prose fiction, play script and literary criticism in 2.1. Try them out on some pieces of text you already know well or are currently studying. Then try them with some you perhaps haven't seen before.

- *Do a basic 'Wide reading' diagram for a text you are studying.* Use the 'Text–Context–Intertext Triangle' and get used to thinking and reading in these terms whenever you have a set text to situate and explore.

- *Sketch the beginnings of an 'Openly Plural Pattern' relating to a text, author, topic or area in which you are interested.* Then decide on two very different configurations you could foreground against the background you have established. Get used to thinking and reading in these terms whenever you have some lines of enquiry you would like to open up.

- *Keep a reading journal.* Make brief notes on what you have read and how you responded at the beginning, and list some things you would like to read and why at the end. This maintains a sense of reading as an unfolding adventure.

- *Don't forget to read 'wildly' as well as widely!* Browsing in book shops, junk shops, on friends' shelves – as well as in the library or on the web – is also an essential part of the mix. This makes for unforeseen yet suggestive connections, re-combinations and extensions, and it helps keep ideas fresh and challenging. It will keep 'English and you' at the edge: pushing the limits as well as consolidating the cores.

Also see: Prelude: Texts in context, literature in history. Part Two: Critical and Creative strategies for analysis and interpretation. Part Three: WORDS ON THE PAGE – PRACTICAL CRITICISM AND (OLD) NEW CRITICISM (3.2); DEVICES AND EFFECTS – FORMALISM INTO FUNCTIONALISM (3.3); **Part Four: Text, context and intertextuality**. A further 'text-centred Square' appears @ 1.2.4.

READING: McCaw 2008: 24–63; Montgomery *et al.* 2007: 7–54; Scholes 2004; Bartholomae and Petrosky 1999.

1.2.5   Library, web, 'home' – an ongoing cycle

> The Library of Babel is a sphere whose exact centre is anywhere within, and whose circumference is everywhere beyond.
>
> Adapted from Jorge Luis Borges, 'The Library of Babel' (1941)

For some students nowadays, the first (perhaps the only) port of call when trying to find out about something is the web. At worst they simply type the words into their general search engine (perhaps Google or straight to Wikipedia) and produce page upon page of more or less similar stuff, most of it useless because repetitive and of uncertain quality and authority. Rather better, they use something more selective like 'Google Scholar'; but the scope is vast and the categories large. Much better, they use one of the dedicated websites listed below or recommended by their lecturers. These will obviously be much more relevant, authoritative and of good quality. But even that is not necessarily to start in the right place.

The best place to start – obvious though it may sound – is with the texts you are studying and the course you are studying them on. To be precise, you should begin with your initial response to a particular text (as sketched in your notes and refined by close reading; see the previous two *actions*) and with the reasons you are studying it (as set out in the course description and developed in lectures and seminars). You start with these things because they are most immediately what you need to know about. It is then some specific task (whether essay question, analysis, presentation or project) that forces you actively to explore that knowledge and make sense of things, for yourself but not on your own. The combination *'text + response'* and *'course + task'* is what establishes your initial bearings in a territory as on a kind of map. These are the basic coordinates of what is here called 'home base' or simply *home*, and they ensure that while you may sometimes feel anxious you need not feel lost. *Home* is where you start your search even before you start your re-search. That is why *HOME* is in pride of place at the apex of the following diagram. Below it and to either side are the two other 'spaces', both actual and virtual that you need to engage with in the course of study: *LIBRARY* and *WEB*. The lists attached to each are worth pondering, as are the interrelations amongst all three and their relation to yourself:

'HOME'
Set texts (scholarly editions)
Close reading and notes
Course description—aims and schedule
Agenda and atmosphere of lectures and seminars
Specific task (question project)
Core personal reference books, anthologies, etc.
Regular bookmarked websites

ACTUAL / VIRTUAL

LIBRARY
Reference section
Author section
Literary Linguistic History
Cultural and Critical Theory
Other subjects

WEB
Recommended websites
General approved gateways
Sites specific to topic
Specialist application
Random search

LIBRARY obviously means books, journals and CDs, while *WEB* basically means websites and other Internet resources. But the two are increasingly interdependent. You can use specialist catalogue and search facilities from within a library and download articles wherever you are; and a web search may lead you to get hold of a book and consult or print off an article. Hence the two-way arrows on all sides with an 'Actual/Virtual' interface at the core. You may even have a Virtual Learning Environment (VLE) which supports lectures and seminars on the intranet, much as the present book is supplemented by a site on the Internet. It is therefore as much the connection as the distinction between actual printed and virtually accessible resources that will be explored here. Further, whatever the medium in play, you are urged to keep on returning *'HOME'*: to constantly remind yourself of the particular text featured and topic assigned ('text + response' and 'course + task').

What follow are lists of the *kinds* of general resource identified with each of the three study 'spaces': Home, Library, Web. (Some extended examples relating to a specific author and text – William Blake's 'London', featured in 2.1.3 and 2.2.2 – can be found @ 1.2.6.)

HOME will typically be made up of:

♦   *A good edition of the text you are studying.* Many editions of standard texts – such as those published by Norton, Bedford, Penguin, Broadview, Longman, Routledge and some university presses – include introduction and notes and sometimes samples of criticism. These give you the best platform for further study.

- *A comprehensive Guide or Companion to English Literature and/or English Language.* Standard examples, frequently revised and updated, are: *The Cambridge Guide to Literature in English*, ed. Dominic Head; *The Oxford Companion to English Literature*, ed. Margaret Drabble; *The Oxford Companion to the English Language*, ed. Tom McArthur, along with standard Histories of Language and Literature referred to on p. 31. These are invaluable for quick and authoritative reference, and fascinating just to dip into and browse around.

- *A good dictionary of English including etymologies and, if possible, historical examples.* This will help you grasp the full range of possible meanings of words, now and in the past, and gauge the precise senses in play at the time of a particular author or text. There are concise single-volume and fuller two-volume editions of the Oxford English, Webster's American and the Macquarie Australian Dictionaries suitable for desk use (avoid the 'Little' and 'Pocket' versions for study purposes). What's more, even from 'home', if you have an Internet link you may be able to get direct access via a university library site to the very fullest version of the *Oxford English Dictionary* (OED) or one of the current corpora of World Englishes: the *Cambridge International Corpus* (CIC) or the *Vienna and Oxford International Corpus of English* (VOICE). Desks are prodigiously extendable through virtual 'desk-tops' nowadays.

- *A couple of the big anthologies in your areas of study*, again for both concerted reading and general browsing. Particularly capacious, frequently updated and in various formats are the *Norton Anthologies of . . . English Literature, American Literature, African American Literature* and *Theory and Criticism*; but there are many other anthologies organised by genre, period, area and theoretical position or critical approach published by Arnold, Blackwell, Broadview, Continuum, Heath, Heinemann, Palgrave, Riverside, Routledge and Open University, Oxford and other university presses.

- *A short dictionary or big encyclopaedia of critical terms.* A couple of my personal favourites amongst the latter are *The Princeton Encyclopedia of Poetry and Poetics* and *The Toronto Encyclopaedia of Contemporary Literary Theory*; but there are many shorter dictionaries of critical terms produced by, say, Penguin, Oxford and Yale that are handy for quick reference. With all or any of these, it is less important to get the latest edition than to use what you have regularly and resourcefully. That means using the Index as well as the Contents pages, and sometimes following your nose rather than the pack.

LIBRARY is an actual place (one of many libraries, general and specialist) you should get used to visiting and browsing as well as searching by catalogue. For often it is the book next to the ones you are looking for (which may not be there anyway) that proves most illuminating. So, along with the general sections for English Literature and English Language – and American and Australian and African and Asian . . . – get used to visiting or sitting in Journals / Periodicals. (The latter may be increasingly available electronically on such systems as JSTOR; but handling some of the paper formats still gives a more direct 'feel' for the communities involved.) Meanwhile, be prepared to go to and check out what's on the shelves in, for example, Art, Drama, Performance, Education, Media, Music, History, Politics, Psychology, Sociology, Ecology, Environmentalism (see 6.2.1. for a fuller array of subjects closely related to English).

WEB
General websites and gateways well worth 'book-marking' and returning to are:

- English Subject Centre, http://www.english.heacademy.ac.uk
- *Contemporary Writers* (British Council), http://www.contemporarywriters.com

- *Intute* (Arts and Humanities: English) http://intute.ac.uk/artsandhumanities/english/ [Resources and tutorials for English Studies].
- *Literary Encyclopedia,* http://www.litencyc.com [Profiles of authors, texts and topics with debates].
- *Literary Resources on the Net,* http://andromeda.rutgers.edu/~jlynch/Lit/ [Gateway to sites on English and American Literature for Higher Education].
- *Project Muse,* http://muse.jhu.edu/ [Large online journals collection with other humanities-wide resources].
- *Voice of the Shuttle,* http://vos.ucsb.edu/ [Comprehensive database for Arts and Humanities].
- *Jstor,* http://www.jstor.org [A large collection of online journal articles to which many institutions subscribe, searchable by discipline, title, author and subject].
- Lexis Nexis, http://www.lexisnexis.co.uk/ [Searchable database for newspaper and magazine materials].
- Online bibliographies: Annotated Bibliography of English Studies, http://abe.informaworld.com; Modern Languages Association, http://collections.chadwyck.co.uk.

Clearly, the resources available for the study of English nowadays are potentially prodigious. And for that reason they may be awfully overwhelming as well as awesomely inspiring. Pragmatically, however, the crucial thing is to recognise that there are indeed distinct yet connected *kinds* of resource at your disposal. There is also a simple yet highly effective cycle that you must go through every time you have a text to study or a task to prepare. In outline it is just a triangle made up of three terms:

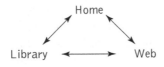

But in principle it is a powerful model for connecting yourself and your subject to the wider (and deeper and infinitely various) worlds of reading and research. And with practice it can become the kind of 'second nature' that enhances and extends your 'first nature' – who and what you were before you started really studying. 'Home', it turns out, is constantly changing and never the same again.

To do immediately . . .

- *Begin to build a 'home base' of your own* – set texts in good editions and a few reference books and big anthologies. Get to know them well by using them often.
- *Go to the library to gather good books about you.* Try this as an experiment. Choose a well-known author or book that you are studying. Using the catalogue, a map of the library and your nose, set out to gather a relevant example of each of the following: (i) another edition of a book you are studying; (ii) another book by the same author; (iii) an entry in a reference book; (iv) a chapter in a book of criticism; (v) a related journal article; (vi) a book by another author at the time; (vii) a book on a related topic from a quite different section of the library. (You may not get examples of all but you will get some.) Spread everything out in front of you. Look at the Contents and Index pages. Flick through and get a feel for the books and journals. There is never everything you need or are looking for in a library. But there is usually more than enough and far different from what you expected.
- *Go to the web through the recommended websites.* Try this as another experiment. Choose a well-known text or author you are studying (the same as previously or a different one). *Don't*

just tap the words into Google or similar but *do* go through some of the recommended websites (those above or recommended by your tutor). See if you can find: (i) a reliable text; (ii) a facsimile of a manuscript or first edition; (iii) a short biography; (iv) a piece of critical writing that interests you; (v) an article from a journal (ditto); (vi) some relevant images and perhaps a reading/ performance. 'Bookmark' or take a note of the sites and 'pages' you visited adding today's date. (The challenge here is *not* to do a random search from scratch.)

♦   *Go through the 'Home–Library–Web' cycle* at least a couple of times in any order with every substantial piece of work you have to do. Remember to start from and return 'Home'.

Also see: Getting your bearings (Action 1); Close reading – wide reading (Action 4); and for more research-related activity, 'Longer projects: lines of enquiry and sample study patterns' (2.3); also @ 1.2.5 for further illustration and examples.

READING: Childs 2008 and Eaglestone 2009 are excellent on sources and resources for the beginning student. Also see Green 2009: 112–28; 175–89 and, for more advanced search methods and research methodologies, Griffin 2005.

1.2.6   Taking responsibility: referencing and plagiarism

[T]hese named meanings are swept towards other names; names call to each other, reassemble, and their groupings call for further naming.

Roland Barthes, *S/Z* (1975)

Good academic writing is neither wholly *dependent* on other people's work (that would make it utterly derivative or mere copying) nor is it wholly *independent* of other people's work (that would make it out of touch and uninformed). Rather, it is richly *interdependent*: it acknowledges what has been done previously by others *and* offers to do something fresh in its own right. Both aspects are essential for a vital academic community. Put another way, the good academic writer is both *responsive* and *responsible*: responsive to others and responsible for themselves. This is what is here meant by 'taking responsibility'. For obviously a great deal – but far from all – of what each of us knows we get to know through other people. So *ac*knowledging the interdependent nature of knowledge is a natural and necessary part of the study process. That is why every formal piece of academic work submitted for assessment is accompanied by some such claim – and disclaimer – as the following:

I hereby certify that this is all my own work and that all sources are fully acknowledged and accurately referenced.

'All my own work' is the claim to independence; 'all sources are fully acknowledged and referenced' is the acknowledgement of dependence. Together, the whole thing adds up to what may be called *a declaration of interdependence*. Linguistically, this kind of statement is known as a performative and, like saying 'I solemnly swear . . .' in a court of law or 'I hereby promise . . .' on a contract, it is meant to do what it says and be legally binding. It also ('hereby') locks the speaker or writer into a specific situation. And that is why such statements are formally sworn or signed and identified with a particular time, place and purpose (in academic work a specific task and course). In fact, when filled in, such an academic declaration of interdependence has all the essential elements of a book reference (Name, *Title*, Place and Date) and is clinched by the addition of a signature. By that mark you both claim what you know and disclaim what you didn't, while also staking your claim to be 'marked' (i.e. assessed) accordingly. Done properly, all this is standard academic practice and perfectly straightforward. Done improperly, it's sloppy scholarship or downright cheating. We return to the latter shortly, with some simple advice on avoiding plagiarism. Before that, however – so as to forestall the problem entirely – there are some essential guidelines on quoting and referencing. Get used to following these and you need never worry about being called either a sloppy scholar or a cheat.

The first thing is to recall the crucial distinction already introduced when **Taking and making notes** (Action 3): between presenting 'other people's words' (within inverted commas) and presenting your own words (without). The point at issue is precisely the distinction between *taking down* what someone else says in a lecture or wrote in a book and *making it up* in your own terms. In this respect, quoting and referencing properly all begin with good notes. If you don't show who said or wrote or thought at that stage, you can hardly know later when it comes to writing things up. At that point, at the writing stage, it's then pretty straightforward. There are basically two ways of presenting *quotation* from other people's work:

1   *Put quotation marks round shorter passages and phrases* that you include in the sentences within the main body of your argument.

2   *Indent longer passages separately* so that they are clearly set apart – and therefore do not need quotation marks too. (Anything over twenty-odd words of prose tends to count as long; even a couple of lines from poetry and plays may get indented.)

(For examples of both, see the page of the critical essay in 2.2.5; also @ 1.2.6.)

The next thing is to choose one of the systems of *referencing* to record your sources. There are two main systems for writing down the bibliographic details of a book (to take the simplest example), and they chiefly differ in the placing of the date. For example, here is that critical book (2.2.5) referenced according to the system of the *Modern Humanities Research Association (MHRA)*, where the date appears towards the end of the entry. (The scheme is modelled more abstractly below):

Childs, Peter, *Reading Fiction: Opening the Text* (London: Palgrave, 2001) pp. 124–5.
Surname, First name, *Title in Italics or Underlined* (Place: Publisher, Date) page numbers.

And here is the same book referenced with a 'date earlier' system, in this case the *Harvard* system used in the book you are reading (again modelled below):

Childs, P. (2001) *Reading Fiction: Opening the Text*. London: Palgrave. pp. 124–5.
Surname, Initial. (Date) *Title in Italics or Underlined*. Place: Publisher. page numbers.

Whichever referencing system you use, the main thing is to recognise the essential simplicity of its principles. Despite all the profusion and apparent confusion of detail, it will identify person, title, place, publisher and page references; the only main difference will be in the placing of the date – towards the end or the beginning. For the rest, it's a matter of punctuation: whether there's a bracket, a comma or a full stop and so forth. So the only thing you have got to do is to *choose one system and stick to it*. Put slightly more formally, *be clear, consistent and accurate*. (Some departments insist on a particular referencing system, just as most publishers have a particular house style.)

Below is a full range of all the kinds of reference – to edited volumes, journals, websites, films and so forth – that you are likely to come across and use in English Studies. Return to this list whenever you have some referencing of your own to do. Don't be put off by all the pernickety detail – the underlying principle is simple. But do get it right and, to repeat, be clear, consistent and accurate. All the examples that follow again relate directly to the critical essay by Peter Childs (2.2.5) or more generally to its subject, Emily Brontë's *Wuthering Heights* (featured in 2.2.3). They are set out as in a full *Bibliography* (the kind that you put at the end of a formal essay): in alphabetical order by surname. The particular system shown here is that of the *Modern Humanities Research Association* (MHRA), in this case with the date towards the end. (That of the *Modern Language Association* (MLA) is slightly different; but further information on both systems is supplied at the end of this action.)

Bakhtin, Mikhail, *The Dialogic Imagination: Four Essays*, ed. M. Holquist, trans. C. Emerson and M. Holquist (Austin: University of Texas Press, 1981).

Brontë, Charlotte, 'Preface' and 'Biographical Notice of Ellis and Acton Bell' [1850] in Brontë, E. 2003), pp. 307–16.

Brontë, Emily, *Wuthering Heights*, ed. R.J. Dunn (New York and London: Norton, [1847] 2003).

Brontë Parsonage Museum and Brontë Society, http://bronte.org.uk. Index.library (consulted 19.12.2010).

Bush, Kate, 'Wuthering Heights', *The Kick Inside*, EMI, 1978; released as single, November 1978 with different videos for UK and US.

Childs, Peter *Reading Fiction: Opening the Text* (London: Palgrave, 2001) pp. 124–5.

Kosminsky, Peter (dir.), *Emily Brontë's Wuthering Heights* (Paramount Pictures, 1992).

Lodge, David, *After Bakhtin: Essays on Fiction and Criticism* (London and New York: Routledge, 1990).

Nussbaum, Martha, '*Wuthering Heights*: The Romantic Ascent', *Philosophy and Literature*, 20, 1996, 362–82.

Oxford Text Archive (searchable text) http://ftp.sunet.se/pub/doc/etext/ota/public/english/bronte/e_wheights.1851 (consulted 02.12.10).

Tepa Lupack, Barbara (ed.), *Nineteenth-Century Classic Women at the Movies* (Bowling Green: Bowling Green State University Press, 1999).

The next thing to get straight is the way you reference things in the course of writing. While the Bibliography that appears at the end of a piece is a list of everything that you have referred to, there are also all the individual references to things as you go along. This is called *annotation* and is basically of two kinds: *in-text notes* in brackets and *out-text notes* with numbers. To be precise:

- ◆ *In-text notes* go within brackets in the main body of the text and are directly keyed to the final Bibliography (which then functions as a list of References); e.g.

  It is now virtually a critical commonplace that 'Critics habitually analyse Brontë's novel in terms of contrasts' (Childs 2001: 124).

- ◆ *Out-text notes* are numbered and refer to a *footnote* at the bottom of the page or an *end-note* at the end of the whole piece, and this note – usually in smaller font – contains full bibliographic information; e.g.

  It is now virtually a critical commonplace that 'Critics habitually analyse Brontë's novel in terms of contrasts'.[2]

  2. Peter Childs, *Reading Fiction: Opening the Text* (London: Palgrave, 2001), p. 124.

Bracketed in-text notes are minimal and strictly informative: they can feature multiple references, e.g. (Childs 2001; Bakhtin 1981), but they don't carry extra comment. They therefore encourage you to keep to the point and identify only the essential materials in the main body of your writing; but they leave no space for further explanation or qualification. Numbered foot- and end-notes can be more expansive and may include extra information or comment (e.g., adding to the above note 'Childs himself concentrates on oppositions within language and takes his cue from Bakhtin as explicated by Lodge; see Bakhtin, M. (1981) *The Dialogic Imagination: Four Essays*, ed. M. Holquist, trans. C. Emerson and M. Holquist, Austin: University of Texas Press and Lodge, D. (1990) *After Bakhtin: Essays on Fiction and Criticism*, London and New York: Routledge'). So out-text notes can open up judicious spaces to develop the fine-root structure of the argument and scholarship; but may also become an undergrowth that obscures or engulfs it. Whether you use in-text or out-text annotation partly depends upon your immediate aim and the space you have; and again your department may have a preferred system. But whichever method you use, again you should stick to just one: *be clear, consistent and accurate*. (Conversely, don't pick and mix and finish up with a hotch-potch of your own devising.)

By now the overall message about referencing should be pretty clear too. If you take and make notes properly in the first place (taking care to distinguish other people's words from your own) and if you annotate carefully as you go along, listing all the works you refer to at the end, then you will be taking full responsibility for your work. You will then be able to sign whatever claim and disclaimer you are required to make with complete confidence. You will show, and your reader will know, which are your words and which are somebody else's. Your declaration of interdependence will be complete and convincing. However, if you *don't* do all of this, it *won't* be. It's as simple – and potentially as serious – as that. So the concluding gesture in this action is by way of warning. Distinguish other people's words from your own and say where they came from . . . it will never apply to you. Don't and it will. Seriously.

ACADEMIC HEALTH WARNING
Plagiarism
is the unacknowledged use of other people's knowledge.
It involves passing off other people's words as your own
whether on purpose – cheating
or by accident – incompetence.
Either way, it can result in the failure of a particular course
or a complete programme.
(So it can spoil far more than your whole day . . .)

To do immediately . . .

- *'Do-it-yourself' experiment in referencing.* Write a few words off the top of your head about what you did last night. Give them a title and turn them into a full reference of the kind Author (you), *Title*, Place of publication (wherever you are), Publisher (make one up), the present year, p. 1 (more if you got carried away). Daft though this may sound, this has all the essential elements of a formal academic reference. Go on to sign and date it, and it will also have all the essential elements of a formal claim to authorship. This is *your* text and says so.
- *'Done-by-someone-else' example of plagiarism.* Now pass your text to someone else and ask them to either (i) write *their* name instead of yours at the beginning of your reference; or (ii) vaguely mention where the text came from but leave the general impression that they wrote it; or (iii) give you your text back without any of your details on and claim to your face that they did it. This is plagiarism and it is rude as well as wrong. Consider how someone else would feel if you did something similar with their work.
- *Re-run a version of the 'Library' and 'Web' activities in the 'To do immediately . . .' section of the previous action (Action 5).* This time fully reference an example of each kind of book, article, website or other resource used. Do this clearly, consistently and accurately using the examples in the above Bibliography as models.

♦   *Take a previous essay or project of your own.* Look at the references and annotation with a
    freshly critical (and picky) eye. Have you been (i) clear, consistent and accurate in your
    referencing; (ii) sparing (effective, efficient, resourceful) in your annotation? If you have not
    used either referencing or annotation, then consider how you could have, perhaps with wider
    reading and research (see Actions 4 and 5).

♦   *Look at some examples of annotation and Bibliography in a range of academic books, journals
    and websites* – new and old, not all of them in English Language or Literature. Notice the
    different conventions of presentation and organisation they use: in-text, foot- and end-notes,
    etc. Consider their fitness for purpose, and whether you might find some of them useful for
    your purposes.

Also see: Taking and making notes (Action 3); Read closely – read widely (Action 4); Library,
web, 'home' (Action 5); and Writing an essay (Action 7); and for discussion of 'responsibility/
responseability', see Part Four: **Writing, reading, response and rewriting**. Further discussion
and examples can be found @ 1.2.6.

READING: Carroll and Williams 2010; Green 2009: 169–73; 87–90; Young 2008; Stott *et al.* 2001;
Durant and Fabb 2005; Coyle and Peck 2001; Childs 2008: 88–94; Ringrose in Wolfreys 2011: 45–53.
For comprehensive guidance – and far more detail than you will need for some time – see the Handbooks
(frequently revised) and websites (constantly updated) of the *MHRA* (*Modern Humanities Research
Association*) and the *MLA* (*Modern Languages Association*).

1.2.7   Writing an essay to make your mark

> The word essay is significant. For Montaigne it retained its fundamental, experimental meaning:
> 'assay', 'attempt', 'test'.
>
> Graham Swift, *Making an Elephant: Writing from Within* (2009)

One way of approaching an essay is as an 'attempt', 'try-out', 'way of trying to say'; for that is
its root sense from the French *essayer*, 'to try', 'to attempt'. This is the exploratory, and in that
sense 'experimental' approach to essay-writing. It emphasises the playfully enquiring side of
essays, and its most famous early exponent, as observed by Swift above, is Michel de Montaigne
in his seriously witty volumes of *Essais* (1572–80, 1588). Another way of approaching an essay
is in terms of 'testing' or 'proving': testing a case, proving an argument and reaching a conclusion.
This relates to the now archaic and specialist sense of 'assay' meaning 'test', 'proof', 'measure',
as with an assayer of gold or gems, someone who establishes their quality and purity. This too
is an 'experimental' approach, but it involves essays/assays as proving grounds and tools for
making cases. It is the more overtly rational and impersonal side of essay-writing and its most
famous early exponent is Francis Bacon in his volumes of *Essays* (1612, 1625). Both kinds of
essay are encouraged in the approach that follows: the essay as 'try-out' and the essay as 'proof'.
For ultimately the two are complementary and may be blended and turn into one another. So
the emphasis here is on essays as 'experimental' forms of writing in the fullest and most flexible
sense. (To gauge what kinds of essay-writer you currently are – and would like to become – do
the exercise @ 1.2.7. This section also includes examples and essays by Montaigne and Bacon.)

Basic structures and strategies What follows is a freshly articulated version of the highly
serviceable *diamond* model of essay structure. The shape offers a visually memorable way of
developing the simple notion of 'beginning, middle and end': opening out from a point of
departure, through full extension of materials and argument in the middle, to gradual
convergence on a point of arrival. Each line of the diamond is elaborated below. This shows

how what may at first seem a mechanically ordered march can be realised in practice as an imaginative dance. For each essay is indeed an experiment in its own right: a fresh 'attempt' as well as a kind of lasting 'proof'. First the basic shape:

Open

State aim

Address question

Identify key words and materials

Explore main body of argument by topics

each distinct . . . 1   2   3   4   5 . . . all linked

each with its point, illustration and comment

which gradually, together, make a case to

extend/intensify materials, refine terms

re-address the question then

draw to a fresh

Close

And now the various ways you can twist, turn and play around with this shape:

Open with a 'quotation', question, provocation, image (verbal, visual) – anything that is arresting and relevant. Getting your reader engaged is crucial.

State the aim of your essay, its overall objectives and range: what it will (and will not) do.

Address the question by acknowledging its particular agenda, which you must engage with even if you are going to disagree (you can shift but must not switch the grounds).

Identify the key words: the technical and theoretical terms that may be strange but often prove less difficult than they seem once you define them, along with the 'ordinary', 'common' words that are slippery and contentious precisely because they are so widely used; **and materials:** the writers, texts, times, places involved; the basic 'who', 'what', 'when' and 'where' that lead into the more complex matters of 'why' and 'how' . . .

Explore the main body of the argument by topics. This often means one topic (point, issue, idea) per paragraph, typically cued by a *topic sentence* saying explicitly what it is and elaborated in the rest of the paragraph through . . .

Illustration from your set text and a **comment** to clinch the analysis and tie it into the argument, perhaps with reference to a critic/theorist, all of which makes each **point** . . .

Both distinct . . . 1 . . . 2a . . . 2b . . . 3 . . . 4 a/b/c . . . 5 . . . **and linked** – a various yet continuous argument supported by *sign-posting* such as 'Here we turn to . . .', 'Another aspect of . . .', 'Firstly . . . Secondly . . . Thirdly . . .', 'X would not agree . . .', 'Though the issue Y, as we now see, is much more complex than that', '. . . all of which brings us to Z'. In other words (your own) . . .

Make a case (it's your argument), **extend or intensify materials** (you can go further in as well as out) and **refine terms** (they don't mean quite – or at all – the same towards the end as they did at the beginning). You therefore need to

Re-address the question in the light and shade of your response throughout. Both it and you and the text and question will have moved in the meantime. So you can finally

Draw to a close that is **fresh** – gesturing back to but not merely repeating your opening. Because you have reached conclusions that could be prepared but not wholly predicted. Because you have approached your essay as an 'experiment' that genuinely 'tries out' as well as 'proves' something. Because your point of arrival is never – quite or at all – what you could have seen at your point of departure. Because it's *your essay*.

For an example and analysis of the opening of a critical essay, turn to **Critical essay +** (2.2.5). This will help you see such a structure and strategy in action, and also offers detailed illustration of what is meant by 'topics' and 'topic sentences', 'linking', 'sign-posting', and so forth.

For guidance on the ways in which **Taking and making notes** and **Reading closely – reading widely** relate to writing in general and essays in particular, see 1.2.3 and 1.2.4.

Library, web, 'home' (1.2.5) shows how a repeated and varied cycle of using these resources can inform a 'home base' defined in the first instance by 'course + task' (in this case, an essay question). All these preceding actions are framed so as to make full allowance for combinations of 'orderly' and 'chaotic', 'rational' and 'imaginative' approaches to study. This is especially important when seeking to maintain a balance – and tension – between the variously experimental models of essay-writing: the essay as 'try-out' and the essay as 'proof'.

For a specifically **'chaotic'** *and* **'orderly' approach to essay-planning**, see @ 1.2.7.

Re-drafting In good writing there is nearly always another stage between the first full draft and the final version that is 'polished off' for submission. (There may well be third and fourth and yet further drafts too.) The following checklist will help during the process of revising and redrafting.

◆ *Put your first draft aside for a while*, preferably for a few days, at least for a few hours. This helps you get some distance and return to it fresh as a reader of your own work, not just the writer who is embroiled in its difficulties and perhaps cannot see wood for trees.

◆ *Re-read the question* and course guidelines to remind yourself of the key terms, issues and materials you should be addressing and the main areas you are operating in.

◆ *Print out a clean copy of your essay,* read it straight through once, then read it through again, pencil in hand. Don't get hung up on detail; look for overall substance and strategy.

◆ *Sort through the big stuff.* Put a tick by parts that are good, a line through those that aren't, a query by passages you are not sure about, and some arrows back or forwards with parts that you think you should move.

◆ *Go through the elaborations of the above 'diamond' model line by line.* See if any of these will help solve the remaining problems and open up possibilities in more engaging and effective ways.

◆ *Concentrate on the core of your essay*, the main argument in the middle. Make sure you can identify 3 . . . 4 . . . 5 distinct yet connected topics. Try some 'reverse engineering': by reducing each part to a single sentence of the form 'This bit is about A and leads to B'; then the next part 'This bit is about B and leads to C', and so on. If you can do this – and A, B and C all relate to the question – then you have a good core to the essay.

◆ *Check each topic* has a reference to or quotation from your main text and a comment from you firmly tying it into the argument and the question, also perhaps a reference to another writer (critic or theorist) you agree or take issue with.

◆ *Adjust the 'sign-posting' to guide your reader through the argument*: 'Firstly . . . secondly . . . thirdly . . .', 'Another aspect of . . .', 'We now turn . . .', '. . . as we see next'.

◆ *Look again at your 'Opening' and 'Close'.* Do they really introduce and conclude what you have argued in the middle? If they seem dull or obscure or simply repetitious, look again at the suggestions for ways in and out that are more engaging. Confirm how far we have come by the end, and suggest there is more you could say.

♦ *Leave time for a final draft* to 'polish off' the whole thing . . .

'Polishing off' There are certain things you must do before considering your essay 'finished' and ready for submission. They affect the overall look and feel of your text: its *texture* and *authority*. It is called 'polishing' and is the last stage of 'polishing off'. Your whole attention at this stage should be on the anticipated effect on your reader. Once your work leaves your hands it ceases to be a piece of writing and becomes a piece of reading. Polish it off with this thought firmly in mind.

Mechanically and visibly – almost at a glance – will the reader see:

♦ enough variety and visible shape in the overall *lay out* of the pages?

♦ clear and consistent *paragraphing*?

♦ *sentences* of varied length and complexity, and questions as well as statements?

♦ fully indented text for *longer quotation*, and quotation marks round *shorter quotation* in the body of the text?

♦ some Names, *Titles* and Dates (proper nouns, typically with capital letters) to suggest you are being specific and grounding your observations in the world of scholarship beyond?

♦ *annotation* that is sparing but sufficient, whether '*in-text*' *(*in brackets) or '*out-text*' (numbered foot- or *end-notes*)?

♦ *referencing* that is full, clear, accurate and consistent, and gathered at the end in a specific *References* section or full *Bibliography*?

♦ evidence of careful *proof-reading* – not just automatic 'spell-checking' – to pick up spellings, punctuation and grammar the latter will miss?

♦ *numbering* of all of your pages, and all of them there?

♦ *a cover sheet* (as required) including your name, student number, title of course and assignment, date, word-length and the crucial (and true) claim that this is all your own work and that all sources are fully acknowledged?

If all these things are done, then your reader will see them. If they are not, then they won't. It's as simple as that.

To do immediately . . .

♦ *Would you like to be more of a 'Try-out' or 'Proof' kind of essay-writer – or what?* To help gauge what kinds of essay-writer you are – and would like to become – use the diagnostic framework @ 1.2.7. Then decide on a couple of practical things you could do to become better at writing essays.

♦ *Try out the 'essay-diamond' and its variants* next time you are *drafting* an essay; and go on to use the checklist for *re-drafting* when you are trying to get it into better shape. Gradually move from thinking of yourself as the writer to someone else as the reader.

♦ *Go through the 'Polishing off' check-list* before you submit your next essay.

♦ *Try planning further essays using a combination of 'chaotic' and 'orderly' approaches.* A simple yet astonishing activity involving two sides of a single sheet of paper and two kinds of fold can be found @ 1.2.7.

Also see: Critical essay + (2.2.5) and Taking responsibility: referencing and plagiarism (1.2.6). For examples of essays by Montaigne and Bacon, see @ 5.2.1.

READING: Fabb and Durant 2005; Peck and Coyle 2005; Young 2008: 79–120; Stott, Snaith and Rylance 2001. Advanced: Sharples 1999; Kress 2003.

1.2.8   Giving a presentation, stimulating a response

> Word is a two-sided act . . . It is precisely the product of the reciprocal relation between speaker and listener.
>
> V. Voloshinov, *Marxism and the Philosophy of Language* ([1930] 1973)

You will almost certainly have to do some live presentations as part of your programmes, individually or as part of a group. Many people find this daunting though it can be invigorating too. This action is designed to help you present yourself and your materials effectively and enjoyably: to get over initial nervousness, avoid the common pitfalls, and come out feeling you have informed and stimulated your audience, not bludgeoned or bored them to death. The initial emphasis is upon individual presentation; extra tips for when presenting as a group are offered later. The particular dynamics of presentations and interviews for jobs are picked up later in the book (6.4).

Shocking to some and cheering to most – though it should surprise no one – this action is premised on the observation that simply reading from a script, word-for-word, with head down and without eye contact, is dull and boring. The core appeal of a live, face-to-face presentation is precisely that: it depends upon an immediate living encounter and a live response; all the faces and bodies are actually present and can respond to one another. Audio-visual supports such as hand-outs, data-projection, retrieved images and recorded sound can be very important. But the crucial difference between doing a presentation and reading all these things in books or looking them up on the web is the speaking voice and palpable presence of the person who is doing the presenting; also the listening and watching presence of everyone else around. In short, it is the *present* in *present*ation that makes all the difference. So it is the *giving* of this 'present' that is the job of presenters, while the job of the audience and viewers is not just to receive but also to respond – always attentively, sometimes actively.

Begin, then, by recalling the most fundamental action when doing English with other people: **Turning up and taking part** (1.2.2). This will remind you about the importance of a fundamentally *dialogic* approach to language even when dealing with an ostensibly *monologic* form such as the presentation. Everyone has to be there, audience as well as presenters, if it is to work. **Taking and making notes** (1.2.3) obviously plays a part in preparing for this kind of work, as for any other. In this case you are best aiming at 'orderly notes' (with headings and sub-headings listed on cue cards or paper) to refer to during the presentation itself; though you may well use combinations of 'chaotic' (clustered, netted and web-like) and 'orderly' strategies in the preparation and early agenda-setting and material-gathering stages. And of course all of this activity should be informed by visits to the **Library and web**, constantly returning **'home'** to the particular 'text + task' and 'context + course' in play – in this case your presentation (1.2.5). Many of the structural and strategic aspects of presentations are the same as for **Writing essays** (1.2.7). So remind yourself of the classic 'diamond' model and its alternatives when thinking about how to open engagingly, develop purposefully, and conclude with the audience still engaged – wanting to know (and ask and say) more. For that, from first to last, is the main point of a short presentation: to stimulate a response. It should inform, it must engage.

The advice that follows is designed to help you do good presentations in your own way but not on your own. It is framed in terms of a *Before*, *During* and *Afterwards* and emphasises practical things you should do (with a few cautionary notes sounded in brackets).

Before:

◆ *Gather your main ideas and materials as a preliminary long-list (or wish-list).* Think how many of these you can realistically cover in the time available. (From the start, don't aim to write everything down or cram everything in.)

◆ *Select what you feel you must present, analyse and discuss yourself – as monologue.* Organise these as provisional headings and sub-headings, quotations and references. Leave room for images and sound where appropriate. (Doing fewer things well, with time for discussion, is far better than doing everything in a rush with no time for what comes up.)

◆ *Consider what might be better approached through group activity – as dialogue.* One or two brief 'question/answer' or 'response' points can be valuable for a change of pace and dynamic. (But they are time-consuming, so introduce them sparingly and strategically.)

◆ *Select some essential materials to go on paper hand-outs or transparencies and power-point*: passages of text for discussion, key quotations, lists of main points, images, references. (Simple and to the point is better than all flash and no substance.) Try to give yourself room for manoeuvre and some paper back-up if the technology fails.

◆ *Check out the room* for size, equipment, audibility and visibility – imagine yourself doing it there. Will your voice – or images – be big enough and 'project'?

◆ *Practise and time your presentation* with all this in mind, gauging then seeing how long each topic or activity takes. Write '1 min', '5 mins', etc. in the margin of your notes to remind you. If possible do this to fellow-students, and more than once if need be.

◆ *Be there in good time and in good shape.* Breathe deeply and compose yourself. You are doing a presentation: it's a kind of performance. (Don't roll up at the last minute, sweating and in a panic.)

During:

◆ *Make sure everything is in place so as to start on time*: that you can be heard and seen; that the technology is working; and that everyone has hand-outs if there are any.

◆ *Aim to establish a good rapport and atmosphere from the first.* Say hello, who you are, and what you aim to do. Energy and enthusiasm go a long way in presentation; as do seriousness and a sense of purpose.

◆ *Open with something interesting*: a quotation, question, image, *brief* anecdote or activity – but nothing wacky, trivial or too long. (You must engage. You don't have to amuse or amaze.)

◆ *Get briskly into the substance of your talk.* Present points that are distinct yet linked. Use clear sign-posting in the form of introductory and summary lists of main points. As with essays, a basic pattern of quotation, comment, analysis/activity for each topic works well.

◆ *Meanwhile – throughout – remember:*
  ◆ Audio-visual aids are there to support your talk and should free you up. (They are not a substitute for it and should not tie you down.) Elaborate, don't duplicate.
  ◆ Keep making eye-contact with your audience from time to time, and do remember to address the people at the back too. (Don't have your head solemnly down in your script, or face turned back to the projection on the wall.)
  ◆ You and everyone else are the vital elements because you are alive and actually there. (The rest you could all get virtually, without anyone else there.)
  ◆ Leave time to breathe, pace yourself, and even move round. (Don't hold your breath or fidget.)
  ◆ As far as possible enjoy yourself. You are allowed to smile!

◆ *Almost finally, draw your presentation to a firm close.* Perhaps recall your opening and what has been learnt since, but also gesture to other possibilities to help cue discussion. (Don't just tail off with 'Well, I guess that's it . . . '. Or stop abruptly: 'Any questions?')

♦ *Finally, be ready to respond openly to questions and suggestions.* Treat this as an opportunity, not a threat. If you have prepared thoroughly there will be plenty of things you didn't have time to fit in or elaborate. (One's peers usually just need some encouragement. They know they probably have to go through this process too.)

Afterwards:

♦ Gather up your script, unused hand-outs and audio-visual bits and pieces.

♦ Weigh up and try to get feedback on how it went: interest, pacing, coherence, audio-visual aids, handling questions.

♦ Tell yourself: however well or badly it seems to have gone, next time will be different – even with the same material. You will never do *that* presentation again with *that* response. That's what makes them both live.

Group presentations   If you are presenting in pairs or groups of three or four, the possibilities multiply but so can the problems. It is therefore important to start getting organised early. You will need to meet at least three times before the presentation itself:

(i)   *to discuss overall emphasis and approach, and to decide who is doing what.* Some people are better at: having ideas, doing research, analysing, arguing, theorising, handling technology, talking, writing . . . Some are leaders, team-players, supporters, followers. Everyone is a particular mix and personality, yet everyone has to present something. Getting the mix of mixes right takes time.

(ii)   *to check on how it's going and what's (not) been done*: where are you up to and what (or who!) needs tweaking?

(iii)   *to have a practice run-through for order*, incorporation of hand-outs/audio-visuals/technology, and timing – then another if need be.

Transitions are a crucial aspect of group presentation. Make sure you move smoothly and clearly from one person (and topic) to another: 'At this point Katie will tell you more about / show you . . .', 'Katie . . .'. Try to conclude with a lively, even if divided, sense of 'We . . .'. You don't have to agree, but you are a group.

---

*For **common assessment criteria** and typical comments on what makes for a 'strong' or 'weak' presentation, see @ 1.2.8. You will usually be assessed for delivery and response as well as structure and substance. So do give a live presentation, don't just read out an essay.

To do immediately . . .

♦ *If you know a course will include an oral presentation, bear this in mind from the beginning.* Organise related notes in readily retrievable forms and take every opportunity to speak, support and listen so as to get a feel for the group and its dynamics.

♦ *If you are doing a group presentation, get yourselves organised well in advance.* Meet at least three times for (i) groundwork and delegation; (ii) checking on progress; (iii) practice run-through.

♦ *Prepare your topic early and practise your presentation in advance, preferably to a friend or fellow-student.* Get used to speaking loud and clear, head up and with occasional eye-contact, using headings on paper or cue-cards, and working in whatever hand-outs, back-projection, images or sound are appropriate. Keep it live!

◆   *Think of yourself as a reasonably informed and well-disposed but potentially bored or confused member of your own audience. Engage and illuminate yourself!* If you can't do it for yourself, you won't do it for anyone else.

Also see: Turning up, taking part (1.2.2); Taking and making notes (1.2.3); Writing an essay (1.2.7); Part Four: **Speech, conversation and dialogue**; Part Six: Towards application and interview (6.4.3).

READING: Stott, Young and Bryan 2001; Carroll *et al.* 2010; Childs 2008: 99–106; Green 2009: 74–7.

1.2.9   Revision: preparing to take an exam

> re-vision – the act of looking back, of seeing with fresh eyes, of entering an old text from a new critical direction.
>
> Adrienne Rich, 'When We Dead Awaken: Writing as Re-Vision' (1971)

Like all educational discourses – lectures, seminars, essays, presentations – exams are worth thinking about critically and creatively, not just doing as a matter of course. What's more, as the above epigraph intimates, this whole matter of 're-vision' can be approached as an opportunity for fresh thinking and synthesis, not just repetition and reinforcement. There are in fact various kinds of exam used nowadays: open-book (where you can consult an unmarked text); take-away (where you get the paper a limited time before and can use a library and other resources); or just plain, traditional one-, two-, or three-hour exam (where you have neither books nor libraries nor flexible time to draw on). This last is still the most common. But whatever the precise type, the fact is that the written exam is a way of showing what you know and can do under controlled conditions. Like the spoken presentation, it demonstrates that you can work towards and complete a specified task within time constraints. Put bluntly, you have to get your act together and be there to do it. So the name of the game with exams is 'preparation and performance'. Or, to use terms that may prove more conducive as well as suggestive, it is a matter of *re-vision and response*: drawing together what you know and responding to what is asked.

Now, you may already have a general feeling that you are 'good' or 'bad' at exams. Either way, there are certain practical things you can do that will make a big difference to how well you do in them and how you go about the whole process of revising for and sitting them. The following guidelines will help. As for that other time-constrained task, **Giving a presentation** (1.2.8), the whole process is best grasped in terms of a *Before*, *During* and *After*. (And again, some cautionary notes are sounded in the brackets.)

Before
◆   *Confirm the organisation and range of the exam-paper early on.* If there are past papers available look at those, but check whether there are changes in text, topic or mark-scheme. This will give you a provisional sense of what you are aiming at.
◆   *Approach the early stages of revision as an opportunity for* **re-vision** *– seeing afresh not just again.* Use a variety of exploratory techniques (e.g. 'chaotic', web and other diagrams) to revisit your earlier notes, essays and analyses in the light of what you have learnt subsequently. What fresh connections and patterns can you now see, configured round what terms and topics?
◆   *Approach the later stages of revision as a time of* **reinforcement**. Here the more 'orderly', horizontal and vertical kinds of note-taking tend to come into their own. (Though some people still prefer working with 'nets', 'webs' and 'trees', etc.) The main thing now is to fix things in the most readily memorable forms.

♦   *A week or so before the exam, try to grasp each area both **minimally** and **maximally**.* *Minimally* means registering the main points on some topic (view of an author, issue, theory) on a single side of paper. *Maximally* means reframing your notes so as to fill, say, eight sides; these represent your combination of fresh 're-vision' and 'reinforcement' based on the rest of your work (essays, lecture notes, notes from books, etc.). The crucial thing is to connect the minimal notes to the maximal notes, perhaps keying them with corresponding 'key terms'. In fact, together, minimal and maximal notes operate like 'key and lock', opening doors and windows on what you know beyond.

♦   *If you have three questions to do, aim for three sides of 'minimal' notes – with 'maximal' notes to match.* (Prepare a fourth as back-up, to be on the safe side and give yourself room for manoeuvre.) Think of these as keys and locks to get at *all* the good things you have gathered and thought. (In any case, don't just settle for a mess and hope for the best.)

♦   *A few days before the exam, practise responding to questions in timed ('exam') conditions.* Use past papers and sample questions as prompts to make you revisit what you know in different ways. Keep sorting through and recombining to put you on your toes and keep stuff fresh.

♦   *The day before the exam, look over your notes and practise recalling from memory what you know and think.* By this stage what you have gathered is what you will draw upon. (But don't stay up working till the early hours going round in ever-decreasing circles.) Sleep on it.

During

♦   *Give yourself time* to look over the whole paper at the beginning, plan each question when you get to it, and read through all your answers at the end. (Don't just go in and start writing straightaway.) But do get on with it once you have got your bearings.

♦   *Respond to each question in turn in its own terms as well as your own.* Recall your 'minimal' notes and use them to access your 'maximal' notes selectively. Identify only those parts that are relevant and work them up to make a considered and coherent response. (Don't just bang down your plan anyhow at first sight of a vaguely relatable question.) Make it clear that any working notes you make in the exam are just that – putting a line through them afterwards.

♦   *Keep an eye on the question and the clock* at the beginning of each paragraph or new section. Leave yourself time to read through each essay as you go or all of them at the end – even if it is just to correct spelling and tweak punctuation.

Afterwards: The first thing most people want to do after taking an exam is forget it. That is one reason why many people never get any better at them. Another reason is that, other than the grade, it is often difficult to get feedback after an exam. Nonetheless . . .

♦   *Take an informed guess at what grade you think you will get* on the basis of what you did. Use the marking criteria supplied against what you can remember doing.

♦   *If your grade is markedly worse or better than you expected*, ask your course tutor or the course leader for some sense of what went wrong or right.

♦   *In any event, think about the ways in which you 'revised', 'recalled' and 'responded'.* What seemed to work? What could you do differently, better, next time?

See @ 1.2.9 for further information and guidance on:

♦   the two main kinds of exam question – essay and text/extract analysis
♦   common assessment criteria for written work, including exams
♦   comments frequently made on 'strong' and 'weak' exam answers.

To do immediately . . .

♦ *If you know a course will include an exam, start taking and making notes with this in mind from the start.* Summarise main issues regularly and generally keep your preparation on the 'orderly' side. You can't 're-vise' a topic if you didn't 'vise' it properly in the first place!

♦ *Select a text, author or issue on which you expect to be examined and organise your thoughts, materials and references on progressively fewer sides of paper.* In particular, try the *minimal* (one-side) and *maximal* (eight-side) method as a 'key and lock' strategy for opening up what is relevant by way of immediate response.

♦ *For the exam itself, respond to the particular questions and tasks as posed.* Don't just bang down your plan or everything you know regardless. Select from your materials and build up an argument or analysis in response to the particular terms of the questions and the texts presented. Meanwhile – because exams are time-tests – keep an eye on it.

Also see: Taking and making notes (1.2.3), Writing an essay (1.2.7) and, for analysis of short texts and extracts, Initial analysis: how to approach a text (2.1). For common kinds of exam question, assessment criteria, and typical comments on 'strong' and 'weak' work, see @ 1.2.9.

READING: Carroll *et al.* 2010; Fabb and Durant 2005: 13–14.

1.2.10 Seriously enjoy studying English

Studies serve for delight, for ornament, and for ability.

Francis Bacon, 'Of Studies' (1625)

If I study, the only learning I look for is that which tells me how to know myself, and teaches me how to die well and to live well.

Michel de Montaigne, 'On Books' (1580)

The four words at the head of this section – the tenth and final 'action' – sum up this whole approach to doing English. Fully grasped, they express what is common and essential to all the preceding nine actions. In some respects none of this is new. Bacon and Montaigne in the above epigraphs sounded a similar note in their own terms some four hundred years ago; and these are still the two main models of essay-writing promoted in the present book (1.2.7). Yet in other respects the subject is still all to play for, and its future – like the future of English, and the particular powers and pleasures people will derive from it – is as yet unmade and far from predictable. *Seriously enjoy studying English* is therefore proposed as a kind of categorical imperative. Though it's offered more by way of open invitation than pressing imposition . . .

Seriously – because you've got to mean it and it's got to mean something to you. Serious does not mean solemn or po-faced; but it does mean taking time and care and having due respect for what you read and for others and yourself. Many of the issues and experiences you will read and write about and discuss are disturbing and sensitive and important: relationships that fail, broken families, war, abuse, isolation, madness, anger, despair, injustice, poverty, dispossession, invasion, global catastrophe, physical pain, mental distress and spiritual anguish. And suffering and death – a lot more suffering and death than you may believe possible or even necessary, especially if you are young and well and perhaps relatively well-off. (You are in a position to study English to an advanced level after all.) But there are many other things, equally important and sensitive, that will be more cheering or comforting, and perhaps inspiring or consoling: visions and versions of love, friendship, understanding, justice, relationships and communities that somehow work, nature – including human nature – that in some way grows, heals itself and becomes whole. Seriously . . .

Enjoy – because literature and language and culture are also about pleasure, playing, celebrating, exploring, experimenting, imagining. They are full of risk and excitement, the unexpected and the refreshing. Sometimes even being nonsensical can be serious – though never self-serious. If you forget all this, you will miss most of the fun and much of the point of reading and writing. Both are deeply demanding. But they are also highly rewarding. Learning to read more attentively and sensitively – in a word, critically – is satisfying. So, for all the sheer hell of it sometimes, is managing to write or say something that has never been said before and is worth saying, because you really need to say it and it really needs saying. In a word, creating. Because words are toys as well as tools, and language is inherently creative and literature is singularly so. Seriously enjoy . . .

Studying – because it is far more than just reading or even writing. It is also reflecting hard on what you do, finding out things you did not know previously, and making sense of the familiar in fresh ways. It is about searching far and wide as well as re-searching (looking again, afresh) at what is near and only partly or apparently known. Library–Web–'Home'; 'Home'–Web–Library . . . the cycle goes on and yet never wheels back to quite – or at all – the same place. Chance and close encounters crop up along the way, even when on a pre-set, long-haul mission, quest, project. Roads not taken are always more numerous than those that are. And as each makes all the difference, sooner or later, you have to express a preference. That requires critical discrimination and judgement as well as creative engagement and imagination: an analytical and historical understanding of the object of study as well as active participation as a lived and living subject. Seriously enjoy studying . . .

English – because from first to last, this is the language we *use* as well as the name of the subject we *study*. It is what we *ourselves* say and write 'here and now' as well as what we hear and read *other people* having said and written 'there and then', in other periods and cultures as well as our own. In short, this is both a 'many Englishes' and 'one English' view of its subject. In long, it's very much an ongoing project: *person*ally speaking, 'English' starts where each of us does, slightly or very differently, with the kinds of language we habitually use and know; *institution*ally speaking, 'English' is whatever your department on good authority and probably with a broad consensus says it is; though even then individual members – including you – may see and say it differently: linguistically, literarily, culturally, critically, creatively, historically, contemporarily . . . And so on to other languages and literatures and cultures that are notionally 'not-English', but may become so through translation and both influence and be influenced by the many and various things that still, continuously, from last to first, make 'English' one and many, more or less similar but always different . . .

Seriously enjoy studying English

To do immediately . . .

♦ *Go briskly through each of the first nine actions in turn.* What, in your own words – using any kind of English you want – does each really mean to you? What piece of no-nonsense advice would you give to yourself about, say, turning up and taking part, using the library and web, writing an essay, giving a presentation, and so forth?

♦ *Consider in what ways you **seriously enjoy** studying English.* (Think of particular texts, activities, courses, approaches.) How *serious* (committed, industrious) are you about English, and what are some of the issues it raises that are *serious* (important, significant) to you? What in particular do you get *enjoyment* from in doing English – reading novels, writing essays, doing presentations, researching, working on your own or as part of a group . . . ? Consider how you might take your English studies more seriously and get more enjoyment from them.

♦   *Now you are **doing** English, where are you **going** with it?* Answers will range from what you are doing next in your particular course to what you are doing next in your programme as a whole. Beyond that stretch questions about what you are doing and where you are going in the rest of your life . . . The latter may not seem to be pressing questions at the moment, especially if you are near the start of a programme. But sooner or later they will be. So, apart from checking how what you are studying now relates to what you may be studying later, take a few minutes to turn to the last part of the present book: Part Six. Taking it all further: English and the Rest of Your Life. Later if not sooner, you will be seriously glad that you did.

Also see: Which 'Englishes' (1.1); Theory in practice (3.1); ETHICS, AESTHETICS, ECOLOGY (3.9); English again, afresh, otherwise (6.2); and @ 2.3 Media, language, power and pleasure; @ 4 Aesthetics and pleasure.

READING: Knights and Thurgar-Dawson 2006; Scholes 1985, 1998; Barthes 1966; Kristeva 1971; McCaw 2006; Eaglestone 2009: 145–51; Bennett and Royle 2009: Chs 23, 32.

1.3   FIELDS OF STUDY

Here we take a closer look at the the three main 'fields' in which English is currently studied. For convenience, these are distinguished as LANGUAGE, LITERATURE and CULTURE (this last including Communication and Media). Such labels are crude. But they are initially useful in that they agree with the recent history of the subject and the currently recognised institutional divisions within and around it. That is, individual English courses (and sometimes whole degree programmes) tend to concentrate on 'language' and/or 'literature' and/or 'culture, communication and media'. (The repeated and/ors are a reminder that some courses and most programmes do a mixture, though invariably with a particular emphasis.) At the most obvious level, these distinctions can be observed in the various names we find in prospectuses and over departmental corridors. Aside from the relatively plain and all-purpose *English* and *English Studies*, the current favourites are *English Language & Literature*; *English & Cultural Studies*; *English & Communication*; and so on. Significantly, these names are increasingly hybrid (often projecting English and *or* as something else). The combination *English and Creative Writing* has been introduced in the Prelude and will be carried through in Part Two. (See 6.2 for an overview of 'English *and* or *as* other subjects' and @ 1.4 for an historical overview of the main configurations.)

A couple of things should be clarified about the notion of 'fields' used here. First, these are better conceived as *force fields* rather than the kind of fields we find in farming. They operate as ceaselessly shifting and mutually shaping energies, not as spatially fixed and mutually exclusive areas. In this sense a 'field' is a force we bring to bear on a particular material, or the conditions in which we place that material. It is also the force exerted by that material. What one person sees and uses primarily as 'language' another may see and use primarily as 'literature', and yet another may see and use primarily as an instance of 'culture' (or communication or media). For instance, think of an extract from a novel and the lyrics of a pop song: e.g., Austen's *Pride and Prejudice* (5.3.2) and Queen's 'Bohemian Rhapsody' (5.1.5). Each can be grasped as a series of words (language); as a form of verbal play (literature); and as representation of things going on in the rest of the human world (culture). At the same time, the properties of the material itself predispose (though they do not absolutely predetermine) the ways in which we use and understand it. A novel tends to be read silently and in solitude; a pop song tends to be heard and (if supported by a video or performance) seen, often in the company of other people. We may also be predisposed to classify *Pride and Prejudice* as (classic) literature and 'Bohemian Rhapsody' as (popular) culture. However, the fact the novel can be made into a successful high-street film (and thus shift in medium and cultural location) while the words and music of the pop song have achieved such 'classic' status that they will be readily recognised by most readers of this book (and can thus legitimately be studied as instances of contemporary lyric/poetry) reminds us that these categories are flexible and to some extent arbitrary. What we see in a text is partly a function of what we look for. What it *is* partly relates to what is *done* with it. That is why it is useful to approach all texts, at least initially, as potential instances of language and literature and culture. For only by grasping the complex interconnections amongst the latter concepts can we wield them effectively, together, as analytical tools.

The following brief example should help fix the above points. We focus on just one line: 'I wandered lonely as a cloud' (the first line of Wordsworth's poem of that name; see 5.4.1). This is used to show how the analysis of a text can operate at a variety of levels, and that, taking all these levels together, we can develop a complexly multilayered comprehension of that text in context and in relation to other texts. The main fields LANGUAGE, LITERATURE and CULTURE are signalled to the left. Meanwhile, the terms *Rhetoric*, *Intertextuality* and *Discourse* have been inserted into the gaps to the right. These simply confirm the overlap between the three fields, while also pointing to other ways in which the analysis might be configured. More will be said about all these levels and terms in Part Two. For the moment, simply note the multilayered nature of these analyses:

'I wandered lonely as a cloud'

LANGUAGE: 'I' is a first person singular pronoun (subject); 'wandered' is a simple past tense (verb); 'lonely as a cloud' is an adverbial phrase of manner and comparison. Grammatical structure: (traditional) subject–verb–adverb; (functional): participant–process–circumstance

Rhetoric

LITERATURE: Opening of lyric poem; octosyllabic; embellished by pastoral simile; influential Romantic image of 'poet' and 'poetry'

Intertextuality

CULTURE: Pastoral individualism; 'idle' country classes; subsequently clichéd view of poetry frequently cited and very variously 'sited' in other texts (e.g. 5.4.1)

Discourse

Clearly, then, even a single line of a text may act as the focus for a highly varied yet intricately interrelated set of analytical operations. It can be described at a variety of levels using a variety of *linguistic*, *literary* and *cultural* terms. Picking up those other terms featured to the right, we might also say that every text can be analysed in terms of RHETORIC (its organisation of information and its power to persuade); **intertextuality** (its relations to other texts) and **discourse** (the particular way of saying and seeing and the values it projects). But whatever the terms and techniques used, it is crucial to observe that analysis can be undertaken in a variety of dimensions and directions and with various frames of reference in mind. It is equally crucial to recognise that all these 'levels' or 'dimensions' contribute to the building of what is notionally a single edifice: a full yet flexible critical understanding of the text. Thus we may roll all the above comments on the first line of Wordsworth's 'I wandered lonely as a cloud' together to produce something like the following.

> This text is organised round the notion of the poet as solitary individual, hence the prominence of the first person singular pronoun in the first word and the use of the adverb 'lonely'. The verb 'wandered' (as distinct from, say, 'walked' or 'marched') implies an aimless ramble where there is neither the pressure of work nor a firm destination to direct it. The simile 'lonely as a cloud' points both to the wanderer's aloneness and, at the same time, his oneness with nature. This line is often cited as a quintessential instance of 'poetry'. To be more precise, it exemplifies a certain kind of Romantic pastoral poetry in which some supposedly special and sensitive soul comments upon and communes with nature. However, the susceptibility of this line to ironic and parodic treatment is a measure of just how particular, even peculiar, that vision of poetry and the poet is. Certainly this version of poetry stands at some distance from the largely urban scenes and the highly technologised and commercialised situations we encounter in much of modern life. For all these reasons, Marxists, Feminists and Postmodernists would all have different tales to tell about – and with – this material. In fact, the cultural value of this line is endlessly renegotiable, depending upon the texts with which it is identified and the discourses in which it is made to figure (see 'Daffodils?' 5.4.1). Compare it, for instance, with Dorothy Wordsworth's *Journal* entry about the same outing, where other people are present and some are working. Or compare it with the poetic parody, where it is the gendered dimension of the text's mode and moment of reproduction that is wittily exposed. Meanwhile, the invocation of the text in the advertising copy quite literally 'trades upon' the poem's status as a familiar classic. This is now palpably poem as commodity.

In all these ways, then, even a single line can serve as the site, or act as the focus, for a wide range of analytical and critical activities. Significantly, these activities are both *in*tensive and *ex*tensive. We look hard *at* the text in hand, but we also attempt to see *through* it. We look closely at 'the words on the page', but also try to see them in relation to other texts and as part of a larger world. We look at what the text *is* but also try to see what it *does*. To be sure, none of this absolutely determines the **value** of William Wordsworth's text, or of any of the others touched upon here. Nor does it determine whether we should like it or not. (Revaluation and dis/likes are matters that can only be weighed through discussion, negotiation and exchange. And in any case these are tiny, merely token samples.) At the same time, it should be clear that getting one's initial bearings in terms of language, literature and culture (or rhetoric, intertextuality and discourse) has some real appeal. It allows us to establish fairly firm ground and provisional conditions upon which to frame a more sophisticated analysis. It also allows us to talk in a number of more or less common critical languages without forcing us to agree. The rest, quite properly, is up to us.

Activity

Sketch a linguistic, literary and cultural analysis of the following line of text. Do this in the form of a three-tiered and an integrated analysis like that for the Wordsworth line. The text for analysis – in its entirety – is:

'If I should die, think only this of me'

It can be found in its original form in Brooke's 'The Soldier', and again in Fanthorpe's 'Knowing about Sonnets' (5.1.2). Experiment with ways in which Wordsworth's line 'I wandered lonely as a cloud' and Brooke's 'If I should die, think only this of me' might be read: formed and informed; serious and silly. Look to explore alternative ways in which Wordsworth's, Brooke's or your words might be said and situated, performed and adapted. Then return to gauge how they actually used them in their own times and terms.

(Notice that, like the Wordsworth material, this line is presented as part of a cluster of related materials supported by notes (5.1.2). This should help you gesture to broader contexts and conditions.) Finally, follow up the terms 'rhetoric', **intertextuality** and **discourse** in the index. How might these also be used as tools to analyse one of the above texts?

Discussion

> The field cannot well be seen from within the field.
>
> Ralph Waldo Emerson, *Circles* (1841)

READING: The kind of reading *across* language, literature and culture (and across rhetoric, intertextuality and discourse) practised here is variously called 'literary linguistics', 'stylistics', 'language through literature' and 'literary discourse analysis'. Stimulating introductions are Simpson 1997 and Cook 2004. A good textbook is Montgomery, Durant, Fabb, Furniss and Mills 2012; a comprehensive reader is Carter and Stockwell 2008, and a wide-ranging essay collection is McIntyre and Busse 2010. Collections of essays spanning language and literature with an emphasis on creativity are Maybin and Swann 2006; Goodman and O'Halloran 2006; and Swann, Pope and Carter 2011. For ways in which re-reading across these fields turns into the rewriting of them, see Pope 1995 and Scholes, Comley and Ulmer 2002. This project is carried through below in 2.1–2. Also see @ 3.10.

1.3.1   Language

Language can be provisionally defined as 'words', however made and wherever found. Learning to grasp words, both analytically and actively, is obviously a central part of English Studies. And that *grasping*, it should be stressed, means learning both to take language apart and to put it together again – differently. We *use* as well as *analyse* words. As far as language is concerned, English Studies embraces everything from the teaching and learning of basic literacy skills to the cultivation of advanced skills in comprehension and composition (in reading and writing literary and scientific texts, for instance). It includes a knowledge of specific texts and utterances as well as a sense of how language in general works. Reading and writing are also best developed in conjunction with listening and speaking, with viewing and presenting. In this way language from the outset is situated in a variety of media (not all of which are exclusively verbal) and is used for a variety of purposes (not all of which are narrowly academic).

Every major theoretical position and critical practice in contemporary English Studies may be 'placed' according to its particular view of language. Each position or practice also has its own partially distinctive vocabulary and even style. Thus American NEW CRITICS, Russian FORMALISTS, and some deconstructionists tend, in their various ways, to concentrate on language as a system in its own right: they play up the relations between one word and another, and play down the relations between words and the rest of reality. They emphasise the **text** as a self-sufficient construct, more or less independent of **context**, and textuality as a wor(l)d unto itself. Conversely, a number of historically sensitive and politically motivated approaches associated with MARXISM, FEMINISM and POSTCOLONIALISM are much more committed to exploring word–world and text–context relations. They investigate the ways in which people can be liberated or enslaved by the words they use (or which use them), and they treat language as a form of social power (i.e. **discourse**). PSYCHOLOGICAL critics also emphasise the power of words both to express and repress that which is hidden in the unconscious. POST-MODERNISTS, meanwhile, are more engaged by the shifting relations among words, images and sounds in the contemporary media. They often treat words, and especially printed books, as of diminishing cultural significance.

Of course, many theorists and critics combine two or more positions with respect to language. They also develop distinctive approaches to the relations between, for instance, literary and non-literary or **standard** and 'non-standard' language. Indeed, some linguists contest such distinctions altogether. They use the more neutral terms **text** and **discourse** (without appealing to any essentially literary or non-literary properties) and often prefer to talk of plural **varieties** or versions of English (without insisting on a strict division into standard and non-standard).

For all these reasons, it is important for students of English to develop a good grasp of language, theoretically and in practice.

- What are words? What do we do with them? What do they do to us?
- How and why does language change over time and vary from place to place?
- What's so special (or so common) about the language of each and every one of us?
- Are there really such things as 'literary' or 'standard' language? Or do these change and vary too?

You will not find neat, complete answers in what follows. But you will be encouraged to frame these questions more precisely and to relate them directly to your own experience of using, analysing and reflecting upon words.

What language is and can be

The word *language* derives from Latin *lingua*, through French *langue*, meaning 'tongue'. Conversely, *tongue* is an archaic, ultimately Anglo-Saxon, English word for 'language' (as in 'native tongue', 'foreign tongues'). Either way, language was initially primarily identified with the physical business of **speech**. **Writing**, on the other hand, is invariably a later manifestation of language, both in individual persons and in whole societies. Thus virtually everybody learns to listen and speak before they learn to read and write, and every society is oral before it is literate. Moreover, most people continue to communicate orally even when literacy is widespread, though the relations between oracy and literacy change. For instance, virtually all the readers of this book will use language to talk with other people in corridors, in shops, over meals, in bed and on the telephone as well as to write notes, type essays, write poems, etc. We also routinely use language when listening to the radio and watching TV. This multimedia potentiality of words – their capacity to operate as speech *and* writing, sound *and* sight, in a variety of live *and* recorded modes – is of fundamental significance. It means that words are an extraordinarily versatile and volatile communicative resource. It also means that **variation** and the capacity to generate highly distinct versions of ostensibly 'the same words' are knit into the very fabric of language. That is why some of the activities in the present book work across the speech/writing interface, and involve various kinds of **translation** from one medium to another.

Language is a term which is used to refer to many different things. It is important to be aware which sense is in play at any one time. Language can be:

1   *spoken, written, printed and otherwise recorded words*: notionally a single sign-system but constituted in many materials and media;

2   *the notional totality of all languages*, as well as what is common to them: 'Language' (capitalised and singular);

3   *specific languages* (lower case and plural) e.g., the English, Russian or Yoruba languages;

4   *a distinctive variety, style* or **genre**, e.g., advertising language, journalese, the language of Anglo-Saxon or of Caribbean poetry, old Church Slavonic;

5   *loosely, by extension, modes of non-verbal communication and other sign-systems in general*, e.g., 'body language', 'the language of film – or flowers or music or love or advertising' – even though each sign-system or communicative practice has its own way of saying/seeing/being which is not wholly explicable in terms of a narrowly linguistic model.

(For descriptions of English in particular, as 'one *and* many' – historically, geographically, socially and by medium – see 1.1.)

What language does and what we do with language

The preceding definitions of language are 'essentialist' in that they aim to explain language in terms of what it *is*. Functional or pragmatic approaches, however, set out to explore language in terms of what it *does* and how it is *used*. Here is an overview of functional perspectives. We use language:

♦   *to interact in a wide range of social situations and material contexts*: immediate and face-to-face (typically through **speech**); indirectly in mediated situations (typically through **writing** and print); in the modern audio-visual MEDIA (typically in various permutations of live and recorded, immediate and remote sign-systems – only one of which is verbal language);

♦   *to share and shape information collaboratively, through* **dialogue**, *as well as to transmit and transfer information from one person or group to another, through* **monologue**: we thus use words for, respectively, many-way and one-way COMMUNICATION;

♦   *to converse with the rest of the world, others, ourselves and the language itself*; i.e.

    – the *referential/ideational* function: referring to features or aspects of the rest of the world, whether as objects, persons, events or ideas;

    – the *inter/personal* function: expressing and helping constitute individual identities and social relations, senses of self and other;

    – the *metalinguistic* or *metatextual* function: drawing attention to the nature of language itself and the status of the specific utterance or text, a comment *in* language *on* language.

♦   *to perform a range of functions which may be further distinguished as*:

    ♦ *declarative*: making statements (e.g., 'It is');

    ♦ *interrogative*: asking questions or making requests ('Is it?');

    ♦ *directive/imperative*: giving directions or issuing orders ('Give it me!');

    ♦ *expressive/exclamatory*: expressing emotions ('It is?!').

(Many of these functions are combined in actual practice, resulting in more subtle kinds of **speech act**: inviting, imploring, insulting, threatening, cajoling, etc.)

♦   *in short – for power and for play.*

We use words for all the above functions. The fact that we do not *only* use words – or rarely use words alone – to perform these functions is a reminder that words are always implicated in other communication and sign-systems. Touch, gesture, clothing, car design, cityscapes: these too are ways in which we interact, share and shape, exercise power and explore through play.

The advantage (some would say disadvantage) of a functionalist approach to language is that it is much richer (and messier) than an essentialist approach. Either way, trying to establish what we actually *do* with language always turns out to be a much more demanding and potentially rewarding activity than formulating in the abstract what language *is*.

Language variation and change

All languages change over time and eventually they change into 'other languages'. Common Latin of the Roman Empire transformed into the various modern Romance languages: Italian, French, Spanish, etc. Old English transformed into the various kinds of modern English found in Britain, America, the Caribbean, Africa and India, etc. Relatedly, languages vary from place to place and from one social group to another. Even the language of a single person (her or his idiolect) changes over the course of her or his life and varies according to the company s/he keeps and the situations s/he is involved in. All these processes of change and **variation** are interrelated. It is obviously important for anyone studying English to understand the principles which inform these processes. These pressures for change and variation may for convenience be categorised under four heads: *historically, geographically, socially* and by *medium* (see 1.1). Here we shall review the main reasons language changes, as well as how people change language and language changes people.

CHANGE – A TRANSITIVE AND AN INTRANSITIVE PROCESS

A complex formulation of the whole matter of 'change' is necessary from the outset. This applies as much to change in persons, society, nature and life in general, as to language in particular.

- If we see change as something that just happens of itself, we conceive it *intransitively*, independent of any chain of cause and effect (e.g., 'It changes'; 'You've changed').
- But if we see change as something that is bound up with other processes, we conceive it *transitively*, implicated in chains of cause and effect (e.g., 'It changed them'; 'That experience changed you').

The most sensible and sophisticated understandings of change tend to acknowledge that it is in some sense both intransitive *and* transitive: *intr*ansitive in that we as human beings are never in a position to identify *ultimate* causes and effects; transitive because we as human beings are always able to identify and assign *immediate* causes and effects. Ultimately, change is a sublimely philosophical and spiritual concept; immediately, it is an urgently historical and political matter. Both perspectives are possible and necessary when trying to grasp change in language, as in life in general. Hence the emphasis on 'Changing English Now' in the Prelude and the multiplex framing of the next sentence . . .

Language changes . . . language changes people . . . people change language because:

♦ *language communities move around geographically*: people thereby meet the challenge of new conditions and other language communities with old words used in new ways and new words drawn from other languages and cultures;

♦ *language communities are never socially uniform but are always compounded of 'differences'*: differentiation is most evident along the lines of rank, class, status, gender, occupation, ethnicity, religion, age and education;

- *human societies constantly evolve new modes of production and reproduction, of words as of everything else*: changes in technology and material conditions thus underpin shifts between and mixtures of **speech, writing**, print and the modern electronic MEDIA;
- *the human psyche, whether viewed individually or collectively, is constantly exploring new modes of expression and repression*: psychologically, words exist on the shifting interface between conscious and unconscious states;
- *all signs are inherently split and unstable*: the material forms of words (signifiers) have no direct and necessary relation to the things they represent (signifieds). For instance, the modern English words 'woman' (Anglo-Saxon 'wifman') and 'black' (Anglo-Saxon 'bla(e)c'), have changed in both form and sense over the past thousand years. The former split to give us modern 'wife' and 'woman'; the latter could mean variously 'black', 'shining' or even 'white' – it all depended upon the reflective property of whatever was shining, not any intrinsic colour.

Overall, then, language change is implicated in every other aspect of change: social, technological, physical and biological. Plenty of big questions remain unanswered, of course. Precisely how and why do communities move geographically? societies become differentiated? new technologies arise? psyches express and repress? signs ceaselessly split and re-form? But at least we can now recognise language change to be no isolated or purely self-sufficient process. It does happen *for reasons* not just 'because it happens'. It is implicated in chains of cause and effect. It is, so to speak, a *transitive* process. However, not surprisingly, people differ widely as to who or what causes what effect on whom or what. Some people also persist in the belief that language simply changes of itself, *intransitively*, as a kind of self-sufficing process. The following activities and discussion topics will help you weigh these and related matters for yourself.

The Quick Reference (Appendix A) defines all the common linguistic and grammatical terms, and a linguistic checklist for close reading can be found in 2.1. For a fuller glossary of linguistic terms, see @ Appendix A.

Activities

(a) *Translate and adapt a couple of the following texts* into a variety of English with which you are familiar (spoken or written, formal or informal, literally or freely – as you wish): one of the Old and Middle English poems (5.1.1); πo's 7 'daiz' (5.1.5); Chan Wei Meng's 'I spik Ingglish' (5.1.4).

Go on to make a systematic comparison between your version and the version(s) you translated/adapted with respect to: spelling, punctuation and visual presentation; word choice; word combination and discourse (see the checklist in 2.1).

(b) *Put the questions 'What is it?' and 'What does it do?' to some very different kinds of text.* Use your observations to prime reflection on the distinctions and connections between an 'essentialist' and a 'functionalist' approach to language.
    Suggested genres for comparison are:

  (i) a brief conversational exchange (e.g., student talk 5.3.1);
  (ii) news headlines or photo captions on the same event (e.g., 5.2.6);
  (iii) a brief passage from a novel or short story (e.g., 5.3.2);
  (iv) a short poem, song or advert (e.g., 'Tropical Death' (5.4.5); 'Bohemian Rhapsody' (5.1.5); Clarins skincare advert (5.4.4).

Discussion

(i) A system network is a theory of language as choice. It represents a language, or any part of a language, as a resource for making meaning by choosing.

M.A.K. Halliday, *An Introduction to Functional Grammar* (2004)

(ii) As a writer I know that I must select studiously the nouns, pronouns, verbs, adverbs, etcetera, and by a careful syntactical arrangement make readers laugh, reflect or riot.

Maya Angelou, from *Conversations with Maya Angelou* (1985)

(iii) Language is not decaying due to neglect. It is just changing as it always did.

Jean Aitchison, *The Language Web* (1996, BBC Reith Lectures)

READING: Lively and relevant introductions to language are Goddard 2012 (English in particular) and Trask 1999 and Yule 2010 (language in general). Robson and Stockwell 2004 connects language at large to critical and cultural theory in a practical way; while Mullany and Stockwell 2010 is a resource book (with website) on the English language in particular. Also see Reading for 1.1.

1.3.2   LITERATURE

If you are studying English in tertiary education it tends to be assumed you are doing English *Literature*. And that in turn leads to the common assumption (amongst people outside college at least) that you spend most of your time sitting round making admiring remarks about 'great works of Eng. Lit.': poems by Wordsworth and Keats, novels by Austen and Dickens, and plays by Shakespeare and . . . well, more Shakespeare. Occasionally such assumptions turn out to be true. The equation 'English' = 'Eng. Lit.' = 'a small selection of great authors/works' sometimes still holds. Increasingly, however, such assumptions are likely to prove ill-founded, or at best only partial truths. You may indeed spend some of your time studying, discussing and writing about commonly recognised **classics** belonging to a **canon** of supposedly great works. But this is likely to involve something more historically informed and culturally demanding than mere literary appreciation. It is also likely to focus on authors, works, genres, social movements and even whole national literatures which have little or nothing in common with the popular – and remarkably persistent – vision of 'Eng. Lit.' as a kind of genteel club.

The shifting multiplicity of subjects covered by the term 'English' is explored earlier in 1.1. The historical fact that Literature, narrowly conceived, has only ever been a part of English Studies, broadly conceived, is explored in @ 1.4. In the present section we concentrate on the fact that 'literature' is itself a historically variable and theoretically elastic term. We also review past, present and possible future alternatives to it. To be precise, we consider

♦   the history of the term 'literature', along with cognate terms such as literary, literariness and literate;

♦   the relative usefulness of alternative terms such as rhetoric, poetics, **writing, text, discourse** and performance.

What was, is and can be literature?

The word 'literature' ultimately derives from the Latin *littera*, meaning 'letter of the alphabet'. The word came into English, via court French, in the late fourteenth century and for the next few centuries simply meant 'acquaintance with books' and 'book learning' in general. As such it was virtually synonymous with what we now call 'literacy' (being able to read and write), a word which came into English in contradistinction to 'illiteracy' in the early nineteenth century. Thus a writer in 1581 can talk of 'Ane pure [i.e. poor] man quha [who] hes nocht sufficient literatur to undirstond the scripture' (see *OED*, Literature, 1). By extension, in so far as 'literature' referred to a body of books, as well as the activity of book learning, there was little attempt to distinguish the *kinds* of book. This generalised sense of literature meaning 'anything written on a subject' persists to the present day (e.g., scientific or advertising literature). The only criterion seems to have been that the books be of some value. Thus Hazlitt (*c.*1825) quotes Ayrton as having dubbed 'the two greatest names in English literature, Sir Isaac Newton and Mr Locke' (Williams 1983: 185). Newton was a scientist and Locke a philosopher; so neither of them would fit into the conceptions of 'English literature' which later came to underpin university departments of that name.

In fact it is only since the late eighteenth and early nineteenth centuries that 'literature' has become narrowed in meaning to its current dominant sense of *creative* or *imaginative* writing of a specifically *aesthetic* kind. Thus Dr Johnson in his 'Life of Cowley' (1779): 'An author whose pregnancy of imagination and elegance of language have set him high in the ranks of literature.' Corresponding narrowings and elevations of meaning can be observed over the same period in the terms **artist** (increasingly distinguished from the humbler term artisan) and **author** (increasingly distinguished from the more general term writer). Meanwhile, again relatedly, a category of specifically **fictional** writing was being increasingly distinguished from a category of specifically factual writing (see **realism**), just as story was being separated out from history (see **narrative**). The overall result of these interrelated changes may be summed up as follows.

'Literature', from the late eighteenth century onwards, was narrowed and elevated so as to mean: certain kinds of artistic or aesthetic writing which were reckoned to be especially creative and imaginative, fictional (not factual), stories (not histories), and to be the product of especially gifted or talented writers called authors – in extreme cases geniuses. Conversely, from this new and narrowly 'literary' point of view, all writing that was reckoned to be factual and historical was also implicitly stigmatised as less creative and imaginative – in short, 'non-literary'.

The ramifications of such a division and hierarchy are of fundamental significance. They underpin both the sorting of texts and the sorting of whole subject areas into distinct disciplines. Henceforth (and it is worth repeating that this shift only began to become marked less than two hundred years ago), 'literature' was abstracted from the general continuum of writing practices and book production and put on a special pedestal of its own.

It is the above narrowed and elevated sense of literature which dominated most departments of Literature until quite recently. Now, however, there are signs of a return to Literary Studies, along lines which more and more resemble its pre-Romantic shape. That is, there is a return to a much more capacious view of literature as 'book learning' in particular, and the processes and products of reading and writing in general. This is especially noticeable in the adjacent (and increasingly overlapping) 'field' of Rhetoric and Composition. One symptom of this is that there is now a tendency to talk more neutrally and in less value-laden terms of **texts** (rather than of 'literary works' or even 'poems', 'plays' and 'novels'). Another is that there is a tendency to foreground the social-historical and power dimensions of various kinds of **writing and reading** by characterising them as **discourses** (rather than compulsively sorting them into the categories of 'literary' or 'non-literary', 'fictional' or 'factual'). In all these ways, contemporary Literary Studies – and even more so contemporary Cultural Studies – have challenged recently dominant notions of literature and have sought to put the study of texts of all kinds on a different footing. Partly this has been done with the support of the more rigorous models and methods of text and discourse analysis derived from Linguistics. Partly this has been prompted by more or less explicit and committed political agendas drawn from varieties of MARXISM, FEMINISM and POSTCOLONIALISM. Either way, the result is an approach to literature – and an interrogation of the category itself – which is substantially opposed to the various orthodoxies that dominated the teaching of 'English' (as) 'Literature' for much of the twentieth century. American NEW CRITICISM in its concentration on the literary work, especially the poem, as 'verbal icon' was one such orthodoxy. Russian FORMALISM with its concentration on literariness as the defamiliarisation ('making strange') of ordinary language use and 'routine' norms of perception was another. In the event, whether they have assumed or asserted, resisted or refused the category itself, every one of the approaches represented in Part Three has had something useful to contribute to the debate on literature. So has the rise of Creative Writing sketched in the Prelude.

WHAT IS LITERATURE – OPEN DISCUSSION OR HIDDEN AGENDA?

Contemporary students of English quickly become aware of certain things about the continuing debate on what is or isn't literature. For one thing, they recognise that there is indeed a debate (and sometimes nothing short of a pitched battle) when it comes to defending or attacking, maintaining or modifying, certain versions of 'literature'. For another thing, more immediately and as a matter of academic survival, they are usually adept at working out which lecturers hold which views – and perhaps adjusting their own accordingly. This leaves everyone involved, staff as well as students, with opportunities as well as problems.

- At best, the debates on 'what is(n't) literature' are conducted from the outset, in the open, reasonably and for all to participate in, student or lecturer. Regular forums, position papers and round-tables work well in these respects.
- At worst, there is no debate at all: only more or less secret, undeclared and unargued agendas; a sense of faction or mutual incomprehension amongst the teachers. Students are thus left with the unenviable task of second-guessing what version or vision of literature (or textuality or discourse) particular members of their department expect them to engage with.

The suggestions and questions below will not solve any of these problems, intellectually or institutionally. But they will at least help identify areas of common concern and, perhaps, transform them into common interest. The question of '*What was, is and can be literature?*' can then be recognised as a challenge and an opportunity – not a threat and an obstacle.

Activities

(a)   *What kinds of literature are YOU engaged with*? Go through the following kinds of text and in each case ask how far approaching them as literature is appropriate or adequate. (Some alternative terms and concepts are offered in parentheses.)
Does the kind of literature you are engaged with include:

   (i)   *works which are chiefly designed to be read silently by individuals?*

   (Does a 'literary' approach therefore emphasise reading more than writing?)

   (ii)   *works which are primarily designed to be spoken and performed, heard and seen*, e.g., stage and TV plays, films, scripts of speeches?

   (Does a 'literary' approach draw undue attention to the page rather than the stage or screen? What other approaches through drama and theatre, performance and other MEDIA are possible and perhaps desirable? How practicable are they?)

   (iii)   *texts which are clearly in some sense 'creative', 'imaginative' and 'made-up'* – terms commonly used to designate poems, novels and plays – but which also clearly have instrumental social functions: advertising, news reporting, political speeches? And do these include texts that you 'create' yourself?

   (How far are notions of rhetoric and, say, play more helpful in these areas? Can poetics embrace more than 'poetry' as such? And what about 'creative writing'?)

   (iv)   narratives *of all kinds*: not just novels and short stories, but also instances of auto/biography, history, oral anecdotes and jokes, as well as news and magazine stories (printed and televised), films (documentary and otherwise)?

   (v)   *materials from the popular 'broadcast'* MEDIA (e.g., pulp fiction, soap operas, pop song) as well as materials from elite 'narrowcast' CULTURE (e.g., experimental or avant-garde art works, modernist writing, **classic** drama, ballet and opera).

   (Is 'discourse' a more useful term than 'literature' in such areas? What others are there?)

   (vi)   *texts identified with a supposedly single national culture* (e.g., 'English literature' or 'Literature in English') or with a variety of interrelated cultures worldwide (e.g., American, African, Caribbean, Indian, Australian writing)? How far are these texts in translation?

   (Would POSTCOLONIAL and MULTICULTURAL frames be more fitting?)

(b)   *Literary or non-literary?* Take an actual instance of a supposedly non-literary text (e.g., a bus ticket, a recipe, a news headline, an advert, a note to the milkman, entries in a telephone book). Do two things with and to it.

   (i)   Argue with all the resources and cunning at your disposal that this text is already in some senses creative, imaginative, fictional – in short, '*literary*'.
   (ii)   Relocate and, if you wish, adapt the 'non-literary' text you chose so that it functions as (part of) a plausible poem, play, novel or short story. Add a commentary exploring what you did and why.

Discussion

(i)   Some texts are born literary, some achieve literariness, and some have literariness thrust
upon them.

Terry Eagleton, *Literary Theory: An Introduction* (1996: 7)

(ii) It seems, however, best to consider as literature only works in which the aesthetic function
is dominant.

René Wellek and Austin Warren, *Theory of Literature* (1963: 25)

(iii) Clearly the proper study of literature is – everything else.

Peter Widdowson, 'W(h)ither English?', in Coyle *et al.* (1990: 1228)

READING: Lively and relevant introductions to literature are Eaglestone 2009 and Bate 2011 (both
with an emphasis on 'English Literature'). More wide-ranging and with an emphasis on modern
'literature(s) in English' is Walder 2003 (a critical reader). Widdowson 1999 is a handy theoretical and
historical interrogation of 'literature' as term and concept. For a classic Marxist critique, see Williams
1977: 44–54, and for an influential defence of the 'singularity' of literature see Attridge 2004. A
perceptive array of essays on core topics in literature and criticism is Bennett and Royle 2009. For
further debate, a provocative pairing is Eagleton 1996: 1–14 (British socialist) with Wellek and Warren
1963: 15–53 (American liberal). A revealing critique of changing approaches to literature – in and out
of context, more or less theorised – is Williams 1979 (interviews). 'English literature', in so far as it is
more than just a list of named authors and set texts, tends to be constructed in terms of period (e.g.
Chantler and Higgins 2010) and/or genre (e.g. Cavanagh, Gillis, Keown, Loxley and Stevenson 2010).
'Literatures in English' tend also to be organised geographically by region and linguistically by variety,
e.g Walder 1999 and Thieme 1996 (literary reader). Also see Reading for 1.1.

1.3.3 Culture, communication and media

The complex and sometimes vexed relations between various kinds of Studies – English,
Literary, Cultural, Communication and Media – are reviewed from a historical and institutional
perpective on the website @ 1.4. In the present section we consider how a practical approach
to our subject through Culture, Communication and Media (these terms are differentiated but
taken together as a kind of composite 'field') can help redefine and redirect what we are doing
in the other two fields of LANGUAGE and LITERATURE. We also see that all these relations are
reciprocal. Specifically linguistic and literary approaches have their parts to play, too,
particularly in the precise and sensitive analysis of verbal materials.

In certain limited senses 'English' has always been concerned with culture, communication
and media. Literary critics from Matthew Arnold in the late nineteenth century to F.R. Leavis
and Lionel Trilling in mid-twentieth-century Britain and America, along with many of their
successors to the present day, have often insisted upon the 'cultural' dimension of their mission
(see NEW CRITICISM). For what is 'the English language', they insist, but a quintessential verbal
expression of English (or American) culture? What is 'English Literature' but a splendid way
of communicating that culture as a national heritage or spiritual and aesthetic resource? And
what are manuscript and print but the primary media in which 'the best that has been known
and thought' (to recall Arnold's famous phrase) in that culture have been recorded and
transmitted to future generations? In other words, even the most conventional courses in History
of the Language and Literary Criticism have always been concerned with larger cultural issues.

Or have they?

Depending how you look at it, answers to all the above questions may be a qualified ' yes' followed by 'but . . . ', or a disqualifying 'no'. I'll opt for the former.

♦   *Yes*, 'the English language' may express 'English culture'

but which ENGLISHES: Old, Middle, modern or 'new'? spoken Cumbrian or Caribbean creole? standard printed British or American?

and which versions or sections of those cultures: upper, middle or working class? women or men? the un/employed or the un/educated? Protestants, Catholics, Jews, atheists? non/native Britons, Americans, Australians . . . ?

♦   *Yes*, 'English LITERATURE' has had a central role in communicating culture

but for a long time the latter has been (mis)represented by a highly specific **canon** *of texts*, chiefly by men who were almost exclusively white, middle-to-upper class and Western European in origin or orientation.

♦   *Yes* with an emphasis on the written and printed words

but not much attending to manuscript and print cultures in general (including newspapers, popular magazines, bestsellers and pulp fiction) and only very selectively attending to early oral culture (court songs rather than popular ballads) while roundly ignoring most of contemporary audio and audio-visual cultures (from radio to film, TV, video and, latterly, hypermedia).

Yes, English Studies has always in some sense been concerned with culture, communication and media – *but . . . but . . . but . . .*

The purpose of this section is therefore twofold:

• to provide some definitions of 'culture', 'communication' and 'media' which both embrace and exceed those current in contemporary English Studies;
• to encourage a range of activities and educational practices which are effective and enjoyable, whether the course be nominally in English, Cultural, Communication or Media Studies.

CULTURE as a word derives via French from Latin *cultus*, primarily meaning 'the nurturing of growth'. The root verb is *colere* – to grow. The history of the term is especially complex and fascinating. Six uses of 'culture' are distinguished below, each of which belongs to a distinct line of development and all of which can be traced in current debates on the subject. Culture has previously meant and still can mean:

1   *the tending of growing things, the nurturing of nature.* The earliest English senses of culture are tied up with farming, agri*culture* and horti*culture*. '*Cultivation*' is a closely related word which also initially referred to the cultivation of fields, orchards and gardens, and only later (from the seventeenth century) designated the cultivation of people's minds and manners. This radical connection between 'culture' and 'cultivation' and the tending of natural growth is crucial to traditional (especially Romantic) debates on the relations between 'nature' and 'nurture', and the 'human/nature' debate in general. It is also tapped into by modern ECOLOGICAL critics. In these cases, basically, Culture = Nature + Humanity.

2   *human civilisation, set against (rather than alongside or in harmony with) the rest of nature.* From the eighteenth century onwards it became increasingly common to see human culture, for better and worse, as hardly part of nature at all. In these cases, Culture = Humanity – Nature.

3   *artistic and aesthetic activity of a primarily symbolic kind,* as distinct from artisanal and practical activity of a primarily instrumental kind. Such a narrowing and elevation of the sense of 'culture' is observable from the mid-nineteenth century onwards and is closely paralleled by changes in the senses of LITERATURE and art.

4   *high culture (variously called court, elite or dominant cultures) as distinct from popular culture (variously called folk, mass or sub-cultures).* The tendency latterly, largely through pressure from MARXIST, FEMINIST, MULTICULTURAL and POSTMODERNIST critics, has been to resist such fixed polarities, to recognise genuinely plural cultural differences, and to argue for constant re-valuation.

5   *specific national cultures,* usually in terms of such generalised qualities as 'English reserve' or 'Australian directness', or represented by a few other assorted stereotypes: e.g., 'England' = cream teas, castles and Shakespeare; 'Australia' = the outback, Sydney Opera House and Waltzing Matilda. Such highly selective versions of cultural identity underpin national heritage and tourist industries.

6   *universal or global culture – which may or may not be recognised as rooted in 'the local'.* Thus in the spheres of both high art and the mass MEDIA, it is now common for anything from Van Goghs to cans of Coke and from CDs to soap operas to circulate throughout the world as both aesthetic objects and commodities. Celebrants of POSTMODERNISM hail this, along with the Internet and multimedia in general, as the onset of a qualitatively new global culture. Critics of postmodernism recognise the quantity and ubiquity but question the quality and relevance. POSTCOLONIAL, MARXIST and FEMINIST critics all point to continuing imbalances of power and access with respect to this supposedly 'global' culture. (They might also point out that 'colony' ultimately derives from the same verb *colere*, 'to cultivate', 'to settle', which in its past participle form, *cultum*, gave us the root of *culture* in the first place. Hence the threat of domination – not simply emancipation – through someone else's version of culture.)

These six definitions of 'culture' are neither exhaustive nor conclusive. They often overlap and they sometimes contradict one another. All that is to be expected. Culture is a concept central to so many contemporary debates and practices (including whole disciplines such as English, Art, Sociology and Anthropology) that it would be very surprising if there were anything resembling consensus. Indeed, that is precisely why we are left with the challenge and responsibility of deciding how debates on culture are to be articulated outside as well as within those disciplines.

COMMUNICATION as a word derives via French from the Latin *communicare* meaning 'to share', 'to make common', as well as 'to impart' (information) and 'to convey' (goods). The distinctions among these meanings are worth emphasising because they point to fundamental differences in the theory and practice of a whole range of activities we now call communications. Basically, there are four interrelated ways in which we can conceive of the processes of

COMMUNICATION: one-way; two- or many-way; exchange and change; through medium and context.

1   *In a one-way process,* information is 'imparted' or goods 'conveyed' from one person (or source) to another: addresser to addressee; A → B. In terms of language this corresponds to monologue, and is generally referred to as a uni-directional, linear or transference model of communication. This model is properly used in communications engineering where the aim is to transmit a signal from transmitter to receiver in the purest form possible and with the minimum interference or 'noise'. Monologic, one-way modes are also common in social situations where there are marked differences in *power* and **authority** (e.g., in traditional sermons and lectures, where the preacher or teacher is institutionally empowered to speak for long stretches without interruption or audible response).

2   *In a two- or many-way process,* information is shared, goods are made collectively, and they are in some sense held in common. In terms of language this corresponds to **dialogue**, and is in general referred to as a multidirectional, recursive ('feedback') or interactive model of communication. In this case the emphasis is on communication as a complexly *inter*active process, not simply *pro*active or *re*active. For instance, addresser A talks to addressee B, who then responds but is interrupted by addresser C. Meanwhile, participant D goes out without saying anything but having heard everything (though she wasn't meant to). She is thus, technically, neither addres*ser* nor addres*see*, but is still a very important participant. Such many-way modes of communication are the norm in **conversation**, and in this case the activities of interruption or joining in are not merely 'noise' or 'interference' to be eliminated. They may turn out to be a crucial part of the interaction.

3   *Communication as a process of change as well as exchange.* This applies whether the communication system involved is as obvious as a plane full of people or a ship full of cargo (i.e. transport systems) or as inconspicuous as a trace on a computer screen or a movement of air between a speaker's mouth and a hearer's ear. In any event – in every event – neither the vehicles which carry the 'message' (the MEDIA), nor the materials themselves nor the participants involved are left unchanged by the process. Nothing arrives exactly as dispatched; it may or may not reach its projected destination, and both senders and receivers are never quite – or at all – the same again. Notice, too, that this notion of communication as ex/change has a symbolic or semiotic dimension. Values are *transformed*, never simply *transferred*, once they are communicated. In this respect all communication is a form of **translation** and **re-valuation** in the fullest senses.

4   *Communication also varies markedly according to MEDIUM, context and participants.* It is convenient to distinguish various kinds of communication in these respects, some of which overlap:

   ♦ *face-to-face,* where all participants are 'present' in that they are in the same time and place, share an immediate context and can address one another directly (e.g., most conversation);
   ♦ *mediated,* where one or more of the participants is 'absent' and in a different time or place; the contexts are therefore various and some of the communication must be indirect (e.g., all writing, print and telecommunications, including television and the Internet);

- *'live'*, where participants communicate at the same time but in different places (e.g., a telephone conversation, an instantaneous broadcast). The inverted commas confirm the mediated aspect of the contact;
- *recorded*, where some trace of the message is stored and may be subsequently retrieved. Writing, print, film, audio and audio-visual tape, as well as computer memory and disks are all 'recording' technologies in these respects;
- *verbal*, using words;
- *non-verbal*, not using words, but other signs and sign-systems. (Notice that the treatment of 'verbal' as norm and '*non*-verbal' as marked betrays a word-based, logocentric, bias.)

A couple of further cautions and qualifications may be added. First, all communication is in some sense *interpersonal*, so it can be confusing to talk of specifically interpersonal communication when what is meant is 'face-to-face' interaction. A more precise and useful distinction is that between *inter*personal communication (self with others e.g., 'I' with 'you', 'she' with 'he') and *intra*-personal communication (self with self e.g., 'I' with 'me'). Second, we must beware of treating face-to-face communication as unproblematic and even the norm. Certainly, *face-to-face* communication may be more immediate than *mediated* or *recorded* communication, but it is not necessarily simpler or less problematic. For one thing there are many more codes to cope with in face-to-face communication than in writing or print: 'body language' and context as well as verbal language. For another thing the participants may be physically present in the same time and space; but they may have widely varying premises, aims, values and frames of reference. People are still in some respects **absent** from one another even when they are ostensibly 'present'. Indeed, PSYCHOLOGICALLY, no one is wholly 'present' to (i.e. conscious of) her or him self – let alone to others. What's more, all experiences are mediated by our consciousness and by our perceptual – including biological and technological – apparatuses. Hence the need to understand mediation as both apparatus and process.

MEDIA as a word derives from the plural of Latin *medium*, meaning 'middle' or 'between' (hence 'mediator'as a 'go-between', also *medie*val, coined in the nineteenth century to label the age *between* the classical period and the Renaissance). From the early twentieth century, however, it has become increasingly common to talk of 'the media' (definite article and plural). The media thus understood mean two interrelated yet distinct things:

- *those specifically modern technologies and modes of* COMMUNICATION *which enable people to communicate at a distance*, characteristically through print (especially newspapers and magazines); the various *tele*-communications ('tele-' comes from the Greek word for 'far', hence telegraph/'far-writing', telephone/'far-sound', television/ 'far-sight'), as well as film, video, cable, satellite and the Internet;
- *by extension, the institutions which own and control these technologies as well as the people who work for them* (e.g., newspaper proprietors, TV and film companies, advertising agencies and governments, as well as reporters, camera operators, editors, producers, presenters, etc.).

We may therefore say that the media have both *technological* and *social* dimensions. The emphasis on specifically modern, often contemporary, technologies and organisations is constitutive. Many current courses in MEDIA STUDIES do not reach back to materials much before the mid-nineteenth century and the invention of the steam-driven printing press. Often they concentrate on today's (and as far as possible tomorrow's) most pervasive, influential and popular media. Increasingly these are hi-tech *multi*-media. For all these reasons, notwithstanding their obvious areas of overlap, the models and methods used in Media and Communication Studies can to some extent be distinguished. Media Studies tend to:

- play down face-to-face interaction (e.g., **speech** and **conversation**) and play up technologically mediated modes (e.g., print and TV);
- concentrate on TV drama (soap operas and documentary) and film rather than on stage plays, theatre and live performance;
- within print culture, concentrate on newspapers and magazines rather than on books;
- generally concentrate on broadcast rather than narrowcast media and genres: public letters to 'problem pages' rather than private letters to a friend; bestselling pulp fiction rather than **classics**; general release rather than studio films; magazine and TV advertising rather than poetry; etc.

Mediation is the process whereby one person (or group) handles and passes on perceptions and information to another. Some people claim or pretend that the medium and the mediator can be 'neutral', 'impartial', 'objective' or 'innocent'. This is to ignore or suppress the fact that every transference of information involves a transformation, every exchange a change. There is thus, strictly, no such thing as a mediation (or medium or mediator) which simply presents or reflects reality: all *re-present* and *refract* versions of reality (see **realism**). Again, all **translation** entails *transformation* as well as *transference*.

Activities

(a)   *What kinds of culture does each of the following represent?* Milton's *Paradise Lost* (5.1.3); Tutuola's *The Palm-Wine Drinkard* (5.3.2); Kelman's *How Late it Was, How Late* (5.3.2); Nichols's 'Tropical Death' (5.4.5). Are the cultures represented by each piece adequately definable in terms of: (i) high art or popular culture; (ii) literature or non-literature; (iii) class, gender, ethnicity, nationality, age and education? Go on to put the same questions to texts you are studying.

(b)   *'Great English Writing' or 'Visions of Empire'?* These are the titles of two radio or TV programmes for which you have been asked to script alternative frames and links using the same material. The material is by Chaucer (5.1.1), Defoe and Behn (5.2.2) and Brooke (5.1.2). (Substitute others if you wish.) Sketch two very different scripts then consider what this activity shows about the relations between Language, Literature, Culture, Communication and Media.

Discussion

(i)   a culture is not only a body of intellectual and imaginative work; it is also a whole way of life.

Raymond Williams, *Culture and Society 1780–1950* (1958: 148)

(ii)   there is no document of civilisation which is not at the same time a document of barbarism.

Walter Benjamin, *Theses on the Philosophy of History* VI ([1940] 1970: 248)

(iii)   though cultures have changed and will change poems remain and explain.

W.K. Wimsatt and M. Beardsley, 'The Affective Fallacy' (1949)

in Lodge (1972: 357)

(iv)   communication defined as strict transference of or participation in identical experiences does not occur.

I.A. Richards, *The Principles of Literary Criticism* (1924) (1967: 135)

(v)   a scholarly discipline, like literature, cannot begin to do cultural studies simply by expanding its dominion to encompass specific cultural forms (western novels, say, or TV sitcoms, or rock and roll) [. . .] Cultural Studies involves *how* and *why* such work is done, not just its content.

Lawrence Grossberg *et al.*, Introduction to *Cultural Studies* (1992: 11)

READING: The best way into the major debates in culture, communication and media is through two books of 'keywords': Williams 1983, and Bennett, Grossberg and Morris 2005. The latter is an express continuation and updating of the former, and together they are a powerful reminder that core topics such as 'Art' and 'Experience' 'Utopia' and 'Virtual' – as well as the concepts 'Culture', 'Communication' and 'Media' themselves – cannot be grasped without an understanding of their changing meanings and widely contested values. Even in the twenty-odd years between this pair of books the differences can be traced; and with the aid of the *OED* and other key reference works they can be traced way back and further afield. A relevant Cultural Studies reader is During 2006, and the shorter selection in Rivkin and Ryan 2004: 1233–1308 is useful too. Communication is still served well, in principle, with the 'key words' in O'Sullivan, Hartley, Fiske and Montgomery 1994. For New Media in particular a good practical and theoretical work-out is Lister, Dovey, Giddings, Grant and Kelly 2009 (with website). Bassnett 2003 reviews 'British' identities, while Gilroy 2000, 2004 explore the transatlantic diaspora of the 'Middle Passage / Slave-trade Triangle'. Also see reading for 1.1 and POSTCOLONIALISM AND MULTI-CULTURALISM (3.8).

1.3.4   SUMMARY: KEEPING ON COURSE AND MAKING YOUR OWN WAY

There is no single way of summarising the relations between Language and Literature and both of them and Culture, Communication and Media. Indeed the main point of the previous section has been to demonstrate that all these terms are categories and tools, not fixed 'things' at all. We use them to sort and select, work and play with materials which, depending on the very categories and tools we apply, are transformed into specific subjects of study. To be sure, certain texts or other artefacts, because of what we perceive to be intrinsic qualities, may predispose us to work and play with them primarily as 'literary', 'linguistic', 'cultural', 'communicative' or 'media' materials. Nonetheless, it is still arguable how far such qualities are indeed *intrinsic*, and how far they are *extrinsic*: what they contain or essentially are, or the result of a particular way of looking at and handling them.

Of course, the main frames and terms of reference within which you are expected to approach 'English' (or whatever it is called) have already been set in the design of the course you are taking. Your teachers have already chosen and combined the materials you will study. They have also, implicitly or explicitly, already decided on the models and methods you will use in handling those materials. However, that still leaves you with the fundamental task of recognising what those materials, models and methods are; and then attempting to grasp and wield them for yourself. This can only really happen if you are able to stand back a little from the particular course you are engaged in, and try to see round – and even beyond – it. Hence the following summary questions:

- What *are* the kinds of material you are dealing with?
- How far are they being represented to you as language and/or literature and/or culture? And what *kinds* or *genres* of language, literature, culture?
- Are some kinds of text valued more than others? And what are the implicit or explicit criteria of valuation? Are these texts representative, unusual, the most common, the 'best'?
- Are you concentrating on detailed analysis of 'the words on the page' and/or 'the text in context'? Is the medium (or media) in which it is realised incidental or central to your approach?
- Are there visual or audio-visual dimensions to what you do? Or is the emphasis (and your critical apparatus) primarily verbal?
- Are you handling this material on your own and/or in groups? Does this 'handling' involve practical work: making, remaking and 'publishing' texts (including your own), as well as analysing and describing those of others?
- Is there a 'virtual learning' or Internet-based aspect to what you do?
- Turn to the 'Overview of textual activities as learning strategies' (2.4). Consider which of these you use a lot, a little or not at all. Which might you do more of or differently?

Perhaps use the rest of this page to sketch a view of particular courses or your whole programme in the above terms. And in any other terms you choose . . .

CRITICAL AND CREATIVE STRATEGIES FOR ANALYSIS AND INTERPRETATION

PART TWO

PREVIEW

This part offers some flexible, fully integrated strategies for reading and writing. The emphasis throughout is on responses that are both critical and creative. So *interpretation* here implies the possibility of interpretation through *performance* as well as interpretation through *analysis*. The result may just as well be an adaptation as an analysis of a text, a creative re-writing or a critical re-reading. Examples of all the major genres are featured (Poetry, Prose fiction and Play script) and there is practical analysis of a Critical essay too. The whole approach assumes that interpretation is about making as well as finding meaning.

Initial analysis: how to approach a text (2.1) provides a framework that can be used with any text, more or less at first reading. Beginning with some opening moves (*Notice–Pattern–Contrast–Feeling*) and a series of key questions (*What, Who, When, Where, How, Why* and *What if?*), the reader is shown how to analyse texts in detail while keeping alert to broader possibilities of interpretation. This is a robust and versatile method for close reading: modelled at length with one text, it can be applied to many.

Full interpretation: informed reading, adventurous writing (2.2) takes close reading further: wider and deeper. It shows how to build a comprehensive interpretation informed by knowledge of cultural and historical context and enriched by concerted critical reflection. All these aspects involve using the kinds of critical apparatus found in good editions (hence 'Poetry +', 'Prose fiction +', etc.). There is a multi-layered approach to meanings and effects through four pairs of categories: Language–Text, Literature–Genre and Culture–Context, culminating in Critical–Creative Interpretation. Again, the framework is essentially simple, while the kinds of reading and writing it supports are highly nuanced and infinitely various.

Longer projects: sample study patterns and lines of enquiry (2.3) offers guidelines for framing larger-scale, independent work. This is the kind of work that characterises more advanced study and research: in final-year dissertations and projects and portfolios, for example. The lines of enquiry featured draw on the clusters of texts in the Anthology (Part Five): Poetries, Proses, Voices, Crossings. But they extend in many directions and dimensions, and these study patterns can be used to help frame all sorts of major project, critical and creative.

This part concludes with a two-page spread featuring an **Overview of textual activities as learning strategies (2.4)**: from individual essays and portfolios to group presentations and wikis. Further activities and examples can be found on the book website @ 2.

2.1   INITIAL ANALYSIS: HOW TO APPROACH A TEXT

This is a flexible framework to help you analyse and respond to any short piece of text you meet. Here it will be demonstrated in action with a single text, a poem by William Blake. But exactly the same principles apply – with richly various results – to the analysis of passages of prose fiction, play script and critical writing. These are treated using the same method as in the corresponding part of the website (@ 2.1) and, with the addition of further information on context, they are featured in the next part of the book (2.2). The method has already been introduced in outline in the section on **Close reading** in Part One (1.2.4); so turn back there now if you want a quick overview (esp. pp. 41–2).

What follows is a more detailed, technically precise and conceptually elaborated version of those close reading guidelines. And it is worth emphasising that the method is both simple and complex: easy and quick to recall in principle, it is endlessly fascinating to explore – not just apply – in practice. The opening moves (*Notice–Pattern–Contrast–Feeling*) get the critical reading off on the right footing, on your own terms and with a particular moment of response. The core questions (*What, Who, When, Where, How, Why* and *What if?*) follow through with a comprehensive address to all major aspects of the text. The focus is then firmly on the text as such. Meanwhile, each of those interrogatives entails a critical category of considerable power and reach. The approach overall is therefore beguilingly simple in principle and prodigiously complex in practice. The key terms can be recalled at a moment's notice. Exploring, extending and refining them, however – and retuning each in turn to a different text and moment of reading – can take as long as you like.

To see this initial framework in action straightaway – with the words literally 'framed' in the margins – turn to the poem as marked up below on page 96. Otherwise read straight on and get a grasp of the general criteria first.

If you are working in a group, discuss and compare responses at each stage. What do various people *notice* first, for example, and what *feelings* are aroused? *What* do they say it's about, and *what if* everyone introduced a different change? Detailed discussion of such things can be both reassuring and revealing. It confirms that quite a lot of people read and respond similarly (hence the relative stability of academic communities) and that there is plenty of room for disagreement (hence their vitality).

2.1.1   Opening moves: Notice–Pattern–Contrast–Feeling

NOTICE. *What do you first notice about the text – something that for you stands out?* An image, lay out, point of view, sound effect, overall structure, something familiar, something strange, anything. Whatever it is, it will get you going and establish a point of entry. Comparing yours with other people's confirms that there are many possible ways in.

PATTERN. *Now look for a pattern – something that repeats or is similar.* This might be a repeated word or structure, words that have a similar sound or look or range of meanings, perhaps a consistent way of saying or seeing things. This will help you to begin looking across the piece, to see what holds it together. People perceive many similar and some different patterns, but it is always a moot point precisely what they mean and do.

CONTRAST. *Then look for a contrast – something that varies or is different.* Again this might be at word or phrase level – words that don't usually go together – all the way through to larger ways of organising the text: shifts or switches in point of view, different ways of seeing and saying the world. Interesting texts usually have something dynamic or dramatic about them, some problem or complication, subtle movement or outright conflict. So do groups of people discussing them.

FEELING. *And say something about the overall feeling – mood, atmosphere, tone.* Perhaps it basically feels personal or impersonal, informal or formal, positive or negative, even just simple or difficult. Then again, perhaps particular parts of it are more so than others, and you need a more openly mobile array of terms such as fascinating / disturbing / disgusting, or cool / creepy / chilling, or warm / delightful / surprising, etc. Some such 'feelings', though initially vague and apparently crude, are crucial in holding the reading experience together. Meanwhile, just what 'feeling' means – and how far it is reckoned to be in the text, from the reader or author, or among all of them – is obviously up for debate. (So it's picked up later.)

Notice–Pattern–Contrast–Feeling is an effective and memorable combination of opening moves. The core questions put next are a powerful way of following through, and equally easy to remember. They come down to 6 *Wh and a H.*

2.1.2   Core questions: What, Who, When, Where, How, Why, and What if?

WHAT, basically, is it about? Try to say this in a phrase or two to begin with, and then a full sentence. (Subject matter, topic)

WHAT would you like to know more about? Perhaps there are words you don't immediately understand the meaning of, references to things you don't know, or just things you would like to know more about. (Knowledge, reference)

WHAT kind of text is it? Think of how you would categorise it (e.g. poetry, novel, play) and then of what kind (e.g. lyric poem, romantic novel, comedy of manners) and so on to other texts it reminds you of. (Genre, intertextuality)

WHO is addressing WHOM – 'inside' and 'outside' the text, directly or indirectly? Consider a range between 'internal' narrator and characters and 'external' author and reader. There are always many voices and presences of people in play at various levels and moments. (Addressers and addressees: speaker–listener, writer–reader, presenter–viewer)

WHERE and WHEN is the text located in place and time? Again distinguish between the 'internal' times and places represented *within* the text and the 'external' times and places of when and where it was written or produced. (The latter, contextual and historical information you do not have here initially; it is supplied later. But you may still be able to guess and make inferences on the basis of the text itself.) Take Blake's 'London', for example, the place-name and date ('London' (1792)) in the title of the poem here will conjure up certain images and expectations that will be filled out by such noun phrases as 'midnight streets', 'Chimney-sweeper's cry' and 'youthful Harlot's curse' and further clinched in place by the name (proper noun) 'Thames'. Meanwhile, the choice of verb tense (present, past, future) gestures to certain kinds of time-frame and experience of time: here an insistent present tense that is both particular to then and extendable to anyone who puts themselves in the shoes, eyes, ears and mind of the first-person observer: 'I wander . . . I meet . . . I hear . . .'. (Situation and context, culture and history)

HOW precisely is it done? Consider this at every level of language from the smallest individual feature to the largest overall structure. (Form and style, structure and strategy) In particular, consider each of the following in turn (in this order to begin with, then in any order that suits once you have internalised the categories):

- *visual layout and punctuation:* line organisation and paragraphing; speech marks; etc.
- *sound effects and patterns,* voice and tone (e.g. plosives and assonance; personal/public)
- *kinds of word used,* diction/lexis: common, colloquial, in/formal, technical, exotic, etc.
- *kinds of word group,* phrasing: familiar, unusual or strange collocations, simple or complex noun or verb group – with many/few/no adjectives or adverbs, etc.
- *sentence types and structures:* short/long; simple/complex, in/complete; spoken/written; statement, question, command, exclamation; coordinated or subordinated; etc.
- *overall cohesion and development,* links across text as a 'w/hole', how it comes together or falls apart, moves forward or circles round: *repetition* or repetition with variation (*parallelism*) of items and structures (e.g. 'charter'd', 'marks' and 'In every cry / Infant's cry / voice'); *co-reference* such as 'a woman . . . Joan . . . she'; *deixis* such as 'here . . . there', 'this . . . that', 'now . . . then'; *tense* such as 'I see / saw / will see'; *aspect* such as 'I am meeting' (progressive) and 'I meet' (perfective); and *modality* (possibility, condition, obligation) such as 'I may / can / must / ought to see'); *logical connectors* such as 'and', 'therefore', 'but', 'however', 'or', 'and yet'. Along with all the other features above that help keep things together or apart by being similar or different.

WHY does it seem to have been written – and why do you respond as you do? (Motivation, function, value.) Such questions cannot be answered solely on the basis of 'close reading'; they require further information. But you can still make educated guesses on the basis of the text in front of you. For instance – along with financial gain, social prestige and personal expression – ask yourself:

- Does it seem to have been written to please, amuse, inform, provoke, persuade . . . ? Or what?
- And *are you* pleased, amused, informed, provoked, persuaded . . . ? If so, about what? If not, what else?

WHAT IF the text were changed – in some way similar yet different? (Alternative, hypothesis, comparison) This puts the onus firmly back on readers to respond actively to the text in terms of their own choosing. For example, *what if* the text were

- written from a different point of view?
- written in a style (colloquial, formal, technical) with which you are more familiar?
- updated or done in the manner of another author or the substance of another period?
- adapted for another genre and/or medium (e.g. poetry as prose; novel as play or film; or any configuration of, say, song, feature article, TV news, text-message, tweet, blog . . .)

This initial framework is obviously infinitely extendable, and precisely what you do with it is up to you. But its principles are simple and serviceable, and it proves easy to adapt as well as remember. So – one last time – with a fresh lay out for good measure:

Notice–Pattern–Contrast–Feeling!
What? Who? When? Where? How? Why?
What if?!

And now to the proof of the pudding, which in this case involves the reading of a poem. Read the poem on the next page for yourself, using the surrounding terms as an initial framework. It's worth taking some time over this, then comparing your response with those that follow.

2.1.3   Worked and played example

Notice

Pattern   *Contrast*

Feeling

WILLIAM BLAKE, 'London' (1792)

I wander thro' each charter'd street,
Near where the charter'd Thames does flow.
And mark in every face I meet
Marks of weakness, marks of woe.

In every cry of every Man,
In every Infant's cry of fear,
In every voice, in every ban,
The mind-forg'd manacles I hear:

How the Chimney-sweeper's cry
Every blackning Church appalls,
And the hapless Soldier's sigh,
Runs in blood down Palace walls

But most thro' midnight streets I hear
How the youthful Harlot's curse
Blasts the new-born Infant's tear
And blights with plagues the Marriage hearse.

What?   *Who?*   *When?*   *Where?*
            How?   *Why?*   *What if . . . ?*

Notice–Pattern–Contrast–Feeling: notes towards an analysis

Here is the same text marked up (and re-typed) for examples of the main features. *Repeated words and structures* are in italics. Similar sounds, including rhymes, are underlined. **Contrasting words** are in bold. A couple of items that most people NOTICED and talked about at length are in small capitals. Naturally, some of these features coincide and not all of them are registered. (Otherwise everything would be marked in some way.) The commentary below is organised in terms of the four opening moves and left in note form. It draws directly on a couple of classes who worked on this poem (with thanks to those who took 'Advanced Textual Analysis' with me in 2007–9).

I wander thro' each charter'd street,
Near where the *charter'd* Thames does flow.
And mark *in every* face *I meet*
Marks of weakness, marks of woe.

In every cry of *every* **Man**,
In every **Infant's** *cry of fear*,
In every voice, *in every* ban,
The MIND-FORG'D MANACLES *I hear*:

> How the **Chimney-sweeper's** *cry*
> *Every* blackning **Church** app<u>alls,</u>
> And the hapless **Soldier's** si<u>gh,</u>
> Runs in blood down **Palace** w<u>alls</u>
>
> But most *thro'* midnight *streets I* h<u>ear</u>
> How the youthful **Harlot's** c<u>urse</u>
> <u>B</u>lasts the new-born *Infant's* t<u>ear</u>
> And <u>bl</u>ights with plagues the MARRIAGE H<u>EARSE</u>.

NOTICE: "Regular blocks of text on the page, verse." "Stark imagery, a lot of woe, fear, tears, cries, sighs." "There are many repeated words – 'charter'd', 'marks', 'every' . . . very insistent." "'Mind-forg'd manacles' really stands out . . . They sound intricate and horrible." "That strange phrase 'Marriage hearse' . . . a kind of death-wedding . . . an oxymoron?"

PATTERN (samples in italics): "We have 'In every', three – no four – times in the second stanza, and once in the first – so it really is everyone, universal." "Everyone is a 'the' – not 'a' – a type not an individual." "The verse-form, of course, four lines rhyming *abab*." "There are a lot of other repeated words, 'cry' and 'Infant' as well as 'charter'd' and 'marks'. "The 'I meet' and 'I hear' echo the 'I wander'."

CONTRAST (samples in bold): "The contrast between the Infant's tear and the Harlot's curse – innocent child, angry adult . . . though the Harlot is 'youthful' too." "Not sure if this is a contrast but between the 'I' wandering and everyone else seen and heard." "That 'Marriage hearse' again – marriage and a funeral, together." "The 'mark in every face I meet' is different from 'Marks of weakness, marks of woe', they mean slightly different things . . . and the first one's a verb."

FEELING: "It feels lonely, distressing, there's a lot of suffering." "Dark, threatening, 'midnight streets',' blackening', 'runs in blood'. "It's kind of sing-song but also very dark." "Mad and sad – 'mind-forg'd manacles' and 'Marriage hearse'." "Diseased – 'blights with plagues'."

What, Who, When, Where, How, Why, and What if . . . ? Blake's 'London'

WHAT, basically, it is about. In a phrase: 'Suffering on the streets of London.' In a full sentence: 'Someone is walking the streets of London at night describing the suffering of all the different kinds of people they meet.'

WHAT you would like to know more about. 'What does "charter'd" mean – is it the same as "charted"?' 'Does "ban" mean something different from what it means now?' 'What exactly is a "manacle"?' 'Which "plagues"?'

WHAT kind of text it is. A kind of poem – lyric, ballad. A street scene, 'cries of London'.

WHO is speaking to WHOM. 'Inside' the text everyone is crying or sighing or cursing but no one seems to be actually talking to one another. Everyone is a type of person – Infant, Chimney-sweeper, Soldier, Harlot – not an individual. The 'I' (poetic persona / narrator) is not speaking to any of them but to him/herself or anyone who will listen. Most immediately this is to us, the readers 'outside' the text. We may tend to identify the 'I' within the text with the named author, 'William Blake', outside it.

WHERE and WHEN the text is located in place and time. It's the same with the 'where' and 'when'; they are complexly 'internal' and 'external'. The text is expressly placed in 'London' by the 'Thames', dated '1792' and eventually located on 'midnight streets'. But this is perhaps to collapse the text's date of publication and the time and place represented within it. The poem is in the present tense ('I wander . . . meet . . . hear . . .') so that leaves it open to a sense of immediacy at any time. For the present reader that extends to wherever and whenever you happen to be (with the students then it was Oxford, October 2008).

HOW precisely it is done:
♦ *sound structures* The four-line lyric/ballad verse form establishes a pervasive pattern of eight syllables with four beats each and alternating rhymes (abab cdcd . . .), against which certain phrases are foregrounded through sheer repetition (e.g. 'charter'd', 'in every') and localised alliteration and assonance (e.g. '*Marks of* weakness, *marks of w*oe' – a line with seven syllables, and '*mi*nd-forg'd *ma*nacles').
♦ *visual lay out and punctuation* Four four-line blocks are set down the middle of the page; some words, mainly nouns, are capitalised ('Man', 'Infant's', 'Harlot', etc.). 'In every' is prominent at the beginning of three lines. The colon sets up the second half of the poem.
♦ *kinds of word* Most of the words are short, common and simple; a few may strike us as technical ('charter'd') or archaic (e.g. 'ban', 'Harlot', 'blights').
♦ *kinds of word-group/phrasing* There is frequent use of the noun-group structure 'determiner + adjective + noun(s)', e.g. 'each charter'd street', 'Every blackning Church', 'the hapless Soldier's sigh'; and occasional phrases that are unusually compounded or compressed (e.g. 'mind-forg'd manacles', 'Marriage hearse').
♦ *sentence types and structures* The first verse is two sentences and the next three verses are a single, discontinuous sentence, though they might now be punctuated quite differently (e.g. a full stop at the end of the third verse). All the sentences are declarative (they state or describe), though there is a sense of exclamation in the repeated and prominent 'How the . . .'.
♦ *overall cohesion and development* The text is held together by verse-form, repetition of words and phrase structures, a pervasive emphasis on signs of suffering, and by the fact that all is seen or heard by the same 'I'. There is a clear development from scene-setting in the first verse to climax in the last ('But most . . .').

WHY it seems to have been written – and why you respond as you do. It seems to have been written to provoke, make feel and think, and to disturb as well as delight through the combination of dark material with light lyric. For most modern readers this makes for an apparently simple but constantly vexing response. Certain phrases tend to stick in the mind, especially 'mind-forg'd manacles', and the atmosphere is threatening to the last, 'Marriage hearse'. But as always this will depend upon previous life as well as reading experience: only you can respond for you. Hence the importance of the last, more overtly imaginative question.

WHAT IF the text were changed – in some way similar yet different? The poem might be recast as prose and punctuated differently, or technical or archaic words such as 'charter'd' or 'Harlot' might have more common and current words such as 'licensed' and 'prostitute' substituted for them. Both kinds of change would prompt a freshly creative as well as critical revisiting of the precise meanings and effects of the poem as Blake wrote it. So would a more radical recasting of 'London' in terms of an area that you know or know of: the particular 'Marks of weakness, marks of woe' – cries, sighs and tears – that you come across. This could be realised through image or music as well as poetic or narrative text, and again the results could be compared strategically and in detail with the text that prompted it. After all, the text here designated as 'Blake's "London" (1792)' can be approached as lyric and ballad, aesthetic object and historical document, observed record and imaginative insight. So it can be responded to in *similar yet different*, creative as well as critical, ways. (For examples of this method applied to prose fiction, play script and a critical essay, see @ 2.1.)

The above is an initial analysis of 'the words on the page', 'the text in itself'. It is comprehensive as far as it goes but is still fairly rudimentary: it does not really consider the text in context and is still in note form. In the next section (2.2) these opening moves and core questions are developed through a more complex critical and creative apparatus and, crucially, the text is situated in its cultural and historical contexts, past and present. The result is a much more fully informed as well as formed interpretation. Three more kinds of texts will be fed into the mix: prose fiction, play script and critical essay. The same poem is featured, but now supported by further information, then the focus shifts to the analysis and interpretation of prose fiction.

2.2   FULL INTERPRETATION: INFORMED READING, ADVENTUROUS WRITING

Here we deepen and broaden the initial textual analysis in the previous section (2.1) so as to produce a much fuller and more complex interpretation. To do this, we draw on information about the author's life and times and the cultural and historical contexts, past and present. We also develop a more expressly theoretical framework. The result is the kind of interpretation that might inform a substantial critical essay or creative project, and again there is recognition of the critical and creative dimensions of all responses. The poem featured in the previous section is here treated again, but now with extra information supplied in the form of footnotes (hence 'Poetry +'). This serves by way of prelude. Readers are invited to work through this material for themselves using the further categories and checklists introduced below; they can also compare their findings and makings with examples on the web.

The main focus of this section is on prose fiction. A passage from a novel serves as a fully worked – and played – example, again drawing on material in the footnotes (hence 'Prose fiction +'). This demonstrates the method in action and at length. Further samples of text representing the other main genres then follow, also fully annotated: 'Play script +'; 'Critical essay +'. These too are there to be worked through and played around with using the fully developed method. And again, as with 'Poetry +', the results can be compared with examples supplied on the web. The overall pattern, then, is a mix of experiment and example, practice and comparison. By the end of this section it will be seen that fully critical and creative interpretation needs to be informed as well as formed, based on both knowledge and know-how. This is still a method that requires sensitive and systematic close reading. But it is always in search of supplementary information and insight; so it constantly needs to be extended and retuned. Yet further extensions and elaborations are considered in 'Longer projects' (2.3). But first it is important to have a firm grasp of the concepts and categories of the fully developed method.

2.2.1   Interpretative framework and analytical checklists

There are four major critical and theoretical processes in play in this fully developed method; each is characterised by a pairing of closely related categories. These can be presented diagrammatically as follows, with each pairing representing a different level or stage:

LANGUAGE–TEXT
  LITERATURE–GENRE
    CULTURE–CONTEXT
      CRITICAL–CREATIVE interpretation

What this basically means is that fully critical and creative interpretation involves a grasp of the language of texts in cultural context and in relation to other texts and kinds of text, literary and otherwise. The first three of these pairings add depth and dynamism to the preliminary mapping of English in terms of the fields Language, Literature and Culture (1.3). The fourth pairing represents a practical culmination of the other three in acts of interpretation that are always in some measure, and with varying emphasis, Critical and Creative. In short, interpretation depends upon what we find as well as make.

Each of the above pairs of terms will now be reviewed in turn. There are overarching questions in bold, underpinned by detailed checklists and supplementary questions. Return to these questions and checklists every time you have a text to explore in context, and an interpretation that needs to be both informed and fully formed. To begin with, it's helpful to take all the steps more or less in the present order. The progression from the words of a particular text to words and worlds beyond – like that from close to wide reading (1.2.4) – is often convenient as well as conventional. But once you have got used to them, you can vary the steps to suit the particular text-in-context and your immediate purposes. So in practice, as the diagram also suggests, these pairings can be seen as simultaneously accessible levels, not just successively sequenced stages. Your own approach should eventually be more like an assured yet partly improvised dance up and down a staircase than a one-way more or less passive escalator-ride. *It is* what *you do*.

To see an example of this 'full interpretation' method in action, applied to a particular text-in-context, turn to 2.2.3. Further examples can be found @ 2.2.

LANGUAGE–TEXT

What sort of text is this?
- a whole text, part of a text, one of a series?
- to be spoken, written, printed, electronically communicated?
- with or without images, music, movement, touch, smell, taste?
- a monologue or dialogue, representing one voice/position, or two and more?
- serious, humorous, entertaining, ironic, instructive, persuasive, provocative . . . ?

How is language used?
- *visually* in terms of writing, typography, punctuation, lay out and movement?
- *orally/aurally* in terms of sound, pattern, rhythm, intonation and voice quality?
- *verbally*, with words that are familiar or unfamiliar, colloquial or formal, common or specialised, archaic or contemporary, literal or metaphorical, relating to one or two areas of life or many?
- *grammatically – phrases and word-groups* that are plain and simple or complex and elaborate (e.g. mainly nouns and verbs or with many adjectives and adverbs)? *sentences* that are short or long, simple or complex; coordinated or subordinated; stating, asking, directing, exclaiming . . . ?
- *for overall coherence and cohesion,* so as to hold things together or keep them apart: with words referring to one or two figures (or scenes or ideas) or many? with words that develop an argument, description, story or speech . . . ?

(This section connects to the discussion of 'Language' (1.3.1) and builds on the 'How' in 'How to approach a text' (2.1.2).)

LITERATURE–GENRE

Is there anything recognisably *literary* about this text? Alternatively, to invoke other terms, is there anything about it you would recognise as *imaginative, playful, ambiguous, patterned, formed, made-up, fictional, indirect* . . . ? In any case, think of other texts that it reminds you of and be prepared to debate what you mean by 'literary' in the first or last place.

Are there any specifically *literary* genres, forms and conventions in play?
♦ *mega-genres*, identified by big, familiar categories, e.g. poetry, prose fiction, drama; comedy, tragedy, epic, lyric; . . . ?
♦ *sub-genres*, defined by more than one element: e.g. epistolary novel, humorous short story, love lyric, free verse, concrete poetry, dramatic monologue, realist play, biographical sketch.
♦ *specific instances of genre*, which in any particular case tend to be richly plural and more or less unique, and therefore describable in terms that ultimately only apply to that instance, e.g. 'revenge tragedy mainly in blank verse with a soliloquising hero, ghostly prompt, comic elements, pervasive theatricality and a play-within-a-play' (as a characterisation of Shakespeare's *Hamlet*).
♦ *text- and discourse-types* (other than 'literary'), which are equally recognisable and also have discernible sub-types, though the categories may be less familiar and more mobile, e.g.: face-to-face service encounter (exchange at market stall or supermarket check-out); human–machine communication (cash-point transaction, answer-phone message); public media dialogue (newspaper problem pages; broadcast phone-in).

(This section connects to the discussion of 'Literature' (1.3.2); Formalist and Functionalist concerns with 'literariness' and 'genre' (3.3); and the entry on 'Genre and kinds of text' in Part Four.)

CULTURE–CONTEXT

What kinds of culture (way of life, community, group) are represented?
♦ social, sexual, family, ethnic, religious, educational, occupational . . .
♦ urban, suburban, pastoral, agricultural, industrial, commercial . . .
♦ face-to-face, print, multi-media, virtual . . .
♦ common, 'popular', mass, elite, 'high art' . . .
Conversely, whose vision or version of the world is not *being represented, or is mis- or under-represented?*

How does the text relate to its social and historical contexts?
♦ there and then – at its initial moments of production
♦ here and now – at its current moments of reproduction
So how do you see – and say – yourself in this social and historical dialogue?

(Theoretically, this section connects to the discussion of 'Culture, communication and media' in 1.3.3; to the kinds of culturally and contextually alert – often socially and politically charged – approaches featured in 3.5–9; and to the treatment of Text, context and intertextuality in Part Four.)

CRITICAL–CREATIVE INTERPRETATION

This fourth and final section draws together all the above analyses of language, literature and culture into some sustained attempts at overall interpretation and response. It also picks up the opening moves and core questions from the Initial analysis (2.1.2) and turns them to fresh account. Individual interpretations and responses, as already observed, can take a wide variety of critical and creative forms. They may result in an essay, an extended analysis, a rewrite, an adaptation – or a combination of all of these and more. So, while the interpretations that follow are distinguished as, respectively, 'critical' and 'creative' (as is conventional), it is also recognised that the two processes are interdependent and that each is better conceived as '*critical*-creative' or '*creative*-critical', depending on the aim and emphasis. The distinction is relative, not absolute, and always implies a connection.

Turn your overall response into a CRITICAL INTERPRETATION – essay or analysis. (What can you say *about* the text so as to explore it through *critical explication*?)

1   *Begin again with the basic questions WHO, WHAT, WHEN and WHERE to establish some broad terms of reference.* Who is speaking and being represented and what is happening, in what times and places? Equally importantly, critically, who is *not* speaking and being represented, what is *not* happening but could be? *Extend this to HOW and WHY so as to develop your argument:* how is this done, to what ends and with what effects? Again, the critical question is how *else* this might have been done and with what *other* outcomes? And, as always, looking for persistent *patterns* and *contrasts* – things that hold together or push apart – is a good way to get a provisional sense of overall structure and strategy. For any text of interest is likely to involve tension and conflict or complication leading to some kind of transformation or resolution – rarely a complete solution. Some ends are tied – others are left hanging. (Notice that these are essentially the same questions and suggestions as those in Initial analysis (2.1). The crucial, creatively critical difference here is that they are extended through negation and alteration: . . . *not* . . . *else* . . . *otherwise*.)

2   *Go on to identify specific features of the LANGUAGE and specific aspects of the TEXT that throw light on the 'Who', 'What', 'When', 'Where', 'How' and 'Why'.* Consider especially how the LITERARY (imaginative, playful, fictional) aspects of the text open up possibilities and alternatives and expose problems or contradictions (. . . *not* . . . *else* . . . *otherwise*). What is so fascinating, fulfilling or frustrating about this particular verbal construction of a/the world – this particular 'wor(l)d-view'? For example, how do specific GENRES give us a particular vision or version of the CULTURE(S) being represented? And in the light of social and historical CONTEXTS, there and then, what do you make of it all here and now? (This is to reconfigure and mobilise all the foregoing concepts and categories with a view to an integrated though far from totalised interpretation.)

3   *Come to some provisional conclusions about the significance and value of studying this text in its own time and terms as well as your own.* Initial questions will have been provisionally answered on the basis of information gathered and insight generated so far. But in the process they will have been re-posed in other terms and generated other questions as well as other possible lines of enquiry. The most interesting conclusions round off without closing down. They confirm what has been achieved but still acknowledge alternatives.

Turn your response into a CREATIVE INTERPRETATION: performance or rewrite. (What can you do *with* and *to* the text so as to explore it through *creative experiment*?)

1a)   *'Ex- the text'! Explore, experience, express, exchange, experiment with it – in as many ways as possible.* Begin by realising the words through your most immediately available senses and personal resources, then gradually work out through face-to-face social dynamics to more or less virtual modes of communication and media.

> • Read it out loud • Learn some of it by heart • Play with it on paper or screen • Try it in many voices and shapes • Exchange (and change) it as tx, e-mail, blog • 'Free-write' or 'Riff out loud' round some phrase, line, passage • Find or make a relatable image/pic, sound/song, touch, smell, gesture . . .

Do some of this on your own, some of it with others. Here and there. Now and then.

1b)   *Alternatively, begin again with WHO, WHAT, WHEN, WHERE, HOW and WHY – but put the emphasis on WHAT IF? . . . HOW ELSE? . . . WHY NOT . . . ?!* (cf. 2.1)

What if the words were slightly or very different? How else might things be said, seen, heard, projected . . . ? Why not express, explore, experiment with the almost but not quite or at all said: in the gaps, the margins, the silences . . . ? There will be *patterns* that can be extended, disturbed or reconfigured. There will be *contrasts* that can be inverted, resisted or recast. It is your job both to find and to make them.

2)   *Go on to explore the words and worlds in play, textually and contextually.*
     ♦ *Text Word.* Identify specific features or aspects of the text that have attracted or irritated you: particular words, phrases, lines or passages; recurrent styles, structures, strategies; specific characters, situations or events. Play with them.
     ♦ *Context World.* Follow up any aspects of the context that you wish to draw attention to and perhaps incorporate: the author's life and times, processes of composition, modes and moments of (re)production; subsequent critical reception; current use in education (e.g. your own contact with the text). Play with them.

3a)   *Develop some of these creative experiments into a sustained creative interpretation.* This may take the form of a particular reading, performance, rewrite or 'free-write'. It may begin with the 'Text Word' or 'Context World' but eventually draw on elements of both. Such processes can never be predicted but they can, in part, be prepared for and planned. Often, in the event, it will turn out that you have done one or more of the following – though rarely in a single and pure form. But still it can help to know where you may be heading. For example, you may:

> • *imitate closely* as pastiche • *parody humorously* as critique or celebration • *adapt faithfully or freely* (e.g. novel into play or film; sonnet into problem page) • *'update'* or *'down-date'* (e.g. an old text in new clothes, a new text in old) • *do a 'sequel', 'prequel' or 'interlude'* – after, before or during the present action • *intervene with an inversion or alternative* – writing 'against' or 'across' the grain • *just see what happens ('free write')* and try to shape and point the results later.

(Whatever you do is still likely to turn out to be one or more of the above. Becoming aware of which and how far is a crucial part of the critical process during composition.)

3b)   *Add a critical commentary reflecting on your processes of research, reflection and composition.* Compare the text that you first read with the text that you eventually wrote. You will not have been fully aware of such processes at the time, but they can be partly traced in retrospect and so in some measure made conscious and communicated. Where did you start from and go to, with what dead-ends and back-tracking along the way? How far did you take the *text word* or *context world* routes, or both? What were the 'roads not taken' though perhaps considered? How far did you maintain or transform, adopt or adapt the initial genre and media? To be precise, what were the particular words, strategies, characters, events and issues you picked up on from the initial text? In carrying them over how far – and why – were they con-, sub-, di- or even per-verted? Standing back, what kinds of dialogue (linguistic, literary and cultural) have you felt yourself to be creatively engaged in? How far has your critical understanding of the text you first read been enhanced or enriched by the text you eventually wrote – and *vice versa*?

(Creative practice within formal education almost always requires some kind of critical and reflective commentary on processes of research and composition. The trick is to make such things genuine explorations and explications not excuses and self-justifications.)

Also see: English Literature and Creative Writing (Prelude); Writing and reading, response and rewriting (Part Four); and Creative writing, creativity, re-creation @ 4.

READING: McCaw 2008: 24–41, 98–103; Knights and Thurgar-Dawson 2006; Pope 1995; Wandor 2008: 174–231; 2012; Morley 2007: 88–154 ; Cook in Griffin 2005: 195–212.

READ AND WRITE ON! APPLYING AND EXPLORING THE METHOD . . .

The pages of text featured in the following sections are set out as in a full critical edition. That is, together with the footnotes at the bottom of the page, line numbers and highlighted terms have been added in the right-hand margin. You are invited to read and respond to each of these texts in a variety of ways, though all the time reinforcing and refining the method set out above.

Poetry + (2.2.2) is a reprise of Blake's 'London' that was presented as a plain printed text in the previous Initial analysis (2.1.3). Here it is fully annotated and you are invited to draw on this information while trying out the above method for yourself. You may then compare your interpretation with those on the web @ 2.2.

Prose fiction + (a fully worked and played example) is precisely that: a thorough working-over and playing-around with a passage from a novel. The passage is the opening of Emily Brontë's *Wuthering Heights;* but similar procedures can be gone through with any piece of prose fiction. Again, it is best to try out the method for yourself before seeing what others have made of it with this particular passage.

Play script + features an annotated passage from Oscar Wilde's *The Importance of Being Earnest.* Here you are invited to apply the method to a dramatic text and adapt it accordingly. Comparison can then be made with responses on the web @ 2.4.

Critical essay + is a sample and in some ways exemplary essay. It, too, is annotated for the present purpose, and here you are invited to apply the method to a piece of literary-critical – not just literary-fictional – writing. This entails both rewriting and rereading, so the emphasis is again on the creative as well as critical dimensions of interpretation. Responses for comparison can be found on the web @ 2.5.

2.2.2   Poetry +

Try the above method of full interpretation (2.2.1) for yourself on the following text. Be sure to use the information in the notes on the following page along with the text of the poem itself.

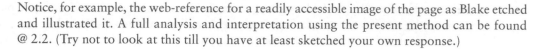

Notice, for example, the web-reference for a readily accessible image of the page as Blake etched and illustrated it. A full analysis and interpretation using the present method can be found @ 2.2. (Try not to look at this till you have at least sketched your own response.)

WILLIAM BLAKE, 'London'

I wander thro' each charter'd street,
Near where the *charter'd Thames does flow.
And mark in every face I meet
Marks of weakness, marks of woe.   4

In every cry of every Man,
In every Infant's cry of fear,
In every voice, in every *ban,
The mind-forg'd *manacles I hear: 8

How the Chimney-sweeper's cry
Every blackning Church appalls,
And the hapless Soldier's sigh,
Runs in blood down Palace walls   12

But most thro' midnight streets I hear
How the youthful *Harlot's curse
Blasts the new-born Infant's tear
And blights with *plagues the Marriage hearse.   16

Notes:

This is one of a series of poems called *Songs of Experience* by William Blake (1757–1827). These were published together with his earlier *Songs of Innocence* in 1794. On the title page they are described as 'Shewing the Two Contrary States of the Human Soul', and are presented in the poetic Introduction to *Songs of Experience* as 'the voice of the Bard! / Who Present, Past, & Future sees'. The volume in which this collection of poems first appeared consists of small pages of ornamented, hand-written etchings that were individually hand-pressed and produced by Blake himself. This poem is illustrated at the top with a picture of a decrepit old man with a stick being led through the streets by a young child; in the right-hand margin another child (or image of the same) is warming hands at a fire. A copy can be found at The Online Blake Archive: http://www.blakearchive.org/blake/. Twenty-seven copies of *Songs of Innocence and of Experience* are known to have existed, each different. Blake wrote and illustrated his own poems, but he made his living as an engraver of catalogues for such companies as Wedgwood pottery. He was a political radical sympathetic to the ideals of the American and French Revolutions and a strongly nonconforming Protestant. He claimed divine inspiration for his art and had visions that informed it.

charter'd (ll.1, 2) The 'liberties of London' and its various City and Guild institutions were assured by royal and parliamentary charters; but they only extended to a wealthy and powerful minority, who were almost exclusively male. Like *mind-forg'd* (l.8), *charter'd* is written with an apostrophe to confirm that the last syllable is not sounded (verbs ending in -*ed* could be at the time, especially in poetry); so when spoken, 'charter'd' sounds very like 'charted' (i.e. mapped). Blake's Notebook of 1792 shows he first tried 'dirty' in place of both these instances of *charter'd*.

ban (l.7) A public proclamation (cf. 'marriage bans') sometimes, as here, narrowed to the negative sense of 'prohibition', 'curse'.

mind-forg'd manacles (l.8) Manacles were chains fastened by forging around the wrists of slaves and convicts; *mind-forg'd* is a compound adjective specially made up by Blake to register a sense of mental anguish and self-inflicted constraint. Blake's Notebook shows that he had previously tried 'german forg'd' instead, presumably as an attack on King George III as a German/Hanoverian monarch and the German mercenaries hired by the Crown.

Harlot's curse (l.14), *plagues* (l.16) Metaphorical and literal references to the sexually transmitted disease, gonorrhoea, which can cause blindness at birth and even death, hence 'Infant's tear' and 'Marriage hearse' (ll.15–16).

2.2.3   Prose fiction +

Read through the following text and then try the method of full interpretation (2.2.1). Be sure to use information in the contextual and historical note along with the passage from the novel itself. A detailed analysis and interpretation using this method is offered in the pages that follow. But try not to look at this till you have at least sketched your own response.

EMILY BRONTË, *Wuthering Heights* (1847) opening

1801.—I have just returned from a visit to my landlord—the solitary neighbour that I shall be troubled with. This is certainly a beautiful country! In all England, I do not believe that I could have fixed on a situation so completely removed from the stir of society. A perfect misanthropist's Heaven—and Mr. Heathcliff and I are such a suitable pair to divide the desolation between us. A capital fellow! He little imagined how my heart warmed towards him when I beheld his black eyes withdraw so suspiciously under their brows, as I rode up, and when his fingers sheltered themselves, with a jealous resolution, still further in his waistcoat, as I announced my name.

"Mr. Heathcliff?" I said.

A nod was the answer.

"Mr. Lockwood, your new tenant, sir. I do myself the honour of calling as soon as possible, after my arrival, to express the hope that I have not inconvenienced you by my perseverance in soliciting the occupation of Thrushcross Grange: I heard, yesterday, you had had some thoughts—"

"Thrushcross Grange is my own, sir," he interrupted, wincing, "I should not allow any one to inconvenience me, if I could hinder it—walk in!"

The "walk in" was uttered with closed teeth and expressed the sentiment, "Go to the Deuce!" Even the gate over which he leant manifested no sympathizing movement to the words; and I think that circumstance determined me to accept the invitation: I felt interested in a man who seemed more exaggeratedly reserved than myself.

When he saw my horse's breast fairly pushing the barrier, he did pull out his hand to unchain it, and then sullenly preceded me up the causeway, calling, as we entered the court—

"Joseph, take Mr. Lockwood's horse; and bring up some wine."

"Here we have the whole establishment of domestics, I suppose," was the reflection, suggested by this compound order. "No wonder the grass grows up between the flags, and cattle are the only hedgecutters."

Joseph was an elderly, nay, an old man, very old, perhaps, though hale and sinewy.

"The Lord help us!" he soliloquised in an undertone of peevish displeasure, while relieving me of my horse: looking, meantime, in my face so sourly that I charitably conjectured he must have need of divine aid to digest his dinner, and his pious ejaculation had no reference to my unexpected advent.

Wuthering Heights is the name of Mr. Heathcliff's dwelling. "Wuthering" being a significant provincial adjective, descriptive of the atmospheric tumult to which its station is exposed in stormy weather. Pure, bracing ventilation they must have up there, at all times, indeed: one may guess the power of the north wind, blowing over the edge, by the excessive slant of a few, stunted firs at the end of the house; and by a range of gaunt thorns all stretching their limbs one way, as if craving alms of the sun. Happily, the architect had foresight to build it strong: the narrow windows are deeply set in the wall, and the corners defended with large jutting stones.

Before passing the threshold, I paused to admire a quantity of grotesque carving lavished over the front, and especially about the principal door, above which, among a wilderness of crumbling griffins and shameless little boys, I detected the date "1500," and the name "Hareton Earnshaw."

Notes:

Emily Brontë's *Wuthering Heights*, her only novel, was first published in three volumes in 1847 under the name of 'Ellis Bell'. Emily died of tuberculosis the following year at the age of thirty. The novel was published in a second edition in 1850 with a Preface and Biographical note by her sister Charlotte, author of *Jane Eyre* (1847), commemorating both Emily and their sister Anne, who wrote *The Tenant of Wildfell Hall* (1848). The 'Brontë sisters' along with 'Brontë country' have since become a powerful composite literary myth and focus for the tourist/heritage industry. This rolls together the West Yorkshire moors, the village of Haworth and the parsonage where they, along with unruly brother Branwell, were brought up motherless by their father Patrick and aunt Elizabeth. They are also the subject, individually and together, of sustained research, criticism and theory, and are widely studied and examined as 'set texts' everywhere in the world that English literature is taught. Emily has recently become much known for her poetry too, first published with the novel in the 1850 edition. *Wuthering Heights* has frequently been adapted into film (e.g. dir. Wyler 1939; dir. Kosminsky 1992; dir. Skinner 1998) and, perhaps most memorably, into a song and video of the same name by Kate Bush (1978). Emily Brontë and *Wuthering Heights* are also featured in the frameworks for Close reading – wide reading (1.2.4).

An Initial analysis of this text in terms of opening moves (*Notice–Pattern–Contrast–Feeling*) and core questions (*What, who, when, where, how, why* and *what if?*) can be found @ 2.1.3. This is freshly synthesised in the Critical and Creative Interpretation below.

Language–Text This text immediately has the look of prose fiction. It is printed from one side of the page to the other (not in the middle, like poetry), there are paragraphs of various lengths, and some of these are clearly indented for speech. The text begins with a date ('1801'), followed by a first-person account of the recent past ('I have just returned . . .'), so we may surmise this is from a personal journal or diary. The text that follows is informative in that it tells us about people, places, times and events (Heathcliff, Joseph, the countryside, Wuthering Heights); but it is also engaging and persuasive in that it invites us to get personally engaged and to view these things in certain ways ('a beautiful country!', 'A capital fellow!'). In fact, as the exclamation marks show, this is an account that is strongly evaluative as well as descriptive. People and things are presented from an emphatically personal, even partial point of view. It is, so to speak, an account 'with attitude'.

This openly evaluative aspect of the text – and by extension the overtly judgmental nature of the narrator – is confirmed by looking closely and systematically at the language. The first clue is the number of words in the opening paragraph that express extremity ('certainly', 'completely', 'A perfect misanthropist's Heaven'). Typically, these are adverbs and adjectives and they have the effect of intensifying feeling from the outset. These are followed by many other adverbs ('suspiciously', 'sullenly', 'sourly') and many other adjectives ('a *jealous* resolution', '*black* eyes', '*closed* teeth', '*peevish* displeasure') which serve to underscore emotionally charged, often negative views of the persons to whom they attach. The same goes for the description of the place later: 'the *excessive* slant of a *few, stunted* firs' and its '*gaunt* thorns'. Meanwhile, the basic choice of verbs and nouns tends to favour those that are highly coloured and dramatic rather than neutral: Heathcliff's black eyes 'withdraw' and fingers 'sheltered' – verbs that express defensiveness, evasion – rather than simply 'did not show', 'were invisible'. Similarly, just about every word that characterises Wuthering Heights the house carries its own freight of embattled strength and defensiveness: 'the *narrow* windows are *deeply* set in the wall, and the corners *defended* with *large jutting stones*'. (Strip out 'narrow' and 'deeply' or replace 'defended' with 'supported' and 'large jutting stones' with, say, 'big uneven bricks' to gauge the precise and cumulative effect of these words.) The fact that the names and natures of the place, Wuthering Heights, and of its owner, Heathcliff, are similarly stern and forbidding is a point to which we return.

Other basic aspects of language and text organisation are worth noting and following up. The meaning of the learned and now faintly archaic word 'misanthropist' may not have been immediately familiar (it means 'one who dislikes people'); while 'station', referring to the location of Wuthering Heights, here carries its root sense of 'where something stands' rather than, as now, where you catch buses and trains. But these are relatively localised, mechanical difficulties; they can be quickly resolved by using a good dictionary (especially a historical dictionary such as the full *Oxford English Dictionary* (OED)).

Much more tricky – because more pervasive and shifting – are matters of style. The basic style here is plain or formal rather than informal: plain in the routine recounting of events (e.g. 'I have just returned from a visit . . .') and formal in the manner of Lockwood's opening address to Heathcliff ('"Mr Lockwood, your new tenant, sir – I do myself the honour of calling . . ."') and in the fact that Lockwood and Heathcliff are both referred to as 'Mr.'; though the old servant is just 'Joseph'. In fact, there is a steadily descending range of styles identified with Heathcliff's response: from the plain and barely civil ' "Thrushcross Grange is my own, sir," he interrupted, wincing'; through the peremptory and imperative ' "–walk in!" '; and so on to the explicit interpretation and virtual translation of the subtext of this by Lockwood, 'The "walk in" was uttered with closed teeth and expressed the sentiment, "Go to the Deuce!"'. We thus descend stylistically from 'high' to 'low' in the course of a couple of sentences: from the strained politeness of the speaker to the downright rudeness understood by the listener. Such effects clearly depend upon dramatic pacing and narrative perspective, so at this point we shift the analysis of language and text into another frame.

Literature–Genre

It is precisely the textual complexity of a first-person narrative that includes dramatic dialogue and insight into people's minds and motives that marks this text as imaginative writing (literature) in general and that species of prose fiction we call 'the novel' in particular. Even if we were not expressly told that this is the opening of a classic novel, we could tell this from its structures and strategies: the switches in who speaks (addresser), who is spoken to (addressee) and what is spoken about (address), as well as the shifts in point of view and perspective. This is a text that openly plays with the activity of telling and showing – it narrates and dramatises. Once these broader aspects of genre are recognised, we can add further distinctions and observe that the mix of wild rural setting and strong feelings promises a kind of raw and passionate pastoral.

We can also get down to further detail about *how* this works as prose fiction: how precisely the narrative and drama unfold, and what room for imaginative play there is in the representation of people and the patterning of events. In addition to the exchange between Lockwood and Heathcliff already considered, we could examine the presentation of the servant Joseph. This begins with what we will already recognise as a couple of characteristically blunt commands from Heathcliff: ' "Joseph, take Mr. Lockwood's horse; and bring up some wine." ' There is then a switch from Heathcliff speaking to Lockwood thinking. Interestingly, the latter is presented as a kind of inner speech, and punctuated with inverted commas, though the narrator's reflection in the accompanying clause (the reporting clause) confirms that this is indeed thought, not speech, that is being recalled: ' "Here we have the whole establishment of domestics, I suppose," was the reflection suggested by the compound order.' This in turn occasions an inference about why the place looks so wild and weed-ridden, again as a kind of recalled inner speech: ' "No wonder the grass grows up between the flags . . ." '. Then there is a direct observation on Joseph that registers the process of gauging how old and well he was ('Joseph was an elderly, nay, an old man, very old, perhaps, though hale and sinewy'). And then we pick up Joseph's response, in words and actions, to Heathcliff's command, along with Lockwood's observation about that: ' "The Lord help us!" he soliloquised in an undertone of peevish displeasure, while relieving me of my horse.' Finally we are treated to an extended inference from Lockwood about Joseph's 'pious ejaculation' and the sour way he looked at him: 'so sourly that I charitably conjectured he must have had need of divine aid to digest his dinner'. The overall treatment of this exchange is therefore both rich and complex in a number of directions and dimensions: it confirms Heathcliff's brusqueness and introduces Joseph's miserable piety (he turns out to be a member of a severely self-denying 'Chapel' sect); it sounds the first note of wildness and lack of care about Wuthering Heights; and it gives us direct insight into the way Lockwood observes and judges people. What's more, it does all this by moving across the dramatic dialogue of direct speech (between Heathcliff and Joseph) while picking up the quasi-dramatic inner speech of the narrator (Lockwood) recalling talking to himself.

The more general point is that we are *presented* with the apparent immediacy of words and actions in a particular place as they unfolded in the past, while also being made aware that all these are being *re-presented* through the memory and words of the narrator as he writes in the present. In other words, we are not only being told something, we are shown that we are being told it. We see the narrator and the act of narration as well as the finished narrative; so we can grasp words and thoughts, not just as past, finished events but also as ongoing processes of thinking and speaking. We, as readers, therefore have the privilege and pleasure of being both *after* the event and *in* it, capable of *seeing* characters and even the narrator, while also being alongside – even apparently inside – them. All this complexity of perspective and potential richness of experience is what we tend to expect from literature. And it is the abiding capacity of certain texts to stimulate and sustain a sense of complexity and richness (though differently realised by different readers at different times) that is the distinguishing mark of all literature that tends to be termed, variously, as 'great', 'classic' or 'canonical' – or at the very least, *worth re-reading*.

Conversely, and almost incidentally, the success of such 'literature' does not much depend upon what is conventionally and stereotypically considered essential to 'literary' language: 'imagery' (metaphor, simile) and what used to be called 'flowery language', usually meaning ostentatious and out-of-the-way expressions ('poetic', 'high flown', 'archaic', 'exotic', etc.). It is more a matter of structure and strategy, complexity of perspective and richness of perception, however these are achieved. To be sure, as already noted, there is highly coloured language at various points throughout this passage: Heathcliff's 'black eyes' that ' withdraw so suspiciously under their brows', which anticipate the rugged, face-like aspect of the place he lives, with its 'narrow windows . . . deeply set in the wall'. There is also the implied wildness and ruggedness that links his name ('Heath' + 'cliff') with the name of the place where he lives ('Wuthering' + 'Heights'). But these metaphorical effects would have much less impact and interest if it were not for the tensions set up between the narrator and the narrative, and the shifts and switches in person, perspective and time. Thus we are expressly told by Lockwood that 'Wuthering Heights is the name of Mr Heathcliff's dwelling, "Wuthering" being a significant provincial adjective, descriptive of the atmospheric tumult to which its station is exposed in stormy weather'; to this he adds the observation 'Pure, bracing ventilation they must have up there at all times'. But the observation on the name, though informative, may also come across as pedantic and patronising (it partly depends how we take the adjective 'provincial' – *OED* tells us it could mean neutrally 'of the provinces' and/or negatively 'not cosmopolitan'). The comment on the windswept location can be read likewise, as a city-dweller's supercilious remark at the expense of those who live in the wild and windy outdoors ('ventilation' is the verbose and probably ironic word he uses). Indeed it is the controlled play of ambiguity and the room for variety of response that many critics see as essential qualities for really good literature and genuinely imaginative fiction. But still the capacity to generate such things is as much a matter of overall structures and strategies as localised devices and effects. Purely verbal imagery and style without narrative and drama will not sustain interest for long. Nor will purely formal textual complexity mean much without reference and relevance to some context: form needs meaning, as much as style needs substance. That is why we now shift focus and deepen the perspective so as to see the language and the literature dynamically in relation to a number of cultural, social and historical frames.

Context–Culture

Questions of the text's relation to its context have to be posed with especial care when the text has become a classic as widely known from film and song or by reputation as *Wuthering Heights*; and even more so when the author belongs to a famous literary family ('the Brontës') whose lives and works are the objects of major tourist, heritage, academic and educational industries that are substantially distinct yet partly overlap. The result is all too easily a kind of mythic composite identity that casually conflates novel and novelist with family and place ('Brontë country'). This myth is fascinating in itself as an instance of the popular imaginary. But it is important to distinguish it from the actual literary, critical, historical and biographical records. The former turns out to be woven from a highly selective and more or less sensational version of the latter. Catching the novel at its actual moment of publication is an essential step in preventing such 'myth-perception' and encouraging genuinely historical understanding.

The very first word of *Wuthering Heights* is a date – '1801' – and this immediately alerts us to a historical complication when read alongside the date on the preceding title page at first publication – '1847'. Evidently the story is set in a time over forty years before it was written and published (it was written just a year or two before publication); and in fact the novel reconstructs the life of a more rural, less industrial time. In this respect, like George Eliot's *Middlemarch* (published 1871–2 yet set in the years before the Parliamentary Reform Act of 1832), it has the benefit of historical hindsight and aesthetic distance: it can offer a cultural overview and social critique. That same original title page also informs us that *Wuthering Heights* is 'A Novel by Ellis Bell' – which is not the name you find above and on any modern edition, 'Emily Brontë'. This palpably reminds us that women writers were viewed patronisingly and with condescension throughout the nineteenth century; so Emily, like her sisters Charlotte and Anne, chose to write under a literary pseudonym that would hide their actual identity and pass as male or female – her sisters chose 'Currer Bell' and 'Acton Bell', respectively.

(Interestingly, the author of *Middlemarch* is still known by her literary pseudonym, 'George Eliot', which could also pass as male or female, rather than her actual name, Mary Ann Evans.) A third significant fact that can be gleaned from the original title page of *Wuthering Heights* is that it was first published as 'A Novel . . . in Three Volumes'. The three-volume ('three-decker') novel became standard throughout the later nineteenth century. Its existence reflects both the massive growth in print output enabled by the introduction of steam rather than hand-presses and the corresponding growth in a novel-reading public, chiefly among the middle classes, particularly women; the novel in three parts was favoured by the circulating libraries because they could hire out three times rather than once for the same book. An important consequence was that novelists tended to structure their novels with the three-volume format in mind: beginning (one), middle (two), end (three); and with an assortment or alternation of narrators by part. All of these considerations have a bearing on the structure and strategies of *Wuthering Heights* as a whole, which has a first volume (which the present passage introduces) that sets up everything very dramatically and a final volume that wraps it all up very (perhaps too) tidily; also another main narrator in addition to Lockwood, the servant Nelly Dean.

In all these ways, just three apparently simple facts gleaned from the original title page of this novel open up whole worlds of difference that could be easily obscured – or completely ignored – if we did not approach the text in context. They give us clues to follow up our initial reading with reading-around, research and reflection. Such 'facts' are not dead and inert but prove live and illuminating: they open up a historically grounded critical understanding of how the novel was conceived by its author and received by its readers then, and by extension how it may be received similarly yet differently by us as modern readers now. They also lead to other questions that have specific social and historical point, and require answers that are culturally framed as well as critically insightful. How come Lockwood has the time and money to withdraw himself from 'the stir of society' and indulge his desire for a 'perfect Misanthropist's heaven' for a while? (He seems to be a type of wealthy city-dweller who can afford an extended stay in the country, observing others but without himself working and getting really involved.) Why does Heathcliff choose – or feel compelled – to let Thrushcross Grange to a tenant? '"I should not allow any one to inconvenience me, if I could hinder it", he interrupted, wincing'. (He may just need the money, but we also find that he is deeply implicated in the personal as well as economic relations of the two main households of the neighbourhood.) To what particular religious persuasion does Joseph belong and perhaps owe his sour-faced piety? (It turns out to be a particularly severe and self-regarding sect of Chapel current in the mid-nineteenth century.)

Finding out about such things is obviously part of the narrative and dramatic appeal of reading the story: what happens next? why do the characters act and react as they do? But finding out more about them – and tracing the relations beyond as well as between the pages of the book – is obviously a major appeal in studying the text-in-context as 'story-in-history'. And naturally, most immediately, this involves study of the novel as it contributes to the present reader's 'story-in-history' in some 'here and now', as well as Brontë's there and then. After all, 'getting away from it all' – whether for a weekend country break, a long-term rent or by owning a country cottage/second home – has an enduring appeal for those who aspire to the pastoral ideal and can afford a life of pseudo-solitude with society as an optional extra. (Notice that Lockwood's position is complex and perhaps contradictory in this respect: he speaks grudgingly of his landlord as 'the solitary neighbour that I shall be troubled with' and yet says 'I do myself the honour of calling as soon as possible after my arrival'.)

The differences between city visitor and country dweller – those who observe and judge and those who act and take part – are writ large in the social and narrative fabric of *Wuthering Heights*. So are the differences between those who observe social proprieties and respect traditional property rights (like Lockwood) and those who flout or subvert them (like Heathcliff). So, too, are the differences and similarities between men and women when it comes to passion inside and outside marriage. At the very opening of the novel we are introduced to just three of the men. We have yet to meet three of the central women: Catherine ('Cathy') Earnshaw, the wild and wilful girl who is Heathcliff's childhood sweetheart and lifelong passion; Isabella Linton, the well-behaved daughter of a well-to-do household; and Nelly Dean, the servant-woman who has known all of them from childhood and acts as the main alternative narrator to Lockwood (to whom she herself tells the tale). All of these, naturally, greatly complicate and extend our sense of the personal, sexual, social and economic relations in play. They also deepen our awareness of the houses and households of 'Wuthering Heights' and 'Thrushcross Grange' as polarised extremes turning on the same cultural and historical axis: the former raw, wild and passionate; the latter decorous, tame and restrained. Significantly – and symptomatically – much of this can be picked up in a close and attentive reading of the opening page or so, refined by systematic analysis and informed by essential knowledge. The same applies to the study of most literature that lasts. Particular interpretations may vary and sometimes whole new approaches come along. But the groundwork in language, literature and culture tends to turn over and return to – even if it offers to reconfigure and recast – much the same words and worlds.

Critical–Creative Interpretations

As usual, for convenience, these are notionally distinguished as *critical interpretation* (typically an essay or analytical commentary) and *creative interpretation* (typically an adaptation or performance). But it is recognised that at any point the one can lead to or turn into or be accompanied by the other. So these categories are treated as permeable and the activities as interdependent. These critical readings are in some way creative. These creative writings are in some way critical. The issue is not so much 'which and whether' – but 'how and how much'?

A critical interpretation of *Wuthering Heights* (essay or analysis), grounded in this passage, might begin by looking for comparisons and contrasts, in this case by weighing the superficial similarity and fundamental difference between Lockwood and Heathcliff. The one is a visitor to the country who claims to be in search of 'a perfect misanthropist's Heaven' and initially thinks that 'Mr. Heathcliff and I are such a suitable pair to divide the desolation between us'; the other is the actual long-standing country-dweller whose glowering presence and downright brusqueness – 'a man who seemed more exaggeratedly reserved than myself' – make Lockwood think again. This contrast also gets us straight to the narrative and dramatic strategy of the piece: everything here is presented as perceived through the more or less polite and civilised, perhaps naïve or condescending, eyes and ears of Lockwood as narrator; what he actually sees and hears are the words and actions of Heathcliff in relation to himself and Joseph. This dynamic of more or less 'civilised' outsider-observer and more or less 'wild' insider-actor offers an axis on which the whole passage (and indeed much of the novel) revolves. So the interpretation could be made to turn on the contrast between the wild and windy, storm-exposed location of Wuthering Heights, home and virtual castle to Heathcliff, and Thrushcross Grange, the more sheltered dwelling of the temporary tenant Lockwood – and again this contrast of the two houses and their respective households extend to the rest of the novel. It is always useful to organise an argument around a fundamental contrast, tension or complication.

A way of developing this contrast would be to focus on the narrative and dramatic strategies as such. While Lockwood is highly self-conscious and deeply judgemental as a narrator, constantly verbalising and explicitly interpreting what he sees and hears, Heathcliff is a man of few words and decisive actions. Thus, as already analysed at length, Lockwood explicitly translates Heathcliff's ' "walk in" . . . uttered with closed teeth as 'express[ing] the sentiment "Go to the Deuce!" '. And Lockwood is similarly vocal about the thoughts that flowed from Heathcliff's curt, two-edged instruction to Joseph: 'Here we have the whole establishment . . . suggested by this compound order'. To these might be added the explicit glossing of the name of Heathcliff's dwelling: ' "Wuthering" being a significant provincial adjective, descriptive of . . .'. All these establish a narrator position that is certainly observant and informative, but also arguably opinionated and pedantic, as ready to verbalise as to judge. Heathcliff, however, is marked by his taciturn gestures, represented more by what he does than what he says – or refuses to say: 'A nod was the answer . . . wincing . . . with closed teeth'; 'he did pull out his hand to unchain it, and then sullenly preceded me'. Lockwood's is an ideas-filled, openly verbal discourse; Heathcliff's is embodied and full of a suppressed passion. The opening is dynamised by the tension between the two and sets the tone as well as scene of the novel.

At this point, to bring in the text–context, story–history dimension, it would be worth confirming that the setting of the novel is emphatically rural and pre-industrial. The present scene is projected as taking place at the turn of the eighteenth century (1801) rather than the mid-nineteenth century when it was written and published. The close of the passage also gestures back to the date '1500' carved in crumbling stone over the door. It is therefore easier to point up the distance and difference between the 'civilised' city (represented by Lockwood) and the 'wild' country (represented by Heathcliff). When Emily was writing, the village of Haworth where she had been brought up in the parsonage was already beginning to show signs of intensive industry (it has been estimated there were some 3,000 looms in the Haworth area by this time); so the contrast between country and city was being eroded. A couple of further observations will help throw light on the oblique relation between story and history and confirm the construct-edness of the fictional world in *Wuthering Heights*. One is that the fictional house of that name (with 'narrow windows . . . deeply set in the wall . . . and the corners defended with large jutting stones') seems to be based on one of that appearance called High Sutherland near the school in Halifax where Emily taught in 1838. Evidently she re-named and projected it out of town and up onto the moors for dramatic effect, for 'atmospheric tumult', as Lockwood has it.

A further observation relates to Emily's character and the preoccupation with solitariness and seclusion that pervades the opening of the novel. According to her sister Charlotte's Preface to the second (1850) edition of *Wuthering Heights*, Emily's 'disposition was not naturally gregarious; circumstances favoured and fostered her tendency to seclusion; except to go to church or take a walk on the hills, she rarely crossed the threshold of home'. This may help explain why Lockwood's resolve to be 'so completely removed from the stir of society' and his preoccupation with Heathcliff as a supposed kindred spirit ('Mr. Heathcliff and I are such a suitable pair to divide the desolation between us') so dominates the opening of the novel. At the same time, it is evidently the difference between the pair of them – the one observing, the other observed; the one acting as narrator of the story, the other enacting its drama – that provides the novel with its tension and multi-levelled appeal. This too, according to sister Charlotte, resonates with a tension she observed in its author: 'Though her feeling for the people round was benevolent, intercourse with them she never sought; nor, with very few exceptions, ever experienced.'

From such contemporary and intimate biographical observation we might proceed, with due caution, to the more or less modern, psychological interpretation that the Lockwood–Heathcliff dynamic plays out an object–subject, outsider–insider word–world dynamic within Emily herself. In this view, it can be seen as a projection of her conflicted psyche that could supplement as well as complement more expressly social interpretations in terms of larger cultural forces and historical changes involving, say, city and country, present and past. In a similar way, in terms of broader theories and models of interpretation, we can steadily move across – we don't have to jump between – Personal–Psychological and Social–Political approaches (see 3.5–9); they can be treated as reciprocally defining not mutually exclusive. Finally, it might be observed that Emily's sister, Charlotte, was writing with the benefit of hindsight, three years after first publication, two after Emily's death; she had read the novel and was now busy (re)introducing and in a sense 'selling' it to a wider reading public. So Charlotte herself, whether she intended it or not, was already part of the process that was turning history into myth, and blurring – even while sketching – the lines between the author's life outside the novel and that of the characters within it. There is no once-and-for-all solution to such problems. A genuinely critical interpretation will not be content to accept one person's view at face value or as the whole story (however intimate or authoritative that view may be) any more than it need privilege one approach and emphasis to the exclusion of all others. A multiplicity of perspective, information and insight is essential. At the same time, each particular interpretation will make its own way through the available materials: drawing attention to specific words and passages with specific analytical tools and techniques, relating them to specific items or kinds of information, and aligning its arguments alongside, against or across certain positions and approaches. It will eventually produce *an* interpretation – not any, many or none. The same – come at by a different route and with partly different resources – applies to the kind of expressly creative interpretation we turn to next.

A creative interpretation of *Wuthering Heights* (performance or rewrite) grounded in this passage might begin with something as simple and direct as *reading the passage out loud* – first with one and then with several voices. This would give an opportunity to experience and experiment with the kind of tone and manner that characterise Lockwood as narrator (reasonable, polite, opinionated, pedantic?) and Heathcliff as his principal object (quietly reserved, noisily gruff, etc.); also to register vocally the narrative transitions from description to dialogue, and speech to thought. A natural extension of this is reflecting on how you might *script the passage as a radio play* (perhaps with voice-over for narrator and sound effects); *a stage play* (what is the dramatic core you could practically present in a theatre?) *or a film for TV or cinema* (what specifically visual textures and camera movement, angles and stances would you use to set the scene or focus action and character?). In each of these modes and media, you would be presented with specific possibilities for interpretation, as well as more or less common questions about overall strategy:

- how do you handle description, action, speech and thought (e.g. Lockwood reflecting on the implications of Heathcliff's double-edged command to Joseph)?
- do you go for 'period feel', updating or a kind of 'universal present' (commercial mainline films tend to go for romanticised naturalism while experimental drama may be minimal or symbolic)?
- what effects do you want to have on your listeners, audience or viewers – what do you want to make them think and feel (sympathy for Lockwood, hostility to Heathcliff, the reverse, or other shifting plays of emotion and indentification)?
- and do you primarily conceive them as for, say, children or adults, a prime-time domestic or specific cinema-going audience (Cliff Richard as the hero of the musical stage show and film *Heathcliff* (1996), for example, filled out Brontë's story with a smash hit family show for all his long-time fans; though it was dubbed 'Wuthering Heights' by some critics).

All of these technical and social considerations about context, receivers and function will have subtle and detailed as well as pervasive effects on how, materially, you interpret the opening of *Wuthering Heights*. Naturally, in the larger scheme of things, this would depend on how you read and interpret the novel as a whole. But a great deal can be achieved in practice as well as principle working with even such a short passage in relative isolation.

Having got one's bearings in the passage (and possibly the novel) as a whole, you can focus on specific *text words* within it and/or extend to particular *context worlds* around it. In this case, at the immediately verbal level, it might be something as intriguing (or irritating) as Lockwood's initial judgement of the place as 'A perfect misanthropist's Heaven' or his condescending comment on ' "Wuthering" being a significant provincial adjective descriptive of the atmospheric tumult'. Or it might be an assortment of ways in which Heathcliff physically responds: 'A nod was the answer . . . wincing . . . with closed teeth . . . sullenly'; or a single significantly charged image: 'gaunt thorns all stretching their limbs one way, as if craving alms of the sun'; or the erotic edge of those 'shameless little boys' (cupids) carved over the doorway. Any of these might provide a growth point for a creative (poetic, dramatic, filmic, photographic . . .) exploration of the issues, devices and strategies of the present passage. Or it might serve to give point to an interpretation that is already on the go.

By extension, any item of contextual information could also serve as the focus for a creative interpretation of the text from outside-in – perhaps to meet one of the 'growth points' coming inside-out. For example, the fact that Emily Brontë wrote under the pseudonym of 'Ellis Bell' might prompt some research (beginning with searching of notes) and further reflection on the generally negative reception of the novel by male reviewers at the time – except by one Sidney Dobell in *Palladium*, September 1850, who observed that, for all its flaws, the novel bore 'the stamp of genius'. (What do *you* find right or wrong, clumsy or inspiring in the present passage? How might you *write a review* of it?) Another example: Emily's sister Charlotte in the Preface to the 1850 edition (already referred to) characterised her as 'not naturally gregarious' and with a 'tendency to seclusion' but added that 'she could hear of them ['the people round'] with interest and talk *of* them with detail, minute, graphic and accurate, but *with* them she rarely exchanged a word' (the emphasis is Charlotte's). How might you combine this perspective on Emily as author 'outside' the novel with that of Lockwood as character-narrator 'inside' it? Again, filmic, theatrical and radio possibilities readily spring to mind (alternating scenes, changes in voice-over, etc.). But so, with a little more thought, do other modes of writing in prose and/or poetry: a blend of fictionalised auto/biography and novel, for instance, perhaps including some of Emily's less famous but increasingly studied poetry. What's more – the possibilities are virtually endless, of course, as are the potential sources and resources – you could easily follow through by drawing on information and insights in Charlotte's 'Biographical Notice of Ellis and Acton Bell' (all good editions of the novel include it). In that, for example, we are given a memorable cameo-image of all three sisters – Emily, Charlotte and Anne – knit tight in 'our own domestic circle . . . wholly dependent on ourselves and each other, on books and study, for the enjoyments and occupations of life'; also how in childhood they made up full-blown myths and stories for – sometimes with – one another. Such images foreground activities of literary cooperation and sharing, together with the legendary close-knit emotional interdependence of the sisters – which in fact, especially later on, was sporadic and uneven, not smooth and continuous. Some things might be made of this too, both in relation to the acts of narrative telling and dramatic showing in the opening of *Wuthering Heights* and in relation to the encompassing myths and histories of 'the Brontës' and 'Brontë country' that compete for the imaginative space around it.

Meanwhile, to realise these interpretive ends – critical as well as creative – all sorts of strategies might be used and other materials invoked and perhaps imitated or emulated.

- ♦ *Sequel, prequel and interlude* – what do you imagine happened before or after the present passage, or might (like the observation on Joseph) be inserted into it? (This could then be compared with what actually happens next and is reported as having happened previously.)
- ♦ *Updating, down-dating and cross-dating* – you could update this opening so it featured a modern landlord and tenant (a student?); or imagine how, say, Dickens, Austen, Sterne or Defoe

might have handled the encounter earlier, in their own times and terms; or consider how it might have been handled later in their idioms by, say, Woolf or Carter, Hardy or Hemingway.

♦ *Responding with, against or across the grain* – you don't have to take Lockwood's word and world at face value (responding with the grain); Heathcliff and Joseph have their say too, and so can you: perspectives and points of view are critically negotiable and, where they don't currently exist but you feel they should, can be created.

For finally, in the end as in the beginning, there are always many more and various ways of responding to a text than 'for' or 'against' it ('good/bad', 'like/dislike' etc.). In fact, there are as many and various responses as there are readers and readings. And all the best (most subtle, sophisticated, demanding, rewarding – in a word, *interesting*) interpretations are creative *and* critical. They re-read *and* re-write *across* the spaces that the text occupies in a variety of contexts, past and present, the author's, the reader's, and many others'. Indeed, the whole aim and rationale of the activity of *interpretation* is to cross and re-cross the text in hand and in mind at certain points, from various angles, on different trajectories. (The word comes from Latin *interpretare*, via French *interpreter*, meaning 'to ask between', 'make a claim').

Also see: 'Critical essay +' (2.2.5), which features Peter Childs's essay on the opening of *Wuthering Heights*; and Close reading – wide reading (1.2.4) and Taking responsibility (1.2.6), which include further work-outs with and references to Emily Brontë and her novel.

READING: For a range of good (and different) critical editions, see Brontë, E. 2007, 1996, 1965; for critical biography, see Gérin 1971, Frank 1992; and for some classic studies, see Eagleton 1975, Showalter 1977 and Gilbert and Gubar 1999; also the site of the Brontë Society at http://bronte.org.uk. (For fuller references see 1.2.4 and 1.2.6.)

2.2.4   Play script +

Read through the following text for yourself, and perhaps out loud with others. Then try the method of full interpretation (2.2.1). Be sure to use the information in the attached notes along with the passage from the play. An Initial analysis is offered in the pages that follow; and a full interpretation using the present method can be found @ 2.2.5. But try not to look at either of these till you have at least sketched your own response.

OSCAR WILDE, *The Importance of Being Earnest* (1895) Act 1

[Jack and Gwendolen have just agreed to get engaged; but they have yet to secure the agreement of her mother, Lady Bracknell. The play is set at the time of writing, in the early 1890s, and the present scene (towards the end of Act 1) takes place in the flat of Jack's close friend, Algernon, a nephew of Lady Bracknell, in London's fashionable West End. * refers to a footnote]

LADY BRACKNELL. (*Sitting down.*) You can take a seat, Mr Worthing. (*Looks in her pocket for note-book and pencil.*)

JACK. Thank you, Lady Bracknell, I prefer standing.

LADY BRACKNELL. (*Pencil and note-book in hand.*) I feel bound to tell you that you are not down on my list of eligible young men, although I have the same list as the dear Duchess of Bolton has. We work together, in fact. However, I am quite ready to enter your name, should your answers be what a really affectionate mother requires. Do you smoke?

JACK. Well, yes, I must admit I smoke.*

LADY BRACKNELL. I am glad to hear it. A man should always have an occupation of some kind. There are far too many idle men in London as it is. How old are you?

JACK. Twenty-nine.

LADY BRACKNELL. A very good age to be married at. I have always been of an opinion that a man who desires to get married should know everything or nothing. Which do you know?

JACK. (*After some hesitation.*) I know nothing, Lady Bracknell.

LADY BRACKNELL. I am pleased to hear it. I do not approve of anything that tampers with natural ignorance. Ignorance is like a delicate exotic fruit; touch it and the bloom is gone. The whole theory of modern education is radically unsound.* Fortunately in England, at any rate, education produces no effect whatsoever. If it did, it would prove a serious danger to the upper classes, and probably lead to acts of violence in Grosvenor Square. What is your income?

JACK. Between seven and eight thousand a year.*

LADY BRACKNELL. (*Makes a note in her book.*) In land, or in *investments*?*

JACK. In investments, chiefly.

LADY BRACKNELL. That is satisfactory. What between the duties expected of one during one's lifetime, and the duties extracted of one after one's death, land has ceased to be either a profit or a pleasure. It gives one position and prevents one from keeping it up. That's all that can be said about land. [. . .] What are your politics?

JACK. Well, I am afraid I really have none. I am a Liberal Unionist.

LADY BRACKNELL. Oh, they count as Tories.* They dine with us. Or come in the evening at any rate. Now to minor matters. Are your parents living?

JACK. I have lost both my parents.

LADY BRACKNELL. Both? . . . To lose one parent may be regarded as a misfortune . . . to lose both seems like carelessness. Who was your father? He was evidently a man of some wealth. Was he born in what the Radical papers call the purple of commerce, or did he rise from the ranks of the aristocracy?

JACK. I am afraid I really don't know. The fact is, Lady Bracknell, I said I had lost my parents. It would be nearer the truth to say that my parents seem to have lost me . . . I don't actually know who I am by birth. I was . . . well, I was found.

LADY BRACKNELL. Found!

JACK. The late Mr Thomas Cardew, an old gentleman of a very charitable and kind disposition, found me, and gave me the name of Worthing, because he happened to have a first-class ticket for Worthing in his pocket at the time. Worthing is a place in Sussex. It is a sea-side resort.*

LADY BRACKNELL. Where did the charitable gentleman who had a ticket for this sea-side resort find you?

JACK. (*Gravely.*) In a handbag.

LADY BRACKNELL. A handbag?

JACK. (*Very seriously.*) Yes, Lady Bracknell, I was in a handbag – a somewhat large, black leather handbag, with handles to it – an ordinary handbag, in fact.

LADY BRACKNELL. In what locality did this Mr James, or Thomas, Cardew come across this ordinary handbag?

JACK. In the cloak room at Victoria Station.* It was given to him in mistake for his own.

LADY BRACKNELL. The cloak room at Victoria Station?

JACK. Yes. The Brighton line.*

LADY BRACKNELL. The line is immaterial. Mr Worthing, I confess I feel somewhat bewildered by what you have just told me. To be born, or at any rate bred, in a handbag, whether it had handles or not, seems to me to display a contempt for the ordinary decencies of family life that reminds one of the worst excesses of the French Revolution.* And I presume you know what that unfortunate movement led to? As for the particular locality in which the handbag was found, a cloakroom at a railway station might serve to conceal a social indiscretion – has probably, indeed, been used for that purpose before now – but it could hardly be regarded as an assured basis for a recognized position in good society.

Notes:

The Importance of Being Earnest (printed in 1899 with the subtitle 'A Trivial Comedy for Serious People') was first performed in 1895 at St James's Theatre in London's fashionable West End (near where the above scene is set). It was unusual in that it was more verbally witty and politically sharp but also more dramatically static than the then-dominant genre of fast-paced and racy farces in the French manner. It did well at the box office though it received mixed reviews: William Archer applauded, Bernard Shaw expressed reservations. It was taken off the stage after sixty-six performances, however, because of its author's trial and subsequent prosecution for homosexual behaviour. This at that time was stigmatised as 'gross indecency', and a criminal offence.

Oscar Wilde – full name Oscar Fingal O'Flahertie Wills Wilde – was born into the Anglo-Irish aristocracy in Dublin in 1854. He studied classics at Trinity College, Dublin and Magdalen College, Oxford and at that time identified himself with the cult of 'Art for Art's sake'. After writing children's stories such as *The Happy Prince* (1888) and a partly autobiographical novel on the relation between sublime art and decadent life, *The Picture of Dorian Gray* (1890; represented below, 5.2.3), he turned to writing for the theatre – very successfully – in the early 1890s. Meanwhile, he was writing critical essays, chiefly on art and politics: 'The Critic as Artist' (a Platonic dialogue in a modern drawing room) and 'The Soul of Man under Socialism' (he was a committed, if highly eccentric, socialist) – both printed in *Intentions* (1891). After his trial, which he lost, Wilde served two years in jail, where he wrote *The Ballad of Reading Gaol* (1898) and *De Profundis* (incomplete and published posthumously). He died, relatively poor and obscure, in Paris in 1900. But his plays, especially *The Importance of Being Earnest*, have been regularly staged ever since his death, and greatly influenced those of Noël Coward; it was turned into successful films in 1952 and 2002, this last starring Colin Firth as Jack/Earnest and Judi Dench as Lady Bracknell. Since the 1970s Wilde has been increasingly studied across all his work, and is now appreciated as a gay, socialist and Anglo-Irish writer, as well as an irrepressible wit and aesthete.

I must admit I smoke. Smoking was chiefly a male preserve, especially amongst the upper classes. The immediate reference here is to cigarettes (Jack has a cigarette case), which in the 1890s were coming into fashion as luxury items. More commonly, smoking featured pipes and cigars were more prestigious.

Modern education. In England at this time 'public' (i.e. private) schools for the wealthy and privileged were beginning to emphasise preparation for the professions alongside the classics, and there was growing recognition that modern workers needed to be literate and technically trained. There was also growing awareness amongst the working class themselves, supported by the emerging Trades Union and Labour Movements, that education was essential for political power and a full life. As a consequence, the highly cultured yet essentially elitist view of mid-Victorian education for the middle and upper classes held by Matthew Arnold (1822–88) was being challenged and in part superseded. Wilde wrote extensively and wittily on the 'over-educated' and with critical edge on the un- or under-educated classes: e.g. 'A Few Maxims for the Instruction of the Over-Educated' (1890) and 'The Soul of Man under Socialism' (1891).

Grosvenor Square. By the 1890s there was already a long-standing history of riots and popular demonstrations in Grosvenor Square, stretching from the Gordon riots of the 1780s onwards. One of the most affluent and fashionable 'addresses' in London (its central garden was kept locked and solely for private use by residents), it became the site of embassies and commissions as well as opulent residences, and therefore a favourite target for public dissent.

Between seven and eight thousand a year. This was over 100 times the annual earnings of a skilled male factory worker (who got a weekly wage of under 30 shillings, £75 per year); a female doing a similar job got less than 20 shillings, £50 a year. But there was not always work the year round.

In investments? (The emphasis is Lady Bracknell's / Wilde's.) This is therefore 'new', more readily available money based largely on business and trade, rather than 'old' money tied up in land. The aristocracy continued to offer social status but were increasingly short of economic clout.

Liberal Unionist . . . Tories Liberals and Tories were the two main political parties in nineteenth-century Britain; the Labour Party was not to have its first MP for another five years, in 1900. Liberals tended to be more economically 'progressive' and identified with business and 'the city'; Tories tended to be more 'conservative' (this became their official name later) and identified with land and 'the country'. Liberal Unionists wanted to keep the Union between Britain and Ireland but supported Irish 'Home Rule', and they inclined to the Tory position in this respect. Hence Lady Bracknell's accommodating but barbed comment.

Worthing . . . Victoria Station . . . The Brighton line Worthing and Brighton, both on the Sussex coast, had become well established as seaside resorts during the nineteenth century. Later in the century, because of the expansion of the railways, they were especially popular as destinations for day excursions from Victoria Station in London. ('Brighton and Back for Three and Sixpence' (1859) is the title of a painting by Charles Rossiter depicting a railway carriage crowded with 'shabby genteel' passengers out for a day excursion.) Brighton had been associated with the stylish and affluent life since before the days of the Prince Regent, later George IV, who had had Brighton Pavilion built, and completed in 1822. Worthing was where Wilde wrote this play in 1894.

The French Revolution. The gesture is obviously dismissive but, in performance and in historical context, has complex and contentious resonances that need listening out for and looking into. Lady Bracknell is referring in very broad terms to the overthrow of the aristocracy and the *ancien régime* by the French first Republic. Slightly more particularly, and more darkly – *And I presume you know what that unfortunate movement led to* – she doubtless intends Jack to recall the sensationalised accounts of 'The Terror' (almost exactly a hundred years earlier) in which some of the nobility, including the king and queen, were guillotined and their lands confiscated. This was the account most famously and influentially circulated by the anti-revolutionary writer Edmund Burke in his *Reflections on the Revolution in France* (1790). An alternative account, sympathetic to the aims of the revolutions in both America and France and expressly critical of Burke's interpretation, is Thomas Paine *The Rights of Man* (1791–2), which in turn helped occasion Mary Wollstonecraft's *A Vindication of the Rights of Woman* (1792). Unlike Burke, Paine and Wollstonecraft were actually in France at the time, and Paine is unique in having had had a hand in drafting the post-revolutionary constitutions of both America and France. Other events that followed and in part flowed from the early example of the French Revolution included the Paris Commune and other mid-nineteenth-century expressions of revolutionary activity across Europe; especially (in)famous were those of 1848, which were the subject of a study by Karl Marx. Lady Bracknell most certainly did *not* intend a direct reference to these revolutions, nor to Paine and Marx – nor would Jack probably have recognised it. But Wilde, who counted himself a 'Socialist' (albeit of a highly idiosyncratic variety), had read all of them and may *well* have intended such an allusion for the alert or like-minded. Certainly he could have expected at least some of his audience to recognise that Lady Bracknell's (and

Burke's) was the traditionally negative and reactionary view of what 'that unfortunate movement led to' – not the revolutionary positive one.

Initial analysis of Wilde passage using 'opening moves' and 'core questions' (2.1.1–2)

Opening moves tend to *notice* such things as: the fact that Lady Bracknell persists in sitting while Jack insists on standing; Lady Bracknell's slightly unexpected responses to Jack's answers; all the seemingly gratuitous detail about trains and seaside resorts; the overall wit and politeness of the piece; the fact that a section has been edited out, hence the [. . .]. (Yes. Unfortunately it had to be trimmed for reasons of space. It contains another five exchanges on the subject of wealth and respectability.) The basic *pattern* discerned is the steady alternation of question from Lady B, answer from Jack, and response from Lady B; and this naturally underpins the overall *contrast* between older, aristocratic (seated) woman and younger, moneyed man (standing). The *feelings* generated are of lightness, cheerfulness and quiet optimism overall – though these are troubled towards the close as the vagaries of Jack's parentage are unpacked. The essential feeling (following from the genre) is comic – with an ironic or even satiric edge.

Core questions produce a similarly serviceable array to get some basic bearings:

- *What?* In very brief, it's about a mother checking out a prospective husband. More fully, it's an interview – an interrogation really – of a younger moneyed man by an older aristocratic woman to see how far he is suitable, economically and socially, to marry her daughter. What modern readers tend to want to know more about is 'Does Lady B care whether he loves Gwendolen?'; was there ever a 'Lady Bracknell' or a 'Duchess of Bolton' (they suspect not); and will it all turn out alright in the end? (they supect or already know it will). For the question 'what kind of text is this?' is quite easy to answer on the surface: It's a witty comedy of social manners. Though there may also be a sense that there is depth to it too.
- *Who?* Lady Bracknell and Jack Worthing in the foreground, of course, and Gwendolen and Algernon off stage at the moment. But beyond and around those are questions of actual actors and audiences (there is always another such layer of make-believe in the theatre); and by extension of Oscar Wilde as author (wit, social critic, story writer, gay man, Anglo-Irishman, and the un/like . . .) and of you, me or someone else as actual readers, writers, responders-to and the un/like. Whether we move inside-out or outside-in, the people involved in plays – producing or responding – all have a tendency to don metaphorical masks and assume roles: to become kinds of *dramatis personae*. It seems to go with the territory.
- *When and Where?* In 1895 at The St James's Theatre in London's West End – first night on February 14th, St Valentine's Day, to be precise. It ran for sixty-six performances and then was pulled as Wilde's trial hit the headlines. He was in Pentonville prison by 25th May and the play was not revived until 1902 (when Wilde had been two years dead) – though it then became an immediate and long-running success. It was, however, published and quickly sold out in 1899. After that it's a matter of the many and various moments and modes of reproduction up to the present. In whatever 'heres and nows' you and I do or don't share.
- *How?* This present text, in a strange yet routine way, is the most immediate crucial link in time and place and person between us. Wilde's play as text (play-script) is the most immediate instance of it, a page or two before this. That, however, would be to limit the 'how' to the words on the page alone. Though we also know, can imagine, project these as moving and speaking bodies in space on stage (with an audience) or flickering screens and speakers at the cinema or

on TV, through DVD or whatever other computerised multi-media interface is in use when you come to read this (also with its own viewers, touchers, tasters . . .). The 'how' is that – this . . . the other variable.

♦   *Why?* 'Whyever not?!' might have been Wilde's wittily evasive answer – sporting with inversion just for the heaven and hell of it. Followed perhaps by some subtle, searching, delightful disquisition – doubtless enchanting some and irritating others – on the intricate, intimate relation between aesthetics and ethics, politics and poetics. Or any other pairing that might sound good enough both to charm and to be truly moral. For, as Wilde himself says, in one of many memorable and ultimately inimitable epigrams: 'If one tells the truth, one is sure, sooner or later, to be found out.' Or, conversely and equally paradoxically, 'I live in terror of not being misunderstood' (see Wilde 'The Critic as Artist' [1891] 1992 : 104). So . . .

♦   *What if?* was obviously second, third – even perhaps first – nature to him. In reading and responding to his work we may be persuaded to think so too. Certainly, we should and shall take him seriously. But not solemnly. And we really must take *his* hypotheses and imaginings otherwise at face value. Or else! For 'Art is the only serious thing in the world. And the artist is the only person who is never serious'. Seriously? (If all else fails – or seems to work too easily – fall back on Action 10: 'Enjoy Studying English Seriously'. You can usually make something from there.)

A full interpretation of this passage from *The Importance of Being Earnest*, using all the stages/levels of Language–Text, Literature–Genre, Culture–Context and Critical–Creative Interpretation, can be found on the website @ 2.2.4.

Also see: **Drama, theatre, film, TV** and **Comedy, tragedy**; (Part Three) GENDER AND SEXUALITY – FEMINISM, MASCULINITY AND QUEER THEORY (3.6); and @ 1.4. Theatre and Film Studies. For Oscar Wilde's and Will Self's 'Pictures of Dorian Gray', see 5.2.3.

READING: On Wilde's play, begin with a good critical edition such as that by Gillespie (Norton 2006).

2.2.5   Critical essay +

Read through the following essay and then use the same method of full interpretation that you have used with other texts (2.2.1). Be sure to use the information in the attached notes along with the passage from the essay itself. The beginning of a full interpretation is offered in the pages that follow, and this is carried through on the web. But try not to look at either till you have at least sketched your own response.

Peter Childs, *Reading Fiction: Opening the Text* (2001)

[This essay is from a chapter in the above collection and is based on the opening of Emily Brontë's *Wuthering Heights*, featured earlier in the present section (2.2.3). The present piece has been slightly reduced, but the words used and the order of the argument are exactly the same as in the original. Comments within square brackets indicate what has been omitted.]

Critics habitually analyse Brontë's novel in terms of contrasts, particularly that between the Heights and the Grange, the Earnshaws and the Lintons. I also want to consider oppositions in *Wuthering Heights*, but in terms of language, not character and location. To do this I will employ some of the concepts of the Russian critic Mikhail Bakhtin whose theories of the novel provide a distinctive approach to the analysis of textual meaning. My starting points from the opening pages of the novel, because their importance will also be evident in the conclusion of my analysis, are the two sentences: 'Thrushcross Grange is my own, sir' (l.19) and 'Wuthering Heights is the name of Mr. Heathcliff's dwelling' (l.43).

At the heart of Bakhtin's theories is the idea of dialogism. Bakhtin believed that nothing has meaning in itself but only in relation to something else. [He emphasises Bakhtin's belief that 'nothing could really be monologic'.] David Lodge writes in *After Bakhtin* (1990: 22) that:

> There is an indissoluble link in Bakhtin's theory between the linguistic variety of prose fiction, which he called heteroglossia, and its cultural function as the continuous critique of all repressive, authoritarian, one-eyed ideologies. As soon as you allow a variety of discourses into a textual space – vulgar discourses as well as polite ones, vernacular as well as literary, oral as well as written – you establish a resistance . . . to the dominant discourse.

Bakhtin therefore roots meaning in the social, though the social is conceived in a special way because Bakhtin's concept of language is as something essentially dialogic: that is, the word is a two-sided act. The words we use come to us already imprinted with the intentions and accents of previous users, and the novel for Bakhtin is a mix of varying and opposed languages in which a number of different types of speech, representing different belief systems, carry on an unresolved battle. Fiction therefore presents a multiplicity of social voices and in studying a novel it is profitable to analyse the range of competing voices. Words have meanings according to the groups that use them and language is always in a state of flux: this potential of language to mean different things is the basis of Bakhtin's dialogism.

So, for Bakhtin there is always an official language in play; one which is generally accepted and sanctioned by society. With *Wuthering Heights* it is possible from this perspective to interrogate the use of names inside and outside the text in terms of a struggle for power, property and possession; not between the Grange and the Heights but between those with and without privilege, those with being the dynastic patriarchs in the Linton and Earnshaw families, and those without being the women and orphans, particularly the first Cathy and Heathcliff.

First of all, names and narrators within and without *Wuthering Heights* seem to reinforce a masculine norm in society. For example in 1847, the first fictional name a reader would have encountered (without knowing it) was the pseudonym under which Emily Brontë published the novel: 'Ellis Bell'. Additionally, the author 'Ellis Bell' employed a male character, Lockwood, as the principal narrating voice. From a Bakhtinian perspective this apparent male authority is undermined first by the fact that Ellis, though it is assumed by many readers to be a male name, is in fact an androgynous name, like Currer and Acton, the names chosen by Charlotte and Anne Brontë; and second, by the introduction of a female narrator who in fact provides and controls the majority of the story that Lockwood tells.

If we next consider the names within the text itself, an initial puzzle is 'Heathcliff'. The character's position as orphan, or perhaps illegitimate son, is reinforced by the lack of an additional name. Heathcliff stands as both first name and surname, but it is at first used only as a forename and therefore an emasculated Heathcliff lacks the father's surname which would represent his masculine power and identity in a property-owning society. This allies his socio-economic position with that of women in 1847, who could neither own property in marriage nor pass on their surname to a child. However, this is undermined by the history of the name that the orphan is given: 'Heathcliff' was the name of the Earnshaws' dead first son, and this connection implies that the illegitimate Heathcliff has a nominal right to inherit the family wealth. It is also an important semantic point that the name 'Heathcliff' has a similar meaning to the name of the Earnshaws' house. Lockwood informs the reader in the opening that '"Wuthering" being a significant provincial adjective, descriptive of the atmospheric tumult to which its station is exposed in stormy weather' (ll.44–6). Similarly the name 'Heathcliff' connotes a lofty windswept place, adding further meaning to Lockwood's previous observation that: 'Wuthering Heights is the name of Mr. Heathcliff's dwelling' (l.43).

[There are then two further arguments about and examples of the significance of names. One is that the first Cathy has a 'name-that-never-was' in that she never actually married Heathcliff and therefore was never actually called 'Catherine Heathcliff'; though she did once passionately declare '"I *am* Heathcliff"'. The other is that 'Heathcliff', as an orphan of unknown parentage, was never able to make a clear distinction between first and last names; this is compared to his suspended state between various versions of heaven and hell. 'In Wuthering Heights', it is observed, 'there is a constant battle over the notions of heaven and hell.']

In conclusion, the last words of the opening I have quoted are: 'Before passing the threshold, I paused to admire a quantity of grotesque carving lavished over the front, and especially about the principal door, above which, among a wilderness of crumbling griffins and shameless little boys, I detected the date "1500" and the name "Hareton Earnshaw"' (ll.54–8). In terms of names and their symbolization of power struggles, as in other ways, *Wuthering Heights* has a cyclical shape. Hareton Earnshaw is the name of the builder of the Heights and it is a new Hareton Earnshaw who, by marrying the second Catherine, born a Linton, brings the novel full circle, by possessing the Heights again. Meanwhile, Heathcliff, the orphan who has become the catalyst and engineer of the book's *revolutions,* has turned away from this secular struggle to a supernatural struggle over heaven and hell.

Notes:

Peter Childs's *Reading Fiction: Opening the Text* (2001) looks at the openings of twenty-four novels in English, from Daniel Defoe's *Robinson Crusoe* (1719) to Hanif Kureishi's *The Buddha of Suburbia* (1990), including, for example, Mary Shelley's *Frankenstein* (1818) and James Joyce's *A Portrait of the Artist as a Young Man* (1916) along the way. The book grew out of a course he was teaching at the time as a Senior Lecturer in English at Cheltenham and Gloucester College of Higher Education. That institution subsequently became the University of Gloucestershire, where he is currently Dean of Research and Professor of Modern English Literature. Previously he taught at Liverpool John Moores University, another institution that had become one of the 'new' British universities from the early 1990s onwards. Childs is a prolific critic and theorist of literature and culture, as well as a committed teacher and text-book writer. His other books include *Texts: Contemporary Cultural Texts and Critical Approaches* (2006) (which looks at modern media texts and discourses, from films and TV shows such as *The Matrix* and *Big Brother* to a popular novel such as *Harry Potter* and a global book-selling site such as *Amazon*) and *The Essential Guide to English Studies* (2008), which was written while he was a UK National Teaching Fellow. (On a more personal note, as someone working at another 'new' university and as a fellow Teaching Fellow, I would like to express my particular thanks to Peter Childs for agreeing to my use of his essay.)

Below is the beginning of a full interpretation of Childs's critical essay in terms of *Language–Text*. The other levels/stages (*Literature–Genre* and *Culture–Context* through to *Critical–Creative Interpretation*) can be found @ 2.2.5, where you will also find an Initial Analysis framed in terms of opening moves and core questions. Compare these analyses and interpretations with your own.

To begin with, it will be useful to refresh your sense of the common structures and strategies used in essays, including the classic *diamond* design (see 1.2.7 **Writing an essay to make your mark**). Consider the precise ways in which Childs opens, develops and closes his essay. Notice how he establishes the initial critical context and his own agenda; how he develops and substantiates specific topics; and how he draws it all to a conclusion while reminding us of where he came in and has gone since. All these aspects are elaborated in the interpretation that follows.

Language–Text This is a critical essay which itself looks at the opening of a novel. The present critical piece comes from a textbook that uses this strategy with a number of novels. It has here been cut and re-joined at a number of points; hence the square brackets enclosing suspension dots [. . .], so as to signal an editorial excision. Even a quick look over the layout and punctuation will confirm a number of apparently simple yet highly significant aspects of this text's structures and strategies. Above all there are the visible signs that it includes other texts: the indented words in a slightly different font size signal an extended quotation, and the snippets of text in inverted commas in the body of the text signal shorter quotations. Meanwhile, the italicised items (*Wuthering Heights* and *After Bakhtin*) signal book titles and inform us of specific sources and authorities. The other items beginning with capital letters are names (proper nouns) that tell us that specific people and places are being referred to: Brontë's novel, the Grange, Lintons, Earnshaws, Mikhail Bakhtin, Mr Heathcliff, etc. In other words, like many kinds of text that report and review things (historical accounts, life stories, news reports), this critical essay is partly made up of references to other texts and of references to the rest of the world. The former are conventionally and here conveniently referred to as literary works (often called 'primary texts', here *Wuthering Heights*) and critical or theoretical works (called 'secondary', here *After Bakhtin*). Though it may also be observed that this is an explicitly theoretical essay, so Bakhtin could also be seen as a 'primary' focus.

Childs's essay, then, draws in a number of selected 'parts' from other texts that represent different discourses and are 'whole' texts in their own rights (a novel, books of theory and criticism). At the same time, his text – held together by the writer's own views and values – offers to make of them a 'whole' text with a coherent argument of its own, and representing an instance of a distinct yet familiar discourse (critical essay and text book introduction). In short, it is visibly a composite *and* cohesive – an intertext yet also a text in its own right. From the reader's point of view, it is there a synthesis that is open to analysis. The same can be said of many – perhaps all – texts. The thing about a critical and critically aware essay is that it not only knows something, it shows that it knows it. It exposes how it is made and what it is made from, even in the making and knitting together.

Such preliminary observations may seem obvious, but they are crucial and often overlooked. What's more, they arise from what we can immediately see, almost without reading the words themselves: indenting for extensive quotation, inverted commas for passing quotation, italics for titles, capitals for names, etc. Such things are worth looking for from the start – much as a musician may quickly look over a piece of music to see what key and time it's in, and where the melody line and chords are, and then the bits where it looks easy or difficult. With a printed text, these features tell us immediately – at a glance – that the text is made up of various materials (the author's own words and those of others, commentary, quotations, names). More teasingly, almost metaphysically, they also intimate how one set of words and worlds (the *present* author's) relate to those of others (what might be called *absent* authors). So in this respect the text in hand is also a product of other texts in mind; it is compounded of presences that gesture to absences.

Practically, meanwhile, all this is also the basic stock-in-trade of essay-writing. Fashioning a cohesive text and coherent argument from a range of heterogeneous materials ('primary' and 'secondary', both fictional and factual) is arguably – with the emphasis on *argument* – precisely what writing essays is all about. To recall our core questions, the big decisions are therefore about *what, who, when* and *where* to quote, *how, how much* and *why* – or *what else* and *why not*? The '*what if?*' is the constant sense that for the writer it could have been otherwise – and that for the reader-as-writer it still can. Grasping these building blocks, actively as well as analytically, is what turns attentive readers into skilful writers. (We return to this aspect in the section on Critical Interpretation later.)

Some more detailed observations on the actual language used by Childs will help confirm what kind of text this is and how it offers itself to be read and used. Again, when singled out for attention, even apparently routine features turn out to be significant. Take just the first two or three words of each of the paragraphs in Childs's essay (ignoring for this purpose the fact that it has been edited to this length): *Paragraph 1* 'Critics habitually analyse . . .'. *Paragraph 2* 'At the heart of Bakhtin's theories . . .'. (Indented quotation: 'There is an indissoluble link in Bakhtin's theory.) *Paragraph 3* 'Bakhtin therefore roots meaning . . . '. *Paragraph 4* 'So, for Bakhtin . . .'. *Paragraph 5* 'First of all . . .'. *Paragraph 6* 'If we next . . .'. *Paragraph 7* 'In conclusion . . .'. Here in miniature, writ small, are the writer's initial devices for guiding the reader through his essay *and* for establishing the basic progression of his argument: from critics in general to Bakhtin in particular; 'first' one thing; 'next' another; and then 'conclusion'. This is what is called *sign-posting* and obviously it is best placed at the very beginning of each paragraph (on the principle that a sign-post halfway down the road is not much use).

If we go on to push just a little further into each paragraph (down the road) we get a clear sense of what each paragraph is about. This is what is called *establishing topic*, and it usually takes place in the first sentence of each paragraph, occasionally the second. In the first paragraph of the whole piece, establishing topic usually takes longer – perhaps two or three sentences – because the writer is just starting out and has to establish broad area as well as specific focus. The result in the present piece is as follows (numbers refer to paragraphs; repeated or related words are underlined to signal cohesion):

1   *First sentence:* Critics habitually analyse Brontë's novel <u>in terms of contrasts</u> . . .
     Second sentence: I also want to consider <u>oppositions</u> in . . . but <u>in terms of language</u>
2   *First sentence:* At the heart of Bakhtin's theories is the idea of <u>dialogism</u> . . .
     Indented quotation about '<u>linguistic</u> variety of <u>prose fiction</u>' in <u>Bakhtin's</u> theory.
3   *First sentence after quotation:* <u>Bakhtin</u> therefore roots meaning in the <u>social</u>
4   *First sentence:* <u>First</u> of all, <u>names</u> and narrators <u>within</u> and <u>without</u> <u>*Wuthering Heights*</u> . . .
5   *First sentence:* If we <u>next</u> consider the <u>names</u> <u>within</u> the text itself, an initial puzzle is '<u>Heathcliff</u>'.
6   *First sentence:* In conclusion, the <u>last</u> <u>words</u> of the opening I have quoted are 'Before passing the threshold . . .'

In this way, we can follow the outlines of the argument simply by tracking the progressive accumulation of key terms. The result can even be summarised in a single sentence, thus:

> Against a critical background that stresses contrasts there is specific attention to oppositions in language and, with the aid of Bakhtin's approach to linguistic variety, there is attention to the names within and without.

More will be said on the ramifications and nuances of this particular argument in later sections. Here I shall just draw attention to three more features of the language of this essay that act as cues for reading and clues to the kind of interpretation involved. The first is the writer's sparing yet strategic and effective use of the first-person singular pronoun: 'I/my'. (I just used one myself.) He uses it at the beginning when setting out his particular emphasis in contradistinction to that of other writers ('I also want to consider opposition . . . but in terms of language', 'My starting points') and again at the end, when gathering his argument for a final distinctive thrust/gesture ('In conclusion, the last words . . . I have quoted are'). In the middle, for the core of his argument, he does not use the 'I' at all. Instead, he keeps his distance with third-person or impersonal forms ('There is', 'It is also an important point') or invokes other people as authorities ('Bakhtin believed', 'David Lodge writes'). Alternatively, when he does want to gather the reader into a more intimate relationship alongside the writer, he does so through the use of the first-person plural, 'we', not the singular (e.g. 'If we next consider'). Such fluidity and flexibility in pronoun use – and therefore manner of address – is an important aspect of writing. It helps establish the writer's tone and relationship with the reader, while allowing for a combination of personal presence and impersonal authority. Such things can be traced in other people's writing and cultivated in one's own. ('One', incidentally, is a slightly archaic but still useful alternative to 'I' and 'we' and 'you'. As long as, like the stereotypical royal, 'One does not overdo it!')

The second feature has to do with words that may be initially unfamiliar and difficult, especially technical or relatively rare terms. A technical one here is *'heteroglossia'*, which is explained in the passage itself. Another is *'androgynous'* which may need looking up, though its broad sense is perhaps recoverable from the context. Such words are part of the demand and therefore the reward of studying. The final feature has to do with whole passages that may initially be difficult. This may be because the sentences are long and complex or because the material is detailed, or the two together. The last sentence of the fourth paragraph ('From a Bakhtinian perspective . . . that Lockwood tells') is perhaps the knottiest in both respects. It contains no fewer than seventy words, an assortment of coordinated and subordinated clauses, and makes a precise and informed point about how each of the Brontë sisters named themselves in print (it includes 'androgynous' too). There is no quick fix with such things: you have to work at them, read the passage over several times till you grasp it, and also recognise that you need to know something. Study *is* demanding. At the same time, it is the job of writers to meet their intended readers half way: they imply if not actually explain what needs to be known (Childs in fact expressly accommodates what 'is assumed by many readers'); and they make sure the sense is sign-posted within the sentence (hence the organisation of points as 'first . . . ; and second', with the semi-colon carefully placed to suggest a semi-independent statement within the same sentence). In short, good readers have to work hard – but good writers will already have done much of the work for them. That is why, as both reader and writer, it is in everyone's interest to pay close attention to the basics of language choice and text organisation: from sign-posting to establishing topic and developing argument.

For further consideration of Childs's essay in terms of *Literature–Genre* and *Culture–Context*, see @ 2.2. This culminates in a full *Critical–Creative Interpretation* that explores alternative ways of framing his argument and alternative arguments altogether. So, again, as throughout the book, the aims of all these activities are themselves both critical and creative: to encourage close reading and detailed analysis; to develop insight that is informed; and to promote theoretical reflection that leads to transformed practice. Learning to really read this essay, you may also learn to write more adventurous and convincing essays of your own.

Also see: Writing an essay (1.2.7) Close reading – wide reading (1.2.4); Library, web, 'home' (1.2.5). Writing and reading, response and rewriting (Part Four); and Critical essay + @ 2.2.5.

READING: On essay-writing: Sharples 1999; Stott and Chapman 2001; Young 2008: Durant and Fabb 2007; McCaw 2008. Bennett and Royle 2009 is a collection of stylish essays. Knights and Thurgar-Dawson 2006 and Bartholomae and Petrosky 2005 have some other critical–creative ideas too. On Bakhtin: Bakhtin 1981, 1999 and Hirschkop and Shepherd 2006. On Emily Brontë, see 2.2.3.

2.3   LONGER PROJECTS: SAMPLE STUDY PATTERNS AND LINES OF ENQUIRY

This section gives guidance on how to go about the kinds of work undertaken for longer or 'major' projects such as extended essays, dissertations, independent study and portfolios. These are often done in the later stages of a programme and they usually involve establishing an area of activity or following up lines of enquiry for yourself. But all advanced work is in some measure independent, requiring personal initiative and resource as well as the ability to research and reflect, so the kinds of skill and insight developed here can help form and inform any substantial piece of work. This section therefore carries forward the actions of *Close reading – wide reading* and use of *Library, web and 'home'* in Part One (1.2.4–5). It just pushes them further in the direction of the kinds of study you might wish to design yourself.

The overall format is the same as for other sections in this part. There are broad guidelines and detailed checklists of a handy, all-purpose kind, and these are followed by particular worked examples and further illustrations. The guidelines and checklists are gathered in the book for ease of reference and regular use; the sample study patterns and specific lines of enquiry are extended onto the web @ 2.4, where they are supplemented from time to time. The essential thing with such projects is to feel you are doing them for yourself but not on your own. The initial idea and much of the impetus must be yours. But you will also probably have a supervisor or tutor to help you refine – sometimes radically revise – the idea, and keep you going as well as on track. The present section is also designed to support but not lead. For 'Taking responsibility', as observed earlier (1.2.6), involves neither utter independence (which tends to be wilful and ignorant) nor utter dependence (which tends to be servile and derivative). It is all about *interdependence*. And so are these last but far from final words on critical and creative strategies for doing English.

'Doing English' afresh, for yourself At this point it makes sense to revisit the initial study frameworks for **Close reading – wide reading** (1.2.4) and **Library, web, 'home'** (1.2.5). The 'Openly plural patterns' of the former (Figure 1.2.4 n) and the 'Home base' of the latter are precisely the kinds of mental and physical 'space' – terrain, *habitus*, work-pattern – you need to set up to sustain an extended piece of work. This is also the point at which your essential skills in **Taking and making notes** (1.2.3) and **Taking responsibility**, referencing properly and avoiding plagiarism (1.2.6) will be really put to the test and on display. **Writing an essay** (1.2.7) provides persistently relevant advice on everything from planning and preparation through redrafting to final 'polishing' off. And again, especially with a longer project substantially of your own devising, it's worth stressing the imperative to **Seriously enjoy . . .** whatever it is you have chosen to do (1.2.10). Enthusiasm and involvement are essential fuel for the longer-distance haul.

2.3.1   From vague idea to viable project

There are some basic things to get straight from the start about a longer project:

- It is perhaps three or four times longer than your average essay – but not infinitely long. It must be 'doable' in the words and time available.
- It will take a lot of sustained effort over a long time (most projects span a term/semester or even a year) and cannot be done in a rush in the last week or two. But it should also not be allowed to swamp your other work.

♦   Choose something you are really interested in. You will need the enthusiasm and energy as fuel to carry you through some of the slog to completion.

Once you have an initial idea – however vague – read and think around it using various kinds of notes to help you home in on something really interesting yet doable. This is where a combination of 'chaotic' and 'orderly' notes comes into its own: doing scatter-diagrams, clusters, webs and potentially endless lists so as to think outside the box to begin with; while also knowing you are going to have to get it to fit *some* kind of box (albeit one partly of your own devising) in the end (see **Taking and making notes**, 1.2.3). When you have this basically interesting yet still probably pretty vague idea in play, the next thing is to get it into shape: to define and refine it. At this point, the *core questions* from **Initial analysis** (2.1.2) come in handy again: What, Who, When, Where, How, Why and What if? And this time the 'What if?' can itself be projected otherwise: into 'What else?' (to make the widest and most inclusive initial sweep) and 'What not?' (to cut back from that and keep it all doable). Go through the following questions systematically to get your initial ideas and materials and methods into better shape:

♦   *WHAT* are some basic texts, genres and topics that you would like to address, at least to start with?

♦   *WHO* are the authors, critics and theorists likely to be central? (Name some and look at some of their work.)

♦   *WHEN* – over what period, between what rough dates – might your project be set in time? (Note *your* time-limit – the deadline – too.)

♦   *WHERE* – in what countries or regions or specific contexts – might it take place?

♦   *HOW* are you going to go about it: using what textual materials (found where or how gathered), and subjected to what critical and creative operations, in the light of what broad approaches or theories? (See Part Two for an initial review.)

♦   *WHY* are you doing all this? This question is often hard to answer at the beginning, but still try to get some preliminary sense of your motivation and orientation. Where in the world has the idea come from, and where do you want to take it?

♦   *WHAT ELSE* – what other materials, authors, topics, theories, methods – *might* be relevant? (Positive and maximal)

♦   *WHAT NOT* to do? What really needs cutting back – or out completely? What is *not* doable . . . impracticable, just too much?! (Negative and minimal)

By this stage you are in a good position to be talking over things with a tutor or prospective supervisor. You have something to *propose*. Sometimes it is decided that projects cannot or should not be taken further. This may be because there is nobody suitable available to supervise them. (Advanced work requires more specialist supervision.) Or it may be because the idea is half-baked and without much serious thought. If you have gone through the above steps and questions for yourself in the first place, you will be taken seriously and suitable supervision sorted out if at all possible. (Most people like to take on a student who has already done some thinking and groundwork. No one is much interested in one who evidently isn't much interested either.)

Once a proposal for a longer/major project has been agreed in principle and a supervisor identified there is usually one last clinching move. It is the drafting, submission and agreement of a *Provisional title*, *Brief description* and (perhaps) preliminary list of *Contents*. (Tutors and prospective supervisors usually help with these.) Here is what they are and do:

♦   *Provisional title* – This is a handy hook to hang the whole thing on in your mind: nothing too fancy in the first place but robust and serviceable. You may distinguish a main title and subtitle later. (NB. Titles can sometimes change substantially. The important thing is to have one you can happily work with.)

♦   *Brief description* – This clarifies for yourself and everyone else the initial who, what, where, when, how and why sketched out above – though not necessarily in that order. A paragraph or two (150–300 words) usually suffices. This may later be turned into an Abstract.

♦   *Preliminary list of Contents* – This typically comes out as some three, four or five chapters or section-headings into which the whole thing can be very provisionally organised. Often names of key authors and texts or genres along with main issues, themes or problems are signalled in chapter headings. You will need some kind of Introduction to set everything up and some kind of Conclusion to round it off.

See @ 2.3 for some illustrations and further comment.

Doing all this can feel like a chore but is really worth it. For once you have got a *provisional title*, *brief description* and *preliminary list of Contents*, the rest is a matter of planning and preparation, pacing yourself over time, submitting sections for your tutor to comment on and (eventually) drawing it all together and to a close. The thing is, if you really plan well and pace yourself, there will still be time for the odd leisurely stroll. This should be above all *your* version or vision of – 'take' on – whatever interests you in 'doing English'. Seriously, enjoy it.

2.3.2   Working and playing from the Anthology

What follow are some brief indications of common kinds of project. These are related to the Anthology in Part Five in the first instance. (Further study patterns can be found on the web and are listed at the end of this section.) The Anthology is organised in three sections along broadly generic lines (*Poetries*, *Proses* and *Voices*) and culminates in a section called *Crossings* which draws together texts from various genres and discourses. Within these sections texts are gathered in clusters, each of which is given a title to signal its organising principles. Typically, these principles are mixed and represent some configuration of period, genre, medium, theme, or approach, e.g.: 'Early English verses' (period plus genre); 'Romance revisited' (genre approached through rewriting); 'Translations / Transformations' (medium, theme and approach). This itself is a useful reminder that even short titles tend to be hybrid; they imply a 'how' as well as a 'what' and possibly a 'why'. So arriving at a working title is a crucial step in organising one's ideas and materials as a writer, and it is essential in giving readers a broad sense of what to expect (see previous section, 2.3.1). The following very brief selection from the Anthology gives a further indication of the range of ways in which projects can be framed:

Performing poetry, singing culture (5.1.5) embraces performance poetry and song. There is an equal emphasis on popular culture (including 'rap' and 'pop') and poetry for studio reading and in print. The focus is modern, contemporary and Western but there is referencing of other periods and culture.

Rewriting Crusoe's Island (5.2.2) takes a classic early novel of trade and empire and places it alongside later rewrites of it: one by a Nobel prize-winning novelist; the other by a student. Other versions of Defoe's *Robinson Crusoe* and of 'desert island' texts are referred to and the whole process of adaptation and continuation is opened up.

War on – of – Terror (5.2.5) begins with very different contemporary responses by journalist-novelists to the '9/11' attacks on the World Trade Center in New York, and goes on to place them alongside later accounts by soldiers of war in the Middle East. There are broader questions about the construction of 'war' and 'terror' in the media.

Dramatising 'English' in education (5.3.1) gathers a transcript of the actual use of English by students along with representations in drama, prose and poetry of how 'English' is constructed fictionally as a subject. The 'Englishes' in play include basic literacy in the Pacific, an Open University mature student and a British Council lecture on Postmodernism.

Daffodils? (5.4.1) features texts relating to William Wordsworth's 'I wandered lonely as a cloud', including his sister Dorothy's account of the event and later rewrites and parodies in poetry and advertising. This project readily extends in many directions: from the nature of poetry in and out of context, and of poets in their own and other people's lives, to the uses and abuses of literature in modern popular culture.

Mapping journeys (5.4.2) connects texts about and maps of the London Underground to ways of mapping space and pacing journeys in other cultures and periods: from a novelistic recreation of the Atlantic slave trade to a poetic rendering of an Australian Aboriginal journey. Its lines of enquiry also connect – strangely yet surely – to medical microscopy and dramatic representations of map-making in colonial Ireland.

This last sampling, in name as in deed, gives an idea of just how far and in how many directions and dimensions an openly enquiring and intellectually adventurous project can go. But even these are only a small sample of the clusters of texts and ideas in the Anthology. And those in turn are only a tiny sample of the projects possible. The list below indicates some of the fully framed sample projects available on the web. But always the onus in such work in the first instance is on you. It is up to you to identify your own interests, and then gradually to follow through in as formed and informed a way as you can manage. The guidelines and checklists in the previous section should help, as may the samples here and the further examples on the web. So – once you have a provisional idea of your own – will a supervisor or tutor. For such work is always ultimately interdependent. But it is immediately independent. And that is where you come in . . .

Sample study patterns and lines of enquiry offered on the web @ 2.3 include:

- *Adaptation and continuation*
- *Children's literature and childhood revisited*
- *Media, language, power and pleasure*
- *English at the edge: further 'limit' cases:*
  - *translating–transforming*
  - *games–playing*
  - *life–work.*

Others are added from time to time, so check what else is there. It may not be identical with what you have in mind (by definition it won't be). But it may help you make up your own mind.

2.3.3   Further strategies for critical–creative writing

There are many modes of 'critical writing' other than those of the traditional essay or analysis; just as there are many modes of 'creative writing' that start with something other than the writer's immediate or remembered experience. In fact, as argued throughout the book and foregrounded in the present Part, it is better to view all writing as in some measure *critical–creative* or *creative–critical*, depending upon emphasis; just as it is better to see reading and writing as continuously interrelated rather than utterly distinct processes. In fact, many of these strategies involve processes of *re-reading* and *re-writing*, and the intrinsically critical *and* creative nature of such activity has been part of the methodology throughout: in the shift from 'What?' to 'What if?' in the framework for Initial analysis (2.1.2) and in the explicit culmination of the Full interpretation (2.2) with 'Critical–creative interpretation'. These approaches are further theorised in the entry on **Writing and reading, response and rewriting** in Part Four.

   Below is a review of the main ways in which texts can be re-read through rewriting, grasped critically through creative engagement. The basic principle is simple. It is the experimental imperative: *change something and see what happens*. In this case, *rewrite the text and compare what you wrote with what you read*. The text may be a short story, novel, poem or play; but it may also be anything from a street sign or snatch of passing conversation to a news report, advert or website. In any event – arguably in every event – you will learn far more by getting actively involved and then standing back to reflect rather than just judging from the outside and a distance. Here, then, are the main ways in which you can rewrite a text and go on to reflect about what you have done. Guidance on the reflective commentary follows: this prompts you to reflect on your own processes of reading and composition as well as compare and contrast the products: the initial text and the text you turned it into. And like the rewriting, they may invoke and involve context, culture, history and the whole familiar gamut of reading round and researching into. The crucial difference here, however, is that you have an active say in the texts and contexts in play.

Alternative summaries and the arts of paraphrase

Summarise the text in a variety of ways so as to draw attention to different aspects of its preoccupations or construction. In the commentary draw attention to the implication of your own methods of paraphrase. For instance, a series of summaries varying between a phrase, a sentence, 50 words, and 100 words can be very revealing in establishing what you consider progressively more or less central in terms of themes, events, figures, strategies, etc. Each of these can then be compared with those of colleagues so as to identify areas of overlap and difference. Devising posters, adverts, songs, trailers and reviews based on the text in hand is another way of exploring summaries. Alternatively, you might 'paraphrase' the text drawing on critical discourses of one of the approaches featured in Part Three: MARXIST, FEMINIST, PSYCHOLOGICAL, POSTSTRUCTURALIST, POSTCOLONIALIST, etc. In all these ways you would learn to treat your own apparently 'merely descriptive' summaries as forms of discourse – and your own apparently 'natural' and 'neutral' discourses as inevitably value-laden ways of categorising, labelling and explaining. Paraphrase might then be recognised not so much as a 'heresy', as certain NEW CRITICS believed (see 3.2), but as a valuable critical tool.

Changed titles, prefaces and openings

Intervene in these areas of the text so as to disturb and reorient them. Aim to cue the reader for a slightly or very different reading experience: one with slightly (or very) different expectations as to **genre, centre** of interest, **discourse,** readership/audience and market (e.g., 'Hamlet' as 'Ophelia's nothing' or 'A further view from the gravediggers').

Alternative endings

Alter the ending of the base text so as to draw attention to some option not explored or in some way foreclosed. Go on to explore the reasons why such an ending was not desirable, advisable or possible in the text at its initial moment of production. Then consider why you, in your own moment of reproduction, opted for it. Notice that, like all the exercises, this is an opportunity to explore historical differences and not simply express personal preferences. (What if Queen Gertrude had *not* drunk the poison? Or if Horatio were disposed to 'speak to th'yet unknowing world / How these things came about' in the manner of, say, Jane Austen, Henry James or Bertolt Brecht?) See Atwood, 'Happy Endings' (5.2.1) for an extended example.

Preludes, interludes and postludes

Extend the text 'before', 'during' or 'after' the events it represents so as to explore alternative points of departure, processes of development, or points of arrival. What overall premises, procedures and aims are highlighted by this strategy? Really playful preludes, interludes and postludes often sport with a variety of historical moments as well as a variety of genres and discourses, and narrative and dramatic strategies. (Notice that Rhys's *Wide Sargasso Sea* is a 'prelude' for Brontë's *Jane Eyre* (see 5.2.3) and that Stoppard's *Rosencrantz and Guildenstern Are Dead* is an 'interlude' for Shakespeare's *Hamlet.*) Bolam's 'Gruoch' raises a voice before, during and after that of Shakespeare's Lady Macbeth (5.1.4). Self's *Dorian* is a kind of 'postlude' (in the vein of 'update') to Wilde's *The Picture of Dorian Gray* (5.2.3).

Narrative intervention

Change some 'turning point' in the **narrative** so as to explore alternative premises or consequences. Also consider ways of reframing the narrative so that the very process of narration is reoriented (e.g., by adding another narrator). This method of exploring continuities and discontinuities, kinds of textual cohesion and perceptual coherence, can be applied to 'histories' as well as 'stories', 'factual' as well as 'fictional' narratives. (What would happen if Friday, not Crusoe, were the narrator in *Robinson Crusoe*: see Holdsworth's version (see 5.2.2 for examples of both). Or if a woman were projected as the author, not Daniel Defoe, as in J.M. Coetzee's *Foe*, 1986?)

Dramatic intervention

Change the direction of a scripted **drama** or transcribed **conversation** by intervening in a single 'move' or 'exchange'. Also consider figures you might reorient or insert so as to alter the emphasis or choice of topic and the course of the action. (Thus, perhaps, someone butting into or out of the supermarket exchange (5.3.1 a) or yet other twists in the scenes from *Educating Rita* (5.3.1) and *The Pillowman* (5.3.3.)

Narrative into drama – drama into narrative

Explore 'showing' through 're-telling', and 'telling' through 're-showing' (see **drama** and **narrative**), and thereby examine the peculiar configuration of **re/presentation** in your text. (There are plenty of adaptations of Austen, Dickens, Twain and Mary Shelley (*Frankenstein*) for stage and screen; while Shakespeare is ceaselessly 're-told' by many more people than Charles Lamb. Experimenting with the possibilities yourself is a good way of tackling the problems of **point of view** and the relation between **foreground** and **background**, also of gauging what is specific to a particular medium. (Notice that the dramatic pieces by Thomas, Beckett, McDonagh and Oswald (5.3.3) all have strong narrative voices: they can be tipped either way; so can the 'novel voices' in 5.3.2.)

Imitation

Cast something in the characteristic manner and form of a particular author, director, period or genre. This is no mere matter of 'slavish imitation', even if such a thing were practically or theoretically possible (which strictly it isn't). For it soon becomes obvious that rewriting, say, some Shakespeare 'in the manner' of Ibsen, Brecht or Churchill (or Austen, or Dickens, or Joyce or Morrison) is no merely superficial exercise in style. It also entails transformations of substance as well. Another's 'word' always implies a whole 'world'. Innumerable writers from Chaucer through Pope and Byron to Tony Harrison have engaged in studied imitation. (A lively variation on this activity is to select a nursery rhyme, contemporary news item, advert or joke, then work it up in the manner and matter of, say, Gothic fantasy, women's magazine romance or postmodern collage.) Self's *Dorian* is both an imitation (updated) and a parody (see next) of Wilde's *The Picture of Dorian Gray* (5.2.3). Shapcott's 'Rose' poems are 'in conversation' with Rilke's, and therefore somewhere between translation and imitation.

Parody

Exaggerate some features of the text, or introduce incongruous (perhaps anachronistic) frames of reference so as to throw its characteristic style or preoccupations into relief. Crude parody is *burlesque*. Subtle parody can be so implicit and ironic that its parodic intent may be all but invisible. Both can be critically and creatively valid – and great fun. Either way, parody can be an act of affectionate celebration of an author's work and need be neither negative nor destructive. In fact, the most searching and revealing parodies are usually those grounded in a mixture of fascination and frustration with the text/author/genre being parodied. (Milton's, Pope's and Byron's mock/heroic verses are bound in peculiarly fruitful, partly parodic relations (see 5.1.3).)

Collage

Gather a diverse and perhaps disparate range of materials directly or indirectly relevant to the text, author or topic in hand: sources; parallels; contrasts; bits of critical commentary; relatable words, images, pieces of music, etc. – often from other periods and discourses. Then select from and arrange these materials so as to make a number of implicit statements, while also opening up the possibility of other interpretations. 'Collage' is neither more nor less than the art of 'sticking together'. As always, the commentary should seek to make explicit what was implicit, and to lay bare the process of composition. Where do *you* want to take the play of **inter-textuality** (see **text**) – and why? See Petrucci, 'The Complete Letter Guide' (5.1.4) for an example; and the 'Media messages and street texts' (5.2.6) for likely materials.

Hybrids and faction

Recast two or more related texts in a new textual mould so as to produce a compound – not merely a mixture. Compounding conventionally 'fictional' and 'factual' texts usually produces 'faction' (in every sense). Alternative metaphors for this process include grafting a new plant from two 'parent' plants to generate a hybrid; or the biological process of cross-fertilisation of species. In any event, experiment with ways of making texts coalesce as well as collide. In this respect the generation of hybrids is distinct from the sticking together of 'collages'. There is more obviously the making of a new and organic whole rather than a mechanical assemblage of old fragments. (For instance, the 'Wordsworth' material (5.4.1) might be spliced and compounded so as to produce a complexly composite text – some of it by those writers and some by you. So might the 'Ageings' and 'Epitaphs' texts (5.4.4–5). Again, the commentary would help reinforce or tease out the various problems and possibilities of interpretation, along with the critical-historical insights the activity entails.)

Word to image, word to music, word to movement, word to . . . ?

This is a catch-all reminder that verbal texts can be very revealingly understood in the attempt to 'translate' and transform them into another medium, sign-system or mode of communication and expression. Film, video, photography, painting and sculpture; all kinds of music; dance, mime and other kinds of performance art; even clothes, architecture, smells, touches and tastes (see the Performance Pieces (5.1.5) for examples sung and chanted). These all offer alternative ways of 're-realising' the actual and potential meanings, effects and values of a particular string of words: long or short, epic or epigram, novel or one-liner, single sound or letter. As always, the possibilities are infinite. But it is still your business to say which you have opened up (or closed down) and why. And it is the business of the commentary to make the implications of this critical-creative process explicit.

Discussion

(i)   Criticism begins with the recognition of textual power and ends in the attempt to exercise it. This attempt may take the form of an essay, but it may just as easily be textualised as parody or countertext in the same mode as its critical object. As teachers we should encourage the full range of critical practices in our students.

Robert Scholes, *Textual Power* (1985: Ch. 1); cf. 1.7,

essays can be experimental 'assays', journalistic reviews, brief position papers, or full mini-theses — all on set or negotiated topics. They can involve different proportions of theory, illustration, analysis and argument; and their 'logics' can be variously linear, dialectical, metaphorical, recursive or self-reflexive. There is no such thing as '*the* essay'.

analyses can be of short complete texts or of extracts from longer works. The objects of study may be previously 'seen' or 'unseen', and may or may not be accompanied by supplementary information on author(s), dates, contexts and conventions, etc. What is analysed may be the state or status of the text, formal, linguistic and ideological structures, the responses of particular readers or the processes of reading and sense-making as such.

portfolios are cumulative samples of a range of work done over a whole course. Common in creative writing, they may also be used to represent a range of analytical, historical and theoretical activities. Portfolios are an opportunity to choose and combine individual pieces and to reflect upon overall development. They work best if there is an element of self-selection by the student.

translation can be done between one language and another or between distinct historical, geographical and social varieties of 'the same language'. It operates on a continuum between literal, word-for-word substitution and fairly free recasting, depending on the relative distances between source and target languages/cultures and the functions of the translation: for specialists or non-specialists; for instruction and/or pleasure, etc. All translation involves the tricky matter of non/equivalence: the fact that different languages have analogous — but never identical — structures and effects. Such problems and possibilities can be explored in a preface, notes and commentary.

course journals involve a cumulative record of what is going into and coming out of a course — or even a whole pro-gramme. Informal or formal, personal or public, individual or collective, purely verbal or accompanied by other materials — a journal acts as a space where the processes of learning (and teaching) can be recorded and reviewed. The whole thing may be handed in and shared, or a selection or summary made. The journal-keeper's control of the journal and what is or is not made public is crucial. Journals often work best when required for completion of a course but not directly assigned a mark.

dissertations/theses (the terms are interchangeable) are in effect extended formal essays, with an emphasis on the learner's role in identifying, investigating and framing a topic of particular interest to her- or himself. The super-visor's role is to help guide the research and shape the overall result. Traditionally, dissertations begin with a speculative 'hypothesis' which is subjected to successive proof ('thesis') and disproof ('antithesis') with the whole thing leading towards an eventual conclusion ('synthesis'). Now, however, this dialectical structure is often replaced by four or five chapters on interrelated issues. These are framed by an introduction and a conclusion and supported by a full scholarly apparatus of notes, bibliography and appendices.

presentations can be done individually or in groups, before just one person (e.g., the lecturer in a tutorial) or before a larger group (e.g., a seminar of one's peers). There tends to be as much emphasis on how, and how well, things are presented as on the information as such. Clearly audi-ble speech, a visibly engaged face and sheer enthusiasm are the basic keys to good presentation. These are greatly helped by well-prepared and rehearsed cues and notes, perhaps on cards (*not* a verbatim script dutifully read out with head down). Handouts, overhead transparencies and posters can be a big help too. So may audio-visual and multimedia aids (though beware of all flash and no sub-stance). Success is perhaps best judged by how much thought, discussion and other activity are generated than by how much the presenter manages to cram in or show off.

editing and publishing involve gathering, comparing, selecting and combining existing materials (manuscript, print, still or moving images, sound-recording, etc.) so as to re-produce and re-present them. The results can be designed and published for a wide or narrow range of readers, audiences and viewers, and may or may not be accompanied by annotation and commentary. The work of scholarly editors and, say, news editors is thus in principle similar; though their materials, tools and aims differ markedly. Either way, editing is one of the most powerful forms of criticism. Student projects generally include a commentary on criteria, procedures and projected 'public'.

information searches involve identifying, selecting and using reference resources appropriate to a specific task such as researching an author, period, genre, social group or event. The task may be 'set' or self-selected, solo or collaborative, and the resources may be paper or electronic – and other people. Given the vast increase in the range and variable quality of modern information sources, along with the relative speed and ease of retrieval, it is becoming more and more important to decide what to select and how to sort it out. The framing of provisional research questions and the selection of appropriate 'key words' are thus crucial. So is the capacity to ignore what seems to be irrelevant for one's immediate purposes.

interviews and questionnaires can elicit information and opinion about issues relevant to a particular text, activity or event (such as a lecture, concert or TV programme). Tasks may include monitoring reader-, listener- or viewer-responses, comparing 'expert' and 'non-expert' informants, and gathering instances of oral history and story. Tools may include pen and paper, tape-recorders and videos. It's a good idea to decide what *you* want to know first, then to seek advice on how to go about gathering the information and presenting the results. Most student work in this area is best seen as small-scale 'pilot studies' rather than full-blown surveys.

imitation and parody involve writing in the manner of a specific writer (e.g., reproducing Dickinson's characteristic verse-form, imagery and punctuation; or Hemingway's characteristic dialogue and action) or rewriting one writer in the terms and times of another (e.g., Austen as though by Woolf, Ibsen as though by Brecht, Eisenstein as though by Spielberg – and vice versa). How far the results are judged to be 'imitative' or 'parodic' depends on the kinds of critical distance perceived between the model and its copy. A commentary may be added to explore such distinctions and to record the processes of re- (and de-) composition.

creative writing, performance and production may begin with one of the other activities (e.g., imitation and parody or adaptation and intervention – or even an information search) and move towards a more free-standing text. They may also begin with a topic or format suggested by someone else (e.g., an instructor); or derive from the writer's, performer's or director's own experience; or be generated by workshops and collective improvisation round a theme or object. But in any event the results will be a compound of the 'found' and the 'made', the old and the new, the individual and the collective. The activity may be as 'critical' as it is 'creative', and again a commentary may be attached to explicate and explore the processes. A selection of student work may be edited and 'published' by the students themselves. This process may itself be a formal, assessed part of the course; or it may basically provide a souvenir and show-case.

adaptation and intervention can involve transferring – and thereby transforming – a text from one genre or medium into another (e.g., verse into prose, novel into stage play or film – and vice versa) even to the point of re-casting plot, beginnings and endings, narrators, characters, etc. At a more detailed level this may entail tinkering with specific choices and combinations of words, sounds, images, etc. The critical–creative nature of these activities spans imitation and parody and creative writing as such. Again, a commentary can be added to explore distinctions and processes explicitly .

web-work – wikis, blogs, notice-boards and other features of the virtual learning environment – can all be used to develop a flexible and variously sharable space. All the other kinds of textual activity are possible – portfolios, anthologies, editions, analyses, searches, translations, adaptations, etc. – but here done virtually with an emphasis on cumulative and retraceable process at various stages and levels, and with multi-media capacity and further links. Group and course-wide co-operation can even extend to cross-institutional and international collaboration. The trick is to start small, with something doable at 'home', and go from there.

Figure 2.1 Textual activities as learning strategies

Discussion (ii)

(ii)   In a post-traditional social universe, an indefinite range of potential courses of action
       (with their attendant risks) is at any moment open to individuals and collectivities.
       Choosing among such alternatives is always an 'as if' matter, a question of selecting
       between 'possible worlds'.

       Antony Giddens, *Modernity and Self-identity* (1991: 29)

(iii) The highest Criticism, then, is more creative [. . .] and the primary aim of the critic is
       to see the object as in itself it really is not.

       Oscar Wilde, *The Critic as Artist* (1891)

READING: The best place to start is with your own rewriting. Try one of the above strategies with a
text you are studying. Fuller arguments, further strategies and copious illustration of the kinds of
rewriting practices featured above can be found in Scholes 1985, Carter and Nash 1990, Hackman and
Marshall 1990, Thomson 1992, Bartholomae and Petrosky 1986, Bassnett and Grundy 1993, Corcoran
et al. 1994, Pope 1995, Scholes *et al*. 1995, Nash and Stacey 1997; Goatly 2000, Knights and Thurgar-
Dawson 2006.

THEORETICAL POSITIONS, PRACTICAL APPROACHES

PART THREE

PREVIEW

This part of the book explores the main theoretical positions available within contemporary English Studies. It shows how these can be used both to approach individual texts and to understand textual and cultural activity in general. The emphasis is on relating varieties of critical theory to varieties of practical activity, and on developing models that really work. The first section (3.1) invites you to get some initial bearings and insists that what ultimately matters is the development of your own positions and orientations. We also consider a general model of textuality and the critical process. This is framed in terms of *producers*, *texts*, *receivers* and *relations to the rest of the world*. The model is illustrated in action with a specific textual focus (Shakespeare's *Hamlet*) and also used as matrix against which to plot the various theoretical positions and critical practices that follow. Each of these is presented through: Overview; Key terms; Major figures and movements; 'How to practise . . .'; Worked example; and Reading.

The positions and approaches featured in this part are:

PRACTICAL CRITICISM and (old) NEW CRITICISM (3.2)
FORMALISM into FUNCTIONALISM (3.3)
PSYCHOLOGICAL approaches (3.4)
MARXISM, CULTURAL MATERIALISM and NEW HISTORICISM (3.5)
FEMINISM, MASCULINITY and QUEER THEORY (3.6)
POSTSTRUCTURALISM and POSTMODERNISM (3.7)
POSTCOLONIALISM and MULTICULTURALISM (3.8)
ETHICS, AESTHETICS, ECOLOGY (3.9)

Activities and Discussion for each of these approaches can be found @ 3, as can an extra section dedicated to LINGUISTICS, STYLISTICS and COGNITIVE POETICS @ 3.10.

3.1   THEORY IN PRACTICE: A WORKING MODEL TO PLAY WITH

The book is not much concerned with 'Theory' (with a capital T) on its own. It is dedicated to Theory-in-Practice: putting various theories (plural) to work as sets of tools, and playing around with them as kinds of serious toy. In fact, we are mainly concerned with theor*ing* (the emphasis is again on the progressive participle) as an openly and to some extent experimental process: seeing what various theories and approaches are good for and bad at, and refining or replacing them accordingly. Often, initially, they will be supplemented with parts of other theories; always the result will be a slightly different or even a fresh synthesis; occasionally – eventually or suddenly – you will generate alternatives of our own. Basically, then, to recall the subtitle of this part of the book, this is all about identifying 'Theoretical Positions' and realising – dynamising, even dynamiting – them as 'Practical Approaches'. The emphasis, as always, is on 'seriously enjoying English' (see 1.2.10), so it is in a spirit of earnest playfulness that we shall here seek in practice, in various ways, to *see through theory*. As anticipated in the Prelude (p. 10), this can be meant in three very different senses:

1   seeing through theories, as through different lenses and apparatuses, so as to see more and differently and better;
2   seeing through the 'merely theoretical' aspects of positions so as to expose obscure jargon and hazy abstraction;
3   seeing through and following up the various projects of theorising (-*ing* again) for ourselves, in whatever directions and dimensions we care – or dare – to develop them.

Together, these positive, negative and alternative senses of 'seeing through theory' should help set the agenda as well as the tone. Some provisional definitions and a big, flexible diagram will help get us going.

THEORY/PRACTICE A DYNAMIC RELATION

• *THEORY* is a natural and necessary extension of thinking. It is about developing big ideas that cover many cases in various circumstances, about framing 'the bigger picture'. Theory tends to be overtly conceptual and abstract. Strong theorising extends practice in ways that were previously unimagined.

• *PRACTICE* is a natural and necessary aspect of action. It is about engaging with particular materials and seeing what works; it is often concerned with the finer detail. Practice tends to be overtly concrete and specific. Strong practice tests and proves – or disproves – existing theories and shows the need for fresh ones.

• *THEORY/PRACTICE* are therefore interdependent. They depend upon a dynamic of *both/and* not just *either/or*: like the blades of a pair of scissors that cross to cut; left and right arms as they come together to embrace. Sooner or later, the one must be braced by the other if both are to be strong. (Theory and practice neither work nor play properly when kept apart.)

Theory/practice are thus like all the other crucial pairs of terms in this book: critical/creative, monologue/dialogue, reading/writing, re-reading/re-writing, etc. They are complementary not opposed, reciprocally defining not mutually exclusive. You can't have or do or be – even think – the one without the other.

The diagram that follows shows a model which will help frame the various theoretical positions and practical approaches that follow. It is adapted from one in M.H. Abrams's influential essay 'Orientation of Critical Theories' in *The Mirror and the Lamp* (1953); also in Lodge (1972: 1–26). Abrams suggests that we may categorise critical positions in so far as they emphasise one of four aspects of the literary-critical process: the *work*, the *author*, the *reader*, the *universe*. In order to make this model more applicable in a contemporary interdisciplinary context, I have modified it as follows. Any text or other human artefact may be understood as a *product* or succession of *products* (Abrams's 'work') and as the result of a number of *processes*. These processes involve three basic elements: *producers* (e.g. authors, artists, performers, publishers – Abrams's 'author'); *receivers* (e.g. readers, audiences, viewers – Abrams's 'reader'); and *relations to the rest of the world* (i.e. everyone and everything else to which the work can be taken to refer or relate – Abrams's 'universe'). Some further detail on each of these key terms will be useful.

Text can be understood both as an array of achieved *products* and as a series of constitutive *processes*. That is why the 'process' arrows in the diagram are double-headed. They converge on and radiate out from the centre and help us see human activity as both 'product-centred' and 'process-oriented'. They therefore remind us that texts/artefacts are not simply fixed 'things'

RELATIONS TO
REST OF THE WORLD
(everything else the text
refers or relates to)
Texts are ABOUT things

P
R
O
C
E
S
S

TEXT AS PRODUCTS
(versions of the text as notes,
drafts, publications, performances, etc.)
Texts ARE things

PRODUCERS   RECEIVERS
(author, artist,   (readers, audiences,
director, performer, etc.)   viewers, etc.)
Texts are MADE   *Texts are RESPONDED TO*

Figure 3.1 A working model of the text as products and processes

but are also items we change and exchange. (This may be called the *product-based* or *object-centred* dimension.)

Producers are featured whenever we understand the text as an expression of the design, intentional or otherwise, of particular authors, artists, directors, etc. By extension these include the 'designs' on the text of collaborating or subsequent publishers, performers, adapters, etc. All producers are therefore in some sense *re*producers in that people always make new things out of existing materials in the language, literature and culture. We never make things from scratch, out of nothing. (This may be called the *expressive* or *maker-centred* dimension.)

Receivers are featured whenever we understand the text through its actual or implied effects on various readers, audiences and viewers. Notice that all 'receivers' are also in some sense re/producers; for we make sense of things actively not just passively. (This may be called the *affective* or *effects-based* dimension.)

Relations to the rest of the world are featured whenever we understand the text to represent, refer or in some way relate to people, places, events, ideas, beliefs in the worlds behind or beyond it. We say the 'rest' of the world because texts, producers and receivers are also part of the world; we might also say 'worlds' (plural) because there are always many realities (psychological, economic, political, ecological, etc.) to which a text can be related. (This may be called the *representational, mimetic, referential* or *relevance-based* dimension.)

There is a further complication, however. We must also recognise that texts exist in time and space. Every one of these products and processes is therefore constituted in a variety of historical moments. That grand abstraction 'the text' is always potentially deceptive. In reality 'the text' always turns out to be both plural and variable – a series of versions (notes, sketches, drafts, editions, performances, etc.) and not a simple and single thing at all. (Think of your own notes and drafts of essays, for instance.) The text in hand is always a *particular* text – and not just any text or every text. The notions of producer*s* and receiver*s* may be similarly pluralised and extended. They can embrace anyone and everyone who has ever had a hand in the transmission, transformation and reception of the text. Meanwhile, as remarked above, 'relations with the rest of the world' entail locations within and gestures towards all sorts of versions and visions of reality. These stretch from the 'then and there' of an initial moment of production to the 'here and now' of a current moment of reproduction and reception (also see 1.2.4 and 2.2).

BASIC THEORETICAL AND PRACTICAL QUESTIONS TO PUT TO ANY TEXT

1 *Text as products*: In what manuscript, printed, performance, film or otherwise recorded versions has this text existed?

2 *Reproduction and reception*: Who has been involved in making and responding to this text at various moments?

3 *Relations to the rest of the world*: What are the various frames of reference and contexts (political, religious, social, etc.) within which this text has been realised historically? What 'world-views' does it represent?

Example: The not-so-strange case of 'Shakespeare's Hamlet'

Here is the above model set to work on a phenomenon known as 'Shakespeare's Hamlet'. The cautious 'scare quotes' round author and title are necessary because, as we quickly see, the whole matter of what we mean by 'Hamlet', whose it is, and where and when it is to be found are themselves the matters at issue. Incidentally, for the purpose of this illustration, it does not matter whether you already know anything about anybody's 'Hamlet'. The same principles can and will be applied to all sorts of other texts and artefacts.

Text as products

'Shakespeare's Hamlet' involves a wide variety of *products* – verbal, theatrical and filmic.

◆   *Verbally*, in a narrow sense, 'Hamlet' exists in three early and substantially distinct printed versions: the First Quarto (1603), based on a transcript of an actual performance and/or actors' scripts; the Second Quarto (1604), a much longer text presumably related to a later performance; and the First Folio (1623), part of the posthumous collection of Shakespeare's plays put together primarily for literary posterity and reading rather than performers. None of these texts bears Shakespeare's signature or is in his hand. All have been used – sometimes singly, often in combination – as the basis for later printed editions.

◆   *Theatrically*, an earlier play called 'Hamlet' (probably written by Thomas Kyd) is known to have existed in the late 1580s. We also know that performances of Shakespeare's earliest version preceded the First Quarto, and various versions have continued to be performed, often highly adapted, from the seventeenth century to the present. Just a few of many notable examples include: a performance for foreign merchants on the deck of an East India Company ship anchored off Sierra Leone (1607–8); Garrick's influential version in which he drops the gravediggers and much of the fifth act as 'indecorous' (1772); Kemble's streamlined version of less than 3,000 lines (early nineteenth century). Meanwhile, outright theatrical parodies, rewrites and extensions are legion. They include Marovitz's *Hamlet: the Collage* (1966; a cut-up, reshuffled version); Stoppard's *Rosencrantz and Guildenstern are Dead* (also 1966, adapted for film 1991, in which two minor characters move centre stage); Hormone Imbalance's *Ophelia* (1979), in which Ophelia is a lesbian and runs off with a woman servant to join a guerrilla commune; Curtis's obscenely funny *The Skinhead Hamlet* (1982) and Jean Betts's *Ophelia Thinks Harder* (1993), in which the heroine acts assertively while the hero dithers.

◆   *Filmically*, 'Hamlet' has existed for film and TV viewers in numerous heavily cut and adapted versions directed by, for instance, Olivier (England, 1947; darkly psychological); Kozintsev (Russia, 1963; darkly political); Zeffirelli (America, 1990; youthfully romantic); as well as the series of half-hour *Shakespeare: The Animated Tales* (English and Russian, 1992; as a brisk folk tale). Again this is to mention only a few.

Producers

'Shakespeare's Hamlet' therefore also involves a wide variety of *producers*, all in their various *moments of production* and *reproduction*. These include: Saxo Grammaticus, the twelfth-century Dane who first recorded but apparently did not invent the Hamlet story; Belleforest, with his retelling of Saxo in the *Histoires Tragiques* (1582, Vol. V); Thomas Kyd, the likely author of the play before Shakespeare; Shakespeare *and* his fellow actors, directors and playwrights (Shakespeare is known to have collaborated closely with all of these as a matter of course, as did virtually all his contemporaries and as do many subsequent theatrical practitioners); Garrick, Kemble, Olivier, Kozinstsev, Zeffirelli, etc. – along with all the people and technologies (actors, designers, camera-crews, editors, etc.) they worked with. In short,

Shakespeare is just one of a vast succession of *re*-producers of 'Hamlet', both named and anonymous. Certainly he is the best known. But he was not the first and assuredly will not be the last.

Receivers

'Shakespeare's Hamlet' therefore necessarily involves a wide variety of *receivers*, all in their various *moments of reception*. In one sense Shakespeare himself was just another receiver of other people's versions. Whether directly or indirectly, he drew upon Saxo's and Belleforest's versions, the earlier play, and a whole host of influences from other areas of language, literature and culture (widely known works on and beliefs in 'melancholy', ghosts and revenge, for instance). Only through those could he in turn re-produce. Moreover, fellow actors, directors and playwrights are likely to have been his first and most formative 'audience'. Performances of the play will then have been heard and seen by a prodigious variety of early seventeenth-century audiences ranging from artisans to aristocracy, 'groundlings' to grandees (Elizabethan theatre audiences were much more socially variegated than their modern counterparts). Thereafter, we must look to moments of reception (and reproduction) as different as: early seventeenth-century foreign merchants at sea off Sierra Leone; the Restoration and eighteenth-century court and city; the nineteenth-century Victorian music-hall; twentieth-century Soviet, British, Italian, US and world cinemas – and any time, anywhere that a TV has been showing one of the many acted or animated versions. What's more, the awesome – some would say awful – fact is that by far the greatest number of modern 'receivers' of 'Shakespeare's Hamlet' are to be found in formal education. These include students, teachers, scholars, critics – in fact anyone and everyone who has studied 'it' in the classroom or lecture theatre, chiefly from the page, occasionally on the stage, and increasingly from the screen.

Relations to the rest of the world

'Shakespeare's Hamlet' thus involves a wide variety of references, representations and kinds of relevance, again in various historical moments and social contexts. These include representations of such matters as: social and psychological order and disorder, families, adolescence, adultery, murder, revenge, love, lust, the supernatural, royalty, nobility, manual labour, scholarship, being a student, returning home, having friends, being alone, and much more. Notice again that all of these issues will be understood slightly or very differently depending on the frames of reference within which they are realised: what they relate to in some contemporary world. These worlds will vary between, say, the late sixteenth and early twenty-first centuries, between post-feudal and post-industrial societies. The world-views in play amongst readers and audiences will vary correspondingly: in *religion* across kinds of Christianity, Buddhism, Islam, agnosticism, atheism, etc.; in *politics* across forms of monarchy, absolutism, democracy and dictatorship; in *psychology/physiology* from a vision of the mind–body based on the elements of fire, air, earth and water, along with their associated 'humours', to interrelations of 'ego' and 'id', or 'Oedipus complexes', desire, the 'semiotic', sexuality, and so on. For this reason, the most personallypressing questions you are likely to put to 'Hamlet' would be: 'what are my views and experiences of social and psychological dis/order, families, monarchy, being a student, returning home, etc.?' And yet inevitably, at the same time, you are likely to wonder about the historical context: 'what views and experiences of social dis/order, psychological disturbance, families, etc. were available, encouraged, prohibited or unthinkable in late sixteenth- and early seventeenth-century London (England, Britain, the rest of the world)?' Similar questions quickly arise about every other time, place and social context within which Shakespeare's (and everyone else's) 'Hamlet' has been realised.

By now it will be clear that 'Shakespeare's Hamlet' is a very complex and changeable phenomenon indeed. In fact, 'it' turns out to be a 'they': an apparently single object turns out, on closer investigation, to be an array of *products* and a series of *processes*. These have been plotted systematically and at length (though still far from exhaustively) in four dimensions: *texts*; *reproduction*; *reception*; and *relations to the rest of the world*. It has also been pointed out that all of these dimensions are characterised by variation in time, place and social space. Consequently, just whose 'Hamlet' this is remains a highly fascinating and deeply contentious matter: Shakespeare's? his predecessors'? his contemporaries'? his successors'? our own? someone else's entirely? That is one reason why we need theoretical models. It is also why, if they are to be of practical use, we need particular materials on which to try and test them. No model or method is universal and omnipotent. Only by bringing materials, models and methods into dynamic relation can we really know the potentialities of any of them.

ONE MODEL LEADS TO ANOTHER . . .

The above model of *text, producer, receiver* and *relations to the rest of the world* can be used in four ways:

- as a practical tool to help analyse a particular text;
- as a theoretical model of how texts in general come into being;
- as a framework in which to 'place' particular critical movements;
- as a matrix to help generate fresh theories and approaches.

Other related yet distinct models can be found in the frameworks for **initial analysis** and **full interpretation** in Part Two and the entry on **text, context and intertextuality** in Part Four. All are used to underpin the 'How to practise . . . ' sections featured in the rest of Part Three.

READING: Good short introductions to literary theory are Culler 1997 and Bertens 2007. Good and practical on language theory is Robson and Stockwell 2005, and so on cultural theory is Hills 2005. The following introduce all the major theories and theorists in turn and are especially recommended: Barry 2002; Selden, Widdowson and Brooker 2005; Castle 2007. Lively theoretical and critical essays on a range of topics are Bennett and Royle 2009; more practical and 'hands-on' is Hopkins 2009. Still provocative and worth reading but now rather dated is Eagleton 2008 (nominally a third edition of his 1983 classic). Excellent anthologies that feature the major writings are, in steadily increasing scale and range: Rice and Waugh 2001; Lodge and Wood 2008; Rivkin and Ryan 2004; Leitch 2010. Handy shorter reference works are Macey 2001; Baldick 2008 and Abrams 2009. Most of these are periodically updated; so also see @ 3. Classic and still useful encyclopedias of theory are Coyle *et al.* 1990, Preminger and Brogan 1993, Makaryk 1993. Newer theorists critiqueing earlier ones (Althusser on Marx, Adorno on Freud, Butler on Kristeva and Foucault, etc.) can be found in Milne 2003. For some of the first and the latest – but evidently far from the last – words on 'Post-theory' and 'theory after theory', see Docherty 1990, McQuillan *et al.* 1999, Eagleton 2003, Schad 2003 (interviews) and Elliott and Attridge 2011 (essays).

'HOW (NOT) TO PRACTISE APPROACH X . . .': A NOTE ON CRITICAL METHOD

For each of the theories and approaches featured in Part Three there is a section called 'How to practise': 'How to practise a Formalist approach'; 'How to practise Feminist and Gendered approaches', etc. Each is followed by an example of that particular critical methodology in action. It should be stressed, however, that in each of these examples I have tried to avoid a merely mechanical application of the method. I deliberately do *not* march straight through each text dutifully noting and ticking off every aspect or feature in strict accordance with the suggested questions. Instead, I seek to weave all or most of the issues mentioned into the fabric of a more subtly variegated (though still I hope integrated) response. Thus I start with the 'How to practise . . .' framework in one hand and with a specific text in the other, but I use the former to help prompt and develop the shape of a response to the latter – not to prescribe its precise design. I treat it as a companion, not a tyrant. That is how I suggest you approach the 'How to practise . . .' sections too. Look to them for a supporting and occasionally guiding presence. But *don't* treat them too slavishly or solemnly. Good methodologies encourage us to be creative as well as critical, playful as well as principled. What you do with those here – as with those for Full interpretation in 2.2 – is up (and down) to you.

3.2 WORDS ON THE PAGE – PRACTICAL CRITICISM AND (OLD) NEW CRITICISM

If you are given a short literary text and asked to respond to 'the words on the page' (without further information or instruction) then this is the kind of approach being adopted.

Overview

Practical Criticism and New Criticism were two highly influential approaches developed during the middle years of the twentieth century in, respectively, Britain and the USA. Both were *text-centred* and required 'close reading' of 'the words on the page'. This was done substantially without reference to context, author's identity and reader's role. Discriminating aesthetic responses and ethical judgements were encouraged among readers. However, students were generally not expected to challenge either the choice of texts (typically, short lyrics and prose extracts from classic English and American authors) or the critic's and teacher's methods and values (these tended to be assumed or asserted rather than explicitly theorised). The New Critics' emphasis on LITERATURE as a series of finished art objects or 'verbal icons' made them suspicious of (and suspected by) more theoretically explicit and linguistically systematic FORMALISTS and FUNCTIONALISTS. New Critics were also opposed to (and by) many kinds of PSYCHOLOGICAL, MARXIST and, latterly, FEMINIST and POSTCOLONIAL CRITICS. They appeared to assume that most literature of note was by white, middle- to upper-class males – but that this fact need not itself be noted or was impertinent. It has been suggested that certain strains of POST-STRUCTURALISM (especially deconstructive criticism) continue the New Critical programme under a different guise; for deconstruction too can sometimes be narrowly text-centred and concerned with paradox, ambiguity and irony (these were all key New Critical concepts). Meanwhile, the general practice of 'close reading' has tended to be technically sharpened by the use of STYLISTICS and politically sensitised by an awareness of language as **discourse**.

Key terms: aesthetic; ambiguity; **art; canon and classic**; criticism; form; **imagery**; irony; LITERATURE; narrator (un/reliable); paradox; **point of view**; structure, including balance, pattern, tension, (organic) unity and integrity, LINGUISTICS, STYLISTICS and POETICS.

Major figures and movements

Practical Criticism as both a critical method and an educational movement was initiated by the publication of I.A. Richards's book of that name in 1929. Its subtitle was 'A Study of Literary Judgement', and it was dedicated to establishing an area of English devoted to LITERARY CRITICISM as distinct from LITERARY HISTORY and philology (historical language study) – both of which had dominated the subject till then. Criticism as such had often been a dilettanteish form of LITERARY APPRECIATION (see @ 1.4). Richards's method was basically simple and is still quite widely practised: 'I have made the experiment of issuing printed sheets of poems [. . .] to audiences who were asked to comment freely in writing upon them. The authorship of the poems was not revealed' (1929: 3). The written responses that resulted, what Richards called 'protocols', then formed the subject of his lectures and subsequently his book. Through detailed analysis of student responses Richards pointed to many aspects of the **reading** process that had previously been ignored or merely assumed. In particular, he stressed the ultimate ambiguity of all words, as well as recurring problems which seemed to prevent a sensitive appreciation of the text, e.g., 'stock responses', 'general critical preconceptions' and 'doctrinal adhesions'. Above all, developing a line of argument initiated in his previous book, *Principles of Literary Criticism* (1924), Richards insisted that the reading of poetry was a searching test of and stimulating aid to the cultivation of 'discrimination' in general and 'literary judgement' in particular.

In his practice Richards was clearly heir to the eminent Victorian poet, critic and educationist Matthew Arnold. Arnold advocated that 'short passages, even single lines' of 'poetry belong[ing] to the class of the truly excellent' can be applied as 'touchstones' to other poetry (*The Study of Poetry*, 1880). It should be added, however, that Richards was generally more interested in understanding the process whereby literary and cultural judgements were formed, rather than in simply imposing them. In this respect Richards can be distinguished from most of his predecessors as well as many of his successors (e.g., F.R. Leavis, also at Cambridge), who tended to assert their judgements rather than explaining – let alone theorising – them. Richards was unusual, too, in his readiness to engage with larger problems of COMMUNICATION, **value** and meaning (e.g., Richards 1924: Chs 4, 21 and Appendix).

In the year of the first publication of *Practical Criticism* (1929), Richards left Cambridge for Peking and then Harvard, where he taught from 1939. This move influenced the development of a partly similar critical movement in English in the United States. This movement came to be called 'New Criticism', after the title of John Crowe Ransom's book of that name (1941). New Criticism and Practical Criticism were to have a pervasive and decisive influence on the critical and classroom practices of the middle years of the twentieth century. In effect, they became orthodoxies which in some quarters persist to the present day. Other key New Critical textbooks were Cleanth Brooks and Robert Penn Warren's *Understanding Poetry* (1939, 4th edn still in print), Brooks's *The Well-Wrought Urn: Studies in the Structure of Poetry* (1947) and William Wimsatt's *The Verbal Icon: Studies in the Meaning of Poetry* (1954). All these texts proclaim themselves in various ways as 'new' criticism in so far as, like Richards, they distinguish their objects and methods from the then 'old' study of literature which concentrated on literary history (including biography) and history of the language (philology) (see @ 1.4.7). However, in a much more exclusive and self-conscious way than Richards, New Critics insisted that the proper object of study was 'the words on the page' and 'the text itself' or (more often and more narrowly) 'the poem itself'. Consequently, they ruled out appeals both to the supposed intentions or even the life of the **author** on the one hand, and to the actual effects of the poem on particular **readers** on the other. These positions were put most forcefully and influentially by William Wimsatt and Monroe Beardsley in two joint essays attacking what they dubbed 'The Intentional Fallacy' (1946) and 'The Affective Fallacy' (1949). In the former they claimed that 'the design or intention of the author is neither available nor desirable as a standard for judging the success of a work of literary art' (Lodge 1972: 335). In the later essay they asserted that 'The Affective Fallacy is a confusion between the poem and its results (what it *is* and what it *does*)' (Lodge 1972: 345).

New Critics developed a distinctive, though not especially systematic, critical vocabulary. Characteristically, a New Critic would look for the overall principle of *organic unity* or *integrated structure* in a work, often a short lyric poem. This would then be related to the detailed 'particulars' and 'textures' of **imagery**. *Tension*, *contrast* and above all *balance* in design as well as *ambiguity* in individual words and phrases were reckoned the hallmarks of a fine piece. Thus the overall aim of *the poem as a whole* was to establish *variety within unity*. Where contradictions remained these could be resolved through *irony* (not really meaning what is said) or *paradox* (maintaining two or more contradictory positions simultaneously). According to Brooks (1947: 12), 'the language of poetry *is* the language of paradox'. New Critics were also flatly opposed to any abstraction of what they called the 'prose sense' of a piece of poetry, especially in the form of paraphrase (which they considered a 'heresy'). Instead, they preferred to concentrate on the 'poetic sense'. In this, like Richards, they opposed a referential, 'scientific' use of language to an emotive, 'poetic' use of language. They thereby perpetuated that split between the sciences and the 'arts' which continues to divide (and bedevil) much of society both inside and outside education.

A further consequence of the elevation of **poetry** was the marginalising of prose and the neglect of drama. When New Critics did treat prose, it was almost exclusively 'literary' prose (short stories and extracts from novels – and not diaries, letters, newspaper stories and adverts). They also concentrated on formal and structural matters of technique such as **point of view**, **characterisation**, narrators (first and third person, partial and omniscient), **narrative** structure and plot. They were not particularly interested in the worlds represented and the novel's or the novelist's relations with the society at the time (i.e. 'relations with the rest of the world'; see 3.1).

How to practise Practical Criticism and New Criticism

Practical Criticism

Concentrate on short unidentified texts, preferably poems and extracts from novels or short stories, and ask people to 'comment freely' upon them. On the basis of the ensuing discussion or short comments in writing, try to pick out insensitive, clichéd and 'stock' responses. Aim to cultivate greater 'critical discrimination' and 'literary judgement'. (Use texts from Part Five if you wish, but for the purpose of this exercise be sure to *ignore* the attached notes.)

New Criticism

Read an unidentified whole poem, a short story or an extract from a play or novel. Then talk or write about it with respect to the following:

- the main tensions or contrasts around which it is organised;
- the overall structuring of argument, plot or imagery (including verse organisation for poetry, and types of narrator, characterisation and points of view for story or play);
- all the imagery, paradoxes, ambiguities and ironies which contribute to the localised texture and overall variety of the text;
- those strategies and devices which, especially towards the close of the text, ensure that it seems to be 'integrated', 'whole' and 'successfully resolved'.

Examples

Read William Wordsworth's 'I wandered lonely as a cloud' (5.4.1) with the above suggestions on 'How to practise Practical and New Criticism' in mind. Be sure to ignore the accompanying notes and the other 'Daffodils' text in the anthology for the purpose of this exercise.

Poem: William Wordsworth's 'I wandered lonely as a cloud' (5.4.1) The Practical Critical aim here would be to see this poem afresh, avoiding the 'stock responses' that its familiarity as a classic Romantic poem have built up. In a more specifically New Critical vein we would observe that the poem is generally organised around tensions between the sad and solitary poet and joyful teeming nature; between the immediate experience of what was seen and the subsequent memory of it. The argument progresses in three stages: from the poet's solitude ('I wandered lonely . . . ') to pleasant communing with nature ('laughing company') to a later moment of reverie ('when on my couch I lie . . . '). Each state dominates one of the verses in turn. Metrically, all the lines are octosyllabic and gathered in verses rhyming 'ababcc'.

Localised ambiguities, especially of imagery, include the observations that even from the beginning the poet is likened to *a part of* nature ('I wandered lonely *as a* cloud') and is therefore not wholly alone and *apart from* it. Notice too that the daffodils and waves are humanised as 'dancing' and 'a laughing company'. The ultimate ambiguity, and perhaps paradox, is that by the close we may not be sure whether the daffodils and waves we have just 'seen' are those of the poet's first moment of vision or his later moments of re-vision: is he – and are we – '[a]long the lake' or 'on my couch'? This may be a paradoxical resolution in that it draws together what are usually recognised as distinct: humanity and nature; inner and outer worlds; past, present and future.

(*Note*: Practical and New Critical readings of this poem would *not* draw attention to many of the historical, biographical, contextual and intertextual aspects featured in the anthology: the redrafting process involving manual and verbal assistance from sister and wife (especially Mary's contribution of 'They flash . . . solitude', ll.21–2); William's transformation of a country ramble evidently involving several people into a solitary act of wandering (see Dorothy's account, 5.4.1); the screening out of 'people working' and thus, perhaps, of any thought that William was not. Nor would Practical and New Critics pay anything but slight – and probably slighting – attention to subsequent *re*-productions of the poem in the forms of Feminist critique and Commercial parody (i.e. the other 'Daffodils' texts in 5.4.1). Such things would be considered irrelevant, 'non-literary' or trivial and could not, it would be argued, contribute to an understanding of 'the poem itself'.)

Prose: Kipling's 'The Story of Muhammad Din' (5.2.1) The overall tension is between the world-views of adult Englishman and Indian child, the worlds of grown-up work and child's play. The story develops fairly simply, from first meeting with Muhammad Din, through the construction, destruction and reconstruction of his toy palaces, to his death. There is just one, first-person narrator throughout, the Englishman, who seems to play a partly enigmatic role.

Localised tensions include: the illicit but tolerated presence of Muhammad Din in the Sahib's room; strain between father and son; the accidental destruction of the child's toy palace, and the doctor's callous remark on 'these brats'. The precise attitude of the Englishman to the Indian boy is hard to pin down: sympathetic and yet distant, fatherly and yet patronising – in a word (paradoxically) im/personal. All these ambiguous perspectives might be inferred from the narrator's references to 'the little white shirt and the fat little body', 'chubby little eccentricity'. Accordingly, the tone is often ironic, a blend of the (mock-)heroic with the trivial (e.g., the self-conscious formality of 'my salutation' and the 'magnificent palaces from the stale flowers').

The story is resolved sharply, by the boy's sudden illness and death. However, the narrator's ambiguously im/personal, sympathetic and yet distant tone is maintained to the very end: 'wrapped in a white cloth, all that was left of little Muhammad Din'.

(*Note*: Practical and New Critics would probably *not* choose this Anglo-Indian tale in the first place: they rarely feature overtly cross-cultural materials. But if they did they would probably not comment directly on such matters as the specifically political and historical dimensions of the colonial relations between English 'sahib' and Indian servants (e.g., 'servants' quarters . . . any command of mine . . . '); the fanciful, make-believe palaces being built from natural and imperial bric-à-brac in the white man's 'garden'; the total absence of women (mothers, wives, sisters); the occluded 'otherness' of 'Mussulman' burial grounds and customs; Kipling's own deeply traumatic childhood and his – and his age's – general tendency to sentimentalise children; the polyglot mixture of languages, English and Indian, while still observing a hierarchy in favour of the former (all the Indian words are overtly 'power' terms: *sahib*, *khitmatgar*, *budmash*, etc.). In short, there would be no obviously POSTCOLONIAL, MARXIST, FEMINIST or PSYCHOANALYTIC dimensions to such a reading.)

Also see: Close reading – wide reading, 1.2.4; Initial analysis, 2.1; DEVICES AND EFFECTS 3.3; STYLISTICS @ 3.10; and above Key Terms p.137.

READING: *Introductory*: Selden, Widdowson and Brooker 2005: 15–28; Rylance in Coyle *et al.* 1990: 721–35; Jefferson and Robey 1987: 24–45. *Core texts*: Ransom, Brooks, Wimsatt and Beardsley, and Schorer in Lodge 1972; *also* Ransom, Brooks, Wimsatt and Beardsley in Leitch 2010; Richards 1924, 1929; Brooks 1947. *Advanced*: Baldick 1996: 64–160; Fekete 1977; Lentricchia 1980.

3.3   DEVICES AND EFFECTS – FORMALISM INTO FUNCTIONALISM

If you are mainly concerned with the literary devices and structures of a text, your approach is broadly 'formal'. If you then ask about the main effects and significance of these devices, your approach becomes more 'functional'.

Overview

Formalist as the name for a specific critical movement is usually identified with 'Russian Formalism'. This developed in Moscow and St Petersburg/Leningrad between 1915 and the late 1920s. The position Russian Formalists adopted was *text-centred* (or, perhaps better, textuality-centred) in that they concentrated on those features that make LITERATURE 'literary' and poems 'poetic'. They also systematically studied the devices of narrative fiction. Their aim was thus less the analysis of particular texts (which was the aim of NEW CRITICS) and more the establishment of general principles and theories. Chief amongst the concepts developed by

Russian Formalists were defamiliarisation and foregrounding. The idea was that literary texts always in some way challenge and change (i.e. 'defamiliarise') all that is dulled by familiarity and habit: they freshen and sharpen perception. Formalists also observed that literary, especially poetic, texts tend to draw attention to certain aspects of the language (notably through imagery, unusual word combinations, sound patterning, metre, rhyme, inverted or unusual word order) and these elements are thereby 'foregrounded' against a 'background' made up of more routine and 'ordinary' language use. Foregrounding is basically any linguistic feature that, for whatever reason, sticks out. Narrative fiction does this on a larger scale through reshuffling time, space and narrator or character perspective.

Functionalism as the name for a specific movement is usually identified with 'Prague School Functionalism'. This was a distinctive outgrowth from Russian Formalism and was centred on Czechoslovakia, and subsequently Estonia, from the late 1920s to the 1960s. Functionalists took the fairly abstract Formalist notions of defamiliarisation and foregrounding and in effect socialised and historicised them. They insisted that these criteria be seen dynamically in relation to changing notions of 'the familiar' and 'background.' Crucially, the latter were now recognised to be constantly in flux. It was argued that there is no fixed norm of perception nor any absolutely 'ordinary' language-use. Consequently, we have no firm grounds on which to plot that which is universally un/familiar or that which is universally in the 'fore-' or the 'back-' ground. Instead, Functionalists argued, we must recognise that the relation between, say, literature and life, or art and reality, is always shifting. What we consider literature or art is, therefore, subject to constant renegotiation and revision.

Russian Formalism and Czech Functionalism only really came to prominence in the West from the 1960s onwards, chiefly as a result of the activities of STRUCTURALISTS and functional linguists.

Key terms: **aesthetics** and **art**; **foreground and background**; defamiliarisation; deviation; **dialogic**; form and function; LITERATURE; **narrative**; poetics; **versification**; RHETORIC; stylistics.

Major figures and movements

Two preliminary warnings should be given about the phrase 'Russian Formalism'. Not everyone associated with the movement was Russian (or constantly based in Russia), and none called themselves Formalist! In fact there were *two* founding groups and movements: the Moscow Linguistic Circle (1915) and the Petrograd – later Leningrad – based group, the Society for the Study of Poetic Language (1916). Members of the former included Roman Jakobson and Petr Bogatyrev; members of the latter included Viktor Shklovsky, Yuri Tynyanov and Boris Eikhenbaum. Several of these (notably Jakobson and Bogatyrev) subsequently moved to Czechoslovakia where they helped found the Prague Linguistic Circle (1926–48). Dominant members of the latter in the 1930s were the Czechs Jan Mukarovsky and Nikolay Trubetskoy; meanwhile Jakobson and René Wellek, another native Czech member of the Prague Circle, emigrated to the USA and became US citizens. In short, the Russian-ness of 'Russian' Formalism was elastic. 'Formalist', meanwhile, was a term of abuse wielded by the opponents – not the proponents – of these groups. The members referred to themselves variously as students of 'linguistics and literature', 'poetics' and, later, 'semiotics'. The name has stuck, however, so we shall stick with it too, though not in a pejorative sense.

Poetry and poetics v. 'ordinary language'

One of the lasting achievements of Russian Formalists was in poetics. Previously, literary historians had gathered and categorised poems in terms of the various periods, genres and traditions they represented. Formalists, however, sought to codify the underlying rules which made poetry 'poetic'. Central to this project was Jakobson's view of poetry as 'organised violence committed on ordinary speech'. That is, poetry both disturbs and re-forms the patterns of routine language. And it does so at three distinct linguistic levels: (i) *sound-structure* (alliteration, assonance, rhyme, metre, etc.); (ii) *choice of words* (metaphor, archaism, varieties of vocabulary, etc.); and (iii) *combination of words* (e.g., unusual collocations, inverted word-order, marked parallelism, ellipsis). (For a glossary explaining and a checklist applying these terms, see Appendix A and 2.1.) Look at the first verse of Blake's 'London', for instance (2.1.3). This would be analysed by Formalists in terms of : (i) sound – the succession of eight-syllable, four-beat lines with rhymes in the second and fourth; (ii) word choice – the mixture of street cries and images of disease, including metaphor (e.g. 'mind-forg'd manacles'); word combination – the insistent repetition of phrases and the striking compound 'Marriage-hearse'. Taken together, all these features effectively commit 'organised violence' in that they both disturb *and* re-form what we would find otherwise in 'ordinary speech'. They draw on ordinary linguistic resources (sounds, choices and combinations of words) but pattern them in other-than-ordinary ways. And that, for Formalists, is chiefly what distinguishes poetic speech from ordinary speech: not choice of special subject matter, or tone, or a special 'poetic' (e.g., archaic) vocabulary – but a formal *re-*design of routine verbal materials. Formalists said something similar of prose and drama in so far as they exhibit more-than-usual design: plot structure; narrative perspective; etc.

It is therefore important to insist on two further distinctions: one made by Formalists themselves; the other by their critics. First, poetics is *not* restricted to poetry as traditionally conceived; there is a potential for 'more-than-ordinary' design in all language. It's simply that poems are more obviously locatable towards one end of a continuum which can also include, say, advertising, political speech-making, sermons, wittily pointed conversations, etc. (see **poetry and word-play**). Second, the very concept of 'ordinary speech' is problematic. Can we say with confidence that it actually exists? Can we point to an actual instance (a conversation amongst students (5.3.1), say, or your last conversation) and say categorically: *that* is ordinary? Ordinary for whom, when and where? Plenty of students would talk in different ways. And if you think your last converation *was* really 'ordinary', then why don't most people speak like that most of the time?! Paradoxically, then, 'ordinariness' is an extraordinarily variable social, geographical and historical matter. As we see shortly, however, this problem was tackled with considerable success by Formalists in so far as they later turned Functionalist. First, however, we must review the other main terms and concepts that early Formalists put in play.

Defamiliarisation in poetry and narrative

Defamiliarisation is a concept that many people find initially useful when asking 'what precisely is it about this text that I find interesting or striking?' The answer, simply yet significantly, is often 'because it makes me see things differently'. Obvious examples are the opening lines of Shakespeare's 'My mistress' eyes are nothing like the sun' (5.1.2) and Dickinson's 'I'm Nobody – who are You?' (5.3.4). In the first, we are treated to an unexpected *non*-compliment about the poet's mistress. In the second, we wonder about the obtrusively capitalised 'Nobody' and the dashingly direct question to 'You'.

Formalists also extended the concept of defamiliarisation to **narrative**. They concentrated on its larger-scale 'techniques' and smaller-scale 'devices'. Shklovsky, notably, argued that the crucial aspect of 'literariness' in the **novel** was its tendency to reshuffle and reconfigure elements of the world. Shklovsky's favourite examples from English literature were Sterne's *Tristram Shandy* and Swift's *Gulliver's Travels*. In the former, the narrator overtly and playfully interrupts, accelerates, delays, expands or digresses from his story till we are sometimes sure of nothing except the act and art of narration itself (see @ 5.2.7). In the latter, the ceaseless disproportions in size or nature between the narrator Gulliver and the tiny Lilliputians or the huge Brobdingnagians constantly draw attention to aspects of life which might otherwise pass unnoticed. For Shklovsky it was precisely this sense of art, and especially the novel, as 'technique' that openly reconstituted the categories of time, space and persons which was paramount. (The NEW CRITIC Mark Schorer made a similar observation in his 'Technique as Discovery' (1948).) In fact both Shklovsky and Schorer thereby proclaim their affinity with specifically Modernist techniques. For writers, artists, and film-makers otherwise as diverse as T.S. Eliot, Joyce, Woolf, Faulkner, Picasso and Eisenstein, it was precisely this project of exposing how a work is put together that marks their work as Modernist. Shklovsky's phrase for this activity was 'baring the device'. This is often cited as the chief characteristic which distinguishes '**realist**' work (where devices are purportedly *not* 'bared') from pre- and post-realist work, whether medieval, Renaissance or modern (where they purportedly *are*). A politically motivated version of 'defamiliarisation' and 'baring the device' can be found in the dramatic theory and practice of Bertolt Brecht, notably his 'making-strange effects' (*Verfremdungseffekte*); also in Benjamin's notion of 'shock' (see MARXISM).

We meet several other fundamental distinctions in early Russian Formalism which later theorists and practitioners have adapted. Eikhenbaum, for instance, developed a view of narrative as *skaz* (in Russian literally, 'the thing *said*'). English equivalents would be the anecdote or 'yarn', where it is precisely the narrator's visible and audible presence, and her or his palpable relations with the characters and actions that constitute much of the tale's dynamic and appeal. With a similar emphasis, Mukarovsky, later, following Tomashevsky, was to develop an influential distinction between *fabula* and *sjuzhet*. *Fabula* is the raw stuff of the narrative imagined as though in chronological sequence, in a continuous space and as yet untold. *Sjuzhet* is the worked-up material of an actual narrative once it has been reconfigured in time and space and been informed by specific narratorial and character voices.

Another influential approach to narrative was that of Vladimir Propp in his *Morphology of the Folktale* (1928). This was more narrowly Formalist in that it concentrated on a body of texts (a collection of classic Russian folk tales) but paid no attention to narrators and narratees. Instead, Propp aimed to discover what he termed 'the underlying principles of the various shapes' (i.e. morphology) of 'the Folk tale' in general. Propp's claims have subsequently been contested with respect to world folk tale in general. His corpus was small and culture-specific; and world story is such a vast and variegated body. Nonetheless, Propp's model and some of his categories have been applied, sometimes very suggestively, in areas ranging from medieval romance to Hollywood feature films, taking in detective fiction, tabloid newspaper stories, cartoons and soap operas on the way. (For further explanation and activities, see **narrative**.)

Foreground and background

But Formalism was not solely concerned with identifying potentially universal structures. Indeed, in so far as it transformed into Functionalism, it came increasingly to focus on particular structures and effects at particular historical moments. The notion of **foregrounding** is a case in point. In the early years of Formalism, drawing on an analogy with the visual arts, 'foregrounding' had referred to those features which are prominent *within* a text in contrast to other elements *within* the text which thereby act as a **background**. Later, Functionalists recognised that there are in fact at least two stages of the foregrounding/backgrounding process: (1) foreground and background *within* the text; (2) foregrounding *of* the text against the background *outside* the text. This may be explained in terms of the initial text–painting analogy. Not only must we see what is prominent *inside* the frame, we must also look *behind and beyond* the frame. Only then can we gauge the overall effect (and material fact) of the picture in relation to the room and building in which it hangs, and by extension the world as a whole. To get 'the whole picture', in the fullest sense, we must look *at, through, behind* and *beyond* it.

Similar refinements and extensions of early Formalist positions characterised Functionalism in general. Defamiliarisation came to be more dynamically braced against a notion of the familiar or routine world which was itself recognised as problematic: historically changing, geographically dispersed, socially variegated and politically contentious. It was recognised that what is familiar or unfamiliar in one period and place, or for one group or person, might not be for another. Moreover, if the whole concept of defamiliarisation is culturally relative, so is the whole concept of 'literariness', of which it was the cornerstone. LITERATURE might be different things to different people(s) – not a universal and eternal form but a range of social-historical functions. Its **values** would therefore be conditional, not absolute.

Form into function

A fully developed version of this Functionalist model can be found in the work of the most influential member of the Prague Linguistic Circle, Jan Mukarovsky. His *Aesthetic Function: Norm and Value as Social Facts* (1936) is a particularly powerful example. As the title makes clear, Mukarovsky was not at all interested in **aesthetics** in some merely formal sense of 'art for art's sake'. He was concerned with aesthetic function: the ways in which aesthetic and social values interrelate according to prevailing 'norms', and shift as those norms shift. For Mukarovsky, what was crucial was whether a work was perceived as having a practical, instrumental function with some other end in mind, or 'aesthetically', as an end in itself irrespective of other purposes. For instance, a picture of a Madonna and child might have a primarily religious function in a certain period or society. But in another, more secular, period or society it might primarily function as an art object or as a tourist attraction. It might also, of course, chiefly function as an educational object of study – in a History of Art course, for example. A church or cathedral or mosque can be perceived as a house of God or as an instance of building techniques and architectural styles or, as with Althusser, an 'ideological apparatus'. A rough clay drinking vessel can become a priceless museum exhibit. It's the same with any text or other artefact you may be studying. How we *see* it will partly depend upon how we are expected to *use* it. Its value is a product of its function. Mukarovsky summarises the situation thus (1936: 6, 60):

> [W]e can never discount the possibility that the functions of a given work were originally entirely different from what they appear to be when we apply our system of values . . . Every shift in time, space or social surroundings alters the existing artistic traditions through whose prism that work is observed.

Mukarovsky also insists that there is no eternally present 'norm' in relation to which the value of a work may be gauged (p. 36): 'A living work of art always oscillates between the past and future status of an aesthetic norm.' In all these respects, Mukarovsky clearly anticipated and, indeed, influenced the reception aesthetics developed by later German reader-response critics such as Iser and Jauss (see **writing and reading**). More immediately, we may recognise some close affinities between positions being developed by Mukarovsky in Czechoslovakia and those being developed by Mikhail Bakhtin in Russia around the same time. For instance, Bakhtin was interested in:

◆ the word as 'a two-sided act' suspended between one language-user and another: words are always 'a site of struggle' between contending **value** systems;
◆ the **dialogic** relations between various moments of production and reproduction: we are constantly refashioning 'another's words in one's own language';
◆ 'chronotopes' (Greek for 'time-topics'), which he conceived as hybrids compounded of formal features of **genres** along with their period-specific aesthetic and social values, all of which change according to time, place and persons;
◆ **carnival** in general and parody in particular, where one set of cultural and aesthetic 'norms' is overthrown by another which is its obverse.

How to practise Formalism . . .

Concentrate on the overall strategies and localised devices whereby a work which is considered LITERATURE demonstrates its 'literariness'. In particular, draw attention to ways in which it:

◆ *defamiliarises habitual perceptions*, prevents merely 'automatic' responses and promotes a fresh view of familiar things;
◆ *commits 'organised violence on ordinary language'* and thereby establishes a more than ordinary sense of poetic or rhetorical pattern, chiefly through manipulations of sound-patterning, parallelism (repetition with variation), antithesis, imagery and inverted syntax;
◆ *foregrounds certain aspects of language within the text* (e.g. imagery, sound-patterning) and effectively assumes or 'backgrounds' others;
◆ *plays around with dimensions of time and space and narration*: obtrudes or obscures the controlling presence of the writer, and generally 'lays bare' the devices of writing.

. . . And how to turn it into Functionalism

Go on to investigate:

◆ the aesthetic and social norms which the text was confirming or challenging at the time;
◆ the various functions the text has served, and effects it has had, at various moments of (re)production and reception;
◆ the processes of **re-valuation** it has been – and continues to be – subject to.

Examples

Draw on the above guidelines to help sketch your own Formalist and Functionalist analyses of each of the following texts. Do this before reading the commentary supplied below.

Poetry and poetics: Shakespeare's 'My mistress' eyes . . .' (5.1.2) A Formalist reading of this sonnet might start by drawing attention to the **versification**: how the rigour of the rhyme-scheme (ababcdcdefefgg) and metre (iambic pentameter) supply a 'poetic' framework, and yet the conversational freedom of the rhythms informs it with a sense of 'ordinary speech'. Formalists might then move to consider the witty contrasts and inversions, and the systematically antithetical, parodic argument. All these features would be cited as evidence of the text's self-conscious 'literariness', and its pervasive defamiliarising of the romantic love experience. A more fully Functionalist reading would compare the various uses the sonnet form is put to here and elsewhere by Shakespeare, with its use by Wyatt, Sidney and Petrarch previously and, say, Milton, Brooke and others subsequently (see other sonnets in 5.1.2). It would also consider the fact that most sonnets were written by men and passed around among men. The emphasis would thus shift from what the sonnet *is* to what it *does*; e.g. boast, complain, insult, praise, show off, insinuate, admonish, celebrate. It would also be important to gauge the various **foregrounds** and **backgrounds** against which this sonnet can be placed and evaluated: the conventional (Petrarchan) image of 'fair' female beauty which it twists and turns in the textual 'foreground', and the changing norms and valuations of female beauty (as well as males' roles as observers and judges) which act as 'backgrounds'. The significance and value of this sonnet could thereby be plotted textually, contextually and intertextually, and in a succession of historical moments.

Prose narrative: Pratchett and Gaiman's 'Good Omens' (5.2.4) Formalists tend to concentrate on prose texts which sport with language, genre and narrative structure. In the *Good Omens* passage they would draw attention to such features as:

♦   the humorous slippage between different time-frames and world-views, from the nostalgically archaic and rural ('slumbering villages . . . honest yeomen') to the patently modern and commercial ('financial consulting . . . software engineering').
♦   the playful mixture of different genres, from documentary journalism ('The surveyor's theodolite is one of the most direful symbols of the twentieth century') through biblical parody ('there will come Road Widening, yea, . . .') to an apocalyptic blend of real estate agent's blurb ('and two-thousand-home estates in keeping with the Essential Character of the Village. Executive Development will be manifest').
♦   the overt act of narration and acknowledgement of the fact that this is one book amongst many ('Most books on witchcraft will tell you . . . This is because most books on witchcraft are written by men').

Functionalists would go on to observe that many of these issues were acutely topical in the late 1980s and early 1990s in Britain, notably the gentrifying and embourgeoisement of the countryside, and the problem of road extension and widening (along with ecological opposition to it). Also acute was – and is – a sense that sensitive male writers might feel the need to apologise for patriarchal literary traditions. Further contextualisation would entail comparison with other contemporary fantasy and neo-Gothic tales, parodic and otherwise. In all these ways, precisely what is being defamiliarised would be recognised as a function of a specific social and historical moment – even while the aesthetic forms and techniques might be recognised as in some sense universal.

Drama: Beckett's 'Not I' (5.3.3) Formalists, like NEW CRITICS, did not devote much attention to drama. In its mode of production on stage or screen, it was less exclusively 'literary' and more obviously and messily social. But when they did treat drama, again they tended to concentrate on Modernist or experimental works. Beckett's *Not I* would be chosen because it committed 'organised violence on ordinary speech' through:

♦   the piling-up of truncated or interrupted phrases without much conventional punctuation or
    sentence-structure;
♦   half-formed thoughts, a sense of 'talking to oneself' and uncertain or scrambled frames of
    reference in time, space and person;
♦   the patent theatricality of Mouth and Auditor, which are clearly roles and devices not
    naturalistic character-parts;
♦   the sheer effort the reader/audience has to put into making familiar sense of what may initially
    seem crazily incomprehensible. (Is 'Mouth' the 'tiny little girl' or the mother? Is this an inner
    dialogue with self or an outer dialogue with an other?)

Functionalists would try to gauge the norms of sense and nonsense prevailing at the time and,
more specifically, trace the historical development and reception of so-called **absurdist** theatre.
Just *how* 'absurd' was it – and is it now – to whom, when and where?

Discussion

(i)   The technique of art is to make objects 'unfamiliar', to make forms difficult, to increase
      the difficulty and length of perception.
                    Victor Shklovsky, *Art as Technique* (1917), in Rice and Waugh (2001: 50)

(ii) Any object and any activity, whether natural or human, may become a carrier of the
      aesthetic function.
                    Jan Mukarovsky, *Aesthetic Function: Norm and Value as Social Facts*
                                                                            (1936: 6)

Also see: 'Initial analysis' into 'Full interpretation', 2.1–2.2; LITERATURE, 1.3.2; RELATIVITIES,
3.7 and LINGUISTICS, STYLISTICS AND COGNITIVE POETICS @ 3.10; and above Key Terms
p. 141.

READING: Introductory: Selden, Widdowson and Brooker 2005: 29–44; Makaryk 1993: 53–60; Carter
and Nash 1990: 1–19. *Core texts*: Eichenbaum, Shklovsky and Bakthin in Rivkin and Ryan 2004; *also*
Todorov, Jakobson and Bakhtin in Lodge and Wood 2008; Eichenbaum, Jakobson and Bakhtin in Leitch
2010; Mukarovsky in Garvin 1964; Bakhtin 1981. *Advanced*: Medvedev and Bakhtin 1978; Volshinov
1973; Mukarovsky 1936; Jameson 1972; Erlich 1981; Holquist (Bakhtin) 2002; Womack and Todd
2002; Bennett 2003.

3.4   MIND AND PERSON – PSYCHOLOGICAL APPROACHES

*If you concentrate on the mental, emotional, personal or unconscious aspects of interpretation,
your approach is broadly psychological.*

Overview

Psychology for our purposes can be initially defined as the understanding of mental and
emotional processes as these relate to language, literature and culture. Psychoanalysis is the
study of these processes in individual people. Psychotherapy is concerned with techniques for
resolving mental and emotional problems and with people realising their full potential. As
distinctly modern practices, psychoanalysis and psychotherapy are primarily identified with
Sigmund Freud (1856–1939). For it was Freud who aimed to put the study of human

consciousness and the unconscious on a scientific footing. However, the analysis and treatment of mental and emotional disorders (as well as debate about the very terms 'mental', 'emotional', 'dis/order', 'ab/normality', 'in/sanity', 'non/sense', etc.) have long and complex histories both before and after Freud. Indeed, one of the main challenges in studying the 'psyche' is choosing the ground upon which we define it. The term derives from Greek *psyche* meaning 'breath' and 'soul' as well as 'mind'. Psyche-ology broadly conceived is thus potentially the study of mental, emotional and spiritual processes.

LANGUAGE, in modern psychological terms, is the primary symbolic system through which we differentiate and categorise the worlds within and around us. For Lacan, the 'subject's entry into language' is the primary condition for the perception of difference. Words are the chief means whereby we distinguish various selves from various others (notably through the personal pronouns 'I, me, my, mine; you, she, he, it, they . . . '). It is also chiefly through language that we assume or are assigned various subject positions, roles and identities (e.g. common nouns such as 'mummy', 'daddy', 'girl', 'boy', 'baby', 'grown-up', 'student', 'lecturer'; and proper nouns such as people's personal and family names). Words are therefore a primary means of both expression and repression. They allow us to say and see certain things but at the same time they prompt us to ignore or fail to recognise others. For this reason, psychologists often pay a great deal of attention to processes of dialogue, especially that between analyst and patient, and in psychotherapy the practice of the 'talking cure'. They also look closely at the psychological implications of word-play, including word association, ambiguities, puns and slips of the tongue. Meanwhile, educational and developmental psychologists engage specifically with the processes of perception and memory and the relations between learning and play, not only in language but also in other forms of symbolic representation and social interaction.

LITERATURE, and more generally writing, figures both as an object of psychological study and as a therapeutic practice. We can study other people's poems, plays, novels, auto/biographies and journals for what these tell us about their 'inner' lives. We can also use these genres and activities to explore our own identities, situations and circumstances. Either way, the focus tends to oscillate between the psychological object (the writer as realised *in* the text) and the psychological subject (the reader or writer's relation *to* the text). Indeed, as with many contemporary approaches, there has been a noticeable shift of emphasis over the past thirty years: from writer to text to reader. The ostensible focus of study is now less likely to be, say, Shakespeare's or Austen's or Dickens's 'mind', or even the 'mind' of the characters Hamlet or Elizabeth Bennett or Pip. It is more likely to be the psychological problems and possibilities realised by these figures in the minds of contemporary audiences and readers. In this respect current psychological approaches have much in common with those of Reader Response and Reception. Fiction in particular becomes a 'space' in which it is not only the writer but also the reader who plays, 'daydreams', and generally explores and experiments with various versions of reality and the interplay of conscious and unconscious states.

CULTURE figures in psychological approaches in a variety of shadowy yet powerful ways. Civilisation as a whole can be seen as the result (the symptom even) of human beings' struggles to control and redirect their basic animal drives and desires. Viewed negatively, culture is thus a sustained act of collective repression: it thwarts and distorts our animal natures and alienates us from our bodies. Viewed positively, culture is a celebration of all that it is to be distinctly 'human': it keeps us sane and safe and also allows us to express and project our bodies in many directions and dimensions. Thus we can conceive of literature, art, clothing, buildings, cityscapes, regimes of work and play (i.e. COMMUNICATION and sign-systems in general) in at least two ways: on the one hand, they conceal, constrict and contain; but on the other hand, they express, extend and explore. Either way, we are obliged to recognise that our understanding of emotional and mental processes is likely to be tied up with our understanding of bodily ('animal') functions, and that neither can be divorced from arguments about what we mean by culture, civilisation and humanity. For all these reasons, it is now common to find psychological dimensions to MARXIST, FEMINIST, POSTCOLONIAL and POSTSTRUCTURALIST approaches. Conversely, there are several kinds of psychological theory and practice specifically inflected in terms of class, sexuality and gender, race and ethnicity, and the post-humanist subject. Psychological processes of expression and repression are thereby related to social-historical processes of oppression and suppression. The personal is recognised to be public and political – and vice versa.

Key terms: **absence and presence; absurd** (see **comedy**); **self and other** (see **auto/biography**); **character**; condensation and displacement; consciousness and the unconscious; content (manifest and latent); desire; dream-work; ego, id and super-ego; expression and repression; lack; transaction; **subjects and agents, identities and roles.**

Major figures and models

Many of the most enduring terms in psychoanalysis were made current by Sigmund Freud. Even where these terms have been subsequently challenged or changed, they still provide a useful initial frame of reference. (They can be followed up further through the index.)

The unconscious and consciousness; repression and expression

The unconscious is everything in our psychological make-up that we are *not* directly aware of: our ultimate biological drives, pre-eminently sex, along with all those formative moments in our personal histories, chiefly from early childhood, which we have forgotten or repressed. By definition, the unconscious is a huge yet hidden power. It drives much of what we do yet remains concealed. Consciousness, meanwhile, is everything about ourselves that we *are* aware of: the sensations and perceptions we can talk about or otherwise express, including those aspects of our personal histories and identities we can recall and explicitly represent. The relation between the unconscious and the conscious is dynamic not fixed. Hence our capacity to *become* conscious of things of which we were previously unaware, as well as the possibility of active 'consciousness raising' in general. Some later writers go on to make direct links between forms of psychological *re*pression, the political *op*pression of certain social groups, and mechanisms of *sup*pression (e.g., censorship) of certain kinds of information (e.g. Macherey 1966; Jameson 1981). They argue in effect for a politicised unconscious. We can – or cannot – realise certain things about our **selves** precisely because of our past and present power relations with **others** (see **auto/biography**).

Manifest and latent contents: condensation, displacement and symbolism

Dreams, for Freud, are 'the royal road to the unconscious'. So too, potentially, are imaginative LITERATURE and **art** in general. In all these areas Freud observed that much more is meant than meets the eye. Put more formally, the obvious 'surface' meaning of a dream (story, play or painting) is a merely *manifest* content. This must be interpreted so as to get at its hidden 'deeper' meaning, the *latent* content. Freud identified three ways in which meanings tend to be embedded and hidden, more or less unconsciously:

♦ *condensation*, where two or more meanings come to bear on the same word, figure or image (e.g. puns, metaphors, a composite person or event in a dream or painting);

♦ *displacement*, where one item stands in for another with which it has some perceived connection (e.g. substitution of opposites or part for whole, say, 'girl' for 'boy' or a ring for the person who wears it);

♦ *symbolism*, where some word, image or object is conventionally identified with a certain meaning or function (e.g. spears with fighting with men, bowls with cooking with women).

This last kind of symbolic meaning is primary for Carl Jung, Freud's one-time collaborator and subsequent critic. It underpinned Jung's notion that dreams and art were storehouses of universal images belonging to a 'collective unconscious' that had been repressed by civilisation. In general, Jung had a more positively celebratory, less negatively suspicious, view of the nature and function of art and literature than Freud. However, the POSTSTRUCTURALIST psychoanalyst Jacques Lacan repudiated the notion of universal symbolism of all kinds. Instead, he insisted that the sign – whether in literature, art or dreams – is inherently unstable and elusive. Consequently, we are always faced by a lack of essential meaning and are constantly engaged in processes of condensation and displacement. There is no ultimate 'deeper', 'latent' content at all – only a ceaseless succession of metaphoric and metonymic substitutions (for Lacan's notion of 'the Imaginary', see **image**).

Myth and psycho-drama; ego, super-ego and id

Several of Freud's dramatic representations of psychological processes have become classics. They draw upon classical **myth** and, like the man himself, have become myths in their own right. The 'Oedipus complex', for instance, was Freud's name for what he saw as a general developmental process: a phase when the male child wishes to kill the father and sleep with the mother. The prototype was Sophocles's *Oedipus the King* where the hero, Oedipus, unwittingly does precisely that. Female children, meanwhile, according to Freud, are particularly prone to 'penis envy'. They are aware of themselves chiefly in terms of a 'lack' of what little boys so visibly have: physically a penis, and symbolically a phallus. Not surprisingly, many FEMINISTS have taken Freud to task over the male-centred myths at the heart of his psychology. In their various ways writers such as Klein, Chodorow, Kristeva and Cixous all argue for quite different configurations of mother–father, mother–daughter and mother–son relations. Characteristically, they equate the 'good mother' figure with a phase of security and undifferentiated 'wholeness' before the threat of separation represented by the father. Some psychoanalytic feminists, following Lacan, also identify the pre-verbal stage of child development with undifferentiated sexuality and semiotic flux, and the verbal stage with differentiated sexuality and symbolic fixity. Feminists have also been quick to question the vision of female 'hysteria' represented in Freud's case history of 'Dora'.

Another psycho-drama which has achieved classic status and common currency in speech is Freud's model of the ego, super-ego and id. This later, three-part model of emotional and mental processes both refined and replaced the earlier two-part model of the conscious and unconscious. Now the psyche was conceived as the site where three, not two, forces are in play. The *ego* (Latin 'I') represents that part of the **self** most concerned to gratify the instinctual drives emanating from the unconscious, now renamed the *id* (Latin 'that', 'that **other**'). Meanwhile, the *super-ego* (Latin 'above-I') is that part of the conscious self which acts as censor and judge. The super-ego regulates what shall be permitted or prohibited by way of expression or repression. It has the function of a kind of 'conscience' or self-censor and is identified by Freud with a socially internalised sense of self. (The ego, meanwhile, is identified with a relatively free, pre-social self.) One advantage of this triadic model of the ego, super-ego and id over that of the binary model of the un/conscious is that it introduces a sense of dynamism within the conscious self. There is now a range of actual and potential 'selves' (plural). The ego is both impelled by the desires of the id from within and imposed upon by the conscience of the super-ego from without. In short, 'I' becomes a site where versions of self and other contend. Henceforth the psychological **subject** is split, the 'individual' is divided, and people's identities can never be wholly identified with their conscious view of themselves.

Freud's models and myths have been extended (or exploded) in many ways. The following have been most influential in English and Literary Studies.

Transactional analysis

As developed by Norman Holland, this is concerned less with what the text tells us about an individual psyche (that of an author or character, say) and more with the text's function as a form of therapy involving both writer and reader. In this view writers supply frameworks and scenarios to which readers respond and relate in their own ways. The text thereby becomes the site not just of one but of many psycho-dramas. In Melanie Klein's terms, the text is 'projected onto' by the reader and thereby becomes 'introjected into' her or his unconsciousness. D.W. Winnicott in *Playing and Reality* (1974) develops a comparable notion of play as the exchange of real or imaginary objects. These *transitional objects* (whether dolls or texts) operate as a kind of 'potential space' in which hopes and fears may be safely realised and released. Such processes clearly have something in common with Aristotle's notion of catharsis as the 'purging' of emotion by the witnessing of a dramatic spectacle (see **comedy and tragedy**). They also partly overlap with reader-response approaches, especially those developed by David Bleich (1978) in his model of 'subjective criticism' as a kind of individual and group therapy (see **writing and reading**).

An overtly socio-psychological approach to learning in general and language-learning in particular was developed by Lev Vygotsky (1934). For Vygotsky language is a form of consciousness which develops through a continuing **dialogue** between the 'inner voices' of the speaker's unconscious **self** and the 'outer voices' of significant **others** in the surrounding world. Learning and development are thus recognised to be *inter*personal as well as *intra*personal processes: articulated on an 'I/we–you' axis as well as an 'I–me' axis. Indeed, the one is a refraction of the other. For Bakhtin, too, words are always caught in the processes of exchange and change that bind people to one another socially. Every transaction (linguistic, educational and psychological) therefore entails a transformation. People are human *becomings* not simply human *beings*. Deleuze (1987) presses a similar point.

Psycho-politics: the personal is political

The progressive socialising and historicising of psychology are a feature of most contemporary approaches. So is a recognition that 'personal politics' cuts both ways. Just as the personal is always political, so the political always has a psychological dimension to it. Michel Foucault (1986: 121ff.), for instance, insists that we understand 'sanity' and 'insanity', 'normality' and 'abnormality', 'sense' and 'nonsense', dialectically and historically. These terms are braced against one another within shifting medical, legal and other **discourses**. They mean subtly or markedly different things at different times. Thus 'madness' is not the same, nor treated the same, amongst medieval mystics, in eighteenth-century French asylums, in Stalinist Russia and in twenty-first-century Manhattan. Diagnosis and treatment also vary according to sex and social status. Sexuality, too, Foucault argues, is inscribed and expressed differently in different cultures. The libido, like the body in general, is subject to various 'economies' (distributions, values) and is perhaps not the universal instinctual drive often implied by Freud.

Others, meanwhile, as already mentioned, point to the need to read psychological *repression* in relation to political *op*pression of powerless groups and the systematic *sup*pression of potentially available means of communication and *ex*pression. (In short, all these '—pressions' are interdependent.) Writers such as Fanon, Freire, Macherey, Williams, Jameson and Žižek see efforts to achieve consciousness as struggles which are personal-political not simply personal. MARXISTS in effect insist on a pluralising and collectivising of Freud's psycho-drama of the 'I', 'above-I' and 'it'. They argue for the recognition of a 'them' and 'us' dimension of 'inner' as well as 'outer' struggle. FEMINISTS too insist on sexually complicated versions of the psyche, even before the gendered differences entailed by the entry into language and the symbolic order. The whole drama of 's/he' (i.e. the psychological subject as 'she' and/or 'he') must therefore be added to that of an otherwise neutered or patriarchally privileged 'I'. So must the dramas (and traumas) of a self-consciously 'queer' psyche in so far as these expose and exceed the limitations of a merely binary view of heterosexuality. 'Colour', too, whatever the precise colours of the actual faces and perceived 'masks' of ourselves and others, inevitably impinges upon the development of each and every one of us as personal-political **subjects** living through POST-COLONIALISM. Study of cultural identification and cross-cultural **differences** is a significant feature of contemporary psychology.

The end(s) of psychology

Finally, in the various debates informing POSTSTRUCTURALISM and POSTMODERNISM, it is the radical instability not only of the psychological subject as person but also of psychology as a discipline and practice which is at issue. That is, psychology too, along with its associated practices of psychoanalysis and psychotherapy, may itself be identified as just one of a range of socially and historically situated discourses. At some point these will be transformed into or superseded by others. After all, modern psychoanalysis and psychotherapy largely took over the 'curative' and 'purgative' functions previously assigned to religion and magic (e.g. confession, spiritual guidance, conscience, exorcism). The question, then, paradoxically, is *What is it that modern psychology itself 'represses'?* What other modes of expression does psychology in some way deny or distort? What alternative disciplines and practices are currently developing inside, alongside and outside psychology? Does the notion of the specifically human 'psyche' as mental, emotional and spiritual entity have a future at all? Is it, for instance, a humanist or post-humanist construct, and does it survive contemporary genetics and bio-technics? Or do we need to think, feel, and generally **imagine** in ways as yet undreamt of – at least in mainstream Western traditions? The method which follows tries to take account of these possibilities too.

How to practise psychological approaches

Begin by considering the text in three dimensions:

♦   what it suggests about the *writer's* emotional, mental and spiritual states and processes, as well as those of her or his time;

- how you as a modern *reader* relate to – and perhaps identify with or project onto – the events, characters and situations represented;
- what the *language of the text* suggests about the nature of expression and repression in general, and the relation of both to our understanding of tensions between conscious and unconscious states.

In all these areas try to take into account the interplay of a range of psychological subjects (writer, reader, text, language) in a range of social and historical moments. Don't imagine there is just one psychological reading. Further research and reflection are clearly necessary, so go on to consider:

- *auto/biography*: what is known about the writer's life, both from her- or himself and from others? What seems to be revealed or concealed in the work in hand? What are we (not) being told, and why?
- *choice of psychological model*: which of the following emphases seems to best answer both the demands of the particular material and your own particular aims:
  - *manifest and latent content*, observing and perhaps attempting to 'decode' the text's strategies of *condensation, displacement and symbolism*?
  - Freudian notions of a tension between *the unconscious and consciousness*; and psycho-dramas such as the *Oedipus complex* and *hysteria*; or the relations between *ego, super-ego and id*?
- *transactional analysis* of teacher–learner and learner–learner as well as writer– reader relations, where the text functions as a 'transitional' object and item of exchange at various moments?
- *post- or anti-Freudian models* of 'the good mother'; lack and desire; self and other; the Imaginary; the subject's entry into language and the symbolic order?
- *social-psychological* differences relating to sexuality and gender, rank and class, ethnicity, religion and MULTICULTURALISM in general.

Finally, consider those aspects of the text and your response to it that are under-represented, misrepresented or completely unrepresented by this kind of psychological approach. What other, potential approaches has it, in turn, repressed or suppressed?

Example

John Clare's 'I am – yet what I am' (5.3.4). Read this in conjunction with the accompanying notes and, if possible, a brief account of Clare's life (e.g. in Head 2006). Sketch a psychological analysis using the above 'How to practise' guidelines before reading on.

A psychological approach to this poem might begin with the writer–text relation (how the poem relates to Clare's life) then move to the reader–text relation (e.g. how you and I relate to the poem). Both might lead to larger inferences about language, the un/conscious, and expression and repression in general, as well as to reflection upon the similarities and differences between early-nineteenth- and twenty-first-century notions of sanity and insanity, normality and abnormality.

'I'dentity crises. The profound sense of self-alienation and estrangement from others that pervades the first two stanzas might be traced back to Clare's adolescence. For it was then that Clare's lifelong love for Mary Joyce, a local farmer's daughter, was thwarted by the intervention of her father. Clare was of farm-labourer stock and apparently not considered a suitable match. It was then, too, in the early 1800s, that land around Clare's native village of Helpstone was

'enclosed' (i.e. taken over by a local landowner for private parkland and conversion to sheep-farming). This resulted in the dislocation, both physical and mental, of many farm-labourers, including Clare and his family. Against all this could be set the idyllic vision projected in the last stanza of early childhood as a time of security and belonging. Such observations might be backed up by appeal to Clare's scattered autobiographical writings (1821–41) as well as to his other poems. Many are marked by the sense of a previously pastoral, almost paradisal, childhood state (real or imaginary) that was subsequently subject to personally traumatic and socially dramatic change. We might therefore venture to say that Clare had trouble maintaining a viable sense of **self** when challenged by **others**: his 'super/ego' fragmented under the pressure of an internal or external 'id'.

But whatever the cause or explanation, it is matter of record that Clare was first admitted to an asylum at Epping in 1837. He escaped in 1841 and tried to walk back to Northampton, believing he was married to his childhood sweetheart. He was then committed to Northampton General Lunatic Asylum. There he lived for the remaining twenty-three years of his life and wrote many poems, including this one (*c.* 1844). All this information may help us explore – even though it can only crudely explain – a number of the poem's recurrent concerns:

- the sense of a self divided against itself ('I am – yet what I am . . . the self-consumer of my woes');
- the absence of comforting others ('friends forsake me like a memory lost');
- a loss of clear distinction between consciousness and unconsciousness ('the living sea of waking dreams . . . '); all that remains is a present sense of longing contrasted with a past sense of belonging: an overpowering desire to fill an irreparable lack.

Thus the whole last stanza (perhaps re-read it now) may be variously interpreted as: (i) yearning for a kind of primordial infantile oblivion; (ii) a vision of a heavenly paradise or utopia; (iii) a throwback to some sexually undifferentiated state; (iv) a desire for reintegration with nature, the 'id' and all that is 'not-I' – a 'death-wish', even.

The 'forming' of desire Psychological readings might move in other directions and dimensions too. Formally, they might point to the expressively irregular rhythms, the moving caesura (right from the first line) and the 'dashing' punctuation. At the same time they would note the controlling, if not calming, influence of the highly regular versification and metre: three stanzas each with six ten-syllable lines, the first with alternating rhymes throughout, the last two concluding with couplets. Such a high degree of patterning might be seen negatively as a symbolic attempt to repress the semiotic flux beneath – a kind of verbal straitjacket. But it might also be seen positively as a saving vestige of civilisation, turning what would otherwise be an anguished animal cry into a recognisably human harmony. A rather different, contextual reading might relate the poem's substance and structure to the sense of 'confinement' experienced in many early nineteenth-century (and later) asylums. This might even be extended to notions of 'enclosure': the privatisation of fields and property resulting in the privation of bodies and minds. In this way the personal would be realised as political, and vice versa. The psychology invoked would be grounded in society and history, not simply in the notion of the universal human psyche. There might also be some recognition that this poem was written over a decade before the birth of Freud and half a century before the formal institution of psychoanalysis. Perhaps, then, the most appropriate contemporary intellectual framework for the poem *at that time* was religious and spiritual (as in its last verse) and not psychological at all (as in the above analysis).

A personal–political response. All this leaves us, as modern readers, with a crucial responsibility. And this cannot be detached from the ways in which we, collectively and individually, respond to the text (i.e. our 'response-ability'). What sense do we make of the poem? More pointedly, what sense does it make of us? Personal responses will vary of course. But if we regard psychological transaction as what takes place between reader and reader as well as between reader, text and writer, then we have an obligation to try to tease out at least some of our responses. Inevitably, some of these will turn out to be idiosyncratic; others may be common; and all are in some sense shareable. (I must leave you to decide which are which, for you, in the following.) Here 'I' go:

> I too, like Clare in the last verse, associate childhood with a time when I 'sweetly slept'. Now I often don't sleep too well. As I get older I also recognise, perhaps with Clare (ll. 11–12), that friends and family can become 'strange', either through death (the ultimate estrangement) or through changing relationships. (When I first drafted this piece in October 1996 I remembered my mother who had died a year previously and a good friend who had died recently. These events were very much part of my immediate response then.) More generally, there is the tricky matter of fears for one's own own sanity, as well as general uncertainty about what 'sanity' and 'normality' actually mean nowadays. After all, I am a member of a species which is gradually tearing itself and the rest of the planet to pieces, notwithstanding claims to scientific rationality and progess. ('Enclosure' too, I recall, was hailed as a mark of progress and civilisation – though by the enclos*ers* rather than the enclos*ed*.) In other words, you don't have to have been in a mental asylum or formally certified as insane to have anxieties about your own and other people's sanity. At the same time, as I reread Clare's last verse, I take comfort from its vision of at least potential harmony and (re-)union. Though whether this is saving illusion or crazy delusion I cannot say.

The relevance of this brief autobiographical excursus to your own response to Clare's poem I must leave you to decide for yourself.

Also see: FEMINISM; POSTSTRUCTURALISM; POSTCOLONIALISM; COGNITIVE POETICS @ 3.10; also above Key Terms p. 149.

READING: Introductory: Wright in Coyle, Peck *et al.* 1990: 764–76; Eagleton (M.) 1996: 131–68; Green and Lebihan 1996: 139–81; Parkin-Gounelas 2001. *Core texts*: Freud, Jung, Trilling and Holland in Lodge 1972; Freud and Lacan in Lodge and Wood 2008; *also* Freud, Lacan, Fanon and Chodorow in Rivkin and Ryan 2004; Winnicott 1974; Kristeva 1984; Holland 1990. *Advanced*: Vygotsky 1934; Deleuze and Guattari 1982 (Anti-Oedipal); Rudynitsky 1993 (Winnicott and Literature); Lacan 2007; Wright 2000; Žižek 2006.

3.5   CLASS AND COMMUNITY – MARXISM, CULTURAL MATERIALISM AND NEW HISTORICISM

If you are concerned with the social and political aspects of interpretation – especially class, status and power in the community – these are approaches you will want to engage with.

Overview

All these approaches are concerned with understanding texts in social and historical context. LANGUAGE is grasped functionally for what it *does*, rather than essentially for what it *is*. LITERATURE is treated as a problematic, even suspect category, especially in so far as it offers as 'universal' and 'natural' writing which appears to underpin privileged, often elitist, views of society. Accordingly, the emphasis of these approaches tends to be broadly cultural and specifically political. CULTURE is recognised as an arena of conflict as well as consensus, a 'space' where differences of interest diverge as well as converge. Access or denial of access to certain modes of COMMUNICATION is also recognised as crucial. Meanwhile, the primary forces of historical change are reckoned to be those of social class as well as latterly, gender and race.

Marxist approaches to language, literature and culture tend to be developed from the models of economic and political change that Marx, Engels and the other founders of Marxism devised, rather than from the relatively few and incidental things they said about literature and art as such. There is thus much attention to:

♦   *modes of production* – the technologies and social relations whereby goods are produced (including the modes of production, publication and transmission of poems, novels, plays, newspapers, films, TV programmes, etc.);

♦   relations between the *economic base* and the *ideological superstructure* – how certain economic organisations of labour and materials affect and are affected by institutions such as the law, religion, education, the MEDIA and the state (e.g. the relations between poverty and illiteracy, control of the media and access to political power);

♦   *power, powerlessness and empowerment* – how far power is maintained by coercion, complicity or consent; and how far those who are subject to dominant world-views have the capacity to assert themselves as agents in their own emancipation.

Cultural Materialism is a form of Marxist analysis chiefly identified with Raymond Williams, Alan Sinfield, Catherine Belsey and others in Britain. It is marked by a committed socialist critique of literary and cultural artefacts and of the institutions that maintain them. **New Historicism** is a related, socially sensitive but less politically committed form of analysis identified with such figures as Stephen Greenblatt, Louis Montrose and others in the USA. The aim of New Historicists is to recognise the power relations in play both in a text's moment of production and in its subsequent moments of re-production (e.g., by academics in universities). Typically, whereas (British) Cultural Materialists tended to emphasise resistant, subversive and sometimes revolutionary readings of texts, their (American) New Historicist counterparts tended to emphasise the ways in which texts and their readers finally 'contain' subversion and promote conformity.

There are very few pure – some would say vulgar – Marxists in academic circles nowadays. But there are many broadly 'Marxian' critics and theorists who would identify with parts of the above agendas. Most do so with an awareness of other socially sensitive and politically motivated approaches, especially FEMINIST and POSTCOLONIAL ones. Marxists also have vexed but often highly productive relations with PSYCHOANALYTIC, POSTSTRUCTURALIST and POSTMODERNIST approaches. Arguments in this area often revolve around differing notions of the subject (conceived as person, subject matter and academic discipline). It all depends how far it (and we) are understood to be individual *and* social, private *and* public, repressed *and* oppressed, coherent *and* dispersed, local *and* global, in *and* out of history.

Key terms: **absence and presence, gaps and silences, centres and margins; foreground and background;** class; **text in context;** CULTURE; **discourse;** HISTORY; **narrative . . . hi/story;** ideology; popular; power; **realism and representation; subject and agent; re-valuation.**

Some major figures and movements

Broadly speaking, there are three distinct yet interrelated approaches to texts practised by critics in the Marxist tradition, each of which we shall treat in turn:

♦   'socialist **realism**', primarily associated with the critical writing of Georg Lukács (1885–1971);
♦   'socialist POST/MODERNISM', primarily associated with the theory and practice of Bertolt Brecht (1898–1956);
♦   'democratic MULTICULTURALISM', spanning contemporary Cultural Materialism and New Historicism, and distinguished by its attention to cultural **differences** and power.

Socialist realism

The Hungarian critic Lukács was chiefly interested in the nineteenth-century novel and the ways in which such 'epic' and 'encyclopaedic' novelists as Dickens, Balzac and Tolstoy could present overarching views of the societies in which they lived. The sheer breadth of these writers' social and historical visions offered imaginary 'totalities'. In effect, they afforded what Lukács termed a 'world-historical' sense of the various classes and sections of society in dynamic tension: caught in the very ebb and flow of social conflict and historical change. **Characters** were thus significant not only as individuals but for their 'typicality', their capacity to express the pressures which their social roles thrust upon them. In short, Lukács read fictions for the social-economic conditions and class conflicts they represented. His attachment to **realism** (or rather 'critical realism') as a mode and the nineteenth-century novel as a historical genre was based upon the assumption that the best art both reflects and refracts history 'as a whole': it holds up a large mirror to social changes and at the same time revealingly tilts it.

Socialist post/modernism

This is a very different kind of political and **aesthetic** vision. Though still discernibly Marxist, it was practised by Brecht. He too aimed for what he termed an 'epic theatre'; but in his case he had in mind a more formal, Aristotelian notion of epic as **dramatic** exchanges framed by **narrative**. More particularly, Brecht practised a politically motivated version of the kinds of defamiliarisation technique theorised by the Russian FORMALISTS. His 'making-strange-device' (*Verfremdungseffekt*) aimed to prevent audiences identifying too readily with the characters and situations presented. Instead, spectators were forced to stand back from the action and appraise it critically, from a distance. Brecht's mixture of narrative and dramatic modes, sometimes punctuated by song, had the same aim: to make viewers pause for reflection, not just empathise emotionally. There is particular attention to clashes between **discourses** so as to produce, not a single and unified illusion of wholeness, but a plural and variegated play of competing realities. Where Lukács stressed totality, Brecht stressed fragmentation. In this respect Brecht practised what Adorno (a theoretician of the contemporary Frankfurt School) preached: a politically charged Modernism. Indeed, in his use of the then-modern media (back-projection of slides, bursts of audio-recording) and in his attempts to be popularly accessible, Brecht can properly be seen as POSTMODERNIST. Certainly he did not indulge in the kinds of 'literary' difficulty and obscurity practised by such 'high' modernists as Joyce, Kafka and T.S. Eliot. All of these writers and their characteristic qualities Lukács stigmatised as symptomatic of bourgeois decadence.

Shocking change

Walter Benjamin, Brecht's friend and commentator, went on to develop the theoretical ramifications of such a politicised post/modernist **aesthetics**. Key elements in this are the concept of *shock* and the practice of brushing **history** *against the grain*. Benjamin maintained that in times of revolutionary change a traditional, neo-classical aesthetics of 'harmony', 'balance', 'organic unity' and 'reconciliation' (the basic NEW CRITICAL position, in fact) was inadequate and likely to prove politically reactionary. He insisted that genuinely revolutionary art needed to effect a radical rupture with the past. It needed to shock readers and viewers into a recognition of the oppression which underpins even the most apparently civilised society. 'There's no document of civilisation which is not at the same time a document of barbarism,' as Walter Benjamin says in his 'Theses on History' (Benjamin [1940] 1970: 248). The job of radical writers and readers was therefore to brush official, dominant versions of history against the grain: to expose the many alternative histories (especially of working-class men and women) that had been muted or suppressed. Benjamin also articulated a crucial POSTMODERNIST view of the relations between **art** and modern technology in his essay 'The Work of Art in an Age of Mechanical Reproduction' (*c.* 1935). There he pointed out that the capacity of modern technology to reproduce images cheaply and accurately in effect disperses the 'aura' surrounding supposedly unique works of art. What was previously exclusive may be made widely available. What belonged to elite culture may circulate in popular culture. Moreover, the 'art object' is more clearly recognised for what it always was – a commodity.

The subsequent progress of Marxist criticism can be seen in terms of a tension between the socialist **realist** and socialist post/modernist positions outlined above. Should history be viewed as a totality or a series of fragments: one grand and continuous narrative featuring the gradual emancipation of the working classes, for instance; or many small and discontinuous narratives involving many intermittent kinds of struggle? How far does the control of contemporary technologies increasingly turn all cultural products into commodities circulating according to (late) capitalist modes of production, reproduction and distribution? What are the possible vantage points and points of leverage outside or within that system? Indeed, is it still possible to 'see' capitalism at all as a distinct and potentially transient phase of social and economic organisation? Or is it already so all-encompassing as to seem 'universal', 'natural' and 'inevitable'? All these questions are answered in various ways by the writers we now review.

Ideological subjects and agents

For a rereading of Marxism through a combination of POSTSTRUCTURALIST and PSYCHOANALYTIC lenses, we must turn to the work of Louis Althusser (1918–90), a political theorist who produced a number of influential modifications of central tenets. Most fundamentally, he distinguished the 'Ideological State Apparatuses' of law, religion, politics and education from the 'Repressive State Apparatuses' of the police and the military, assigning to each sphere a 'relative autonomy' both from one another and from the economic base. This opened the way for a kind of culturalism in which **discourses** tend to be detached from modes of production. Cultural **differences** may then be understood without direct appeal to differences in material conditions. At the same time, Althusser insisted that the humanist notion of the unified and integrated 'individual' (i.e., 'the one who cannot be divided') be radically reformulated. In its place he offered a view of each person as a variegated and shifting configuration of ideological **subjects** (plural). Each member of society is in effect assigned a variety of roles depending on the contexts in which she or he operates. In Althusser's terms, each of us is **addressed** (i.e. greeted and named) by various institutions and thereby 'interpellated' in a variety of 'subject positions'. Crucially, many of these roles or subject positions are not initially of our own choosing. They are thrust upon us and we must then decide to comply and consent, or resist and refuse, perhaps insisting on another role and subject position entirely. A current example in the UK would be the tendency among educational managers to speak of students as 'customers' or 'clients', and lecturers/teachers as 'providers' who 'deliver course-packages'. Meanwhile, all of them/us, including employers and the rest of the public, are addressed as 'stakeholders'. In this way a conspicuously *commercial* model of human relations is being superimposed on a traditionally *educational* process. Those involved may then decide to comply, resist, or assert a preferable alternative. *Pro*-active, as distinct from merely reactive, subjects are sometime called **agents** (see **subject**).

Gaps and silences – the 'not-said'

Pierre Macherey's *A Theory of Literary Production* (1966) initiated an even more marked convergence of Marxist and POSTSTRUCTURALIST models. For Macherey the primary focus of textual study is what the text *does not* – or *cannot* – say (the *non-dit*). Every text can therefore be characterised not only by what it *does* talk about, its expressed subject matter (its **presences**) but also by what it represses or suppresses (its **absences**). The 'unsaid' or 'unsayable' thus constitutes a kind of unconscious upon which the text draws but which, by definition, it cannot wholly bring to consciousness. The role of the critical reader, therefore, is to search for the 'gaps and silences': the figures and events that have been quickly glossed over, marginalised or ignored. What other stories and histories have been displaced or replaced by the very act of telling *this* **hi/story** in *this* way and not another? Clearly, then, though Macherey's method is dialectical, historical and psychological, it is not exclusively Marxist. This can be said of much of the later work in this area. Fredric Jameson's *The Political Unconscious: Narrative as a Socially Symbolic Act* (1981) is a case in point. Like Macherey, Jameson stresses the psycho-political force of texts. **Narrative** structure can be construed as a double-edged act of repression/ oppression as well as expression.

Dominant, residual and emergent ideologies

Similar tensions can be found, variously articulated, throughout British and American writings in a broadly Marxian tradition. Raymond Williams, for instance, worked through from a social democratic commitment to CULTURE as 'the whole way of living of a people' (*Culture and Society 1780–1950*, 1958: 83) to 'an argument [. . .] set into a new and conscious relation with Marxism' (*Marxism and Literature*, 1977: 6). In the latter work in particular, Williams developed a dynamic model of ideology which many students of literature and culture have found very useful. Williams suggests that we see every text (or other cultural practice) as the site in which three phases of ideological development can be traced. These phases he calls *dominant*, *residual* and *emergent* (1977: 121–8):

♦   The *dominant* refers to those aspects of the text which express the socially privileged and central ways of seeing and saying of its age: the dominant discourses *in the present*.
♦   The *residual* refers to those ways of saying and seeing which were once central but have now been superseded and are only evident as vestiges: these were often the dominant discourses *of the past*.

♦   The *emergent* refers to those embryonic growth points which exist only as half-formed potential but which may be perceived as precursors of new ways of saying and seeing: these may become the dominant discourses *of the future*.

In short, every text can be grasped as a site where the discourses of past, present and future meet and contend. We might see *Hamlet*, for instance, as a play where residual feudal models of society are challenged by emergent forms of individualism, with both set against the dominant contemporary model of the nation-state. The emphasis is thus not on texts simply reflecting or representing a single fixed ideology, but on texts refracting ideolog*ies* (plural) as part of a continuing process of struggle. Moreover, following Bakhtin and Voloshinov, Williams points out that such struggles take place in and over words of all kinds. The contest of dominant, residual and emergent ideologies ensures that even a single word, every utterance of that word (e.g. 'woman', 'black', 'God', 'freedom') is a newly configured site for the collision and coalescence of the past and the future in the present.

Cultural Materialists and New Historicists

All practitioners of these approaches work with conceptions of ideology as a dynamic process: texts and language are sites of ideological struggle. The chief differences among them are in the kinds and degrees of political commitment each brings to the task; also in the specific academic institutions and national cultures within which each operates. It is initially tempting, and to some extent useful, to offer the broad equations: Cultural Materialism = British socialist tradition = more positive commitment to conflictual politics; and New Historicism = American democratic tradition = more positive commitment to consensual politics. However, it should also be stressed that contemporary practitioners of all these positions are in some sense eclectic and elastic. Terry Eagleton (UK) and Fredric Jameson (US) may have exchanged comradely blows on their respective analyses of POSTMODERNISM and its relations to 'late capitalism'. But they did so wielding a similarly wide array of models and methods drawn from POST-STRUCTURALISM and PSYCHOANALYSIS. Moreover, many of the most forceful and resourceful proponents of Marxist analysis now operate with an acute awareness of the need to meld it with FEMINIST and POSTCOLONIALIST critical discourses too. Catherine Belsey and Gayatri Spivak are influential in this respect. Alan Sinfield and Jonathan Dollimore, in particular, have further developed cultural materialist agendas in terms of changing modes and models of sexuality in highly charged social and political contexts. The overall result is multiply determined – not crudely reductive – readings. But whatever the labels we apply, one thing is clear: all these writers share a concern not simply with *which* texts are studied and *how*, but also *who* is doing the studying and *why*. The broadly institutional and cultural as well as the narrowly textual dimensions of study are therefore equally emphasised in the method which follows.

How to practise Marxist analyses, as developed by Cultural Materialists and New Historicists

In general, consider the power relations in play within and around the text (i) in its initial moment of production ('there and then'); (ii) in its subsequent moments of reproduction (e.g. 'here and now').

In particular, concentrate on such factors as class, rank, occupation and education, gradually broadening your analysis to take in such complicating factors as *gender, race, nationality and age*. Do this systematically with attention to every major aspect of the text in context and every moment of production and reception. The following checklist will help.

Start with 'the text in hand' (on the screen, in your mind)

♦   How did it get there? Who made it as an object and traded in it as a commodity?
♦   What labour and materials have gone into its making?
♦   What technologies, social organisations and general modes of production and exchange (including publication and distribution) were involved? At what economic and ecological costs?

Move to the immediate context and participants

♦   Where and when are *you* receiving (and thereby reproducing) this text?
♦   Who are 'you', the 'I-who-reads', in terms of class, status, occupation and education; as well as gender, race, nationality and age?
♦   Who are you doing this with? What are the kinds of relation involved: reader–text, learner–learner and learner–teacher? And what kinds of authority and hierarchy are in play?
♦   How would you describe the social and political functions of the programme and institution you are studying in? How far do these accord with your own aims?
♦   In sum, what constructions of the subject (i.e. topic and course as well as yourself as subject) currently apply?

Now consider every major dimension of the 'text as products and processes' (see Figure 3.1):

♦   *author–reader (producer–receiver) relations*:

   ♦   What do you know, or can you infer, about the author's social relations to her or his readers (audience, viewers, etc.)? (Pluralise 's/he' to 'they', where appropriate.) Was s/he in some way dependent or independent?
   ♦   Did s/he make a living from this, or was it a private activity? Did s/he require or hire others to produce and distribute it?
   ♦   What do we know about his or her ideas, tastes, values and beliefs? And do these make any difference to how we understand this text?

♦   *text as products at earlier moments of reproduction*:

   ♦   What were the general modes of economic production and social organisation at the time (e.g. was the society chiefly 'slave', 'feudal', 'bourgeois', 'capitalist')?
   ♦   What were the specifically 'literary' or 'artistic' modes of production and distribution in which this text was implicated (e.g. oral, theatrical, manuscript, print, filmic; libraries, bookshops, studios)? Who owned or controlled them?

♦   *relations to the rest of the world – then and now*:

   ♦   What sections of society are represented as central – or arguably mis- or under- or un-represented? Are there marked gaps and silences?
   ♦   Is the society represented contemporary with that of the author, or before or after, or some other imagined time and place entirely? Does this make for a more or less critical perspective on the author's present?

♦ Which of the ideologies in play would you characterise as *dominant, residual* or *emergent*? And does the writer express or imply a preference?

♦ What relevance to your own times and society does the work seem to have? For instance, does it help you see your relations to other people and to the rest of the world more clearly or differently?

EXAMPLE

Drawing on the above questions and suggestions, sketch an analysis of the representation of Chaucer's Knight in 'The General Prologue' (5.1.1). (Be sure to draw on the accompanying notes as well, if possible supplemented by the notes in a scholarly edition such as *The Oxford Riverside Chaucer*, ed. L.D. Benson 2008: 800–1. Notice that even when you lack further information you can still pose questions about context and history. Do this before reading on.)

The 'value' of Chaucer. A Marxist analysis might start by drawing attention to the specific social and political context in which you are studying, and the fact that you are reading Chaucer in a modern printed textbook. This has an educational function and a price: it is itself both a medium of instruction and a commodity. The social relations, media and technologies involved are therefore very different from Chaucer's initial moments and modes of production. Chaucer probably first read this orally to other members of the court circle of which he was a relatively junior member (he was the son of a wine merchant). Thereafter the text circulated in manuscript copies amongst members of the aristocracy, richer merchants and senior clergy. Straight away, then, we are involved in a complex socio-historical dialogue. We may be left asking how far the 'Chaucer' (or any other author) we are studying is a modern educational subject and capitalist commodity as well as, say, a feudal subject and court entertainer. What are and were the social relations? What are and were the 'values' in play?

An (un)ideal knight. A Marxist might then observe that the Knight is given pride of place as the first pilgrim to be introduced, thus confirming his status as the most senior pilgrim. This is also, at least at first glance, an idealised and perhaps flattering image of knighthood: 'He was a verray, parfit gentil knyght' (l.72). All this is conventional and perhaps socially conformist. However, on further investigation, the image of the knight perhaps turns out to be not so simple and stable. And here we may bring parts of the historical background into the foreground. For one thing, by this time in the late fourteenth century, crusading knights were relatively outmoded as well as economically and militarily irrelevant. They were being displaced by yeomen archers and footsoldiers in fighting, and by members of the moneyed merchant classes in the economy. Chivalry was thus largely a *residual* social form. It belonged to the older feudal order, even though it still exerted a powerful symbolic force. For another thing, reading 'between the lines' of the text, we can identify significant gaps and silences. We are told the knight was 'At Alisaundre . . . whan it was wonne' (l.51). What we are *not* told is that 'Alexandria, in Egypt, was conquered by Peter I (Lusignan) of Cyprus on 10 October 1365 and abandoned a week later, after great plundering and a massacre of its inhabitants' (*Riverside Chaucer* 2008: 801, n. 51). Merely to note this is to brush Chaucer's history *against the grain*. It raises the possibility of a negative reading of the Knight as a mercenary, and may also make us wonder whether Chaucer was being ironic in his view of 'many a noble armee' (l.60).

Christians v. heathens: from the Crusades to the Gulf War and beyond. There also remains the ideologically vexed matter of Chaucer's specifically Western European version of medieval

Christianity. Did he wholly approve of those who 'foughten for oure feith' against the '|
(ll.49, 66)? As another historical note tells us, 'only campaigns against Moslems, s<
(Russian Orthodox), and pagans are enumerated' (*Riverside Chaucer* 2008: 80|
Perhaps, then, we are justified in discerning a routinely 'anti-oriental' slant to Chaucer's world-
historical reality? Obviously no amount of scrutinising of these few words on the page and the
extract out of context will give us answers. But a reading in context will begin to. A reading
of the whole of 'The General Prologue' would clearly help too. For there we see Chaucer
formally and critically distancing himself from all these observations by placing them in the
mouth and mind of himself represented as a naïve and perhaps gullible narrator.

We might then proceed to compare late medieval and modern world-views. One thing this
might indicate is just how pervasive and deep-seated were (and are) certain Christian and
Western antipathies to Muslims and Orientals. We might even draw tentative analogies between
medieval crusades and the 1992 Gulf War. Even the archaic and euphemistic names for the
Western forces marshalled against Iraq ('Desert Shield') smacked of a latter-day crusade, and
this imagery was widely reinforced in many of the accounts in the Western popular media. Such
an appeal to a medieval/modern analogy would be a characteristic move for Cultural
Materialists and New Historicists alike. It would be all the more acute in the wake of the attack
by Islamic extremists on the World Trade Centre in New York in 2001 and subsequent Western
armed interventions in the Middle East. (It would probably be put and received differently in
Britain and the USA, too.) Either way, such a transhistorical gesture would complete the
interpretive cycle by reading the past both in and through the present. The critical–political
and textual–contextual project would thus be integrated but still open and ongoing.

Also see: Close reading – wide reading, 1.2.4; Full interpretation, 2.2; FEMINISM; POST-
COLONIALISM; Key terms above p.163 and @ 3.5.

READING: *Introductory across all*: Haslett and Brannigan in Wolfreys 2001: 67–83; Selden, Widdowson
and Brooker 2005: 82–115. Frow and Wayne in Coyle *et al.* 1990: 708–21; Hawthorn 1996. *Core
texts*: Marx and Engels, Benjamin, Brecht and Willima in Lodge and Wood 2008; *also* Gramsci,
Althusser, Greenblatt, Foucault Sinfield and Žižek Rivkin and Ryan 2004; Brecht 1964; Benjamin 1970;
Williams 1958, 1977; Jameson 1981; Veeser 1989; Eagleton and Milne 1995. *Advanced*: Osborne
2005 (Marxism); Higgins 1999 (on Raymond Williams); Jenkins 2003 (New History); Milner 2002
(Cultural Materialism).

3.6   GENDER AND SEXUALITY – FEMINISM, MASCULINITY AND QUEER THEORY

*If you are concerned with the nature and representation of women and men – especially
realisations of gender, sexuality and desire – these are approaches you will want to engage with.*

Overview

Feminism is a politically motivated movement dedicated to personal and social change.
Feminists challenge the traditional power of men (patriarchy) and revalue and celebrate the
roles of women. Feminism is informed by critical–political agendas which cut across subject
areas and are not limited to education. LANGUAGE and LITERATURE are, ultimately, not treated
separately but recognised as part of a larger and deeply contentious CULTURAL project. In these
respects Feminism both influences and is influenced by MARXIST and POSTCOLONIAL

approaches. Many Feminist writers also have a strong interest in PSYCHOLOGICAL models and methods, especially those which wrest the human subject from a narrowly patriarchal, substantially Freudian frame. Whether as post-Freudians or anti-Freudians, they seek to develop more positively woman-centred and gender-sensitive critical and therapeutic practices. It used to be common to distinguish psychoanalytically inclined (French) Feminists from more socially and historically inclined (Anglo-American) Feminists. Now, however, though these emphases partly persist, the internationalising of the women's movement has led to a much more flexible and eclectic approach amongst Feminist critics. Notwithstanding, it can still be useful to further distinguish a variety of Feminisms (plural). Current practitioners can often be described in so far as they adopt one of the following positions or a combination of them:

♦ *socialist Feminist* – expressly configured with Marxism and CULTURAL MATERIALISM;
♦ *black Feminist* and *women of colour* – often drawing on and contributing to expressly Postcolonial or MULTICULTURAL agendas;
♦ *radical separatist Feminist* – often expressly aligned with the lesbian movement;
♦ *bourgeois or liberal Feminist* – concerned with selected 'images' of relatively privileged women, but not with the **representation** (in every sense) of working-class women and women of colour or with lesbian and gay politics as such.

Gender and sexuality are related but partly distinct areas. Studying them entails investigating not only cultural constructions of women and men, but also the shifting relations and changing evaluations of heterosexuality and homosexuality in general. Some feminists complain that Gender Studies represents a dilution and diffusion – even a neutralising – of sexual politics. Others maintain that it is more open, plural and less dogmatic, and that it also makes more space for lesbian and gay perspectives. It makes more space for men too. Either way, these approaches have much common as well as some disputed ground. Both were initially concerned with 'images of women', extending latterly to 'images of men' and 'gays'. Soon, however, critics and scholars set about recovering and re-valuing previously marginalised traditions or suppressed works by women, gays and/or lesbians themselves (for a note on the changing politics of 'gay', 'lesbian' and 'queer' as names, see below, p.167). Latterly, there has been an emphasis on seeing patterns of sexuality in complexly plural rather than simply polarised ways. Contemporary 'queer' approaches, in particular, insist on the potential for an active assertion and performance of kinds of homosexuality beyond – not just between – current heterosexual models.

Key terms: **auto/biography, selves and others; canon** (alternative, new orthodox); **difference** . . . (re-)**valuation**; gender; power; reproduction (biological and economic); romance; sex; sexuality; **writing and reading, response and rewriting** (resistantly, as a wo/man).

Some major figures and movements

Crucial to any work in this area is an initial distinction between 'sex' and 'gender'.

♦ *Sex* refers to our physiological make-up and those *biological* **differences** which determine us as *female* or *male*: differences of chromosomes, genitals, hormones.
♦ *Gender*, however, refers to our social make-up and those *culturally constructed* differences which distinguish us as *feminine* or *masculine*: differences of dress, social role, expectations, etc.

We are all *born* female or male; but each of us *learns* to be feminine or masculine according to our experience of the prevailing social norms. Thus, sexually, women (not men) are equipped to conceive, carry and give birth to children. However, these functions do not necessarily mean that women and men have to be stereotyped along the following gender lines:

'FEMININE'?	'MASCULINE'?
emotional	rational
private and personal (interior)	public and impersonal (exterior)
home- and child-centred	job- and task-centred
quiet	noisy
passive	active
beautiful	strong
smooth	rough
arts and education	sciences and engineering

Such mutually reinforcing binary oppositions underpin many people's expectations of what it is to be a girl/woman and a boy/man. They also underpin dominant notions of how women and men speak and write, and what subjects or areas of life they speak and write about. Thus, stereotypically, in **conversation** men talk louder (often about sport and politics), swear more and compete with one another; whereas women talk more quietly and more 'properly' (often about children and relationships) and they support one another. In terms of **genres**, again stereotypically, men like war stories and perhaps pornography, whereas women like romances and perhaps domestic soap opera. Clearly these stereotypes do partly correspond to observable patterns. Equally clearly, however, they by no means apply to all men and women. Nor do they apply to all historical periods and cultures, or to all parts of nominally 'the same' society. Thus the Victorian middle and upper classes may have idolised women as 'the softer sex' and 'angels in the house'. But this characterisation did not extend to the female factory workers who in clothing, manners and even tasks were often virtually indistinguishable from the males. Similarly, and equally complexly, Westernised women and men may affect the appearance of equality by wearing 'unisex' clothing (e.g. jeans); but this does not guarantee equality as an economic fact. Nor, conversely, does the wearing of the yashmak and their exclusion from public office prevent many Moslem women from having great matriarchal power over the family within the domestic sphere. Gender differences are therefore always inflected with other MULTICULTURAL differences of period, class, caste, nation, religion, age and familial role. That is why many people working in this area concentrate on attitudes to modes of *sexual reproduction*, broadly understood (e.g. representations of puberty, menstruation, conception, contraception, pregnancy, abortion, birth and child care), as well as the gendering of modes of *economic production* (e.g. nursing, secretarial and housework gendered as primarily 'woman's work').

But there is an increasing recognition that a conceptualising of issues based solely on sexual reproduction and gender roles is not enough. Obviously *homo*sexuality needs to be added to the various *hetero*sexual equations. But even that, though crucial, is potentially limiting, and all too easily recuperated as a 'queer'/'straight' dichotomy. A further term and distinction is required. **Sexuality**, as currently defined, refers to sexual orientation and the play of desire across a wide range of objects, subject positions and practices. As Eve Kosofsky Sedgwick puts it in her highly influential *Epistemology of the Closet*:

> Other dimensions of sexuality, however, distinguish object choices quite differently (e.g., human/animal, adult/child, singular/plural, autoerotic/alloerotic) or are not even about object

choice (e.g., orgasmic/non-orgasmic, non-commercial/commercial, using bodies only/using manufactured objects, in private/in public, spontaneous/scripted).

(1990: Introduction, Axiom 2)

Battles of (and for) the sexes. Contrary to casual opinion, there has always been an acute awareness that women and men are expected to play distinct roles, and an equally acute awareness that they often fail or refuse to conform. Alternatives are sometimes explored too. Chaucer's 'Wife of Bath's Prologue and Tale' and Shakespeare's *The Taming of the Shrew* as well as his Sonnets are but three instances of earlier classic texts by men in which traditional gender roles are inverted and sported with. Among the ancient Greeks, Socrates was gay, Sappho was a lesbian, and they both wrote of love partly in those terms. Christine de Pisan's *City of Ladies* (c. 1405) is a learned and witty attack on the assumptions of medieval patriarchy and a celebration as well as a defence of the unrecognised achievements and supposedly superior morality of women. Mary Wollstonecraft's *A Vindication of the Rights of Woman* (1792) is a powerful plea for social reform of women's lot at a time when the restitution of middle-class *men's* rights was being trumpeted. Ibsen, too, scandalised bourgeois propriety with his head-on tackling of the nineteenth-century 'woman question' in *A Doll's House*. Virginia Woolf, most famously in *A Room of One's Own* (1929), acted as feminist literary echo to the work of the suffragettes in the 1920s. In particular she pointed to the lack of education, leisure and opportunity which hitherto had precluded most women from writing, and also began to re-construct a female literary tradition (e.g., Behn, 5.2.2). A little later, Simone de Beauvoir in *The Second Sex* (1949) offered a political and philosophical history of women as the institutionalised **other** relative to dominant notions of the male **self**.

All these writers confirm that there has long been an acute awareness, and sometimes a political consciousness, of the constraints of gender roles as well as a need to establish more positive conditions and roles for women in particular. Sexuality, too, male and female, has repeatedly been at issue. Witness the various 'obscenity' trials and *causes célèbres* that have rocked the literary establishment over the past century: Oscar Wilde's imprisonment for homosexuality (1895); the banning of Marguerite Radcliffe Hall's sympathetic and now classic study of lesbian experience, *The Well of Loneliness* (1928); the attempt at continuing expurgation of D.H. Lawrence's *Lady Chatterley's Lover* (1959–60), also now a novel and film classic; the attempted prosecution of Allen Ginsberg's 'Beat' bible *Howl* (1956) for obscenity; the attempted prosecution of the director of Howard Brenton's *The Romans in Britain* (1980) for sexually explicit and politically abrasive analogies between the Roman invasion of Britain and British 'occupation' of Northern Ireland, both conceived as homosexual rape. Many other cases could be cited. All attest to attempts to police the boundaries between LITERATURE (or **art**) and life, as well as to deep anxieties about explorations and exhibitions of sexuality. (Oscar Wilde can be followed up at 2.2.4 and 5.2.3.)

Foucault's *The History of Sexuality* (Vol. 1, 1976) is a primary reference here. It laid the foundations for an understanding of social regimes and institutions in terms not only of explicitly heterosexual and homosexual practices, but also of implicitly homo*social* or homo*phobic* expectations. Thus everything from the organisation of schooling, health care and prisons to dress codes and dietary regimes might underwrite certain kinds of male or female identification and 'bonding' as acceptable or unacceptable: to be embraced (homosocial) or shunned (homophobic).

Clearly, then, 'sexual politics' is no new thing, especially if we take this to include 'the policing of sexuality' as well as 'the battle of the sexes'. Most immediately, however, it is to the Women's Liberation and Gay Rights movements initiated in the late 1960s and 1970s that most people look for the roots of contemporary Feminism, Gender and Sexuality Studies. Below we retrace these roots through the fields of Language and Literature.

'GAY', 'QUEER' AND A NOTE ON THE POLITICS OF LANGUAGE

Since the 1970s the term 'gay' has been widely used to refer to homosexual women *and* men but, latterly, may be reserved for homosexual men alone. 'Lesbian' is increasingly the preferred term for homosexual women. Both 'gay' and 'lesbian', however, are currently covered by the assertively up-front use of 'Queer', as in 'Queer politics' and 'Queer reading and writing' *by* some homosexuals *of* themselves. 'Queer' then becomes a positively charged term for homosexuality, deliberately challenging the negatively charged sense of the earlier and persistent anti-homosexual or homophobic usage of the term (cf. 'queer-bashing'). Meanwhile, some people continue to bemoan the associations of both 'gay' and 'queer' with homosexuality, nothwithstanding the fact that both have had such associations in the larger culture or in subcultures since at least the sixteenth century.

LANGUAGE is a common place to start exploring the ways in which women and men are culturally constructed through **discourse** and not just biologically determined. We may distinguish four main kinds of approach, all of which to some extent overlap:

♦   The Anglo-American and Australasian approach (represented by such writers as Lakoff, Spender, Miller and Swift, and Tannen) tends to be more practical and overtly political: language is seen as 'man-made' or at least 'man-centred' and it is the task of the feminist language-user to overthrow that order and construct one fairer to women.

♦   The French approach (represented by such writers as Kristeva, Irigaray and Cixous) tends to be more theoretical and politically elusive, and emphasises PSYCHOANALYTIC models. Here language is seen as the primary system wherein we learn to construct ourselves and others through **differences** of all kinds, including those of gender. It is therefore the task of each of us to renegotiate our **subject** positions and gender identities as best we can.

♦   'Black', 'ethnic' or 'postcolonial' approaches (represented by such figures as Hurston, Fanon, hooks, Smith and Spivak) often combine political and psychological emphases: language is seen as the primary site where gender identity is further vexed by combinations of Western and indigenous versions of patriarchy and matriarchy.

♦   Gay and lesbian writers (represented by such figures as Rich, Butler, Kosofsky Sedgwick and Dollimore) attempt to wrest the whole notion of differences constructed on *hetero*sexual lines from its pride of place. Instead they propose radically revised notions of what it is (not) to be, and read and write, from a range of assertively – but often deliberately elusive and evasive – 'queer' positions.

In practice, much of the best contemporary work on language, gender and sexuality (e.g. that by Cameron, Coates, Mills and Weedon) attempts to take cognisance of many, if not all, of the above perspectives. For this reason, the following review of topics offers a synthesis rather than a segregation of approaches.

The gendered entry into language and the symbolic order

In learning a language, we learn to label ourselves and others as 'girl' and 'boy', 'daughter' and 'son', 'sister' and 'brother', 'mummy' and 'daddy', 'aunty' and 'uncle', etc. This process of differentiation is strongly gendered in fundamentally binary ways. As a result, we may learn to ignore or repress differences within and the common ground between what nominally pass as 'masculine' or 'feminine': the 'feminine *within* the masculine', for instance, and vice versa.

We may also play down sexual differences and preferences which are not just negatively neither (neuter), but alternatively and positively **other**.

Names and titles

Many languages, including English, have a distinctly 'patrilineal' skew to the ways in which they assign family names and titles denoting status. Family names are invariably drawn from the male rather than the female line. Thus my mother's 'maiden name' was Parsons and *her* mother's 'maiden name' was Stephenson and *her* mother's 'maiden name' was Grimwood. But you could not possibly know that from the surname Pope which appears on the front of this book. *That* was my father's name, and *his* father's, and *his* father's . . . In this way, women's identities and *matri*lineal traditions in general are relatively 'hidden from history'. Titles, too, are generally distributed in ways which betray a gender imbalance. In English, males will be addressed as 'Mr' (short for 'Master') throughout their lives, whether they marry or not. Females, however, are still usually addressed as 'Miss' when girls and unmarried, and then they become 'Mrs' when they get married. In other words, women are sorted into the categories single/available (Miss) and married/ unavailable (Mrs), whereas men (Mr) are not. Nor has the relative newcomer 'Ms' solved all the problems. Though technically this simply signals 'female', regardless of marital status, it is commonly understood by many people to mean 'feminist'. Such is the persistent power of patriarchy. Indeed, it is only when women acquire professional status as 'Dr', 'Professor', 'Your honour', etc. that they achieve titular equality with men. And then of course we encounter the pointed matter of how many female doctors, academics and judges there really are: (see 'Qualification in need of further qualification' @ 6.3.1).

'Unmarked' men and 'marked' women

Imbalances between masculine and feminine terms are pervasive in English, as in many languages. Usually this takes the form of the masculine term being privileged as 'normal' (unmarked) and often positive, while the corresponding feminine term is 'abnormal' (marked) and often negatively loaded. Familiar examples of masculine as norm are 'man' and 'mankind' (not 'wo/mankind') ; 'the man in the street' and 'chairman' (cf. archaic 'Madam chairman' and modern 'chairperson'). Examples of masculine as positive and feminine as negative are 'master' (cf. 'mistress'); 'dog' (cf. 'bitch'), as well as a motley host of words for genitalia: cock (cf. cunt); chest (cf. tit), etc. Moreover, notwithstanding the clamour for and against politically correct pronouns, it is still not hard to find people who believe that the masculine pronoun 'he' is perfectly acceptable even when the person referred to may be male or female (e.g.,'The student . . . he . . . '). For some the shift to 'he or she' (sometimes written 's/he') or the plural 'they' seems to be curiously unthinkable.

Women and men in conversation

Robin Lakoff in a pioneering book called *A Woman's Place* (1975) claimed that in **conversation**, compared with men, women tend to (i) use more 'hedges', continually qualifying what they say ('It's *sort of* hot', 'I'd *kind of* like to', 'I guess'); (ii) be super-polite ('Would you please . . . ', ' . . . if you wouldn't mind'); (iii) add on 'tag questions' ('Pete is here, *isn't he*?'; 'We'll go, *shall we*?'); and (iv) generally answer questions with a quizzical rise in intonation (e.g. in response to the question 'When shall we meet?' the answer 'Around eight o'clock?'). You may feel there is some truth in these observations. However, later researchers (e.g., Tannen 1992) point out that much still depends upon education, class and ethnicity, as well as temperament.

Sexist syntax

The combination and ordering of words always carry implications for focus and emphasis. The order of precedence in 'Mr and Mrs', 'male and female' and even 'he or she' may *seem* natural; but try reversing these items and consider whether that seems 'natural' too. Conversely, notice the order of deference in the formula of address 'Ladies and gentlemen'. Often it is the overall organisation of the text which betrays a sexist bias in favour of the male subject or the masculine viewpoint. Hence this characteristic story opening from the UK tabloid newspaper the *Sun*: 'A terrified 19-stone husband was forced to lie next to his wife as two men raped her yesterday' (see Cameron 1998: 17).

Writing as a wo/man

It is sometimes maintained that women and men have different styles of writing and, by extension, different thought processes. Luce Irigaray and Hélène Cixous, for instance, have argued that there is a distinctive form of 'womanly speech/writing' which they call, respectively, *parler femme* and *écriture féminine*. Both of them partly take their cue from Virginia Woolf's praise of Dorothy Richardson's development of 'the psychological sentence of the female gender' (1923; see Cameron 1998). The general characteristics of such 'womanly writing/speech' are reckoned to be long and loosely coordinated sentences, fluid changes of topic, a resistance to 'linear' logic and, implicitly, a woman-centred focus on inner feelings and personal relationships. Set against this are the presumably archetypal characteristics of 'manly writing': tightly controlled and heavily subordinated sentences, orderly and linear progression of topic, and a man-centred focus on external actions and public relationships. Three important qualifications need to be made, however:

1   Irigaray insists that ultimately only biological women have facility in 'parler femme', whereas Cixous suggests that men too can open up the 'féminine' in themselves and their 'écriture' (e.g. Joyce, Mallarmé);

2   many women writers from the fifteenth century to the present have cultivated a 'plain' or supposedly 'manly' style;

3   there therefore remains a big question about how far so-called 'womanly writing' is tied up with contradictory notions of Modernism and sexual essentialism. Is it a period-specific phase posing as a universal determinant?

LITERATURE, as the above review confirms, is clearly not separated from a fundamental concern with language by most feminists. Nor is it divorced from a larger CULTURAL and political project. Nonetheless, there are distinctive historical phases and critical emphases within feminist and gender-based literary studies. These may be identified under several heads, as long as we remember that these 'heads' sometimes argue amongst themselves and may or may not belong to the same, constantly metamorphosing 'body'.

Gendered literacies and genre

Most women for most of human history have not been allowed or encouraged to learn to read or write. And when they have become literate this has often equipped them to do no more than keep household accounts, write letters and diaries, and perhaps read the Bible and novels in the vernacular (e.g. English). Women have thus often been denied 'higher' or more specialised learning in the CLASSICS (Latin and Greek) and in the sciences. The results of all this have been complex and many-edged. Though long discouraged from making substantial contributions to traditional **genres** such as poetry and drama, women developed facility in both reading and writing the 'newer', and initially notionally inferior genre of the **novel** (see **narrative**). They also cultivated forms of recording the interiorised **self** (through diaries) and personal interactions with **others** (through letters) which have latterly been recognised as pre-eminently – but not exclusively – 'feminine' modes of writing (see **auto/biography**).

Representations of women by men

An initial and enduring emphasis in feminist literary studies has been on **images** or **representations** of women in work by male writers. Given the relative absence of women writers from the traditional male-dominated **canon**, this focus was at first inevitable. So, too, was an early insistence on the ways in which male writers mis- or under-represent women. Modern male writers, chiefly novelists, such as D.H. Lawrence, Ernest Hemingway, Henry Miller, Phillip Roth and Norman Mailer, were the primary targets in the pioneering polemical work by Kate Millett (*Sexual Politics*, 1970). These men were roundly attacked for representing women as stereotypes, often 'sex-objects'. At the same time, 'images of women' criticism was being extended to earlier bastions of the male canon such as Chaucer, Shakespeare and Milton (e.g., Germaine Greer's *The Female Eunuch*, 1970). Behind and informing all these works were discerned a number of powerful patriarchal stereotypes, many of them ultimately identified with **biblical** women. In addition to the main polarities of woman as sinful temptress (the Old Testament Eve, Adam's 'spare rib') and woman as holy mother (the New Testament Mary, 'full of grace' or a grieving *mater dolorosa*), there were woman as whore (Salome, the whore of Babylon) or silent or subjected woman (Ruth, Martha). It is still common, and often useful, for readers to read with a critical eye trained on precisely such stereotypes, whether they are reading *Beowulf* or 'the Beats'. Increasingly, however, it is recognised that male writers do not always simply misrepresent women; they may also renegotiate and challenge the stereotypes. They may well be exploring masculinity and their own sexuality too (see Hall 2002).

Rediscovering and revaluing women's writing

The next phase of feminist criticism and research (sometimes called *gynocriticism*) tended to concentrate less on men's representations of women than on women's struggle to represent themselves. The few established female novelists (Austen, the Brontës, George Eliot, Gaskell and Woolf) have been radically reread, and the numerous previously marginalised or ignored female writers (Bradstreet, Behn, Butts, Manley, Wollstonecraft, Mary Shelley, Edgeworth, Barrett Browning, Dickinson, Stein – to mention just a few) have been investigated afresh or for the first time. Their work was also widely published and promoted, notably by presses such as Virago, Pandora and the Women's Press. Since then there has been a considerable commitment to publishing and studying contemporary women's writing, often with an eye trained on specifically female traditions which conventional LITERARY HISTORY had patronised or ignored. Foundation texts in this deliberate and often daring reshaping of the literary landscape include Ellen Moers's *Literary Women* (1976), Elaine Showalter's *A Literature of their Own* (1977), Sandra Gilbert and Susan Gubar's *The Madwoman in the Attic* (1979), Joanna Russ's *How to Suppress Women's Writing* (1983), Dale Spender's *Mothers of the Novel* (1986) and Jane Spencer's *The Rise of the Woman Novelist* (1986). Nor is this simply a matter of putting women in the existing picture. The effect has been to switch the picture and shift the focus entirely. Thus there was a thoroughgoing critical and historical revaluation of such social phenomena as 'being single', marriage, child-bearing and rearing, madness and hysteria, and widowhood. The institutions of religion, education, the law and medicine have been especially explored for the ways in which they relate to women's (and men's) powers over their bodies, minds and property.

Reading and writing by or as a wo/man

Latterly, there are signs that the issues of women's writing, including the activities of women writing and reading, have opened out again. Do you need to be biologically a woman to write or read 'as a woman'? Is to be a woman or a man to be locked into certain kinds of sympathy and antipathy? Or is it a matter of learning to identify with certain **subject** positions within and around a given text – and therefore of potentially unlearning and relearning? In short, can women *and* men re(en)gender themselves as certain kinds of writer and reader? Whatever the answers, the point is precisely that there is room for potential agreement, as well as persistent disagreement, about who, under what social, political and psychological circumstances, where and when, can claim to write or read *by*, *for* or *as* a woman (see e.g. Jardine and Smith 1987; Cameron 1998; Mills 1994): and *by*, *for* or *as* a man (e.g. Castle 2002, Knights 2007).

Becoming our bodies ourselves

There are several ways in which 'the body' features in contemporary cultural debates and practices. The fact that these debates and practices are central to but not peculiar to Feminism, Gender and Sexuality Studies is a measure of the liveliness of the 'bodies' in question. Especially influential are Judith Butler's *Bodies that Matter* (1993), Susan Bordo's *Unbearable Weight: Feminism, Western Culture and the Body* (1993), and Donna Haraway's 'A Manifesto for Cyborgs: Science, Technology and Socialist Feminism' (1990) (e.g. in Leitch 2010).

♦   Women's bodies have long been **represented** as objects of male desire and of the 'masculine gaze' in practices ranging from high **art** nude portraiture to popular advertising, and from rape to pornography. It is one of the primary purposes of feminism to reclaim and celebrate that body as an active **subject/agent** in its own right.

♦   Appeals to or displays of the body promise an actuality and **presence** which are supposedly beyond words. According to certain feminist PSYCHOANALYSTS, bodies defy or defer not only a 'logocentric' (word-centred) world-view but more particularly celebrate a pre-Oedipal semiotic flux before, alongside and even against the symbolic 'order of the father' (i.e., phallo-logocentrism).

♦   More practically and urgently, the body is a site of disease and sickness (including eating disorders and AIDS); and it is women's and men's bodies that are intervened in or extended, often differently, by everything from surgery (medical and cosmetic) and contraception (internal and external) to tattooing, hair-styling and clothing.

The body is therefore the ultimate site and sign for all **discourses** on gender, sex and sexuality. Therefore it is crucial how far the body is taken to underwrite and guarantee versions not only of femininity and masculinity (i.e., gender) but also of hetero- and homosexuality. Time and again the argument is whether men and women are 'necessarily', 'essentially', 'biologically' one thing or another. Are we as human *beings* always already some version of 'feminine' or 'masculine' and 'female' or 'male'? Or are we still in the process of *becoming* something and someone else – alternative, other, plural?: (See e.g. Braidotti 2002.)

How to practise a feminist analysis sensitive to gender and sexuality

Begin by considering the roles and representations of women and men as they affect your understanding of the text (i) in your immediate context; (ii) in its initial moment of production. More particularly, consider:

♦ *the sexual composition and orientation and gender roles of the group or course in which you are studying.* How evident are these in terms of the texts and topics highlighted; social hierarchies and dynamics; the kinds and patterns of contribution? For instance, are the atmosphere and critical agenda discernibly feminist or anti-feminist, and hetero- or homosexual?

♦ *the kinds of women and men represented within the text.* Is there a sense of tension between and within the sexes? What kinds of women's and men's roles and relationships are *not* represented – and are either unspoken or even 'unspeakable' (i.e. taboo)? Pay special attention to representations of: family; occupations outside and within the home; gendered ways of speaking, dressing and behaving; clothed and naked bodies; sexual activity; childbirth and child care; single or married states; other commercial, legal, medical, educational, military and religious institutions as they bear on women and men differently (e.g., the army, clergy, schools, hospitals); complicating factors of class, ethnicity, age and other cultural differences.

♦ *the sex, sexual orientation and gender expectations of the writer.* Are these ascertainable from the text or from external (e.g. auto/biographical) sources? How far are we justified in identifying the author's subject position with any of those offered by the text? What aspects of, say, genre, narration, characterisation and imagery prevent such a ready author–text identification?

♦ *the gender roles and sexual practices current at the time.* Can the text be read as a form of sexual expression, repression or negotiation? What behaviour seems to have been considered 'proper' or 'normal', and how far are such proprieties and norms reinforced or challenged?

♦ *your own reading and writing practices as a wo/man.* How far do you think gender differences and sexual preferences affect the way *you* relate to this text: whom you identify with and what you look for and value? Again, consider complicating factors such as class, ethnicity, age and temperament.

Go on to investigate other relatable texts by women and men at the time, as well as other media and modes of representation. How did women and men feature in the performing or visual arts, for instance, either as producers or as objects of representation? How relatively powerful or powerless were women and men, gays and lesbians with respect to publication and broadcasting? How much have things changed now?

Example

Read Adrienne Rich's 'Dialogue' (5.3.4) with the above 'How to practise' questions and suggestions in mind. Go on to compare your responses with the following.

Feeling a way into the conversation. The poem is a dialogue of a particularly open and teasing kind. There is general uncertainty about the nature of the relationship between the narrator and the speaker. The shifting indeterminacy of the 'I's and 'she's makes for an especially enigmatic encounter. In fact the whole thing seems to be more of a monologue than a dialogue: there are no 'you's, for instance, and only one 'we'. Perhaps, then, it is the dialogue with us the readers which is most insistent. We are privy to the action but excluded from any sure knowledge of what it means. As a result, precisely how we read this poem in terms of gender and sexuality (and much else) very much depends upon who and what we reckon we are. It also, of course, depends upon what we infer from the text, and what we may know about the author (a little information about Adrienne Rich is supplied in the supporting notes). I shall therefore begin with some tentative questions:

♦   Is the 'old ring' a token of past friendship, a 'marriage' ring perhaps?
♦   How do we respond to the persistence and natural violence of 'our talk has beaten / like rain against the screens'? or the studied distance of 'we look at each other'?
♦   Is the second, repor*ted* 'I' (who speaks in italics) talking of another event and relationship altogether? If so, why is the first, repor*ting* 'I' so obsessed by the memory of what was said as to 'live through [it] over and over'?
♦   Could it be, then, that what is being so elusively spoken of in italics in fact refers to the relationship between the two participants? or does it refer to another?

At this point most readers pause for further reflection and introspection. They may also reach for information about the writer, or at least a sense of who s/he is. Often they return to the brief biographical notes.

Going public through discussion. Here are some observations on my experience of studying this poem in sexually mixed groups. These are the kinds of 'answer' usually forthcoming once people have formulated something like the above questions for themselves. Overtly heterosexual readers (often men) who have no knowledge of or perhaps interest in Adrienne Rich usually persist in the view that the second speaker is speaking of another, female–male relationship, and that she is talking about this to the first. However, readers sensitive to homosexuality (often women) who are aware of Rich's radical feminist and subsequently assertively lesbian stance tend to read the poem quite otherwise: as a comment on a female–female relationship, probably between the two present participants, the narrating 'I' in the first part and the speaking 'I' in the second part. But other readings are possible too, and these may be voiced by a range of women and men. Perhaps we should not assume the 'I'dentity of either narrator *or* speaker with Adrienne Rich. Or perhaps we should treat this as a dramatised dialogue between two parts of the self: one observing and the other observed. In any event, as the discussion continues there remain many suggestions and questions in play. Is the 'sex' in question ('I don't know / if sex is an illusion') the biological difference between female and male? the social gender difference? the sexual act? What kind of subject, gendered and otherwise, is the 'I' who asks 'whether I willed to feel / what I had read about'? The willing victim of romantic or of radical feminist literature, perhaps?

A 'Rich' tradition. Our sense of the contexts of writing and reading could be important too. Rich has lived through a period of changing gender roles and continuing sexual revolution.

Reading the poem around 1967, when it was first published and when Rich had not yet 'come out' as a lesbian, might have entailed a 'heterosexual' response. Reading it in *Poems Old and New* in 1984, when she had 'come out', might have prompted another (perhaps suggesting a 'repressed lesbian'). Reading it in Carol Rumens's controversially titled collection of *Post-feminist Poetry: Making for the Open* (2nd edn, 1987) might even have suggested a *post*-feminist or a *post*-lesbian reading (whatever one might understand those to mean). But whatever your own reading of 'Dialogue', one thing at least should be clear. Gender differences and sexual preferences are themselves caught up in the ongoing dialogue *between* and *within* specific writers and readers. The image and fact of 'woman' or 'man' are never simply a given but always in part remade. Rich, herself, has famously referred to this process as 're-vision' (see 1.2.9).

Also see: PSYCHOLOGY; CULTURAL MATERIALISM; POSTCOLONIALISM; for the Brontës 2.2.3 and 2.2.5; for Wilde 2.2.5 and 5.2.3; and above Key Terms p. 164 and @3.6.

READING: *Introductory*: Benstock, Ferris and Woods 2003; Selden, Widdowson and Brooker 2005: 115–43, 243–66; Robbins 2000; Belsey and Moore 1997; Stimpson and Sedgwick in Greenblatt and Gunn 1992: 251–70; Eagleton (M.) 2003. *Core texts*: de Beauvoir, Kolodny, Rich, Wittig, Cixous, Gilbert and Gubar, Haraway, Smith, Zimmerman, Bordo, Rubin, Sedgwick, Butler, Berlant and Warner, and Halberstam in Leitch 2010; *also* Woolf, Foucault, Irigaray, Spivak and Heng in Rivkin and Ryan 2004; *also* Feminist Collective and Haraway in Rice and Waugh 2001; Woolf 1929; de Beauvoir 1949; Kristeva 1984. *On language*: Tannen 1992; Mills 1995; Cameron 1998 (anthology). *On literary history and theory*: Showalter 1977; Gilbert and Gubar 1999; Moi 2002. *Masculinities*: Castle 2002; Hall 2002; Jardine and Smith 1987; Whitehead 2002; Knights 2007. *Gay/Queer*: Sedgwick 1990; Dollimore 1991; Butler 1993; Sinfield 1994 (on Wilde). *Advanced*: Weedon 1999; Glover and Kaplan 2000; Célélestin, DalMolin and de Courtviron 2003; Lechte and Zournazi 2003 (Kristeva); Braidotti 2002 (Irigaray and Deleuze); Butler 2006.

3.7 RELATIVITIES – POSTSTRUCTURALISM AND POSTMODERNISM

If you tend to see texts not so much as 'things' or 'objects' but as shifting relations *and* ongoing projects, *then these are areas of theoretical activity you will want to get involved in.*

Overview

Poststructuralism and Postmodernism are two relatable yet distinct contemporary movements. Both are concerned with the radical instability of subjects (whether conceived as human subjects, subject matters or whole disciplines) and both celebrate kinds of openness, plurality and difference in systems of all kinds. Both are also devoted to the play of indeterminacy within and around meanings. But these two movements are also distinct. Poststructuralism grows out of an academic milieu in Linguistics, Anthropology and Philosophy and is primarily concerned with LANGUAGE. Postmodernism grows out of an artistic and literary milieu and is primarily concerned with global COMMUNICATIONS and the commercial multi-media. *Post*structuralism and *post*modernism are both clearly terms that depend on prior concepts for their definition (i.e. Structuralism and Modernism). As with *post*colonialism, however, we must recognise that the prefix 'post-' can mean 'after' in at least two senses: 'after and distinct from' as well as 'after and a result of'. That is, Poststructuralism can be seen as a radical break with Structuralism as well as a natural extension of it. The same can be said of Postmodernism's relation to

Modernism and Postcolonialism's relation to Colonialism. We therefore need to know what is being succeeded or superseded in each case.

Structuralism is a grab-bag of a term stuffed with a wide range of writers and writings: the structural anthropology of Lévi-Strauss; the formal linguistics of Saussure and of Chomsky; the early writings of Barthes and Derrida; and the writings of the much earlier Russian FORMALISTS as rediscovered and translated in the West during the late 1960s and early 1970s. What all these writers and writings have in common is the understanding of phenomena (words, poems, narratives, myths, customs, social practices) not as discrete entities but as parts of larger structures or systems. The emphasis is on making sense of things as signs in larger sign-systems, and on perceiving the ways in which one sign-system relates to another. Hence the close association of structuralism with semiotics/semiology, the study of sign-systems.

Poststructuralism is chiefly associated with the later writings of Barthes, Derrida and Foucault and is 'post-' in that it both extends and to some extent explodes the premises of Structuralism. Whereas a structuralist approach would tend to treat a sign-system as a complete, finished, potentially knowable whole with a notional **centre**, a *post*structuralist approach would tend to treat a sign-system as an incomplete, unfinished and ultimately unknowable fragment with many potential centres or no centre at all. We may therefore say that Structuralism concentrates on 'whole systems' whereas Poststructuralism concentrates on the 'holes in systems'. Put yet another way, where Structuralism concentrates on 'sense-making' activities, Poststructuralism concentrates on 'nonsense-making activities' or, perhaps better, 'the making of sense other-wise'.

Poststructuralism is probably best known for the analytical techniques of *deconstruction*. This involves breaking down a text (or other artefact) into its constituent **differences** and identifying its notional centre, then exploring the procedures whereby certain of these are preferred or 'privileged'. A characteristic deconstructive move is to invert differences and to point to what is marginalised or absent, thereby setting up alternative centres or challenging the notion of centres altogether. Poststructuralists in general, and deconstructors in particular, are especially fascinated by **absences, gaps and silences** and are keen on offering radical inversions (some would say perversions) of the relations between foreground and background.

Postmodernism involves something relatable yet distinct. *Modernism*, its precursor, can be broadly characterised as an early twentieth-century literary and artistic movement with an aesthetic opposed to that of nineteenth-century 'classic realism'. Modernists in English include such figures as Joyce, Woolf, T.S. Eliot, W.B. Yeats, Carlos Williams, Stevens and Beckett. All of these writers developed strategies of 'non-realist' representation involving collage, montage, pastiche, 'stream of consciousness', multiple points of view, and other kinds of highly self-conscious, reflexive and apparently fragmentary techniques. What most of these modernists also have in common is their implication in a 'high art' view of CULTURE and their concentration on a traditionally literary medium: the written word. It is in these latter respects that Postmodernism most obviously both extends and explodes the premises of Modernism. Postmodernism is broadly populist rather than narrowly elitist in appeal, and tends to be multimedia rather than purely literary in materials. At the same time postmodernist texts deploy many of the strategies of Modernism and promote an aesthetic which is still palpably non-realist. Thus we find that collage, montage, pastiche, multiple viewpoint, reflexivity and open intertextuality are also characteristic of such pre-eminently postmodern discourses as advertising, popular music, game and chat shows, magazines and magazine programmes, TV and tabloid news reporting, interactive video, computer games and the World Wide Web. In fact just about any aspect of modern life has a potentially 'postmodernist' edge to it in so far as it is concerned with the self-conscious production, projection and consumption of reflexive **images** of all kinds, especially those in the commercial, global domains. By this definition, shopping malls and Disneyland are typical postmodern 'texts'.

Relations between and reactions to Poststructuralism and Postmodernism vary greatly. Some see the two as complementary aspects of a kind of intellectual– commercial 'New Ageism', and get correspondingly excited or irritated. Others see them as utterly distinct in origin and trajectory. Meanwhile, political critiques proliferate. Poststructuralism is attacked by some MARXIST, FEMINIST and POSTCOLONIAL critics as a kind of hyper-sceptical game which is finally debilitating and self-defeating. If all differences and centres are arbitrary, then what grounds are there for morally and politically informed preferences? Others, however, recognise the ground-breaking or at least ground-clearing power of deconstruction to challenge all supposedly 'neutral' differences, 'natural' hierarchies and fixed centres. Postmodernism, meanwhile, is regularly mauled for its complicity with various brands of capitalism, patriarchy and neo-colonialism. Though some critics do point to the potentially subversive power of postmodernist texts in so far as such texts expose and sport with the superficial artifice and glaring contradictions of contemporary life rather than smoothing them over and concealing them.

Key terms: COMMUNICATION and MEDIA; FORMALISM INTO FUNCTIONALISM; **absence and presence, gaps and silences, centres and margins**; **aesthetics**; **author** (death of); **differences**; **image**; metatextuality; **realism and representations**; signs; **subject**; translation.

Major figures and models

We now review the main concepts and figures associated with Poststructuralism and Postmodernism in turn. As usual, this is basically a checklist designed to prompt activities and further reading.

Saussure and sign-systems

The concept of the sign composed of 'signifier' and 'signified' is fundamental to Structuralism and Poststructuralism alike. Saussure made it the basis of his General Linguistics and thereby opened up the way for an understanding of COMMUNICATION in terms of sign-systems in general. In Saussure's view, words do not simply mean things in themselves. Words are the product of systematic yet shifting relations between sounds in air or marks on paper (signifiers) and those aspects of experience which those sounds or marks are taken to refer to (signifieds). There is therefore no necessary reason why the English words 'tree', 'blue' and 'walk', for example, should mean what they do (after all, other languages have different words corresponding to comparable phenomena). Rather, words 'mean' by virtue of an assumed and broadly agreed relation amongst people who 'speak the same language' and therefore draw on the same sign-system. At the same time, there is always a tension between any particular instance or utterance of a word (the 'parole') and the language system viewed as a whole (the 'langue'). Particular people or groups of people always mean slightly – sometimes very – different things by ostensibly the same word. In the above cases the precise meanings would depend on your experiences of 'trees', 'blue' and 'walk' and the contexts in which you routinely meet and use these words. In short, signs are parts of apparently stable but ultimately moving sign-systems.

Many of the crucial differences between Structuralist and Poststructuralist positions can be placed in relation to one of these two polarities.

Structuralists tend to emphasise systems as closed 'wholes'.
Poststructuralists tend to emphasise the 'holes' within and around open systems.

Lévi-Strauss and a structural model of culture

The anthropologist Claude Lévi-Strauss developed a model which sought to systematise understanding of symbolic interaction within CULTURES. His model is basically structuralist in that he used sets of fundamental oppositions such as 'nature v. civilisation', 'wild v. domestic' and 'raw v. cooked' to produce an overview of how whole societies interact coherently. For Lévi-Strauss, all cultural artefacts and practices have not only a functional but also a symbolic dimension. Everything from pots and buildings to gesture, costume and field layout thereby become 'goods for thinking with' (*bonnes à penser*). The systematic interrelations among these artefacts and practices also encourage a kind of 'thinking by analogy' (*bricolage*). For instance, pots and spears may be associated with, respectively, feminine and masculine in a given culture, and both pairs of terms may then be accommodated within a larger structural opposition relating 'nurture' (maintaining civilisation) and 'nature' (keeping the wild at bay). Lévi-Strauss also pointed to the ways in which myths, dramas and narratives in general rehearse and resolve the contradictions experienced within societies, thereby allowing cultures to maintain a sense of coherence. Lévi-Strauss's approach to myth is similar to Propp's approach to folktale in that both are looking for the constant, underlying structures that relate one narrative to another. They are less interested in the idiosyncrasies of various versions or the peculiar pressures which make each telling in context to some extent unique. In this respect structuralist models have much in common with FORMALIST models, which they partly draw upon.

Barthes and the opening up of modern myths

Barthes was a structuralist who always had strong poststructuralist tendencies. His early *Mythologies* (1957) was heavily influenced by Saussure and Lévi-Strauss. The concluding section on 'Myth today' argues for an extension of sign-theory so as to recognise myth, including narrative and drama, as what Barthes calls 'second-order sign-systems'. That is, not only are they chiefly made of words (a 'first-order sign-system'); they are also made of strings or frames of words which can be aligned with certain **genres** of verbal experience ('second-order sign-systems'). A simple example would be the formulas 'Once upon a time . . . ' and ' . . . and they all lived happily ever after'. These are made up of a series of individual verbal signs ('Once', 'upon', etc.). However, taken together as strings of words, they also signal the beginning and ending of a traditional kind of children's story. Such attempts at formal systematisation recur in Barthes's theoretical work, and they often have a 'totalising' (and therefore structuralist) air about them – attempting to embrace, if not explain, everything. Another instance is his 'Introduction to a Structural Analysis of Narrative' (1977: 79–124). Significantly, however, Barthes's own analytical practice often belies or exceeds his theorising. Many of the essays in *Mythologies* are lively and more or less *ad hoc* meditations on contemporary popular culture: 'The Face of Greta Garbo', 'The new Citroën' and 'Strip-tease'. They offer playful and often inspiring sallies into what was then a new terrain. And their cumulative effect is to suggest much more that CULTURE is plural, hybrid, many-centred and ultimately 'non-totalisable'. In this Barthes confirms the strongly poststructuralist side to his project. There is a similarly suggestive disjuncture in his later work *S/Z* (1970). This offers a highly complex and elaborate overview of the processes of **reading** and interpretation in terms of just five codes (proairetic, hermeneutic, semic, symbolic and referential). However, again, in Barthes's own daring and virtuoso readings these codes are seen converging and diverging, coalescing and exploding in ways which are decidedly *post*structuralist rather than structuralist. There is always a sense that the system is open and in process.

Derrida, decentring and deconstruction

Derrida is the philosopher who has probably done most to challenge dominant Western notions of 'wholeness' and 'centre' in symbolic structures of all kinds, especially in language. Proceeding from the structuralist insight that all meaning is constituted through the interplay of **differences** (Saussure had remarked that language is 'a system of . . . differences without positive terms'), Derrida argues that all meanings are ultimately 'deferred'. (The ambiguity of the French *différance* allows him a pun on 'difference' and 'deferral'.) According to Derrida, there is never an encounter with meaning as such, simply a ceaseless play of differences between those terms which are present and those which are absent. Put another way, we only understand things by understanding what they are not. Moreover, in any given culture there is a tendency to assume a hierarchy of differences, to imply preferences. Thus in dominant Western traditions it is common and conventional to privilege 'white' before 'black', 'male' before 'female', 'up' before 'down', 'reason' before 'the senses', 'the whole' before 'the part', 'presence' before 'absence', 'centre' before 'margin', and so on. These are all instances of what Derrida and other poststructuralists would term 'violent hierarchies'. It is thus the role of *deconstructive* thinkers not simply to invert these hierarchies (for example by now privileging 'black' before 'white' or 'female' before 'male') but actually to reopen the play of differences round the terms and to resist the lure of merely binary thinking. In the above examples this means radically rethinking our notions of the 'colour' spectrum (both in the physical and the social sense); recognising the plurality of possible gender roles as well as permutations of homo- and heterosexuality; and generally opening up a relativistic sense of alternative – not simply opposed – differences and centres.

Much of Derrida's work is concentrated upon the domain of linguistic philosophy – even while he attacks many of its premises. Characteristically, he is concerned with the vexed relations between **speech** and **writing** and the effect of trying to 'decentre' the human **subject** from the core of philosophical debate. He also offers the challenge of a non-Western approach to issues of **reality and representation** (including problems of **absence and presence,** and non/sense) which is not simply its traditional obverse, i.e. Eastern. Put another way, Derrida explores the problems and possibilities of 'sense-other-wise' – beyond the binary principle of sense *or* nonsense. Significantly, this project is seen as too radical by right-wing political commentators who accuse deconstructionists of the destruction of civilised (Western) values. Meanwhile, overtly MARXIST, FEMINIST and POSTCOLONIAL commentators sometimes complain of Derrida's apparent philosophical distance from pointedly political issues. Either way, Derrida's deconstructive techniques, like all tools, remain politically powerful or powerless depending upon who they are wielded by and how.

Foucault, discourse and historical discontinuity

Foucault was chiefly concerned with the interrelations of knowledge and power, especially the ways in which legal, medical and religious **discourses** operate to produce changing perceptions of what it is to be 'normal' or 'deviant' ('sane' or 'insane', 'law-abiding' or 'criminal'). Along with Barthes, Foucault was also committed to exploding the dominant Western notion of the **author** as the sole source, origin and guarantor of a text's meanings. Instead, they proposed that the concept 'author' be treated as a historically variable and politically contested site. They also shifted the focus to **texts** in **context** as **intertextual** constructs, insisting that cultures are expressed *through* not simply *by* writers and producers. Foucault articulated various influential historical models of **self** and **other** as well as a radically dis/continuous view of history which has been very influential with NEW HISTORICISTS. He resists the notion that history can ever be understood, let alone told, within a single narrative frame. Instead, he argues, we must recognise that the many localised narratives of history, like the many discourses of culture, do not add up to a single coherent whole. History is always fractured and off balance. Indeed, Foucault emphasises that what most often arrests us in history is a sense of radical rupture with the past. It is the *dis*continuity rather than the continuity of history which is significant.

Lyotard and the postmodern condition

Lyotard made a comparable attack on what he called the 'grand narratives' (*grands récits*) in *The Postmodern Condition: A Report on Knowledge* (1979). By grand narratives Lyotard means all those overarching intellectual schemes which purport to offer a totalising frame in which to understand some aspect of modern life. The Enlightenment belief in progress, Darwinian evolutionism, MARXIST political and economic history, and Freudian PSYCHOLOGY are all seen as potentially repressive and regressive forces in so far as they limit what he calls 'intensities and energies'. Whatever their avowed aims, all these forms of knowledge may become straitjackets within which the human body and mind are restrained. In place of such 'grand narratives' Lyotard argues for a politics of 'small-scale narratives' (*petits récits*), working from the immediate and the local, and without aspirations to any totalising – and potentially totalitarian – grasp of the whole. In the field of **discourse** this means that Lyotard is committed to what Wittgenstein calls 'language games': people playing their roles with all the energies and resources at their disposal – even to the point of bending or breaking the rules and insisting that another game be played – but at no time believing that theirs is the only game, or that there is some grander mega-game of which all games are simply a part.

Another dimension of Lyotard's vision of the postmodern condition is his attention to the implications of contemporary global communications. Given our increasing capacity to bring fragments of the 'far' near and to incorporate fragments of the 'past' in the present, he argues that *all* knowledge thereby becomes at once global *and* local, timeless *and* timely. Contemporary humanity has thus done something radically paradoxical with the perception of space and time. This line of thinking is taken to its logical (some would say illogical) extreme in the work of Baudrillard. He argues that modern COMMUNICATIONS and MEDIA (including computer-assisted editing and transmission techniques) have become so pervasive and sophisticated that we can no longer claim to have a view of 'the **real**' untouched by human hand, mind or machine. Instead we are treated to composite images of images of images – without any guarantee of an 'untouched' reality beyond. These '**images** without originals' Baudrillard calls *simulacra*. Thus, most memorably, he argued that in a sense the 1992 Gulf War did not really take place for most people in the West. Its communication through an elaborately mediated mix of real life and simulation meant that for many the events existed in 'virtual reality' and 'cyber-space'. It could all just as well have been a daily dose of hi-tech war stories and disaster movies. This provocative perspective he and others – notably Žižek – probed still further with the hauntingly iconic images of 9/11 (compare 5.2.5).

Postmodernism attacked and defended

Perhaps not surprisingly, there are many who take exception to this view of the postmodern world. They see the implications and consequences of global communications more positively, as potentially emancipating rather than enslaving, heightening and extending rather than dulling and constraining our senses of reality – virtual and otherwise. Some, however, attack the very notion of 'the postmodern'. Eagleton and Harvey suggested that Postmodernism is finally little more than a fancy label for 'late Capitalism' (see MARXISM). Meanwhile, Said, Spivak and others pointed to the *laissez-faire* complicity of the concept with neo-colonialism and 'coca-colaisation', as well as its casually unreconstructed stereotypes of gender and sexuality (see POSTCOLONIALISM and FEMINISM).

And yet there are those such as Jameson, Hutcheon and Bhabha who see 'the postmodern condition' as something we should neither dismiss nor acquiesce in. Rather, we must play *in* and work *through* it, engaging actively with its strategies in order to redirect its political agenda. Hutcheon for example draws attention to the productively disruptive effects of much postmodern practice in writing, art and the media. She cites numerous instances of parody, collage and non- or anti-realist representations and performances where there is a sense of creative critique from within a postmodernist **aesthetic** – not simply an uncritical wallowing in consumer culture. More particularly, Hutcheon points to the radical and potentially liberating view of history as **faction** rather than 'fact'. She argues that alternative histories, both actual and potential, can only be generated once the illusion of a single overarching story (Lyotard's 'grand narrative') is fractured, dispersed and re-formed. She is especially interested (as is Waugh) in the capacity of supposedly 'fictional' writers and other imaginative artists to blur and redraw the boundaries between **fact** and **fiction**, notably in the genre she terms 'historiographic metafiction' and latterly her work on adaption. Hutcheon also places considerable emphasis on the critical and creative powers (as well as the responsibilities) of **readers**, audiences and viewers. She observes that people generally take what is most useful and helpful for themselves, and ignore or reject what they judge irrelevant or harmful. Overall, then, Hutcheon argues for a recognition of the opportunities as well as the risks of living *through* the postmodern moment: exploring and experimenting, not simply coping or copping out. In this respect her position resembles that of Benjamin and Brecht much earlier. For they too urged culturally aware and politically active engagement with all the contemporary media resources at their disposal. And they too counselled against lofty indifference, reactionary disaffection or indulgent immersion.

The account of Poststructuralism in this section emphasises its primarily philosophical concerns. For a specifically psychoanalytic framing of related issues to do with fragmented and displaced subjects, especially Lacan's notion of 'lack', see PSYCHOLOGY; also **subject identity and role**.

How to practise Poststructuralism in a postmodern moment

Begin by considering the various kinds of **subject** in play: the *subject matter* of the text in hand; the *academic subject* within which you are studying it; some sense of yourself as a *human subject* constituted in terms of gender, ethnicity, class, education and personal history. This serves as a preliminary reminder of the interrelated structures and moments within which you and the text are currently constructing meaning. Go on to consider the following:

Differences, binary and plural:
- *What are the main contrasts and tensions*, especially the binary oppositions, through which the text seems to operate (e.g. nature v. artifice; passion v. reason; men v. women; human v. machine; order v. disorder; past v. present; individual v. society; etc.)?
- *Which polarities seem to be preferred before their opposites*, thus establishing a perceptual hierarchy (e.g. passion before reason, past before present)?

♦   *What other, plural differences* does the text appear to express or suppress (e.g. other ways of seeing and saying 'the same thing' differently)?

Centres and margins, de-centring and re-centring:

♦   *What is assumed to be central* within the text (e.g. a certain time, place and set of participants; a particular aesthetic, moral, economic or political premise)?

♦   *What is treated as marginal or ignored completely* but might nonetheless offer a related yet alternative centre of interest and valuation (e.g. other previously merely implied or excluded places and participants; other relatable times and places; alternative aesthetic and moral premises)?

♦   *Is there in fact any limit to the number of different centres* you can perceive within and around the text? And how do you, individually and collectively, arrive at preferring some before others?

Closed and open structures, 'wholes' and 'holes':

♦   *Try to describe the text as a 'whole'*, complete and unified in itself. Do the same for the language (or other sign-system) in which it is realised. (In effect, this means saying: 'The text is wholly X', 'The language is wholly Y', and so on.)

♦   *Now try to see the text as a series of 'holes'* through which can be glimpsed fragments of other words and worlds. Do the same for the language (or sign-system) in which it is realised. (In effect, this means saying: 'Through this text I get glimpses of texts A and B to which it is similar or relatable. Through this sign-system I get glimpses of other relatable sign-systems.')

Narratives, 'grand' and 'small', local and global, **factional** and **metafictional** (this is where we go more obviously 'postmodern'):

♦   *Are there any larger 'narratives'* (general, psychological, political, scientific or religious frameworks and regimes) which the text seems to draw on or contribute to? In what sense could it be viewed as an episode in a global cultural history?

♦   *Or would you rather see it on a smaller scale*, as a configuration of peculiarly local and to some extent unique effects?

♦   *How far is the text categorisable* as fiction or fact, story or history? Or would you rather categorise it as factional and hi/story? Why?

♦   *Does the text comment on itself* (metatextually)? Or is such reflection and self-reflexivity also the prerogative of the reader, audience or viewer (e.g. you)?

Example

Read the text of Queen's 'Bohemian Rhapsody' (5.1.5) with the above 'How to practise . . .' guidelines in mind. If possible, listen to a recording and watch the original video promo or a 'live' performance too (all readily available on the Internet). Then compare your responses with those below.

Preliminary reflection on the kinds of 'subject' in play within and around 'Bohemian Rhapsody' produces, for me, something like the following. Textually, this is a song about a marginalised figure, an outcast: the protagonist seems to be a 'poor boy' who faces a death sentence for murder. In this respect it is similar to a number of rock songs which express alienation and disaffection. Contextually, from a present perspective, 'Bohemian Rhapsody' is strongly identified with Queen's singer, Freddie Mercury, who died of AIDS in 1991, when the song was re-released. This fact has tended to reinforce the 'tragic' sense of the song as well as, perhaps, the gendering of its protagonist. Meanwhile, from my own subject position as a white, middle-aged, male lecturer in English (and an old Queen fan), I am aware that there are attitudes and perspectives that may not be shared by all present readers. The mere inclusion in this book of the words of a pop song may grate with more traditional proponents of 'Eng. Lit.' ('It may be English – but is it Literature?!'). This particular choice of song may also clash with the musical interests and tastes of younger, perhaps predominantly female students.

The general point is that all the above 'subjects' (the subject matter of the text and the subject positions of both performer and interpreters) are all implicated in an understanding of 'Bohemian Rhapsody'. Each and all might serve as focuses for a systematic enquiry into not only *what* the song means but also *how* it means. What are the conditions whereby this text operates in the world? What are the social and textual structures and relations within which it can be sited – or cited and sighted? Anything like a comprehensive answer would therefore need to consider the interplay between a number of verbal, musical and (in performance) visual codes. It would also need to engage with a variety of specific yet shifting discourses – commercial and educational, popular and academic. In what follows I shall concentrate on the words of the song as reproduced in 5.1.5. However, as occasion demands, I shall pick up the broader concerns signalled above. A poststructuralist reading must necessarily recognise that all structures are interrelated yet open, while a postmodern response cannot be limited to words alone.

If we plot the overall structure of the text of 'Bohemian Rhapsody' in terms of binary oppositions we come up with something like this:

> 'real life' versus 'fantasy'; life versus death; 'I' (murderer) versus 'he' (murdered); individual versus society; solo voice versus chorus; angels versus devils; aggression versus apathy . . .

This is initially useful because it offers an overall conceptual grid within which to structure an interpretation. Ultimately, however, it is limiting. For what such simple, fixed oppositions fail to catch are the plural and shifting differences that are in play. For instance, 'Mama, (I) just killed a man' involves three (not two) participants: one spoken to ('Mama'), one speaking (I, understood), and one spoken about ('a man'). Meanwhile, the singer modulates – sometimes gradually, sometimes abruptly – through a whole array of postures and emotions (again not just two). He is by turns languorous, aggressive, defiant, terrified, pathetic and apathetic. Binary structures may be a good place to start. They are rarely a good place to end.

In terms of what is explicitly **centred**, the dominant subject position of the text is emphatically male: 'poor boy' (x 4), 'just killed a man', 'silhouetto of a man', 'Galileo'. This is reinforced by the fact of a male singer and an all-male band – and perhaps by me as a male commentator. However, there is also a marginal yet strong female presence signalled by the repeated appeals to 'Mama' and 'mama mia'. Moreover, still other, non-binary possibilities are opened up by the recognition that Freddie Mercury affected an alternately or simultaneously 'gay–macho' persona in performance. He did this increasingly overtly between 1975, when the single was first released, and 1991 when it was re-released. As a result, the gendering of both performer and performance shifted noticeably over a decade and a half, just as it may still do between one viewer/listener/reader and another. Hetero- and homosexual interpretations are never absolutely circumscribed. They are always renegotiable.

'Bohemian Rhapsody' is an apparently finished yet in reality open structure in other ways. It is obviously complete and 'whole' in that it lasts six minutes and physically sounds much the same every time you hear it (in Part Five it occupies a determinate space on the paper and is framed as an entire text). It also has a discernible beginning, middle and end. The song opens and closes simply and quietly, but there is a hell of a lot going on in the middle (including full diabolic/angelic chorus and extended instrumental solos). There is an overall sense of narrative and dramatic structure, too: 'I' (the 'poor boy') is telling others (notably the chorus and us) of the terrible thing he's done and the punishment that awaits him. There are also several key phrases repeated over the course of the piece, many of them passed between singer and chorus, notably 'poor boy', 'any way the wind blows', 'mama (mia)', 'easy come. easy go', 'let me (him, you) go'. In all these ways textual cohesion and a degree of perceptual coherence are achieved.

At the same time the text obviously falls apart in various ways. It is full of 'holes'. For one thing, the 'I' who speaks/sings is either highly variable or inconsistent. He switches from aggression to apathy, terror to languor, with little notice or apparent cause. It is also unclear whether anything has really progressed by the end, or indeed whether the whole thing, as the opening lines ask, is 'real life' or 'fantasy'. (Do 'Galileo', 'piccolo' and 'magnifico-o-o-o-o', for instance, relate to anything else or even to one another – except as a series of similar sounds?)

For a combination of all the above reasons we may therefore say that this text is at once 'whole' *and* 'full of holes'. It is a determinate structure with partly coherent meanings and it is teeming with indeterminacies and discontinuities.

'Bohemian Rhapsody' draws upon a variety of 'grand narratives' in that it can be readily aligned with certain recognisable genres and scenarios. It rehearses a classic, perhaps distinctively modern, confrontation between the individual and society: the outsider pitted against everybody else. The 'poor boy' figure obviously keys into popular images of angry and apathetic young men, rebels with and without causes. It also hints at a combination of the figure on death-row with that of the Faust-like damned soul ('Too late. My time has come . . . '). In all these respects this text can be 'placed' generically and intertextually: it can be viewed as an episode in a larger cultural history. At the same time, this particular text offers a peculiar and to some extent unique configuration of effects. It is a highly distinctive 'small narrative' in its own right. Historically, 'Bohemian Rhapsody' was among the first cooperations between a rock band and full orchestra. It was innovative in its use of a full-length promotional video incorporating computerised graphics. In addition, as already mentioned, the sense of the song was given a bitterly ironic twist because of the fate of the singer. The anticipated death of the 'poor boy' and that of Freddie Mercury through AIDS have tended to be confused in the popular imagination. The death in the song gets mixed up with the death of the singer. Fiction lends itself to fact, and vice versa. The two combined make up the factional hi/story that is the rock legend that is 'Queen'.

Also see: FORMALISM, PSYCHOLOGY, key terms (p. 176) and @ 3.7.

READING: *Introductory*: Wolfreys 2001: 33–46, 117–51, 261–92; Selden, Widdowson and Brooker 2005: 62–81, 144–217; Green and Lebihan 1996: 49–90. *Structuralism*: Hawkes 2003; Sturrock 2003. *Poststructuralism (Deconstruction)*: Norris 2002; Weedon 1996 (and Feminism); Allen 2003 (Barthes); Royle 2002 (Derrida); Colebrook 2002 (Deleuze). *Postmodernism*: McHale 1992; Waugh 1992; Wheale 1995 (critical reader); Cahoone 1996 (anthology); Connor 1996; Bertens and Natoli 2002, Malpas 2004. *Core texts*: de Saussure, Barthes, Foucault, Derrida, Lyotard, Baudrillard in Lodge and Wood 2008; *also* Nietzsche, Bataille, and Deleuze and Guattari in Rivkin and Ryan 2004; *also* Habermas in Leitch 2010. *Advanced*: Norris 2007 (post-poststructuralist); Baudrillard 2006 (post-postmodernist).

3.8   ETHNICITIES – POSTCOLONIALISM AND MULTICULTURALISM

If you are concerned with the ongoing effects of colonialism and with the experience of living in an expressly multicultural world, these approaches will help you think about ethnicity *in terms of culture, history and politics as much as birth and race.*

Overview

Awareness of the colonial and postcolonial dimensions of English Studies has massively increased over the past few decades. So has recognition of the fact that most English-speaking countries (including Britain, America, Australia and New Zealand) are fundamentally multicultural and in some senses always have been. Signal moments in the modern raising of consciousness were the Civil Rights and 'Black Power' movements of the late 1960s and 1970s in the USA. In the UK the consequences of the British Empire and subsequently the Commonwealth came home (both literally and metaphorically) from the late 1950s onwards: by 1990 around five million people from the former colonies (chiefly the West Indies, Africa, India, Pakistan and Hong Kong) had emigrated to the 'motherland' in search of work and a better life. In Australia and New Zealand, meanwhile, since the 1970s at least, the position of indigenous Aboriginal and Maori peoples previously displaced or dispossessed by European settlers has been prominent on political and educational agendas (though as with their counterparts, the Native Indians of America, sometimes more has been said than done). One of the most recent and radical sites of postcolonial change in the English-speaking world is South Africa. The system of 'apartheid' (a Boer word meaning separation/segregation) was formally overthrown in 1994.

Such prodigious changes have important implications for English Studies. We are experiencing a huge shift in the ways we construct and approach our **subjects** of study, as well as in the ways we perceive ourselves as certain kinds of ideological subject, geographically and historically. Along with FEMINISM and GENDER STUDIES, postcolonialism and multiculturalism have arguably done more to transform our sense of who we are and what we are about than any other recent intellectual and political movements. Throughout the English-speaking world debates about the role of English in education regularly become embroiled in arguments about national or regional identity, 'mono-' or 'multi-' culturalism, majorities and minorities. In every domain of language, literature and culture there is an acute tension and sometimes a flat contradiction between globalising processes of standardisation and localising processes of differentiation. Thus in English LANGUAGE studies there is currently much attention to the following:

New Englishes of the former British colonies, chiefly in Africa, the Caribbean, India, Australasia and the Pacific rim. These 'new' Englishes include varieties such as pidgins and creoles as well as alternative national **standards** (e.g. Rhys 5.2.3 and Nichols 5.4.5), though in fact most of them have been around for a long time. The most notable and powerful old 'new' English is none other than American English, which has its roots deep in colonial history and its branches moving in a palpably multilingual atmosphere (including Spanish, French and Native American languages). There is now a strong interest in notions of global dispersal (diaspora) and differentiation. This is in part in reaction to *World or International English* as a kind of global standard. This is primarily written and printed, and substantially American in spelling, vocabulary and grammar. It is commonly used for international communication in science, technology, business and education, and has a kind of colloquial counterpart in the voice of the American popular media (notably Hollywood films, TV, adverts and pop songs). These too have a remarkably global reach. Locally, English may be conceived as a 'killer language', endangering indigenous varieties even as it enables global communication.

Kinds of ill/literacy. In so-called 'Third World' or 'developing' countries the ability to read and write, often in English, is a rare skill and a prized commodity. Basic illiteracy is a continuing problem. Meanwhile, in so-called 'First World' or 'developed' countries there are signs that literacy (i.e., reading and writing skills, as such), may be decreasing both in practice and prestige. Partly this is a consequence of an increasing emphasis on visual and audio-visual modes of COMMUNICATION, rather than on the written and printed word alone. Meanwhile, the gulf between the barely literate and the sophisticatedly 'computer literate' continues to widen.

In LITERARY studies, too, postcolonial and multicultural agendas are having profound effects:

'English Literature' is currently being transformed into 'Literature(s) in English', or 'Literary Studies' or 'Literary and Cultural Studies', dropping the 'English' completely. This tends to happen even where there is no formal change of departmental name or programme title.

The conventional Anglocentric and Anglo-American **canons** *of literary* **classics** *are being recast* in the shapes of a wide variety of national and regional cultures. Caribbean, African, Australian, New Zealand, Canadian and other literatures (themselves always hybrid) now commonly feature as courses and programmes in their own rights. So too do national, regional and ethnic writings in English from within the British Isles, from Ireland, Wales, Scotland and indigenous Caribbean and Asian communities; as do the work and traditions of Black American, Spanish, Chicano, Jewish and other groups of writers within the USA (e.g. 5.3.3 and 5.4.5).

There is an increasing recognition of non-Western-European **genres** *of writing, oral performance and cultural production.* Legends, histories, laws, fables, anecdotes, oratory, song, chant, song-and-dance are all making their way on to a transformed cultural agenda, and thereby challenging the dominant Western neo-classical division of literature into the mega-genres of poetry, prose and drama (see 5.1.5). The latter often don't fit the hybrid forms of oratory, writing and performance that characterise many pre-colonial, colonial and post-colonial verbal arts. The printed novel, for instance, is being recognised as just one, distinctively Western form of **narrative**. All this is also prompting a revised awareness of the nature of pre-print oral and manuscript cultures within the Old and Middle English periods. Anglo-Saxon oral-formulaic elegies and battle-poems turn out to have a surprising amount in common with modern Caribbean 'dub' poetry.

Texts in **translation** *are now much more likely to be 'set' in English and Literary Studies* (e.g. 5.4.3). Classic writers of the modern Western European theatre such as Ibsen, Pirandello and Brecht have been naturalised as legitimate 'Eng. Lit.' subjects for quite a while. Also now classic in their way are translations of the works of such writers, chiefly novelists, as Allende and Márquez from Central and South America, Kundera and Havel from Eastern Europe and Chang from Asia. The challenge in all these cases is to grasp the nature of translation as, in its broadest sense, an activity of transformation: between cultures as well as languages. Easy access can lead to appropriation as well as assimilation. The possibility of radical misinterpretation because of an ignorance of local social and historical conditions has to be recognised.

In terms of broader CULTURE there is a corresponding relativising, and to some extent a challenging, of exclusively Western European models:

The **classical** *heritage of Greece and Rome now tends to be seen alongside many other, sometimes older 'classical' cultures.* The Middle and Far East, India, China and Japan, as well as the largely oral cultures of Africa and the Americas (North, Central and South) also have their highly elaborate, distinctive and often extremely powerful philosophies, sciences and world-views.

Christianity and the **Bible**, in particular, must be seen in relation to other religions and their associated **myths**, stories, symbolism, belief systems and holy books. There is especial interest in and investigation of those forms of religious organisation and spiritual insight which were displaced by the deliberate dissemination of the Bible as part of the 'civilising' project of colonisation (e.g. Seminole chants 5.1.5 and Marshall-Stoneking 5.4.2).

Overall, then, postcolonial and multicultural perspectives entail a radical reconfiguring of English Studies, not a mere tinkering with it. The following are some of the most persistent questions and the most prominent figures in this lively and important area of debate (for references see Reading at the end of this section):

◆ *How deep is skin-deep?* When does ethnicity become racism? When does patriotic pride become nationalist paranoia? (Fanon, Gates, Young).

◆ *What happens when 'the empire writes back'?* Or when people(s) attempt to forget or reclaim some of their many pasts? (Rushdie, Ashcroft, Griffiths *et al.*, Gates).

◆ *Where and how are we to locate the many and various 'centres' and 'margins' of culture?* Can we ever expect these to be more than provisional and contested? (Bhabha, Said).

♦ *What desires and dangers are involved when we try to recognise people(s) as other?* Can we be so sure our selves are unitary and stable in the first place? And when does a respect for cultural difference tip into a covert sense of separation/segregation? (Kristeva, Morrison, Spivak).

♦ *Can anyone ever 'speak for' and in every sense* **represent** *someone else?* (a member of one ethnic group representing another, for instance?) If people aspire to look and sound like one another, then who is 'mimicking' whom? Whose 'mask' is in play? In whose language does 'the subaltern' (dependent subordinate) speak? (Spivak, Minh-ha, Bhabha).

♦ *What of community and consensus, personal expression and collective celebration?* Or is it all division and conflict, personal repression, public oppression or secret suppression? Can we reject certain imperialist (and aristocratic and patriarchal) aspects of the Western European humanist and Enlightenment models of human nature, while building on its project of justice, reason and democracy? (hooks, Hall, Norris).

Key terms: ENGLISH/Englishes (1.1); LANGUAGE; LITERATURE; CULTURE; **absence and presence . . . centres and margins; auto/biography and travel writing, self and other; canon and classic;** colonialism (post- and neo-); **similarity and differences;** ethnic, ethnocentric (e.g. Anglocentric, Eurocentric); literacy and illiteracy; native; orality; orientalism; race, racism; **standards and varieties; translation**.

Major issues and models

The terrain we are traversing is uneven and shifting. It can be both frustrating and fascinating, dangerous as well as delightful. (For a white, male, middle-aged, British-born university teacher of English there are peculiar perils as well as privileges in this area. You will have your own.) There are, moreover, no absolutely reliable and impartial 'maps'. I have simply set up some signposts and ask you to follow these as long as seems helpful – then look for or set up others.

Colonisation – a varied and ongoing process

'Colonisation' is the activity of making colonies. 'Colonialism' is the system of having colonies. Both terms ultimately derive from the Latin *colonia*, meaning 'farm' or 'settlement'. Both therefore also share a common root with the word 'culture', through Latin *colere* (past part. *cultum*) – 'to grow' (see CULTURE). As currently used, colonisation (the active noun we shall stick with here) is an all-purpose term which can embrace many different relations amongst peoples and things and places. In British colonisation alone we may distinguish the following kinds and stages from the twelfth to the twentieth centuries:

♦ *'internal' colonisation within the British Isles* by England of Wales, Ireland and Scotland, involving successive 'plantations' of English settlers and displacements or 'clearances' of natives from the Western Isles to the Highlands; also 'enclosures' of common land and evictions of natives within England;

♦ *'external' colonisation beyond the British Isles* in what became successively the British Empire and (from 1931) the Commonwealth. External colonies may also be further distinguished according to the ways in which they came into being:

  ♦ initial trading relations eventually leading to imperial administration (India from the seventeenth-century East India Company to the twentieth-century Raj);

- dissident religious communities, primarily of tradespeople (e.g. the Pilgrim Fathers – and Mothers and Children – who settled New England in America from the 1620s);
- farming and mining communities of settlers, living and working largely on their own (as in New Zealand) or with the more or less enforced labour of natives or slaves (in South Africa, other parts of Africa and the Americas);
- slave transportation and enforced labour on a large scale (from West Africa to the Caribbean and North, Central and South America);
- convict transportation and penal colonies (e.g. Botany Bay in Australia, so-called because of an earlier natural history survey by James Cook *et al.*).

It is important to recognise the shifting permutations and complex interdependencies of all these aspects of empire. Trading relations could lead to imperial control (as in India). A first phase of religious foundation might be succeeded by a welter of other kinds of settler, including slave and then migrant labour (as in North America). Farming and mining might initially be undertaken by white settlers, but then draw on native and slave labour (as in South Africa). Even the term 'plantation' has shifted in sense. Initially it referred to '*trans*planting of people'; only later, by association, was the sense extended to plantations of fruit, sugar cane and cotton.

The internal–external dynamic of the processes of colonisation within and beyond Britain and America must also be appreciated. Many of the people who were the first English settlers (farmers, miners, craftspeople and traders, as well as soldiers and sailors) emigrated out of necessity or compulsion, not out of choice. Often they had been dispossessed in Britain as a result of land enclosures and clearances (especially in Ireland, Scotland and the Home Counties). Alternatively, or as well, they had been left un- or under-employed during the Industrial Revolution, chiefly as a result of the mechanisation of the cotton and wool mills, the mines and farming. Religious dissenters fled persecution as much as they sought new communities. Criminals were 'transported' abroad (e.g., to Australia); and many of the soldiers and sailors of the empire were either 'pressed' (i.e. forced) into military and naval service, or took up arms abroad as an alternative to unemployment or starvation at home. Thus the history of empire and exploitation *beyond* the British Isles is continuous with the history of empire and exploitation *within* the British Isles. This helps explain the complex and often vexed relations between the colonisers abroad and the colonial authorities back in Britain. It was not only the colonis*ed* who had some bones to pick with their British masters and mistresses.

The slave-trade triangle

The classic British–American example illustrating the interdependencies of empire is the 'slave-trade triangle' which linked Britain to West Africa and both to the West Indies and the Americas (see Appendix D). Ships from Britain would head for West Africa with a load of supplies (including guns) for the settlers and their allies and trinkets for the natives. In West Africa, they would pick up African slaves, spices, animal skins and ivory and take them all to the Caribbean and America. Once there, the slaves would be sold and set to work on the sugar-cane, cotton and fruit plantations. Sugar, molasses and rum, as well as raw cotton, would then be taken back to Britain for manufacture, sale and 'home' consumption or export. And so back round again. The whole 'triangular' operation had, in theory at least, an elegance, simplicity and efficiency which made it a model of economic resource management. Unless, that is, you happened to be an African captured, enslaved, transported and, if you survived the appalling voyage, quite possibly worked to death. The slave traffic across the Atlantic has resulted in this phase of slavery being referred to as 'the Middle Passage' and its defining space (after Paul

Gilroy) as 'the Black Atlantic'. (See 5.2.2 for a cluster of perspectives on slaves and slavery. *Oroonoko* (*c*. 1681) is about this very 'slave-trade triangle'; as is Phillips 5.4.2.)

America, too, has thus been in both colonial *and* postcolonial states since the arrival of the Europeans, and arguably well before. Native American Indians were – and in some sense remain – the colonis*ed*; though their own earlier tribal wars and empires complicate the picture further. Meanwhile, white Western European settlers in America (notably the English and French) were colonis*ers* then changed their status by breaking away from their respective homelands to set up nations of their own. They also subsequently broke away from one another, notably in French- and English-speaking Canada.

Colonisers, colonised and slaves

Theoretically as well as practically, it is important to distinguish the various participants in the processes of colonisation:

- the colonis*ers*, 'foreigners', those who initially come from elsewhere;
- the colonis*ed*, 'natives', those who were born in the place (from Latin *natus* – 'born'; cf. *nat*ion);
- slaves, who were often neither colonisers nor colonised but forcibly brought from elsewhere, and therefore were both 'foreign' and 'non-native' in their new place.

It is also important to observe that over time the families of colonisers may become second-, third- and fourth-generation *settlers*, and therefore are also 'natives' in that they too were 'born' there. Settlers may also have interbred with the initial natives, thus complicating issues still further. Moreover, taking a still longer historical view, we must also recognise that many of the colonis*ed* have themselves at some time been colonis*ers* (displacing and perhaps dispossessing other peoples). Colonis*ers*, too, may well have been colonis*ed* at some point in their past. Thus in Britain the Normans colonised the Germanic tribes who themselves had colonised the Celts. In South Africa the English and Dutch (Boers) colonised the Zulus, who themselves had colonised earlier tribes and nations 'native' to the southern grasslands. In this respect no people is in absolute terms either 'native' or 'foreign' to a place. We are all in some sense visitors, temporary tenants. Put another way, everybody is involved in various stages of post/colonialism, before, during or after the event. Hence the optional slashed form (/) in the term itself. An alternative is to consider any and every phase as in some sense *mid*-colonialism. As with wars, there is always one going on somewhere.

To some extent, then, the labels 'coloniser' and 'colonised' may be swapped around over time and from place to place. Colonisation is a varied and ongoing process. Yet it is crucial to recognise that, over any given period and in any given place, some people, often whole peoples, have indeed been colonis*ers* while others have most certainly been colonis*ed*, and perhaps enslav*ed* too. Thus in the past five hundred years many (native) African, American and Asian peoples have been at the sharp end of colonisation while others (chiefly Western Europeans and their descendants) have been doing the sharpening and cutting. There are, therefore, crucial distinctions to be maintained between those 'doing' and responsible for colonisation and those 'done to' and affected by it. History *does* involve actions and reactions as well as interactions and interrelation. This latter point may seem to be obvious and laboured. However, it would not seem so in the context of certain kinds of NEW HISTORICIST and POSTMODERNIST approach where agency, causality and responsibility threaten to dissolve into an amorphous mass of relations without determination or discrimination. In short, to repeat, some people were – and are – more colonis*ing* than colonis*ed*. To pretend otherwise is in effect to tell *no* **hi/story** while affecting to tell *every* or *any* hi/story. And we always tell *some* hi/story. The point is to realise that that is precisely what we are doing: to reflect upon our knowledge, remedy our ignorance, and recognise the inevitable partiality of our points of view and subject positions.

Postcolonialism, as such, can be broadly and theoretically defined as 'what grows out of and away from colonialism'. Like POSTSTRUCTURALISM and POSTMODERNISM, the term expresses a state which is both continuous with and distinct from that which it succeeds. Postcolonialism, more narrowly and historically defined, is usually understood to refer to the state of those countries which achieved formal political independence from Britain (and from other Western European powers such as Spain, France, Portugal, Holland, Belgium and Germany) from the mid-twentieth century onwards. As far as Britain is concerned, many of these countries became – and some still are – members of the British Commonwealth (first recognised in 1931). However, as the above more complex and flexible definitions of post/colonialism imply (embracing the simultaneous presence of both colonial and postcolonial states), Britain and America can be characterised as being in both colonial *and* postcolonial conditions virtually since the beginning of modern history. In this respect, the most recent, successful independence movement by a British colony *within* Britain was that of Eire (Southern Ireland) in 1922. Scotland and Wales gained a regional Parliament and Assembly, respectively, at the beginning of the twenty-first century. Britain's most recent colonial 'war' was with Argentina over the Falkland Islands/Malvinas in 1982. Meanwhile, in 1997, Hong Kong was handed back to China; though the British government again refused to give back Gibraltar to Spain. Relations amongst Britain, Spain and Gibraltar remain unresolved.

Neo-colonialism (meaning 'new-style' colonialism) generally means the exercise of international power through economic and commercial rather than military means. The USA and Japan are currently often accused of neo-colonialism because of their dominance in world markets and their power to make other countries economically dependent. The World Banking System, especially the International Monetary Fund, is also arguably neo-colonial in its power to maintain the dependence of many 'Third World' countries through control of their debts and trade alliances.

Multiculturalism can be briefly defined as 'awareness of the distinctively plural and hybrid nature of *all* CULTURES'. I put the case like this, slightly provocatively, because it is impossible to point to any culture which has been, is or is ever likely to be, 'single and pure' (i.e. *mono*cultural). Historically, those who have seriously sought to maintain the myth of a pure culture have been rabble-rousing ideologues (e.g. Hitler). There are, however, various views of what multicultural can mean. It can mean:

♦ *multiracial*, in which case the emphasis is on perceived differences in people's 'colour', hair texture and physical build (white, black, yellow, etc.). *Race* is the core term here, a concept that is still heavy with nineteenth-century notions of fixed human physiological types, particularly the mistaken belief that different peoples (African, Caucasian, Asiatic, etc.) have fundamentally different physical and mental capacities. Hence the negative charge of the term 'racism'.

♦ *multi-ethnic*, where the emphasis is more on people's social organisation and cultural practices (e.g. dress and marriage customs) rather than their physiological make-up. *Ethnicity* (derived from Greek *ethnos*, meaning 'nation') therefore avoids the biological determinism of the term 'race' and recognises the fact that people can be born into a certain group but that they may subsequently take up the cultural practices of another group. Ethnicity offers the possibility of cultural change and variation; race implies biologically determined fixity. (Compare the crucial distinction in GENDER STUDIES between biologically determined sex and socially constructed gender.) Ethnicity is a term which is positively valued. *Ethnocentrism*, conversely, is negatively charged because it refers to the tendency to privilege or **centre** one culture before others, which thereby become marginalised or ignored (e.g. Anglocentric, Eurocentric).

- *cultural* **differences** *of all kinds*, including differences of class, rank, caste, sexuality, gender, occupation, region, age, dis/ability, etc. – as well as race and ethnicity. Though broad and potentially bland, this extended sense of multiculturalism has the great advantage that it does not concentrate upon one cultural difference to the potential exclusion of others. It recognises cultural differences to be plural and complexly interrelated (also see CULTURAL MATERIALISM and FEMINISM).

Finally, it should also be noted that multiculturalism is a term that can be used in a superficial, merely expedient way. It can be used to promote the sense that everyone should simply 'get on' with one another – regardless of persisting disparities in access to education, work, housing, health care, etc. Then the concept papers over the cracks in a fundamentally unequal system. Some purportedly 'multicultural' programmes may encourage a kind of sham or fragile consensus, but without addressing the real (largely economic) causes of conflict. It also depends upon whose interests are really being served by the maintenance or dissolution of existing cultural differences. Such, in outline, are the problems and the possibilities facing all purportedly multicultural initiatives from Northern Ireland to the former Yugoslavia, from inner city London to outer city Johannesburg. *Whose* version or vision of multiculturalism, *for whom* and *why*?

Literacy, illiteracy and language policies

Questions of who can read, write and speak what kinds of thing in what language ('native' and/or English and/or another) inevitably bulk large in postcolonial contexts. They did under colonialism too. However, both literacy and language policies are all too easily ignored or obscured in a narrowly 'literary' approach to texts. The *fact* of reading and writing is readily assumed and forgotten by those who have long been in on the act. So are the privileges and prejudices of those who routinely and perhaps exclusively use English. (See Which 'Englishes'?, 1.1 and English in Education @ 1.4.6.) Answers to such problems, as we see shortly, vary greatly from place to place. The underlying issues, however, have much in common:

- *How far are the languages of the European colonisers (English, French, Spanish, Portuguese, Dutch and German) permanently tainted in the eyes, ears and minds of colonised non-Europeans?* Can the English word 'black', for instance, ever be fully cleansed of its dominant associations with 'evil', 'dirt' and 'darkness', and the word 'white' ever be invested with dominant associations other than those of 'goodness', 'innocence', 'light' and 'cleanliness'? What would this do to everything from pictorial representations of God as an old white man to advertising slogans for washing powders promising 'whiter than white' cleanness?
- *What are the practical alternatives to English (French, Spanish, etc.) from amongst the native languages of the various states of Africa, Asia and the Americas?* What are the immediate and the long-term dis/advantages of teaching people to read and write as well as speak these languages, especially when resources of all kinds (including those for basic literacy) are so scarce?
- *What are the 'internal' implications* for regional, tribal, caste and national identity if any single language (European or indigenous) is chosen to the exclusion of others?
- *What are the 'external' implications* of a presence and voice on the international stage which is 'English' or native? Can a workable compromise be fashioned?

These are persistent questions facing educationists, language-planners, governments and companies worldwide. Because they cut across so many areas of language, literature and culture,

ENGLISH	NATIVE LANGUAGE(S)
Associated with British Empire and/or American neo-colonialism	Associated with indigenous social structures and institutions
Identified with local power elite	Identified with local powerlessness
Learnt artificially through formal education	Learnt naturally through routine social interaction
Mainly for reading and writing – print culture	Mainly for speaking and listening – oral culture
Part of public, official sphere; international power	Part of personal, informal sphere; ethnic solidarity
Access to global learning and communication	Access to local learning, customs and communication

Figure 3.2 Postcolonial problems and possibilities with English

refractions of them can be found elsewhere throughout the book (see 1.2; **accent and dialect** and **standards**). Figure 3.2 presents a theoretically polarised view of the dilemmas. In practice, people invariably come up with compromises and hybrid solutions. In post-independence Tanzania, Kenya and Malaysia, for instance, English is no longer an 'official' language but it is still widely used. In India, English shares 'official' status with Hindi, Urdu and several other languages and is often valued for its external, non-sectarian status. In Nigeria English has 'official' status, along with Igbo and Yoruba; but there continues to be very pointed argument about the harm it does or benefits it brings to the literacy of indigenous cultures. In any given instance, we are likely to find a mixture of arguments from both sides. The result, in principle or practice, 'officially' or otherwise, will be a hybrid situation. Interestingly, much the same principles apply to all kinds of bi- or multilingual groups and institutions, large and small – from individual families, schools and neighbourhoods to international companies and whole countries.

Renaming and remapping

One of the first acts of any explorer, conqueror or coloniser (the terms are at first fluidly interchangeable) is to name the places he (and it usually is a he) 'discovers'. The fact that the places he 'discovers' have been known and inhabited by native peoples for generations, and that many names for the places already exist, is generally overlooked or accounted of merely incidental interest. Somebody's 'New World' is always somebody else's 'Old World'. Visitors invariably 'find' what the locals had never lost – or had not lost yet anyway. But what *were* the many and varied names of the 'Americas' (North, Central and South) before Amerigo Vespucci's first name was applied to all of them – prefaced by some approximate latitudinal markers? 'New England' before the recently arrived Englanders named it 'New'? 'Australia' before it blew Europeans there from the north (the name comes from the Latin for 'south wind' – *auster*, *australis*)? And, once there, what were the tribal names of 'Aborigines' for themselves before the visiting Europeans called the natives that in the belief they had found a more 'primitive' and 'original' kind of human animal? (The European word is a conflation of Latin *ab origine*, meaning 'from the beginning'; just one of their own tribal names was 'Koori'.) Put the other way round, did you know that 'Aotearoa' was one of the Maori names for 'New Zealand' before the Dutchman Abel Tasman visited and renamed it in the seventeenth century? Or that 'Kentucky' is Iroquois for 'meadow land', and 'Kansas' and 'Arkansas' are Sioux for 'land of the South Wind people'? That 'California' and 'Texas' derive from the Spanish for, respectively, 'earthly paradise' and 'allies'? (See Appendix D.) In all these ways, the suppression or the survival of particular place-names, and the ceaseless processes of renaming, give us glimpses in miniature of tiny fragments of continuing, invariably contentious, histories.

Maps, too, are symbolic as well as practical tools. For many people born in Britain in the 1950s (e.g. me) there are variously proud or perplexed memories of maps of the world liberally coloured in pink (the colour reserved for the British Empire and Commonwealth). There was also curiosity about the extremely straight, geometrical and patently non-natural, national boundaries of most of the African states. Only later did I realise just how arbitrary and 'sharp', in every sense, was the mid-nineteenth-century 'carving up' of Africa by Western European powers. Now, however, I am constantly reminded of the long-term consequences for the self-(in)sufficient (non-)economic development of many of these nations in the modern world. On a still grander scale, there is the understandable but still unsettling fact that most maps of the world before the early twentieth century were made by Western Europeans with an eye to Western Europe as the **centre**, visually as well as figuratively. After all, if you think the world revolves around you, that's how you draw it. More technically, the traditional 'Mercator' (conical) projection of the globe, dominant from the seventeenth century, had a strong tendency to exaggerate the relative size of Western Europe. More recent projections such as that by Winckel represent the world more accurately in terms of actual land area. The effect has been to shrink Western Europe to less than half its former size relative to, say, Russia or Africa. On large-scale maps Britain almost disappears completely.

In all these ways, through processes of renaming and remapping, Western Europeans have left their marks, both physical and figurative, on the shape of the modern post/colonial world. To be sure, post-independence governments were often quick to *re*-rename their countries and cities, even if they couldn't always do much about the actual redrawing of their borders. Thus Rhodesia (named after Sir Cecil Rhodes) was renamed Zimbabwe; Salisbury its capital was renamed Harare; though these were only two of the previous local options. 'South West Africa' was named 'Namibia'; though this had no exact relation to any preceding cultural–political configuration. Each one of these acts of (re)naming and (re-)mapping, whether by colonisers or de-colonisers, is thus historically highly specific and motivated by politically distinct agendas. One thing is clear about all of these processes, however. The signs on buildings, roads and maps may change and even 'return', but they never point to exactly the same places or peoples. The pointing is always going on in a different social context and historical moment. This is a principle that applies as much to actual signs as to notional ones. Issues of renaming and remapping, whether understood literally or metaphorically, are also central to such activities as **translation** and **travel-writing** (see Mapping journeys, 5.4.2 and Translations/Transformations, 5.4.3).

White selves and black others: some cases of mis-, under- and non-representation

In general terms, we tend to brace a sense of our **selves** against our sense of everyone and everything else we are not (i.e. **others**). In ethnic terms, this means that specific cultural groups tend to define themselves by reference to other groups they are not. Thus a Jew is aware s/he is not a Gentile; a Christian is aware s/he is not a Jew or Moslem. And countless British jokes sport with the supposed differences between 'this Englishman, this Irishman, this Scotsman and this Welshman'. Of course, the basis of all such distinctions is ethnic stereotypes of a generally negative but occasionally positive kind: the Jew may be God-fearing or God-challenging, family-minded or acquisitive; the Scot may be wildly drunken or a hyper-sober Presbyterian, generous or mean; and so on. Add physiological features to these caricatures and you quickly get racial stereotyping (the sallow-faced, hook-nosed Jew; the fierily red-haired Scot).

There are obviously deeply psychological as well as social dimensions to these processes. The person who reckons her- or himself to be 'pure white' has necessarily only been able to do this by taking on board an equally extreme image of 'pure black'. S/he is thus totally locked into a process of self-definition which actually needs the 'other' to maintain the fixed dynamic of that definition. The inverse applies, of course. 'Pure black' consciousness (i.e. *negritude*) actually needs an internalised and externalised sense of 'pure whiteness' to maintain *its* self-definition.

'WHITE'	*'BLACK'*
civilisation (*corruption*)	barbarism (*innocence*)
culture (*as repression*)	nature (*back to true*)
soul (*trapped in* body)	body (*expresses soul*)
Christian (*v. Christian v. Jew v. Islam*)	heathen (*other religions*)
God (the *vengeful father*)	devils (*other gods*)
reason (*narrow rationalism*)	feeling (*intuition*)
intellectual (*cerebral*)	sensual (*in touch with body*)
mental activity (*white collar*)	manual activity (*worker*)
sexual restraint (*repressed*)	sexual freedom (*expressed*)
cleanliness (*obsessive*)	dirt (*natural*)
science (*inhuman*)	superstition (*folk wisdom*)
medicine (*mechanical*)	magic (*holistic*)
classical music & dance	popular music & dance
print culture (*lifeless*)	oral culture (*lively*)
reserved (*up-tight*)	savage ('*cool*')
self (*as other*)	other (*as self*)
culturally 'normal'	'ethnic'
familiar	exotic
intellectual games	athletics
'First' World	'Third' World
'Rich North'	'Poor South'
computing & hypermedia	print literacy
developed, independent	underdeveloped, dependent
future . . .	past . . .

Figure 3.3 Dominant colonial and neo-colonial mind-sets (*and some muted alternatives*)

Similar processes are at work when people talk approvingly or disapprovingly of someone or something as being, say, 'English through and through', 'all-American', 'genuinely Russian' or 'typically Japanese'. In all these cases, there is some strongly implied obverse ('not at all English', 'un-American', etc.) which underwrites the observation.

The model offered in Figure 3.3 shows a dominant Western European mind-set and cultural frame. This model is deeply embedded in colonialism and persists in modified form into postcolonialism. Such binary oppositions are commonly invoked or implied when people adopt a simplistically 'black-and-white' approach to ethnicity. (Some 'muted' mind-sets and cultural frames are supplied italicised in brackets. These point to alternative views that were and are available; though notice that these too may easily become polarised.) The first polarities are chiefly identified with the earlier stages of empire. The later ones are more recent and demonstrate just how remarkably resilient and pervasive such modes of thinking, seeing and saying can be.

It was a founding axiom of European colonialism, and one of the declared rationales of its civilising mission, that 'the black man is the white man's burden'. The dominant polarities featured obviously underwrite this view of the coloniser as basically a helper, nurturer and guide for the colonised. Such polarities also clearly extend from the colonial to the postcolonial and neo-colonial worlds (in 'Third World/Development Aid' programmes, for instance). At the same time we must recognise the complex relations between these black-and-white oppositions and those identified with, for instance, masculine and feminine (see GENDER STUDIES, p. 165) and upper (or middle) class and working class. Thus even in terms of crudely dominant discourses, there are complications in the ways we must frame notions of race and ethnicity. These frames must be superimposed on those relating to sexuality and gender, class and rank, as well as education, religion, region, and the like. In short, even leaving aside the matter of actual times, places and names, it makes a huge difference whether we think of a white or a black person as, say, female, middle class and Muslim or male, working class and Christian. And of course the complications multiply prodigiously once we add in 'muted' and 'alternative' dimensions of all these superimposed and, in reality, ceaselessly shifting frames (for related work on other kinds of multicultural, political and philosophical **difference**, see MARXISM, FEMINISM and POSTSTRUCTURALISM).

How to practise postcolonial approaches in a multicultural world

General frames

Begin by putting yourself 'on the map', both geographically and historically. Where in the world are you? Where did your family and people you know come from – when, where and why? What, for instance, was their likely relation to the 'slave-trade triangle' between Britain, Africa and the Caribbean/Americas? (See the maps in Appendix D and Activity (b) in 1.1 for detailed suggestions.) More particularly, consider:

♦   *the various phases of post/colonialism (including neo-colonialism) in which you are directly or indirectly implicated.* How far do you identify yourself with coloni*ser*s or with coloni*sed*? within or beyond the British Isles, Western Europe, America, Australia? within or beyond whatever centre(s) you identify as 'home'?

♦   *the kinds and degrees of multiculturalism in which you are directly or indirectly implicated because you live where, when and how you do.* Representatives of what ethnic and other cultural groups do you routinely (or rarely) come into contact with? Which do you only know through the media (TV, films, newspapers, magazines)?

Go on to reflect upon the kinds of LANGUAGE you use and the kinds of LITERATURE you are studying with an eye and ear to their post/colonial and multicultural implications:

♦ *What* **varieties** *of English (including accents and dialects) do you use? What* **standard** *do you identify with* – British, American, Indian, Caribbean, etc.?
♦ *Would you categorise the texts you are currently studying nationally, internationally or in some other way* (e.g. as English or American or Australian Literature; Literature in English; English Studies; Comparative (Commonwealth, Postcolonial) Literature; Women's Writing; Literary or Textual Studies)?

Specific text

Notice that versions of the above questions can be put to any text, whether or not it has an obviously post/colonial, ethnic or multicultural dimension to it. (Revising views of what is obvious is itself part of the project.)

Where in the world did – and does – the text come from? Who wrote or produced it – for whom, where, when, why and how? *Is it noticeably ethnocentric* (e.g. Anglo-, Euro-, Afrocentric) in the people and places it represents, or in the communicative and media circles in which it moves?
  (All the following questions may focus initially on ethnicity; but they should be extended and complicated so as to acknowledge other differences of class, rank, gender, sexuality, age and education, etc.):

♦ *Which persons or peoples are centred, marginalised or ignored – geographically and socially?* Do you feel that any group is over-, under-, mis- or un-represented? (What if roles were reversed, say, or background figures were moved to the foreground?)
♦ *Are racial or ethnic stereotypes reinforced or challenged?* For instance, how far do physiological build and physical appearance (complexion, hair, bone structure, dress, body language) support a particular cultural 'placing' and, perhaps, moral evaluation? Who are realised as 'selves' – near and known, familiar and perhaps 'normal'? And who are realised as 'others' – far and foreign, unfamiliar and perhaps exotic or grotesque?
♦ *How far does the text seem to assume or assert some of the dominant 'black-and-white' polarities presented above* (e.g. culture v. nature; reason v. feeling; science v. superstition; Christian v. heathen)? And how far does it seem to offer 'muted' positions, or explore genuinely alternative possibilities (perhaps by shifting or completely switching the terms of the argument)?
♦ *Are there any genres or cultural frames of reference which are unfamiliar to you?* For instance, are there any distinctions between or confusions of, say, literature and performance, story and history, or fiction and fact, which you find striking? And are there stories, myths, legends, religious imagery, world-views you've never encountered before?
♦ *How might you interpret (and perhaps even rewrite) the text so as to make its post/colonial and multi/cultural dimensions more – or differently – 'obvious'?* Because every text is always already in some sense both post/colonial and multi/cultural, this is quite properly a matter not only of the initial writing but also of subsequent reading and rewriting.

Example

Read Billy Marshall-Stoneking's 'Passage' (5.4.2) with the accompanying notes and above questions and suggestions in mind. Then compare your responses to those below.

'In' but not 'of' English. The first thing that strikes me about this text is that English is being talked about as an optional medium. The act of using it is commented upon explicitly and thereby foregrounded: 'The oldest man . . . speaks to me in English'; 'We speak to each other in English'. Implicitly, somewhere in the background, is the sense that another language might be used, one that would not prompt such surprise, one that would perhaps suit 'the oldest man in the world' and the occasion better. And yet, because this text is written in English, we are reading and understanding it. It is still proving serviceable. English brings you and me and the narrator and the oldest man into contact. We understand them – after a fashion. But perhaps only after a fashion. For the strong implication of the poem, reinforced by the notes, is that the 'other', unmentioned yet potentially more expected, language is 'Aboriginal'. That, clearly, is the culture *of* which the oldest man speaks, albeit *through* the verbal medium of another.

But there are other signs of an interplay of cultures: apparently slight yet subtle intimations of sights and sensations. From the very first line our attention is drawn to the seemingly unexceptional fact that 'The oldest man in the world wears shoes'. To you and me, who probably wear them most of the time, this is nothing strange. Yet again, as with the insistent presence of 'English', the foregrounding of 'shoes' presence implies a significant absence. Other footwear maybe? Or perhaps rather, again taking our cue from the notes and any other cultural knowledge we have of these traditionally far-roaming, fast-moving peoples, the fact that we might expect no shoes at all. The implied absence is most likely bare feet. The same presumably goes for the fact that 'He rides in motor cars'. Notice that it doesn't say he 'drives' or 'has' (i.e. owns) a car, but that he 'rides' in them, as though there is a certain distance between him and the machine. (This distance is confirmed by the use of the more formal, now archaic phrase 'motor car'.) The oldest man's relation to motor cars evidently involves neither control nor possession – simply use. Presumably it's the poet's car. At the same time, the oldest man seems perfectly capable of handling it all. He even, in his own way, seems to be totally in harmony with the machine; or at least well able to resist and respond to it: 'He rides in motor cars. / His body: fluid, capable – a perfect shock absorber.'

Re-mapping hi/story. Meanwhile, we too are in for some shocks as, in the company of this pair, 'we bounce over the dirt track in the back / of a four-wheel drive'. For this may not just be a 'dirt track' that the four-wheel drive is bouncing 'over'. The oldest man has already begun to 'name . . . Names'. Perhaps there is something we are missing – or messing up.

> 'That tree is a digging stick
> left by the giant woman who was looking for honey ants;
> That rock, a dingo's nose;
> There, on the mountain, is the footprint
> left by Tjangara on his way to Ulamburra;
> Here the rockhole of Warnampi – very dangerous – '

And so he 'names Names' and, in effect, re-maps the landscape for his listener in the car. And incidentally for us too. Perhaps it is we who are the lucky ones because this is not in an Aboriginal language but in English. This way we can follow the 'Passage'. It leads us through legends otherwise almost certainly inaccessible to us; and it leads us to a vision of the landscape, both physical and mythical, we could not otherwise have. Because for me certainly, and for you quite probably, none of these 'Names' and none of these stories is familiar. We therefore have to piece meanings together, to make some coherent sense of plants ('That tree'); minerals ('That rock'); animals ('a dingo's nose'); people ('the giant woman', 'Tjangara'); places ('Ulamburra', 'Warnampi' – or are these personal names too?). To us such traces may be barely decipherable. We have no frame of shared story or history in which to place them. We do not even know how many, if any, of these legends are based on what we would distinguish as story (anthropomorphic myth, folktale, fable) or history (the oral record, albeit refashioned, of some actual settlement, some actual events). Indeed, we cannot at all be sure whether or how well our conventional Western distinctions between 'story' and 'history' will hold up in this world. For this is a kind of oral narrative, and perhaps a mix of 'hi/story' Westerners are not now familiar with (though its principles would probably have been familiar enough to the Anglo-Saxons and the Native American Indians who sang and listened to their own legends, histories and lore). Moreover, those casually assumed categories 'mineral', 'plant', 'animal', 'place', 'person', may also turn out to be impositions of alien, or at least inappropriate, mind-sets and cultural frames. For the general drift and continuous flow of the hi/story we are being told and the whole shape and shift of the landscape we are having fashioned for us may suggest some quite different world-sense: one in which it is the intuited wholeness – not the analytical discreteness – that is being rehearsed and realised.

Tell-tale singsong. In fact, it is through this verbal rehearsal that all this – and this sense of 'allness' – is being realised. The world is being given coherent shape, meaning and purpose by the very act of telling the tale. The landscape is being, in every sense, 'animated' by the teller – even as the features of that landscape act as prompts for him in the telling:

> 'This is the power of the Song.
> Through the singing we keep everything alive;
> through the songs the spirits keep us alive.'

This is, then, a reciprocal, symbiotic relationship. The Song keeps everything alive; while the singer (and by extension singers-along and listeners) are all part of the 'us' that 'the spirits' through the songs 'keep alive'. It is a model of the world and a function of singing many people in the West are not now very familiar with. It is a hi/story within a poem – and perhaps a science within an art – that we may therefore learn a lot from.

Old worlds for new. But of course there is not one 'we' but at least two. There's the 'we' within the poem (the oldest man and his interlocutor, the poet-narrator) and there's you and me and other people outside it. Certainly, in a crucial imaginative sense, for the duration of our reading of the poem, we all bob along as a kind of capacious, collective 'we': 'We bump along together in the back of the truck . . . We speak to each other in English.' 'We' all do in some sense communicate, we share things. At the same time, 'we' are all of us in some crucial respects different. In the poem, for instance, 'The oldest man in the world' is distinguished from 'the newest man in the world'. And the latter acknowledges that 'my place [is] less exact than his'. Perhaps the newest man is literally on unfamiliar terrain, lost even. But perhaps, too, he feels himself to be more lost in the world – or at least less sure of his 'place' in the one they are currently in – than his older companion. And here again the supplementary notes, including a very brief biography, might help us refine, point and 'locate' our interpretation. Billy Marshall-Stoneking is an American who has adopted and adapted Australian, especially Aboriginal, ways. Perhaps, then, what he is making us privy to is his own sense of dislocation, inadequacy even, when confronted by an 'older' member of one of the ethnic groups he is beginning to identify with. After all, it seems that the poet-listener, like us, needs to be told these things about the land/spirit-scape he is in. Maybe he knows more of the myths, legends and hi/stories than you or I do. But he evidently knows much less than 'the oldest man' he listens to. We may therefore be left wondering a variety of things by the end of the poem. For by now the last lines have built up a stronger pressure behind them, and acquired a more subtly ambiguous resonance than the first time we met versions of them near the beginning:

> We speak to each other in English
> over the rumble of engine, over the roar of the wheels.
> His body: a perfect shock absorber.

Maybe the oldest man has an effective way of dealing not only with the rumble and roar of the car, but also with the 'rumble' and 'roar' of modern Western life. We have already been told explicitly by him that 'the Dreaming does not end; it is not like the whiteman's way'. So very likely the shock his body is able to absorb is the 'shock of the new' (to use Toffler's phrase) as well as the literal bump and bounce of motor cars. And very likely it is this quality of resilience as well as the sense of being sure of the world and one's place in it that the poet-listener admires and perhaps even wishes to emulate.

Also see: CULTURE, COMMUNICATION, MEDIA; key terms p. 186; @ 3.8.

READING: *Introductory*: Ashcroft, Griffiths and Tiffin 2000; Boehmer 2005. *Core texts*: Hurston, Hughes, Fanon, Achebe, Ngugi, Said, Anderson, Spivak, Christian, Smith, Bhabha, Gates, hooks, Gilroy, Hardt and Negri in Leitch 2010; *also* Brathwaite, Morrison, Anzaldua, Loomba, Okonkwo in Rivkin and Ryan 2004. *Anthologies and readers*: Williams and Chrisman 1993 (postcolonial); Ashcroft, Griffiths and Tiffin 2002 (postcolonial); Gates and McKay 2005 (African American); *Advanced*: Quayson 2011; Parry 2004; Diedrich, Gates and Pedersen 1999 ('Middle Passage' / Slave Trade Triangle); Sollors 2008 (ethnic Modernism); Young 2004 (reader); Tuhiwai Smith 1999 (research methodologies).

3.9   THE NEW ECLECTICISM? ETHICS, AESTHETICS, ECOLOGY . . .

If you are seeking a fresh and powerful theoretical synthesis, a combination of ethical, aesthetic and ecological perspectives may help. This may not be the particular configuration you want, but it will remind you of how approaches can be critically recombined and even created. These are steps towards a – if not the – 'new eclecticism'.

The aim of this final section is not to have the last word on theory. But it is to put in a word (four of them, in fact) for certain ways of going about things. It is offered as a contribution to a continuing conversation on what theorising the subject (and being a subject who actively theorises) is and may yet be. It also seeks in various ways to 'see through' the current Post-positions (Poststructuralism, Postmodernism, Postcolonialism, Post-theory) with their predominant sense of belatedness, of being 'after' rather than 'during' or 'before' the event. Above all this is an invitation to readers to review and reconfigure the options for themselves, while also cueing some of the key terms and topics in Part Four.

The kind of **eclecticism** referred to here is not really another '-ism'. It is not a distinct movement, model or even method. Rather, it is the pragmatic activity of gathering and selecting, refining and adapting, whatever tools and techniques work with the materials and task in hand. The root is Greek *ekleigin*, meaning 'to select' or 'to elect', which are the Latin forms that came into English. 'Eclectics' was the name for a loose association of early Greek philosophers (second and first centuries BCE) distinguished by their attempts to synthesise a variety of idealist and materialist philosophies (Aristotelian, Platonic, Stoic, Epicurean); and they were praised or censured depending whether the effort was judged worthwhile. 'Being eclectic', it should be observed, is still considered a good or a bad thing. Again it all depends whether the results are reckoned significant and satisfying. By definition, therefore, the present eclecticism is only 'new' in so far as it helps draw attention to existing practices that are readily recognised but usually unacknowledged. For the fact is that virtually all the most powerful and persuasive contemporary approaches turn out to be mixtures, compounds or hybrids and, however principled, in some measure 'impure' – in a word eclectic. Examples are the convergence of psychoanalytic, postmodern and poststructural perspectives in a nominally 'postcolonial' critic such as Bhabha, with feminist and Marxist inflections in another nominally 'postcolonial' critic such as Spivak;

or the capacious theoretical resource and nimble rhetoric of such opponents and proponents of Postmodernism as, say, Eagleton and Jameson (avowedly Marxist) and Hutchcon and Weedon (avowedly Feminist). All these writers are eclectic in that they continue to refine and develop – they do not simply impose – their particular syntheses. The present reader is enjoined to do the same.

Ethics is a handy, hold-all term for systematic attention to matters of right and wrong, responsibility, justice, and, by extension, all kinds of **value**. At its broadest ethics embraces moral and cultural 'atmosphere' or 'ethos' (whence ethics). All approaches to the subject are inevitably ethical in so far as their practitioners propose or presuppose a better rather than a worse way of looking at and doing things. In the case of overtly social-historical approaches such as Marxism, Feminism and Postcolonialism, the ethical imperative is linked to more or less explicit political agendas associated with class, gender, sexuality, race and ethnicity. In the case of more narrowly text-based approaches such as New Criticism, Formalism and Post-structuralism (especially deconstruction), the ethical dimension is usually implicit in attitudes to verbal devices and textual structures: what counts as coherent and unified, or as acceptably discontinuous and heterogeneous. Meanwhile, the most persistent general rationale for the reading and study of LITERATURE is fundamentally ethical as well as aesthetic: that it cultivates a sense of imaginative tolerance, a capacity to see many points of view; reading 'opens up horizons' and 'broadens the mind'. To be sure, such an argument has its problems: not all students and teachers of English are automatically full of sweetness and light. (The commandants of the Nazi death camps, we should recall, still enjoyed high art.) None the less, it is a widely held conviction that the very process of seriously engaging with complex and demanding work is inherently good for you. Bakhtin, for example, argues that the capacity to be fully responsive to a work (i.e. 'response-able') also helps readers sharpen their sense of 'responsibility' (see p. 276), and related arguments are made by many critics committed to Reader Response and Reception Aesthetics (see **writing and reading, response and rewriting**). Some such positions are held by defenders and proponents of liberal – and liberating – education as various as Ricoeur, Nussbaum, Hillis Miller, Kearney and Levinas (see Reading below).

Meanwhile, in pragmatic approaches to LANGUAGE there is a long-standing engagement with issues of power and responsibility. The teaching of RHETORIC, for instance, whether ancient or modern, directly addresses the relation between information and persuasion. In ancient Greece and Rome this was in the context of oratory and an oligarchy, which excluded women and depended on slave labour. Today it is more likely to be in the context of a broader-based democracy with communications dominated by the multi-media. But both kinds of Rhetoric are expressly concerned with what it means, in the fullest sense, to use language 'well' or 'badly': in the ethical service of what is true and good and not just for aesthetically pleasing effects and politically expedient ends. Similar concerns are expressed in current movements such as Critical Discourse Analysis and Critical Language Awareness (Hodge and Kress, Fairclough, Tannen, Cameron and others) and, latterly, Ethical Linguistics (especially Wales). There are two main areas of attention:

♦ *Critical awareness of the ideological implications of using certain words, structures and varieties of language.* This includes (a) sensitivity to sexual and racial discrimination in language, and recognition of the loaded nature of such choices as 'terrorist/freedom-fighter', 'fanatic/believer/infidel', 'we/they', 'them/us', etc.; (b) a grasp of the implications of grammatical structure when identifying causes, attributing agency and assigning responsibility for actions and events (notably the differences among active/passive, transitive/intransitive, nominalised and verbalised structures; see Appendix A); and (c) awareness that sometimes simply using a technically specialist variety of language – even a particular language (English, say) – may serve to exclude some interested parties while consolidating the power of others. In this respect **translation**, both broadly and narrowly conceived, between specialist varieties as well as between whole languages, is a crucial issue. As it is in . . .

♦   *Conduct of interviews, consultations and negotiations; the drafting of contracts, agreements, records and other official documents.* Such activities are particularly significant in legal, medical, educational and other professional or bureaucratic encounters (getting a job or advice, receiving treatment, being legally sentenced, resolving a dispute, etc.); but they arise in any **discourse** situation where information and opinion need to be elicited, facts established and action taken. In such cases it is acutely obvious that speech *acts*: it has real, serious and sometimes life-threatening or -saving consequences. The crucial consideration is how far the COMMUNICATION is one-, two- or many-way (i.e. based upon **monologue** or **dialogue**), and whether the controlling dynamic is conceived as 'top-down', 'bottom-up' or 'across' (e.g., expert–lay, doctor–patient, police–suspect, lecturer–student, provider–customer, citizen–citizen, person–person). With written and printed documents there is the added matter of specialised literacy skills (legal, financial, medical, etc.) and the technology used in recording and retrieving information. Meanwhile, underpinning all of these activities are processes of official certification and professional accreditation. Linguistically, these have a palpably performative dimension to them: you can't be an officially recognised doctor, lawyer, teacher or whatever unless you have the appropriate 'bit of paper'. Documents such as passports, visas and work-permits can in some circumstances be essential to survival as well as employment.

In all these ways, language not only reflects and underwrites but in effect enacts and embodies power relations. Words are tools or weapons and may be wielded in ways that are more or less ir/responsible and more or less un/just. They are at the very heart of processes of legitimation and validation, and are therefore subject to covert control and connivance, as well as being the objects of open re-negotiation and re-valuation.

But values are shifting and complex, and one kind of value judgement tends to get mixed up with another. As a result, any approach to language and/or literature tends to entail not only a particular ethics but also a particular **aesthetics**. That is, for better and worse, the sense of what is good or bad *ethically* (morally, politically) tends to get mixed up with a sense of what is good or bad *aesthetically* (formally, perceptually). There is therefore a fundamental, and often undeclared, ambiguity about virtually all talk of 'good' or 'bad' writing, as of 'good' or 'bad' art. Does this mean writing that is morally good or bad for you? technically good or bad in its execution? a good or bad **representation** or **image** of something that already exists in the world (and therefore in some sense in/accurate or in/adequate)? a good or bad **performance** or work of **imagination** in its own right, and therefore un/successful at creating its own world? or a mixture of all of these? To be sure, casual talk of 'good' and 'bad' writing or art can be confusing and unproductive; it smacks of dilettantism and idle opinionating. However, careful consideration of the interrelations among various kinds of value is absolutely essential if there is to be any sense of an integrated subject as well as any claim to integrity in its study.

Aesthetics, importantly, can carry its broadly plural and ultimately radical sense of 'study of the conditions of sensuous perception' (the meaning favoured by Kant, from the Greek root *aisthetes*, 'those who perceive through the senses'). Conversely, 'the Aesthetic' need not be limited to the narrower, essentially singular sense of 'the idea of the beautiful' that underwrote the predominantly elitist and escapist 'art for art's sake' movement of the late nineteenth century. All that will be added here is that it is tempting to venture some kind of compound approach to value that we might call 'Aesth-ethics'. The emphasis then is upon the tensions within and between various value systems, their points of convergence as well as divergence. 'Aesth-ethically' speaking, for instance, we may observe that many of the critical approaches reviewed in previous sections entail a distinctive aesthetics as well as ethics. (Put another way, each has a distinctive poetics as well as politics.) NEW CRITICISM, for instance, celebrates certain kinds of textual 'wholeness' and 'unity' produced by the paradoxical resolution of 'tensions' and 'ambiguities'. It tends to be neo-classical and 'High' Modernist in temper and conservative in politics, and works best with lyric poetry and shorter fiction. Traditional forms of MARXISM, however – represented by Lukács and Goldmann – are dedicated to 'totalising' and 'world-historical' visions of social reality built along lines of class-conflict; they tend to favour large-scale, encyclopaedic fiction in a realist mode. Meanwhile, more experimental forms of Marxism and CULTURAL MATERIALISM (represented by Brecht and Benjamin) are far more committed to fragmented and discontinuous dramatic and narrative forms (even when nominally 'epic'); and they propose a more dynamically revolutionary vision of political change through 'shock' and 'making strange'. FORMALISTS, on the other hand, may concern themselves chiefly with perceptual defamiliari-sation and linguistic deviation; but they rarely take the turn back from form to function, and text to context enjoined by their FUNCTIONALIST successors. POSTSTRUCTURALISTS and POSTMODERNISTS, likewise, may in various ways be politically elusive, submissive or subversive. It all depends how far the instability of the **subject** is conceived as an individual, collective or collaborative matter and whether the play of **difference** in verbal, intertextual and cross-media space is merely self-reflexive or prompts critical reflection on the world beyond. Finally, FEMINIST and POSTCOLONIAL approaches are particularly notable for the wide range of ethical-aesthetic and political-poetic agendas they address; also the sheer variety of theories and disciplines they draw upon and reconfigure. They are therefore 'eclectic' in the fullest, most flexible and contentious sense of the word. So is the approach – and final key term – featured next.

   Ecology is the study of the evolving interrelations among natural – including human – systems, also the systems themselves. The 'eco-' part derives from Greek *oikos*, meaning 'household' or 'home', a root which ecology shares with *economics* (in which case all economics is in some sense 'home economics'). The difference is that eco*logy* designates 'study', 'knowledge' or 'understanding' (from Greek *logos*) whereas eco*nomics* designates 'control', 'management' or 'direction' (from Greek *nomia*). The persistent challenge, in fact, is to bring the two together to produce a kind of 'understanding-management' or 'knowledgeable-control': economics informed by ecological awareness, and an ecology that is economically viable. Crucially, this depends upon the definitions of 'household' or 'home', and a recognition that these differ from culture to culture and vary over time. (For the crucial learning cycle Library, web, 'home' see 1.2.5.) The Latin counterpart of Greek *oikos* was *habitus*, which also carried a range of senses from 'human habitation' to 'natural habitat'. In Darwin's *The Origin of Species* (1859), for instance, 'inhabitants' is regularly used to refer to any organism – human, animal or plant – that occupies a common space. For the Greeks, *oikos* was a similarly capacious and flexible concept. At the very least it covered everyone 'under the same roof' and, so to speak, 'held by the same house' (not just the householder as the nominal owner of the property). More generally, it embraced not only the immediate, 'nuclear' family of parents and children and the larger, 'extended' family of grandparents, uncles, aunts and cousins etc., but also the servants and slaves as well as the livestock and the attached gardens and fields. All belonged to and were identified with the *oikos*. This was therefore a model of community based not just upon blood and family ties but on a sense of place and shared space. Nor was it limited to humans; though it was certainly centred on human social organisation. The combined human–animal, house–field sense of the archaic notion of 'eco-'/*oikos* (like that of Latin *habitus*) is worth stressing. For it is often casually assumed that ecology is simply a faddish word for biology or nature and, conversely, that economics is a purely human affair. In reality, however, the two activities are intimately and intricately interconnected. They are deeply coloured by the politics of their particular historical moment, too. As already mentioned, Greek 'households' were organised hierarchically in terms of men, women and slaves; just as Roman 'households' were circumscribed by notions of citizenship and empire. Modern 'ecology' movements may be aligned with the 'green' politics of a just and sustainable global economy based on 'fair' rather than 'free' trade. But similar arguments may be appropriated, especially by advertisers, to underwrite a mere back-to-nature 'organic' lifestyle for the rich who consume – not the poor who produce.

That said, the implications for a fully ecological–economic grasp of the subject (in principle any subject) are prodigious. The central focus then becomes a complex phenomenon we might call *humanity-in-nature* and *nature-in-humanity* (rather than, say, *human nature* viewed as a separate and privileged entity in a narrowly Humanistic sense); and the main issues have to do with kinds of relation and interchange, and dynamic processes of evolution and becoming (rather than, say, essence, identity and fixed states of being). Radical Ecology therefore shares with POSTSTRUCTURALISM a concern with the interrelations amongst notionally whole systems in so far as these are perceived to be open and in process and to have indeterminate or multiple centres. It shares with POSTMODERNISM a concern with the human/nature/technology interface; with FEMINISM and Queer Studies a concern with the 'naturalness' or otherwise of current models of both GENDER and SEXUALITY (especially the nature of the body, reproduction and contraception); and with POSTCOLONIALISM a concern with what it is to be 'native' and have 'roots' or a sense of 'belonging' or, conversely, what it is to be 'rootless' or '*en route*' – displaced, migratory or nomadic – moved by a sense of 'longing'. The three main strands of the present section may therefore be woven together thus:

- ◆ **Ethics** is concerned with principles of justice, right and responsibility that lay claim to some degree of common and ultimately universal applicability – whether based on shared reason, humanity, the sanctity of life, humility before god or death, or scientific laws. Crucially, such principles are always tested and put to the proof by contact, often collision, with values and belief systems that are relatively local and historically specific but which themselves often claim to be absolute.

- ◆ **Aesthetics** is concerned with the realisation of kinds of wholeness and satisfaction in perception and experience, commonly expressed as a tension between gestures towards some ultimate totality or infinity on the one hand and immediate impulses towards finite yet intensely charged particulars on the other. This may also involve the tension between a formal aesthetic that claims some kind of ideal purity and unity, and various functional aesthetics that are felt in practice to be irreducibly plural and concrete.

- ◆ **Ecology**, meanwhile, is concerned with an integrated, notionally holistic view of human–natural systems, even though at any point in time or space these systems – whether nominally organic or mechanical – are seen to be open and evolving. They are in process of becoming yet other systems.

There are two things, then, that characterise all these projects: (i) a concern with kinds of wholeness and universality and with values that are in some measure held in common; (ii) a recognition that values differ and vary, and are arrived at by processes of valuation that involve conflict as well as cooperation. Hence the persistent need for methods that are capacious and flexible, generous yet principled. Hence, here, the argument for a kind of **eclecticism** the defining characteristic of which is precisely the attempt to gather a whole host of different approaches and synthesise them in ways that are significant and satisfying. Though it should be added that this is necessarily always in some way unique to each person and occasion. And, of course, the present reader may have objections to all of this. Isn't it limply 'liberal' or merely 'pragmatic'? or perhaps far too 'radical'? or simply, most tellingly – with the emphasis on the negative –

eclectic?! But that's fine too. For you will then have to state clearly just what your own grounds for gathering, selecting and synthesising materials and methods and models are – and if not *ethically*, *aesthetically* and *ecologically* in the present senses, then in others you prefer. And if not these terms, then yet others of your own finding and fashioning. For there are plenty to choose from in the previous sections, and plenty more in the next part of the book. Equally importantly, there are plenty *not* in this book and, perhaps most important, some *not yet* in any book or essay or discussion at all. Unless or until, that is, someone decides to write or say them. You, for instance.

Returning to English Studies in particular, we see that many of these issues have been around in one form or another for a long time. A fundamentally ethical commitment to the cultivation of discriminating judgement and powers of right action, over and above mere matters of taste and appreciation, is a persistent strain in the subject. This is a project to which figures as various as Arnold, Richards, Leavis, Williams, Eagleton, Haraway and Spivak all contribute, albeit with radically different aims and agendas. Meanwhile a broadly ecological concern with human/nature and people/place relations is a deep-rooted and perennial feature of the subject, implicit in some of its Classical origins and explicit in much of its Romantic legacy. What follows, therefore, is a kind of 'ecological' checklist of terms and topics. It is dedicated to what might be called (somewhat cumbersomely) *re-valuations and re-presentations* of *people in place in time*. But really, like all the other checklists, if it helps prompt some exploration and argument it will have served its turn. (Notice that the questions and suggestions that follow can – and in some ways must – be addressed to yourself and to others as well as to the text in hand. For those are properly ecological and eclectic moves, too.)

◆ *Household, family and community* (*oikos* and *habitus*). Are the 'households' based on property, land, rank, blood ties, friendship, occupation? and are they with or without servants, animals, etc.? Are the families one-parent, nuclear, extended . . . ? What of the other overlapping communities based on street, neighbourhood, farm, village, work, recreation, network, etc.? Overall, is there a sense of 'home' or 'homelessness', literal or metaphorical? (In the work of the Brontës, for instance, most famously in *Jane Eyre* and *Wuthering Heights* (see 2.2.3), it is the larger household, including such figures as adopted relatives, servants and governesses, that is the primary social unit and focus; it is not 'family' in a narrowly blood-based, and still less a modern 'nuclear', sense. Thornfield Hall, the Heights and Thrushcross Grange are all more populous and various than the latter alone, and also extend through the buildings to the landscapes beyond.)

◆ *Identity and identification: 'roots' or 'routes'*. Is there a sense of rootlessness or of being '*en route*', perhaps as a migrant or nomad – and is this experienced as a good or bad thing? Relatedly, are there strong identifications between a character and an environment, or a mood and a place? (The latter is sometimes, following Ruskin, negatively referred to as the 'pathetic fallacy'; it may be more positively conceived as the 'genius or spirit of place', *genius loci*.) Alternatively, are there strong antipathies and marked disjunctures between persons and places – perhaps the sense of a hostile environment, whether threatening nature or alienating society? Often, in fact, the dynamic arises from a sense of belonging to – and longing for – different places, times and social spaces. (Slave narratives offer particularly poignant and vexed images of be/longing; but such strains can be traced in virtually all auto/biography and travel writing (see 5.2.2 and 5.4.2) and ultimately in most projections of people in – and out of – place and time; e.g. Wordsworth and Clare, 5.4.1 and 5.3.4.)

◆ *Life and death, time and change, pattern and rhythm*. How are the fundamental cycles of birth, life and death realised? And what of the fundamental activities of eating, drinking, sleeping and sex? Is the passage of time gauged by sun and stars, light and dark, changes of sea or river, the revolving seasons? Or is it tied to work schedules, the social and religious round, clock-time and calendars? (Often, in fact, there is a mixture of 'natural' and 'artificial' cycles in play.) Go on to gauge how far the text not only represents but actually embodies and enacts a certain rhythm or pattern of life (in its formal organisation, for instance); also consider how far this is similar to your own way of life. (An extreme example would be the Seminole chants, 5.1.5, with their ritual celebration and commemoration of human birth and death in terms of the regular turning of the heavens, the seasons and the social round. Another, equally extreme, is Beckett's *Not I*, 5.3.3, in which there is radical uncertainty about what story and history the 'Mouth' tells and how it stands in relation to the rest of its body and life – or indeed whether it is already dead or disembodied.)

♦   *People a part of – or apart from – Nature?* How far is humanity represented as a part of or apart from the rest of nature, in harmony or at odds with it? And is 'Nature' conceived as a hospitable or hostile force? Either way, are natural forces conceived as 'internal' to humanity and generated from within, or 'external' and imposed from without? All this can be expressed in terms of three major and recurrent topics in literary and cultural history:

1   *Versions of pastoral.* Stereotypically, *pastoral* is a **genre** in which shepherds in particular (Latin *pastor* = shepherd) or country-dwellers in general are represented in an idyllically idealised state of simplicity and innocence, far from the complex ills and excesses of court or city. Sometimes this gets inflected in terms of paradisal garden states, before the Fall. Alternatively, country folk are presented as brutal and backward, country bumpkins or boorish peasants. In biblical terms they may live in a wild state of nature, after the expulsion from the Garden of Eden. In social terms, pastoral images of a 'back-to-nature' kind often underwrite a sense of organic community and belonging: 'a place for everyone . . .'. But sometimes this impression is offset by counter-images of nature red in tooth and claw, of primitive life as nasty, brutish and short, and, socially, by an oppressive sense of old-fashioned, semi-feudal hierarchy: '. . . and everyone in their place'. Typically, in many a piece it is the movement *between* these states that drives the plot and informs the main issues. In Shakespeare *The Tempest*, for instance, the ethereal Ariel and the earthy Caliban represent two very different aspects of 'nature' *vis-à-vis* their master, the aristocrat-magician Prospero. Contemporary versions of pastoral on TV include everything from garden 'make-overs' to travel programmes and 'castaway' challenges.)

2   *The city as second nature.* Here alternatives tend to be framed in terms of the delights and distresses of urban living as a whole, without recourse to rural comparisons. Above all it is the capital city, the Metropolis, that is seen as an interlocking system of worlds within worlds, an intricate network of cultures and sub-cultures. Thus, as both myth and lived reality, a city such as London (or Paris or New York or Sydney or Delhi or Tokyo) tends to feature as the hero, the villain, or the chorus of the piece in a variety of ways. There are two extreme views and a host of intermediate permutations. The most persistent scenario or schema is one in which the city is hailed from afar as a place of individual opportunity and social mobility, 'the bright city lights', 'where it's at'. As such, it offers an enticingly cosmopolitan array of high art and popular culture, conspicuous consumption, and the seething busy-ness of a multicultural melting-pot (this is the world in which Baudelaire's and Benjamin's typically male *flâneur* moves as in his natural element – street-wandering and people-watching). But on further acquaintance and reflection the city often turns out to be a place of personal loneliness and social alienation, naked acquisitiveness and financial vulnerability. Its inhabitants are either rootless and restless or fragmented into ghettos, and

they are dogged as much by the threat of the low-life (crime, violence, drugs, vagrancy) as by the tawdry promise of the high-life. (Familiar examples are the urban worlds of Blake's 'London' (2.1.3), Dickens's *Bleak House*, Batman's 'Gotham City' and Irvine Welsh's *Trainspotting*. Moreover, again, it is the clash or transition between these two visions of the city – the rich promise of freedom and opportunity and the bleak threat of decadence or degradation – that serves to motivate the plot, point the theme, and test and reveal character. In Hollinghurst's *The Swimming-Pool Library*, 5.3.4, for example, it is precisely the tension between 'those formative landscapes, the Yorkshire dales, the streams and watermeads of Winchester' and 'the sexed immediacy of London life . . . the sex-sharp little circuits of discos and pubs' that sounds the key-note of a life that is exhilaratingly yet enervatingly divided – superabundant in some ways, mean in others.)

3   *Science Fiction: Utopias and Dystopias*. The genre of Science Fiction has been particularly influential in offering representations of imaginary places that are variously utopian and dystopian. 'Utopia', from Greek *ou-topos*, is strictly 'no-place'. However, following Thomas More's coining of the term for his imaginary travelogue of that name (1516), it has come to mean an imaginary *ideal* place. Dystopia was a term coined later to designate an imaginary *horrible* place. And in fact, depending on one's point of view, most Utopias have a potentially dystopian dimension to them. The challenge is to decide which is which and for whom. Philip K. Dick's *Do Androids Dream of Electric Sheep?*, 5.2.4, for instance – filmed as *Blade Runner* – offers a vision of a world in which it is difficult to tell the difference between humans and machines. Humans may be callous, calculating and lacking in sympathy – in a word 'machine-like'; whereas humanoid robots, androids, may be more 'sensitive' to conditions and simulate human sympathy and desire. Indeed, 'andies', as they are familiarly called, have responsibilities without rights, and duties without legitimate desires; so they tend to excite the sympathy of readers. A similar problem is rehearsed in Mary Shelley's *Frankenstein*, a work centrally concerned with the relation between the obsessed and then disgusted scientist and the wretchedly alienated 'creature' he has fashioned. Moreover, in both Shelley and Dick the finger points squarely at humanity's inhumanity to other humans (slaves, servants, the under-class), while also exposing humanity's ultimate flouting of natural laws and waste of natural resources. Such are the consequences of power without responsibility, economic control without ecological understanding. A related ethical and ecological issue is broached in Le Guin's *The Left Hand of Darkness*, 5.2.4. There we are offered an appealingly Utopian or – depending how you see it – appallingly Dystopian vision of a world in which SEXUALITY is optional and negotiable, as is the responsibility for actually bearing and giving birth to children. On the planet Gethin this happens because there is a physiological and psychological state of 'Kemmer', which can tip to male or female for either party depending on the precise stage and dynamic of the relationship. So either partner can produce an egg and become 'female' for a while. This tendency can also be induced by drugs. For better and worse this is medical engineering and a genetic Utopia/Dystopia in one of its more beguiling guises.

The final two topics relate to issues already raised under POSTCOLONIALISM, particularly in relation to (re-)naming and (re-)mapping (see pp. 191–2). Here they are inflected in ways that are more specifically ecological and ethical, though in any given application no less political and historical. And again questions are addressed not only to the text and task in hand but also to the persons doing the handling. For, as always, it is the resulting dialogue and dynamic *between* text and reader that is most revealing – not one or other as a fixed and isolated point of reference.

♦   *Local and global.* How far is the text conceived – and do you conceive yourself – in pointedly local or broadly global terms? Where does it – and do you – seem to be speaking from and for in the first place? and on further reflection in the last or another place? For even such apparently neutral and neatly balanced terms as *local* and *global* are always loaded. What is judged 'local' (from Latin *locus*, place) can be as big or small, as inclusive or exclusive, as whatever and whoever you choose to 'locate' within it. The local is thus always already implicated in the global (i.e., the planet at large); just as the global is always constituted by a multiplicity of localities. The notion of *global*, meanwhile, like that of 'the world', very much depends upon who is drawing the 'whole' thing, from where and why. (The maps of the Britain, the USA and 'the world' in Appendix D are no exception. Re-visit them and consider which places have been put in or left out and why; also see Local and Global Community @ Prologue.)

♦   *Nation states and international relations.* Is there a markedly or self-consciously 'national' or 'international' dimension to the text – or to the present reader(s)? For 'nation', too, is a loaded term. It shares a root with *native*, meaning 'born somewhere'; and yet not everyone born in a place has equal claim to being a citizen. For *nationality* (i.e. formal citizenship) may be variously inherited or acquired. Meanwhile, *national borders* are where screening takes place; and *national security* and *the national interest* can be invoked to cover everything from internal dissent to external threat, the public good and official secrets, freedom of speech and suppression of information. Against and alongside these 'national' concerns are braced all things 'international': *international* trade, military and political agreements of a more or less binding kind; *international* pressure, understanding and opinion of a more or less informal nature. Moreover, even nominally international organisations (from the United Nations to the International Monetary Fund) include and privilege some nations while excluding and marginalising others. As a result, *inter/national* relations always turn out to be more partial and less comprehensive than they may initially appear. Historically, they are contingent on the development of the modern nation state from the sixteenth to the twentieth centuries; and latterly, increasingly urgently, the development of supplementary or compensatory international bodies. (Such issues are a matter of constant concern in the areas of migration, citizenship and employment; e.g. Tan, 5.2.1. They become horrifically acute in the event of acts of international terrorism and war; see esp. McEwan and Roy, 5.2.5 War on – of – Terror.)

How to practise eclectically . . . ?!

By definition there is no single way of 'being eclectic'. But it is worth considering that your present practice is already likely to be in some measure a mixture (whether deliberate or accidental). It makes sense to develop a more theoretically considered and resourceful array of practices. The following advice builds on that given at the beginning of this part of the book, on 'How (not) to practise approach X' (p. 136).

♦   Draw on any and every available resource – but be selective when drawing them together.

♦   Be prepared to adapt, synthesise and extend – not just adopt, repeat and explain.
Recognise and to some extent respect existing disciplinary boundaries – but be ready to cross and re-draw them at need.

♦   Know that even the most apparently 'pure' theory turns out to be 'mixed' in practice; and even the most apparently 'comprehensive' practice turns out to be theoretically 'partial'. (The present plea for eclecticism is no exception.)

♦   Some theories and practices are certainly better than others – if not absolutely then for particular purposes.

♦　　The 'best' theorising, however – with the emphasis on doing it – is something you have a hand and say in putting together yourself, with others as well as on your own.

Closing words – open discussion

(i)　(a) On my return home, it occurred to me [. . .] that something might perhaps be made out on this question by patiently accumulating and reflecting on all sorts of facts which could possibly have any bearing on it.

　　　　　　Charles Darwin's Introduction to *The Origin of Species* (1859: 1)

　　(b) *The Origin of Species*, with its passionate and intense sympathies, open and inclusive approach to all phenomena, and its seemingly inexhaustible range of applications and concerns, provides a model of the ecological knowledge we continue to need.

　　　　　　Jeff Wallace's Introduction to *The Origin of Species* (1998: xxiii)

(ii)　You could see your own house as a tiny fleck on an ever-widening landscape, or as the center of it all from which the circles expanded into the infinite unknown. [. . .] At the center of what? [. . .] Begin though, not with a continent or a country or a house, but with the geography closest in – the body.

　　　　　　Adrienne Rich, 'Notes Towards a Politics of Location' (Rich 1996; and see @ Prologue)

(iii)　[W]e cannot stand aside from the popular discourse of value. [. . .] Very many language-users hold passionate convictions about what is right in language, and conversely about what is wrong with it. [. . .] we must acknowledge people's genuine concerns about language, understand the desires and fears that lie behind their concerns, and try to work with them not against them.

　　　　　　Deborah Cameron, *Verbal Hygiene* (1995: 235–6)

(iv)　To follow through the question of democratic agency, we need to move towards an analysis of the contradictory identifications of which we are capable. This means turning the search for roots – the desire for a fixed centre of identity – into a search for routes out of the prison-house of marginality,

　　　　　　Kobena Mercer, 'Back to my Routes' (1990) in Procter (2000: 292)

(v)　What are poets for in our brave new millennium? Could it be to remind the next few generations that it is we who have the power to determine whether the earth will sing or be silent?

　　　　　　Jonathan Bate, *The Song of the Earth* (2001: 282)

(vi)　Imagining what it is like to be someone other than yourself is at the core of our humanity. It is the essence of compassion, and it is the beginning of morality.

　　　　　　Ian McEwan, from the *Guardian,* 15 September 2001 (see 5.2.5)

(vii)　We are always in a zone of intensity or flux which is common to [. . .] a very remote global enterprise, to very distant geographical environments.

　　　　　　Gilles Deleuze and Claire Parnet, *Dialogues* (1988: 112)

(viii)   A map of the world that does not include Utopia is not worth even glancing at, for it leaves
out the one country at which Humanity is always landing.
Oscar Wilde, 'The Soul of Man under Socialism', *Intentions* (1891)

READING: Given the **eclectic** nature of the present enterprise, reading should be wide-ranging and open to chance as well as, where appropriate, deep and deliberate. The 'wide-and-close reading' dynamic modelled in 1.2.4 should be pushed up to and beyond current limits; and the cycle of 'Home'/Library/Web modelled in 1.2.5 should be gone through several times in various directions and dimensions. The lines of enquiry and sample study patterns sketched for longer projects in 2.3 suggest some of the ways forward and around, pushed still further in 'English at the edge' @ 2.3. In fact, being deliberately 'eclectic' (i.e. deeply curious *and* wide-ranging *and* selective) is rather more about openness of attitude (you want to see things afresh and from where you are) and about multiplicity of methods (a judicious combination of 'orderly *and* 'chaotic' ones) than about any pre-given substance or content other than an initial interest and provisional focus. Both the latter will and should shift – even switch – as the lines of enquiry multiply and the object of research itself is subject to a project of re-search and re-vision. As a result, all and any of the Readings for the previous theoretical positions/practical approaches can come into play, alongside or against one another. A quick reminder of some powerful prefixes and a preferred verbal suffix may help – as may a table that invades the margins and can be readily extended:

RE-	INTER-	TRANS-	CO- COM- CON-	MULTI-	-ING
(again / afresh)	*(between / among)*	*(across / through)*	*(with / against)*	*(many / multiple)*	B
Re-vision	Inter-view	Trans-port	Co-operate	Multiply	E
Re-member	Inter-pret	Trans-form	Compare. . .	Multi-	C
Re-cycle	Inter-change	Translate	Compete	national	O
Re-search	Interested (dis-)	Transgress	Consent	cultural	M
Re-create	Interesting (un-)	Trans-national	Conflict	disciplinary	I
. . . ?	. . . ?	. . . ?	. . . ?	. . . ?	N
					G . . . ?

Five prefixes and a suffix in search of another word . . .

The result of some such re-vision, interplay (etc.) when brought to bear on particular materials (texts, images, events) will by definition – in the act of defining its peculiar and singular object/subject/project, including some of what was previously ignored or rejected ('abject') – exceed any narrowly mechanical dialectic of *either/or* leading to a more or less predictable synthesis. The synthesi*sing* (again with an emphasis on the *-ing*) will rather be a becoming of *both/and*: *both more than and different from* what was first planned, hypothesised or even imagined.

All that said but never absolutely done, the present 'eclecticism' has been (re)configured from the interplay of three broadly designated and overlapping areas: ethics, aesthetics and ecology. 'New' or 'old' or both and more is for you to decide (in principle, it may be all as 'old as the hills' but still be as 'new' as the particular hills and valleys or plains you inhabit with other people now – which are particularly ugly or beautiful or a mixture or, worst of all, a matter of utter indifference). The following Readings (plural) therefore will be stacked in parallel and may be read across. For a change. To help *Change 'English' Now* again – afresh (see Prelude). Preferably, for the better. As far and as close as you can see. In your own time and place, in your coming to terms with others. It's up and down – and over – to you.

	ETHICAL	AESTHETIC	ECOLOGICAL
Introductory	Palmer 1992 Cameron 1995	Armstrong 2000 Dewey 1954	Garrard 2007 Bate 2001
Core texts	Nussbaum and Levinas in Rice and Waugh 2001 Kristeva and Žižek in Lodge and Wood 2008 Habermas and Bourdieu in Leitch 2010	Certeau and Bordo in Leitch 2010 Kearney and Rasmussen 2001 (Reader) Cazeaux 2000 (Reader)	Buell 1995 Glofelty and Fromm 1996 (Reader) Coupe 2000 (Reader) Williams. Weeks and Buell in Lodge and Wood 2008, Rich and Kincaid in Rivkin and Ryan 2004
Advanced	Haraway 1998 Critchley 1992 Eaglestone 1997 . . .	Joghin and Malpas 2003 Balshaw 1998 Deleuze and Guattari 1982 . . .	Buell 2005 Brooker and Thacker 2003 James 1999; Pepper 1993 Guattari 1992 . . .

KEY TERMS, CORE TOPICS

PART FOUR

PREVIEW

This consists of twenty entries featuring over sixty key terms. These are 'core' topics in that they recur in critical discussions of all kinds and are not the exclusive property of a single model or method. You will therefore find them throughout the book highlighted in bold. Indeed, words such as **author, character, image, poetry, standard(s)** and **text** are central and significant precisely because people either assume what they mean or argue about what they can mean. Paradoxically, then, what is 'common' about such terms is precisely their differences: the different roles they are made to play in various critical discourses. (**Discourse** is also such a term and therefore included too.) Each entry comprises:

- a preliminary definition, usually in the first sentence;
- an indication of the areas of LANGUAGE, LITERATURE and CULTURE, and the various theoretical positions and critical approaches to which it most readily relates (keyed to Parts One and Three);
- further distinctions and qualifications;
- illustrations and activities framed so as to be applicable to any text, but also keyed to the anthology of sample texts in Part Five;
- points for discussion and further reading.

Entries on further key terms and core topics can be found on the companion website @ 4. These are listed at the end of the present part, where you are also invited to gather further entries and build a critical dictionary of your own.

ABSENCE AND PRESENCE, GAPS AND SILENCES, CENTRES AND MARGINS

All the concepts gathered here have to do with the fundamental matter of understanding what *is* there in terms of what *isn't*: gauging the 'thisness' of something against all the 'thatnesses' which it is not. In dialectical terms, this is called the activity of negation. Arguably, all thought involves some such process organised round the double-edged question 'What is/n't it?' However, the concepts featured here have become especially prominent in POSTSTRUCTURALISM and the activity of *deconstruction* in particular.

Derrida has argued that Western thought systems are dominated by the notion of ultimate 'presence' and 'essence'. That is, 'truth' and 'facts' are treated as phenomena that can be positively identified and are ultimately knowable. This contrasts with Eastern thought systems (and some Western philosophical and mystical traditions) where there is greater emphasis on what can *not* be identified and is ultimately *un*knowable. Derrida illustrates this Western preoccupation with presence by observing that most Western philosophers of language, and indeed most linguists, tend to privilege **speech** before **writing**, as though speech is a primary and writing a secondary manifestation. They imply that speech is more obviously tied to an authenticating source and palpable presence (the speaker), whereas writing can more readily exist without the writer present. Derrida challenges this conventional wisdom by insisting that it is writing – not speech – which is the more characteristically linguistic mode. For, he argues, all words are always by definition *not* the things they refer to, but substitutes for them. The word 'tree' is not a tree, but stands in for it. Language is not primarily about presences at all, but about absences. Moreover, as many writers on COMMUNICATION are quick to add, there is no such thing as a pure unmediated event, 'the event in itself'. The apparently simple matter of being present at an event is no guarantee that a participant will have a full, let alone an impartial, grasp of what is going on. Given their personal histories and temperaments, as well as their immediate aims and expectations, participants are never strictly present in the same way.

In PSYCHOLOGICAL terms, too, the absence of our unconscious from our conscious selves ensures that we are never completely 'self-evident'. We are more than and different from what we know. With this in mind, the notion of **gaps and silences** was developed by Macherey in his *A Theory of Literary Production* (1966). For Macherey the primary focus of textual study is what the text *does not* or *cannot* say (the *non-dit*). That is, every text can be characterised not only by its expressed subject matter (its presences) but also by what it represses psychologically and suppresses politically (its absences). The role of the critical reader, therefore, is to search for the 'gaps and silences': reading between the lines and filling the embarrassed or pregnant silences. What figures and events have been quickly passed over or ignored? What other stories and histories have been partially displaced or utterly replaced by the very act of telling *this* story (or history) *this* way? Macherey explores the 'unsaid' or 'unsayable' in, for instance, *Robinson Crusoe* (see 5.2.2), tying this work in with the construction of a white colonising self (Crusoe) established at the expense of a a black colonised **other** (Friday). He also gestures towards hi/stories of empire and slaves either inevitably unwritten or deliberately ignored. Jameson develops related insights in *The Political Unconscious* (1981).

The concept of **centres and margins**, along with the activities of decentring and recentring, can be usefully introduced at this point. MARXISTS, FEMINISTS and others have long talked about 'marginalised' as opposed to 'dominant' groups. However, it is to POSTSTRUCTURALIST writers such as Derrida that we chiefly owe an interest in the activities known as decentring and, by extension, recentring. The basic principles are simple and follow from the previous explication of absences and presences and gaps and silences. By *centring* we mean the act of placing certain persons, places, times, issues and perceptions at the centre of attention – and thereby marginalising or ignoring others. By *decentring* a text, critical readers and writers actively dislocate what was assumed to be at the centre of attention and draw attention to something inside or outside the text which they feel throws a revealing light across it. In *Hamlet* an instance of such 'internal' decentring might mean drawing attention to the go-betweens Rosencrantz and Guildenstern (as Stoppard does in his play) or to Ophelia and Gertrude (as do many FEMINISTS). 'External' decentring might mean turning to critical receptions of the play or, say, investigating the role of actual gravediggers (featured theatrically in Act V sc. i) in the early seventeenth century – or even analysing a series of classic TV ads for some cigars called 'Hamlet' (see 3.1). Another instance of de- and recentring is Jean Rhys's *Wide Sargasso Sea*. This centres attention on the earlier life of the mad and largely absent Mrs Rochester of Charlotte Brontë's *Jane Eyre* (see 5.2.3).

   The theoretical terminology of de- and recentring, like that of deconstruction in general, can be forbiddingly dense. But the practice can be both simple and powerful. Here's a suggested procedure:

DE- AND RECENTRING TEXTS (cf. discourse questions, p. 227)

1 *Identify the presumed centre of the text*: the one the author seems to be preoccupied with, or the one critics invite you to concentrate on.
2 *DEcentre it so as to draw attention to marginal or ignored figures, events and materials.* Try decentring in two dimensions, *internally* and *externally*, drawing attention to other possibilities within and outside the text in hand.
3 *Recognise that you have thereby REcentred the text.* Weigh the implications of what you have done for an understanding of the text as you first found it. Also notice that you have produced another configuration which can itself be challenged and changed, and further de- and recentred in turn.

There is, strictly, no single 'end' or ultimate 'point' to the process of de- and recentring: there are always multiple absences which will help us realise a presence. Nor is there just one gap or silence which can be detected within the noisy fabric of a text. The value of such an activity, however, is that it encourages us to grasp texts **creatively** as well as critically. We weigh what they are or seem to say in relation to what they are not or might have said differently. We grasp texts, so to speak, not only as 'wholes' but also as configurations of 'holes'.

Activity

Consider how far a text which interests you is in some sense about the tension between 'absence' and 'presence'. Go on to apply the three-part procedure for *de- and recentring*. (Suggested focuses in Part Five: 'They flee from me' (5.1.1); *How Late it Was, How Late* (5.3.2); *Not I* (5.3.3).)

Discussion

(i) Play is the disruption of presence. [. . .] Play is always play of absence and presence.
Jacques Derrida, 'Sign, Structure and Play in the Discourse of the Human
Sciences' (1978) in Lodge and Wood (2008: 233)

(ii) Things fall apart; the centre cannot hold;

William Butler Yeats, 'The Second Coming' (1921); also in the title of
Achebe's novel (see 5.4.5)

Also see: POSTSTRUCTURALISM; **foreground, background; difference and similarity**.

READING: Bennett *et al.* 2005: 201–3; Pope 1995: 14–30, 162–80. *Core texts*: Macherey 1966; Jameson 1981; Spivak 1987; Derrida in Lodge and Wood 2008.

ACCENT AND DIALECT

Accent and dialect are aspects of language **variety**. They therefore vary from place to place, over time, according to social context and depending on medium (see 1.1.1). Speaking 'with an accent' means pronouncing words in a way which is nationally, regionally or socially distinctive; hence speaking English with a Southern, Russian, Irish, New York or upper-class accent. In this respect everyone has an accent. Speaking or writing 'in dialect', however, is more than a matter of accent alone. It also involves choices and combinations of words which are distinctive, if not peculiar, to the vocabulary and grammar of a particular region or social group. Thus speakers of English will pronounce the same words ('How are you?', for instance) with a variety of accents. However, only when they use distinctive choices and combinations of words would we describe them as using dialectal forms (stereotypically, such greetings as 'G'day' in Australia; 'Wotcha!' in parts of London). For a fuller sense of dialectal variation in English across the whole range of word choice and word combination, as well as accent/pronunciation (here represented by variations in spelling), see πo and Meng (5.1.5 and 5.1.4), Tutuola and Achebe (5.3.2, 5.4.5) and Fugard (5.3.3) and Kelman (5.3.2).

Accents and dialects sometimes get ranked hierarchically in relation to a socially privileged **standard**. In Britain it is common to place accents against 'Received Pronunciation' (RP) and to place the language as a whole (including dialects) against 'BBC English' or, more archaically, 'the Queen's English'. In the USA and Australia, however, there is far less identification of a specific regional accent with power, privilege and status. No one state tends to dominate the various 'network' (i.e. media) standards which operate. What's more, it should be observed that people everywhere routinely switch from one variety to another, depending on the social situation and topic. The 'local' variety tends to be used in informal conversation and implies a sense of solidarity. Meanwhile the 'standard' variety tends to be used whenever there is an increase in formality, where printed documents are involved and where there is a stronger sense of power. In this respect, most speakers of English and other languages are at least *di-glossic*, routinely shifting between two varieties: local and national. Indeed, most speakers are *hetero-glossic* in that they readily switch amongst many varieties, depending on age, education, peer group, gender, class and ethnicity, as well as on region. The term sociolect is sometimes used to refer to all these other kinds of social language variety, the term dialect being reserved for purely regional variety.

Selected versions of accents, dialects, sociolects and even instances of other languages are often used in novels, plays, films, adverts and songs. They signal a specific regional, class, national or ethnic identity. Perhaps the most persistent and predictable instances occur in TV and radio adverts. On British TV and radio, for instance, upper-class and markedly 'Queen's English' accents are used to sell insurance, banking, lean cuisine and expensive cars; 'regional' and working-class accents are used to sell beers (Australian matiness an optional extra), junk food and washing powders (though even then the sales pitch is often clinched by a final voice-over invoking the authority of another, more 'standard' variety). Plays, novels and stories, too, often give at least a passing flavour, and sometimes a full taste, of people speaking and writing in ways which are 'other-than-standard' (though even then they are usually braced against a standard printed or spoken form which is assumed to be the norm). Classic examples include: Shakespeare's *Henry V* (for 'stage' Welsh, Scots, Irish and French); Gaskell's *North and South*, Dickens's *Hard Times*, Lawrence's *Sons and Lovers* (for Northern English working class); Hardy's 'Wessex' novels (for rural West Country); also Faulkner's *As I Lay Dying*, Hurston's *Their Eyes Were Watching God*, Walker's *The Color Purple* and Morrison's *Beloved* (5.4.5) (for varieties of English from the American Southern States). Synge's *Playboy of the Western World* and Thomas's *Under Milk Wood* have been especially influential stage and radio play versions of respectively, Irish and Welsh varieties of English (see 5.3.3). For current Irish and Scots varieties, see Doyle (5.3.2), Leonard (5.1.4) and Kelman (5.3.2).

In Britain, novels, plays and films by Roddy Doyle, James Kelman, Mike Leigh and Hanif Kureishi and Monica Ali have done much to put contemporary urban Irish, Scottish, London-based and Asian varieties on the literary and media map. Soap operas, comedy programmes and other TV series such as *Coronation Street* and *EastEnders* have done something similar, though with different degrees of stereotyping. Meanwhile, the accents of *Neighbours* and *Home and Away* virtually *were* Australian English for legions of TV-watching non-Australian English-speakers the world over. Bands such as Simply Red and the Pogues as well as comedians such as Ricky Gervais, Jimmy Carr, Billy Connolly and Victoria Wood have (or have had) noticeably 'regional' accents and images. Many Hollywood films also include voices other than those of white Anglo-Saxon Americans, notably black, Hispanic and Native American Indian. Remarkably few, however, get beyond stereotyped roles and marginal or token presences. Rap, hip hop and other 'street' styles, similarly, have given wide currency to certain aspects of 'youth' and 'black' cultures while always open to the risk of being commodified and stereotyped accordingly.

Finally, it should be noted that each one of us has a particular idiolect. An idiolect is the distinctive and to some extent unique configuration of language varieties peculiar to each person. It is our personal repertoire – a kind of verbal fingerprint – with the difference that our *verbal* resources not only grow but also change in pattern over the course of our lives.

(For the specialised meaning of 'accent' as the accentual stress in verse, see **versification**.)

Activity

Consider how regional accents and dialects (or sociolects) are represented and what they signify in a novel, poem, play, film, TV programme or advert with which you are familiar. Alternatively, concentrate on one of those referred to above or featured in Part Five: e.g., Leonard's 'This is thi . . . news' (5.1.4); Nichols's 'Tropical Death' (5.4.5); 'πo's '7 daiz' (5.1.5). How far are the formal differences simply matters of pronunciation/spelling or of word choice and combination? Go on to consider what kinds of social and cultural identity are being projected, against what kinds of assumed or asserted background.

Discussion

> Mrs Durbeyfield habitually spoke the dialect [Dorset]; her daughter, who had passed the Sixth Standard in the National School under a London-trained mistress, spoke two languages: the dialect at home, more or less; ordinary English abroad and to persons of quality.
>
> Thomas Hardy, *Tess of the d'Urbervilles* (1891: Ch. 3)

Also see: Which 'Englishes'? 1.1; **discourse; standards and . . . varieties.**

READING: Montgomery *et al.* 2012: Section 2; Mullany and Stockwell 2010: 118–25, 192–9. *Core text*: Trudgill and Hannah 1994.

AUTHOR AND AUTHORITY

'Author' is now commonly used to refer to an individual writer who is supposed to be the ultimate creator of some especially valued text, often of a LITERARY kind. A more all-purpose and less prestigious term is **writer**. Generally speaking, 'author' is to 'writer' as artist is to 'artisan': authors and artists are assumed to be supreme and sublime individualists; writers and artisans to be practical, humdrum and generally serviceable. Such a view of the author/artist is problematic, however. It is also a relatively modern and in some respects predominantly Western view. In earlier periods, as in many other cultures today, we find that the concept of authorship was and is far more tied up with notions of collective *authority* and received wisdom. In Chaucer, for instance, 'auctors' (authors) were those who followed and in large measure translated previous 'auctoritees' (authorities, sources). Meanwhile, many contemporary African, Caribbean and Australasian writers draw upon corresponding traditions and roles voicing public rather than private concerns. The dominant modern Western view of the author must therefore be seen relatively, both historically and cross-culturally. It is characterised by five main assumptions:

1   the assumed primacy of the individual and of her or his experience as a guarantee of authenticity (hence the popular belief that authors work in splendid or miserable isolation);

2   an emphasis on the written word, as well as a generally 'logocentric' view of the creative process of composition;

3   the belief that authors make things up spontaneously out of their own heads;

4   the related belief that authors are very special people and in extreme cases 'geniuses';

5   the view that all readers have to do is be receptive and reverential.

Some people, however, hold quite different views of the nature and function of authorship in particular, and of the processes of **creativity** and cultural production in general. They would counter each of the above assumptions by emphasising:

1a   the primarily social role of the author/artist in representing common and collective experiences, often appealing to precedent and tradition; also the fact that writers, performers and artists often work in close association with other people;

2a   the pervasive interpenetration of cultural activities across many media (e.g., illustrated book, performance pieces, theatre, film), with the written word sometimes playing a minor role;

3a   the fact that authors are *reproducers* and always in some sense transform previously existing materials (i.e. the current resources of language, literature and culture); they do not create out of nothing or simply 'out of their heads';

4a   the belief that everyone constantly communicates things of significance and worth – they do not need to be special to do this;

5a   an insistence that readers, audiences and viewers also have a crucial role to play in the negotiation and construction of meanings and values.

POSTSTRUCTURALISTS, moreover, would argue that there is never a fixed, ultimately identifiable source or 'origin' for anything. There is therefore no single 'author' or absolute 'authority'. POSTMODERNISTS, meanwhile, would add that the very notion of 'authorship' has a narrowly literary as well as quaintly archaic ring to it: most media production now is palpably collaborative and decreasingly dependent on the written or printed word. 'Authenticity' (i.e. genuineness), they would further claim, has been dissolved into a succession of competing **images** and persistently plural points of view.

For all the above reasons, the question of whether the author (i.e., the concept of the author) is 'dead' or 'alive' is frequently raised in contemporary literary and cultural studies, most famously by Barthes and Foucault. Viewing the matter historically, we are also obliged to think about such matters as the impact of literary copyright and the nominal ownership of printed works from the seventeenth century onwards. Before that, writers did not 'own' their printed words and consequently could not derive direct profit from them. More recently, we may wonder what place 'authors-as-individual-creators' have in the collaborative wor(l)ds of the Internet and the hypermedia. This in turn may prompt us to revalue traditional, anonymous or collective cultural practices such as folktales, oral histories and anecdotes. In social and political terms, we may ask how far we see writers as isolable and self-creating individuals or as social roles and ideological **identities** interacting with others. In PSYCHOLOGICAL terms, we may ask how far we see writers as sources of expression or sites of repression. Related questions arise about LANGUAGE in particular and CULTURE in general. How far are we the active users (the 'authors') of our own words and worlds, and how far do they use and in effect 'author' us?

Activity

Authors, Writers, Producers, Directors, Performers, Practitioners . . . ?   Which of the following are commonly thought to be produced by 'an author':
(a) classic novel; (b) pulp fiction; (c) computer manual; (d) sonnet; (e) magazine advert; (f) TV soap opera; (g) theatrical performance; (h) movie; (i) news story; (j) greetings card message; (k) your last essay? In each case consider everyone who might be involved in the processes of (re)production and what other terms might be substituted or added.

Go on to select one anonymous work and one work with a known author and consider how important it is to know precisely who wrote or performed it. Do you put different questions to work by A. Nonymous? (Comparison between 'Maiden in the mor lay' (5.1.1) and Wordsworth's 'I wandered lonely . . . ' (5.4.1) works well here.)

Discussion

the birth of the reader must be at the cost of the death of the author.
                                        Roland Barthes, *The Death of the Author* (1968) (1977: 148)

Also see: 3.1; PSYCHOLOGICAL; POSTSTRUCTURALIST and POSTMODERNIST; **art; auto/ biography; canon; creative writing; subject; writing.**

READING: Bennett and Royle 2009: 19–27; Parrinder1991; Bennett 2005; Mitchell 2008; Wandor 2008 (in creative writing). *Core texts*: Barthes and Foucault in Lodge and Wood 2008.

CANON AND CLASSIC

'The canon' refers to a body of privileged and prescribed texts which are assumed to be of 'classic' status and therefore automatically worthy of study. The matter of what texts are to be admitted to the canon, or of whether there ever has been or should be a fixed canon at all, has been especially contentious in English Studies over the past few decades. So, relatedly, has the matter of whether texts can be distinguished as 'classic' or 'popular'. Often this comes down to the matter of what counts as LITERATURE, and whether we ultimately need that category either.

Canon derives from a Greek word meaning either 'measuring rod' or 'list'. Both meanings were taken over and eventually conflated by early Christianity. 'Canon law' referred to rules or decrees of the Church; 'the canon' was a list of those books of the **Bible** officially accepted as genuine along with, later, those works of the Church fathers approved as **authoritative** and orthodox. All these were studiously distinguished from *apocryphal* works, which were reckoned to be fake, and *heretical* works, which were reckoned blasphemous and put on 'the forbidden list'. Since the split at the Reformation, the Roman Catholic Church has continued to recognise as canonical eleven books of the Bible that Protestants reject as apocryphal. Saints, meanwhile, are formally 'canonised' once they are added to the official list of the (s)elect. From the outset, then, whether conceived as official rules or as lists, canons and canonisation are characterised by at least two features: concerted institutional control and a high degree of inclusivity/ exclusivity.

The notion of the canon as a list of *secular* privileged books dates from the seventeenth century. Initially it referred to those works accepted as genuinely by a particular author (e.g., 'the Shakespeare canon'). More recently, debate over what shall be recognised, celebrated and taught as 'the canon of English Literature' has generated a great deal of heat if not always a lot of light. Most immediately, this comes down to the practical matter of who and what shall be 'set texts' on courses in schools, colleges and universities. The institutions involved include:

1) exam and syllabus-setting committees, 2) lecturers and teachers
3) publishers, editors, marketing managers, 4) librarians and stock-purchasers
5) critics and reviewers, 6) students and other book purchasers.

At the critical and ideological core there is invariably a complex of debates over what shall be deemed to constitute the national heritage or international identity of, say, England, Britain, America or Australia. At the same time there are contributory, often conflicting, debates on the nature of the ENGLISH language, **standard** or otherwise, as well as argument over precisely what literature might or should be. The outcome of all these debates varies greatly. It very much depends on whether there is a predominantly monocultural or MULTICULTURAL conception of what it means to be 'English', 'American', 'Australian', etc. There are pressingly practical dimensions to the problem too. On the one hand, considerations of cost, copyright, availability and sheer familiarity often weigh heavily in favour of the well-known (if not always well-loved) text. On the other hand, fresh texts (old as well as new) are brought to prominence and people really do welcome a change if it seems to be in a promising direction. Either way, the assumption or assertion that 'the canon' (singular and definitive) has always simply been 'there', a universal and timeless entity, is a convenient but misleading myth. 'English Literature' itself has hardly been around as an educational subject for more than a century (see @ 1.5). How could any of its texts be that 'set'?!

The concept **classic** tends to work in tandem with that of canon. Writers and their works get dubbed 'classic(s)' when they are reckoned first- (not second- or third-) class. It is also usually insisted that they have 'stood the test of time' (though this still leaves the question of precisely how long, whose time, and what kinds of test). Moreover, 'classics' invariably tend to be defined in contradistinction to other work which is labelled variously as 'minor', 'common' or (underscoring an implied elitism) 'popular'. The ancient writer Gellius, for instance, talks of the *classicus scriptor* (classic writer) who by definition is *non proletarius* (not common/proletarian) (see *OED* classic). In fact, this value-laden and socially hierarchical sense of classic was carried over from Greek and Latin so that from the sixteenth century onwards 'the Classics' became the usual term to refer to the study of Greek and Latin culture as a whole, as distinct from later vernacular cultures. Thus in many a neo-classical battle of the books, classics were invariably identified with 'the ancients' as opposed to 'the moderns'. However, it was not long before vernacular writers such as Dante in Italy and Chaucer, Spenser, Shakespeare and Milton in England were also hailed as classics. This especially tended to happen with poets in so far as they could be shown to use classical (i.e. Greek and Latin) models *and* to represent the beginnings of modern national literary traditions. In this way the appearance of a continuous tradition was forged between older and newer literatures and social orders.

FEMINISTS, however, continue to point out that these were largely patriarchal orders; and POSTCOLONIAL critics have added that they were white and Western European too. For, until very recently, the charge that the traditional literary canon was largely stocked with classics by 'Dead White European Males' (*DWEMs* for short), though crudely put, was hard to deny. MARXISTS, meanwhile, would insist on inserting a class component into the equation (perhaps 'DWE Middle-to-Upper Class Males'). In all these cases the consequences have been both radical and far-reaching. Not only have there been concerted critiques of previously established writers with respect to gender, ethnicity and class; there has also been a prodigious amount of work in the rediscovery and reappraisal of neglected traditions of women's, black and working-class writing. (For further information on these, turn to sections 3.5–8.) At any rate, it is now necessary to think in terms of opposed or alternative traditions, and to talk of *plural* or *open canons*: lists of texts and lines of development which were previously ignored or crossed out and now cross and re-cross according to the logics of **difference** and similarity and **self** and other.

But even this is only one side of the canon debate. Strictly, the other side is no canon at all. A symptom of this is that during the late twentieth century it became increasingly common to talk of many more things than authors and books as 'classics'. In the MEDIA and in popular CULTURE generally, we readily speak of classic cars, races, films, pop songs and soap operas. Indeed, in POSTMODERN discourses 'classic' has come to mean little more than 'something that used to be popular' (or more cynically, 'something being commercially recycled'). However, in principle, such a charge may be as easily levelled at the 'recycling' of Shakespeare on stage and on exam syllabuses as at the latest TV re-run of *Friends* or a re-mix of 'Bohemian Rhapsody'. Indeed, whether you are inclined or required to treat any of these materials as 'canonical', 'classic' or otherwise is very much the point at issue. It is also the point of the openly ambiguous invitation to 'fire canons yourself' in the activity which follows.

Activity

What *ten* texts would *you* put in a first-year course introducing a degree programme called 'English Literature', 'Literature in English', 'English Studies' or 'Literary and Cultural Studies'? (You choose the course title and emphasis too.) Go on to review and perhaps revise your choices and combinations of text in the light of the criteria below. Have you 'covered' or sought to represent instances of:

♦ mega-genres such as poetry, drama and prose (including the novel and short story)?
♦ genres ancient and modern such as comedy and tragedy, epic and lyric; auto/biography, travel writing, science fiction and romance?
♦ writings and performances in English from, say, Australia, New Zealand, India, Africa, America, the Caribbean, England, Ireland, Scotland, Wales?
♦ influential texts in English translation; e.g., by Ibsen, Brecht, Allende, Márquez?
♦ various periods and movements: fifth century to the present, Anglo-Saxon to postmodern?
♦ various social groups distinguished by gender, class and ethnicity?
♦ various media – spoken, written, printed, audio-visual?

Go on to consider the possibility of introductory courses based not so much on 'set' texts or 'coverage' but on, say, skills, techniques, theories, approaches, practices of reading and writing and research (see 2.4 for some possibilities).

Discussion

(i)   The great English novelists are Jane Austen, George Eliot, Henry James and Joseph Conrad – to stop for the moment at that comparatively safe point in history.
          Frank R. Leavis, *The Great Tradition* (1948) (1972: 9, opening sentence)

(ii) The challenge, then, is not simply to supplant the 'ecclesiastical' canon with the 'emergent' transgressive canon, but to rethink the relation of both on the basis of what it means to be 'cultured' or indeed educated.
          Homi Bhabha, *Times Higher Education Supplement* (24 January 1992)

Also see: LITERATURE; **bibles; genre; poetry and word-play**.

READING: Bennett *et al.* 2005: 20–2; Walder 2003: Section 1; Guillory in Lentricchia and McLaughlin 1995: 233–49; Strickland in Coyle *et al.* 1990: 696–707. *Core texts*: Leavis 1948; Showalter 1977; Said 1993; Bloom 2000.

CHARACTER AND CHARACTERISATION

Character can be provisionally defined as 'the construction of a fictional figure', and characterisation as 'the literary, linguistic and cultural means whereby that figure is constructed'. Character is a central concept in traditional approaches to narrative, especially novels, plays and film. That is why the meaning and value of the term are often merely assumed or asserted. There is also a common tendency simply to describe fictional characters as though they really existed and to forget that the matter at issue is often the *kinds* of character represented and the *process* of characte*risation*. For all these reasons it is important to grasp the various things that may be implied by character, and to recognise that characterisation is both a creative and a critical activity. It is also important to know that many approaches are critical of the very concept of character as such.

   Character derives from a Greek word meaning 'to engrave, to inscribe' and currently has three main meanings:

1   the distinctive nature, disposition and traits of a real person (e.g., 'My children have/are quite different characters');

2   the particular role played by a fictional figure in a novel, film or play (e.g., 'Hamlet is a character in Shakespeare's play of that name');

3   a letter of the alphabet or other graphic device (e.g., 'The printer picked up each character and put it in its box').

Together, all three meanings remind us that 'a character' can be everything from a real person (whatever we mean by that) to a fragment of printed language – a personal identity and a textual entity. The first two definitions also remind us that discussions of character inevitably require us to negotiate the relation between **real** and **imagined** persons, and between **fact** and **fiction**. One answer is to treat all characters, 'real' or 'imagined', as the products of **discourse** and **representation**. It then depends upon the precise frames of reference (physical, biological, psychological, social, historical, philosophical, etc.) within which we construct our notions of reality and what it is to be a person. More particularly, it obliges us to engage with the relations between people's personal **stories** (including auto/biographies) and more public and general **histories**. Indeed, if people are in reality already 'playing parts' and adopting psychological and social **roles**, it becomes a fascinating question just how far we can distinguish characters in LITERATURE from characters in the rest of life. What *are* the differences between playing the roles of, say, father, son, partner and lecturer in a film and playing those roles in fact? To be sure, there are crucial differences of consequence and responsibility. But formally and ideologically – in terms of how and why we play these roles – there is obviously much interdependence and mutual influence. 'She feels as if she's in a play – she is anyway', as the Beatles put it in 'Penny Lane'.

For these reasons not all critics are happy with the notion of 'character', as such. MARXIST, FEMINIST and POSTCOLONIAL critics often prefer to talk about people as 'sites of struggle', 'subjectivities', 'ideological subjects', 'identities', 'representatives of dominant or muted positions', 'instances of competing discourses', 'voices', 'bodies', 'stereotypes', 'antitypes', etc. Character in a traditional sense is not a central and effective part of their critical lexicon. Indeed, for many contemporary critics the concept of character is far too tainted by humanist assumptions about the unity and sanctity of 'the individual' and the alleged universality of human nature to be of much use. For such critics the concept of character may serve as a point of departure, but it is rarely a point of arrival. Resistance to and deconstruction of 'character' is even more emphatic among writers with a POST/STRUCTURALIST or a POSTMODERNIST bent. They have little time for a construct so tied to notions of the individual as a pre-given centre or for notions of 'convincing characters' tied to limiting notions of **realism**.

Notwithstanding such a barrage of alternatives, certain traditional ways of describing character and characterisation prove remarkably resilient and, if handled with care, serviceable. Characters may thus still be described as:

♦   *rounded or flat*, following E.M. Forster's *Aspects of the Novel* (1927): 'rounded' characters are interiorised, psychologically complex and develop (e.g., Paul Morel in *Sons and Lovers*, Seth in *Beloved*); 'flat' characters are known through exterior appearance, are apparently simpler and perhaps predictable – the latter are often also called *caricatures* (e.g., Jonson's Volpone, Dickens's Mr Pickwick).

♦   *individuals* or *types* (on closer inspection, most characters turn out to be both). Chaucer's and Shakespeare's major characters are often described as a mixture.

♦   *character-narrators* or *character-actors*: telling the tale or being told by it (Jane in *Jane Eyre* is a character-narrator, whereas Edward Rochester is a character-actor; these relations are reversed in *Wide Sargasso Sea*: see 5.2.3).

◆   **points of view** that switch, get mixed or compounded according to the various narrative and dramatic strategies in play (Jane Austen and Beckett represent what may be termed, respectively, 'realist' and 'modernist' ways with character and point of view).

But whatever terms you use to describe characters, it will be clear that the emphasis should largely be on character*isation*: the *kinds* of character and the *ways* in which characters are constructed. Crucially, from a critical point of view this is as much a matter of how the reader *sees* the characters as how the writer *says* them. Meanwhile, as many of the approaches referred to earlier suggest, it is sometimes arguable whether we should talk of 'characters' as such at all.

Activity

Concentrate on a group of figures from a novel, play, film, auto/biography, history or news story and suggest how they might be approached by (a) a MARXIST; (b) a FEMINIST; (c) a POSTCOLONIAL critic. How compatible are such approaches with analyses of characterisation based upon, say, 'rounded' and 'flat' characters, 'caricatures', 'individuals' and 'types', 'point of view' (see above)? Which critical terms and frames do you prefer? (Atwood's 'Happy Endings' and Kipling's 'Muhammad Din' are suggested focuses in Part Five, 5.2.1.)

Discussion

(i)   Character is arguably the most important single component of the novel.

David Lodge, The Art of Fiction (1992: 67)

(ii)   Characters are imaginary identities constructed through reports of appearance, action, speech and thought.

Brian Moon, Literary Terms: A Practical Glossary (1992: 10)

Also see: **auto/biography; narrative; foreground . . . point of view; subject.**

READING: Bennett and Royle 2009: 63–70; Lodge 1992: 66–9. *Core texts*: Forster 1927; Booth 1961; Belsey 2002: 56–84.

COMEDY AND TRAGEDY, CARNIVAL AND THE ABSURD

Briefly, comedy is what makes us laugh and has a happy ending; tragedy is what makes us sad and has an unhappy ending; carnival is a kind of riotous festival, and the absurd is what perplexes and confounds us. All these terms offer ways of categorising *kinds* or **genres** of experience. They are applied chiefly but not exclusively to LITERATURE, and chiefly but not exclusively to **drama**. Comedy and tragedy are primarily associated with CLASSICAL and neo-classical approaches to drama derived from Aristotle's *Poetics* (*c.* 330 BC). Carnival and the absurd have more specifically modern antecedents. Carnival and the carnivalesque owe their critical currency to Bakhtin's interest in popular festival forms in literature, notably in his *Rabelais and his World* (1968). The absurd and absurdism are most often encountered in the phrase 'the theatre of the absurd' and still owe their currency to a highly influential book of that name by Martin Esslin (1961). The three kinds of concept gathered in this entry are on different trajectories in different frames of reference. They therefore entail different **aesthetics** and politics. Nonetheless, it is highly instructive to approach them as a relatable cluster; for they are commonly used to map, and sometimes to redraw, the same textual terrain.

Comedy and tragedy are braced against one another in a clear hierarchy by Aristotle: comedy inferior, tragedy superior. This order and emphasis are deliberately reversed in the present entry. **Comedy** derives from Greek *komos-oidos*, meaning 'revel-song', and initially referred to events associated with fertility rituals and the festival of Dionysus. According to Aristotle, who treats it slightly and slightingly (*Poetics*, Chapters 4 and 5), comedy has the following ingredients:

- *happy endings* and an overall progression from disorder to order, chaos to harmony;
- *characters of inferior moral quality, usually of lower social status* (slaves, artisans, traders, etc.);
- *a spectacle of what is ridiculous but laughable*, and therefore causes no pain.

To this must be added a catalogue of comic sub-genres which have subsequently been developed and distinguished (even though in any particular instance we invariably meet a mixture):

- *comedy of humours*, based on exaggeration of supposed physiological types: sanguine, melancholic, phlegmatic, choleric (hence 'humorous' = 'funny');
- *comedy of manners*, based on affectations in social appearance and behaviour;
- *romantic comedy*, involving fantastic adventures and often a love interest;
- *pastoral comedy*, invoking idyllic or idiotic images of country living, especially amongst romantically prettified or grotesquely uglified shepherds;
- *satiric comedy*, exposing and censuring faults, usually involving sex and acquisitiveness, often set in a corrupt city or household;
- *black comedy*, a dark kind of satire, often with an uncertain sense of morality and a sharp sense of *absurdity* and perhaps with a *carnivalesque* feel (see below).

Comedy is not limited to plays, of course, or to literature. Comedy was and is a common feature of the **novel** well before and after Fielding's witty characterisation of his *Tom Jones* (1749) as 'a comic epic poem in prose'. Meanwhile, comedy in verse – sometimes softened to irony, sometimes sharpened to satire – is evident in English from well before Chaucer to well after Byron. *Comics* (plural), we should also note, refers to a couple of popular and until recently academically neglected genres: comic strips and comedians. Printed *comic strips* appeared in newspapers during the late nineteenth century and soon grew to occupy whole publications (i.e. full-blown comics) in their own right. Though long associated with children's or childish reading, neither the comic nor its descendant the modern graphic novel/book is necessarily trivial or even funny. In fact, much of the best contemporary work on **narrative** and popular verbal-visual culture concentrates on precisely these genres. 'Comics' in the sense of *comedians* ('stand-up', 'alternative' or otherwise) are also increasingly recognised as significant focuses of study. Along with TV 'sitcoms' (i.e. situation comedies), they often foreground and sport with shifts in contemporary **discourse**. The study of jokes in particular has featured centrally in various kinds of PSYCHOLOGICAL analysis virtually since its inception (e.g., Freud's *Jokes and their Relation to the Unconscious*, 1905). It is also a focus for much significant work in discourse analysis (e.g., Chiaro 1992). All in all, then, Aristotle may have had the first word on certain aspects of comedy. But he doesn't necessarily have the last laugh.

Tragedy derives from the Greek *tragos-oidos* ('goat-song') and initially referred to festivals to Dionysus in which a he-goat was sacrificed. Tragedy is treated at much greater length and with much greater seriousness than comedy by Aristotle (*Poetics*, Chapters 6–19). According to him, it has the following characteristics (notice that the first three are directly antithetical to those of comedy above):

♦   unhappy endings and a progression from order to disorder, harmony to chaos;

♦   characters of superior morals, usually of high social status: kings, nobles, etc.;

♦   a spectacle which 'arouses pity and fear' but which, being not real but a **representation**, 'purges' these emotions harmlessly (a process called *catharsis*);

♦   a plot built around a 'downturn' (*cata-strophe*) and eventual recognition of a true, appalling state of affairs;

♦   a hero or heroine (the *protagonist*) who is basically noble but eventually undone by some tragic flaw (*hamartia*), often in the form of excessive pride (*hubris*), as well as by some implacable force such as destiny or fate, usually represented by the gods;

♦   a figure who stands out against the protagonist (the *antagonist*) as well as a chorus which comments morally, often prophetically, upon the unfolding action;

♦   'the representation of an action that is complete and whole' (Chapter 7).

Legions of critics (including droves of students) have sought to apply Aristotle's criteria to plays called tragedies. The results range from the brilliant to the banal. Routine analyses dutifully plod through the play in hand duly noting the presence – or lamenting the absence – of catharsis, hamartia, hubris, catastrophe, etc. (invoking the Greek names seems to give the stamp of authority). However, more adventurous and genuinely critical analyses tend to brace themselves *against* the framework supplied by Aristotle. They probe the concepts themselves and ask such questions as: precisely who or what is responsible for the catastrophe? Why is pride accounted a fault? What would happen if pity and fear were redirected rather than purged? What social and political forces are being passed off as fate or the will of the gods? In this way the nature and function of tragedy may be identified not simply with the play itself, treated as an isolated artefact, but with specific social-historical conditions and ideological frameworks (e.g., particular state and family structures, the relative positions of nobles, citizens and slaves, men and women, natives and foreigners) as well as with specific kinds of myth, religion and morality.

Another important consideration is the fact that most post-classical plays are palpably 'mixed' in mode. They commonly alternate and often fuse elements of tragedy and comedy so as to produce **tragi-comedy**. For instance, Shakespeare's *Hamlet*, though nominally a tragedy, includes comic gravediggers/clowns, a fussy and funny old pedant (Polonius) as well as a protagonist, Hamlet himself, who ceaselessly sports with sense and bitterly plays the fool. Conversely, tragi-comic mixtures and fusions characterise nominal 'comedies' such as *As You Like It* and *The Tempest*. Another matter that plays havoc with classical distinctions between tragedy and comedy has to do with changes in underlying social structure. For obviously an aesthetic hierarchy based upon a distinction between the tragically noble high life and the comically ignoble low life can only hold as long as it is underwritten by a corresponding political hierarchy. Once the middle and working classes become socially prominent and politically aware, the old model becomes a straitjacket or is irrelevant. We see this happening in Ibsen's and Chekhov's plays. There the focus is on stresses and strains within the bourgeois family. Classical distinctions between comedy and tragedy, along with their associated aesthetics and politics, simply do not apply.

The absurd, following Esslin's *The Theatre of the Absurd* (1961), refers to a group of mid-twentieth-century playwrights, notably Ionesco, Beckett, Pinter and Albee. These writers exploit silence as much as speech, absence as much as presence, and incoherence rather more than coherence. Esslin emphasises the ways in which they all explore kinds of il/logic and non/character, actionless plot and indeterminate setting, especially by comparison with the then-dominant form of 'well-made play'. (The latter characteristically had a clear beginning, middle and end, a readily recognisable theme, and often presented 'realistic' figures in middle-class surroundings such as drawing-rooms.) Beckett's *Not I* (5.3.3) is an instance of absurdist theatre. It shows a spotlit 'Mouth' pouring forth a continuous monologue on a minimally set stage while a shadowy figure ('the Auditor') looms to one side. But explorations of 'the absurd', generally conceived, extend much wider and much further back than certain kinds of mid-century drama. The movement has close **aesthetic** links with Surrealism and Expressionism (notably Kafka) and philosophical links with the existentialism of Camus and Sartre. All these movements can be characterised by their scepticism about conventional reason and their attempts to embrace, and sometimes celebrate, 'meaninglessness' as a condition. In fact, we can readily see absurdism as part of the general il/logic of modernism where the supposed certainties of family, state and religion are crumbling and isolated individuals are trying to piece together some sense against an ostensibly nonsensical background. In this respect, Eliot's *The Waste Land* (1922) and Joyce's *Ulysses* are not a little 'absurd'. And so, in quite different veins, are Heller's *Catch 22* (1961) and Irving's *The World According to Garp* (1978). 'Nonsense verse', and 'nonsense writing' in general, may also be cited at this point. Lewis Carroll's *Alice* books (1865, 1871) are amongst the most famous fictionalised celebrations of paradox and nonsense. So is Edward Lear's nonsensical take on life, which is pushed in yet other bizarre directions by Don Barthelme (5.2.1). Deconstructive critics have an especial interest in these works, as in forms of paradox and absurdism generally. They argue – and often seek to demonstrate in their own manner of writing – that every model of reason depends upon the covert release and control of its opposite (unreason, nonsense, absurdity). McDonagh's *The Pillowman* (5.3.3) is an especially traumatic as well as theatrically dramatic instance of black comedy sporting with a nightmare of unreason.

Carnival and 'the carnivalesque' are concepts identified with more socially and politically engaged, less philosophically detached, kinds of nonsense. The term derives from the Italian *carne-vale* (literally 'a farewell to flesh') and primarily refers to the Shrovetide festival in which Christians feast and revel before Lent and a period of enforced abstinence. In Europe during the Middle Ages and the Renaissance, as in South American and some other countries now, carnival was an occasion for street parties and pageants. Sometimes these led to riots and uprisings. This is how Bakhtin defines 'carnival' as a critical concept in *Rabelais and his World* (1968: 10):

> [C]arnival celebrates the temporary liberation from prevailing truth and from the established order: it marks the suspension of all hierarchical rank, privileges, norms and prohibitions.

Politically, carnival is seen as an expression of popular culture opposed or alternative to an official order which it inverts and sports with. Physically, it is the celebration of the body over all that habitually constrains it. This **aesthetically** and politically charged notion of carnival has had considerable impact in many areas of literary and cultural studies, especially those where popular forms and practices are braced against (or within) elite structures and contexts. Indeed, the key critical and political question is just how far carnivalesque elements are contained by – or exceed and break open – the frames within which they operate. (Broadly speaking, NEW HISTORICISTS tend to concentrate on 'containment' while MARXISTS and CULTURAL MATERIALISTS point to the possibilities of radical rupture, even revolution; see 3.5).

Meanwhile, what we might call the 'mock-carnivalesque' is rampant in TV advertising, pop videos and many other forms of POSTMODERN cultural activity. But there the fantasy offer of individual freedom, bodily fulfilment and a universal Utopia is always a prelude to purchase. We are only invited to play if we can pay.

Activity

(a)   *Explore a text which is nominally a comedy or a tragedy with Aristotle's criteria in mind (see above)*. How helpful or inhibiting do you find these criteria? What aspects of the text tend to get neglected by starting at these points?

(b)   *Drawing on the above definitions, identify a text which you consider in some way 'absurd' or in some way 'carnivalesque'.* Would it be just as useful to call them, say, 'comic', 'tragic' or 'tragi-comic'? Likely texts from Part Five include: Byron (5.1.3), Leonard (5.1.4), Barthelme and Carter (5.2.1), Holdsworth (5.2.2), Hoban (5.2.4), Russell and Jacobson (5.3.1), Doyle and Kelman (5.3.2), Thomas and McDonagh (5.3.3), Peters and Heineken (5.4.1), Bryson (5.4.2), Nichols (5.4.5).

Discussion

(i)   The tragedy of [any] period lies in the conflict between the individual and the collectivity, or in the conflict between two hostile collectivities within the same individual.
        Leon Trotsky, *Literature and Revolution* (1924: Ch. 8; 'any' replaces 'our')

(ii)   [A]t the centre of European man, dominating the great moments of his life, there lies an essential absurdity.
        André Malraux, *The Temptation of the West* (1926) (see Cuddon 1999: 968)

Also see: CLASSICS; **aesthetics**; **drama**; **genre**; **poetry and word-play**.

READING: Bennett and Royle 2009: 96–116; Stott 2005; Critchley 2002; Cuddon 1999: 148–60, 926–36; Chiaro 1992. *Core texts*: Aristotle in Leitch 2010; Williams 1966; Bakhtin 1968; Esslin 1961.

DISCOURSE AND DISCOURSE ANALYSIS

'Discourse' is a commonly, sometimes casually, used term in the humanities and social sciences. It can mean everything from 'language understood as a form of social interaction and power' to 'a distinctive way of seeing and saying the world'; from dialogue in general to conversation in particular. As far as English Studies is concerned, use of the term discourse (along with **text**) has at least served to cut across conventional distinctions between LANGUAGE and LITERATURE. Both, it is strongly implied, can only be grasped in relation to one another and as forms of COMMUNICATION in specific CULTURAL contexts. Talk of language and literature (or, say, film and TV) as discourse therefore tends to occur in approaches which are socially and historically oriented, and often politically motivated (e.g., MARXISM, FEMINISM, POSTCOLONIALISM). 'Discourse' also tends to cut across conventional fact/fiction distinctions, encouraging us to treat all texts as in some sense *factional* (see **realism and representation**) and to see all *hi/stories* as potentially related (see **narrative**). Discourse is therefore one of the common terms which points to closer relations between History and English as subjects.
     For the sake of clarity, I shall distinguish five main meanings of discourse:

1   a formal treatise or dissertation (archaic); e.g., Descartes's *Discourse on Method*;
2   stretches of language above the level of the sentence (i.e. paragraphs, whole **texts**), with the emphasis on verbal cohesion and perceptual coherence;
3   **dialogue** in general or **conversation** in particular, primarily associated with the kind of discourse/conversation analysis currently extended into work on pragmatics;
4   communicative practices and 'ways of saying' which express the interests of a particular social-historical group or institution. In this case we tend to speak of discourses (plural) as distinct and often competing forms of knowledge and power (e.g., discourses of the law, medicine, science and education);

5   *discours* as used by theorists of **narrative** to refer to the narrational process of the story, especially the interaction between narrator and narratee, as distinguished from the '*histoire*', the narrative product as though independent of the telling.

Given such a variety of potential meanings and applications, it is not surprising that people sometimes use the word discourse vaguely or confusedly. We shall concentrate on senses (3) and (4); for these are the most common senses in contemporary Literary and Cultural Studies. They may be summed up by the formula: *Discourse = text in context = power in action*. (Sense (2) will be invoked in so far as it encourages us to explore whole texts or interactions in detail.) The main issues can be framed as a series of questions to put to any text.

DISCOURSE QUESTIONS

♦ What ways of saying and seeing the world are being assumed or asserted?
♦ What power relations are in play within and around the text in context?
♦ What alternative ways of saying and seeing the world are thereby being marginalised or ignored?
♦ What if the whole text-in-context were said, seen and done differently?

Thus we may consider the words and music of the British (or any) national anthem as an instance of intertwined discourses. Take the first line: 'God save our gracious queen'. This is marked in terms of religion ('God'), aristocracy ('queen'), social decorum ('gracious') and gender ('queen' again). In terms of context, the anthem as a whole is sung chiefly at the openings of national sporting and ceremonial occasions connected with Britain. All these features combine to make this a particularly powerful and privileged instance of language-in-action, text-in-context. We might call this a 'nationalistic' or 'patriotic' discourse. In order to explore and expose this discourse more fully, we might then consider whose ways of saying and seeing are *not* being represented in the British national anthem, and how *else* sporting and other public events might be – and indeed are – celebrated. For clearly there are many who would resist using or refuse to use the configuration of religion, monarchy, nationalism, gender and social decorum that it offers. Muslims, Buddhists, atheists, republicans, socialists, anarchists, internationalists, feminists, gays, and many others – all might (and often do) have different songs to sing and occasions to celebrate. Notice, too, that even if we stick with just the words of the national anthem (the 'text itself') but put them in a different context, their function and value can change dramatically. This happened with versions of 'God Save the Queen' by the punk group the Sex Pistols as well as by the rock group Queen. The former version was banned by the BBC (much as Roseanne Arnold's version of 'The Stars and Stripes' caused an uproar in America), while Queen's version drew attention to the band themselves along with gay politics (i.e. 'Queen(s)'). In all these ways we can see discourse as a function of language-in-action and text-in-context. And arguably we can only fully grasp this process if we also see the possibility of language activated differently, in different contexts and serving different interests.

A further brief example will help clarify what is meant by **discourse analysis** when applied to **speech and conversation** (more analytical detail can be found in that particular entry). In the 'Supermarket exchange' (5.2.6) the following features would be observed:

♦   *At the macro-textual level*, the social roles and power relations in play between the customer and the cashier: these would be analysed in terms of sex, age, ethnicity, class, education and personal temperament, as well as the general historical context and the immediate occasion of the encounter (Friday night shopping in central Oxford is obviously different from Sunday morning shopping in downtown Johannesburg).

♦   *At the micro-textual level*, the specific alternations of elicitation (the customer seeking a response) and silence (the cashier failing or refusing to respond); more particularly, the customer's gradual progression from relatively depersonalised and indirect statements ('There's a mistake here') to pointedly personal accusation (notably, the shift from passive to active structures in the last two moves: 'A mistake has been made' to 'You've made a mistake').

Taken together, these two macro- and micro-textual approaches to the text provide the basic framework within which a more extensive and intensive discourse analysis could be developed. And again there would be attention to text in context and language in action. The analysis would therefore be functional, not simply formal.

Activities

(a)   *Put the above 'Discourse Questions' to a cluster of texts which treat ostensibly the same topic* (e.g., nature, love, war, death, marriage, the family, colonialism). How far do the various discourses in play in effect constitute a variety of subjects? (Suggested focuses in Part Five are: 5.4.2 (nature); 5.4.4 (age); 5.4.5 (death); 'terrorism' (5.2.5).)

(b)   *Analyse an instance of conversational exchange, scripted or unscripted, for the ways in which it constitutes power relations* (e.g. 5.3.1–2).

Discussion

(i)   But discourse is just a fancy name for language, isn't it?
First-year student on 'Language, Literature,Discourse I', Oxford, 1994

(ii)   this model of literature as social discourse [is] . . . socially responsible and progressive, and educationally useful.
Roger Fowler, *Literature as Social Discourse* (1981: 199)

Also see: LANGUAGE; **addresser–address–addressee; genres; speech and conversation; subject . . . role.**

READING: Mills 1997; Cook 1994; Coulthard 1984. *Readers*: Jaworski and Coupland 1999; Schiffrin *et al.* 2001. *Core texts*: Foucault in Leitch 2010; Fairclough 2008.

DRAMA AND THEATRE, FILM AND TV

All these areas prove both attractive and awkward for students of English, especially of English LITERATURE as traditionally conceived. They are attractive because they challenge the exclusivity of the 'words on the page' notion of textuality and draw attention to spoken word, (along with moving bodies, music and many other things) on the stage and screen. They are awkward for the same reason, because they are not primarily written or printed texts but audio-visual performances, live or recorded. The intellectual ramifications are explored in the entries on **speech, text** and **writing**.

We begin with some general distinctions and connections between drama and **narrative**. It is conventional and often convenient to contrast *drama* (the activity of acting, showing and presenting) with *narrative* (the activity of telling, reporting and representing). This can also be put in terms of who talks to whom. In drama we are most conscious of an addresser–addressee relation, persons speaking and spoken to. In narrative we are most conscious of the address itself, what is being related and spoken about. Basically, then, we may say that drama operates on an 'I/we–you' axis, while narrative focuses on 's/he', 'they' or 'it'. Characters are *dramatised* in so far as they appear to speak in their own persons; they are *narrated* in so far as someone else (a narrator) speaks for and of them. Some modern theorists, prompted by Aristotle, distinguish *mimesis* (drama) and *diegesis* (narrative).

At the same time it is important to recognise drama and narrative as points on a continuum rather than mutually exclusive categories. Narrators may be visible 'up front' (and therefore dramatic), most obviously in first-person narratives such as autobiography and in dramatic monologues (e.g., Robert Browning's). Conversely, dramatised characters constantly report on (and therefore narrate) various aspects of their own and other people's experience. Figure 4.1 summarises both the distinctions and connections between drama and narrative:

DRAMA	<< >>	*First-person narration*	<< >>	*NARRATIVE*
acting, showing, presenting		dramatic monologue autobiography		telling, reporting representing
addresser–addressee				address
'I/we – you'				's/he, they, it'
mimesis				diegesis

Figure 4.1 Distinctions and connections between drama and narrative

We now turn to drama, theatre, film and TV in turn.

Drama derives from Greek *draein* (to do, to act) and means any kind of 'acting'. Acting, notice, has the dual sense of 'playing **roles**' and 'performing an action'. Acting can therefore take place on *and* off the stage/screen, in *and* out of a specially designed play or performance space. In short, dramas can happen in **fiction** *and* in **fact**. Hence the common yet potentially confusing reference to 'real-life dramas' and 'dramatic rescues', where actual events are being referred to and simply heightened through an implicit appeal to fictional genres. Conventional Literary Studies courses often 'do drama', but they usually do so in a substantially text-based sense, and concentrate on **classic** plays for the stage. 'TV and radio drama' may be familiar enough categories in programme guides; but in the UK at least they rarely feature beyond the occasional recognition of Dylan Thomas's *Under Milk Wood* as a radio play (see 5.3.3), and passing recognition of, say, Denis Potter and Mike Leigh as TV dramatists. In fact, drama is often the last and least fully represented element in the traditional Lit. Crit. trinity of 'poetry, prose and drama'. (Arguably, the anthology of voices in Part Five (5.3) is no exception.)

Theatre derives from Greek *thea* (spectacle) and *theon* (spectator). Specifically theatrical events always require a special 'play space' where the significantly named 'show' can take place. Theatre also invariably entails some division between actors and audiences, players and spectators. This is the case even if the boundary is sometimes blurred or deliberately transgressed, as with bouts of audience participation. Theatres and the theatrical events played in them are commonly distinguished in terms of their staging: arena, in the round, thrust, proscenium arch (also called 'picture book' and 'fourth wall removed'), Brechtian (e.g., with staging devices and stage-hands open to view), studio and promenade. All these practical considerations of building and space feature prominently in full-blown Theatre Studies courses, as do the economic as well as the aesthetic dimensions of scenery, lighting and costume. So do economic considerations of location, access and cost, along with the precise social composition of actors and audiences. These aspects of theatre may be treated cursorily or not at all in specifically literary courses.

Film is the name for particular MEDIA products (i.e. individual films) as well as the material from which they are made (i.e. film). Films are usually further distinguished according to a variety of criteria:

◆ *director and/or main actor*, e.g., Eisenstein's *Battleship Potemkin*, Chaplin's *Modern Times*, Ridley Scott's and/or Harrison Ford's *Blade Runner*.
◆ *technology*, e.g., celluloid or plastic film; 8 mm, 16 mm or 36 mm film width; silent movies, 'talkies', fully synchronised sound-track, computer-assisted effects, etc.
◆ *country and period*, e.g., Hollywood 1940s, French 1960s, contemporary Chinese.
◆ **genre**, e.g., cowboy, disaster, B movie, *film noir*, teen, spoof, art, porn, science fantasy, road, 'feel good', etc.

Notice, too, that 'film' can be both noun and verb. Like 'writing' (but unlike 'literature') 'film' can therefore more easily designate a process as well as a product. This is convenient because many courses in film emphasise the making and the viewing of films as cumulative activities.

Film is now widely recognised as an important element in English Studies. Often this is at the level of film adaptations of literary classics: Olivier's and Branagh's versions of Shakespeare's *Henry V*, Passolini's and Kurosawa's versions of *Macbeth*, Lean's versions of Dickens's *Great Expectations* and Forster's *A Passage to India*, and more recently film adaptations of Ishiguro's *The Remains of the Day*, Ondaatje's *The English Patient* and McEwan's *Atonement*. However, increasingly (albeit belatedly), it is being recognised within English Studies that film is a medium, mode of representation and art form in its own right; as are the implications of the fact that much of world cinema is either produced in English (notably in Hollywood) or is available dubbed in English or with English subtitles. All this makes for variously close, tense or suspicious relations amongst practitioners of English and Film Studies. The materials and methods of these subjects can be seen as complementary or incompatible (see @ 1.10).

Television (Greek–Latin for 'far-seen') has been a major and growing component in both students' and teachers' leisure-time experience since the 1950s. Along with films, pop music, magazines and newspapers (all the chief elements of the popular MEDIA), TV constitutes probably the most common source of information and entertainment, and the most common frame of CULTURAL reference for most people in contemporary Western (and many non-Western) societies. And again, like film, a great deal of TV is produced in English (notably in the USA, UK and Australia) or is readily dubbed in English. There are therefore all the attractions – as well as the perils – of a kind of English-speaking-media-imperialism. In fact, for a long time many people professionally involved in English Literature have adopted a posture of indifference or downright hostility to TV and the other popular media. NEW CRITICS in America and Leavisites in Britain all basically agreed that 'TV was bad for you'. 'Watching too much TV' was (and is) held responsible for everything from alleged illiteracy and inarticulacy to passivity and time-wasting, as well as general irreverence for authority and a supposed decline in moral standards. The fact that television was and is also, at least potentially, an opportunity for wider participation in democracy, visual literacy, greater awareness of other regions and nations, and offers a rich array of new genres of information and entertainment was not always recognised.

TV and film are readily confused because of their reliance on similar audio-visual media, and the fact that plenty of films are shown and seen on TV. However, TV is distinct from film – and both are distinct from video and Digital Versatile Disk (DVD) – in a number of crucial respects, just as handwriting is similar to but distinct from print. These differences are worth pointing up.

Mode of production: TV uses video or live-relay cameras rather than film cameras: the audio-visual quality and texture are different. TV studios tend to work on series rather than one-offs; they have relatively stable teams and predictable products.

Mode of transmission: TV is characteristically broadcast ('over the air') rather than narrow-cast; though satellite and cable TV are modifying these patterns of distribution. So are TV recall and view on demand, and DVD and downloads.

Mode of reception: TV is commonly part of the routine hubbub at home and, like radio and music, may be part of the background 'noise'. It is not a special spectacle received publicly in the darkness and silence of the cinema. The viewing unit for TV is often, say, part of an evening rather than a specific item. Meanwhile, 'channel hopping' is not an option in the cinema – though concentrated, uninterrupted viewing is.

Genres. TV **genres** are remarkably various; they include soap operas, game and chat shows, phone-ins, police- and hospital-based series, situation comedies, sports, documentaries, nature programmes, news, pop, adverts and recyclings of cinema films. TV genres are typically 'open' and 'continuing' (rather than 'closed' and 'one-off') because of their programming in series and serials. They are also remarkably hybrid in form and function (e.g., 'police/crime' programmes = actual recordings + commentary = documentary 'reality' + 'chase' thriller with moral; TV talent shows = performance + competition, with celebrity panel + public vote).

Activities

(a)   *Showing and/or telling?* Use the above 'Drama>><<Narrative' model (Figure 4.1) to explore the ways in which a particular text may be considered 'dramatic' and/or 'narrative', depending on how you look at it. (Suggestions in Part Five: Kipling, Carter, Atwood or Eggers (5.2.1); Dick, Hoban, Le Guin or Pratchett and Gaiman (5.2.4); Thomas, Beckett, McDonagh or Oswald (5.3.3).)

(b)   *Cross-media and cross-genre adaptation.* Try adapting part of a novel or short story into a script for stage, radio, TV or film. Alternatively, do the reverse. Add a commentary explaining your decisions and exploring the problems and possibilities encountered. Include comment on the following aspects:

   ◆ what is medium-specific to each version and what 'translates' fairly easily;
   ◆ how far the switch in medium prompts a shift in genre;
   ◆ who is speaking, thinking, feeling and looking at corresponding moments;
   ◆ how far there is a discernible authorial voice or directorial 'presence'.

(Suggestions in Part Five: Atwood (5.2.1); Dick, Hoban or Le Guin (5.2.4) or Pratchett and Gaiman (5.2.4); *Noah's Flood* or *The Tempest* (@ 5.3.2).)

Discussion

(i)   Deadly Theatre approaches the classics from the viewpoint that somewhere, someone has found out and defined how the play should be done.

   Peter Brook, *The Empty Space* (1968) (1972: 17)

(ii) It will never be adequate simply to impose a literary analysis on television entertainment without fully understanding the institutions of television, its mode of address and how it is received.

   Ros Coward, 'Character and Narrative in Soap Operas', in MacCabe
   (1988: 169–70; substitute 'film' or 'drama' for 'television' if you wish)

Also see: MEDIA; **speech, conversation and dialogue; narrative**; Voices, 5.3

READING: Montgomery *et al.* 2012: Section 6; Wallis and Shepherd 2002; Stam 2005; Fiske 1987; Hutcheon 2006. *Core texts*: Brecht 1964; Benjamin 1970; Brook 1968; Boal 1992; Bordwell and Thompson 2002.

FOREGROUND, BACKGROUND AND POINT OF VIEW

All of these terms have to do with visualising a text from a variety of perspectives and in a variety of dimensions. The **foreground** is what appears closest and most prominent to someone; the **background** is what appears remotest and most inconspicuous. **Point of view** refers to the vantage point from which a particular event is seen and, by extension, heard, felt and otherwise perceived. Partly relatable concepts, though with a decidedly POSTSTRUCTURALIST turn, can be found in the entry on **absence and presence**. The terms featured in the present entry derive chiefly from the theory of perspective in art and architecture and from the psychology of visual perception. As we shall quickly 'see', a 'way of seeing' invariably turns out to be a 'way of saying', and vice versa.

First, a couple of simple – or apparently simple – illustrations. In Leonardo da Vinci's *Mona Lisa* we might say that the top half of a woman is in the foreground, and a dark landscape is in the background. In Shakespeare's *Hamlet*, we might say that the prince of that name is in the foreground (and literally front-stage in the soliloquies) while the go-betweens Rosencrantz and Guildenstern are in the background. Ophelia, we might add, occupies a kind of middle ground. However, a little further reflection confirms that the foreground–background relation is not quite as simple and stable as it first seems. What we 'see' in a picture (or text) is partly what we are predisposed to see or read into it. It also depends how we are inclined to 'frame' the picture, physically and ideologically. Thus what is firmly in the foreground for one reader, viewer or audience – or for one period or social group – may not be for another. Reconsider Leonardo's *Mona Lisa*, also called *La Gioconda*. If you were interested in landscape rather than portraiture you would concentrate on – and thereby foreground – the background. If you were a dressmaker or historical costumier you might ignore the famous smile but concentrate on the clothes. A MARXIST could look at the painting and the main thing at the front of his or her mind might be the painter's dependence on wealthy patrons both for subjects and support (La Gioconda was the wife of a rich merchant Zanoki del Giocondo). Alternatively, all sorts of NEW HISTORICISTS might be taking a sideways glance at the rest of the Louvre (where the painting hangs) and contemplating its shift in function from royal palace to state museum. A FEMINIST, meanwhile, might be vigorously wrestling with and trying to re-vision one of the most teasing instances of woman as a 'specular subject/object' – both gazing and being gazed at. A POSTMODERNIST, however, might be busily comparing 'the original' with all the versions of the painting reproduced in books and magazines and on T-shirts; for **images** of the Mona Lisa are used to help sell everything from Italian spaghetti (she eats it in one advert) to a classic British TV arts programme (*The South Bank Show*, where she made a cartoon appearance in the credits): 'Will the "real" Mona Lisa stand up please . . . !'

Similarly revised observations might be made about the apparently simple foreground–background relation in *Hamlet* (see 3.1 and @ 3.1). For one thing, a specific critic or director might actually draw attention to Rosencrantz and Guildenstern, or to Ophelia, and thereby put them in the foreground and 'in a spotlight'. In fact this is precisely what Stoppard does in his play *Rosencrantz and Guildenstern are Dead* (1966) and Jean Betts does in her *Ophelia* (1995). Meanwhile, critics of all hues and persuasions do much the same in their 'rewrites' of *Hamlet* (as of other texts); for what are most critical essays but the highly selective quotation

FOREGROUNDS, BACKGROUNDS AND POINTS OF VIEW

◆ Who and what stands out? What people and events? What linguistic features and textual structures? (Standing out against what assumed backgrounds: social and historical; linguistic and literary?)

◆ Whose points of view and which perspectives seem to be preferred? Whose and which seem to be marginalised or ignored? And what shifts and switches in point of view do you experience between, say, narrator and characters?

◆ How do foreground–background relations change over the course of the text? And in what contexts has the text been seen and used at different moments in history?

◆ Is there anything which *you* would actively like to *direct* attention to – even if the text itself does not seem to *draw* attention to it?

and foregrounding of certain 'aspects', 'dimensions of' and 'perspectives on' the play? Here, then, are some general questions which can be put to any text. They help to draw attention to the *perceptual* and *cultural* dimensions of what is never a merely visual issue.

Background is also familiar to students of English Literature in the phrases 'the historical (or social) background' and 'background reading'. In both cases there is a strong implication that LITERATURE is somehow distinct or detachable from the social and historical conditions in which it is produced and received; also that the primary object of study is 'the **text** in itself', with the **context** (including **intertextual** relations) being treated as secondary or even optional. Clearly, a case can be made for the usefulness of such distinctions. NEW CRITICS and FORMALISTS assert or assume them all the time. However, it should be noted that the equation 'foreground = literature = primary text' and 'background = society/history = context' *is* a position, and is in fact just one position amongst many. Virtually all the other positions and approaches surveyed in Part Two would challenge that equation and the oppositions and hierarchies it presupposes. MARXISTS, FEMINISTS and POSTCOLONIAL critics, in particular, would insist on seeing all writing (not just that privileged as 'literary') as being produced and received *in* – not above, to one side or in front of – history and society. Nonetheless, the practical necessity of having to focus on *some*thing (not just *any*thing) inevitably means that some kind of foreground–background relation is implied. The point, therefore, is to decide which one, and as far as possible to make the theoretical 'grounds' of our particular 'fore-' and 'back-' explicit.

Foreground and the activity of **foregrounding** were concepts given prominence and a particular twist in stylistics by Paul Garvin (1964). He used these words to translate Czech *aktualisace* (literally 'actualising'), as used by the 1930s Prague School (see 3.3). For Mukarovsky and Havranek, foregrounding/*aktualisace* occurs whenever a linguistic item, device or strategy draws attention to itself against the assumed background norms of the language. The result is a fresh perception both of the event represented and of the nature of language itself. Foregrounding is thus the textual mechanism whereby defamiliarisation occurs. Routine examples of foregrounding abound in jokes and puns where the ambiguity or incongruity of a particular item suddenly draws attention to itself (e.g., 'A: But I am trying. B: Yes, very!' or 'A: My dog smells awful. How does yours smell? B: With his nose', or such quips as 'Today I got up at the crack of lunchtime'). Another, more structural kind of foregrounding can be equated with rhymes, songs and **poetry** in general, in fact wherever there is some heightening of sound-pattern (see **versification**). In the written or printed word, visual presentation and punctuation can also be foregrounded by, for instance, omitting commas and full stops and using line-breaks to control the reader's attention instead.

The term deviation is also sometimes used to describe instances where the routine norms and expectations of the language are bent or broken, deliberately or accidentally (e.g., e e cummings' 'anyone lived in a pretty how town' or my 3-year-old daughter's 'Mummy has *her*-grain' – modelled on '*mi*graine'!). The problem with 'deviance' analysis, however, is that it presupposes that people have the same norms and expectations (also see Appendix A).

Points of view can also be identified with a variety of positions 'within' and 'outside' the text. It is useful to distinguish the following:

- actual **author**'s attitudes and values, e.g., Defoe's, Brontë's;
- **narrator**'s point of view, e.g., Robinson Crusoe's, Jane Eyre's;
- **character**'s point of view; e.g., Friday's, Rochester's;
- implied **reader**'s point of view, most overtly in the 'dear reader' mode of address;
- actual reader's **responses**, e.g., what you and I actually see or look for.

What most engages us as readers or viewers, however, is *shifts or switches in point of view*: the ways in which the attitudes and values of author, narrator, characters and readers (actual as well as implied) ceaselessly diverge or converge, collide or coalesce. An absolutely fixed point of view, like a static relation between foreground and background, is basically boring.

Activities

(a)   Put the questions on 'Foregrounds, Backgrounds and Points of View' (p. 233) to a text you are studying. (Suggestions from Part Five are: the texts in 'Slave narratives' (5.2.2), 'Romance revisited' (5.2.3) and 'War on – of – Terror' (5.2.5).) Go on to read the entry on **absence and presence, gaps and silences, centres and margins** and consider whether anything is lost or gained by this switch in critical perspective.

(b)   Think of an alternative title or caption for a text, painting or photo with which you are familiar. Consider how far you have thereby realigned the implied foreground–background relations and the implied points of view.

Discussion

(i)   Saying what happened is an angle of saying.
Seamus Heaney on *The South Bank Show* (1991) (cited in Simpson 1993: 1)

(ii)   the function of poetic language consists in the maximum foregrounding of the utterance.
Jan Mukarovsky and P. Havranek, 'Standard Language and Poetic Language' in Garvin (1964: 19)

Also see: FORMALISM INTO FUNCTIONALISM; **absence and presence; character; narrative; subject.**

READING: Wales 2011: 156–7; Simpson 1993; Short 1996: 17–24; Fowler 1996: 160–84. *Core texts:* Eichenbaum and Jakobson in Leitch 2010; Shklovsky in Rivkin and Ryan 2004; Booth 1961.

GENRE AND KINDS OF TEXT

Genres are kinds, categories or types of cultural product and process – including texts. The word derives, through French, from Latin *genera* (pl.), where it simply means 'kinds' or 'types'. Love sonnets, absurdist drama, shopping lists and disaster movies are all genres of text. By extension, we can also talk about genres of everything from chats over coffee to job interviews, and from pizza packaging to shopping malls. The main thing is that there should be some basic similarity of form and function in the kinds of cultural product or activity, notwithstanding all the differences there inevitably are between one item and another. At the broadest, then, analysis of genre has to do with the fundamental activity of perceiving differences and similarities. For students of English it mainly has to do with perceiving the relations between one text and another, i.e. **intertextuality**.

Genre as a term and concept is chiefly known to students of LITERATURE through such traditional categories as **poetry, novel** and **drama**. These are best seen as capacious and flexible mega-genres. Each can be broken down into sub-genres:

- poetry into epic, lyric, ballad, sonnet, haiku, epigram, free verse, concrete poetry, etc. (see **versification**);
- novel into picaresque, epistolary, journals, realist (social or 'magical'), stream of consciousness, etc. (see **narrative**);
- drama into **comedies, tragedies,** street theatre, naturalist, **absurdist,** etc.

Such labels are a recognised and useful part of the vocabulary of literary criticism. Thus, it is helpful to recognise that all the poems in 5.1.2 are sonnets, that Beckett's *Not I* (5.3.3) is an instance of absurdist drama, and that what links the otherwise highly diverse writings of Mapping journeys (5.4.2) is that they are all kinds of 'travel narrative'. Some important qualifications and extensions need to be made, however; for the whole matter of genres and sub-genres is much more fascinating and volatile than these relatively familiar, apparently fixed categories seem to imply.

RE-GENERATING GENRES . . .

Several deliberate decisions were made about the gathering and sorting of texts in the Anthology in the present book (Part Five). All have some bearing on matters of genre.

- The recognised mega-genres of poetry, prose and drama are respected but also stretched and supplemented in the three parts; hence, respectively: poetries, including song and performance (5.1); proses, including life-writing and news (5.2); voices, including drama, conversation and dialogue in the novel (5.3).
- There is a recognition of relatively established generic classifications (e.g., heroic and mock-heroic verse, 5.1.3) as well as more recent ones (e.g. street texts, 5.2.6).
- The crossings section (5.4) is an attempt to demonstrate that gathering and grouping texts is a matter of making as well as finding relations. 'Genre' is something we *do* as well as *see*.

Any named instance of a genre always turns out to be in some sense mixed, hybrid or impure; at the very least it can always be categorised in a variety of ways. Thus Shakespeare's 'My mistress' eyes' (5.1.2) can be characterised and categorised not only as a sonnet but also as a satire on women, a rhetorical display and a parody; Beckett's *Not I* (5.3.3) might be categorised as comedy and/or tragedy (depending how it is performed), minimalist theatre or modernist stream of consciousness.

Genres are constantly changing so as to produce new variations on old modes as well as substantially new configurations. Thus the *romance* was initially a chivalric tale of love and war in the Romance languages (hence the name); but subsequently it came to be the name for any story with a love (but not an erotic or pornographic) interest. Romances can now take forms as various as sentimental Mills and Boon novelettes, A.S. Byatt's highly meta- and intertextual period piece *Possession* (1990) and most of the films featuring Meryl Streep. Meanwhile, the relatively modern genre of *science fiction* has moved from being the apparently exclusive preserve of what has been called the 'men and machines' movement (Verne, Wells, Asimov, Aldiss; latterly *Star Wars*, and *Blade Runner*) towards what might be more properly, though still inadequately, labelled *fantasy fiction*. Moreover, now the emphasis tends to be on FEMINIST and/or ecological agendas, often mixed in with variously *utopian* or *dystopian* visions of the future and meditations on the present. Examples include work by Le Guin, Lessing, Piercy, Russ and Carter; and early precursors include Mary Shelley's *Frankenstein*.

Such constant generation of old/new genres should not surprise us. Genre shares its root *gen-* (meaning 'growth', or 'creation') with such words as *gen*erate, *gen*eration, and *gen*der. Genres which didn't come and go, change and grow, wouldn't be proper genres at all. (Other radical and ongoing shifts in generic classification are recorded in the entry on auto/biography **and** travel writing.)

Genres are by no means limited to LITERATURE *narrowly conceived, or even* LANGUAGE *broadly conceived: they are a characteristic of all kinds of* CULTURAL *product and* COMMUNICATIVE *activity.* Thus we routinely recognise and speak of different genres of music as, say, pop, folk and classical. And then, once more, we can go on to subdivide, blend and extend these 'kinds' so as to produce or recognise sub-genres. For pop perhaps: rock 'n' roll, rhythm 'n' blues, soul, punk, funk, rap, heavy metal, etc; as well as compounds such as 'folk-rock' or – an off-the-cuff coinage I overheard recently – 'rap and roll with a funky rhythm and a touch of Jah Wobble'. (You can doubtless think of and make up many more. DJs do all the time.) In the same fertile and potentially highly nuanced vein, we can talk about different genres, sub-genres and 'cross-genres' of soap opera, game or chat show, police series, news programme, disaster movie, dance craze, and so on.

The basic principles relating to genre are therefore few and simple, even though particular instances always turn out to be complexly variegated:

♦ One instance of a text or activity is or is not like others in certain respects.
♦ It is mixed or fused with others in certain configurations.
♦ It is always on the point of turning away from or back towards another.
♦ Genres – when not fixed and fossilised – are constantly coming and going, changing and growing.

Activities

(a)   Concentrate on one of the texts you are studying (or a text featured in Part Five) and consider some of the ways in which it can be categorised. How stable or debatable are these categories? And which would you say are recognised 'genres'?

(b)   *Re-genring.* Try interpreting the same short text as though it belonged to quite different genres and could therefore be 'placed' in quite different contexts and intertextual relations. (Suggestions from Part Five include treating *each* of the texts in ''I'dentity in the balance' (5.3.4) or 'Versions of ageing' (5.4.4) as though it were (a) part of an advert (for what?); (b) part of a psychological case history (what's the problem?); (c) part of an overheard conversation (with whom? in what context?). Go on to identify what marks it as, in fact, belonging to a particular genre.)

Discussion

(i)   Genre is reborn and renewed at every new stage in the development of literature, and in every individual work of a given genre.

Mikhail Bakhtin, *The Dialogic Imagination* (1981: 321)

(ii) Thus redefined and democratised, not only is the term [genre] enjoying renewed currency in literary discourse; it also shows signs of becoming a general cultural buzzword, used in contexts increasingly remote from literary criticism.

David Duff, *Modern Genre Theory* (2000: 2)

Also see: **discourse; auto/biography and travel writing; canon comedy; and tragedy, carnival and the absurd; drama and theatre; narrative in story . . . ; text, context and intertextuality.**

READING: Hopkins 2009: Part 4; Preminger and Brogan 1993: 456–8; Wellek and Warren 1963: 226–37. *Core texts*: Bakhtin 1981; Duff 2000 (anthology).

IMAGES, IMAGERY AND IMAGINATION

An **image** can be strictly visual (e.g., a painting, a photo) or, by extension, it can be a verbal representation of something visual (e.g., a description in a novel). **Imagery** refers to figurative or metaphorical language invoking a comparison or likeness, chiefly in poetry or 'poetic' writing. **Imagination**, meanwhile, can be provisionally defined as the capacity to conceive, 'grasp' or 'see' things, both in a visual and in a more general intellectual sense. Taken together, then, all the terms in this entry have something to do, at least initially, with ways of seeing and saying, and with issues of **representation**, verbal, visual and otherwise. The terms image, imagery and imagination are also obviously central to many people's idea of what is going on in LITERATURE and the arts in particular, as well as CULTURE in general. They crop up regularly in discussions of everything from **poetry** and **film** to LITERARY and CULTURAL theory, and in the latter they arise in everything from CLASSICAL to PSYCHOANALYTICAL approaches. What follows is a historical overview of the interrelations among the terms image(s), imagery and imagination (including imaginative and (the) imaginary). This is framed so as to encourage interdisciplinary and multimedia perspectives, while also observing the specificity of these terms in distinct discourses. (For other 'visualising' metaphors, see **foreground, background and point of view**; also **absence . . . margins.**)

   Image came into English, via French, from Latin *imago* during the thirteenth century. The word already had various potential meanings, each of which has been realised and become prominent in English at successive historical moments. The cumulative result is that 'image' can now mean at least five things: *physical likeness*; *mental construct*; *figurative language* (i.e. imagery); *optical effect* and *perceived identity*. We shall consider each of these in turn.

♦   *Image as physical likeness or visible copy*, e.g., a painted or photographic representation of people and places, or a perceived resemblance ('She's the very image of her mother').

♦   *Image as mental construct or 'idea'*, usually of something which only really exists *as* an idea, and may therefore be an illusion or (more negatively) a delusion. This divided sense relates to a variety of persistent debates in aesthetics, philosophy and religion about the nature of images: are they pleasing or harmful? true or false? divinely or diabolically inspired?

◆ *Image as 'imagery' – figure of speech, trope ('turn', 'twist'), figurative language in general.* **Imagery,** as such, is usually further distinguished in terms of metaphor, simile and personification: *metaphor* (from Greek *meta-pherein* – 'over-carry') refers to the implicit 'carrying over' of sense from one area to another, implicitly talking about one thing in terms of something else (e.g., 'She's a doll', 'He's a real pig' – when said of a person, not of a doll or a pig!). Metaphors are themselves further distinguished as

- *dead* and relatively routine, e.g., 'He's hard-faced', 'Think straight!'
- *live* and striking, e.g., 'He's marble-eyed', 'Think bent for a change!'
- *extended* and perhaps *mixed* or *compounded*, depending how coherent and successful the extension is judged to be: e.g. Hamlet's 'Whether 'tis nobler in the mind to suffer / The slings and arrows of outrageous fortune / Or to take arms against a sea of troubles, / And by opposing end them' (Act III, sc i).
- *metonymic*, in so far as there is a substitution of a part for the whole (e.g., 'motor' when used to mean 'car', 'hand' meaning 'worker') and where something physically connected is involved (e.g., 'the White House', 'the Kremlin' and 'Downing Street' when used to refer to the US, Russian and British governments).

simile (from Latin *similis* – 'like') refers to an explicit and overtly controlled comparison, characteristically signalled by such words as 'like', 'as', 'seems', 'appears', 'compare', 'recalls' (e.g., 'Like a ferret up a drain-pipe', 'as happy as the day is long', 'Shall I compare thee to a summer's day?'). Similes may also be dead, live and extended.

personification, conferring human attributes and identities on inanimate or non-human entities (e.g., 'This is a friendly (threatening, snobbish, etc.) place'; 'That vodka grabs you by the throat'). When personification involves an address *to* something as though it were a person, the device is called apostrophe (e.g., in odes such as Shelley's 'O wild West Wind, thou breath of Autumn's being'). When personification involves an address *by* some non-human speaker, the device is called *prosopopoeia* (e.g., the speaking cross in the Anglo-Saxon *Dream of the Rood*, as well as riddles of the 'I am . . .' type). Sustained personification can result in *allegory* (e.g., the Giant Despair and Hopeful in Bunyan's *The Pilgrim's Progress*, or Grumpy, Bashful, Dopey and co. in Disney's *Snow White and the Seven Dwarfs*).

All these aspects of imagery are fundamental to LANGUAGE of all kinds, spoken and written. They are not limited to poetry in particular or literature in general. Thus for a long time they were studied as aspects of RHETORIC (see @ 1.4.6). In fact it was only NEW CRITICS and some FORMALISTS during the earlier twentieth century who tended to limit the study of imagery to specifically literary texts, especially poetry (see 3.2–3). Modern **discourse analysis** and a renewed interest in rhetoric is resulting in a much greater attention to the figurative nature of non-literary texts, including conversation (see READING below).

◆ *Image as a specifically technical, optical effect.* The sense here is of what results from the projection of light through a lens or film on to paper or a screen, or the assembly of pixels on a TV or computer screen. This sense of image is obviously tied up with transformations in visual technology from the mid-nineteenth century onwards, notably photography, film, television, video and, latterly, computerised multi-media.

◆ *Image as projected or perceived identity, public reputation* (as in 'brand image', 'company image', 'creating the right image'). This usage has become current, and in some areas of life dominant, largely through the huge growth in the institutions of advertising, marketing and

COMPANION @ WEBSITE

public relations. These discourses permeate many areas of life, especially in the postindustrial societies. It is also common to talk of 'self-image', largely because of the influence of popular PSYCHOLOGY.

Imagination is a term somewhat out of favour in critical circles now. However, imagination is a concept with a complex history and constantly renegotiated meanings so there is every reason to believe that (like the related, equally out-of-favour but resilient term **creativity**) it will have a valuable future too. 'The Imagination' has at various times been visually likened to a mirror, window, lens and eye – all-seeing, opaque, partially sighted or blind. It has also been hailed as the site or source of everything from utter delusion to sublime revelation (see Kearney 1994, 1998). The huge problem – and fascinating challenge – is of course that we are trying to define an object by means of the tool which is that object. We are trying to imagine imagination! Most immediately, it involves trying to do what we're trying to do throughout this book: define language with language. The most famous and influential attempt at a verbal definition of imagination in English Literature is doubtless that offered by the poet and philosopher Samuel Taylor Coleridge in his *Biographia Literaria* (1817: Ch. 14). There Coleridge explains, at length, that by 'the name of imagination' he means: 'the balance or recognition of opposite or discordant qualities: of sameness, with difference; of the general, with the concrete; the idea, with the image; the individual, with the representative; the sense of novelty and freshness, with old and familiar objects; a more than usual state of emotion, with more than usual order . . .'. Many things can be said about Coleridge's definition of imagination. One is that it was much prized and promoted by NEW CRITICS (e.g., Brooks 1947: 12). Such an elegant array of balanced antitheses admirably suited their views of both **aesthetics** and politics as processes of resolving tension through paradox. Another is that this vision of imagination would be substantially challenged by critics engaged in developing more conflictual, oppositional – or simply alternative – models of aesthetics and politics. In short, MARXIST, FEMINIST, POSTCOLONIAL, POST-STRUCTURALIST and POSTMODERNIST writers would all tend to imagine the form and the function of imagination differently. (Hence the invitation to critique Coleridge and imagine some other possibilities in Activity (b) below.) Here just a couple of brief notes will be added to bring the story of images and the imagination up to date.

The Imaginary (*l'Imaginaire*) is given a special status in the PSYCHOANALYTICAL model developed by Lacan. For him the Imaginary is the name of the non-differentiated state (and stage) of the unconscious before the psychological **subject** enters into language and the symbolic order. For Lacan, in the Imaginary there is not yet a clear distinction between, for instance, 'I' and 'you', subject and object, person and thing, child and mother, masculine and feminine, body and mind, physical image and conceptual idea. The Imaginary is also a kind of reservoir of the unconscious which the psyche may draw upon throughout life, chiefly in the form of 'images'; though these are always a skewed refraction (never a direct reflection) of the psyche's 'imaginary' resources.

Meanwhile, Baudrillard, a postmodernist philosopher and cultural critic, has effectively abolished 'images' in any traditional sense. He insists that we now live in an age when the whole concept of the image is in crisis. Because of the sheer speed, accuracy and proliferation of images in the modern audio-visual media, and because of the incredibly enhanced editing techniques of the computer-assisted multi-media, we have reached a point when it becomes hard to be sure that the image is a copy of anything in the rest of the world, or that there is an 'original' version of the image itself. This concept of the image-without-reference and the image-without-an-original Baudrillard calls a *simulacrum* (cf. Benjamin 1970: 219–53). Thus Baudrillard argues that we may have seen and heard countless 'simulacra' of the 1992 Gulf War in the media. But they were so highly mediated at every stage (from computer-guided and camera-tracked missile systems to computer-simulated reconstructions in the media) that we could easily be lulled into believing that a war was not really going on: that the whole thing was a military exercise or another hi-tech disaster movie. The virtual iconicity of the visual image and the fantastic plasticity of the popular imaginary were drawn together in two provocative critiques of representations of 9/11 by Baudrillard and Žižek (both 2002). These continue to resonate with subsequent representations of the 'War on – of – Terror' (see 5.2.5).

Activities

(a) *Ways of saying and seeing*. Compare a poem with an advert, or an extract from a novel with a news report, and consider the various kinds of 'image' and 'imagery' in play. What are the relations between the verbal and the visual? When does a 'way of saying' become a 'way of seeing', and vice versa? (Suggestions for comparison in Part Five are the 'Daffodils' texts (5.4.1); the Clarins advert and the other (anti-)ageing texts (5.4.4), and the reports of terrorism and war (5.2.5).)

(b) *Rewrite Coleridge's definition of 'imagination'* (see above) so as to challenge his assumptions about aesthetics and politics. How, for instance, might some of the writers referred to in Part Three *other than* New Critics view the roles and resources of the imaginative writer or artist?

Discussion

(i) Some readers are constitutionally prone to stress the place of imagery in reading [. . .] and even to judge the value of the poetry by the images it excites in them.
I.A. Richards, *Practical Criticism* (1929: 15)

(ii) The phenomenal impact of the communications revolution in our century has meant a crisis of identity for imagination. [. . .] one can no longer be sure who or what is actually making our images – a creative human subject or some anonymous system of reproduction.
Richard Kearney, *Poetics of Imagining: Modern to Postmodern* (1998: 7)

Also see: 2.3; **foreground, background and point of view; realism and representation**; sign and sign-system.

READING: Preminger and Brogan 1993: 556–75; Wellek and Warren 1963: 186–211; Kearney 1994, 1998; *Core texts*: Jakobson and Lacan in Lodge and Wood 2008; Barthes 1977: 32–51; Benjamin 1970: 219–52; Baudrillard 1995, 2002; Žižek 2002.

NARRATIVE IN STORY AND HISTORY: NOVEL, NEWS, FILM

Narrative can be provisionally defined as telling stories, true or false, factual or fictional, in any medium. The term *narration* is sometimes reserved for the process of telling stories, as distinct from the product of the activity, the narrative proper. Such capacious definitions are handy because they encourage us to recognise as narratives and narrations all sorts of products and processes: from anecdotes and jokes to adverts and news stories, from short stories to blockbuster novels, from comic strips and cartoons to full-length feature films (and their sequels), from your most recent account of what happened yesterday (in conversation, diary or blog) to full-blown printed histories, auto/biographies and TV documentaries. Narrative is any activity which results in a story being told and an event represented and reported. Such a perspective therefore allows us to see the printed novel and short story (the narrative **genres** most often featured in LITERATURE courses) as simply two amongst many story-telling modes. To offset exclusively literary and verbal emphases, we also look at narrative in history and news, including film, TV and video. The following model is useful when approaching any instance of narrative as part of a communicative process of narration.

actual writer ↔ 'external' narrator ↔ character as narrator ↔ narratee ↔ actual reader

This may be explained as follows. The *actual writer* is the historical person as we conceive of him or her independently of the text s/he wrote (e.g., the living, breathing Dickens, Brontë). The *'external' narrator* is the selective image of her or himself the writer projects in the text (how Dickens or Brontë chooses to present him/herself). The *character-as-narrator* is a figure who both relates and participates in the action (e.g., Pip in *Great Expectations*, Jane in *Jane Eyre*; also see **character**). The *narratee* is the implied addressee of the narrative, the kind of person it appears to be primarily directed at (most explicit in the 'dear reader' mode of narrative, but implicit in every narrative). *Actual readers* are you and me and anyone else every time we engage with a particular narrative. The two-way arrows (↔) are important. They remind us of the potential bi- or multidirectionality of all acts of writing and reading. Thus, actual writers define themselves through dialogue with their narrators, while actual readers may or may not cooperate with the role of narratee they are offered. A narrative is therefore not so much a given 'thing' as the constant negotiation and realignment of a variety of actual readers and writers through a variety of narrators, characters and narratees. This means that the points of view and centres of attention of a narrative are never absolutely fixed. The teller tells the tale; but no one ever puts up with simply being 'told'. The reader, audience or viewer has a part to play too.

NARRATIVE TELLING AND DRAMATIC SHOWING

The basic distinction between *narrative* (what is told, reported and represented) and *drama* (what is shown, enacted or presented) is reviewed under **drama**. So is the fact that, characteristically, narrative emphasises the address: what is spoken about, the **subject** positions 'she', 'he', 'they' and 'it'. Drama, meanwhile, emphasises the addresser–addressee relation: people speaking and spoken to, the subject positions 'I', 'we' and 'you'. (See addresser–addressee @ 4.)

Structural aspects of narrative

Many of the most valuable terms and techniques for the analysis of narrative structure have been provided by FORMALIST and STRUCTURALIST approaches. The most common are listed below. A few words should be added by way of caution, however. Not all of these terms are mutually compatible nor are they always glossed in the same way. The very emphasis on structure as something supposedly 'whole' and 'neutral' would be challenged by many POSTSTRUCTURALIST critics, as well as by those who occupy politically explicit positions. That said, the following distinctions still prove both valuable and durable:

Story and plot. Story is *what* is told, the abstractable subject matter. *Plot* is *how* it is told, the actual treatment given to the material. Thus we might list the main characters and events of *Great Expectations* or *Blade Runner*; but that would not tell us how they were actually put together. The plot is what motivates and organises the raw story material.

Fabula and sjuzet (from early Formalist approaches). *Fabula* is the raw narrative events as they would usually be chronologically sequenced outside a particular telling. *Sjuzet* is the particular chronological sequencing and structural logic of a specific telling.

Discours and skaz. Discours (French) and *skaz* (Russian) are tales where the teller is prominent and openly acknowledged (e.g., in the first person and/or with a character-as-narrator). Both are distinct from *histoire* (French) or *historia* (Russian), which are narratives where the presence of the narrator is invisible or unacknowledged. Approximate English equivalents are, respectively, 'yarn' or 'anecdote' as distinct from (impersonal) 'report' or 'account'.

Narrators (also see 'narration' above) are commonly distinguished as:

♦ *first person*, speaking as an 'I', or *third person*, speaking only of others, as 'she', 'he', 'they';
♦ *omniscient* and all-knowing, or *partial* and limited;
♦ *reliable* or *unreliable*, projecting themselves as trustworthy or not.

Narrative episodes are commonly distinguished as:

♦ *beginnings*, *middles* and *ends* – points of opening, development and closure;
♦ *essential* ('kernels', 'nuclei'), i.e. episodes which substantially advance the action;
♦ *optional* ('catalysers', 'satellites'), which elaborate but do not advance action;
♦ *kinetic* – concentrating on action, movement and transformation;
♦ *static* – concentrating on description, state and atmosphere.

Characters are commonly distinguished in terms of the ways they are constructed, how far they are: individuals or types; 'rounded' or 'flat'; psychologically interiorised or externally observed (see **character and characterisation**).

Points of view are usually initially identified with specific narrators and characters, but always eventually involve exploration of the positions and values held by actual writers and readers (see 'narration' above). Critical attention is frequently trained upon shifts and switches in perspective, and collisions and coalescences of identity against a variety of frames of reference which may be internal or external to the text (see **foreground, background and point of view**).

All of the above terms can be used to analyse the structural aspects of narrative in a variety of verbal and visual media, whether in stories or histories, novels or news reports. Care must be taken, however, to respect the structural capacities and generic traditions of the medium (see **drama and theatre, film and TV**); also to recognise that a formal analysis must ultimately take account of functions if it is to engage with **texts** in **context** (see 2.2). With that in mind, we now turn to particular kinds or modes of narrative: history, the novel and film. Clearly, these are not mutually exclusive categories. There are plenty of historical novels and historical films (e.g., period pieces and documentaries). Meanwhile, both the novel and film have their own histories implicated in various media and social-historical moments: the novel arose from print technology and culture during the early modern period; film arose from photographic and audio-visual culture over the past century. Here we concentrate on the narrative dimensions of history, the novel and film. At what points do they converge and diverge as kinds of story?

History and **story** derive from exactly the same root, Latin *historia*. That in turn derives from the Greek *histor*, meaning 'a form of knowing'. This joint derivation points to an underlying sense in which history and story are basically two aspects of the same process. Both involve the fashioning of narratives which form ways of knowing the world. Indeed, in English and other European vernaculars it is only from the sixteenth century onwards that 'history' begins to be systematically distinguished as a way of knowing the actual past through factual narratives from 'story', which was a way of knowing everything else through fictional narratives. Concurrently, **fact** and **fiction** were themselves being more rigorously distinguished (see **realism and representation**). Before that, the words 'histoire', 'historie' and 'storie' were used almost interchangeably. If one looks for a modern equivalent it is most likely to be the coinage 'faction'.

All this may strike modern readers as less strange if it is recalled that most medieval and many classical histories, chronicles and annals began with references to, respectively, Christian and pagan gods, **myths** and legends, then ran up to their own present through more recognisably 'historical' materials, often rounding off with a moral or divine vision of the world to come. The same ample view of history (including what to non-believers are fictional myths and legends) characterises the **Bible**, especially the Old Testament as a history of the Jews. All that need be added here is that there is a growing recognition that the writing and reading of histories (i.e. narrative accounts of what supposedly actually happened) have a great deal in common with the writing and reading of narratives of all kinds, whether supposedly true or not. In fact, an interdisciplinary grasp of **discourse, genre** and **rhetoric** – along with narrative – has recently done much to reconfigure relations between English and History as academic subjects (see @ 1.4.7).

The **novel** was so called because of the perceived 'newness' of the genre in the eighteenth and nineteenth centuries. Novels can be broadly characterised as long narratives in prose dealing chiefly with contemporary life. All these features together distinguished them from the main literary genres recognised previously by neo-classical writers, namely, drama (comedy and tragedy) or poetry (epic and lyric). Prose romance was well developed earlier (e.g., Malory's *Morte D'Arthur*); but this dealt with fantastic, usually mythic or legendary materials. In fact, the formal 'newness' of the novel consisted largely in its capaciousness and flexibility: it accommodated all or flouted any of the previously recognised genres. Socially, the novel was tied to the rapid consolidation of a new class of readers, the bourgeoisie. Technologically, it was deeply dependent upon the consolidation of print culture. In all these respects (formally, socially and technologically) the rise of the novel is therefore best seen in conjunction with the rise of that other relatively 'new' phenomenon, *newspapers*. These too came into their own in the eighteenth and nineteenth centuries. These too were built from narratives in prose, appealed to much the same readership and depended upon the same print technology. The crucial and constitutive difference was that, whereas novels were presumed to be broadly fictional, newspapers were presumed to be broadly factual (see **realism**).

Most early and many later novels can be further categorised in terms of:

♦ *the established literary genres they adapt and blend* (often parodically), notably, romance, **comedy, tragedy** and heroic drama (e.g., Behn, Manley, Fielding, Sterne, Richardson, Dickens);
♦ *the extra-literary genres they draw upon and mimic* (and thereby eventually **canonise** as literary modes), notably, journals, diaries, letters, travelogues, confessions, conduct books of manners (e.g., Defoe, Richardson, Smollett, Austen);
♦ *formal devices and structural strategies* (see 'Structural Aspects of Narrative' above and the highlighted entries), namely, first or third person, partial or omniscient and un/reliable narration; **point of view**; emphasis on action or states, plot or **character**; techniques of **realism and representation** (e.g., 'classic realist', 'stream of consciousness', etc.).

Film and TV are sequential visual media, unfolding in time as well as in space. They are therefore especially amenable to narrative. Film is built up out of discrete frames which are then shown rapidly so as to provide the impression of continuous movement. In this respect films are like comics and moving strip cartoons (which are themselves a significant narrative form), as are animated films as such. TV is formed from patterns of electro-magnetic impulses (now usually stored digitally) which produce a continuous 'flow'. Both film and TV are now accompanied by sound-tracks which enable the synchronised reproduction of images, speech, music and sound effects. The overall consequences for the representation of narrative are profound. *Image–music–word* is the larger parcel we must learn to unpack when analysing story-telling in these media. And again it is convenient to distinguish technical, formal and social dimensions of the narrational process. (The emphasis here is upon film; so also see **drama . . . TV.**)

Technically, the basic minimum filmic unit is the *frame*, a continuous series of which builds up into a single *shot*. Shots are variously distinguished as: still, panning, tracked or hand-held; long, medium, medium-close or close-up; full-body, half-body or talking-head; shot–reverse shot (i.e. action–reaction); from above, below or eye level; etc. All this material is edited by *cutting* and *splicing* with other shots from the same or different cameras so as to produce a *sequence*. A series of sequences makes up the film as a whole. Technical complications include the fact that a single finished frame can be a composite superimposition of several frames or be modified by computer graphics. Meanwhile, the 'whole film' may exist in a variety of cut and uncut versions. The capacity to select and re-combine parts of a film, virtually at will or whim, is a particular feature of Digital Versatile Disks (DVD) and now routine even on mobile phones.

Formally, like all narratives, films are characterised by shifts and switches in time, place and participants. Development is only rarely strictly chronological and almost never limited to a single scene and a single perspective. Much more often the narrative proceeds through jumps in time and space (ellipsis); perhaps includes flashback, flash-forward or repetition; and generally establishes a variety of points of view – identifying with certain camera positions, focusing on certain figures, etc.

Socially, film is distinguished by specific modes of production and distribution and specific moments of reception. In the cinema proper, these include the high-street general release cinema chain or specialised studio cinema. Films on TV get around differently, of course – through commercial or public broadcast; satellite or cable narrowcast; in certain scheduled slots; and often retrievable on demand. There is clearly a big difference between watching a big screen from a row of special seats in the dark and lounging around amongst the clutter and clamour of a domestic front room. All these contexts fundamentally affect both the kinds of story that get told in various kinds of film and TV, and the ways in which viewers engage with those stories. Basically, TV narratives tend to be more open-ended, recursive and diffuse (soap operas and situation comedies are the classic case). Meanwhile cinematic film narratives tend to be more closed, progressive and concentrated (one-off feature films are the model here).

Finally, brief mention will be made of two very different models that have proved particularly useful in the study of popular narratives of all kinds – whether spoken or printed, on film or TV. Vladimir Propp, in his influential *Morphology of the Folktale* (1928), developed a model of thirty-one narrative 'functions' (in effect stereotypical actions) based on the analysis of a corpus of Russian folktales. He distinguished such roles as 'hero', 'helper', 'dispatcher', 'villain' and 'princess' and argued that these function in folktales in predictable ways. Typical examples are: function 25 – a difficult task is proposed to the hero; function 26 – the false hero or villain is exposed; function 31 – the hero is married and ascends the throne. Similar roles and functions can be found in popular narratives from Superman comics to feature films such as *Star Wars* and *The Dark Knight* and TV soaps and series such as *EastEnders* and *Mad Men*. This supports the view that popular narrative is substantially formulaic in nature. It perhaps also underwrites the general observation that 'there are only six or seven basic plots in the world' (though, significantly, people tend to disagree on precisely which these are!).

William Labov, in his *Language in the Inner City* (1972), developed a simple yet remarkably durable model for describing the structure of oral narratives. He studied the story-telling patterns of chiefly black vernacular culture in inner city New York and developed a schema that has been widely observed in many kinds of narrative, oral and otherwise. Labov observes that every act of story-telling tends to involve six stages. These are, in order, abstract, orientation, complicating action, evaluation, resolution, coda. Here they will be illustrated by snatches from a story I recently heard in a pub:

1   *Abstract* (preface, link in) – 'Yeah. Something like that happened to me.'
2   *Orientation* – 'There was this guy who lived by the works . . . '
3   *Complicating action* – 'But then you know what happened . . . '
4   *Evaluation* (can be pervasive) – 'He was sooooo stupid . . . '; 'Isn't that cool!'
5   *Resolution or result* – 'Anyway, no one saw him again.'
6   *Coda* (link out) – 'So there you go. Whose round is it?'

(Fuller applications and discussion can be found in Brumfit and Carter 1986: 119–32 and Toolan 2001: 143–70.)

Activities

(a)   *Draw on one or more of the models/checklists supplied above to help analyse a narrative and a process of narration which interests you.* That is, use one of these: narration as process (actual writer . . . actual reader); structural aspects of narrative; narrative in film and TV (technical, formal and social); Propp's model of popular story; Labov's model of oral story-telling. (Suggestions: Atwood's 'Happy Endings' (5.2.1), Dick's *Do Androids Dream . . . ?* (*Blade Runner*) (5.2.4) or Marshall-Stoneking's 'Passage' (5.4.2).)

(b)   *That's history! What's news?* Compare two news reports of the same event (e.g., 5.2.5). How precisely does each build it into a different news story, and in effect construct a different event? In particular, compare the ways in which these stories begin, develop and close; the arguments or agendas they address; and how they handle people, places and time as well as action, speech and evaluation. Which account would be of greater value as a historical document? Writing a history of what?

(c)   *Adapting beginnings and endings.* Speculate how you would film and edit the opening and closing sequences of a novel or short story with which you are familiar (or one of the short stories in 5.2.1). Be sure at some point to consider all the main *technical*, *formal* and *social* dimensions referred to above.

Discussion

(i)   Caring nothing for the division between good and bad literature, narrative is international, transhistorical, transcultural.
Roland Barthes, 'Introduction to the Structural Analysis of Narratives'
(1977: 79)

(ii)   There is the time of the thing told and the time of the telling . . .
Christian Metz, *Film Language: A Semiotics of the Cinema* (1974: 18)

Also see: FORMALISM INTO FUNCTIONALISM; POSTSTRUCTURALISM; POSTMODERNISM; auto/biography; character; drama and theatre, film and TV; foreground, background and point of view; realism and representation: fiction, fact, faction and metafiction.

READING: Kearney 2002; Montgomery *et al.* 2012: Section 5; Bennett and Royle 2009: 54–62; Prince 1987 (reference); Pope 1995: 70–119; Bhabha 1990; Toolan 2001; Bordwell and Thompson 2003; Cartmell and Whelehan 1999. *Core texts*: Propp 1928; Barthes 1977: 79–124; Onega and Landa 1996 (reader); McQuillan 2000 (reader).

POETRY AND WORD-PLAY

This entry is in part a plea for 'play' in advanced English Studies, both as something we study and something we do. It focuses in particular upon *word-play*, that is, play within and around language. It also proposes that *poetry*, though certainly the most prestigious and sometimes the most complex form of verbal play, is still just one of the many forms that it can take. Jokes and witty remarks (including puns and figurative language) are obvious instances of word-play in which most of us routinely engage. But it is also possible to regard a large part of all language use as a form of play. Much of the time speech and writing are not primarily concerned with the instrumental conveying of information at all, but with the social *inter*play embodied in the activity itself. In fact, in a narrowly instrumental, purely informational sense most language use is no use at all. Moreover, we are all regularly exposed to a barrage of more or less overtly playful language, often accompanied by no less playful images and music. Hence the perennial attraction (and distraction) of everything from advertising and pop songs to newspapers, panel games, quizzes, comedy shows, crosswords, Scrabble and graffiti. Much of this language has designs upon us as well as itself: the play is ultimately designed to make someone pay. There is a commercial as well as an **aesthetic** incentive. For all these reasons, this entry does not concentrate upon poetry narrowly conceived, but on word-play broadly conceived (including poetry). More specific attention to poetry as a **genre, versification** and **imagery** will be found in those entries.

Word-play can occur at all levels of LANGUAGE: sound, visual presentation, word, grammatical structure, genre and context. It also occurs in all areas of **discourse**: the media, education, law, medicine, the family, etc. Indeed, in so far as discourses are conceived, following Wittgenstein (1953) and Lyotard (1979), as distinct kinds of 'language game' (however seriously played), certain kinds of 'word-play' are constitutive of discourses as such. We shall therefore review each of the levels of language in turn, even though in any given instance we usually find more than one level in play (see 2.1 for a corresponding linguistic checklist and Appendix A for definitions).

Sound-play (using phonology) arises whenever the sounds of the language become a source of pleasure in themselves, usually through repetition with variation. In simple cases the result is a kind of 'word-music' with a strong rhythm but with little semantic sense, e.g., 'Hickory, Dickory, Dock', 'Humpty, Dumpty . . . ', 'With a hey-nonny-no', 'Oop-oop-be-doop', 'Bee-bop-a-lula', 'Showaddywaddy'. Commonly these elements function as refrains or choruses: they offer points where everyone can join in. Hence their frequency in popular songs and children's rhymes. More elaborate and extended sound-play usually entails complex relations with word meaning and grammatical structure. Alliteration, assonance, stress, **rhythm**, **rhyme** and **metre** may then supply a framework of sound-patterning which underpins or counterpoints everything else (see **versification**). Poetry and song offer the most complex and varied examples (see Shakespeare's 'My mistress' eyes' and Agbabi's 'Problem pages' (5.1.2) and, if possible, listen to Queen's 'Bohemian Rhapsody' and the Flobots' 'No Handlebars' (5.1.5). But advertising, too, draws upon many of the same playful features: e.g., 'Beanz Meanz Heinz', 'You can with a Nissan'; 'Lipsmackinthirstquenchinacetastin . . . Pepsi!'; 'Coke. It's the Ree-a-l thing' (sung variously). The main difference is in the kinds and degrees of sophistication involved, and the 'games' we feel we are being invited to play. After all, it's not only Coke, Heinz and Queen who have 'designs' on us. So has Shakespeare and every other writer.

Visual play uses the letters, shapes, spaces and colours on the page or screen to form patterns in their own right/write. Punctuation, font styles, letter sizes, line breaks, overall layout and design: these are all areas where the sheer materiality of the written or printed word is what attracts or sustains our attention – from tight sonnet-nuggets (5.1.2) through evenly spaced quatrains (2.1.2) to the more flexible shapes of free verse and magazine advertising (5.4.1) and newspaper – especially tabloid – copy. The editorial sophistication of the modern, computer-assisted multimedia also means that it is increasingly common for words not only to accompany images but actually to transform into them. 'Logos' are already a well-established area of word-as-image design. But film titles and credits also routinely superimpose upon or fade and merge into the action. So do the ceaselessly re-forming names and identities of everything from news programmes to whole TV channels (the constantly metamorphosing '2' of BBC 2 and the '4' of Channel 4 are two familiar instances from the UK). Graffiti on advertising hoardings are simply one of the more graphically resistant responses to a designedly graphic stimulus (5.2.6).

Lexical ('word') play arises where single words or lexical items are swapped around and even chopped up so as to remind us that they are both perpetually mobile and infinitely divisible. Crosswords, Scrabble and many TV and radio quizzes depend upon precisely this volatility and versatility at the level of 'individual' words (words which in the event turn out to be highly 'dividual'!). Playing with parts of words often involves an exploration and informal awareness of their morphology. Characteristically, however, these tend to be framed as word-*games* (narrowly conceived) rather than word-*play* (broadly conceived). Usually the questions are of the who, what, when and where type and can be answered by 'slot-filling' (the quiz equivalent of linguistic 'cloze' tests). Genuinely innovative and amusing panel shows are characterised by a healthy disregard for the question as posed – as well as a healthy irreverence for the questionmaster who poses. The contributors digress at will and the final score is totally irrelevant or an utter travesty. And that, arguably, is the difference between genuine word-*play* and a (mere) word-*game*. Poetry, we may add, also only becomes really significant when it constitutes a form of play with words – and by extension with the world – never simply a word-game.

Interestingly one of the most common kinds of lexical humour, the pun, is often looked down upon in academic discourse. Evidently this is because the pun destabilises the rules of sound-meaning, sporting in the spaces between signifier and signified (see sign). It thereby threatens the very fabric of certain kinds of rationalistic argument. It is sigificant, therefore, that many POSTSTRUCTURALIST, PSYCHOANALYTIC and FEMINIST critics have reinvested the pun with a measure of seriousness while also striving to maintain its free-booting irregularity. Derrida's pun on '*différence/différance*' (i.e. **difference**/deferral) is perhaps the most famous example. But there are many more: Lacan's 'hommelette/omelette' (little man/scrambled egg), Cixous's 'sorties' (way(s) out), Irigaray's 'specular/speculate' and Rich's 're-vision' are simply a few. In all these cases being 'punny' is both a happy accident and a deliberately ambiguating move. All these writers seek to disturb and re-form – not merely reflect – the polished surfaces of academic discourse. Naturally, those who admire that polish decry such writers and continue to demean the pun. Yet both Shakespeare and Joyce were utterly inveterate 'punsters', as legions of critics have noted with distaste or delight.

Structural play (sporting with syntax and cohesion) arises whenever there is a pleasurable sense of tension set up and maintained across larger linguistic structures, even across whole texts. Take the first few lines of Hamlet's 'To be or not to be' speech (Act III, sc. i). In this case, not only is there a sustained sound-play built upon the tension between a regular underlying pattern of pentameter blank verse and the alternately halting and flowing rhythm of the speech. There is also a complex web of metaphors ('take arms', 'sea of trouble', 'to sleep', 'to dream') which itself threatens to come apart even as it seems to come together. Joyce's *Ulysses* and Beckett's *Not I* (5.3.3) also sport with expectations about conventional sentence structure and conventional perceptual coherence. They thereby **foreground** clipped and elliptical structures and in effect defamiliarise our sense of the world.

Contextual and **intertextual** play arise whenever we recognise that a text is being sited and cited differently. For ultimately every text can be aligned with a wide and potentially contradictory range of **genres** and can be located in a wide and potentially contradictory range of **contexts**. Take Mary Shelley's *Frankenstein, or the Modern Prometheus*, for instance (@ 5.2.4). Depending upon the critical discourse in which we cite/site it, this can be categorised as: science fiction; gothic tale; moral tract; novel of ideas; epistolary novel; and so on. Most immediately it functions as 'example on a textbook website'. In addition, mindful of the many later film adaptations and the popular mythology of Frankenstein as the type of 'mad scientist', we may note the 'play' of attention between the various moments of (re-)production of the text. The bit reproduced for the present book may thus be braced against all the other versions that are absent (see **absence and presence**). This is just one way in which there is a degree of 'play' opened up in the spaces within and around a text. Genre and context are not simply 'givens'. They are the product of a kind of 'give and take'. It is also at this point that word-play most obviously gives way to what may be called 'world play' – a sense of the world as a place which is not simply found but also perpetually remade (see **creativity . . . re-creation**).

Activities

(a) *In what ways might each of the following texts be considered in some sense 'playful'*: student talk amongst friends (5.3.1); the Clarins advert (5.4.4), Petrucci's poems (5.1.4)? In each case review all the main levels of language: sound, visuals, individual words, larger structures, genre and context (see 2.2. for an analytical framework and checklists).

Go on to consider any other text which interests you as in some ways 'playful'.

(b) *Is there any common feature or quality of the various 'poems' in section 5.1 that* would allow you to say categorically 'Poetry is X and does Y' or, conversely, 'Poetry is *not* A and does *not* do B'? Weigh the implications of your answer for the study of poetry in particular and texts in general. The two very different kinds of poem by Agbabi – tabloid sonnet (5.1.2) and 'rap' performance piece (5.1.5) – are a good place to start. Then perhaps move to the two very different 'river' poems by Gross (5.1.5) and Oswald (5.3.3).

(c) *Discipline or pun-ish!* Attack or defend the practice of punning in academic disciplines such as English (for instances, see above). Do so in as po-faced or punny a manner as you see fit.

Discussion

(i) Play is the disruption of presence. [. . .] Play is always play of absence and presence.
Jacques Derrida, 'Structure, Sign and Play in the Discourse of the Human Sciences' (1966) in Lodge and Wood (2008: 223)

(ii) We need to alter our definitions of language to give proper recognition to the importance of language play. For only in this way can we reach a satisfactory understanding of what is involved in linguistic creativity.
David Crystal, *Language Play* (1998: 8)

Also see: **absence and presence; aesthetics; comedy and tragedy, carnival and the absurd; creative writing, creativity, re-creation; image, versification: rhythm, metre and rhyme.**

READING: Montgomery *et al.* 2012: Section 4; Crystal 1998; Cook 2000; Attridge 1988, 2004. *Core texts*: Wittgenstein 1953; Bakhtin 1968; Kristeva 1972; Lyotard 1979; Cixous and Derrida in Lodge and Wood 2008.

REALISM AND REPRESENTATION: FICTION, FACT, METAFICTION

All the terms featured here concern the relation between what people consider 'real' and what goes on in cultural representations of that reality. How do literature and art relate to the rest of life? What makes one work 'fictional' and another 'factual'? Is this the same as saying works are 'true' or 'false'? And how stable are such categories as 'fiction' and 'fact' (or 'true' and 'false') from culture to culture, period to period, and even person to person? In any case, do we always have to measure artistic and literary works by their capacity to imitate faithfully some supposedly pre-existent reality? Can't we also think of them as *making* their own realities?

In this entry, we see why it is important to distinguish reali*ty* (the general and ultimately unknowable notion of 'what is') from reali*sms* (specific aesthetic movements which at various times have claimed to represent that reality accurately). We also see that fiction and fact not only turn out to be variable and mutually interdependent categories; they sometimes even turn into one another. Hence the use of the hybrid term 'faction', as well as the attention to texts which flaunt their own status as fictions (i.e. 'metafictions').

Realism in LITERATURE usually refers to one of two things:

- *classic nineteenth-century realism*, as in novels such as Austen's *Pride and Prejudice* (5.3.2) or plays such as Ibsen's *A Doll's House*. Such realism usually entails detailed attention to the routine texture of social life, a narrator who is nominally invisible, and language which does not draw attention to itself. All this gives the impression of a direct, unmediated engagement with the characters and the action. This is sometimes called 'bourgeois realism' by MARXISTS because of the emphasis on middle-class families and values.

- *any movement which claims to offer a fresh, supposedly more faithful view of reality*, and thereby replace a preceding view of reality that has become conventionalised. In this respect almost every major literary or artistic movement (Neo-classical, Romantic, Modernist or POSTMODERNIST) claims to offer a higher or deeper reality than the one preceding it. So invariably do the movements that supersede it.

Clearly, it all depends what we understand by reality in the first place. *Reality* derives from the Latin word *res*, meaning 'thing'. Thus whenever we privilege one view of things to the exclusion of all others we 'reify' it. More precisely, we may say that a certain vision or version of reality always exists in relation to some conceptual *frame of reference*. This in turn presupposes some evaluative *frame of preference* (i.e. what we prefer to acknowledge as real – the kind of reality we consider valid). An obvious example of this is the fact that the various critical approaches featured in Part Three (NEW CRITICAL, PSYCHOLOGICAL, POSTSTRUCTURALIST, etc.) all frame ostensibly 'the same thing' (a **text**) in markedly different ways. Moreover, not only do they see 'it' differently; they also argue about where 'it' ends and something else begins: where text becomes **context**, and where one text becomes another, **intertextually**. By extension, the kind of literary and aesthetic realism you prefer very much depends upon the kind of reality you recognise and value. Thus it is perfectly possible to see 'documentary realism' in photography, cinema, TV, the novel and news as being utterly natural and neutral *or* as being utterly contrived and unconvincing. It all depends how you view the illusion that the camera, reporter or observer are simply there by accident, and the implication that there has been no selection, organisation, editing or distribution. So-called 'Reality TV', for example, is carefully staged and highly edited. Conversely, you may see Joyce's *Ulysses* (1922) or Woolf's *The Waves* (1931) or Faulkner's *The Sound and the Fury* (1929) as the most 'realistic' novels you have ever come across (notwithstanding their reputation as deeply difficult Modernist texts associated with 'stream of consciousness' techniques). Again, it all depends how you reckon your own consciousness works. And in all these cases it depends what *norm of reality* you recognise as **background** to the *form of realism* in the **foreground**.

Representation has two distinct yet connected meanings:

♦ *verbal description and visual depiction*, e.g., the pictorial representation of a landscape or the written representation of someone's speech (in a novel, say);
♦ *acting on behalf of someone or something, standing in for them*, e.g., proportional representation as a form of government, the US House of Representatives, or a sales representative who sells on behalf of a business.

It is important to grasp both the distinction and the connection between these two meanings of representation. Painting a landscape is not necessarily the same as acting on behalf of it. Recording someone's speech is not necessarily the same as speaking on behalf of them. And yet, at the same time, there is clearly some sense in which offering a certain vision of a landscape and offering a certain version of someone's words *is* a way of standing in for that landscape or person. The one kind of representation relates to – even if it is not identical with – the other. The following questions are framed with this in mind. They can be put to cultural activities and political institutions in general, as well as to texts in particular.

QUESTIONS OF 'REPRESENTATION'

♦ Who is representing whom or what, when, where, how and why?
♦ Who or what is being *mis*represented, *under*-represented or *un*represented?
♦ Who and what is present in or absent from the text, image or institution?
♦ Who and what is treated as central, marginal or non-existent?
♦ What frames of reference (and preference) is it – and are you – appealing to?
♦ How else might ostensibly the 'same' people and things be represented?
♦ Or would a really radical re-representation put quite other people and things in play?

(See Core questions, 2.1.2, and the related questions on **absence and presence** and **discourse**.)

Fiction has had a complicated triple sense since its first appearance in English (from French) in the fourteenth century. It could – and still can – mean:

1 imaginative literature or creative writing in general;
2 prose narrative in particular, especially the **novel** and short story;
3 something 'made-up' in the sense of being deceptive, a counterfeit (i.e. a mere or sheer fiction).

Such an ambiguous, and on balance suspicious, attitude to the 'made-up' nature of fiction is at least as old in the West as Plato. Plato would have banished poets from his ideal republic precisely because they invented things which, strictly, never had been or could be (Greek *poiesis* simply meant 'making-up', 'fashioning'; just as 'fiction' derives from another, Latin word meaning 'to fashion' – *fingere*). Something similar happened in practice during the Stalinist era in Russia and at the time of the Cultural Revolution in China. In both cases only certain officially approved forms of 'socialist realism' were encouraged (typically, these represented heroically progressive workers and pathetically decadent bourgeois reactionaries). Everything else was dubbed 'fictional', in the negative sense of being deceptive and deluded, and promptly suppressed.

Another awkward aspect of the term fiction is that, especially from the nineteenth century onwards, it has tended to be crudely set against its supposed opposite, 'fact'. If something is not a fact then apparently it's a (mere) fiction or, by this time used almost synonymously, a 'fancy'. At the same time, and for the same reasons, **story** was being increasingly distinguished from *its* supposed opposite, **history** (see **narrative**). The problem in all these cases, of course, is precisely how far we can actually distinguish fiction from fact and story from history in any particular instance. A further twist in the tale of 'fiction' is that in modern high-street bookstores and local libraries the most fundamental division is that between Fiction and *Non*-fiction (not between Fiction and Fact). This is presumably because in these contexts it is fiction which is the most sought-after and numerous category, so *that* becomes the privileged term. Non-fiction is its merely shadowy inversion – and Fact has disappeared completely.

Faction (i.e. fact + fiction) is the term preferred by some writers when seeking to challenge casually extreme notions of fact versus fiction, truth versus falsehood, and reality versus imagination. Hi/story (with a slash) is sometimes preferred for the same reasons: it avoids a simplistic opposition of story to history. In all these cases it then becomes a matter of deciding what *kinds* and *degrees* of fiction/fact and story/history are in play in any particular instance. Questions of absolute truth thus tend to modulate into questions of relative power and knowledge. Reality is always in some measure an effect of discourse – a form of realism. It is not an entirely pre-existent phenomenon. Such processes are especially highlighted in science fiction (see 5.2.4); for there it is science as the current guarantor of fact and reality that is subjected to most telling interrogation as itself a form of contentious fiction (i.e. faction) or fantasy.

Metafiction involves the activity of revealing and sporting with the processes of fiction-making even while you are engaged in them. It is a comment *on* fiction *in* fiction, just as metalanguage is a comment *on* language *in* language. A famous early example of metafiction is Sterne's *Tristram Shandy* (1760–67; see @ 5.2.7). There the narrator constantly reminds us of the options both writer and reader have as the story is built before our eyes. Devices include a blank page for the reader to fill in, a line-drawing of how a stick was flourished, and the author's constant admission that there are far more events **absent** from the novel than can possibly be represented in it. More classic modern examples are Fowles's *The French Lieutenant's Woman* (1969), where the novelist offers us alternative, un/happy endings from which we may choose (the film adaptation offers us a film within a film). Atwood's 'Happy Endings' (5.2.1) sports still more overtly with beginnings and middles as well as endings.

But the process of self-reflexivity in writing is by no means limited to fiction in a narrow or a broad sense. What FORMALISTS call 'laying bare the device' and what Brecht, in a more politically charged vein, calls 'making strange' occurs in writing and communication of all kinds. **Theatre**, for example, is full of instances of the playwright, director and performers drawing attention to the very theatricality of the stage play. Famous instances include the play within the play in *Hamlet* ('The Mousetrap') and the plays of Brecht himself. Another instance is the childhood flashback and narrated mime in McDonagh's *The Pillowman* (5.3.3). We might call this 'metatheatre': comment on the theatre in the theatre. **Poetry**, too, is virtually by definition metalinguistic in that it calls attention to its own language through sustained processes of foregrounding, notably in **versification** and **imagery**. Narrative poets such as Chaucer and Byron also remind us of the insistent presence of their narrators.

The fact (!) is that any text which at some point calls attention to the fact (!!) that it is a made object can be called 'metatextual' (as here!!!). Even the routine apparatus of avowedly factual textbooks – the acknowledgements, preface, contents, chapter divisions and titles, notes, bibliography, the covers, the title – are constant reminders that a text cannot but expose to view some of its own processes of making. Thus, to be wholly consistent, we should perhaps recognise the category *metafaction* as something which goes on in all kinds of text, whether they are nominally categorised as fiction and/or fact. The same applies to the titles and credits of films and TV programmes – whether feature or documentary. The text in question may or may not overtly present itself as a made-up object. But nothing can stop alertly critical readers and viewers from drawing attention to precisely these aspects of its manufacture and mediation. In this respect, metatextuality, like **intertextuality**, is something we do as much as something we find.

Activities

(a)   *Realisms (plural)*. Compare an extract from a supposedly 'classic realist' text with an extract from a supposedly 'post/modernist' text (e.g., *Pride and Prejudice* (5.3.2) with *How Late it Was, How Late* (5.3.2)). On what grounds might you claim that each both is and isn't 'realistic'?

(b)   *Represented and mis-, under- or un-represented?* Put the above 'Questions of Representation' to any text which interests or irritates you. (Comparing McEwan and Roy, 5.2.5, works powerfully here.)

(c)   *Faction, hi/story, metafiction* . . . Attack, support or suggest alternatives to these critical coinages with reference to specific texts you are studying.

Discussion

(i)   But realism is itself just a matter of convention [. . .] and no one device is inherently more realistic than another.

Ann Jefferson, 'Russian Formalism' in Jefferson and Robey (1986: 34)

(ii)   modern realism [. . . has] developed in increasingly rich forms in keeping with the constantly changing and expanding reality of modern life.

Erich Auerbach, *Mimesis: The Representation of Reality in Western Literature* (1946: 554)

Also see: FORMALISM INTO FUNCTIONALISM; POSTSTRUCTURALISM AND POSTMODERNISM; **auto/biography; discourse; foreground, background and point of view; image . . . imagination; narrative in story and history: novel, news and film.**

READING: Mitchell in Lentricchia and McLaughlin 1995: 11–22; Williams in Lodge 1972: 581–91; Montgomery *et al.* 2012: Chapter 23. *Core texts*: Auerbach 1946; Williams 1983: 134–5, 257–62, 266–9; Hutcheon 1989; Currie 1995 (reader).

SPEECH, CONVERSATION AND DIALOGUE

'Speech' means both the activity of speaking and the thing which results (e.g., a speech). Like **writing**, the other major dimension of LANGUAGE, speech is both process and product. It is important to stress, however, that speech and writing are analogous but not identical activities. Speech is made from sounds in air (phonological material), while writing is made from marks on paper or plastic, etc. (graphological material). Speech is more continuous with its **context**, whereas writing has a semi-independent existence as **text**. Speech tends to be more immediate and ephemeral, writing to be more remote and permanent. Some such broad distinctions between speech and writing are initially useful. However, they also need to be qualified in view of developments in audio-visual COMMUNICATIONS and MEDIA technology since the late nineteenth century. We now routinely use such apparatuses as the telephone (Greek 'far-sound'), as well as photography, radio, film, television (Greek 'far-vision'), video, and a whole host of computer-assisted interfaces. All these technologies have tended to scramble and reconstitute traditional distinctions between speech and writing. Speech, too, can now be recorded and edited like any written or printed text. It too can travel or be broadcast over vast distances in space and time. For this reason the lists of the properties and structures of speech that follow are carefully qualified. (Corresponding lists can be found in the entry on **writing**.)

SPEECH IS CHARACTERISTICALLY (but not always):

♦   *immediate, transitory and often spontaneous* – unless it is scripted, recorded or broadcast and thus obviously mediated;

♦   *face-to-face and tied to a single shared context* – but with non-shared contexts if, say, talking on the telephone or watching TV;

♦   *potentially dialogic, two- or many-way and interactive* – though ostensibly 'live' speeches in lectures, sermons and political speeches can be resolutely monologic and seem anything but 'live'; conversely, letters, magazine problem-pages and TV chat shows – including studio-audience participation and viewer phone-ins – can be palpably two- or many-way;

♦   *learnt 'naturally' by nearly everybody without special training* – though literacy, too, can come to seem 'natural' in certain communities.

THE STRUCTURES OF SPEECH are therefore characteristically (but not always):

♦   *deeply embedded in other, non-verbal aspects of face-to-face* COMMUNICATION, from eye contact, posture and gesture all the way through to the size of the room and the nature of the occasion (though an ostensibly 'live' speaker can still avert eyes, read the speech and ignore the audience; conversely, professional news presenters, DJs and game-show hosts cultivate a wide range of face-to-face – even 'in-your-face' – strategies);

♦   *heavily dependent on context-sensitive words*, e.g., 'I', 'you', 'this', 'that', 'here', 'over there', 'now', 'in a moment' (though informal written communications such as postcards, personal letters and casual e-mail also exhibit many of these features, along with many of those listed below);

♦   *pervasively organised by variations in stress and intonation*, often resulting in words being drawn out or clipped; e.g., 'I r-e-e-ally like *that*! D'you?' (though as these printed examples show, there are partly corresponding resources available in written spelling, punctuation and visual presentation);

♦   *full of suspended, mixed or reduced grammatical structures*, often with an emphasis on loose grammatical *coordination* ('And . . . And . . . But . . . '). Other common features of spoken grammar include:

   – *false-starts, half-formed restatements* and *reinforcements* as speakers switch structures in mid-flow (e.g., 'Perhaps, if you'd be . . . Or rather, would you . . . ');

   – grammatically pared down structures with *ellipsis* of subjects and auxiliaries (e.g., 'Going tomorrow?' rather than 'Are you going tomorrow?');

   – *fillers* like 'erm' and 'ah', *phatic communicators* like 'you know' and *tag questions* like ' . . . isn't it?' – these last two being quick checks that the listener is listening.

♦   *frequent sharing or interrupting by different speakers*, as the listener anticipates and 'completes' or cuts across and deflects what the first speaker was saying, e.g., 'A: He's a real . . . B: – bastard? A: Yeah.' (Though typed 'conferencing' on the Internet can be full of such things too, see @ 5.2.6.)

Speech thus characteristically features all of the above properties and structures. The fact that it doesn't always – and that writing, print and the modern audio-visual media do sometimes – simply adds richness and variety to the possibilities. We therefore have to approach each instance of speech or writing on its own terms, keeping general models in mind but also with a sensitivity to specificities. It will also be clear from the foregoing that some spoken language can be **monologic** and 'one-way' in tendency. Examples are conventional lectures, sermons, political speeches and news bulletins. Equally clearly, however, the great majority of spoken language tends to be **dialogic** and 'two-' or 'many-way' (see 1.2.2). We now concentrate on the most common and characteristic of dialogic speech modes: conversation.

Conversation is the usual word for spoken interaction of all kinds. These range from passing banter and informal chats to formal interviews and interrogations. *Conversation analysis* concentrates on verbal interaction involving two or more present participants. The following analytical scheme is commonly used, though terminology sometimes varies. (The illustrations are drawn from the conversation at the supermarket checkout (5.2.6), which is also analysed in the entry on **discourse analysis** pp. 227–8.)

CONVERSATIONAL STRUCTURES, ranked from larger to smaller, are:

interaction – the encounter as a whole (customer and cashier at supermarket);
transaction – negotiation of a particular topic (the bill and change);
exchange – a minimal round of initiation and response (e.g., first two lines);
turn – one person's turn at speech (e.g., 'There's a mistake here');
move – a particular move within the turn (e.g., 'Excuse me').

CONVERSATIONAL STRATEGIES, both verbal and non-verbal, include:

- who opens and who closes, and how;
- who nominates the topic and appears to direct the transaction;
- who initiates and responds, who listens and supports;
- frequency and fluidity of turn-taking;
- who interrupts or 'completes' another's words;
- precise patterns of question, statement, command and exclamation, as well as more indirect speech acts (e.g., statement as query, invitation as command).

All these strategies are creatively deployed and can be analytically retraced in the transcript of Student talk amongst friends (5.3.1). In fact, when we analyse any instance of conversation with the above structures and strategies in mind, one thing quickly becomes clear.

CULTURE IS A CONTINUING – SOMETIMES CONTENTIOUS – 'CONVERSATION', because . . .

- Conversation proceeds dynamically, through divergence as well as convergence, conflict as well as cooperation.
- Conversation enacts the negotiation of personal relationships and relations of power.
- Any specific interaction is just one part of a continuing conversation which, strictly, has no absolute beginning or absolute end – only provisional, though decisive, points of opening and closure.
- Conversation is therefore part of that larger dialogue we call, variously, society, **history** and CULTURE.

Dialogue has two further, more specialised meanings, aside from the senses of conversation and interaction in general: (i) the fictional representation of speech in novels, plays and films (e.g., 'a piece of dialogue', 'to script some dialogue'); (ii) the dialogic principle as developed by Bakhtin, in which every utterance or text responds to a previous one and anticipates a succeeding one. We briefly treat each in turn.

Dialogue as the fictional representation of conversation in novels, plays and films The most common questions put to this kind of dialogue are 'How authentic, natural or realistic is this dialogue?' or ' How much like ordinary, non-fictional speech is it?' Some cautions need to be issued however:

1. Most fiction writers have never especially aimed to represent non-fictional speech faithfully in the first place – nor have most of their readers and audiences expected it. (This goes for most of Chaucer, Shakespeare, Milton and Dickens, to mention only 'classic' writers.)
2. Most writers and readers work quite happily within highly conventionalised expectations of how people speak (and act) in the various **genres**: romance, novel of manners, detective novel, Elizabethan tragedy or comedy, Victorian melodrama, *film noir*, cowboy film, TV police series, etc. All entail distinctive verbal and visual modes, hence their instant recognisability and openness to parody.
3. There is a vast difference between a crafted *script* and a *transcript* of spontaneous conversation, as is demonstrated by comparing the transcript of conversation (5.3.1) with any of the scripts in the rest of that section (esp. 5.3.3).
4. Even spontaneous speakers in routine conversation still speak in and through various roles. People in 'real' life also 'play parts'. Even spontaneous discourse is in that sense already partly 'made up'.
5. We therefore need a model of conversation which is sensitive to role-playing and speech genres and discourses of all kinds – in fact as well as in fiction. That is why the above checklists are framed so as to be equally applicable to spoken language wherever we engage with it: in our own speech and that of others, in and out of fiction, on and off the page, on and off the stage or screen.

The dialogic principle as developed by Bakhtin

Bakhtin's grandest claim is that 'To *be* means to communicate *dialogically*' (*Problems of Dostoevsky's Poetics*, 1984). By this he means that everyone and everything is bound up with everyone and everything else in a ceaseless process of exchange and transformation. More specifically, Bakhtin observes that 'we always use another's words in our own language' and that 'every word is a site of struggle', a 'multiaccentual' space where people's voices are perpetually contending with those of others (1981: 303ff.). Bakhtin also observes that 'every word is directed towards an answer and cannot escape the profound influence of the answering word that it anticipates' (1981: 280). There is always some **addressee** projected by every **addresser**. Our dialogues are therefore not only backward-looking (to other people whose words we are using and reacting to) but also forward-looking (to future responses that we expect, fear or desire). Bakhtin's especial interest in the **novel** arose because it was there that he reckoned writers were most free to experiment with the 'multi-voicedness' (heteroglossia) of human society; there too that he traced those forms of indirect speech whereby a narrator subtly slips into the words and **point of view** of a character. Arguably, such processes are not limited to the novel, nor even to fiction as such. They may characterise the ways in which we adopt and adapt language and sign-systems in general. Academically speaking, they are as routine and crucial as the ways we note or quote other people's words, whether directly or indirectly (see 1.2.3, 1.2.6).

Activities

(a)   *Monologues as dialogues, and vice versa.* Consider the ways in which any text is always in some sense a combination of monologue (one-way communication) AND dialogue (two- or many-way communication) – depending who you think is talking with or to whom, when, where and how. (Suggested focuses are Wyatt's 'They flee from me' (5.1.1), Kelman's *How Late it Was . . .* (5.3.2) and Jacobson's 'The Post-modern Lecture' (5.3.1).)

(b)   *Tran/scripts.* Compare a transcript of spontaneous conversation with a play, film or TV script (e.g., 5.3.1–2). Use the above checklists of features of speech and conversation to help you do this. Go on to consider how the transcript might be 'tidied up' so as to look like a crafted script. Conversely, consider how the script might be 'roughed up' so as to sound like spontaneous conversation.

Discussion

(i)   For the smallest social unit is not the single person but two people. In life too we develop one another.

> Bertolt Brecht, 'A Short Organon for the Theatre' (1948: part 58)

(ii)   What living and buried speech is always vibrating here!

> Walt Whitman, *Leaves of Grass* (1871: no. 8)

Also see: Voices 5.3; LANGUAGE; COMMUNICATION; **addresser . . . addressee; drama and theatre; writing . . . response and rewriting**.

READING: Mullany and Stockwell 2010: 79–84; Crystal 2003: 288–7; Burton 1980; Herman 1995. *Core texts*: Bakhtin 1981; Tannen 1992; Carter 2004.

STANDARDS AND STANDARDISATION, VARIETIES AND VARIATION

Is there such a thing as 'standard English' or does all English change over time and vary from one place or person to another? Does standardisation mean 'making uniform' or 'improving' – and can it be applied as easily to speech as to writing and print? Is one variety of language more 'correct' and 'proper' than another – or should we rather look at language in terms of appropriateness, context and communicative function? How does one variety become recognised as standard and can processes of variation turn any variety into a 'standard' for certain people and certain purposes? These are the questions addressed in this entry. We start with questions

ENGLISH AND ENGLISHES – ONE AND MANY

Many of the general principles underpinning the present entry and that on **accent and dialect** are introduced in 1.1 and 1.3. Those sections also include illustration.

rather than answers because the whole area of standards and standardisation, varieties and variation is complex and contentious. Snap answers simply increase the confusion and snappiness.

Standard (noun and adjective) is a term with a complicated and potentially confusing history. The plural 'standards', for instance, is often tossed around as though it were a singular and everyone knew what it/they meant. Three basic meanings of standard can be distinguished:

1   average, routine, common, without frills (as in 'standard model', 'standard fare');

2   prescribed measure of quantity or quality, degree of excellence (as in British Standards Authority, the International Gold Standard);

3   the flag or other emblem around which people rally and express their solidarity, often in the face of an enemy (as in 'the royal standard', 'raising the standard' and 'standard bearer'). This is the earliest, twelfth-century sense.

Standards (plural), as already mentioned, has been loosely applied from the mid-nineteenth century onwards to everything from education and industry to appearance and morality (e.g., academic standards, manufacturing standards, standards of dress, moral standards). This sense obviously arises from a confusion of senses (2) and (3) above. The notion of 'prescribed measure' thus gets mixed up with a notion of 'social value', as well as a general sense of people 'rallying round' something or other. Equally obviously, this new sense of standards strenuously avoids sense (1), meaning average, routine or what is common.

It is against this background, then, that we must place the first explicit references and appeals to Standard English as well as Received/Standard Pronunciation which began to appear from the mid-nineteenth century onwards (see *OED* and Williams 1983: 296–9). In both these cases there is evidence of a concerted attempt to distinguish a certain prescribed or approved form of language (in the mid-nineteenth century principally that of the British private boarding schools and the London-based professions) from the forms used routinely and commonly by other sections of the British populace at large. Alternative names for Standard English in Britain are 'the Queen's/King's English' and 'BBC English'. (The latter refers to state-sponsored radio and TV, both of which were also massively dominated, especially in their early days, by upper-middle-class speakers from the South of England.) Clearly, then, any notion of Standard English was from the first heavily implicated in specific historical, geographical, social and technological conditions. Alternative names were *not*, for instance, 'Commoners' English' or 'Manchester Evening News English'. Similar inbuilt partialities relate to the notion of Received Pronunciation: 'received' by whom, how, when, where and why? The form of the passive participle (received) assumes we either already know or wouldn't be so rude as to enquire.

The following brief survey will help provide a historical framework for changing notions of standard English. It supplements that in the general Chronology (Appendix C). The emphasis here is social and political. Linguistic illustrations can be found in 1.1 and throughout Part Five.

Anglo-Saxon: beginning and end of a 'King's English'

Britain's polyglot foundations are laid down at this stage (fifth–eleventh centuries): Celtic and Germanic languages and dialects meet and to some extent mingle. Latin continues to be the international language of official religion (Christianity), learning and letters as it had been previously in the Roman Empire. 'Englisc' first appears as the name applied to a group of related Germanic dialects, notably those of the Angles and Saxons, during the ninth century (see pp. 16–17). The first 'King's English' as such is identified with King Alfred (*c*. 848–*c*. 900) and centred on his Wessex court at Winchester in Southern England. This 'Saxon' variety is braced against other, more Northerly, chiefly 'Anglian' varieties associated with the Danelaw as well as against the Celtic languages of Cornwall, Wales, Ireland and Scotland. For a time, 'Alfredian English' is consolidated through a programme of educational reform, including translations from Latin and the keeping of the *Anglo-Saxon Chronicle*. But then, as a consequence of the Norman Conquest (1066), this potentially 'standard' variety is overlaid and superseded by another based on Norman French.

Medieval many-tonguedness and a hierarchy of functions

The linguistic pecking order for much of the Middle Ages in Britain is as follows:

◆   *Latin* is used in speech and writing for higher religious, educational and administrative purposes, especially in international contexts.
◆   *Norman French and then Parisian French* are used in speech and writing for national and cross-Channel administration by 'nobles' and 'royautee' at 'court(e)' and in the 'parlement' (all the highlighted words derive from early French).
◆   *English* is used chiefly in speech (rarely in writing) for immediate and local purposes amongst peasants, artisans and merchants (the majority of the populace), and is only used by the higher clergy and nobles when teaching, preaching to and administering this 'third estate' (the first two being Church and Knighthood).

In fact English only really begins to make it back on to manuscript as the written word during the fourteenth and fifteenth centuries, and then it is much 'Latinised' and 'Frenchified'. In many respects it has all the hybrid nature and semi-official status of a creole. Only towards the end of this period do laws and parliamentary business begin to be publicised in English. Meanwhile, Northern, Midland, Southern and other regional differences persist in both language and literary forms. But then, for technological and social reasons, everything shifts again.

Early Modern: printing, the state, and the politics of 'correction'

Spelling is increasingly standardised over this period (fifteenth–eighteenth centuries), chiefly through the influence of the printing presses. Most of these are concentrated in London (Caxton sets up the first one there in 1476–77). Again, therefore, the Southern, London-based variety associated with court, parliament and business is the one that is adopted as a model. In handwriting, however, people continue to spell in a wide variety of ways, often inconsistently and idiosyncratically. Even the national bard (1564–1616), blissfully oblivious of subsequent appeals to him as an authority on all things English, blots his copy-book and signs himself in legal documents variously as 'Shackspere', 'Shagspere', 'Shaxper' and even 'Shaxberd'.

   The other major factors in moves both towards and (eventually) away from the concept of a single 'standard' in language are tied up with the development of Britain as a nation-state and imperial power. Britain is by now, notionally at least, a single nation-state presided over by a court and parliament based in England. It is also the centre of a rapidly growing empire, already with territories, settlements or strong commercial interests (chiefly based on slavery and plantations) in America, the Caribbean, India, Africa and, latterly, Australia and New Zealand. The internal–external tensions of this situation can be felt in the sphere of language. Anxiety begins to be expressed about the 'purity' of the English language. From the late seventeenth century onwards, it becomes common, even fashionable, for middle-to-upper-class writers to declare that the language is becoming 'barbarous', 'uncivilised' and 'improper', and therefore needs 'regulating', 'correcting' and 'improving'. Printed grammars, word-lists and dictionaries soon appear, and there are repeated calls for the setting up of an 'Academy', as the French had done, to prescribe rules and to outlaw certain usages.

Later Modern: Standard English, empire and an explosion of varieties

Steam printing presses pour forth more – and more diverse – materials. The United Kingdom is nominally 'United' in 1801, notwithstanding continuing pressure for various forms of regional and national devolution. Successive phases of industrial revolution throughout the nineteenth century prompt crises in social organisation and corresponding demands for political reform (notably through Chartism, the formation of trade unions and the Labour Party). This is also the empire upon which the sun never sets and upon which the gun – as well as legions of colonial administrators and Christian missionaries – never cease to train. It is against this social and political background that we must trace the rise, from the mid-nineteenth century onwards, of appeals to 'Standard English':

- ♦ 'English' is first raised as the 'standard' (flag, emblem, symbol) of empire, not so much as an actual linguistic entity, but in an ongoing attempt to confer social solidity and ideological solidarity upon an ideal. 'Standard English' is offered as something that everyone should rally round and respect or protect.
- ♦ Meanwhile, Queen Victoria, who has a German mother and husband (both Saxe-Coburgs), also has a strong German accent. The 'Queen's English' is therefore a notional rather than an actual model. Nor is such a state of affairs that unusual. The first languages of many of the kings and queens of England have not been English at all. The real 'King's/Queen's English' often turns out to have a strong Norse, Norman, French, Dutch or German accent.
- ♦ In Ireland, Wales and Scotland, there is wide-scale imposition of – as well as resistance to – 'Standard English' as a compulsory school subject. For it systematically displaces other native dialects and whole languages. Beyond Britain, there is corresponding displacement of other native languages, ranging from Swahili and Urdu to Navaho and Koori (an Australian 'Aboriginal' tongue).
- ♦ The mass of the population are offered a version of literacy and a vision of national heritage designed to help them fulfil their roles as productive factory and office workers, or efficient colonial administrators.
- ♦ At the same time, the ground is being prepared for the planting of other 'standards' and the unfurling of banners proclaiming other versions of civilisation . . .

Contemporary standards – global and local varieties

America, India, the Caribbean and Australia now all boast their own 'standard' Englishes. Each of these is to a greater or lesser degree distinct from what must now be specified as *British* Standard English. The differences span the whole linguistic range from accents and spelling through vocabulary and grammar to contexts and communicative functions. For the most part these standards are mutually intelligible and this has huge potential advantages for certain kinds of international communication (see 'Standard World English?' below). But the **differences** between these standards are manifold, and an apparently slight difference can speak volumes, socially and culturally. For all these reasons, the appearance of such volumes as Webster's *American Dictionary* (1828), *Indian and British English: A Handbook* (1970) and Ramson's *Australian National Dictionary* (1988), to cite just three, is arguably as linguistically and ideologically momentous as the appearance of, say, Dr Johnson's *Dictionary of the English Language* (1755) if not the *OED* (1928).

A NON/STANDARD NOTE

The crude division of English into 'standard' and 'non-standard' forms is rare in linguistic circles now. This is because the term 'non-standard' is especially inadequate when it comes to distinguishing amongst such widely different phenomena as colloquialism, swearing, **accents**, **dialects**, pidgins and creoles. The tendency, therefore, is to talk of *all* forms of language (*including* 'standards') as **varieties**.

Varieties are the linguistic *products* of difference; they are constituted by differences according to person, place, medium, context and function. **Variation** refers to the historical *processes* of differentiation; it embraces shifts and switches within the usage of an individual – even within a single speech – as well as large-scale change across whole language communities. Varieties and variation are therefore alternative ways of seeing the same thing as, respectively, product and process. We can thus explore various Englishes at a given moment, synchronically (e.g., now *or* at a certain moment in the fourteenth century); and we can explore them as they change over time, diachronically (e.g., *between* the fourteenth century *and* now). Either way, we avoid loosely value-laden talk of 'standards' as though these were above history. A 'standard' is itself a variety subject to continuing variation. It arises and increases or decreases in influence and prominence according to need and demand.

We therefore conclude much as we began, with problems and possibilities rather than a bogus final solution. Here the focus is on what is increasingly being talked of as a new Global Standard – 'World English'. Though again, as with earlier notions of the Queen's or King's English, it is a moot point how far this really exists as a linguistic entity or is being raised as an ideological 'standard' around which various parts of the world are supposed to rally. (Also see Figure 3.2, p. 191: Postcolonial problems and possibilities with English.)

'STANDARD WORLD ENGLISH'?

Good for international communication?
  Bad for local, regional and national identity?
Good for formal functions and writing in print?
  Bad for informal functions and for other dialects and languages in print?
An ideal to aspire to – a utopian dream?
  An undesirable impossibility – a dystopian nightmare?

Activity

Non/standard, im/proper, in/correct? All the following texts might be cited as instances of 'non-standard' or even 'incorrect' and 'improper' English: talk amongst friends (5.3.1); Leonard's 'This is thi . . . news' (5.1.4); Nichols's 'Tropical Death' (5.4.5); Doyle's *Paddy Clarke* (5.3.2). (Add or substitute any others you wish.) In each case consider other ways in which you might describe these texts so as to be more discriminating and less judgemental. What alternatives are there to the crude dichotomies non/standard, in/correct and im/proper?

Discussion

(i)   Certaynly it is harde to playse eueryman by cause of dyuersitie and chaunge of langage.
William Caxton, Prologue to *Eneydos* (his translation of *The Aeneid*) (1490)

(ii) Nationally, in Britain at least, proper English is a social view of who the proper English are; internationally, proper English cannot be divorced from a view of cultural and political domination.
Ron Carter, *Keywords in Language and Literacy* (1995: 123)

Also see: Which 'Englishes'? 1.1; LANGUAGE; **accent and dialect**; **canon**; change; **speech**.

READING: Maybin and Swann 2010: 76–110; Crystal 2003: 298–393; Montgomery *et al.* 2012: Section 2; Crystal 1997; Williams 1983: 296–9; Maybin and Mercer 1996: 275–310. *Core texts*: Milroy and Milroy 1999; Goodman and Graddol 1996: 141–238 (readings); Pennycook 1994, 2007.

TEXT, CONTEXT, INTERTEXTUALITY

Briefly, a text is any instance of a verbal record; the context is everything around the text; intertextuality refers to the text's relation with other texts. The concept of 'text' is now shared by many areas of LITERARY, LINGUISTIC and CULTURAL Studies. In fact, it is one of the crucial terms which allows these subjects to interrelate and to maintain a sense of some common object of study. They are all in some sense dealing with texts. The problem, as with any widely used term, is that people in different subjects tend to mean rather different things by it. We can thus distinguish two basic senses of text, one narrow, the other broad.

Text as any record of a verbal message

All the following are texts in this sense: a handwritten letter; a printed newspaper or magazine; a book of any kind; a written or printed novel, poem or play; a recording or transcript of a conversation. Texts are thereby distinguished on the one hand from *un*recorded language in the form of spontaneous **speech and conversation**, and on the other hand from messages in *non*-verbal codes such as painting, photography, music and architecture. This sense of *text as verbal record* is the one favoured by most linguists and the one favoured here. However, it should be added that some self-consciously 'literary' critics shun the term 'text' altogether. They complain of it being too indiscriminate or technical-sounding and prefer to talk more selectively and exclusively of literature in general and of poems, novels and plays as such. In fact, there is no reason we should not do both.

Text as any instance of the organisation of human signs

This much-extended sense of text embraces everything from poems, adverts and films to paintings, photos, shopping malls and whole cityscapes. The only limits seem to be that the 'text' in question should be a cultural object produced by people rather than a natural object untouched by human hand or mind. This definition is *not* favoured here on the grounds that if virtually everything is a text the concept has no analytical power at all.

We now turn to the relation between **texts** and their **contexts** and between one text and other texts (i.e. **intertextuality**). The intrinsic and possibly inextricable relations amongst these three concepts can be gauged by the fact that con*text* and inter*text*uality both have the core 'text' embedded within them. Moreover, the word text derives from the Latin verb *texere* meaning to weave and the noun *textus*, meaning 'tissue', 'weaving', 'web' (hence the related English words *text*ile and *text*ure). Texts are therefore perhaps best conceived as intermittent and extensible structures formed by a weaving together of strands. Like the World Wide Web – itself a contemporary kind of electronic mega-text made up of many interweavings – texts are wholes full of holes: always apparently somewhere and at the same time both everywhere and nowhere. In fact, the harder and closer you look *at* a text (paper or electronic), the more you find yourself looking *through*, *round* and *beyond* it. Its **presence** always implies and in a sense requires its **absences**. Like a bell, it rings out by virtue of the space where it is not. More practically and pointedly, we may add that *set texts* (i.e. prescribed reading) always turn out to be far from 'set' in the sense of solid and immovable. They have always been set by somebody for specific purposes. Other texts might have been set for similar or different reasons (see **canon**).

Context (Latin for 'with-text') refers to all those physical and cultural conditions whereby a text – or, for that matter, anything else – comes into being. It is analytically convenient to distinguish four kinds of interrelated context:

♦ *context meaning immediate situation*, e.g., whenever and wherever you are reading this book, a particular course;
♦ *context meaning larger cultural frame of reference*, e.g., the society, language community and general historical moment in which that reading is taking place;
♦ *contexts of (re)production*, e.g., when, where and by whom this book was sketched, drafted, read, redrafted, edited, published;
♦ *contexts of reception*, e.g., who uses it when, where, how and why.

(Notice that the term *co-text* is sometimes used to refer to other words and images in the immediate vicinity of the text. Thus if this entry is treated as a text, the co-text is the rest of the book.)

All these overlapping yet non-identical contexts must be taken into account if we are to attempt to grasp a text fully, functionally as well as formally (see 3.1 for applications to *Hamlet*). We must therefore learn to see a text not only *in* but in some sense *as* its contexts. The same goes for the next dimension of textuality.

Intertextuality (Latin for 'between-texts') is the general term for the relation between one text and another. It is analytically useful to distinguish three kinds of intertextual relation: explicit, implied and inferrable.

Explicit intertextuality comprises all the other texts that are overtly referred to and all the specific sources that the writer has demonstrably drawn upon. Thus we might cite T.S. Eliot's *The Waste Land* with its annotated references to Shakespeare's *The Tempest* and its acknowledged debts to a mixture of Christian and Sanskrit texts as an instance of explicit intertextuality.

Implied intertextuality comprises all those passing allusions to other texts (including texts in the same **genre**) and all those effects (especially ironic and satiric) which seem to have been deliberately contrived by the writer so as to be picked up by the alert and similarly informed reader. One instance might be the first line of *The Waste Land* and its ironic inversion of the opening of line of Chaucer's *General Prologue*: 'April is the cruellest month' as against Chaucer's 'Aprille with his shoures soote [sweet]'. By definition, *implied* intertextuality is always more subtle and indirect – and less easy to prove – than *explicit* intertextuality.

Inferred intertextuality refers to all those texts which actual **readers** draw on to help their understanding of the text in hand. These need not have been in the writer's mind – or even existed at the time. It is their status in the reader's mind that matters chiefly here. Thus we might compare the fragmentary collage effects of *The Waste Land* with Cubist or Surrealist art contemporary with the poem; but we might also compare or, more likely, contrast them with analogous POSTMODERN techniques in TV advertising and pop videos (where it is precisely the recognisable rather than the recondite nature of the allusions that usually engages us). We might also choose to read the poem through Eliot's own essay-writing on Shakespeare, or bring it into collision with, say, current FEMINIST or POSTCOLONIAL readings of *The Tempest*. The fact is that we can make sense of a text by comparing and contrasting it with just about any other. The point, of course, is to make the comparison or contrast significant. Inferred intertextuality is therefore at once the most open and the most demanding kind of textuality. It is more a critical technique than a textual object: a process of intertextual weaving rather than a finished web.

Activities

(a)   *Is there a text in this text?!* Choose a text from Part Five (or anywhere else) and consider: (a) all the various contexts in which it is implicated; (b) all the other texts – or kinds of text – to which it can be related intertextually. What, then, are the grounds upon which you might build a concept of 'the text itself'?

(b)   *Kinds of intertextuality*. Look at one of the clusters of texts in 'Crossings' (5.4) or put together a cluster of your own. Either way, try to describe the relations amongst these texts in terms of the three kinds of intertextuality distinguished above: explicit, implied and inferred. How distinguishable are they in practice?

Discussion

(i)   Depending on one's position, the term 'text' either serves to democratise English Studies, which was previously dominated by a study of literary 'works', or it serves to undermine the judgments of the past, which have established a canon of literary works.
Ron Carter, *Keywords in Language and Literacy* (1995: 155)

(ii)   In our century there are people who write as if there were nothing but texts.
Richard Rorty, 'Consequences of Pragmatism' (1982: 139) in Hawthorn
2000 (190)

Also see: Close reading – wide reading 1.2.4; Full interpretation 2.2; NEW CRITICISM; POSTSTRUCTURALISM; LINGUISTICS, STYLISTICS AND COGNITIVE POETICS @ 3.10; **absence and presence; foreground and background; writing . . . rewriting.**

READING: Wales 2001: 81–3, 210–11, 390–2; Bennett and Royle 2009: 28–34; Birch 1989: 5–44; Toolan 1992. *Core texts*: Barthes 1977: 155–64; Kristeva 1984.

TRANSLATION AND LITERATURE IN TRANSLATION

Translation is the realising of meanings and effects in one language that correspond in some way to the meanings and effects realised in another. 'Translation' refers to both the process of translating and the product of that process ('a translation'). Translation studies, meanwhile, is the academic study of the theory, history and practice of translation. It relates to the professional practice of translators and interpreters and the commercial business of publishing translations; but its chief purpose is to reflect upon and investigate those processes in a historical and cross-cultural perspective. Translation and by extension translation studies are important for a full understanding of English Studies for various reasons:

◆ Globally, many teachers and learners of English have more than one language and, for many, English is not their first language. Thus, deliberately or unconsciously, they regularly operate *across* or *between* languages. This involves translation broadly conceived. The same happens with code-switching within what is notionally the same language.

◆ Even for the many students whose first and perhaps only language is English, there are many historical and contemporary varieties of English (e.g., Anglo-Saxon and Afro-Caribbean) which in some measure require translation into an English with which they are more familiar.

◆ Translation into and out of English, whether for specialist technical purposes such as science and engineering or for general public and commercial use in the media (e.g. news, advertising, dubbing and subtitling of films and TV), is a widespread activity and major source of employment. Some of this is now done by machines (i.e. computer translation); but most is done by more or less professional, often part-time translators.

◆ Many central cultural documents such as the Bible, the Koran and and the epic poetry of Homer are *only* known to most users of English through translation. Within Departments of English alone, this list extends to plays by such writers as Ibsen and Brecht, novels by Proust, Calvino and Marquez, and the work of a great many theorists, from Aristotle to Artaud and Kant to Kristeva.

The traditional notion of translation ranges from word-for-word substitution to translation for the general sense. With poetry especially, there is the additional matter of whether the form of the original is carried over from the 'source' to the 'target' language. This is a particular challenge in that many languages (or different historical stages of the same language) have intrinsically different sound and grammatical structures, and quite distinct poetic traditions (see **versification**). This may be illustrated with a Modern English translation of the Old English poem, 'Wulf and Eadwacer' (5.1.1). The translation offered here is fairly 'literal' (word-for-word); but the word-order has been changed to suit the syntax of Modern English. Thus *Willao hy hine þecgan* becomes 'They will capture him' and not, as in the original, 'Will they him capture' (Old English relied more on word-endings than word-order for its grammar). Meanwhile, the Modern English version occasionally manages to retain the alliterative and stressed manner of the original: 'For my péople it is like a présent. They will cápture him if he cómes.' But this is much more localised and haphazard than the systematic, structural deployment of such features in the Old English. All this, however, is to stay at a relatively formal level, translating 'words on the page'.

Current translation studies would tend to emphasise the text in context and the broader CULTURAL and COMMUNICATIVE dimensions of translation. It would also acknowledge the partial *un*translatability of texts from one language to another in so far as the cultures those languages express and in which they are embedded are distinct and non-equivalent. Here, for instance, there is a potentially unbridgeable gap between the 'source' text and the 'target' text: the former recorded on manuscript by Christian clerics and initially conceived for oral performance, perhaps with musical accompaniment, at some social gathering; the latter as reproduced here in a printed textbook for silent study or discussion in class. At the same time, translation studies would endorse the attempt to search for correspondences, counterparts and analogies between one language, culture and moment of (re)production and another, even while observing that exact equivalence is impossible. Take line 5 of 'Wulf and Eadwacer', for instance. Old English *faest* meant 'secure' or 'strong' and survives in the slightly archaic phrase 'to make fast' (e.g. with a rope). It does *not* mean 'fast' in the modern sense of 'quick', 'rapid'. (This is an example of what translators call 'a false friend', a word with similar look and sound but different sense.) However, in the present translation it should be observed that in fact *none* of the above terms has been used to render *faest*. Instead, the translator (in this case me) has opted for a noun carrying the sense of 'secure' ('stronghold') but not the adjective itself as in the Old English. Some such process of push and pull – or shift and switch – among grammar and sound and sense goes on in all translation that seeks to register correspondences (not simply record equivalences). A more subtle and complex issue attaches to the Old English word *fenne* (literally 'with the fen'), also in line 5. For the Anglo-Saxons the word 'fenn' referred to boggy and dangerous tracts of land of which there were then many; it had the additional connotation of 'forbidden' and 'illegal' because the fen was where many outlaws lived to avoid detection and arrest. In the present poem the 'fen' location therefore reinforces the sense of an illicit relationship between Wulf and Eadwacer. Nowadays, however, since 'the fens' have been extensively drained and farmed, they are more likely to refer to lush, canal-crossed meadows and, for tourists at least, to connote waterways plied by boats and summer evenings at the pub. Again, then, even with a single, virtually identical word such as 'fen(n)', there are richly different worlds in play between one historical moment and cultural context and another. To grasp such complexities systematically is the task of what translation theorists call the 'Polysystems' approach, which is a branch of semiotics. In practice it is what every skilled and experienced translator attempts to do every time s/he grasps one wor(l)d and tries to turn it into another. The success or otherwise of this is then a matter for the many kinds of reader and user of the particular translation to decide. For in this respect there are vast differences between the needs and demands of, say, a five-year-old child, a specialist student and a general reader. Translation is a matter of function as well as form.

Finally, on a practical as well as a theoretical note, it may be observed that 'translation' is itself a word that may be variously translated. It derives from the past participle, *translatum*, of Latin *transferre*, 'to carry across'. It therefore bears close comparison with, on the one hand, the word 'dialogue' (from Greek *dia-logos*, 'across-word') and, on the other, the word 'metaphor' (from Greek *meta-pherein*, 'change-carrying'). Either way – or, rather, both ways – *trans-lation* involves a highly complex and suggestive sense of exchange (dialogue) and change (metaphor). It is never a mere 'transference', in the sense of simply moving an object from A to B, but is always a *transformation*, in which A *becomes* B along the way.

Activities

(a)   Consider the relations amongst the 'Rose' poems by Shapcott and Rilke in 5.4.3. Go on to attempt a translation into an idiom of your own from the French or English. What precisely are the similarities and differences? And what does this activity show about translation as a kind of transformation?

(b)   Compare the passages from Friel's play *Translations* and Sebald's novel *Austerlitz* with the 'Rose' 'poems' by Shapcott and Rilke (5.4.3). How might you relate the politics of translation to the poetics of translation? And do you always care (or notice) whether something is translated?

Discussion

(i)   What is really best in any book is translatable – any real insight or broad human sentiment.
                                Ralph Waldo Emerson, 'Books' in *Society and Solitude*, 1870.

(ii)   Translation is a form of transfusion. It's fresh blood, fresh air, good for the heart.
                                George Szirtes, *An English Apocalypse*, 2001.

Also see: **Writing, reading, response and rewriting; bibles;** 'Translation' (as learning strategy) 2.4; 'Translation/transformation' (anthology) 5.4.3; English at the edge @ 2.3.4.

READING: Bassnett 2002; Baker 2009; Lefevere 1992. *Core texts:* Venuti 2000 (reader).

VERSIFICATION: RHYTHM, METRE AND RHYME

Versification covers all those aspects of the formal organisation of sounds that characterise verse. These range from localised matters of alliteration and stress through more pervasive patternings of rhythm, metre and rhyme to larger structural matters of genre (e.g., sonnet, ballad, and free verse). The principal focus here is **poetry**; but all these features grow out of the routine resources of the language. Similar devices and strategies can therefore be found in the design of speech and writing of all kinds, from oratory to advertising. *Metrics* and *poetics* are terms sometimes used to designate partly similar areas. Metrics, however, is restricted to the analysis of 'measures' or 'feet' within the line of verse ('metre' – also spelt 'meter' – derives from the Greek word for 'measure' which also gives us the *metr*ic units cent*imetre*, kilo*metre*, etc., and gas *meter*, i.e gas-measurer). Poetics, meanwhile, has a more capacious sense than versification alone. It embraces formal patterning in language of all kinds, and includes rhetorical organisation in drama and narrative (Greek *poiesis* simply meant 'fashioning', 'making').

What we 'measure' in English poetry very much depends on the basic resources of the language. ENGLISH is fundamentally a Germanic language. Therefore, like other Germanic languages such as Dutch, German, Danish, Norwegian and Swedish, its basic sound-structure is built upon the presence or absence of stress (i.e. stressed or unstressed syllables). In this respect English differs from CLASSICAL and Romance languages such as Greek, Latin, French and Italian, which are organised chiefly round principles of syllable length (i.e. long or short syllables). Consequently, if we return to the oldest substratum of English verse, Anglo-Saxon poetry, we find it is organised on the principle of a regular number of stresses to the line (four), regardless of the number and length of intervening unstressed syllables. Another convention was that two or three of these stressed syllables had to begin with the same sound (i.e. alliterate). The opening lines of the poem 'Wulf and Eadwacer' (5.1.1) may therefore be measured or 'scanned' as follows (/ = stressed syllable; x = unstressed syllable; v = a marked medial pause or 'caesura'; <u>underlining</u> marks structural alliteration):

```
     /   x   /    v    / x  x  / x
   Wulf, min Wulf      wena me thine

    /  x  x / x   v    / x  /  x  x
   seoce gedygan      thine seldcymas

     /  x  x  /    v    / x   / x x x
   murnende mod        nales meteliste
```

The overall result is what is called stressed (or accentual) alliterative verse. Moreover, in that such poetry was primarily performed live and drew on a repertoire of half-line units (variations on all the above half-lines appear in other Anglo-Saxon poems) it is also called oral-formulaic poetry.

This kind of heavily stressed metre with structural alliteration was a powerful tradition in early English verse. Later medieval variations on it can be found in *Piers Plowman*, *Pearl*, and the Chester *Noah* (see @ 5.1.1 and @ 5.3.1). Furthermore, accentual verse – with or without structural alliteration – has been recognised as a powerful resource by many later writers across a whole range of 'Englishes'. Poets as various as Burns and Hopkins (5.1.2) in the eighteenth and nineteenth centuries, and Dylan Thomas (5.3.3), Walcott, Brathwaite, Dabydeen, Hughes and Heaney in the twentieth century, have all expressly acknowledged the influence of early accentual 'makers' on their own poetic craft.

However, accentual/stressed metre is only half of the history of English verse, albeit the older half. Another principle of metrical organisation has also been at work for a long time, usually in harness and productive tension with accentual metre. This is the principle of 'syllabic' or 'quantitative' metre (often accompanied by end-rhyme) and it became part of the native tradition most obviously and influentially through the work of Geoffrey Chaucer. Unlike his contemporaries, the authors of *Piers Plowman* and *Pearl*, Chaucer mainly adopted French and Italian metrical models. The result was a verse structure based on a regular number of syllables per line (usually eight or ten syllables, hence octo- or decasyllabic) and rhyme schemes ranging from the couplet to complex patterns such as 'rhyme royal' (seven decasyllabic lines rhyming ababbcc). Here are the first two lines of Chaucer's description of the Knight (5.1.1). Like many of *The Canterbury Tales*, these are in decasyllabic couplets and have been marked accordingly (the caesura pause is again marked 'v' and rhymes are in italics; notice that the final 'e' of 'time' is sounded and that of 'Trouthe' elides with the vowel in 'and', as is usual with adjacent vowels):

```
1    2     3   4 v 5    6 7 8  9  10
A Knight ther was    and that a worthy man
```

```
 1   2  3 4 5  6   7 8    9 10
That fro the time that he first bigan
```

```
 1 2 3  4   v  5 6 7    8 9 10
To riden out,    he loved chivalrie
```

```
 1   2     3 4 v  5 6   7  8  9 10
Trouthe and honour,    fredom and curteisie
```

Notice that where there is alliteration it is inconspicuous and localised rather than emphatic and structural. The following couplet from Pope's *The Rape of the Lock* (5.1.3) has a similar underlying decasyllabic structure. Here, however, I have extended the analysis so as to register a sense of the rhythm which also informs the lines. This particular pattern of 'unstressed + stressed' syllables is called by the CLASSICAL name 'iambic', though strictly in Greek and Latin this signalled a pattern of 'short + long' syllables. (Notice, too, that the uprights, |, mark the boundary between one metrical 'foot' and another; here the basic unit is an iamb, so the whole line is called iambic pentameter – five iambic feet.)

```
x    / |x  / |x  / |x  /  | x  /
1    2  3  4  5  6 7  8    9  10
And now unveiled the toilet stands displayed
```

```
        x   / | x  / |  x   / | x / | x  /
        1   2  3  4  5   6 7 8  9  10
        Each silver vase in mystic order laid
```

BUT WHY BOTHER TO 'SCAN' VERSE?

Marking up lines of verse in these ways initially looks cumbersome and unnecessary. However, done systematically and sensitively, 'scanning' quickly proves to be both relatively straightforward and remarkably illuminating. Certainly, it helps give visible structure to the word-musics we hear (it's a kind of metrical oscilloscope). It also provides a firm basis for more subtle explorations both analytically and in performance. See Discussion (ii), below for Dr Johnson's views on the matter.

As the above examples show, it is wisest to conclude that writers of English from the later Middle Ages to the present have had basically two principles of metrical organisation at their disposal: stressed and perhaps alliterating; and quantitative syllabic and perhaps rhymed. Indeed, more often than not the result has been various blends of the two, and what usually goes under the handily hybrid name of 'accentual-syllabic metre'.

Rolling everything together, we may say that most verse gives us syllabic and/or stressed regularity varied by the flexible sense of a speaking voice. At the same time, language as sound interplays with language as syntax, and both are braced against the play of meaning as such. Some such comments can be made on most kinds of verse. For verse, virtually by definition,

FINDING YOUR 'FEET'

There are five basic measures or 'feet' recognised in the scanning of English verse. Each of them involves a particular combination of unstressed (x) and stressed (/) syllables.

```
            x /    x   /   x /    x /
```
Iambus – e.g., again,   unveil, reverse, discuss (Think of further examples)

```
        /   x   /  x    /   x   / x
```
Trochee – e.g., happy, never, heartless, discus, etc.

```
        x  x  /    x x  /   x  x /   x x   /
```
Anapaest – e.g., entertain, repossess, hurry up, disapprove, etc.

```
            /    /    /   /   /   /   /  /
```
Spondee – e.g., heart break, wine glass, Big Mac, Disc-World, etc.

```
        /  x x    /  x x  /  x  x / x  x
```
Dactyl   – e.g., happiness, pulverise, orchestra, discotheque, etc.

The art of the poet chiefly lies in getting her or his 'feet' mixed up in variously elegant or arresting ways. At best the effect is of a kind of word-dance. The art of the analyst (and the perfomer) lies in retracing the steps.

tends to be both orderly and resourceful, economic and expressive. Something of the kind may certainly be said of just about every sample of English verse in the anthology up to the mid-twentieth century, as well as many up to the present. Moreover, absolutely any verse (including 'free verse') – if it is to be at all recognisable *as* verse – must have at least some corresponding principles of regularity and flexibility, unity and variety, order and expressiveness. The principles may be those of visual design organised for silent reading and sustained meditation. Or they may be those of sound patterning organised for live performance and immediate response. They may also be a mixture depending upon the expectations, media and resources in play. But some such general principles will be in operation, even though much of the actual appeal will always depend upon how they are realised in any one instance. Hence the following guidelines for you to apply (and modify) as you see and hear fit.

Versification checklist

What makes you think it's verse?

Appearance on the page – stacked down the middle in regular blocks, or with a freer, more 'spaced-out' look (at any rate not running prose-like from margin to margin)?
A kind of music to the ear, and the way it trips or tears from the tongue – a more than usual sense of sound-patterning, and perhaps more effort in articulation?

Structure of the line:

♦ a regular or irregular number of *stresses* per line? How many, how often?
♦ a regular or irregular number of *syllables* per line? What kinds, in what patterns?
♦ systematic and structural or occasional and opportunistic use of *alliteration*?
♦ systematic or occasional use of *rhyme*? Or half-rhyme (e.g., 'bend/bind')?
♦ regular or variable *break(s)* or *pause(s)* ('caesura(e)') within the line?

Relation between verse line and sentence structure. Is there

♦ *run-over* (enjambment) of sentence structures from one line to the next?
♦ *end-stopping* so that the line-end coincides with a clause or sentence break?
♦ *tension* between the verse music and the rhythm of the speaking voice?

Larger verse structures and patterns in groups of lines. Are there

♦ *rhyming couplets*, *quatrains* rhyming abab, or other configurations (e.g., abaabbcc)?
♦ eight-, ten- or twelve-*syllable* lines, repeated or alternating?
♦ two-, three-, four- or five-*stress* lines, repeated or alternating?

Recognisable **genres** and 'kinds' of verse, for instance

♦ *ballad/lyric forms* – usually in four-line verses (quatrains) with alternating rhymes (abab) and with four or three stresses per line; more 'literary' versions may be syllabically regular; e.g., Blake (2.1.3), Gray (5.4.5).
♦ *blank verse* – regular accentual-syllabic verse, often iambic pentameter, but without rhyme or structural alliteration; e.g., Milton's *Paradise Lost* (5.1.3).
♦ *sonnet* – characteristically, a fourteen-line poem (occasionally sixteen) broken into units of eight and six lines (octave and sestet) or three quatrains and a couplet. Metre is generally iambic

pentameter, but rhyme-schemes can be very various; e.g., Petrarchan (abbaabba cdecde), Spenserian (abab bcbc cdcd ee), and Shakespearean (abab cdcd efef gg): see 5.1.2 and 5.4.4. Brooke's sonnet (5.1.2), for instance, rhymes ababcdcd efgefg.

- *free verse* – a modern hybrid form which picks up various structural principles in passing (by turns perhaps stressed, syllabic, alliterating, (half)rhyming, end-stopped or running over) but without establishing a single consistent pattern; e.g., poems by Peters (5.4.1), Fanthorpe (5.1.2), Rich (5.3.4), Nichols (5.4.5); songs by Queen and the Flobots (5.1.5).

- *concrete poetry* and *word-as-image* – where the very shape of the words on the page or their movement on the screen imitates a particular object or action (e.g., a dove-shaped poem on a dove; a fast-moving 'express' sign). Also common in TV advertising and computer-assisted text/image design, poetic precursors include work by Edwin Morgan and George Herbert. Here, see the visual layout of the Seminole chants (5.1.5) and Agbabi's 'Problem Pages' (5.1.2).

Activities

(a) *Reading out, listening and analysing.* Read out loud and listen to one of the following pairs of poems (or another pair of your own choosing). Go on to analyse each poem in turn using the above 'Versification Checklist'. How far do the poems use similar or different resources for similar or different effects? (Suggested pairings are: Wyatt and Shakespeare (5.1.1, 5.1.2); Milton and Byron (5.1.3); Wordsworth and Peters (5.4.1); Brooke and Fanthorpe (5.1.2); Gross (5.1.5) and Oswald (5.3.3).

(b) *Prose-poetry.* Take some short passages of prose (e.g. the media texts in 5.2.6) and set them out on the page as various kinds of 'poem'. In each case, consider how changes in typeface, line-spacing and punctuation might reinforce the rhetorical strategies and imagery in play. (See the Seminole chants (5.1.5) and Agbabi's 'Problem Pages' in 5.1.2 for some ideas.)

Poetry-prose. Write out the poems by Bolam (5.1.4) and Rich (5.3.4) as continuous prose stretching from one side of the page to the other. What has been lost (or at least changed) by doing this? Go on to experiment with free verse structures alternative to those in the initial poems. Perhaps try a 'cut-out' poem like Petrucci's 'The Complete Letter Guide' (5.1.4).

Poetry-song-performance. Listen to then read the lyrics of a popular song (e.g., The Flobots' 'No Handlebars' or Queen's 'Bohemian Rhapsody' (5.1.5)). How much – or how little – of the sound-effect of the piece depends on the words on the page as distinct from the words in performance? In what ways do you need to supplement the above 'Versification Checklist' to accommodate these features?

Discussion

(i) Although in children's verses the linguist or literary critic may see and analyse patterns of rhythm, repetition and grammatical parallelism, children themselves as they grow older are increasingly likely to see these verses as telling stories, creating images, and [. . .] as a means of social interaction.

Guy Cook, *Language Play, Language Learning* (2000: 31)

(ii) However minute the employment may appear, of analysing lines into syllables, and whatever ridicule may be incurred by a solemn deliberation upon accents and pauses, it is certain that without this petty knowledge no man can be a poet; and that from the proper disposition of single sounds results that harmony that adds force to reason, and gives grace to sublimity.

Samuel Johnson, *Rambler* 88 (19 January 1751)
cited in Butler and Fowler (1971: 348)

Also see: 4.2; **creative writing; foreground, background; poetry and word-play.**

READING: Carper and Attridge 2003; Hobsbawm 1996; Preminger and Brogan 1993: 768–83; Short 1996: 106–67. Easthope 1983; Fabb 1997. *Core texts*: Brathwaite 1984; Kristeva 1984; Jakobson in Lodge and Wood 2008.

WRITING AND READING, RESPONSE AND REWRITING

Writing can be briefly defined as the activity of making verbal marks on paper or some other substance (stone, wood, plastic, computer screen, etc.); also what results (i.e. a piece of writing). **Reading** is the activity of engaging with those verbal marks and, again, what results (i.e. a reading). **Response** is a more capacious process. It includes reading but also embraces other forms of reaction and interaction, from listening and viewing to the initiation of a counter or alternative action. **Rewriting** is a fourth term added here so as to point up the relations among the other three. It reminds us that in some sense every *writing* is a *re*writing of what has been read (heard, seen) previously; while every *reading* is a *re*writing of what has been written. All these activities involve forms of response that may be variously reactive, interactive and proactive. All these activities, including response, can therefore be regarded as part of a continuous yet differentiated process elsewhere called **re-creation** (see **creative writing**). An understanding of this dynamic interrelatedness is crucial if we are to grasp the critical–creative nature of what it is we do whenever we set pen to paper or fingers to keyboards *and* when we focus our eyes on a page or a screen. Some finer, further distinctions are necessary before we proceed.

Writing and reading can be processes as well as products, attributes as well as events. This is evident grammatically because both these words can function as verbs *and* nouns *and* adjectives:

◆ writing and reading as *processes*, e.g., 'She's writing. I'm reading' (present progressive verbs);
◆ writing and reading as *products*, e.g., 'The writings of . . . ', 'a reading of . . . ' (nouns, plural and singular);
◆ writing and reading as *attributes*, e.g., 'A writing course', 'a reading journal' (adjectives).

Another important feature of the verbs 'to read' and 'to write' is that they can be both *transitive* and *intransitive*. That is, we can read and write something to someone (transitively, with objects and persons in mind) or we can just read and write (intransitively, as ends in themselves). Thus

◆ 'I'm writing a card to my friend', 'My daughter is reading a book to her dolly' (both *transitive*, with functional structure: Participant 1 – Process – Object – Participant 2);
◆ 'I'm writing', 'She's reading' (both *intransitive*, with functional structure: Participant – Process).

All this gives us plenty of room for manoeuvre when it comes to deciding what it is we are actually doing when we read and write.

WRITING AND READING – OR LITERATURE – OR TEXT? Which are you doing?

Writing and reading, taken together, are extremely versatile concepts. As shown above, they can refer to things, to attributes of other things, and to activities. Meanwhile, as activities, they can be ends in themselves or have objects and aims beyond themselves.

LITERATURE, however, has a narrower range of senses and grammatical functions. This may or may not be a good thing, depending on how you look at it. 'English Literature', for instance, usually refers to certain privileged kinds of fictional writing, and does not include everything written and read in English. Moreover, 'literature' can only function as a noun and an adjective – not a verb. Thus we may talk of 'great literature' and 'the scientific literature on this subject' (both nouns) and of 'literature courses' and 'literature searches' (both adjectives). However, we cannot say 'Shakespeare *literatured* this play . . . ' or 'She's *literaturing* his play and then going to *literature* an essay on it'.

Text too has distinctive possibilities and problems. Certainly, talk of 'texts' does not pre-empt the matter of which writings are to be privileged as 'literary'; nor does it limit discussion to the written or printed word (we can talk of audio- and audio-visual texts which may not be, strictly, 'written' or 'read' at all). Nonetheless, the term text still implies a certain fixity, an emphasis on achieved product rather than ongoing process. Partly this is because, like 'literature' but unlike 'writing' and 'reading', 'text' usually functions as a noun. It has, however, become common to speak of 'texting' a message; so 'text' now routinely operates as a verb. It is also interesting to observe that this technologically and socially driven change, brought about by changes in the nature and use of mobile phones, took place in a matter of years (between the first and the second editon of this book in fact). Such is the speed with which transformations in language, even at the level of grammar, can occur as responses to broader social and technological changes.

    For all the above reasons, it is important to distinguish precisely what it is we think we are doing. *Writing and reading? Literature? Texts?* How we answer can make a real **difference**. It may also imply some real **preferences**. (For further implications, see LITERATURE and text; also 'Change – a transitive and intransitive process', pp. 6, 69).

Writing occurs in various MEDIA: *handwriting, print and electronic modes.* The term is here being used, as is common, to cover verbal marks in all three. However, we should remember that these are to some extent distinct COMMUNICATIVE technologies with distinct yet variable functions and values. Whether people handwrite or type a letter, for instance, makes a big difference in terms of perceived (im)personality and (in)formality. Moreover, configurations of manuscript, print and screen CULTURES are constantly shifting in relation to one another; they are not fixed. Contemporary instances would be the pseudo-handwritten mass-reproduced advert (affecting informality and intimacy); the handwritten fax to a friend (a kind of electronically mediated but still personalised letter) and e-mail conferencing and text-messaging (which often have the interrupted structure and interactive feel of conversation, as well as the dashingly elliptical and exclamatory style of postcards; see @ 5.2.6 and @ 5.2.8).

    Writing and reading are activities similar to but different from speaking and listening. The written and spoken words draw on the same underlying sign-system (i.e. verbal language); but they are realised in different materials with distinct properties and potentialities. Writing is made from graphological material (visible marks on paper, or whatever), while speech is made from phonological material (audible sounds in air). With these distinctions in mind, here is a review of the characteristic properties and structures of writing. This should be read in conjunction with that for **speech**, where some further qualifications are included.

WRITING IS characteristically (but not always):

- *a more permanent record* than memory alone, and often more 'finished' than speech;
- *faceless and detachable from particular occasions and places* – relatively 'context-free' (though every **text** is read in some **context** and can be placed in a variety of **intertextual** frames);
- *initially 'one-way'* (**monologic**) – only 'two-way' (**dialogic**) after a delay;
- *learnt deliberately*, usually through specialised teaching (mere exposure to writing is not enough to produce literacy);
- *dependent on special writing materials and apparatuses* such as quills, pens, inks, animal skins, paper, printing-presses, typewriters, computers (the more technologically advanced the apparatus, the more expensive it is in capital terms).

THE STRUCTURES OF WRITING are thus characteristically (but not always):

- *self-sufficient and free-standing*, because the written or printed word alone has to do much of the work of contextualising;
- *dependent on full and explicit references*, with an inbuilt tendency towards the past tense (e.g., Cecily, Nathaniel and Charlotte were in Brighton in October 2011) rather than their context-sensitive equivalents in the present tense (e.g., 'They're here now');
- *heavily reliant on punctuation, visual presentation and additional words*, where stress and intonation would serve to point the sense in speech (e.g., 'He greeted the baby with a strangely cooing and sickeningly patronising "Hell-O-oo!"');
- *ostensibly 'fully-formed' and with an emphasis on the 'finished' product*: there is usually little surviving evidence of the redrafting process (including back-tracking, hesitation and changes of direction);
- *uninterrupted and with a tendency towards monologue and a single-voiced discourse*; even though writers can and do invoke other voices and discourses – as do critical and creative readers.

This last point brings us back to the dynamic interrelation of the activities of writing and reading, particularly the fact that reading is always a form of *rewriting*. The rest of this entry is devoted to variations on this theme.

Reception theorists (who explore forms of Reception Aesthetics) insist that a text does not simply exist in itself (as NEW CRITICS maintained) but that it exists as part of a shifting relation with readers over time. The text is a constantly re-forming construct. Thus Hans Robert Jauss sees the text historically, on a changing *horizon of expectation* which is defined by the meeting of the historical moments of the text and reader. As with a real horizon where sky meets land or sea, the relation between text and reader constantly changes as we travel through time and space. For Jauss, therefore, there is no single fixed point of reference, no absolutely imperative original meaning, but rather a succession of *moments of reception*, each one affected by the expectations, tastes and aims of the 'receivers' (for changing reception of *Hamlet* over time, see 3.1).

   Wolfgang Iser is another German reception theorist, but he takes a rather different tack. Iser talks more abstractly and somewhat less historically about the relations between texts and readers that share the same cultural frame. He is less interested in changes in reception over time and more interested in how a contemporary reader responds to a contemporary text. Chief among Iser's tools for modelling the text–reader relation are the following concepts (see 'narration process' under **narrative**):

♦   *implied reader* – the reader apparently intended by the author and implied by the text as a role which actual readers are invited to fill;
♦   *'blanks and vacancies'* – those areas of openness and indeterminacy in the text which actual readers fill according to their own capacities and orientations (cf. Macherey's **gaps and silences**);
♦   *affirmative negation* – the dialectical activity of meeting such blanks, vacancies and indeterminacies creatively as well as critically: through reading, readers make sense of them**selves**; they do not simply make sense of the text as **other**.

Iser's model of critical–creative reading has been deservedly influential. Its major drawback is that it often assumes readers who substantially share the world-view of the text they are reading. Furthermore, on closer inspection, this 'ideal reader' often turns out to be white, Western European and male. The tools of reception **aesthetics** can be extremely useful. But the politics which informs that aesthetics still determines what horizon is expected and what kind of material is assumed to fill the blanks and vacancies. MARXIST, FEMINIST and POSTCOLONIAL readers all tend to be 'receptive' to different possibilities.

   Reader-response critics are another broadly identifiable group of (chiefly American) writers engaged with readers and ways of reading. Many of these critics have a more PSYCHOLOGICAL and less aesthetic emphasis than their German counterparts. Norman Holland, for instance, conceived of the text–reader relation as a transaction much like that between analyst and analysand. For Holland, moreover, it is as much the text which analyses the reader as the reader who analyses the text. The text is thereby seen as a site for the projection of anxieties and hopes, and is understood in terms of its therapeutic functions and effects, not in terms of intrinsic meaning. David Bleich, another American practitioner of reader-response, extended this transactive model of response into the arena of group work. Bleich explores not only the effects of a text on individuals but also the processes whereby groups cooperate and negotiate meanings with the aim of arriving at a consensus – even if in practice this is not achieved. In these respects Bleich's models and techniques of '(inter)subjective criticism' are far more subtle and powerful than, say, Stanley Fish's notion of 'interpretive communities' (i.e. academic groups who share reading practices and values). The problem with the latter is that there is little recognition of the process whereby fundamental conflicts and differences arise between and within various groups of readers. Nor is much attention paid to variation in reading practice, whether from one group or person to another, or even from one reading to another by the same person. Relatedly (though he is not strictly a *reader*-response critic), Harold Bloom talks of the relation between one *writer* and another in terms of an Oedipal scenario: 'strong' writers deliberately 'misunderstand' and thereby both rewrite and overthrow their predecessors (who are conceived as threatening father-figures). However, Bloom does not include readers on his 'map of misprision'. Nor does he much consider models of the individual as a social **subject**, other than those supplied by Freudian psychology.

   For other models of the individual reader as a self-divided subject and an **identity** constantly involved in processes of dispersal and redefinition we must turn to POSTSTRUCTURALIST and POSTMODERNIST theorists. Meanwhile, for frames in which to practise specifically 'resistant', 'oppositional' or 'alternative' readings we must turn to Marxist, feminist and postcolonial writings (see below). All these movements in their various ways challenge politically loaded idealisations of 'the reader' or 'readers', as though s/he or they simply exist as some undifferentiated mass in an ahistorical vacuum. Hence the framing of the following questions.

'THE READER' . . . WHICH READERS?

These questions can be put to any text and to anyone reading. The insistence on past and present moments of reception is a reminder that there are always more readers and readings than one.

Who could read at all there and then? Who can read here and now? What are the implications of these kinds and degrees of il/literacy for what got and gets written?

How were (and are) readers distinguished by class, gender, ethnicity, region, nation, religion and education? And what of the specific kinds of reading practice in play then and now (public and out loud, solitary and silent, for pleasure, instruction, analysis . . .)?

How likely was (and is) a common response given the cultural make-up of the readership? Are utterly consensual *or* utterly conflictual readings ever possible?

How does one person's reading (and one person reading) influence another? And where does this leave the notion of a 'purely personal response'?

At what point does the activity of reading turn into that of (re)writing? In the head when reading? Afterwards on reflection? In conversation when describing and evaluating? In a written essay or analysis? In selective quotation? In finding or fashioning a particular edition? In a concerted critique, adaptation, updating, parody, intervention . . . ?

(For influential case studies which show how such questions can be put to a range of specific historical materials, see J.J. McGann, *The Beauty of Inflections*, 1988.)

The following theorists have also contributed to the notion of reading as rewriting in literary and cultural studies.

Roland Barthes made an influential distinction between 'readerly' (*lisible*) and 'writerly' (*scriptible*) texts. Readerly texts offer the reader the pleasure (*plaisir*) of total immersion in and identification with a supposedly self-sufficient and closed fictional world (examples would be Mills and Boon romances and certain kinds of 'classic **realism**'). Writerly texts offer the reader the joy/ecstasy (*jouissance*) of participation in the construction of a fictional world which is openly in process and always in the making (examples would be everything from Sterne's *Tristram Shandy* and Joyce's *Ulysses* to interactive story-books and virtual reality games; see **metafiction**). Subsequently, however, Barthes modified this distinction. He recognised that it is also the reader (not only the author or the text) who controls how far a text shall be read as 'closed' or 'open', 'readerly' or 'writerly'. Thus even the most apparently complete, self-sufficient and non-playful text (e.g., a telephone directory) can readily be recognised as 'writerly'. We simply need to draw attention to its distinctive apparatuses and discourses and its manifold uses (from finding telephone numbers and addresses to propping up shelves and demonstrating strong-arm techniques). Conversely, even the most apparently incomplete and open text can be substantially filled in and closed down so as to be made 'readerly' (e.g., critical commentaries on Sterne and Joyce). Barthes partly covered this eventuality when he later observed that the same piece of literature could be approached as a finished 'work of art' (French *œuvre*; Latin *opus*) or as a 'text' (in this case invoking its ancient meaning of 'a tissue', 'texture', 'a web'; see **text**). Hélène Cixous makes a relatable distinction with respect to what she calls *écriture féminine* ('feminine writing'). Initially she claimed that there is a kind of writing characterised by its openness, fluidity and apparent fragmentariness which can be identified with women (e.g., Woolf and Dorothy Richardson). Later Cixous allowed that such writing is gendered rather than sexed, and can be identified with the 'feminine' in men too.

RESPONSE-ABILITY IS RESPONSIBILITY

Aesthetic responsiveness = Ethical responsibility
Personal response = Interpersonal response-ability (after Bakhtin, see below)

Mikhail Bakhtin is another critical theorist who challenged any hard-and-fast distinction between the activities of reading and writing. His insistence that words are 'sites of struggle' defined in the dialogic interplay between competing discourses and voices, means that every utterance is Janus-like. It looks both back and forwards: back to past utterances to which it is a response, and forwards to future utterances which it anticipates in response. In this way, for Bakhtin, *response-ability* or 'answerability' is the prerogative of both writers and readers alike. Bakhtin also stresses the ethical *responsibility* as well as the historical *response-ability* of every utterance we make (both senses are covered by Russian *otvetstvenost*). Such a view of response-ability/reponsibility has little in common with an exclusively individualist view of 'personal response'. For Bakhtin, responses can never be purely 'personal' (in the sense of being 'wholly authenticated by one's own experience' and expressed 'in one's own words') precisely because one's own experience *and* words are always already implicated in those of others (what he refers to as 'another's words in one's own language'; see FUNCTIONALISM). Self is always expressed through – never simply against – **other**. Apparently personal responses always turn out to be interpersonal too.

Jacques Derrida is a theorist who has greatly influenced contemporary models of reading and writing in yet other ways. Above all, he insists that both writers and readers, because they use and are used by LANGUAGE, are involved in the continual displacement and deferral of meanings. The ceaseless play of differences within and between words, within and between texts, ensures that there is no fixed point of departure *or* arrival in the process of writing–reading, and therefore no stable distinction between writer and reader. Instead we are treated to a fascinating play of possibilities in interpersonal and intertextual space. Derrida also suggests that it is precisely the play between present words and absent things that is the motivating force informing most activities of writing and reading (see **absence and presence**). Whether as writers or readers, we are all involved in the endlessly fascinating yet ultimately frustrating task of trying to knit presences out of absences: looking *at* a text only to find ourselves looking *through* it. Writing – like speech – always turns out to be full of w/holes.

Resistant readers and reading otherwise. Many overtly political writers propose strategies of reading that can be variously described as 'resistant', 'counter' or 'alternative'. (The mere beginning of such a list might include: hooks, Brecht, Benjamin, Bhabha, Macherey, Hall, Cixous, Eco, Fetterley, Hutcheon, Kristeva, Mills, Said and Spivak.) For convenience, three kinds of response can be distinguished, though in any particular reading or reading practice there may well be a mixture:

♦ *Passive or submissive reading* involves reading 'with the grain' of the text, accepting its perceived values and versions of reality. This may be more positively framed as 'receptive' reading.
♦ *Oppositional or counter-reading* involves reading 'against the grain' of the text, aiming to invert or subvert its meanings. This may also be termed 'aggressive' or 'assertive' reading, depending upon how it is valued.

♦   *Alternative or negotiated reading* involves reading neither 'with' nor 'against' the grain of the text, but flexibly and with a sense of challengeable and changeable critical agendas. This may also be termed 'shifty' or 'subtle' reading, depending upon what precisely goes on in practice and why.

Critical reading into critical–creative rewriting

In more radical versions of reading practice it is recognised that readings lead to rewritings in deed not just in the head. At this point, therefore, we must turn to such critical–creative genres as adaptation, imitation, parody, collage and intervention; also to **creative writing** and **re-creation** as such. Crucially, these are not only activities which specially designated **authors**, **artists** and other kinds of creative practitioner engage in. They are tried and tested genres of academic writing (usually including a commentary) which can very profitably and pleasurably be used to complement the traditional academic essay and analysis. (For practical guidance see 'Further strategies for critical–creative writing' 2.3.3.) All that need be added here is that such modes of re/production encourage interpretation and performance in the fullest sense. They thereby fundamentally reconfigure the relations between reading and writing, on the one hand, and criticism and creativity, on the other. Response is thus realised as something we negotiate and make together – not simply something each of us 'has'.

Activities

(a)   *Transforming texts*. For a range of activities exploring writing as both product and process, with an end in view and as an end in itself, see:

   ♦ **speech**, activity (b) – spontaneous conversation into crafted scripts;
   ♦ **narrative**, activity (c) – adaptation of novels and films for screen;
   ♦ **versification**, activity (b) – permutations of poetry, prose and performance.

(b)   *Being a responsive and responsible reader*. Apply some of the terms and techniques introduced above to a text you are studying or one from Part Five: i.e. moments of reception and horizons of expectation (Jauss); implied reader, blanks and vacancies, affirmative negation (Iser); writerly and readerly, work (of art) and text (Barthes); response-ability and dialogue (Bakhtin); feminine writing and reading as a woman (Cixous); passive, oppositional and alternative readers/readings.

(c)   *Critical reading as critical–creative rewriting*. Use one or two of the 'Further strategies for critical–creative writing' (2.3.3) to explore a text which interests or irritates you. Be sure to add a commentary.

Discussion

(i)   Writing is teachable: it is an art that can be learned rather than a mysterious ability that one either has or does not have.

   Robert Connors and Cheryl Glenn, *The St Martin's Guide to Teaching Writing* (1995: v)

(ii)   The word is a two-sided act [. . .] every utterance is suspended between the utterance to which it responds and the response which it anticipates.

V.I. Voloshinov, *Marxism and the Philosophy of Language* (1973: 86ff.)

(iii)   The goal of literary work (or literature as work) is to make the reader no longer a consumer, but a producer of the text.

Roland Barthes, 'From Work to Text' (1977: 163)

Also see: LITERATURE; Critical and Creative Strategies (Part Two, esp. 2.2 and 2.3.3); **absence and presence; foreground and background; speech; text** and COGNITIVE POETICS @ 3.10.

READING: McCaw 2008; Oatly in Gavins and Steen 2003; Crystal 2003: 256–83; Holub 1984; Johnson in Lentricchia and McLaughlin 1995: 39–49, 321–38; Bennett 1995 (reader on reading); Pope 1995 (reading as rewriting); Fischer 2001, 2005; Rivkin and Ryan 2004: Part 3. *Core texts*: Barthes, Iser and Eco in Lodge and Wood 2008; Knights and Thurgar-Dawson 2006.

YOUR OWN ADDITIONS AND MODIFICATIONS

This is a reminder to continue adding items which you yourself find useful and necessary. For clearly there are plenty of common – and some not so common – terms not featured in this book which you may feel to be equally or more significant. There will probably be some of the definitions you would like to take issue with too. In this respect, Part Four should be regarded simply as a beginning. Extend, refine and replace it as you see fit.

Further entries on the companion website @ 4 feature the following terms and topics:

- ◆ **Addresser, address, addressee**
- ◆ **Aesthetics and pleasure, art and beauty**
- ◆ **Auto/biography and travel writing: selves and others**
- ◆ **Bibles, holy books and myths**
- ◆ **Creative writing, creativity, re-creation**
- ◆ **Difference and similarity, preference and re-valuation**
- ◆ **Multimodal, cyber and hypertexts**
- ◆ **Subject and agent, role and identity**

ANTHOLOGY

PART FIVE

PREVIEW

This part of the book consists of short texts and extracts for discussion, analysis and other activities. A wide variety of Englishes is represented, past and present, 'literary' and 'non-literary', spoken, written and otherwise recorded. The aim is to provide handy resources for a variety of courses and to encourage interdisciplinary study. All these materials are featured in the illustrations and activities in the other parts of the book. A list of authors, texts and topics is supplied on the Contents page, and these can be followed up further in the Index. Much of the material is organised in three areas:

◆   *Poetries*
◆   *Proses*
◆   *Voices*

There is therefore a recognition of the traditional and still serviceable distinction between poetry, prose and drama. At the same time there is an attempt to extend and complicate these categories. We recognise other, relatable kinds of text and performance which are often treated separately or excluded altogether.

   The remaining material is organised in groups of texts by topic or theme. It consists of

◆   *Crossings* (5.4)

All texts are identified by author(s) or producer(s), date of first publication and date of composition where this is significantly different and known. As far as possible, texts are complete. Extracts from longer works are briefly contextualised. The accompanying notes supply further information on context as well as cross-references to particularly relevant terms, issues and approaches featured elsewhere in the book. All this supporting apparatus is important, it is suggested, if we are to *study* texts and not just *read* them.

Further texts can be found in the Supplementary anthology @ 5.

5.1   POETRIES

5.1.1   Early English verses

Old English lament (anon.), 'Wulf and Eadwacer', before 975

Leodum is minum swylce him mon lac gife;
willao hy hine þecgan, gif he on þreat cymeð
Ungelic is us.
Wulf is on iege, ic on oþerre.
Faest is þaet eglond, fenne biworpen.   5
Sindon waelreowe weras þaer on ige
willao hy hine aþecgan, gif he on þreat cymeð
Ungelic is us.
Wulfes ic mines widlastum wenum dogode;
þonne hit waes renig weder and ic reotugu saet,   10
þonne mec se beaducafa bogum bilegde,
waes me wyn to þon, waes me hwaeþre eac lað
Wulf, min Wulf, wena me þine
seoce gedydon, þine seldcymas,
murnende mod, nales meteliste.   15
Gehyrest þu, Eadwacer? Uncerne earmne hwelp
bire wulf to wuda
þaet mon eaþe toslite þaette naefre gesomnad waes,
uncer giedd geador.

Translation:

For my people it is like a present.
They will capture him if he comes with a troop.
We are apart.
Wulf is on one island, I am on another.
It is an island stronghold wrapped round by the fens.   5
Fierce and cruel are the people there on that island.
They will capture him if he comes with a troop.
We are apart.
For my Wulf I have sorrowed from afar.
When it was rainy weather, and I sat bereft.   10
When the bold warrior laid his arms about me.
it was a joy to me, and it was also a pain.
O Wulf, my Wulf, my longing for you
and the rareness of your coming has made me ill.
My spirit grieves me more than the lack of food.   15
Eadwacer, do you hear me? A wolf will carry
our sorry whelp to the woods.
That may easily be sundered which was never solemnised
Our song together.

This oral-formulaic poem is a fragment of a larger, lost whole. It is in alliterative, stressed metre (see **versification**) and West-Saxon dialect, and survives in a single manuscript in one of the four main Anglo-Saxon poetry anthologies, the 'Exeter Book' (compiled *c.* 975). Interpretations and **translations** vary markedly, largely depending on whether the poem is read as a **monologue** or a **dialogue**, and whether there is judged to be the same or a new speaker from line 16. It used to be assumed that Anglo-Saxon poets were all men; but this belief has recently been challenged. As a **genre** this poem can be categorised as 'complaint', 'elegy' and 'riddle'. The þ (a 'thorn') is derived from the Germanic runic alphabet and had the sound 'th', as had the modified Anglo-Saxon ð. Both persisted to the fifteenth century.

(For a parallel text with a somewhat different translation, see Richard Hamer, *A Choice of Anglo-Saxon Verse*, London, 1970: 82–5; and for discussion of **translation** see pp. 264–5.)

Medieval lyric (anon.), 'Maiden in the mor lay', *c.* 1320

Maiden in the mor lay,
In the mor lay;
Sevenight fulle,
Sevenight fulle,
Maiden in the mor lay;   5
In the mor lay,
Sevenightes fulle and a day.

Welle was hire mete.
What was hire mete?
The primerole and the –   10
The primerole and the –
Welle was hire mete.
What was hire mete?
The primerole and the violet.
Welle was hire dring.   15
What was hire dring?
The chelde water of the –
The chelde water of the –
Welle was hire dring.
What was hire dring?   20
The chelde water of the welle-spring.

Welle was hire bowr.
What was hire bowr?
The rede rose and the –
The rede rose and the –   25
Welle was hire bowr.
What was hire bowr?
The rede rose and the lilye flour.

1. mor – moor, wilds. 8. Welle – (pun here?) good / the well; mete – food. 10. primerole – primrose. 15. dring – drink. 17. chelde – chilled, cold. 22. bowr – abode.

This enigmatic poem survives in a single manuscript from the early fourteenth century. It looks and sounds to have been composed for song and perhaps dance, maybe as a 'carole' to be joined in at various moments by different people (part-song refrain, 'round', etc.). Interpretations vary widely. The 'maiden' has been seen as pagan fertility goddess, nature spirit, the Virgin Mary and a dead woman, real or imagined. At any rate, the bishop of Ossory in Ireland declared it was not suitable for singing by any of his priests. (For text and notes, see R.T. Davies (ed.) *Medieval English Lyrics*, London 1966: 102, 320–1.)

GEOFFREY CHAUCER, from 'The General Prologue to the Canterbury Tales', ll.43–72, c. 1385–92

A KNYGHT ther was, and that a worthy man,
That fro the tyme that he first bigan
To riden out, he loved chivalrie,   45
Trouthe and honour, fredom and curteisie.
Ful worthy was he in his lordes werre,
And therto hadde he riden, no man ferre,
As wel in cristendom as in hethenesse,
And evere honoured for his worthynesse;   50
At Alisaundre he was whan it was wonne.
Ful ofte tyme he hadde the bord bigonne
Aboven alle nacions in Pruce;
In Lettow hadde he reysed and in Ruce,
No Cristen man so ofte of his degree.[. . .]   55
At mortal batailles hadde he been fiftene,
And foughten for oure feith at Tramyssene
In lystes thries, and ay slayn his foo.
This ilke worthy knyght hadde been also
Somtyme with the lord of Palatye   65
Agayn another hethen in Turkye;
And everemoore he hadde a sovereyn prys.
And though that he were worthy, he was wys,
And of his port as meeke as is a mayde.
He nevere yet no vileynye ne sayde   70
In al his lyf unto no maner wight.
He was a verray, parfit gentil knyght.

49. hethenesse – heathen lands. 51. Alisaundre – Alexandria. (All the places named in lines 51–66 were places in what is now the Middle East and Eastern Europe where English knights campaigned in the fourteenth century.) 52. bord bigonne – sat in the place of honour. 63. In lystes – in formal duels; ay – always. 64. ilke – same. 66. Agayn – against. 70. vileynye – rudeness, like a 'villein' / peasant. 71 no maner wight – any sort of person. 72. verray – true; parfit – perfect (complete); gentil – noble (of spirit and/or rank).

Chaucer (*c.* 1343–1400) was variously courtier, squire, tax-collector, court poet, and knight of the shire and member of parliament for Kent. His patrons included John of Gaunt, Richard II and Henry IV. 'The General Prologue' survives in over eighty manuscripts from before the mid-fifteenth century. It is written in a South-East Midland, London-based **dialect** that is relatively familiar to modern readers because it came to underpin the printed **standard** favoured at court and in the capital. The

versification in decasyllabic rhyming couplets was influenced by later medieval French and was quite new in English at the time. Now, however, such a verse-form is more familiar than those below, which in fact follow an earlier, Germanic, alliterative and stressed tradition. Chaucer's knight has been variously interpreted as chivalric ideal, mercenary and representative of Western European Christian civilisation or barbarism. For sample analysis, see MARXISM, Example pp. 162–3. (For text and notes, see L.D. Benson (ed.) *The Riverside Chaucer*, Oxford, 2008.)

SIR THOMAS WYATT, 'They flee from me', c. 1535

They flee from me, that sometime did me seek,
With naked foot stalking in my chamber,
I have seen them, gentle, tame and meek,
That now are wild, and do not remember
That sometime they put themselves in danger   5
To take bread at my hand; and now they range,
Busily seeking with a continual change.

Thanked be fortune it hath been otherwise,
Twenty times better; but once in special,
In thin array, after a pleasant guise,   10
When her loose gown from her shoulders did fall,
And she me caught in her arms long and small,
Therewith all sweetly did me kiss
And softly said, 'Dear heart, how like you this?'

It was no dream, I lay broad waking,   15
But all is turned, thorough my gentleness,
Into a strange fashion of forsaking;
And I have leave to go, of her goodness,
And she also to use newfangleness.
But since that I so kindly am serv'd,   20
I would fain know what she hath deservèd.

Wyatt (*c.* 1503–42) was an influential courtier and diplomat at the court of Henry VIII. He was twice imprisoned in the Tower of London (1536, 1541), the first time possibly for an affair with Anne Boleyn, the king's wife. This poem may allude to that incident. The text used here is taken from the Egerton MS (*c.* 1536) which is probably written in the **author**'s own hand. The poem may initially have been a song for musical accompaniment by lute. The poem was later anthologised in Tottel's influential miscellany *Songs and Sonets* (1557). There it is given the title 'The Lover Showeth How He is Forsaken of Such as He Sometimes Enjoyed'. Tottel's last line reads 'How like you this, what hath she now deserv'd?' (For both versions, see Abrams 2000, Vol. I: 529–30.)

5.1.2   Sonnets by various hands

WILLIAM SHAKESPEARE, 'My mistress' eyes' (Sonnet 130), written c. 1594–9, pub. 1609

My mistress' eyes are nothing like the sun;
Coral is far more red than her lips' red;
If snow be white, why then her breasts are dun;
If hairs be wires, black wires grow on her head.
I have seen roses damasked, red and white,   5
But no such roses see I in her cheeks;
And in some perfumes is there more delight
Than in the breath that from my mistress reeks.
I love to hear her speak, yet well I know
That music hath a far more pleasing sound;   10
I grant I never saw a goddess go;
My mistress, when she walks, treads on the ground.
    And yet, by heaven, I think my love as rare
    As any she belied with false compare.

William Shakespeare (1564–1616) – successful theatre shareholder, director, actor and playwright – only seems to have cared to see his **poems**, not his plays, through the press (e.g., *Venus and Adonis* (1593) and *The Rape of Lucrece* (1594) as well as *Sonnets* (1609)). At that time printed plays had little prestige as LITERATURE. In the 1590s, when sonnets were a very fashionable **genre**, Shakespeare was well known for 'his sugared sonnets' among private friends, according to a contemporary, Frances Meres. A decade later Shakespeare had them printed, with an enigmatic dedication: 'To the onelie begetter of these ensuing sonnets, Mr W.H. . . . '. This particular sonnet is about the so-called 'Dark Lady', as are most of sonnets 127–54. Other sonnets are addressed to or are about one or more male youths. For another Shakespeare sonnet, see 5.4.4. For a sample analysis of the present sonnet, see FORMALISM, Example pp. 145–6.

JOHN MILTON, 'When I consider how my light is spent'

WHEN I consider how my light is spent,
    Ere half my days, in this dark world and wide
    And that one talent which is death to hide
    Lodged with me useless, though my soul more bent
To serve therewith my maker, and present
    My true account, lest he returning chide,
    'Doth God exact day-labour, light denied?'
    I fondly ask: but patience to prevent
That murmur soon replies, 'God doth not need
    Either man's work or his own gifts; who best
    Bear his mild yoke, they serve him best, his state
Is kingly. Thousands at his bidding speed
    And post o'er land and ocean without rest:
    They also serve who only stand and wait.

John Milton, Sonnet XVI, first published 1673, from *The New Oxford Book of Seventeenth-Century Verse*, cd. Alastair Fowler, Oxford: Oxford University Press, 1992, pp. 427–8. For note on Milton, see *Paradise Lost* (5.1.3).

PATIENCE AGBABI, 'Problem Pages' (responses to Shakespeare's and Milton's sonnets)

TWO   LOVES   I   HAVE

Dear Patience, I am a poet who writes for the stage and thus typecast a performance poet. Yet my plays are on the GCSE syllabus so my verse will stand the test of time. My sonnet sequence, addressing a white man and black woman, aims to dress old words new. My publishers claim it will confound the reader but I suspect homophobia/racism. Please help!

I empathise. When will people stop categorising and embrace the page-stage, black-white, heterosexual-homosexual continuum? I applaud your literary range! But who is the reader? Seek critical advice and/or ditch your publisher for one who'll take risks. Your solid reputation will help.

MY   LIGHT   IS   SPENT

Dear Patience, I am a middle-aged, respected white, male poet, neoformalist yet reformist, who is losing his sight, and therefore losing sight of his poetic vision, whose ultimate aim is to implant and cherish in all people the seeds of virtue and public civility. Not writing is death but to write in perpetual darkness is also death. And I lack companionship with women.

I wish more poets shared your ambition. Poetry has long been afraid to admit its wants to change the world. Invest in a dictaphone that transcribes. You may begin to compensate with your other five senses, especially your sixth sense, insight, that will rekindle love of writing. And women.

These prose-poems are two of Agbabi's fourteen 'Problem Pages', which cross aspects of the sonnet form with the advice to readers ('agony aunt') column of popular tabloid journalism. The first writes back to Shakespeare's sonnets (e.g. sonnet 130 above and sonnet 19 in 5.4.4); and the second writes back to Milton's sonnet XVI above. Over the series as a whole she also responds to Surrey, Wroth, Smith, Wordsworth, Keats, Barrett Browning, Hopkins, Frost, McKay, St Vincent Millay, Brooks and Jordan. For an example of Agbabi's oral performance poetry and a biographical note, see 'Give me a word', 5.1.5. (Text from Agbabi, *Bloodshot Monochrome*, Edinburgh: Canongate, 2008, pp. 34, 36.)

GERARD MANLEY HOPKINS, 'The Windhover', written 1877, pub. 1918

[*Tips on reading*. This can be a perplexing poem until you get into the swing of sounding it out loud and relish the sense of the French-derived words: 'minion' – darling; 'dauphin' – prince-in-waiting; 'chevalier' – knight; 'sillion' – furrow. The two marks over 'sheer' and 'plod' in line 12 are Hopkins's indications of especial stress, though weighing where to place the stresses is a major part of the poem's overall challenge. A windhover is a kestrel, a small falcon that hovers then suddenly swoops.]

I caught this morning morning's minion, king-
   dom of daylight's dauphin, dapple-dawn-drawn Falcon in his riding
   Of the rolling level underneath him steady air, and striding
High there, how he rung upon the rein of a wimpling wing
In his ecstasy! then off, off forth on swing.   5
   As a skate's heel sweeps smooth on a bow bend: the hurl and gliding
   Rebuffed the big wind. My heart in hiding
Stirred for a bird, — the achieve of, the mastery of the thing!

Brute beauty and valour and act, oh, air, pride, plume, here
   Buckle! AND the fire that breaks from thee then, a billion   10
Times told lovelier, more dangerous, O my chevalier!

   No wonder of it: shéer plód makes plough down sillion
Shine, and blue-bleak embers, ah my dear,
   Fall, gall themselves, and gash gold vermilion.

While studying at Oxford, Hopkins (1844–89) was greatly influenced by the **aesthetic** ideas on sensuous beauty of his tutor, Walter Pater, and the conversion to Catholicism of his mentor, Cardinal Newman. Hopkins subsequently became a Jesuit priest, writing but not publishing poetry; first publication was in 1918, long after his death. The heavily alliterative, stressed verse-form is partly modelled on early English poetic forms (cf. 5.1.1), and the wrenching of sense is an attempt to register what Hopkins calls 'inscape'. This is a sensuously intense realisation of the 'thisness' of a specific event or identity, ultimately leading to an acute apprehension ('instress') of God in all things. Hopkins's subtitle for this poem is 'To Christ our Lord'.

RUPERT BROOKE, 'The Soldier', written December 1914, pub. June 1915

If I should die, think only this of me:
   That there's some corner of a foreign field
That is for ever England. There shall be
   In that rich earth a richer dust concealed;   4
A dust whom England bore, shaped, made aware,
   Gave, once, her flowers to love, her ways to roam,
A body of England's, breathing English air,
   Washed by the rivers, blest by suns of home.   8

And think, this heart, all evil shed away,
   A pulse in the eternal mind, no less
Gives somewhere back the thoughts by England given,
   Her sights and sounds; dreams happy as her day;   12
And laughter, learnt of friends; and gentleness,
   In hearts at peace, under an English heaven.

Brooke (1887–1915) was educated at a public (i.e. fee-paying private) school (Rugby) and Cambridge University. He is usually referred to as a 'Georgian' poet because of his mixture of patriotism and pastoralism. He died of dysentery and blood poisoning on a troop ship on the way to Gallipoli. Winston Churchill, in a 'Valediction' in the London *Times* (1915), used the occasion of the poet's death and the posthumous publication of his poems a month later to reinforce a recruitment drive (see Abrams 2000, Vol II: 2051):

> The thoughts to which he gave expression in the very few incomparable war sonnets which he has left behind will be shared by many thousands of young men moving resolutely and blithely forward into this, the hardest, the cruellest, and the least-rewarded of all the wars that men have fought. They are a whole history and revelation of Rupert Brooke himself. Joyous, fearless, versatile, deeply instructed, with classic symmetry of mind and body, he was all that one would wish England's noblest sons to be in days when no sacrifice but the most precious is acceptable, and the most precious is that which is most freely proffered.

Compare next text(s).

URSULA A. FANTHORPE, 'Knowing about Sonnets', 1986

Lesson I: 'The Soldier' (Brooke)
[The task of criticism] is not to redouble the text's self-understanding, to collude with its object in a conspiracy of silence. The task is to show the text as it cannot know itself.
                                       Terry Eagleton, *Criticism and Ideology*

Recognizing a sonnet is like attaching
A name to a face. *Mister Sonnet, I presume?*
   If I
And naming is power. It can hardly
Deny its name. You are well on the way
To mastery. The next step is telling the sonnet
What it is trying to say. This is called Interpretation.
   If I should die
What you mustn't do is collude with it. This
Is bad for the sonnet, and will only encourage it
To be eloquent. You must question it closely:
What has it left out? What made it decide
To be a sonnet? The author's testimony
(If any) is not evidence. He is the last person to know.
   If I should die, think this
Stand no nonsense with imagery. Remember, though shifty,
It is vulnerable to calculation. Apply the right tests.
Now you are able to Evaluate the sonnet.
   If I

That should do for today.
>*If I should die*
>>And over and over
The new white paper track innocent unlined hands
>*Think this. Think this. Think this. Think only this.*

Fanthorpe (b.1929) was Head of English at Cheltenham Ladies' College, a prestigious private girls' school. Eagleton (b.1943) is a British MARXIST critic and Professor of English at the University of Manchester. His *Criticism and Ideology* was published in 1976. (Text from U.A. Fanthorpe, *Selected Poems*, London, Penguin, 1986: 112.)

5.1.3   Heroics and mock-heroics

JOHN MILTON, from *Paradise Lost* Book IV, ll.549–81, 1667

[At the gates of heaven, the angel Uriel is telling the archangel Gabriel that a devil (Satan) seems to have escaped from hell.]

Betwixt these rocky pillars Gabriel sat,	
Chief of the angelic guards, awaiting night;	550
About him exercised heroic games	
The unarmed youth of heaven, but nigh at hand	
Celestial armoury, shields, helms, and spears,	
Hung high with diamond flaming, and with gold.	
Thither came Uriel, gliding through the even	555
On a sunbeam, swift as a shooting star	
In autumn thwarts the night, when vapours fired	
Impress the air, and shows the mariner	
From what point of his compass to beware	
Impetuous winds. He thus began in haste.	560
Gabriel, to thee thy course by lot hath given	
Charge and strict watch that to this happy place	
No evil thing approach or enter in;	
This day at height of noon came to my sphere	
A spirit, zealous, as he seemed, to know	565
More of the almighty's works, and chiefly man	
God's latest image: I described his way	
Bent all on speed, and marked his airy gait;	
But in the mount that lies from Eden north,	
Where he first lighted, soon discerned his looks	570
Alien from heaven, with passions foul obscured:	
Mine eye pursued him still, but under shade	
Lost sight of him; one of the banished crew,	
I fear, hath ventured from the deep, to raise	
New troubles; him thy care must be to find.	575
To whom the winged warrior thus returned:	
Uriel, no wonder if thy perfect sight,	
Amid the sun's bright circle where thou sit'st,	

> See far and wide: in at this gate none pass
> The vigilance here placed, but such as come   580
> Well known from heaven;

Milton (1608–74) – poet, pamphleteer, and classical and biblical scholar – was also a staunch Protestant, parliamentarian and anti-royalist. He probably began composing *Paradise Lost* when he was Secretary of Foreign Tongues to the Council of State, between the period of the 'Commonwealth' and before the Restoration of the monarchy (1660). Milton regularly wrote in and **translated** from Latin, Italian and English. He composed most of his hybrid Christian and neo-classical epic *Paradise Lost* in his head, when he was blind. The text was written down by his wives Katherine (d.1658) and Elizabeth and by his daughters (cf. William Wordsworth and his female amanuenses, 5.4.1). Milton's heroically biblical and neo-CLASSICAL manner, Latinate diction and sentence-structure, as well as his blank **verse** were to prove very influential. See Milton's sonnet 'On his blindness' (5.1.2) and compare Byron's *The Vision of Judgement* (5.1.3).

ALEXANDER POPE, from *The Rape of the Lock*, Canto 1, ll.121–48, pub. 1714

[A young woman of high society, Belinda, does her make-up, assisted by her maid, Betty. 'Toilet' refers to 'toilette', the contents of the dressing-table.]

> And now, unveiled, the toilet stands displayed,
> Each silver vase in mystic order laid.
> First, robed in white, the nymph intent adores,
> With head uncovered, the cosmetic powers.
> A heavenly image in the glass appears;   125
> To that she bends, to that her eyes she rears.
> The inferior priestess, at her altar's side,
> Trembling begins the sacred rites of Pride.
> Unnumbered treasures ope at once, and here
> The various offerings of the world appear;   130
> From each she nicely culls with curious toil,
> And decks the goddess with the glittering spoil.
> This casket India's glowing gems unlocks,
> And all Arabia breathes from yonder box.
> The tortoise here and elephant unite,   135
> Transformed to combs, the speckled and the white.
> Here files of pins extend their shining rows,
> Puffs, powders, patches, Bibles, billet-doux.
> Now awful Beauty puts on all its arms;
> The fair each moment rises in her charms,   140
> Repairs her smiles, awakens every grace,
> And calls forth all the wonders of her face;
> Sees by degrees a purer blush arise,
> And keener lightnings quicken in her eyes.
> The busy Sylphs surround their darling care,   145
> These set the head, and those divide the hair,
> Some fold the sleeve, whilst others plait the gown;
> And Betty's praised for labours not her own.

Pope (1688–1744) was one of the first professional **authors** to make a living, eventually, as a poet and **translator** (notably of **classical** epics, satires and pastorals from Latin and Greek). He was famous for his satires on the contemporary literary scene and on fashionable London life (London was already the centre of a fast-growing empire based on trade and slavery). These satires were generally mock-heroic in manner and often used decasyllabic couplets (see **versification**). The immediate occasion of *The Rape of the Lock* was the uninvited cutting of a lock of hair belonging to an aristocratic 'belle' (Lady Arabella Fermor) by an aristocratic 'beau' (Lord Petre). The action caused a feud between the two families and the poem was designed to help effect a reconciliation; also to demonstrate 'What mighty contests rise from trivial things'. First published in a two-canto version in 1712, the success of the piece prompted Pope to expand it into a five-canto version (pub. 1714). The above passage is from the latter. (Compare 'Clarins' cosmetic advert 5.4.4.)

ELIZABETH HANDS, 'A Poem, on the Supposition of an Advertisement appearing in a Morning Paper, of the Publication of a Volume of Poems, by a Servant Maid', 1789

The tea-kettle bubbled, the tea things were set.
The candles were lighted, the ladies were met;
The how d'ye's were over, and entering bustle,
The company seated, and silks ceased to rustle:
The great Mrs. Consequence opened her fan,   5
And thus the discourse in an instant began
(All affected reserve and formality scorning):
'I suppose you all saw in the paper this morning
A volume of *Poems* advertised – 'tis said
They're produced by the pen of a poor servant-maid.'   10
'A servant write verses!' says Madam Du Bloom:
'Pray what is the subject – a Mop, or a Broom?'
'He, he, he,' says Miss Flounce: 'I suppose we shall see
An Ode on an Dishclout – what else can it be?'
Says Miss Coquettilla, 'Why, ladies, so tart?   15
Perhaps Tom the footman has fired her heart;
And she'll tell us how charming he looks in new clothes,
And how nimble his hand moves in brushing the shoes;
Or how, the last time that he went to May Fair,
He bought her some sweethearts of gingerbread ware.'   20
'For my part I think,' says old Lady Marr-joy,
'A servant might find herself other employ:
Was she mine I'd employ her as long as 'twas light,
And send her to bed without candle at night.'
'Why so?', says Miss Rhymer, displeased: 'I protest   25
'Tis pity a genius should be so depressed!'
'What ideas can such low-bred creatures conceive?'
Says Mrs Noworthy, and laughed in her sleeve.
Says old Miss Prudella, 'If servants can tell
How to write to their mothers, to say they are well,   30
And read of a Sunday *The Duty of Man*,
Which is more I believe than one half of them can;

I think 'tis much properer they should rest there,
Than be reaching at things so much out of their sphere.'
Says old Mrs Candour, 'I've now got a maid   35
That's the plague of my life – a young gossiping jade;
There's no end of the people that after her come,
And whenever I'm out, she is never at home;
I'd rather ten times she would sit down and write,
Than gossip all over the town every night.'   40
'Some whimsical trollop most like,' says Miss Prim,
'Has been scribbling of nonsense, just out of a whim,
And, conscious it neither is witty or pretty,
Conceals her true name, and ascribes it to Betty.'
'I once had a servant myself,' says Miss Pines,   45
'That wrote on a wedding some very good lines.'
Says Mrs Domestic, 'And when they were done,
I can't see for my part what use they were on;
Had she wrote a receipt, to've instructed you how
To warm a cold breast of veal, like a ragout,   50
Or to make cowslip wine, that would pass for Champagne,
It might have been useful, again and again.'
On the sofa was old Lady Pedigree placed,
She owned that for poetry she had no taste,
That the study of heraldry was more in fashion,   55
And boasted she knew all the crests in the nation.
Says Mrs. Routella, 'Tom, take out the urn,
And stir up the fire, you see it don't burn.'
The tea things removed, and the tea-table gone,
The card-tables brought, and the cards laid thereon,   60
The ladies, ambitious for each others' crown,
Like courtiers contending for honours, sat down.

Hands (flourished *c.* 1789) had herself been a servant maid and subsequently a blacksmith's wife. The present poem may therefore be in part **autobiographical**. It appeared in a collection of her verse, much of which is also mock-heroic in manner and in couplets, that was published by private subscription in Coventry in 1789. Little else is known about her. (The present text comes from R. Lonsdale (ed.), *Eighteenth-Century Women Poets*, Oxford, Oxford University Press, 1990: 425–6.)

GEORGE GORDON, LORD BYRON, from *The Vision of Judgement*, ll.121–44, 1822

[Sitting by the gate of heaven, Saint Peter is told of the recent death of King George III.]

XVI

Saint Peter sat by the celestial gate,
    And nodded o'er his keys; when lo! there came
A wond'rous noise he had not heard of late –
    A rushing sound of wind, and stream, and flame;
In short, a roar of things extremely great,
    Which would have made aught save a saint exclaim;
But he, with first a start and then a wink,
Said, 'There's another star gone out, I think!'

XVII

But ere he could return to his repose,
   A cherub flapp'd his right wing o'er his eyes –
At which Saint Peter yawn'd, and rubb'd his nose:
   'Saint porter,' said the Angel, 'prithee rise!'
Waving a goodly wing, which glow'd, as glows
   An earthly peacock's tail, with heavenly dyes;
To which the Saint replied, 'Well, what's the matter?
Is Lucifer come back with all this clatter?'

XVIII

'No,' quoth the Cherub; 'George the Third is dead.'
   'And who is George the Third?' replied the Apostle;
What George? what Third?' 'The King of England,' said
   The Angel. 'Well! he won't find kings to jostle
Him on his way; but does he wear his head?
   Because the last[1] we saw here had a tussle,
And ne'er would have got into heaven's good graces,
Had he not flung his head in all our faces.'

[1] Louis XVI of France, who was guillotined in 1793 during the Revolution.

Byron (1788–1824) – aristocrat, traveller, part-time revolutionary, sensualist and poet – is very difficult to disentangle from the madcap myth of himself which he so assiduously cultivated. Hence the notion of the 'Byronic hero'. Byron is still by far the best known of the English Romantic poets in mainland Europe, where he, like the Shelleys, travelled extensively. In Britain, however, he is now relatively under-studied compared to Wordsworth, Coleridge and Keats – who are much less well known elsewhere. Byron had an 'insider–outsider' view of the British ruling elite: 'insider' because he was himself an aristocrat and once member of the House of Lords; 'outsider' because he was an avowed republican and never returned to England after 1816. Byron's *The Vision of Judgement* was a satiric **response** to the British Poet Laureate, Robert Southey's poem of the same name. Southey had both elegised and eulogised the mad, blind, tyrant King George III upon the latter's death (1820). In the preface, the Poet Laureate had attacked Byron, along with Percy Shelley, as members of 'the Satanic School' of poets. Compare Shelley's 'Sonnet: England in 1819' (@ 5.1.2), also on George III.

5.1.4 POETRY THAT ANSWERS BACK

ROBYN BOLAM (published as Marion Lomax), 'Gruoch', 1996

[Gruoch is the Gaelic name of the historical Lady Macbeth; the last syllable is pronounced as in Scots 'loch'.]

I have a name of my own. Gruoch –
a low growl of desire. He'd say it
and crush me against his throat. Gruoch –
his huge hands stroking my hip-length hair,
grasping it in his fists, drawing it taut
either side of my arms in ropes,   5
staked like a tent. He'd gasp when

folds slipped open, succulent
as split stems, to welcome him in.
How I held him, squeezed the sorrow   10
of no son out of him – for Lulach
was only mine, fruit of first union –
of Gillecomgain, forgotten by time.

He brought me Duncan as a trophy,
sweet revenge for my father's slaughter.   15
Upstarts never prosper. I was the true
King's daughter, Gruoch – uttered in wonder.
Seventeen years we reigned together through
keen seasons of hunger, feasting one to other.
War nor wantons wrenched him from me: 20
Gruoch – a whisper, sustaining fire.

He died before the battle with Malcolm:
obsequies cradled in a dry bed.
My mouth meandered down his body –
but it was winter, no bud stirring.   25
Gruoch – despairing: our death rattle.

Bolam (b. Newcastle, England 1953) grew up in Northumberland and has close family links with
Scotland. She is Professor of Literature at St Mary's College, Strawberry Hill, London, where she
teaches Renaissance drama and creative writing. The present poem comes from her collection *Raiding
the Borders* (written under the name of Marion Lomax, Newcastle: Bloodaxe, 1996: 17). Her note
on the historical background (p. 64) reads: 'Gruoch was directly descended from Kenneth III of
Scotland (murdered by Malcolm II to secure the throne for his grandson, Duncan). She married
Macbeth *c*.1032, either when she was pregnant with her son (Lulach) by her first partner,
Gillecomgain, or soon after his birth. Lulach succeeded to the throne in August 1057 on the death
of Macbeth (who slew Duncan and was, in turn, killed by Duncan's son, another Malcolm).' Such
information may help when studying the poem. But a vigorous and sensitive reading, preferably
aloud, is the best way to get to grips with it.

TOM LEONARD, 'This is thi six a clock news', 1983

this is thi
six a clock
news thi
man said n
thi reason
a talk wia
BBC accent
iz coz yi
widny wahnt
mi ti talk
aboot thi
trooth wia

voice lik
wanna yoo
scruff. if
a toktaboot
thi trooth
lik wanna yoo
scruff yi
widny thingk
it wuz troo.
jist wanna yoo
scruff tokn.
thirza right
way ti spell
ana right way
ti tok it. this
is me tokn yir
right way a
spellin. this
is ma trooth
yooz doant no
thi trooth
yirsellz cawz
yi canny talk
right. this is
the six a clock
nyooz. belt up.

'Leonard was born in Glasgow in 1944 and still lives there.' The text and this last line are taken
from M. Hulse, D. Kennedy and D. Morley (eds) *The New Poetry*, Newcastle upon Tyne, Bloodaxe,
1993: 71, 346. Originally published in Tom Leonard, *Unrelated Incidents* (1983).

CHAN WEI MENG, 'I spik Ingglish', 1996

I speak English
To a foreign friend —
'I don't understand what you're trying to say!'
'How come? I spik Ingglish what!'

I spik Ingglish   5
In Home —
'Hungry? You want fried lice or mee?'
'I eat Can-tucky cheeken, can or not?'
'Listen! Study Ingglish, earn more manee.'

I spik Ingglish   10
In School —
'Everybody read — sing sang sung.'
'I sing Maly hab a litter lamb.'
'Attention! School close at one.'

I spik Ingglish   15
In Work
'You know, the komputer cannot open, izzit?'
'I donno, got pay or not?'
'Remember – customer is always light, pease.'

I spik Ingglish   20
In Shop –
'Hello, can I hepch you?'
'I looksee first'
'Buy now! they is vely cheep and new.'

I spik Ingglish   25
Everywhere
Understand?

Chan Wei Meng (born *c.* 1975) was a student from Singapore studying English in New Zealand at the University of Otago in 1996. She wrote this as part of her **response** to the mixture of **standard** and creolised **varieties** encountered in a course on Caribbean–British poetry, including the poem by Nichols (5.4.5). (Published by kind permission of the author.)

MARIO PETRUCCI, four poems in process, 2002

(i)   *The Complete Letter Guide*

I have just heard about your intended
engagement to Mr Bird. I must just write this line

to congratulate you. I will just write this short note
to say how deeply affected I was at the untimely death

of your Chihuahua. It is a very difficult thing for me
to say anything to you about the loss you have sustained.

I am convinced you will bear it like a man. I enclose
the bill for the repair to my car caused by the collision.

(ii) *Mutations*

Little Bo-Peep has lost her sheep
Little Bo-Peep has lost her sheep
Littler Bo-Peer hes lost her shep
Littler Boy-Pep hees lost der shep
Littler Boy, Peep ees lost yer ship   5
Littler Boy, Peep his lust fer seep
Litter Boy, Keep h lust fer sheep
Titter Boy, lest ah keep yer wheep
Titter Boy, mah Keepe yoer heep
Sitter Boy, dah km Reepe yor heep   10
Titter Toy, de Reape komt ni yor sheep

Witter Boy – de Beaper kontim yor sheepe
Bitter Boy – de Reaper kom in yor sleepe.

(iii)   *Reflections*

Bees will sting like a razor
The air will be clear as glass
A nut, tough as a tax-form
Hills as old as hats

Trees will be sturdy as girders   5
Hares, scheme-brained;
A feather as light as helium
Coal will be almost as black

as a space-time singularity.
Pie will be easy as numbers   10
Clockwork regular as citizens
And the button, that big red button

as bright as a child.

(iv)   *Trench*

Sniper, Sniper, in your tree –
has your eye closed in on me?
Did your sights hot-cross my head
before you chose young Phil instead?
If looks could kill, would I be dead?

Sniper, Sniper, the one you get
doesn't hear your rifle crack.
They're saying here that you've the knack.
They're telling me I've lost a bet –
they say I'm dead. I just don't know it yet.

Petrucci (b.1958 in London of Italian parents) is a physicist, ecologist, poet, performance artist and teacher, and the author of such collections as *Shrapnel and Sheets* (1996) and *Lepidoptera* (1999). He was the first writer-in-residence at the Imperial War Museum, London, and is currently a Royal Literary Fund Fellow. They demonstrate what Petrucci terms a 'poeclectic' method of gathering and blending, adopting and adapting, materials from various sources in a range of styles and formats. His aim is 'a multi-faceted identity through a play of voices' (see www.nawe.co.uk.HEforum Autumn 2001, Issue 2). In particular, (i) is a 'cut-up' produced by splicing and re-presenting different parts of a guide to letter-writing; (ii) is what *might* happen if the first line of a familiar nursery rhyme were subject to apparently random genetic variation (hence the title 'Mutations'), or if a computer generated seemingly arbitrary sequences (Edwin Morgan's 'The Computer's First Christmas Card' is another example; see Morgan, *Collected Poems*, 1985); (iii) draws together various inversions of idioms based on similes; and (iv) has a telescopic sight superimposed upon it to represent the medium and context in which the poem was first sighted/sited/cited – read through a rifle-sight at the end of a hall in the Imperial War Museum, with heads of passers-by crossing the field of vision. (Four poems are from M. Petrucci *Flowers of Sulphur*, London: Enitharmon Press, 2002.)

5.1.5   PERFORMING POETRY, SINGING CULTURE

SEMINOLE CHANTS:

(i) *Song for the Dying*

Come back

Before you get to the king-tree

Come back

Before you get to the peach-tree

Come back

Before you get to the line of fence

Come back

Before you get to the bushes

Come back

Before you get to the fork in the road

Come back

Before you get to the yard

Come back

Before you get to the door

Come back

Before you get to the fire

Come back

Before you get to the middle of the ladder

Come back

(ii) *Song for Bringing a Child into the World*

let
the
child
be
born

circling around   You day-sun
you wrinkled skin   circling around
circling around   you daylight
you flecked with gray   circling around
circling around   you night sun
you wrinkled age   circling around
circling around   you poor body

These are anonymous translations of songs and rituals of the Native American Seminole tribe from Florida and Oklahoma, who use the Hitchiti language. Initially conceived for oral delivery, probably for more than one voice, these chants are best explored and initially 'interpreted' that way too. The visual layout is as in *Native American Songs and Poems: An Anthology*, Boston, Dover, 1996, pp. 1–2, from which the present texts come.

PATIENCE AGBABI, 'Give me a word', 2000

Give me a word
any word
let it roll across your tongue
like a dolly mixture.
Open your lips
say it loud
let each syllable vibrate
like a transistor.
Say it again again again again again
till it's a tongue twister
till its meaning is in tatters
till its meaning equals sound
now write it down,
letter by letter
loop the loops
till you form a structure.
Do it again again again again again
till it's a word picture.
Does this inspire?
Is your consciousness on fire?
Then let me take you higher.

Give me a noun
give me a verb
and I'm in motion
cos I'm on a mission
to deliver information
so let me take you to the fifth dimension.
No fee, it's free,
you only gotta pay attention.
So sit back, relax,
let me take you back
to when you learnt to walk, talk,
learnt coordination
and communication,
mama
dada.
If you rub two words together you get friction
cut them in half, you get a fraction.
If you join two words you get multiplication.
My school of mathematics
equals verbal acrobatics
so let's make conversation.

Give me a preposition
give me an interjection
give me inspiration.
In the beginning was creation

I'm not scared of revelations
cos I've done my calculations.
I've got high hopes
on the tightrope,
I just keep talking.
I got more skills than I got melanin
I'm fired by adrenaline
if you wanna know what rhyme it is
it's feminine.
Cos I'm Eve on an Apple Mac
this is a rap attack
so rich in onomatopoeia
I'll take you higher than the ozone layer.
So give me 'W' times three
cos I'm on a mission
to deliver information
that is gravity defying
and I'll keep on trying
till you lose your fear of flying.

Give me a pronoun
give me a verb
and I'm living in syntax.
You only need two words to form a sentence.
I am I am I am I am I am
bicultural and sometimes clinical,
my mother fed me rhymes through the umbilical,
I was born waxing lyrical.
I was raised on Watch with Mother
The Rime of the Ancient Mariner
and Fight the Power.
Now I have the perfect tutor
in my postmodern suitor,
I'm in love with my computer.
But let me shut down
before I touch down.

Give me a word
give me a big word
let me manifest
express in excess
the M I X
of my voice box.
Now I've eaten the apple
I'm more subtle than a snake is.
I wanna do poetic things in poetic places.
Give me poetry unplugged
so I can counter silence.
Give me poetic licence.

and I'll give you metaphors that top eclipses
I'll give megabytes and mega mixes.

Give me a stage and I'll cut form on it
give me a page and I'll perform on it.
Give me a word
any word.

Agbabi, born in London in 1965 to Nigerian parents and educated at Oxford University, is a performance poet with a 'rap' background (she can be heard and seen on the web at youtube.com and elsewhere) who also responds creatively to work from previous eras: her 'Wife of Bafa', based on Chaucer's Wife of Bath, is one example; another is her prose poems writing back to earlier sonnet-writers through 'problem pages' (see 5.1.2). 'Give me a word' is the Prologue to her *Transformatrix*, Edinburgh: Canongate, 2000.

QUEEN, 'Bohemian Rhapsody' 1975, re-released 1991

Is this the real life
Is this just fantasy
Caught in a landslide
no escape from reality
open your eyes
look up to the skies
and see . . .
I'm just a poor boy   poor boy
I need no sympathy
because I'm easy come easy go
little high little low
any way the wind blows
doesn't really matter to me
to me . . .
Mama. Just killed a man. Put a gun against his head. Pulled my trigger. Now
    he's dead
Mama. Life'd just begun. But now I've gone and thrown it all away
Mama. 00-00-00-00. I didn't mean to make you cry.
If I'm not back again tomorrow. Carry on carry on. Nothing really matters
Too late. My time has come.
sends shivers down my spine. Body's aching all the time
Goodbye everybody. I've got to go.
gotta leave you all behind and face the truth
Mama. 00-00-00-00 (anyway the wind blows). I don't want to die.
I sometimes wish I'd never been born at all

    [*Instrumental*]

I see a little silhouetto of a man
              scaramouche scaramouche
              will you do the fandango
              thunderbolt and lightning

very very frightening me
Galileo Galileo
Galileo / Galileo
Galileo piccolo
magnifico-o-o-o-o
I'm just a poor boy
nobody loves me

He's just a poor boy
from a poor family
spare him his life
from this monstrosity

Easy come easy go
will you let me go

Bismillah no
we will not let you go
let him goooooo . . .
Bismillah no we will not let you go
let him goooooo . . .
Bismillah no we will not let you go
let me go   will not let you go
let me go   let you go
never never never never never
never never let me go-o-o
no no no no no no no no no
Oh mama mia, mama mia, let me go

Beelzebub has a devil set aside for me, for me, for MEEEEE

[*Instrumental*]

So you think you can stone me and spit in my eye
So you think you can love me and leave me to die

Oh baby
Can't do this to me baby
just gotta get out
just gotta get right out of here

[*Instrumental*]   Oh yeah Oh yeah Oh yeah . . .

Nothing really matters
anyone can see
nothing really matters
nothing really matters
to me . . .

any way the winds blows . . .

'Bohemian Rhapsody' (1975) is a six-minute rock opera and now recognised as a pop **classic**. It has been continuously available for over two decades (*Queen's Greatest Hits*, including this track, was in the UK charts for eleven years). This song was re-released in 1991, the same year it was featured in a famous 'singalong' scene in the film *Wayne's World*. This was also the year the lead singer, Freddie Mercury, died of AIDS, thereby reinforcing the **tragic** and **mythic** status of the song. The fact that many people reading the above words will 'hear' 'Bohemian Rhapsody' and perhaps even 'see' Queen (in video promo or in concert) is a measure of just how deeply this piece is embedded in contemporary popular culture. (For sample analysis, see POSTMODERNISM, Example pp. 181–3).

Compare: 'I'dentity in the balance, 5.3.4.

πo, '7 Daiz', 1996

Wun e-wa mor.	
Wun e-wa mor	
Wun e-wa mor Finish.	
No hev kuppachino.	
No hev kuppachino hee-a.	5
Nex' shop.	
Nex' wun.	
Wayt-kofi onli.	
You Grik unch-ya.	
O – gee. O —gee-z!	10
Yoo awl da taym brok Ali.	
Yoo awl da taym brok.	
No unyon. No letus. No baykon.	
No munni.	
Yoo awl da taym brok Ali.	15
Yoo awl da taym brok.	
Wotz yoo o'ra?	
Yes pliz —thair?	
Wotz yoo o'ra?	
Bool-shee'!	20
Toogeta?	
O'sep-aat?	
On da rol?	
On da bret?	
Solt on? Solt on?	25
Poot solt on?	
Liv it.	
Liv it. Loo-i!	
Liv it.	
Detz yooz.	30
Da udda wun not yooz.	
O'rayt. O'rayt.	
Wun e-wa mor.	
Wun e-wa mor Finish	
Aagen. Aaagen.	35
Toomoro.	

'πo' (b.1951) is a Greek-Australian performance poet who lives and works in Melbourne. For all its initial strangeness on the page, the whole thing quickly becomes clear if you try to read it out loud. Its graphology is an attempt to represent a distinctive English phonology. The differences from standard Australian, British or American **varieties** are wholly matters of **accent** not **dialect**: pronunciation not vocabulary or grammar. In terms of **genre**, this is a dramatic **monologue**. Compare Leonard's 'This is thi six a clock news' (5.1.4). (Text from P. MacFarlane and L. Temple (eds) *Blue Light, Clear Atoms: Poetry for Senior Students*, Melbourne, Macmillan, 1996: 194–5.)

THE FLOBOTS, 'No Handlebars', 2007

I can ride my bike with no handlebars
No handlebars
No handlebars

I can ride my bike with no handlebars
No handlebars
No handlebars

Look at me, look at me
hands in the air like it's good to be
ALIVE
and I'm a famous rapper
even when the paths're all crookedy
I can show you how to do-si-do
I can show you how to scratch a record
I can take apart the remote control
And I can almost put it back together
I can tie a knot in a cherry stem
I can tell you about Leif Ericson
I know all the words to "De Colores"
And "I'm Proud to be an American"
Me and my friend saw a platypus
Me and my friend made a comic book
And guess how long it took
I can do anything that I want cuz, look:

I can keep rhythm with no metronome
No metronome
No metronome

I can see your face on the telephone
On the telephone
On the telephone

Look at me
Look at me
Just called to say that it's good to be
ALIVE
In such a small world
All curled up with a book to read
I can make money open up a thrift store

I can make a living off a magazine
I can design an engine sixty four
Miles to a gallon of gasoline
I can make new antibiotics

I can make computers survive aquatic conditions
I know how to run a business
And I can make you wanna buy a product
Movers shakers and producers
Me and my friends understand the future
I see the strings that control the systems
I can do anything with no assistance
I can lead a nation with a microphone
With a microphone
With a microphone
I can split the atoms of a molecule
Of a molecule
Of a molecule

Look at me
Look at me
Driving and I won't stop
And it feels so good to be
Alive and on top
My reach is global
My tower secure
My cause is noble
My power is pure
I can hand out a million vaccinations
Or let 'em all die in exasperation
Have 'em all healed of their lacerations
Have 'em all killed by assassination
I can make anybody go to prison
Just because I don't like 'em and
I can do anything with no permission
I have it all under my command
I can guide a missile by satellite
By satellite
By satellite
and I can hit a target through a telescope
Through a telescope
Through a telescope
and I can end the planet in a holocaust
In a holocaust
In a holocaust
In a holocaust
In a holocaust
In a holocaust

I can ride my bike with no handlebars
No handlebars

No handlebars

I can ride my bike with no handlebars
No handlebars
No handlebars

The Flobots are an American rock and hip-hop band that formed in Denver, Colorado in 2000. 'No Handlebars' is a track from their album *Fight with Tools* (2007) and became a very popular hit single in the Modern Rock charts the following year. The song features a solo male voice and the music has an insistent rhythm and steady crescendo, which culminates in shouting and distortion and then finishes quietly. It can be heard widely on the web.

PHILIP GROSS, 'Severn Song', 2009

The Severn was brown and the Severn was blue —
not this-then-that, not either-or
no mixture. Two things can be true.
The hills were clouds and the mist was a shore.

The Severn was water, the water was mud
whose eddies stood and did not fill,
the kind of water that's thicker than blood.
The river was flowing, the flowing was still,

the tide-rip the sound of dry fluttering wings
with waves that did not break or fall.
We were two of the world's small particular things.
We were old, we were young, we were no age at all,

for a moment not doing, nor coming undone —
words gained, words lost, till who's to say
which was the father, which was the son,
a week, or fifty years, away.

But the water said *earth*, and the water said *sky*.
We were everyone we'd ever been or would be
every angle of light that says *You*, that says *I*,
and the sea was the river, the river the sea.

Gross was born in Cornwall in 1952. A widely published poet and a writer of children's fiction, he collaborates closely with musicians, dancers and visual artists and has taught in education at every step from nursery to PhD. He is currently Professor of Creative Writing at the University of Glamorgan, South Wales. The above poem is inscribed '(for *John Karl Gross*)' and is the last poem in his collection *The Water Table*, Tarset: Bloodaxe, 2009: 64, which won the T.S. Eliot Poetry Prize for that year.

5.2   PROSES

5.2.1   Short stories, fables and flash fiction (complete)

RUDYARD KIPLING, 'The Story of Muhammad Din', 1888

Who is the happy man? He that sees in his own house at home, little children crowned with dust, leaping and falling and crying —

Munichandra, translated by Professor Peterson

The polo-ball was an old one, scarred, chipped, and dinted. It stood on the mantelpiece among the pipe-stems which Imam Din, *khitmatgar*, was cleaning for me.

'Does the Heaven-born want this ball?' said Imam Din deferentially.

The Heaven-born set no particular store by it; but of what use was a polo-ball to a *khitmatgar*?

'By Your Honour's favour, I have a little son. He has seen this ball, and desires it to play with. I do not want it for myself.'

No one would for an instant accuse portly old Imam Din of wanting to play with polo-balls. He carried out the battered thing into the veranda; and there followed a hurricane of joyful squeaks, a patter of small feet, and the *thud-thud-thud* of the ball rolling along the ground. Evidently the little son had been waiting outside the door to secure his treasure. But how had he managed to see that polo-ball?

Next day, coming back from office half an hour earlier than usual, I was aware of a small figure in the dining-room — a tiny, plump figure in a ridiculously inadequate shirt which came, perhaps, half-way down the tubby stomach. It wandered round the room, thumb in mouth, crooning to itself as it took stock of the pictures. Undoubtedly this was the 'little son'.

He had no business in my room, of course; but was so deeply absorbed in his discoveries that he never noticed me in the doorway. I stepped into the room and startled him nearly into a fit. He sat down on the ground with a gasp. His eyes opened, and his mouth followed suit. I knew what was coming, and fled, followed by a long, dry howl which reached the servants' quarters far more quickly than any command of mine had ever done. In ten seconds Imam Din was in the dining-room. Then despairing sobs arose, and I returned to find Imam Din admonishing the small sinner who was using most of his shirt as a handkerchief.

'This boy,' said Imam Din judicially, 'is a *budmash* — a big *budmash*. He will, without doubt, go to the *jail-khana* for his behaviour.' Renewed yells from the penitent, and an elaborate apology to myself from Imam Din.

'Tell the baby,' said I, 'that the *Sahib* is not angry, and take him away.' Imam Din conveyed my forgiveness to the offender, who had now gathered all his shirt round his neck, stringwise, and the yell subsided into a sob. The two set off for the door. 'His name,' said Imam Din, as though the name were part of the crime, 'is Muhammad Din, and he is a *budmash*.' Freed from present danger, Muhammad Din turned round in his father's arms, and said gravely, 'It is true that my name is Muhammad Din, Tahib, but I am not a *budmash*. I am a man!'

From that day dated my acquaintance with Muhammad Din. Never again did he come into my dining-room, but on the neutral ground of the garden we greeted each other with much state, though our conversation was confined to '*Talaam, tahib*' from his side, and '*Salaam Muhammad Din*' from mine. Daily on my return from office, the little white shirt and the fat little body used to rise from the shade of the creeper-covered trellis where they had been hid; and daily I checked my horse here, that my salutation might not be slurred over or given unseemly.

Muhammad Din never had any companions. He used to trot about the compound, in and out of the castor-oil bushes, on mysterious errands of his own. One day I stumbled upon some of his handiwork far down the grounds. He had half buried the polo-ball in dust, and stuck six shrivelled old marigold flowers in a circle round it. Outside that circle again was a rude square, traced out in bits of red brick alternating with fragments of broken china; the whole bounded by a little bank of dust. The water-man from the well-curb put in a plea for the small architect, saying that it was only the play of a baby and did not much disfigure my garden.

Heaven knows that I had no intention of touching the child's work then or later; but, that evening, a stroll through the garden brought me unawares full on it; so that I trampled, before I knew, marigold-heads, dust-bank, and fragments of broken soap-dish into confusion past all hope of mending. Next morning, I came upon Muhammad Din crying softly to himself over the ruin I had wrought. Some one had cruelly told him that the *Sahib* was very angry with him for spoiling the garden, and had scattered his rubbish, using bad language the while. Muhammad Din laboured for an hour at effacing every trace of the dust-bank and pottery fragments, and it was with a tearful and apologetic face that he said, '*Talaam Tahib,*' when I came home from office. A hasty inquiry resulted in Imam Din informing Muhammad Din that, by my singular favour, he was permitted to disport himself as he pleased. Whereat the child took heart and fell to tracing the ground-plan of an edifice which was to eclipse the marigold-polo-ball creation.

For some months the chubby little eccentricity revolved in his humble orbit among the castor-oil bushes and in the dust; always fashioning magnificent palaces from stale flowers thrown away by the bearer, smooth water-worn pebbles, bits of broken glass, and feathers pulled, I fancy, from my fowls — always alone, and always crooning to himself.

A gaily-spotted seashell was dropped one day close to the last of his little buildings; and I looked that Muhammad Din should build something more than ordinarily splendid on the strength of it. Nor was I disappointed. He meditated for the better part of an hour, and his crooning rose to a jubilant song. Then he began tracing in the dust. It would certainly be a wonderous palace, this one, for it was two yards long and a yard broad in ground-plan. But the palace was never completed.

Next day there was no Muhammad Din at the head of the carriage-drive, and no '*Talaam, Tahib*' to welcome my return. I had grown accustomed to the greeting, and its omission troubled me. Next day Imam Din told me that the child was suffering slightly from fever and needed quinine. He got the medicine, and an English doctor.

'They have no stamina, these brats,' said the doctor, as he left Imam Din's quarters.

A week later, though I would have given much to have avoided it, I met on the road to the Mussulman burying-ground Imam Din, accompanied by one other friend, carrying in his arms, wrapped in a white cloth, all that was left of little Muhammad Din.

Born in Bombay of well-to-do English parents, Kipling (1865–1936) was sent to private school in England at the age of six and had a miserable childhood. On returning to India in 1882 he worked as a journalist and short-story writer on the *Civil and Military Gazette*, which was read by the Anglo-Indian community. The above story first circulated there before being printed in the collection *Plain Tales from the Hills*. Kipling's stories, poems and novels – including *Barrack-Room Ballads* (1892), *The Jungle Books* (1894, 1895), *Kim* (1901) and the *Just So Stories* (1902) – are remarkable for their variety and versatility; also for their critical, teasing and sometimes enigmatic visions of empire and colonialism. After 1898 Kipling visited South Africa regularly. In 1907 he became the first English writer to receive the Nobel Prize for Literature. POSTCOLONIALISM has prompted a thorough revision of Kipling's significance. (For sample analysis, see NEW CRITICISM, Example ii, pp. 139–40.)

DON BARTHELME, 'The Death of Edward Lear', 1971

The death of Edward Lear took place on a Sunday morning in May 1888. Invitations were sent out well in advance. The invitations read:

> *Mr Edward LEAR*
> *Nonsense Writer and Landscape Painter*
> *Requests the Honor of Your Presence*
> *On the Occasion of his DEMISE.*
> *San Remo*   *2:20 a.m.*
> *The 29ᵗʰ of May*   *Please reply*

One can imagine the feelings of the recipients. Our dear friend! is preparing to depart! and such like. Mr. Lear! who has given us so much pleasure! and such like. On the other hand, his years were considered. Mr Lear! who must be, now let me see . . . And there was a good deal of, I remember the first time I (dipped into) (was seized by) . . . But on the whole, Mr. Lear's acquaintances approached the occasion with a mixture of solemnity and practicalness, perhaps remembering the words of Lear's great friend, Tennyson:

> Old men must die,
> Or the world would grow mouldy

and:

> For men may come and men may go
> But I go on forever.

People prepared to attend the death of Edward Lear as they might have for a day in the country. Picnic baskets were packed (for it would be wrong to expect too much of Mr. Lear's hospitality, under the circumstances); bottles of wine were wrapped in white napkins. Toys were chosen for the children. There were debates as to whether the dog ought to be taken or left behind. (Some of the dogs actually present at the death of Edward Lear could not restrain themselves; they frolicked about the dying man's chamber, tugged at the bedclothes, and made such nuisances of themselves that they had to be removed from the room.)

Most of Mr. Lear's friends decided that the appropriate time to arrive at the Villa would be midnight, or in that neighbourhood, in order to allow the old gentleman time to make whatever remarks he might have in mind, or do whatever he wanted to do, before the event. Everyone understood what the time specified in the invitation meant. And so, the visitors found themselves being handed down from their carriages (by Lear's servant Giuseppe Orsini) in almost total darkness. Pausing to greet people they knew, or to corral straying children, they were at length ushered into a large room on the first floor, where the artist had been accustomed to exhibit his watercolors, and thence by a comfortably wide staircase to a similar room on the second floor, where Mr. Lear himself waited, in bed, wearing an old velvet smoking jacket and his familiar silver spectacles with tiny oval lenses. Several dozen straight-backed chairs had been arranged in a rough semicircle around the bed; these were soon filled, and later arrivals stood along the walls.

Mr. Lear's first words were: "I've no money!" As each new group of guests entered the room, he repeated, "I've no money! No money!" He looked extremely tired, yet calm. His ample beard, gray yet retaining patches of black, had evidently not been trimmed in some days. He seemed nervous and immediately began to discourse, as if to prevent anyone else from doing so.

He began by thanking all those present for attending and expressing the hope that he had not put them to too great an inconvenience, acknowledging that the hour was "an unusual one for visits!" He said that he could not find words sufficient to disclose his pleasure in seeing so many of his friends gathered together at his side. He then delivered a pretty little lecture, of some twelve minutes' duration, on the production of his various writings, of which no one has been able to recall the substance, although everyone agreed that it was charming, graceful and wise.

He then startled his guests with a question, uttered in a kind of shriek: "Should I get married? Get married? Should I marry?"

Mr. Lear next offered a short homily on the subject of Friendship. Friendship, he said, is the most golden of the affections. It is also, he said, often the strongest of human ties, surviving strains and tempests fatal to less sublime relations. He noted that his own many friendships constituted the richest memory of a long life.

A disquisition on Cats followed.

When Mr. Lear reached the topic Children, a certain restlessness was observed among his guests. (He had not ceased to shout at intervals, "Should I get married?" and "I've no money!") He then displayed copies of his books, but as everybody had already read them, not more than a polite interest was generated. Next he held up, one by one, a selection of his watercolors, views of various antiquities and picturesque spots. These, too, were familiar; they were the same watercolors the old gentleman had been offering for sale, at £5 and £10, for the past forty years.

Mr. Lear now sang a text of Tennyson's in a setting of his own, accompanying himself on a mandolin. Although his voice was thin and cracked frequently, the song excited vigorous applause.

Finally he caused to be hauled into the room by servants an enormous oil, at least seven feet by ten, depicting Mount Athos. There was a murmur of appreciation, but it did not seem to satisfy the painter, for he assumed a very black look.

At 2:15 Mr. Lear performed a series of actions the meaning of which was obscure to the spectators.

At 2:20 he reached over to the bedside table, picked up an old-fashioned pen which lay there, and died. A death mask was immediately taken. The guests, weeping unaffectedly, moved in a long line back to the carriages.

People who attended the death of Edward Lear agreed that, all in all, it had been a somewhat tedious performance. Why had he seen fit to read the same old verses, sing again the familiar songs, show the well-known pictures, run through his repertoire once more? Why invitations? Then something was understood that Mr. Lear had been doing what he had always done and therefore not doing anything extraordinary, Mr. Lear had transformed the extraordinary into its opposite. He had, in point of fact, created a gentle, genial misunderstanding.

Thus the guests began, as time passed, to regard the affair in an historical light. They told their friends about it, re-enacted parts of it for their children and grandchildren. They would reproduce the way the old man had piped "I've no money!" in a comical voice, and quote his odd remarks about marrying. The death of Edward Lear became so popular, as time passed, that revivals were staged in every part of the country, with considerable success. The death of Edward Lear can still be seen, in the smaller cities, in versions enriched by learned interpretation, textual emendation, and changing fashion. One modification is curious, no one knows how it came about. The supporting company plays in the traditional way, but Lear himself appears shouting, shaking, vibrant with rage.

Barthelme (1931–89), short story writer and novelist, was born in Philadelphia and brought up in Texas. His 'The Death of Edward Lear' first appeared in *The New Yorker* in 1971 and was subsequently included in his frequently reprinted *Sixty Stories* (1981). Initially hailed as 'absurdist' (or 'weird') and latterly as 'postmodernist', the present piece also confirms Barthelme's relation to a long tradition of 'nonsense' writing. But every story breaks fresh ground and all defy glib categorisation. (Text from D. Barthelme, *Sixty Stories*, London: Penguin, 1993: 364–7.)

MARGARET ATWOOD, 'Happy Endings', (complete short story), 1984

John and Mary meet. What happens next? If you want a happy ending, try A

A.   John and Mary fall in love and get married. They both have worthwhile and remunerative jobs which they find stimulating and challenging. They buy a charming house. Real estate values go up. Eventually, when they can afford live-in help, they have two children, to whom they are devoted. The children turn out well. John and Mary have a stimulating and challenging sex life and worthwhile friends. They go on fun vacations together. They retire. They both have hobbies which they find stimulating and challenging. Eventually they die. This is the end of the story.

B.   Mary falls in love with John but John doesn't fall in love with Mary. He merely uses her body for selfish pleasure and ego gratification of a tepid kind. He comes to her apartment twice a week and she cooks him dinner, you'll notice that he doesn't even consider her worth the price of a dinner out, and after he's eaten the dinner he fucks and after that he falls asleep, while she does the dishes so he won't think she's untidy, having all those dirty dishes lying around, and puts on fresh lipstick so she'll look good when he wakes up, but when he wakes up he doesn't even notice, he puts on his socks and his shorts and his pants and his shirt and his tie and his shoes, the reverse order from the one in which he took them off. He doesn't take off Mary's clothes, she takes them off herself, she acts as if she's dying for it every time, not because she likes sex exactly, she doesn't, but she wants John to think she does because if they do it often enough surely he'll get used to her, he'll come to depend on her and they will get married, but John goes out the door with hardly so much as a goodnight and three days later he turns up at six o'clock and they do the whole thing over again.
   Mary gets run down. Crying is bad for your face, everyone knows that and so does Mary but she can't stop. People at work notice. Her friends tell her John is a rat, a pig, a dog, he isn't good enough for her, but she can't believe it. Inside John, she thinks is another John, who is much nicer. This other John will emerge like a butterfly from a cocoon, a Jack from a box, a pit from a prune, if the first John is only squeezed enough.
   One evening John complains about the food. He has never complained about the food before. Mary is hurt.
   Her friends tell her they've seen him in a restaurant with another woman, whose name is Madge. It's not even Madge that finally gets to Mary: it's the restaurant. John has never taken Mary to a restaurant. Mary collects all the sleeping pills and aspirins

she can find, and takes them and half a bottle of sherry. You can see what kind of a woman she is by the fact that it's not even whiskey. She leaves a note for John. She hopes he'll discover her and get her to the hospital in time and repent and then they can get married, but this fails to happen and she dies.

John marries Madge and everything continues as in A.

C. John, who is an older man, falls in love with Mary, and Mary, who is only twenty-two, feels sorry for him because he's worried about his hair falling out. She sleeps with him even though she's not in love with him. She met him at work. She's in love with someone called James, who is twenty-two also and not yet ready to settle down.

John on the contrary settled down long ago: this is what is bothering him. John has a steady respectable job and is getting ahead in his field, but Mary isn't impressed by him, she's impressed by James, who has a motorcycle and a fabulous record collection. But James is often away on his motorcycle, being free. Freedom isn't the same for girls, so in the meantime Mary spends Thursday evenings with John. Thursdays are the only days John can get away.

John is married to a woman called Madge and they have two children, a charming house which they bought just before the real estate values went up, and hobbies which they find stimulating and challenging, when they have the time. John tells Mary how important she is to him, but of course he can't leave his wife because a commitment is a commitment. He goes on about this more than is necessary and Mary finds it boring, but older men can keep it up longer so on the whole she has a fairly good time.

One day James breezes in on his motorcycle with some top grade California hybrid and James and Mary get higher than you'd believe possible and they climb into bed. Everything becomes very underwater, but along comes John, who has a key to Mary's apartment. He finds them stoned and entwined. He's hardly in any position to be jealous, considering Madge, but nevertheless he's overcome with despair. Finally he's middle-aged, in two years he'll be bald as an egg and he can't stand it. He purchases a handgun, saying he needs it for target practice – this is the thin part of the plot, but it can be dealt with later – and shoots the two of them and himself.

Madge, after a suitable period of mourning, marries an understanding man called Fred and everything continues as in A, but under different names.

D. Fred and Madge have no problems. They get along exceptionally well and are good at working out any little difficulties that may arise. But their charming house is by the seashore and one day a giant tidal wave approaches. Real estate values go down. The rest of the story is about what caused the tidal wave and how they escape from it. They do, though thousands drown. Some of the story is about how the thousands drown, but Fred and Madge are virtuous and lucky. Finally on high ground they clasp each other, wet and dripping and grateful, and continue as in A.

E. Yes, but Fred has a bad heart. The rest of the story is about how kind and understanding they both are until Fred dies. Then Madge devotes herself to charity work until the end of A. If you like, it can be 'Madge', 'cancer', 'guilty and confused', and 'bird watching'.

F. If you think this is all too bourgeois, make John a revolutionary and Mary a counterespionage agent and see how far that gets you. Remember, this is Canada. You'll still end with A, though in between you may get a lustful brawling saga of passionate involvement, a chronicle of our times, sort of.

You'll have to face it, the endings are the same however you slice it. Don't be deluded by any other endings, they're all fake, either deliberately fake, with malicious intent to deceive, or just motivated by excessive optimism if not by downright sentimentality.

The only authentic ending is the one provided here:

John and Mary die. John and Mary die. John and Mary die.

So much for endings. Beginnings are always more fun. True connoisseurs, however, are known to favour the stretch in between, since it's the hardest to do anything with.

That's about all that can be said for plots, which anyway are just one thing after another, a what and a what and a what.

Now try How and Why.

Atwood (b. Ottawa, 1939) is a poet, critic and editor as well as novelist and short story writer. Her novels include *Surfacing* (1972) and *The Handmaid's Tale* (1985), a futuristic dystopia about a woman whose sole function is to breed. She is the editor of the *The New Oxford Book of Canadian Verse in English* (1983) and the author of the influential and controversial *Survival: A Thematic Guide to Canadian Literature* (1972), where she argues that Canadian Literature recurrently deals with notions of survival and projects 'a collective victim mentality' (see Thieme 1996: 356–74). Moving between **realism** and **metafiction**, her **creative** work has a strong critical edge to it, particularly with respect to GENDER, SEXUALITY and nationality. The text is from Hermione Lee (ed.) *The Secret Self 1: Short Stories by Women*, London, 1991: 381–4.

ANGELA CARTER, 'The Werewolf', 1979

IT IS A northern country; they have cold weather, they have cold hearts.

Cold; tempest; wild beasts in the forest. It is a hard life. Their houses are built of logs, dark and smoky within. There will be a crude icon of the virgin behind a guttering candle, the leg of a pig hung up to cure, a string of drying mushrooms. A bed, a stool, a table. Harsh, brief, poor lives.

To these upland woodsmen, the Devil is as real as you or I. More so; they have not seen us nor even know that we exist, but the Devil they glimpse often in the graveyards, those bleak and touching townships of the dead where the graves are marked with portraits of the deceased in the naïf style and there are no flowers to put in front of them, no flowers grow there, so they put out small, votive offerings, little loaves, sometimes a cake that the bears come lumbering from the margins of the forest to snatch away. At midnight, especially on Walpurgisnacht, the Devil holds picnics in the graveyards and invites the witches; then they dig up fresh corpses, and eat them. Anyone will tell you that.

Wreaths of garlic on the doors keep out the vampires. A blue-eyed child born feet first on the night of St John's Eve will have second sight. When they discover a witch – some old woman whose cheeses ripen when her neighbours' do not, another old woman whose black cat, oh, sinister! *follows her about all the time*, they strip the crone, search for her marks, for the supernumerary nipple her familiar sucks. They soon find it. Then they stone her to death.

Winter and cold weather.

Go and visit your grandmother, who has been sick. Take her the oatcakes I've baked for her on the hearthstone and a little pot of butter.

The good child does as her mother bids – five miles' trudge through the forest; do not leave the path because of the bears, the wild boar, the starving wolves. Here, take your father's hunting knife; you know how to use it.

The child had a scabby coat of sheepskin to keep out the cold, she knew the forest too well to fear it but she must always be on her guard. When she heard that freezing howl of a wolf, she dropped her gifts, seized her knife and turned on the beast.

It was a huge one, with red eyes and running, grizzled chops; any but a mountaineer's child would have died of fright at the sight of it. It went for her throat, as wolves do, but she made a great swipe at it with her father's knife and slashed off its right forepaw.

The wolf let out a gulp, almost a sob, when it saw what had happened to it; wolves are less brave than they seem. It went off lolloping disconsolately between the trees as well as it could on three legs, leaving a trail of blood behind it. The child wiped the blade of her knife clean on her apron, wrapped up the wolf's paw in the cloth in which her mother had packed the oatcakes and went on towards her grandmother's house. Soon it came on to snow so quickly that the path and any footsteps, track or spoor that might have been upon it were obscured.

She found her grandmother was so sick that she had taken to her bed and fallen into a fretful sleep, moaning and shaking so that the child guessed she had a fever. She felt the forehead, it burned. She shook out the cloth from her basket, to use it to make the old woman a cold compress, and the wolf's paw fell to the floor.

But it was no longer a wolf's paw. It was a hand, chopped off at the wrist, a hand toughened with work and freckled with old age. There was a wedding ring on the third finger and a wart on the index finger. By the wart, she knew it for her grandmother's hand.

She pulled back the sheet but the old woman woke up, at that, and began to struggle, squawking and shrieking like a thing possessed. But the child was strong, and armed with her father's hunting knife; she managed to hold her grandmother down long enough to see the cause of her fever. There was a bloody stump where her right hand should have been, festering already.

The child crossed herself and cried out so loud the neighbours heard her and came rushing in. They knew the wart on the hand at once for a witch's nipple; they drove the old woman, in her shift as she was, out into the snow with sticks, beating her old carcass as far as the edge of the forest, and pelted her with stones until she fell down dead.

Now the child lived in her grandmother's house; she prospered.

Carter (1940–92) was born in Sussex, lived in Japan for a while and was writer-in-residence at universities in America, Australia and Britain. Variously identified with 'magical realism', 'feminist fantasy fiction' and modern 'gothic', her work – which includes journalism and essays – resists pigeon-holing. Her novel *Wise Children* (1991), for example, sports with a medley of literary and popular culture (Shakespeare, theatre, variety show, TV and film), as told through the language-and-life-loving reminiscences of one of a twin double-act. Carter had a long-standing interest in classic and not-so-classic fairy tales and a commitment to restoring less well-known versions, e.g. *Fairy Tales* (1990). The present tale – which blends materials from Little Red Riding Hood and vampire as well as werewolf stories – is one of an influential collection that includes retellings and transformations of 'Bluebeard' and 'Beauty and the Beast'. (Text from A. Carter, *The Bloody Chamber*, London: Vintage [1979], 2006: 126–8.)

AMY TAN, 'Feathers from a thousand li away', prologue from *The Joy Luck Club*, 1989

The old woman remembered a swan she had bought many years ago in Shanghai for a foolish sum. This bird, boasted the market vendor, was once a duck that stretched its neck in hopes of becoming a goose, and now look! – it is too beautiful to eat.

Then the woman and the swan sailed across the ocean many thousands of li wide, stretching their necks towards America. On her journey she cooed to the swan: 'In America I will have a daughter just like me. But over there nobody will say her worth is measured by the loudness of her husband's belch. Over there nobody will look down on her, because

I will make her speak only perfect American English. And over there she will always be too full to swallow any sorrow! She will know my meaning, because I will give her this swan – a creature that became more than what was hoped for.'

But when she arrived in the new country, the immigration officials pulled her swan away from her, leaving the woman fluttering her arms and with only one swan feather for a memory. And then she had to fill out so many forms she forgot why she had come and what she had left behind.

Now the woman was old. And she had a daughter who grew up speaking only English and swallowed more Coca-Cola than sorrow. For a long time now the woman had wanted to give her daughter the single swan feather and tell her, 'This feather may look worthless, but it comes from afar and carries with it all my good intentions.' And she waited year after year, for the day she could tell her daughter this in perfect American English.

Tan was born in Oakland, California in 1952, shortly after her parents emigrated from China to the USA. She worked as an administrator of programmes for disabled children and later as a reporter and editor, visiting China for the first time in 1987. On her return she finished this, her first novel, trying out many parts with a weekly writers' group. Following its adaptation as a film by Oliver Stone (1991) and adoption on many US literature syllabuses, often in the category 'MULTICULTURAL literature', Tan wrote of being delighted but also, in the words of her 1996 article of that name, 'In the **canon** for all the wrong reasons' (see Charters and Charters 2001: 722–5). (Present text from Amy Tan, *The Joy Luck Club*, London, Granada, 1994: 17.)

DAVE EGGERS, 'What the Water Feels Like to the Fishes', 2005

Like the fur of a chinchilla. Like the cleanest tooth. Yes, the fishes say, this is what it feels like. People always ask the fishes, "What does the water feel like to you?" and the fishes are always happy to oblige. Like feathers are to other feathers, they say. Like powder touching ash. When the fishes tell us these things, we begin to understand. We begin to think we know what the water feels like to the fishes. But it's not always like fur and ash and the cleanest tooth. At night, they say, the water can be different. At night, when it's cold, it can be like the tongue of a cat. At night, when it's very very cold, the water is like cracked glass. Or honey. Or forgiveness, they say, ha ha. When the fishes answer these questions – which they are happy to do – they also ask why. They are curious, fish are, and thus they ask, Why? Why do you want to know what the water feels like to the fishes? And we are never quite sure. The fishes press further. Do you breathe air? they ask. The answer, we say, is yes. Well then, they say, What does the air feel like to you? And we do not know. We think of air and we think of wind, but that's another thing. Wind is air in action, air on the move, and the fishes know this. Well then, they ask again, what does air feel like? And we have to think about this. Air feels like air, we say, and the fishes laugh mirthlessly. Think! they say. Think, they say, now gentler. And we think and we guess it feels like hair, thousands of hairs, swaying ever so slightly in breezes microscopic. The fishes laugh again. Do better, think harder, they say. It feels like language, we say, and they are impressed. Keep going, they say. It feels like blood, we say, and they say, No, no, that's not it. The air is like being wanted, we say, and they nod approvingly. The air is like getting older, they say, and they touch our arms gently.

Eggers (b. Boston, MA., 1970), the co-founder of a radical publishing house and an educational writing project for children, first became widely known for his semiautobiographical *A Heartbreaking Work of Staggering Genius* (2000). The above piece of 'flash' fiction is one of his *Short Short Stories*, London: Penguin, 2005: 5–6.

5.2.2   Slave narratives by name

APHRA BEHN, from *Oroonoko, or The Royal Slave*, 1688

[The narrator is a young white woman who is the daughter of a man appointed to be Lieutenant General of (British) Surinam, later (Dutch) Guyana.]

I ought to tell you that the Christians never buy slaves but they give 'em some name of their own, their native ones being likely very barbarous and hard to pronounce; so that Mr. Trefry gave Oroonoko that of Caesar, which name will live in that country as long as that (scarce more) glorious one of the great Roman; for 'tis most evident, he wanted no part of the personal courage of that Caesar, and acted things as memorable, had they been done in some part of the world replenished with people and historians that might have given him his due. But his misfortune was to fall in an obscure world, that afforded only a female pen to celebrate his fame; though I doubt not but it had lived from others' endeavors, if the Dutch, who immediately after his time took that country, had not killed, banished, and dispersed all those that were capable of giving the world this great man's life, much better than I have done. And Mr. Trefry, who designed it, died before he began it, and bemoaned himself for not having undertook it in time.

For the future, therefore, I must call Oroonoko Caesar, since by that name only he was known in our western world, and by that name he was received on shore at Parham House, where he was destined a slave. But if the King himself (God bless him) had come ashore, there could not have been greater expectations by all the whole plantation, and those neighboring ones, than was on ours at that time; and he was received more like a governor than a slave.

Behn (1640–89) was one of the first women writers in English to make a living as a professional writer, chiefly of plays such as *The Rover* (1677) and of prose fiction such as *Oroonoko*. The latter begins as a harem romance on the west coast of Africa and ends as an indictment of slavery in the West Indies and the Americas. Its narrative as told by a white English woman thus retraces the contemporary slave-trade triangle (see map p. 400). Behn was herself probably in the West Indies and Surinam in earlier life, and there is much that is **historical** and **factional**, as well as perhaps **autobiographical**, about her account. (Text from Abrams 2000, Vol. I: 2193.)

DANIEL DEFOE, from *Robinson Crusoe*, Ch. 24: 'I Call Him Friday', 1719

[The shipwrecked hero records his first encounter with the man who is to become his servant.]

His face was round and plump; his nose small, not flat like the Negroes', a very good mouth, thin lips, and his fine teeth well set, and white as ivory. After he had slumbered, rather than slept, about half an hour, he waked again, and comes out of the cave to me, for I had been milking my goats, which I had in the enclosure just by. When he espied me, he came running to me, laying himself down again upon the ground, with all the possible signs of an humble, thankful disposition, making a many antic gestures to show it. At last he lays his head flat upon the ground, close to my foot, and sets my other foot upon his head, as he had done before; and after this, made all the signs to me of subjection, servitude, and submission imaginable, to let me know how he would serve me as long as he lived; I understood him in many things and let him know I was very pleased with him; in a little time I began to speak to him and teach him to speak to me; and first, I made him know his name should be Friday, which was the day I saved his life; I called him so for the memory of the time; I likewise taught him to say 'Master,' and then let him know that was to be my name; I likewise taught him to say 'yes' and 'no' and to know the meaning of them; I gave him some milk in an earthen pot and let him see me drink it before him and sop my bread in it; and I gave him a cake of bread to do the like, which he quickly complied with, and made signs that it was very good for him.

Defoe (1660–1731) – journalist, novelist, tradesman and travel-writer – wrote the highly successful *Robinson Crusoe* and quickly followed it with the *Further Adventures of Robinson Crusoe* (1720) and *Moll Flanders*, the story of a (repentant) thief, prostitute and opportunist (1722). Along with the Bible and Shakespeare, *Robinson Crusoe* became one of the favourite and **classic texts** of the British Empire and was, until recently, read by most English children in full or in one of the many abridged versions. Defoe is also recognised as one of the 'fathers of the English novel'.

GEOFF HOLDSWORTH, 'I call him Tuesday Afternoon', 1994

He was a strange, comical fellow, an ungainly, rather squat figure with plump limbs, and, as I estimated, in his early forties. He was possessed of an arrogant countenance and showed little warmth of spirit, and yet, he seemed to have traces of femininity in his face, and elements of the assertive independence of an African about his countenance, especially on those rare occasions when he smiled. His hair was thin and wispy, not dark and thick; his forehead was narrow and creased from squinting into the sun, and his small pig-eyes were a dull lifeless grey. His skin was white; not the pleasing tinted offwhite of the Spanish visitors I had encountered, but an alarming, sickly white, interspersed with patches of bright red. His face was round, yet long; his nose short and sharp as an arrow head, and his large lip-less mouth revealed crooked yellow and brown teeth.

Having narrowly escaped the head hunters' attack of last week, it was only a matter of time before their return, but Tuesday Afternoon (the first time I set eyes on him, and thereafter, my nick-name for this simpleton) seemed oblivious to this threat. Observing this odd fellow's strange behaviour for over a week, I was convinced that, unless I made an effort to warn him of the impending danger, he was doubtless going to die. As my previous attempts at communication had proved disastrous, I took it upon myself to attempt some form of sign language. When I approached him he was doing something to one of his goats which defies description. Thankfully, on seeing me he stopped what he was doing and made some incomprehensible noises which I took to be a form of greeting. In an effort to instill a sense of urgency and warn him his life was threatened, I mimicked the warlike gestures of the head hunters and prostrated myself on the ground before him in the manner of someone who had been mortally wounded. This was obviously not working: his only reaction was to smile like an imbecile, point to himself and mumble something like 'masta'. Frustrated, yet undeterred, I gesticulated further by grabbing one of his feet, setting it on my head and drawing my forefinger across my throat to indicate exactly what would happen to him should he remain. My exhortations were, however, all in vain. Again he grinned like an idiot, repeatedly pointed to himself and said 'masta' over and over. He then offered me some disgusting bread and warm white liquid which, just to humour him, I ate. Realising that any further attempts at communication would be futile, and that 'I masta' in his strange language probably means 'I am an idiot', I reluctantly left Tuesday Afternoon to his fate.

Holdsworth (b.1948), an undergraduate student at Oxford Brookes University, wrote this in 1994 as part of a **rewriting** exercise (plus commentary) on the preceding passage from *Robinson Crusoe*. Also see: 2.3.3 and Pope 1995: 99–113.

J.M. Coetzee, *Foe*, 1986

[This version of the Crusoe story features a female narrator, Sue Barton, and a central but 'tongueless' Friday. Meanwhile, Defoe as author (the 'Foe' of the title) is represented as lurking enigmatically and elusively somewhere in the background. The three passages that follow are taken from near the beginning, round the middle, and the very end of the novel. The inverted commas round the first two passages are identified with Sue Barton as narrator. Their disappearance at the end leaves the precise identification of the narrator open.]

(i) 'For readers reared on travellers' tales, the words *desert isle* may conjure up a place of soft sands and shady trees where brooks run to quench the castaway's thirst and ripe fruit falls into his hand, where no more is asked of him than to drowse the days away till a ship calls to fetch him home. But the island on which I was cast away was quite another place: a great rocky hill with a flat top, rising sharply from the sea on all sides except one, dotted with drab bushes that never flowered and never shed their leaves. Off the islands grew beds of brown seaweed which, borne ashore by the waves, gave off a noisome stench and supported swarms of large pale fleas. There were ants scurrying everywhere, of the same kind we had in Bahia, and another pest, too, living in the dunes: a tiny insect that hid between your toes and ate its way into the flesh. Even Friday's hard skin was not proof against it: there were bleeding cracks in his feet, though he paid them no heed. I saw no snakes, but lizards came out in the heat of the day to sun themselves, some small and agile, others large and clumsy, with blue ruffs about their gills which they could flare out when alarmed, and hiss and glare.' [. . .]

(ii)
'Dear Mr Foe,
  'Some days ago Friday discovered your robes (the robes in the wardrobe, that is) and your wigs. Are they the robes of a guild-master? I did not know there was a guild of authors.
  'The robes have set him dancing, which I had never seen him do before. In the mornings he dances in the kitchen, where the windows face east. If the sun is shining he does his dance in a patch of sunlight, holding out his arms and spinning in a circle, his eyes shut, hour after hour, never growing fatigued or dizzy. In the afternoon he removes himself to the drawing room, where the window faces west, and does his dancing there.
  'In the grip of the dancing he is not himself. He is beyond human reach. I call his name and am ignored, I put out a hand and am brushed aside. All the while he dances and he makes a humming noise in his throat, deeper than his usual voice; sometimes he seems to be singing.
  'For myself I do not care how much he sings and dances so long as he carries out his few duties. For I will not delve while he spins. Last night I decided I would take the robe away from him, to bring him to his senses. However, when I stole into his room he was awake, his hands already gripping the robe, which was spread over the bed, as though he read my thoughts. So I retreated.' [. . .]

(iii)
Sand rises in slow flurries around my feet. There are no swarms of gay little fish. I enter the hole.
  I am below deck, the port side of the ship beneath my feet, feeling my way along beams and struts soggy to the touch. The stub of candle hangs on a string around my neck. I hold it up before me like a talisman, though it sheds no light.
  Something soft obstructs me, perhaps a shark, a dead shark overgrown with pulpy flowers of the sea, or the body of a guardian wrapped in rotting fabric, turn after turn. On hands and knees I creep past it.

I had not thought the sea could be dirty. But the sand under my hands is soft, dank, slimy, outside the circulation of the waters. It is like the mud of Flanders, in which generations of grenadiers now lie dead, trampled in the postures of sleep. If I am still for more than a moment I begin to sink, inch by inch.

I come to a bulkhead and a stairway. The door at the head of the stairway is closed; but when I put a shoulder to it and push, the wall of water yields and I can enter.

It is not a country bath-house. In the black space of this cabin the water is still and dead, the same water as yesterday, as last year, as three hundred years ago. Susan Barton and her dead captain, fat as pigs in their white nightclothes, their limbs extending stiffly from their trunks, their hands, puckered from long immersion, held out in blessing, float like stars against the low roof. I crawl beneath them.

In the last corner, under the transoms, half buried in sand, his knees drawn up, his hands between his thighs, I come to Friday. I tug his woolly hair, finger the chain about his throat. 'Friday,' I say, I try to say, kneeling over him, sinking hands and knees into the ooze, 'what is this ship?'

But this is not a place of words. Each syllable, as it comes out, is caught and filled with water and diffused. This is a place where bodies are their own signs. It is the home of Friday.

He turns and turns till he lies at full length, his face to my face. The skin is tight across his bones, his lips are drawn back. I pass a fingernail across his teeth, trying to find a way in.

His mouth opens. From inside him comes a slow stream, without breath, without interruption. It flows up through the body and out upon me; it passes through the cabin, through the wreck; washing the cliffs and shores of the island, it runs northward and southward to the ends of the earth. Soft and cold, dark and unending, it beats against my eyelids, against the skin of my face.

Coetzee was born in 1940 in Cape Town, South Africa. After a period studying and teaching in the United States, he returned to Cape Town in 1972, where he taught in the university's Department of English for the next thirty years (a period spanning apartheid and its formal abolition in 1994). Coetzee won the Booker Prize for fiction twice, with *The Life and Times of Michael K* (1983) and *Disgrace* (1999), and won the Nobel Prize for Literature in 2003. He has a persistent, subtle and searching commitment to writing that crosses and reconfigures the relations among fiction, history and life-writing, and he has also written essays on literature, translation, post/colonialism and censorship, e.g. *White Writing: On the Culture of Letters in South Africa* (1988) and *Stranger Shores: Essays 1986–1999* (2001). He currently lives in Adelaide, South Australia. (The above passages are taken from J.M. Coetzee, *Foe*, London: Penguin, 1987: 7, 92, 156–7, respectively. Compare Defoe and Holdsworth above.)

5.2.3   Romance revisited

CHARLOTTE BRONTË, ending of *Jane Eyre*, 1847

[Edward Rochester and Jane Eyre are drawn together, after many trials, tribulations and separations, by hearing one another's voices calling to them from the air. Rochester has been blinded and crippled trying to save his 'mad' first wife from a fatal fire. Jane Eyre is the narrator.]

Reader, it was on Monday night – near midnight – that I too had received the mysterious summons: those were the very words by which I replied to it. I listened to Mr Rochester's narrative, but made no disclosure in return. [. . .]

'You cannot now wonder,' continued my master, 'that when you rose upon me so unexpectedly last night, I had difficulty in believing you any other than a mere voice and vision, something that would melt me to silence and annihilation, as the midnight whisper and mountain echo had melted before. Now, I thank God! I know it to be otherwise. Yes, I thank God!'

He put me off his knee, rose and reverently lifted his hat from his brow, and bending his sightless eyes to the earth, he stood in mute devotion. Only the last words of the worship were audible –

'I thank my Maker, that, in the midst of judgement, He has remembered mercy. I humbly entreat my Redeemer to give me strength to lead henceforth a purer life than I have done hitherto!'

Then he stretched his hand out to be led. I took that dear hand, held it a moment to my lips, and then let it pass round my shoulder: being so much lower of stature than he, I served both for his prop and guide. We entered the wood and wended homeward.

FEMINISTS and others have long argued about the 'progressive' or 'conservative' dimensions of: Jane Eyre as a **character**; *Jane Eyre* as a **novel**, and Charlotte Brontë as an **author** (a succession of **films** further complicates perceptions). These three (or four) elements inevitably tend to get mixed up, but nonetheless need to be carefully distinguished. The first-person fictional narrator, Jane, uses a classic instance of the 'dear reader' mode of **address** to an implied reader. (See next text for another view of Edward Rochester and the (not so) 'mad' Mrs Rochester.)

JEAN RHYS, from *Wide Sargasso Sea*, 1968

[The narrator is Edward Rochester, a well-to-do Englishman visiting the West Indies. Antoinette is his wife, a Creole woman, who gradually finds herself stretched to breaking point between two communities. She is the 'mad' Mrs Rochester whom we never see in Brontë's *Jane Eyre*, above.]

'Did you hear what that girl was singing?' Antoinette said.

'I don't always understand what they say or sing.' Or anything else.

'It was a song about a white cockroach. That's me. That's what they call all of us who were here before their own people in Africa sold them to the slave traders. And I've heard English women call us white niggers. So between you I often wonder who I am and where is my country and where do I belong and why was I ever born at all. Will you go now please. I must dress like Christophine said.'

After I had waited half an hour I knocked at her door. There was no answer so I asked Baptiste to bring me something to eat. He was sitting under the Seville orange tree at the end of the veranda. He served the food with such a mournful expression that I thought these people are very vulnerable. How old was I when I learned to hide what I felt? A very small boy. Six, five, even earlier. It was necessary, I was told, and that view I have always accepted. If these mountains challenge me, or Baptiste's face, or Antoinette's eyes, they are mistaken, melodramatic, unreal (England must be quite unreal and like a dream she said).

Rhys (1894–1979) was herself part Creole. She was born in Dominica and came to England at the age of 16. Her 'prequel' to *Jane Eyre* is now recognised as a **classic** instance of the de- and **recentring** of a mainstream Western novel. Antoinette is in effect the **absence** of Brontë's novel turned into a **presence**: a dead **silence** endowed with speech and life. (Text from J. Rhys, *Wide Sargasso Sea*, Harmondsworth, Penguin, 1972: 85.) Compare Holdsworth's response to Defoe's *Robinson Crusoe* (5.2.2), and Bolam's response to Shakespeare's *Macbeth* (5.1.4).

OSCAR WILDE, *The Picture of Dorian Gray*, [1890] 1891

[It is London's fashionable West End towards 1890. Lord Henry Wotton is visiting his friend Basil Hallward, a painter. Basil is painting a picture of the young man, Dorian Gray, who is present posing for it.]

Lord Henry looked at him. Yes, he was certainly wonderfully handsome, with his finely-curved scarlet lips, his frank blue eyes, his crisp gold hair. There was something in his face that made one trust him at once. All the candour of youth was there, as well as all youth's passionate purity. One felt that he had kept himself unspotted from the world. No wonder Basil Hallward worshipped him.

"You are too charming to go in for philanthropy, Mr. Gray–far too charming." And Lord Henry flung himself down on the divan, and opened his cigarette case.

The painter had been busy mixing his colours and getting his brushes ready. He was looking worried, and when he heard Lord Henry's last remark he glanced at him, hesitated for a moment, and then said, "Harry, I want to finish this picture to-day. Would you think it awfully rude of me if I asked you to go away?"

Lord Henry smiled, and looked at Dorian Gray. "Am I to go, Mr. Gray?" he asked.

"Oh, please don't, Lord Henry, I see that Basil is in one of his sulky moods; and I can't bear him when he sulks. Besides, I want you to tell me why I should not go in for philanthropy."

"I don't know that I shall tell you that, Mr. Gray. It is so tedious a subject that one would have to talk seriously about it. But I shall certainly not run away, now that you have asked me to stop. You don't really mind, Basil, do you? You have often told me that you liked your sitters to have someone to chat to."

Hallward bit his lip. "If Dorian wishes it, of course you must stay. Dorian's whims are laws to everybody, except himself."

Lord Henry took up his hat and gloves. "You are very pressing, Basil, but I am afraid I must go. I have promised to meet a man at the Orleans. Good-bye, Mr Gray. Come and see me some afternoon in Curzon Street. I am nearly always at home at five o'clock. Write to me when you are coming. I should be sorry to miss you."

"Basil," cried Dorian Gray, "if Lord Henry Wotton goes, I shall go too. You never open your lips while you are painting, and it is horribly dull standing on a platform and trying to look pleasant. Ask him to stay. I insist upon it."

"Stay, Harry, to oblige Dorian, and to oblige me," said Hallward, gazing intently at his picture. "It is quite true, I never talk when I am working, and never listen either, and it must be dreadfully tedious for my unfortunate sitters. I beg you to stay."

"But what about my man at the Orleans?"

The painter laughed. "I don't think there will be any difficulty about that. Sit down again, Harry. And now, Dorian, get up on the platform, and don't move about too much, or pay any attention to what Lord Henry says. He has a very bad influence over all his friends, with the single exception of myself."

Dorian Gray stepped up on the dais, with the air of a young Greek martyr, and made a little *moue* of discontent to Lord Henry, to whom he had rather taken a fancy.

Wilde (1854–1900) first published a shorter version of this novel in *Lippincott's Monthly* (July 1890), which immediately drew criticism for its supposedly 'decadent' content. He responded with a Preface in Frank Harris's *Fortnightly Review* a few months later, and published a fuller book version with Ward, Lock and Company in April 1891. The present text is from Chapter

2 of the latter, as printed in *The Picture of Dorian Gray*, ed. M.P. Gillespie, New York: Norton, 2007: 17–18. The Preface has been taken as a kind of manifesto for late nineteenth-century 'aestheticism' and 'art for art's sake' ever since. It begins – and continues and concludes – thus: 'The artist is the creator of all beautiful things. / To reveal art and conceal the artist is art's aim. / The critic is he who can translate into another manner or a new material his impression of beautiful things. / The highest as the lowest form of criticism is a mode of autobiography. / . . . There is no such thing as a moral or immoral book. Books are well written, or badly written. That is all . . . Diversity of opinion about a work of art shows that the work is new, complex and vital . . . All art is useless.' (pp. 3–4). For a fuller account of Wilde, including his reputation for homosexuality and trial for obscenity, see the notes attached to *The Importance of Being Earnest* (1895) in 2.2.4. For a modern adaptation, see Self's *Dorian* next.

WILL SELF, *Dorian: An Imitation*, 2002

[It is London in the early 1990s. Baz, an installation artist, Dorian, his model, and Sir Henry Wotton, an upper-class man about town, are all watching the first version of 'Cathode Narcissus': Baz's multi-screen video installation featuring Dorian dancing.]

Inside the dark studio the nine monitors were sharply outlined. Across their faces, hissing with static, the fluid images of Dorian presented a cascade of motion. There was a soundtrack as well, an insistent thrumming beat entwined with a breathy fluting. Dorian was transfixed for a few moments, but then he moved closer and began to sway in time with his own televisual images. Nine naked Dorians and one clothed. In synchrony, youth and the images of youth waltzed to the heavenly and eternal music of self-consciousness.

'Well, whaddya reckon?' Baz blurted out from the shadows, and Dorian turned to see him and Wotton, their faces soiled with lust.

'He's absolutely superb,' Wotton answered, 'and this afternoon has become remarkable since I encountered your faun.'

'I think I've caught him at just the right point –'

'Oh, indeed you have, Baz, he's like a ripe grape dusted with yeast.' Wotton made as if to pluck one of the monitors and eat it.

Dorian felt uncomfortable with the way the older men were speaking; was it at cross-purposes, or did they regard him and the video installation as entirely interchangeable? 'How long will these tapes last, Baz?' he asked.

'It's hard to say . . . Certainly years, if not decades, and by then they can be transferred to new tapes, and so on – for ever, I guess.'

'So these' – Dorian gestured – 'will remain young for ever, while I grow old, then die?'

'Yeah, well,' Baz snorted derisively. 'You can't copy bodies – yet.'

'I wish it was the other way round,' Dorian said, and to support the throwaway nature of the remark, he picked up a black wind-cheater which was slung over a chair and headed for the door, calling over his shoulder, 'You coming, Henry?'

'Er . . . yuh.' Wotton stirred himself, as did Baz.

'What about the piece, Dorian?' he pleaded. 'I need to do two more recordings for the soundtrack. I *must* do them.'

'Well, if you must.' Dorian's whole tone had hardened since he'd seen the installation. 'Personally I'm jealous of the bloody thing – it's already hours younger than me.'

Self (b.1961, London) writes for and broadcasts in a wide range of media, along with novels. With the photographer David Gamble, he produced *Perfidious Man* (2000) as a witty critique of contemporary masculinity. The present extract is taken from *Dorian: An Imitation*, London: Penguin, 2003: 22–3. Later in the novel the videos are transferred to DVD and mass-marketed. The novel is an updated response to Oscar Wilde's *The Picture of Dorian Gray* (1890–1), for which see the previous passage.

5.2.4 Science and fantasy fiction: genre and gender

PHILIP K. DICK, from *Do Androids Dream of Electric Sheep?*, 1968

[Rick Deckard is a police officer and bounty hunter who 'retires' (i.e. terminates) escaped androids – familiarly known as 'andies'. He is visiting a museum with another police officer, Phil Resch, whom he thinks may in fact be an 'andy' too. Their task is to retire a female android who/that is posing as the opera singer, Luba Luft. The painting referred to is Edvard Munch's *The Scream*.]

They arrived at the museum building, noted on which floor the Munch exhibit could be found, and ascended. Shortly, they wandered amid paintings and woodcuts. Many people had turned out for the exhibit, including a grammar school class; the shrill voice of the teacher penetrated all the rooms comprising the exhibit, and Rick thought, That's what you'd expect an andy to sound – and look – like. Instead of like Rachel Rosen and Luba Luft. And – the man beside him. Or rather the thing beside him. [. . .]

At an oil painting Phil Resch halted, gazed intently. The painting showed a hairless, oppressed creature with a head like an inverted pear, its hands clapped in horror to its ears, its mouth open in a vast, soundless scream. Twisted ripples of the creature's torment, echoes of its cry, flooded out into the air surrounding it; the man or woman, whichever it was, had become contained by its own howl. It had covered its ears against its own sound. The creature stood on a bridge and no one else was present; the creature screamed in isolation. Cut off by – or despite – its outcry.

'He did a woodcut of this,' Rick said, reading the card tacked below the painting.

'I think,' Phil Resch said, 'that this is how an andy must feel.' He traced in the air the convolutions, visible in the picture, of the creature's cry. 'I don't feel like that, so maybe I'm not an –' He broke off, as several persons strolled up to inspect the picture.

'*There's Luba Luft.*' Rick pointed and Phil Resch halted his sombre introspection and defence; the two of them walked at a measured pace toward her, taking their time as if nothing confronted them; as always it was vital to preserve the atmosphere of the commonplace. Other humans, having no knowledge of the presence of androids among them, had to be protected at all costs – even that of losing the quarry.

Holding a printed catalogue, Luba Luft, wearing shiny tapered pants and an illuminated gold vestlike top, stood absorbed in the picture before her: a drawing of a young girl, hands clasped together, seated on the edge of a bed, an expression of bewildered wonder and new, groping awe imprinted on the face.

Dick (1928–82) is widely recognised as one of the **classic** American writers of modern science fiction. He died a few weeks before the release of the film based on the present novel, *Blade Runner* (1982), directed by Ridley Scott and starring Harrison Ford as Rick Deckard. It includes a scene corresponding to that from Chapter 14, featured here.

URSULA LE GUIN, from *The Left Hand of Darkness*, Ch. 7, 1969

From field notes of Ong Tot Oppong, Investigator, of the first Ekumenical landing party on Gethen/Winter, Cycle 93 E.Y. 1448

I theorize about the origins of Gethenian sexual psychology. What do I actually know about it? Otie Nim's communication from the Orgoreyn region has cleared up some of my earlier misconceptions. Let me set down all I know, and after that my theories: first things first.

The sexual cycle averages 26 to 28 days (they tend to speak of it as 26 days, approximating it to the lunar cycle). For 21 or 22 days the individual is *somer*, sexually inactive, latent. On about the 18th day hormonal changes are initiated by the pituitary control and on the 22nd or 23rd day the individual enters *kemmer*, oestrus. In this first phase of kemmer (Karh. Secher) he remains completely androgynous. Gender, and potency, are not attained in isolation. A Gethenian in first-phase kemmer, if kept alone or with others not in kemmer, remains incapable of coitus. Yet the sexual impulse is tremendously strong in this phase, controlling the entire personality, subjecting all other drives to its imperative. When the individual finds a partner in kemmer, hormonal secretion is further stimulated (most importantly by touch – secretion? scent?) until in one partner either a male or female hormonal dominance is established. The genitals engorge or shrink accordingly, foreplay intensifies, and the partner triggered by the change, takes on the other sexual role. [. . .] Normal individuals have no predisposition to either sexual role in kemmer; they do not know whether they will be the male or the female, and have no choice in the matter (Otie Nim wrote that in the Orgoreyn region the use of hormone derivatives to establish a preferred sexuality is quite common; I haven't seen this done in rural Karhide.) [. . .] If the individual was in the female role and was impregnated, hormonal activity of course continues, and for the 8.4-month gestation period and the 6- to 8-month lactation period this individual remains female. The male sexual organs remain retracted somewhat, and the pelvic girdle widens. With the cessation of lactation the female re-enters somer and becomes once more a perfect androgyne. No physiological habit is established, and the mother of several children may be the father of several more.

Le Guin (b.1929, Berkeley, California) is the author of much, now **classic**, science and fantasy **fiction** for both children and adults. Along with a concern with GENDER AND SEXUALITY, as here, her work shows a recurrent interest in the nature of story-telling, and the relations between **story and history** and **fiction and fact**. The present novel, for instance, opens with the following statement from one 'Genly Ai, First Mobile on Gethin/Winter': 'I'll make my report as if I told a story, for I was taught as a child on my homeworld that Truth is a matter of the imagination. The soundest fact may fail or prevail in the style of its telling: like that singular organic jewel of our seas, which grows brighter as one woman wears it and, worn by another, dulls and goes to dust. Facts are no more solid, coherent, round, and real than pearls are. But both are sensitive.'

RUSSELL HOBAN, *Riddley Walker*, 1980

[A child, Riddley Walker, is being told a story about 'The Other Voice Owl of the World' by a man who calls himself 'the Listener'. The language represents a kind of archaic South-western rural English written as it might be said and heard. Strange and almost incomprehensible though it may seem when first read silently from the page, saying it out loud a few times will make it much less so.]

The Lissener and the Other Voyce Owl of the Worl
There wer the Other Voyce Owl of the Worl. He sat in the worl tree larfing in his front voice
only his other voice wernt larfing his other voice wer saying the sylents. He had a way of saying
them. He said them wide and far where he begun them he said them tyny when they come close.
He kep saying the sylents like that in his other voice and when he done it the sylents wer swallering
up the souns of the worl then the owl wer swallering the sylents.

No I knowit he wer doing it. He wer trying to swaller all the souns of the worl then there wunt
be no mor worl becaws every thing wud foller the soun of its self in to the sylents then it wud be
gone. What the owl had in mynd wer to get it all swallert then fly a way. He only done it at nite
he thot hewd get some of it swallert every nite and til he gone the woal worl a way.

No I knowit what the owl wer doing only a kid. He dint have no eyes he lissent all the time.
When he heard the owl saying the sylents in his other voice he heard the sylents swallering up the
souns of the worl littl and big from the wind sying in the trees to the ants crying in ther hoals.
The kid knowit the owl wer trying to say the woal worl a way and he knowit wer on him to stop
the owl so he begun to lissen every thing back. He lissent them far and wide where he begun them
he lissent them tyny when they come close. The eye of the goat and the dants in the stoan and the
beatl digging a grave for the sparrer. He lissent them in to his ear hoals he kep them all safe
there. The foot steps of the mof and the sea foam hissing on the stran he lissent every thing back.

The kid dint keap the souns of the worl in his ear hoals only at nite he kep them safe til morning.
When the cock crowt in the middl nite it never foolt him nor when it crowt agen befor 1st lite. He
kep them souns safe in his ear hoals til the day stood up and the cock of the morning crowt every
thing a wake. Then the kid unheard the souns and they gone back where they livet. The kid wer
larfing at the owl but the owl dint know it he thot he done a good nites work. He sat in the worl
tree grooling and smarling all day thinking he wud get the woal worl gone only he never done it.

The rivvers run
My storys done

Hoban was born in Pennsylvania in 1925 and settled in London in 1960. A novelist and writer
of children's literature, he is known for his experimental way with words and narrative. The
scenario for the present novel is a kind of post-apocalyptic Britain reduced to mere survival
and a primitive but still remarkably resourceful speech. The present story is told round a fire
on a derelict site. Hoban's 'worl'-view is more pervasive and arguably more persuasive, even
if initially more perplexing, than the institutionally reduced language of 'Newspeak' in Orwell's
Nineteen Eighty-Four (1949) and the sub-cultural argot of 'Nadsat' in Burgess's *A Clockwork
Orange* (1962). The book has now achieved classic not just cult status. (Text from R. Hoban,
Riddley Walker, London: Picador, 1982: 82–3.)

TERRY PRATCHETT and NEIL GAIMAN, opening of *Good Omens*, 1991

The Oxfordshire plain stretched out to the west, with a scattering of lights to mark the
slumbering villages where honest yeomen were settling down to sleep after a long day's
editorial direction, financial consulting, or software engineering.

Up here on the hill a few glow-worms were lighting up.

The surveyor's theodolite is one of the most direful symbols of the twentieth century. Set
up anywhere in open countryside, it says: there will come Road Widening, yea, and two-
thousand-home estates in keeping with the Essential Character of the Village. Executive
Developments will be manifest.

But not even the most conscientious surveyor surveys at midnight, and yet here the thing was, tripod legs deep in the turf. Not many theodolites have a hazel twig strapped to the top, either, or crystal pendulums hanging from them and Celtic runes carved into the legs.

The soft breeze flapped the cloak of the slim figure who was adjusting the knobs of the thing. It was quite a heavy cloak, sensibly waterproof, with a warm lining.

Most books on witchcraft will tell you that witches work naked. This is because most books on witchcraft are written by men.

Pratchett, as it says on the inside **auto/biographical** blurbs of several of his **comic** fantasy novels: 'was born in 1948 and is still not dead [. . . He is] on average a sort of youngish middle-aged. He lives in Somerset with his wife and daughter, and long ago chose journalism as a career because it was indoor work with no heavy lifting. Beyond that he positively refuses to be drawn. People never read these biographies anyway, do they? They want to get on with the book, not wade through masses of prose designed to suggest that the **author** is really a very interesting person [. . .] Occasionally he gets accused of literature.' Pratchett is also the author of the hugely popular *Discworld* series. Gaiman, Pratchett's co-writer here, has much less to say for himself but is no doubt equally un/interesting. For sample analysis, see FORMALISM, Example p. 146. (Text from T. Pratchett and N. Gaiman, *Good Omens*, London, Corgi, 1991.)

5.2.5   War on – of – terror

IAN McEWAN, 'Only love and then oblivion', from the *Guardian*, 15 September 2001

Emotions have their narratives: after the shock we move inevitably to the grief, and the sense that we are doing it more or less together is one tiny scrap of consolation.

Initially the visual impact of the scenes – those towers collapsing with malign majesty – extended our state of fevered astonishment. Even on Wednesday, fresh video footage froze us in this stupefied condition, and denied us our profounder feelings: the first plane disappearing into the side of the tower as cleanly as a posted letter; the couple jumping into the void, hand in hand; a solitary figure falling with a strangely extended arm (was it an umbrella serving as a hopeful parachute?); the rescue workers crawling about at the foot of a vast mountain of rubble. In our delirium, most of us wanted to talk. We babbled by e-mail, on the phone, around kitchen tables. We knew there was a greater reckoning ahead, but we could not quite feel it yet. Sheer amazement kept getting in the way. The reckoning, of course, was with the personal. [. . .]

This is the nature of empathy, to think oneself into the minds of others. These are the mechanics of compassion: you are under the bedclothes, unable to sleep, and you are crouching in the brushed-steel lavatory at the rear of the plane, whispering a final message to your loved ones. There is only one thing to say, and you say it. All else is pointless. You have very little time before some holy fool, who believes in his place in eternity, kicks the door, slaps your head and orders you back to your seat. 23C. Here is your seat belt. There is the magazine you were reading before it all began.

The banality of these details might overwhelm you. If you are not already panicking, you are clinging to a shred of hope that the captain, who spoke with such authority as the plane pushed back from the stand, will rise from the floor, his throat uncut, to take the controls.

If the hijackers had been able to imagine themselves into the thoughts and feelings of the passengers, they would have been unable to proceed. It is hard to be cruel once you permit yourself to enter the mind of your victim. Imagining what it is like to be someone other than yourself is at the core of our humanity. It is the essence of compassion, and it is the beginning of morality.

McEwan (b.1948, Aldershot, England) is a novelist and short story writer who has won many prizes for his prose fiction, e.g., *First Love, Last Rites* (1975), *The Cement Garden* (1978), *The Child in Time* (1987) and *Atonement* (2001). He also wrote the screenplay for *The Ploughman's Lunch* (1983). He was amongst the first postgraduates from the programme in **Creative Writing** at the University of East Anglia and won the Booker Prize for *Amsterdam* in 1998.

ARUNDHATI ROY, from 'The Algebra of Infinite Justice', from the *Guardian*, Saturday Review, 29 September 2001

The world will probably never know what motivated those particular hijackers who flew planes into those particular American buildings. They were not glory boys. They left no suicide notes, no political messages, no organization has claimed credit for the attacks. All we know is that their belief in what they were doing outstripped the natural human instinct for survival or any desire to be remembered. It's almost as though they could not scale down the enormity of their rage to anything smaller than their deeds. And what they did was blow a hole in the world as we knew it. In the absence of information, politicians, political commentators and writers (like myself) will invest the act with their own politics, with their own interpretations. This speculation, this analysis of the political climate in which the attacks took place, can only be a good thing.

But war is looming large. Whatever remains to be said, must be said quickly.

Before America places itself at the helm of the 'International Coalition Against Terror', before it invites (and coerces) countries to actively participate in its almost godlike mission – 'Operation Infinite Justice', until it was pointed out that this could be seen as an insult to Muslims, who believe that only Allah can mete out infinite justice, and was renamed 'Operation Enduring Freedom' – it would help if some small clarifications are made. For example, Infinite Justice/Enduring Freedom for whom? Is this America's War against Terror in America or against Terror in general? What exactly is being avenged here? Is it the tragic loss of almost 7,000 lives, the gutting of fifteen million square feet of office space in Manhattan, the destruction of a section of the Pentagon, the loss of several hundreds of thousands of jobs, the bankruptcy of some airline companies and the dip in the New York Stock Exchange? Or is it more than that?

In 1996, Madeleine Albright, then UN Ambassador to the United Nations, was asked on national television what she felt about the fact that 500,000 Iraqi children had died as a result of US economic sanctions. She replied that it was 'a very hard choice', but that all things considered, 'we think the price is worth it'. Madeleine Albright never lost her job for saying this. She continued to travel the world representing the views and aspirations of the US government. More pertinently, the sanctions against Iraq remain in place. Children continue to die.

So here we have it. The equivocating distinction between civilization and savagery, between the 'massacre of innocent people' or, if you like, 'a clash of civilizations' and 'collateral damage'. The sophistry and fastidious algebra of Infinite Justice. How many dead Iraqis will it take to make the world a better place? How many dead Afghans for every dead American? How many dead children for every dead man? How many dead mujahideen for each dead investment banker?

Roy (b.1961, Delhi) trained as an architect and is now a journalist, political activist, film-maker and story-teller. Her first novel, *The God of Small Things* (1997), won the Booker Prize for Fiction. The above piece is from an article which appeared in the *Guardian*, Saturday Review,

29 September, 2001, eighteen days after the attack on the World Trade Center ('9/11'), and was later reprinted in Roy's book of the same name, *The Algebra of Infinite Justice*, London: Penguin, 2nd edn, 2002: 223–5. Her work can be followed at www.weroy.org.

NICK BARTON, *Voices from the Battlefields of Afghanistan* (I) – from the air, 2007–8

For perhaps 50 per cent of our engagements, you probably don't see anyone [the pilots are firing at buildings or tree-lines]. If it subsequently came out in an int [intelligence] report that five women were killed in a building you had fired on, you would feel absolutely terrible. Fortunately I have not had any of those. We [the British Apache pilots] have probably only had one example of it and he [the pilot] was completely right to do it [to open fire]. They'd had two guys firing a mortar out of one end of the building and, on the other side, inside the building, there had been two women. It was in self-defence under the correct Rules of Engagement and, prior to firing, he had checked the building and not seen any women. It would be difficult to take but I suppose one must console oneself in that he had done everything right at the time. We have good squadron camaraderie and attitude to debriefing. After a mission, we will debrief everything and we will talk about it. This helps with our drills and improving our support to the troops as well as dealing with difficult scenarios.

I have been in a night-time scenario in Nad Ali that, taken out of context, could be seen to be quite damning from our gun footage. Our guys had been contacted. They had been caught in an ambush, which they had pre-seen but could not get the Rules of Engagement to engage on. They were subsequently contacted and they swiftly dropped two 500-pounders from a B1 [bomber] because that was all they had on station. They were pretty sure they got one [Taliban], but they were still tracking another with an ISTAR [intelligence, surveillance, targeting, acquisition and reconnaissance] asset. They tracked him for over a K and a half through the fields. We were on high readiness from Bastion – a ten-minute flight time – and were woken up and launched as soon as the initial contact occurred.

When I arrived on station at approximately three in the morning, I had one guy in the middle of the maize-field. It took quite a while picking him up at night. When I actually saw him, I had no doubt in my mind that this guy was one of the original men from the ambush, still rapidly on the run in the middle of a field using the high crops as cover. I was flying at about 2,000 feet with night-vision goggles on. I had all the Rules of Engagement and fired, and I made sure I did it pretty clinically. That sounds shocking. I fired a burst of twenty [rounds], then readjusted and then I fired probably eighty or a hundred rounds at him. Once you have caught him, once he is on the run, you make sure you hit him really hard. You just want to be professional and clinical.

We video everything we do and watch it not only to improve our weaponeering, but also to record every engagement for any Rules of Engagement questions or investigations. Taken out of context, without any background, this footage would be quite shocking in its cold harshness. The fact that we video everything does put the crews under additional pressure in a way that, perhaps, the rest of the Army does not face.

This and the next passage are accounts by serving members of the British forces fighting in Afghanistan between August 2007 and August 2008. This account is given by Captain Nick Barton of the Army Air Corps and is taken from *Spoken from the Front: Real Voices from the Battlefields of Afghanistan*, ed. Andy McNab, London: Bantam Press, 2009, pp. 309–10. The editor of the collection, Andy McNab (who added the square brackets), has been a serving member of the British SAS (Special Air Service) and is a writer of best-selling war fiction.

SIMON PANTER, *Voices from the Battlefields of Afghanistan* (II) –
on the ground, 2007–8

We may have got one on the first burst. We were firing SA80 [assault rifles] and LMG [light machine-gun]. They had AKs and RPGs. We had surprised them. A little bit of a fire-fight ensued and then I thought: We have to take the bull by the horns here and dispatch the Taliban. So we concocted a quick plan. With the remainder of the section giving fire support, me and another lad, Private Patrick Casey, pepper-potted along the ditch and encountered a Taliban just fifteen to twenty metres in front of us. We hadn't seen him initially. I killed him: I shot him with my rifle. At this point I thought: Bloody hell, they're getting a bit close. So I put the bayonet and a fresh mag on, and as I was doing that I saw some movement in front. I chucked a grenade towards the initial area where the Taliban were and after that we didn't really get any incoming fire back from them. Then one of the lads spotted a Taliban running to our left. He fired and I fired and the Taliban dropped. But I didn't know whether he had gone to ground or not. Then I spotted him again in the ditch about twenty metres away. I fired some more rounds and he was down. I jumped into the ditch towards him. He still had his weapon – an AK variant – in his hand and he was still breathing. I had my bayonet fixed and I bayoneted him, straight in the chest. Several times. We were taught in training: once you shoot, then bayonet them because they have been known in the past to jump up behind you after feigning death or injury. So it's always good to make sure they're dead. He was probably in his late twenties, no more than thirty. He was in black with a black tie around his middle and he had chest webbing on as well. The first guy was dressed exactly the same.

To our right flank, the company were still having a bit of a bun-fight with the Taliban. I think the Taliban we encountered had been trying to sneak up on the main company and ambush them from the flank but they got surprised by us because they didn't know we were there. Then we had a quick chat. Me and Casey went up towards the position where we had first seen the Taliban. And there was another Taliban in there. He may have been injured but he still had a weapon with him so he was shot. I shot him. That was for the time being. We had a mini re-org to call the rest of the section in, covering all our arcs, doing a head count and re-arming.

While this was going on, a fourth member of the Taliban opened up on us, again from the ditch. This was three or four minutes after we thought the fire-fight had ended. He was firing with AK: it was automatic gunfire from under a hundred metres. So now we fired back at that Taliban position. I said to one of the guys who had an ILAW [interim light anti-tank weapon] rocket launcher: 'Fire at that position.' He couldn't get the damn thing to work so I took it off him and fired at the position, and all the other guys fired everything we had for a couple of minutes. We didn't get any return fire so we assumed he was killed in that initial volley, from less than a hundred metres away. I thought: I'm not going to send any guys up to confirm the death for safety reasons.

Then we searched for the [three] dead Taliban. Two of the guys looked like they were foreign fighters. These were the guys dressed in black. They were maybe Iranian or Pakistani. We found grenades on their bodies and mobile phones. They had two grenades and a mobile phone each. And we took notebooks from them with phone numbers in. The third guy looked like he was local Afghan. He was wearing brown traditional Afghan dress. He had a red sash round his waist and a turban that was off at the time. He was the guy with the RPG beside him.

I had killed people in battle before but never as close as this. You very rarely see the Taliban. They are usually at a distance and well hidden. I sat down at the end and said: 'Fucking hell, lads. You only normally read about this shit but we've actually done it.' Then we cleared things up and got the Afghan National Army. They did a search and took the weapons off them [the dead] and then it came over the radio that the fire-fight had died out at the other end.

This and the previous passage are accounts by serving members of the British forces of fighting in Afghanistan between August 2007 and August 2008. This account is by Colour Sergeant Simon Panter of the Royal Anglian Regiment and is taken from *Spoken from the Front: Real Voices from the Battlefields of Afghanistan,* ed. Andy McNab, London: Bantam Press, 2009: 231–3. Also see note to previous item.

5.2.6 MEDIA MESSAGES AND STREET TEXTS

This is a sample of the kinds of message that populate public spaces: on posters, in print, on screens, via public address systems and in graffiti. The emphasis is on formulaic language and persistent text-types, and variations of them. Actual instances are infinitely various and the text-types themselves are constantly evolving, depending upon available technology, immediate context and personal resourcefulness. So the present sample is simply indicative. It is designed to support initial study (which may be both critical and creative) and be supplemented by anything else that comes to mind or hand. Further examples can be found @ 5.2.6.

PERSONAL AND NOT-SO-PERSONAL ADS

(i)   *Attractive male*, 38, fair hair, hazel eyes, non-smoker, seeks relationship with warm affectionate Lady. Photo, please.

(ii)   Artistic, feminine Eurasian lady, petite, single, looking for non-smoking man for lunch time Malay/Chinese meals. Go 'Dutch' maybe more if friendship develops. Box No 432.

(iii)   Mother seeking good-looking educated girl for clean-shaven Sikh male, cultured, US citizen, 40, 5ft 11 in, divorced. Hotel management, studying/accountancy.

(iv)   BRIGHTON BIKER, 36, hairy, large motorcycle, seeks bored housewife for wild rides while the kids are at school.

(v)   LEMON CAKETTE seeks professional man for afternoon tea.

(i) and (ii) come from 'free' local newspapers, respectively, *Oxford Star*, 8.11.1990 and *Adelaide Advertiser*, 7.6.1996; (iii) from *India Today*, 30.4.1992; (iv) and (v) from *Private Eye*, 27.3.1992. The formulae 'X seeks Y' or 'X seeks Y for Z' persist on web-based dating sites, as do variants on 'I am . . . , You are . . . ', supported by detailed profiles.

CASH-MACHINE AND CHECK-OUT EXCHANGES

(i)   [At an automated bank service outlet – 'hole-in-the-wall machine']

WELCOME!
Please insert your card and enter you personal pin number.
* Warning – Never use a temporary card reader.
If suspicious, contact bank *

[*You insert card and quickly tap in your number*]

ERROR! Please enter your personal pin number.

[*You tap it in more carefully*]

Which service do you require?

>   Cash   Mobile phone top-up   <
>   Cash with receipt   Mini-statement   <

[*You press 'Cash with receipt'*]

Select the amount you require.

Please note. This machine only has units of £20 today.

>   10   20   <
>   30   40   <
>   50   100   <

[*You really wanted '30', hesitate, and press '40'*]

Please wait. Your request is being processed.

Your cash is being counted.

[*Money issues from slot. You check there are two £20 notes*]

Please wait for your receipt.

Would you like another service?

>   YES   NO   <

[*You take your receipt, press 'NO' and go*]

WELCOME!
Please insert your card and enter you personal pin number.
* Warning – Never use a temporary card reader.
If suspicious, contact bank *

The various pathways through – and possible 'exchanges' with – this and other automated systems are both 'closed' and 'open': narrowly determined in the range of mechanical cues and actions permissible, yet still subject to wide variations in actual human **dialogue** and **response**. Exploring and experimenting with these through a combination of transcripts and scripts proves very revealing. The same thing can be done with:

(ii)   [*At a supermarket checkout*]

CUSTOMER: There's a mistake here [*holds out hand with change in*].
CASHIER: Pardon?
CUSTOMER: A mistake's been made.
CASHIER: [blank look]
CUSTOMER: You've made a mistake.
CASHIER: What's wrong?

This is the kind of transcript of a snatch of conversation (overheard in a supermarket in Oxford) which, when 'tidied up' and represented as a script, is useful when analysing routine **discourse** (as it is there in Part Four). It can also be used as a basis for role play and **rewriting**. How might *you* handle this – or a mistake made by an automatic 'weigh-and-pay' machine?

ANSWER-PHONE MESSAGES AND CALL-CENTRE SCRIPT

(i)   Hi! This is Alan Jenkins here. Sorry I'm not in just now – but if you'd like leave your name and number after the beep, I'll get back to you just as soon as I can. Thanks a lot. See ya. [*Pause*] Here comes the beep, I hope . . . [Long pause, crackle, Bang, beeeeeeeep]

(ii) Welcome to National Rail Enquiries. Please note that your call may be recorded for monitoring and training purposes.

If you are travelling today and want to confirm train times and tickets, please press 1 to connect to our automated train-tracker service. For information on rail travel to the 2012 Olympic Games, please press 2. For all other information, please press 3 or hold for one of our customer service representatives.

[*You press 3*]

To ensure your call is answered by the correct service representative, please select from one of the following options:

If you are travelling today and need information on train times or stations and train companies, please press 1. If you are travelling on another . . .

[*You press 1*]

We are currently experiencing a high volume of enquiries. Please hold and your call will be answered by the soonest available adviser.

[*You hold. Sound of music.*]

(iii) Good evening. My name is David and I am calling to tell you how you can pay less for your fuel bills this winter. Most of them are going up as you probably know. Could I ask whether I am talking to Mr Blondel and who currently supplies your electricity and gas . . .

STREET: SIGNS, GRAFFITI, WORD-ART

This is a sample of messages seen or heard round Oxford railway station during 2010–11.

(i)   Sport-free zone!
Come in and have
a quiet pint and a bite
if you are fed up
with football!!!

(ii)
SMALL CHANGE?
Just keeps him on the street . . .

[Photograph of homeless man and dog]

LIFE CHANGE!
By putting your change in an OxPat collecting box
you **can** change lives for the better.

(iii)   If I had known on earth
        What I know here . . .   . . . I would not have lived
                                        the way I did.

(iv)   This is a security announcement. Due to the current heightened levels of tension, customers
        are asked to be extra vigilant. Any suspicious activity should be reported to the police or
        a member of the railway staff. Thank you.

(v)   MIND THE GAP

(i) was hand-painted on a huge lampshade put outside a pub during the (soccer) World Cup in
2010 and the (rugby) World Cup in 2011. (ii) was from a poster inside the station and featured
a black-and-white photograph of a homeless man and dog begging, seen from above and to
one side. (iii) was sprayed on a poster for burgers and fries on a bus-shelter outside the station.
(iv) was announced over the public address system at Oxford station at various times between
April and August 2011, and could have referred to the threat of international terrorism and/or
the recent street riots in England. (v) is a long-standing (and often-parodied) caution delivered
at British rail and underground stations; this one was painted in big yellow letters on the
platform.

5.3   VOICES

5.3.1   Dramatising 'English' in education

STUDENT TALK AMONGST FRIENDS (transcript), c. 1997

[Three female students are having tea and cake together on a Sunday night. They are all round
the same age (twenty) and share a house in Carmarthen in mid Wales. Two of the speakers (S1
and S2) are from the South-west of England and one (S3) is from South Wales.]

S2: Oh those Cherry Bakewells look lovely.
S1: They do don't they.
S3: Don't they. Oh they were . . . [lowers voice] [inaudible]
S1: Gorgeous aren't they.
S3: Shall we save it for a cup of tea?
S2: [laughs] Yes.
S1: All right then.
S3: Sound like a right mother don't I.
S2: [laughs]
S1: You do.
S2: Well they would go smashing with a cup of tea wouldn't they.
S1: Oh they would.
S2: Yeah.
S3: Cup of tea and a fag.
S1: [laughs]
S2: Cup of tea and a fag missus. We're gonna have to move the table I think.
S1: Yeah. Do you like this ta– this table she's constructed of erm boots and a book?

S2: [laughs]
S3: Ah. That's brilliant.
S1: Hey. That's really good there look.
[laughter]
S2: And it's got the Milky Way wrapper.
[rustling noises]
S1: That's right.
S2: As that little extra support.
S3: I like Sunday nights for some reason. [laughs] I don't know why.
S2: [laughs] Cos you come home.
S3: I come home + . . .
S2: You come home to us.
S3: . . . + and pig out.
S2: Yeah. Yeah.
S3: Sunday is a really nice day I think.
S2: It certainly is.
S1: It's a really nice relaxing day.
S2: It's me earring.
S3 [inaudible]
S2: 's me earring.
S3: Oh. Lovely. Oh. Lovely.
S2: It's fallen apart a bit. But
S3: It looks quite nice like that actually. I like that. I bet, is that supposed to be straight?
S2: Yeah.
S3: I reckon it looks better like that.
S2: And it was another bit as well, was another dangly bit.
S3: What + . . .
S2: Separate
S3: . . . attached to + . . .
S2: The top bit.
S3: . . . + that one.
S2: Yeah. So it was even.
S1: Mobile earrings.
S3: Oh.
S2: [laughs]
S3: I like it like that. It looks better like that.

On the page, at first glance, this transcript based on a tape-recording of informal conversation can look bitty and incoherent. But when read over and out loud a few times (ideally with one person for each voice), it becomes clear that there is an intricate interplay of individuals and a group interdependence is being built up. Partly this has to do with a shared world of references and activities, and partly it has to do with shared words: words passed back and forth, swapped, suspended, reinforced, and elaborated. ('. . . + . . .' indicates an interrupted but sustained speech). Common objects and much laughter are obviously crucial. This is conversation as open dialogue rather than covert monologue. Individual displays of wit add spice, but the basic dynamic is one of collaborative participation-observation and cumulative 'co-creation'. Such things are only partly recoverable from the transcript (the words on the page); they could only be fully experienced and appreciated there and then, *in the event*. That said, in such cases, it may well be argued that we are dealing with 'the art of talk', even 'a poetry of talk'. (These last two phrases and the above transcript from the CANCODE corpus of conversational English are reproduced and analysed by Ronald Carter in his *Language and Creativity: The Art of Common Talk*, London, Routledge, 2004: 6–9, 102–9.)

WILLY RUSSELL, from *Educating Rita,* Act I, Scene 1, first stage performance Royal Shakespeare Company, 1980; film 1983

[Rita is a 'mature student' who has enrolled on an Open University course in English. Frank has been assigned as her tutor.]

RITA: You've got to challenge death an' disease. I read this poem about fightin' death . . .

FRANK: Ah – Dylan Thomas . . .

RITA: No. Roger McGough. It was about this old man who runs away from hospital an' goes out on the ale. He gets pissed an' stands in the street shoutin' an' challengin' death to come out an' fight. It's dead good.

FRANK: Yes, I don't think I know the actual piece you mean . . .

RITA: I'll bring y' the book – it's great.

FRANK: Thank you.

RITA: You probably won't think it's any good.

FRANK: Why?

RITA: It's the sort of poetry you can understand.

FRANK: Ah. I see.

[RITA *begins looking idly round the room.*]

FRANK: Can I offer you a drink?

RITA: What of?

FRANK: Scotch?

RITA: [*going to the bookcase*] Y' wanna be careful with that stuff, it kills y' brain cells.

FRANK: But you'll have one? [*He gets up and goes to the small table.*]

RITA: All right. It'll probably have a job findin' my brain.

FRANK: [*pouring the drinks*] Water?

RITA: [*looking at the bookcase*] Yeh, all right. [*She takes a copy of 'Howards End' from the shelf.*] What's this like?

[FRANK *goes over to* RITA, *looks at the title of the book and then goes back to the drinks.*]

FRANK: *Howards End*?

RITA: Yeh. It sounds filthy, doesn't it? E.M. Foster.

FRANK: Forster.

RITA: Oh yeh. What's it like?

FRANK: Borrow it. Read it.

RITA: Ta. I'll look after it. [*She moves back towards the desk.*] If I pack the course in I'll post it to y'.

[FRANK *comes back to the desk with drinks.*]

FRANK: [*handing her the mug*]: Pack it in? Why should you do that?

[RITA *puts her drink down on the desk and puts the copy of 'Howards End' in her bag.*]

RITA: I just might. I might decide it was a soft idea.

FRANK: [*Looking at her*]: Mm. Cheers. If – erm – you're already contemplating 'packing it in', why did you enrol in the first place?

RITA: Because I wanna know.

FRANK: What do you want to know?
RITA: Everything.
FRANK: Everything? That's rather a lot, isn't it? Where would you like to start?

Russell (b.1947) left school at 15, saw himself as 'a kid from the 'D' stream, a piece of factory fodder' (Russell 1988: 162). He then did a variety of manual jobs, including hairdressing, but saw a play by John McGrath and decided to become a playwright. He is also the author of *Shirley Valentine* (1987) and many other scripts for stage and TV. In the film of the present play Julie Walters played Rita, and Michael Caine played Frank. Russell was awarded an honorary MA in 1983 by the Open University in recognition of his work as a playwright. (Text from W. Russell, *Educating Rita and Other Plays*, London, Methuen, 1988: 172–3.)

LLOYD JONES, *Mister Pip*, 2006

[Matilda, a young girl on an island in the Pacific, is being taught to understand English through readings from Dickens's *Great Expectations* by Mr Watts, the only white person on the island. Matilda later relays the story – and the English – to her mother at home.]

Great Expectations was next. We knew that. We followed Mr Watts with our eyes. We watched him pick the book up from his desk. Mabel's mum saw it too. She whispered something to Mr Watts behind her hand. We heard him say, 'Yes, of course. Of course.' We saw him gesture to an empty desk and Mabel's mum sat down to be read to from the greatest novel by the greatest English writer of the nineteenth century.

Over and above my own enjoyment I had to listen very carefully because later that night my mum would want an update on Pip. I paid special attention to Mr Watts' pronunciation. I liked to surprise my mum with a new word she didn't know. What I didn't know at the time was all of us kids were carrying instalments of *Great Expectations* back to our families. [. . .]

A rimy morning was the phrase I decided to bring home with me. I used it now to create the picture of Pip carrying the pork pie and files off to the convict Magwitch waiting in the marshes. 'It was a rimy morning . . .'

I paused, wickedly, in the dark for my mother to ask what it meant. All she did was to breathe more sternly as if she knew my mind and what I was up to.

Earlier in the day I had stuck up my hand for the very first time. I didn't wave it around like Mabel did. I waited patiently until Mr Watts nodded. I started in the usual way.

'My name is Matilda.'

'Yes, Matilda,' said Mr Watts.

'What is a rimy morning?'

'A rimy morning is a frosty morning. It is a word you don't hear much anymore.' He smiled. [. . .]

But that was the last time she asked to hear an instalment from *Great Expectations*. And I blame 'a rimy morning'. Although she didn't say so I knew she thought I was showing off; and that I was biting off a bigger piece of the world than she could handle with language like 'a rimy morning'. She didn't want to encourage me by asking questions. She didn't want me to go deeper into that other world. She worried she would lose her Matilda to Victorian England.

Jones (b.1955, New Zealand) is a novelist and short story writer who won the Commonwealth Writers' Prize for Best Book (2006) for the present novel, which is here taken from *Mister Pip*,

London: John Murray, 2008: 27–30. This creative (and educational) re-use of Dickens's *Great Expectations* (1860–1) is worth comparing with Peter Carey's novel *Jack Maggs* (1997), which recasts the story through Magwitch, the convict returned from Australia. For the opening of Dickens's novel in which Pip introduces himself, see below, 5.4.5.

JEREMY JACOBSON, 'The Post-modern Lecture', 1999

Dr Martin Lindsey Minelli laconically muses on modernity
He is precise and roundabout,
He is bony and sparse,
He is milk-made:
His hair, his eyebrows, his eyelashes are as milky as milk;   5
He is wrapped in milk paper
And his mouth spurts out sentences like an udder.
They splash on the table, spread out, then gather in puddles.
Long tongues lusting after theory
Lap them up but the words spurt so fast,   10
The puddles become a pool, the pool a lake.
The audience take to boats and bob up and down on a foam of phrases,
Scooping up curdled words from the deep with buckets.

There are more names than words:
Names upon names: 15
Foucault and Fiedler,
Kristeva, Kuhn and Klinkowitz,
Barthes, Baudrillard, Britten and Bhabha;
Bhabha is the most beloved of Dr Minelli's names –
Who is this Bhabha?   20
Ali Baba of the thieves or Babar the Elephant Bhabha?

My boat has sprung a leak, torpedoed by a sharp quotation;
I try to bail out the coagulating names but they stick in my bucket;
I sink in a language bog, gulping.
The words are rancid in my mouth,   25
They take me in.

Jacobson (born in Cornwall) works for the British Council as a programme organiser for Language and Literature. The text comes from *Poetry as a Foreign Language*, ed. Martin Bates, East Linton: White Adder Press, 1999: 100, which, as its subtitle indicates, includes many poems connected with the teaching and learning of English as a Foreign or Second Language. Also see POSTMODERNISM and, for Homi Bhabha, POSTCOLONIALISM.

5.3.2 Novel voices

JANE AUSTEN, opening of *Pride and Prejudice*, 1797, pub. 1813

It is a truth universally acknowledged, that a single man in possession of a good fortune, must be in want of a wife.

However little known the feelings or views of such a man may be on his first entering a neighbourhood, this truth is so well fixed in the minds of the surrounding families, that he is considered as the rightful property of some one or other of their daughters.

'My dear Mr. Bennet,' said his lady to him one day, 'have you heard that Netherfield Park is let at last?'

Mr Bennet replied that he had not.

'But it is,' returned she; 'for Mrs Long has just been here, and she told me all about it.'

Mr Bennet made no answer.

'Do you not want to know who has taken it?' cried his wife impatiently.

'You want to tell me, and I have no objection to hearing it.'

This was invitation enough.

'Why, my dear, you must know, Mrs Long says that Netherfield is taken by a young man of large fortune from the north of England; that he came down on Monday in a chaise and four to see the place, and was so much delighted with it that he agreed with Mr Morris immediately; that he is to take possession before Michaelmas, and some of his servants are to be in the house by the end of next week.'

Austen (1775–1817) was a rector's daughter who lived most of her life in moderately well-to-do circumstances in Hampshire. According to one commentator, 'Her life was conspicuous for its lack of event – allowing **biographers** to make it a study in quiet contemplation or quiet frustration' (Ousby 1992: 49). Her novels are sometimes referred to as 'classic **realist**', but are notable for their subtle shifts in **point of view**, irony and 'rounded' **characterisation**.

AMOS TUTUOLA, from *The Palm-Wine Drinkard*, 1952, pub. 1987

[A man hears the character and destiny of his son interpreted by the Babalawo ('doctor') on the basis of the child's 'esent'aye' – literally 'footprint in the earth'. Two other 'characters' have already been predicted in this way.]

But then it was 'the great grief which droops the heads of elders' for Kimi Adugbo when he heard the bad 'esent'aye' of his child that morning. He was so sad that his mouth rejected food and drink, and great depression overwhelmed him immediately. Even the grief was overmuch for him so that he was unable to thank the Babalawo when he was leaving for his house that morning. After a few days, however, Kimi Adugbo accepted his fate and then he continued to be as cheerful to the people as he was before the 'esent'aye' of his child was read to him.

When Kimi Adugbo's child became eight days old, he reluctantly gave him a name which was ALAGEMO. The meaning of this name 'Alagemo' is chameleon worshipper. But Kimi Adugbo named this his child in proverb, 'The Agemo dancer said that he had done all he could to train his child how to dance. But if he does not know how to dance, that will be his fault.'

Moreover, his child was born in the month of Agemo. But now it is known that the prince of Oba chose the destiny of poverty and wretchedness, the daughter of the Otun Oba chose the destiny of harmful brawls, while the boy of Kimi Adugbo chose the destiny of the multifarious evil characters from Creator before the three of them were coming to earth.

Tutuola's tales are largely based upon Yoruba traditions circulating orally in his native Nigeria. The underlying conception of **character** and the whole pacing and texture of the **narrative** (including frequent appeals to the **authority** of proverbs) are far different from those in the Western mainstream novel. So are the **myths** and social practices referred to – here surrounding the act of naming. (Text from A. Tutuola, *The Palm Wine Drinkard*, London, Faber & Faber, 1987: 18–19.)

RODDY DOYLE, from *Paddy Clarke ha ha ha*, 1993

[The story of Paddy Clarke, a ten-year-old in Dublin in 1968. Paddy/Patrick is the narrator.]

They always talked during The News; they talked about the news. Sometimes it wasn't really talk, not conversation, just comments.
—Bloody eejit.
—Yes.
  I was able to tell when my da was going to call someone a bloody eejit; his chair creaked. It was always a man and he was always saying something to an interviewer.
—Who asked him?
  The interviewer had asked him but I knew what my da meant. Sometimes I got there before him.
—Bloody eejit.
—Good man, Patrick.
  My ma didn't mind me saying Bloody when The News was on. The News was boring but sometimes I watched it properly, all of it. I thought that the Americans were fighting gorillas in Vietnam; that was what it sounded like. But it didn't make any other kind of sense. The Israelis were always fighting the Arabs and the Americans were fighting the gorillas. It was nice that the gorillas had a country of their own, not like the zoo, and the Americans were killing them for it. There were Americans getting killed as well. They had helicopters. Mekong Delta. Demilitarised zone. Tet Offensive. The gorillas in the zoo didn't look like they'd be hard to beat in a war. They were nice and old looking, brainy looking, and their hair was dirty. Their arms were brilliant; I'd have loved arms like that. I'd never been on the roof. Kevin had, and his da had killed him when he found out about it when he got home, and he'd only been on the kitchen roof, the flat bit. I was up for the gorillas even though two of my uncles and aunties lived in America. I'd never seen them. They sent us ten dollars, me and Sinbad, one Christmas. I couldn't remember what I got with my five dollars.

Doyle was born in Dublin in 1958. While lecturing he wrote his first **novel** *The Commitments* (1988), which was adapted into a **film** with music in 1991. (Text from R. Doyle, *Paddy Clarke ha ha ha*, London, Secker and Warburg, 1993: 226–7, which won the Booker Prize that year.)

JAMES KELMAN, *How Late it Was, How Late*, 1994

[The story of an unemployed ex-convict who returns to his native Glasgow, goes blind and finds himself out on the street.]

Ah fuck it man stories, stories, life's full of stories, they're there to help ye out, when ye're in trouble, deep shit, they come to the rescue, and one thing ye learn in life is stories, Sammy's head was fucking full of them, he had met some bastards in his time; it's no as if he was auld either cause he wasnay he was only thirty-eight, he just seemed aulder, cause of the life he had led; when ye come to think about it, the life he had led. [. . .] Maybe he should go to Glancy's. It was an idea. Bound to be some cunt there that would lend him a couple of quid; even auld fucking Morris behind the bar, that crabbit auld bastard, even he would help Sammy out surely to fuck. Nay eyes man know what I'm saying nay fucking eyes! Jesus Christ almighty! Okay relax. The traffic was fierce but and he had to cross this road and there was nay chance of crossing this road, no on his fucking tod, it wasnay fucking possible; out the question.

Patience was a virtue right enough.

Patience. Come on ya bastards! He started kicking his heel against the kerb, keeping his head down for some reason. I'm blind, he said in the offchance somebody was there. Cause there was bound to be. Nay takers but. Patience, ye had to learn it. How to just bloody stand there. What was that song . . . ? Fucking song man what was it again?

Voices at last. He kicked the kerb again. Could ye give me a hand across the street? he said.

What?

I cannay see. I'm blind.

Ye're blind?

Aye.

Kelman was born in Glasgow in 1946 and still lives there. *How Late it Was, How Late* won the 1994 Booker Prize. This prompted much heated (but not always illuminated) comment on the novel's allegedly gratuitous swearing. There was also much more or less overt disapproval of its realisation of a Glaswegian **accent** (compare Leonard, 5.1.4), and a cry for **standards** to be maintained in language, behaviour and much else. (Text from J. Kelman, *How Late it Was, How Late*, London, Secker and Warburg, 1994: 52–3.)

5.3.3   Voice–play, dream–drama

DYLAN THOMAS, *Under Milk Wood: A Play for Voices*, radio broadcast 1954

[Dreams, dreamers and voices mingle in the night sky over a Welsh seaside town.]

FIRST VOICE

From where you are you can hear, in Cockle Row in the spring, moonless night, Miss Price, dressmaker and sweetshop-keeper, dream of

SECOND VOICE

her lover, tall as the town clock tower, Samson-syrup-gold-maned, whacking thighed and piping hot, thunderbolt-bass'd and barnacle-breasted, flailing up the cockles with his eyes like blowlamps and scooping low over her lonely loving hotwaterbottled body . . .

MR EDWARDS

Myfanwy Price!

MISS PRICE

Mr Mog Edwards!

MR EDWARDS

I am a draper mad with love. I love you more than all the flannelette and calico, candlewick, dimity, crash and merino, tussore, cretonne, crepon, muslin, poplin, ticking and twill in the whole Cloth Hall of the world. I have come to take you away to my Emporium on the hill, where the change hums on wires. Throw away your little bedsocks and your Welsh wool knitted jacket, I will lie by your side like the Sunday roast.

MISS PRICE

I will knit you a wallet of forget-me-not blue, for the money to be comfy. I will warm your heart by the fire so that you can slip it in under your vest when the shop is closed.

MR EDWARDS

Myfanwy, Myfanwy, before the mice gnaw at your bottom drawer will you say

MISS PRICE

Yes, Mog, yes, Mog, yes, yes, yes.

MR EDWARDS

And all the bells of the tills of the town shall ring for our wedding.
[*Noise of money-tills and chapel bells*]

Thomas (1914–53) was a charismatic reader of his own poetry and also a script-writer for BBC radio. *Under Milk Wood* (first broadcast 1954) is one of the **classics** of radio **drama** precisely because it blends highly visual **imagery** with highly musical **speech**. It also both reinforced and at the same time humorously mocked a stereotypical image of Welsh people and Anglo-Welsh accents. There is hardly any Welsh as such in the play, and Thomas lived the second half of his short life outside Wales, chiefly in London. (Text from D. Thomas, *The Dylan Thomas Omnibus*, London, Phoenix Orion, 1995.)

SAMUEL BECKETT, opening of *Not I*, performed 1972 (author's stage directions)

Stage in darkness but for MOUTH, upstage audience right, about 8 feet above stage level, faintly lit from close-up and below, rest of face in shadow. Invisible microphone. AUDITOR, downstage audience left, tall standing figure, sex undeterminable, enveloped from head to foot in loose black djellaba [North African cloak], with hood, fully faintly lit, standing on invisible podium about 4 feet high shown by attitude alone to be facing diagonally across stage intent on MOUTH, dead still throughout but for four brief movements where indicated. See Note.

---

[1] Movement: this consists in simple sideways raising of arms from sides and their falling back, in a gesture of helpless compassion. It lessens with each recurrence till scarcely perceptible at third. There is just enough pause to contain it as MOUTH recovers from vehement refusal to relinquish third person.

As house lights down MOUTH's voice unintelligible behind curtain. House lights out.
Voice continues unintelligible behind curtain, 10 seconds. With rise of curtain ad-libbing
from text as required leading when curtain fully up and attention sufficient into:

MOUTH: . . . out . . . into this world . . . this world . . . tiny little thing . . . before its
time . . . in a godfor- . . . what? . . . girl? . . . yes . . . tiny little girl
. . . into this . . . out into this . . . before her time . . . godforsaken hole
called . . . called . . . no matter . . . parents unknown . . . unheard of . . .
he having vanished . . . thin air . . . no sooner buttoned up his breeches
. . . she similarly . . . eight months later . . . almost to the tick . . . so no
love . . . spared that . . . no love such as normally vented on the . . .
speechless infant . . . in the home . . . no . . . nor indeed for that matter
any of any kind . . . no love of any kind . . . at any subsequent stage . . . so typical
affair . . . nothing of any note till coming up to sixty when– . . .
what? . . . seventy? . . . good God! . . . coming up to seventy . . . wandering in
a field . . . looking aimlessly for cowslips . . . to make a ball . . . a few
steps then stop . . . stare into space . . . then on . . . a few more . . . stop
and stare again . . . so on . . . drifting around . . . when suddenly . . .
gradually . . . all went out . . . all that early April morning light . . . and
she found herself in the – . . . what? . . . who? . . . no! . . . she! . . . [*Pause and
Movement.*[1]] . . . found herself in the dark . . . and if not exactly . . .
insentient . . . insentient . . . for she could still hear the buzzing . . .
so-called . . . in the ears . . . and a ray of light came and went . . . came
and went . . . such as the moon might cast . . . drifting . . . in and out of
cloud . . . but so dulled . . . feeling . . . feeling so dulled . . . she did not
know . . . what position she was in . . . imagine! . . . what position she
was in! . . . whether standing . . . or sitting . . . but the brain– . . . what? . . . kneeling?
. . . yes . . . whether standing . . . or sitting . . . or kneeling . . .
but the brain – . . . what? . . . lying? . . . yes . . . whether standing . . .
or sitting . . . or kneeling . . . or lying . . . but the brain still . . . still . . . in a
way . . . for her first thought was . . . oh long after . . . sudden flash . . .
brought up as she had been to believe . . . with the other waifs . . . in a
merciful . . . [*Brief laugh*] . . . God . . . [*Good laugh*] . . .

Beckett (1906–89), best known for *Waiting for Godot* (1953), is commonly labelled an **absurdist** dramatist with a tendency, especially in his novels, to use Modernist 'stream of consciousness' techniques. He is also generally considered a non- or anti-**realist** writer. Such labels are initially useful. However, they also conceal (or indirectly reveal) questions about what one considers to be 'normal' or 'real' in the first place. They also beg questions about the relations between **identities** and **roles** on and off the stage. Even an ostensibly incoherent **text** can be made sense of in some **context** and some **intertextual** frame of reference. Every **foreground** has a variety of immediate and remote **backgrounds**. Every **monologue** presupposes or prompts a **dialogue**. Beckett won the Nobel Prize for Literature in 1969. (Text from S. Beckett, *Collected Plays*, London, Faber & Faber, 1992: 376–7.)

ATHOL FUGARD, from *Boesman and Lena*, performed 1969

[A coloured woman and man share the memory of an enforced eviction from *pondoks* (shanty shacks) by *donner* (bulldozers).]

LENA: It was the same story for all of us. Once is enough if it's a sad one.
BOESMAN: Sad story? Those two that had the fight because somebody grabbed the wrong *broek* [trousers]? The *ou* [guy] trying to catch his donkey? Or that other one running around with his porridge looking for a fire to finish cooking it? It was bioscope, man! And I watched it. Beginning to end, the way it happened. *I* saw it. *Me.*
The women and children sitting there with their snot and tears. The *pondoks* falling. The men standing, looking, as the yellow *donner* pushed them over and then staring at the pieces when they were the only things left standing. I saw all that! The whiteman stopped the bulldozer and smoked a cigarette. I saw that too.

[*another act* [*i.e. he 'play-acts' as he has previously*]]

'Ek se' [Hey, pal], my baas . . . !' He threw me the *stompie* [cigarette butt]. 'Dankie, baas.'
LENA: They made a big pile and burnt everything.

Fugard (b.1932) developed his plays through 'poor **theatre**' conditions with groups from black townships in South Africa. *Boesman and Lena* was written at a time when apartheid was vicious and public criticism of injustice by blacks or whites (let alone both together) was far more dangerous to the individuals concerned than to the state. The play is a modern **tragi-comedy** of resilience in the face of systematic brutalisation. It celebrates the forging of **identity** even when people are treated as nonentities. The translated **dialect** words derive chiefly from Dutch Afrikaans. (Full text in D. Walder (ed.) *Athol Fugard: Selected Plays*, Oxford, Oxford University Press, 1987: 228.)

MARTIN McDONAGH, *The Pillowman*, 2003

[Katurian, an author being held on suspicion of carrying out child murders like those depicted in his stories, recounts the story of his own childhood. Theatrically, this whole scene is framed within an interrogation in which his two interrogators are still visible on stage.]

SCENE TWO

Katurian, sitting on a bed amongst toys, paints, pens, paper, in an approximation of a child's room, next door to which there is another identical room, perhaps made of glass, but padlocked and totally dark. Katurian narrates the short story which he and the mother, in diamonds, and father, in a goatee and glasses, enact.

Katurian Once upon a time there was a little boy upon whom his mother and father showered nothing but love, kindness, warmth, all that stuff. He had his own little room in a big house in the middle of a pretty forest. He wanted for nothing: all the toys in the world were his; all the paints, all the books, paper, pens. All the seeds of creativity were implanted in him from an early age and it was writing that became his first love: short stories, fairy tales, little novels, all happy, colourful things about bears and piglets and angels and so forth, and some of them were good, some of them were very good. His parents' experiment had worked. The *first part* of his parents' experiment had worked.

The Mother and Father, after caressing and kissing Katurian, enter the adjoining room, and leave our sight.

It was the night of his seventh birthday that the nightmares first started. The room next door to his own room had always been kept bolted and padlocked for reasons the boy was never quite sure of but never quite questioned until the low whirring of drills, the scritchety-scratch of bolts being tightened, the dull fizz of unknown things electrical, and the muffled screams of a small gagged child began to emanate through its thick brick walls. On a nightly basis. (*to Mother, in a boy's voice*) 'What were all those noises last night, Mama?' (*normal voice*) he'd ask, after each long, desperate, sleepless night, to which his mother would ever reply . . .

Mother Oh little Kat, that's just your wonderful but overactive imagination playing tricks on you.
Katurian (*boy's voice*) Oh. Do all little boys of my age hear such sounds of abomination nightly?
Mother No, my darling. Only the extraordinarily talented ones.
Katurian (*boy's voice*) Oh. Cool. (*normal voice*) And that was that. And the boy kept on writing, and his parents kept encouraging him with the utmost love, but the sounds of the whirrs and screams kept going on . . .

In the nightmare semi-dark of the adjoining room, it appears for a second as if a child of eight, strapped to the bed, is being tortured with drills and sparks.
. . . and his stories got darker and darker and darker. They got better and better, due to all of the love and encouragement, as is often the case, but they got darker and darker, due to the constant sound of child-torture, as is also often the case.
Light in the adjoining room fades out. The Mother, Father and child can no longer be seen. Katurian clears all the toys etc. away.
It was on the day of his fourteenth birthday, a day he was waiting to hear the results of a story competition he was short-listed for, that a note slipped out from under the door of the locked room . . .
A note in red writing slips under door. Katurian picks it up.
. . . a note which read: 'They have loved you and tortured me for seven straight years for no reason other than as an artistic experiment, an artistic experiment which has worked. You don't write about little green pigs any more, do you?' The note was signed 'Your brother', and the note was written in blood.
Katurian axes into the next-door room.
He axed through the door to find . . .
Lights rise on Mother and Father alone in room, with drills and taped noises as described.
. . . his parents sitting in there, smiling, alone; his father is doing some drill noises; his mother doing some muffled screams of a gagged child; they had a little pot of pig's blood between them, and his father told him to look at the other side of the blood-written note. The boy did, and found out he'd won the fifty-pounds first prize in the short-story competition. They all laughed. The second part of his parents' experiment was complete.
The Mother and Father lie down to sleep side by side on Katurian's bed. Lights fade on them.
They moved house soon after that and though the nightmare sounds had ended, his stories stayed strange and twisted but good, and he was able to thank his parents for the weirdness they'd put him through, and years later, on the day that his first book was published, he decided to revisit his childhood home for the first time since he's left. He idled around his old bedroom, and all the toys and paints still littered around there . . .
Katurian enters the adjoining room, sits on the bed.
. . . then he went into the room beside it that still had the old dusty drills and padlocks and electrical cord lying around, and he smiled at the insanity of the very idea of it all, but he lost his smile when he came across . . .
The bed feels terribly lumpy. He pulls the mattress off to reveal the horrific corpse of a child . . .

. . . the corpse of a fourteen-year-old child that had been left to rot in there, barely a bone of which wasn't broken or burned, in whose hand there lay a story scrawled in blood. And the boy read that story, a story that could only have been written under the most sickening of circumstances, and it was the sweetest, gentlest thing he'd ever come across, but what was even worse, it was better than anything he himself had ever written. Or ever would.

Katurian takes a lighter and sets the story alight.

So he burnt the story, and he covered his brother back up, and he never mentioned a word of what he had seen to anybody. Not to his parents, not to his publishers, not to anybody. The final part of his parents' experiment was over.

Lights fade in adjoining room, but rise slightly on the bed where his Mother and Father are still lying.

Katurian's story 'The Writer and the Writer's Brother' ended there in fashionably downbeat mode, without touching upon the equally downbeat but somewhat more self-incriminating details of the truer story, that after he'd read the blood-written note and broken into the next-door room it was, of course . . .

The child's corpse sits bolt upright in bed, breathing heavily.

. . . his brother he found in there, alive, as such, but brain-damaged beyond repair, and that that night, whilst his parents were sleeping, the fourteen-year-old birthday boy held a pillow over his father's head for a little while . . .

Katurian suffocates his Father with a pillow. His body spasms, then dies. He taps his Mother on the shoulder. She opens her sleepy eyes to see her open-mouthed dead husband.

. . . and, after waking her a moment just to let her see her dead blue husband, he held a pillow over his mother's head for a little while, too.

Katurian, face blank, holds a pillow over his screaming Mother's head. Her body spasms wildly, but he forcefully keeps the pillow down, as the lights slowly fade to black.

McDonagh was born to Irish parents in London in 1970, and currently lives between there and New York. His first plays, the 'Leenane Trilogy' (1996–7), are black yet lyrical comedies of homicidal life and death in a semi-mythical, brutalised and commercialised rural Ireland that the author has imagined but hardly visited. He wrote the screen play for *In Bruges* (2009), which follows the comic and grotesque responses to Belgium of two hit-men forced to take a holiday there while waiting for their next commission – which turns out to be one killing the other. Theatrically, McDonagh's work can be aligned with Artaud's 'Theatre of Cruelty'; linguistically and lyrically with Synge's hard-bitten humorously carnivalesque flights about Ireland (picked up in McDonagh's 'Aran Island Trilogy, 1996–); and filmically with the violently black humour of Tarantino. In the present play, *The Pillowman*, the violent farce (here more violent than farcical) is placed in an unnamed Middle European totalitarian state and framed as an interrogation. It was first performed at the National Theatre in 2003. The above passage is the whole of Scene 2 and is taken from M. McDonagh, *The Pillowman*, London: Faber & Faber, 2003: 31–5.

ALICE OSWALD, *Dart*, 2002

[A voice recreates the experience of the river Dart through those who work and live by it.]

(And then I saw the river's dream-self walk
down to the ringmesh netting by the bridge
to feel the edge of shingle brush the edge

of sleep and float a world up like a cork
out of its body's liquid dark.
Like in a waterfall one small twig caught
catches a stick, a straw, a sack, a mesh
of leaves, a fragile wickerwork of floodbrash,
I saw all things catch and reticulate
into this dreaming of the Dart
that sinks like a feather falls, not quite
in full possession of its weight)

I wake wide in a swim of
seagulls, scavengers, monomaniac, mad
rubbish pickers, mating blatantly, screaming

and slouch off scumming and flashing and hatching flies
to the milk factory, staring at routine things:

looking down the glass lines: bottles on belts going round bends. Watching out for breakages,
working nights. Building up prestige. Me with my hands under the tap, with my brain coated in
a thin film of milk. In the fridge, in the warehouse, wearing ear-protectors.

I'm in a rationalised set-up, a super plant. Everything's stainless and risk can be spun off by
centrifugal motion: blood, excrement, faecal matter from the farms

have you forgotten the force orders the world's fields
and sets all cities in their sites, this nomad
pulling the sun and moon, placeless in all places,
born with her stones, with her circular bird-voice,
carrying everywhere her quarters?

I'm in milk, 600,000,000 gallons a week.

processing, separating, blending. Very precise quantities of raw milk added to skim, piped into
silos, little screwed outlets pouring out milk to be sampled. Milk clarified milk homogenised and
pasteurised and when it rains, the river comes under the ringmesh netting, full of non-potable
water. All those pathogens and spoilage organisms! We have to think of our customers. We take
pride in safety, we discard thirty bottles either side of a breakage. We've got weights and checks
and trading standards

and a duck's nest in the leat with four blue eggs

and all the latest equipment, all stainless steel so immaculate you can see your soul in it, in a
hairnet, in white overalls and safety shoes.

It's a rush, a sploosh of sewage, twenty thousand cubic metres being pumped in, stirred and
settled out and wasted off, looped back, macerated, digested, clarified and returned to the river.
I'm used to the idea. I fork the screenings out – a stink-mass of loopaper and whathaveyou, rags
cotton buds, you name it. I measure the intake through a flume and if there's too much, I waste
it off down the stormflow, it's not my problem.

When you think of all the milk we get from Unigate, fats and proteins and detergents foaming up and the rain and all the public sewers pumping in all day, it's like a prisoner up to his neck in water in a cell with only a hand-pump to keep himself conscious, the whole place is always on the point of going under.

So we only treat the primary flow, we keep it moving up these screws, we get the solids settled out and then push the activated sludge back through. Not much I can do.

I walk on metal grilles above smelly water, I climb the ladder, I stand on a bridge above a brown lagoon, little flocs of sludge and clarified liquor spilling over the edge of the outer circle. The bridge is turning very slowly, sweeping the spill-off round and I'm thinking illicit sneaking thoughts – no one can see me up here, just me and machinery and tiny organisms.

I'm in charge as far as Dartmoor, the metabolism of the whole South West, starting with clouds and flushing down through buildings and bodies into this underground grid of pipes, all ending up with me up here on my bridge – a flare of methane burning off blue at one end of the works and a culvert of clean water discharging out the other end, twenty BOD, nine ammonia, all the time, as and when

Oswald (b.1966) currently lives in Devon near the river Dart. This long combination of poetry and prose follows the course of the river from where it springs to where it flows into the sea. The present passage is from just over half way along. In her preface, the author describes the process of composition thus: 'This poem is made from the language of people who live and work on the Dart. Over the past two years I've been recording conversations with people who know the river. I've used these records as life-models from which to sketch out a series of characters – linking their voices into a sound-map of the river, a songline from the source to the sea. There are indications in the margin where one voice changes into another. These do not refer to real people or even fixed fictions. All voices should be read as the river's mutterings.' The poem was composed as part of the Poetry Society's Poetry Places project funded by the Arts Council of England's 'Arts for Everyone' scheme; it won the T.S. Eliot Poetry Prize. In 2009 she published *A Sleepwalk on the Severn* and *Weeds and Wildflowers* which may also be compared with Gross's 'Severn Song', 5.1.5 (Text from Alice Oswald, *Dart*, London: Faber & Faber, 2002: 28–30.)

5.3.4 'I'dentity in the balance – selves and others

JOHN CLARE, 'I am', composed *c.* 1844, pub. 1865

> I am – yet what I am, none cares or knows;
>   My friends forsake me like a memory lost;
> I am the self-consumer of my woes –
>   They rise and vanish in oblivion's host
> Like shadows in love-frenzied stifled throes   5
> And yet I am, and live – like vapours tost
>
> Into the nothingness of scorn and noise,
>   Into the living sea of waking dreams,
> Where there is neither sense of life or joys,
>   But the vast shipwreck of my life's esteems   10

Even the dearest that I love the best
Are strange – nay, rather, stranger than the rest.

I long for scenes where man hath never trod
 A place where woman never smiled or wept
There to abide with my Creator, God,   15
 And sleep as I in childhood sweetly slept,
Untroubling and untroubled where I lie
The grass below – above the vaulted sky.

Clare (1793–1864) was the son of an agricultural labourer and himself one in youth. At that time the village of Helpston, Northamptonshire, where they lived, was 'enclosed' (i.e. parcelled up into private fields for farming and parkland) and the Clares were uprooted and left without regular work. Also at that time, Clare's relationship with a local farmer's daughter, Mary Joyce, was ended by her father. Clare apparently never adjusted to these calamities, even though he subsequently married, had children and achieved a passing literary success as a 'peasant poet'. Literacy was elementary or non-existent amongst farm labourers. 'Literariness' in such a person was judged remarkably quaint. From 1837 to 1841 Clare was in a private asylum in Epping. He escaped and walked back to Northampton, believing he was married to Mary Joyce. From 1841 till he died he was confined to Northampton General Lunatic Asylum. There he wrote this poem, which was posthumously published. For sample analysis, see PSYCHOLOGICAL APPROACHES, Example, pp. 153–5. (Text from G. Summerfield (ed.) *John Clare: Selected Poems*, London, Penguin, 1990: 311.)

EMILY DICKINSON, 'I'm Nobody' (c. 1861)

I'm Nobody! Who are you?
Are you – Nobody – too?
Then there's a pair of us?
Don't tell! They'd advertise – you know!

How dreary to be Somebody!
How public – like a Frog –
To tell one's name – the livelong June
To an admiring Bog!

Dickinson (1830–86), poet, Puritan, sceptic and recluse, was born and lived all her life in Amherst, Massachusetts. This is the text of the poem as retrieved from Dickinson's manuscripts and was not one of the handful of poems published in her lifetime. An activity exploring this text and other published versions of the poem, in and out of context, will appear @ 2.4. (Text from *The Complete Poems of Emily Dickinson*, ed. T. Johnson, Faber & Faber: London, 1970.)

ADRIENNE RICH, 'Dialogue', 1967

She sits with one hand poised against her head, the
other turning an old ring to the light
for hours our talk has beaten
like rain against the screens
a sense of August and heat-lightning   5

I get up, go to make tea, come back
we look at each other
then she says (and this is what I live through
over and over) – she says: *I do not know*
if sex is an illusion   10

I do not know
who I was when I did those things
or who I said I was
or whether I willed to feel
what I had read about   15
or who in fact was there with me
or whether I knew, even then
that there was doubt about these things

Rich, b.1929 in Baltimore, USA, has been strongly influential as poet, essayist and political commentator in the development of radical FEMINIST, and latterly lesbian feminist, writing. Her work is marked by a special interest in reclaiming LANGUAGE, exploring oppressive and repressive **silences** and in urging a re-vision of past, present and future hi/stories. For sample analysis, see FEMINISM, Example pp. 173–4. (Text from C. Rumens (ed.) *Making for the Open: Post-feminist Poetry*, 2nd edn, London, 1987: 73.)

ALAN HOLLINGHURST, from *The Swimming-Pool Library*, 1988

Though I didn't believe in such things, I was a perfect Gemini, a child of the ambiguous early summer, tugged between two versions of myself, one of them the hedonist and the other – a little in the background these days – an almost scholarly figure with a faintly puritanical set to the mouth. And there were deeper dichotomies, differing stories – one the 'account of myself', the sex-sharp little circuits of discos and pubs and cottages, the sheer crammed, single-minded repetition of my empty months; the other the 'romance of myself', which transformed all these mundanities with a protective glow, as if from my earliest days my destiny had indeed been charmed, so that I was both of the world and beyond its power, like the pantomime character Wordsworth describes, with 'Invisible' written on his chest.

At times my friend James became my other self, and told me off and tried to persuade me that I was not doing all I might. I was never good at being told off, and when he insisted that I should find a job, or even a man to settle down with, it was in so intimate and knowledgeable a way that I felt as if one half of me were accusing the other. It was from him, whom I loved more than anyone, that I most often heard the account of myself. He had even said lately in his diary that I was 'thoughtless' – he meant cruel, in the way I had thrown off a kid who had fallen for me and who irritated me to distraction; but then he got the idea into his head: does Will care about anybody? does Will ever really *think*? and so on and so forth. 'Of course I fucking think,' I muttered, though he wasn't there to hear me. And he gave a horrid little diagnosis: 'Will becoming more and more brutal, more and more sentimental.'

I was certainly sentimental with Arthur, deeply sentimental and lightly brutal, at one moment caressingly attentive, the next glutting him with sex, mindlessly – thoughtlessly. It was the most beautiful thing I could imagine – all the more so for our knowledge that we could never make a go of it together. Even among the straight lines of the Park I wasn't thinking straight – all the time I looped back to Arthur, was almost burdened by my need for him, and by the oppressive mildness of the day. The Park after all was only stilted countryside, its lake and trees inadequate reminders of those formative landscapes, the Yorkshire dales, the streams and watermeads of Winchester, whose influence was lost in the sexed immediacy of London life.

Hollinghurst (b.1954) taught English at the Universities of Oxford and London before becoming deputy editor of *The Times Literary Supplement*. His *The Swimming-Pool Library* (here from pp. 4–5 of the Penguin edition) draws together the narratives of two 'queer'/'gay' men (the terms themselves are part of the matter at issue): William Beckwith (born 1958 and featured here) and Lord Nantwich (born 1900). Through their overlapping yet palpably discontinuous and unreliable stories, sometimes conflating the **self** and **other** of the two narrators, the novel refracts a complex and contentious **history** of SEXUALITY in Britain spanning much of the twentieth century. Though stopping short of a direct address to AIDS, it has become something of a contemporary 'gay' **classic** (see Wolfreys 2001: 200–60).

5.4   CROSSINGS

5.4.1   Daffodils?

WILLIAM WORDSWORTH, 'I wandered lonely as a cloud', 1804

> I wandered lonely as a cloud
>   That floats on high o'er vales and hills
> When all at once I saw a crowd
>   A host, of golden daffodils;
> Beside the lake, beneath the trees,   5
> Fluttering and dancing in the breeze.
>
> Continuous as the stars that shine
>   And twinkle on the milky way,
> They stretched in never-ending line
>   Along the margin of a bay: 10
> Ten thousand saw I at a glance,
> Tossing their heads in sprightly dance.
>
> The waves beside them danced, but they
>   Outdid the sparkling waves in glee:
> A poet could not but be gay   15
>   In such a jocund company:
> I gazed – and gazed – but little thought
> What wealth the show to me had brought.
>
> For oft when on my couch I lie
>   In vacant or in pensive mood,   20
> They flash upon that inward eye
>   Which is the bliss of solitude;
> And then my heart with pleasure fills,
> And dances with the daffodils.

Wordsworth (1770–1850) dictated early drafts to Mary, his wife, and then to Dorothy, his sister, between 1802 and 1804. This poem was first published without the third verse in *Poems, in Two*

Volumes (1807). According to William's own notes which were dictated to Isabella Fenwick forty years later (1842–43), 'The best two lines in it are by Mary' (quoting ll.21–2). This poem has subsequently become one of the most popular and **classic** lyrics in English, as well one of the most influential examples of what Romantic poets do and of what **poetry** in general is. (For sample analyses, see 1.3 and 3.1, PRACTICAL CRITICISM, Example pp. 139.)

DOROTHY WORDSWORTH, *Grasmere Journals*, 15 April 1802

We got over into a field to avoid some cows – people working, a few primroses by the roadside, wood-sorrel flower, the anemone, scentless violets, strawberries, and that starry yellow flower which Mrs C. calls pile wort. When we were in the woods beyond Gorbarrow park we saw a few daffodils, close to the water side. We fancied that the lake had floated the seeds ashore and that the little colony had so sprung up. But as we went along there were more and yet more and at last under the boughs of the trees, we saw that there was a long belt of them along the shore, about the breadth of a country turn-pike road. I never saw daffodils so beautiful, they grew among the mossy stones about and about them, some rested their heads upon these stones as on a pillow for weariness and the rest tossed and reeled and danced and seemed as if they verily laughed with the wind that blew upon them over the lake, they looked so gay ever glancing ever changing.

Dorothy Wordsworth's *Grasmere Journals* (1800–3) were written without thought of publication and were not published till after her death in 1855. Their substance was freely shared with her brother William, often supplying him with prompts, reminders and even phrasing for his poetry. (Text from Abrams 2000, Vol. II: 391.)

LYNN PETERS, 'Why Dorothy Wordsworth is Not as Famous as her Brother'

'I wandered lonely as a . . .
They're in the top drawer, William,
Under your socks –
I wandered lonely as a –
No not that drawer, the top one.   5
I wandered by myself –
Well wear the ones you can find.
No, don't get overwought my dear,
I'm coming.

'One day I was out for a walk   10
When I saw this flock –
It can't be too hard, it had three minutes.
Well put some butter in it.
– This host of golden daffodils
As I was out for a stroll one –   15

'Oh you fancy a stroll, do you?
Yes all right, William, I'm coming.
It's on the peg. Under your hat.
I'll bring my pad, shall I, just in case
You want to jot something down?'   20

(from the *Virago Book of Wicked Verse*, London, 1992)

TV ADVERT for lager: 'Heineken refreshes the poets other beers can't reach'

Scene: A handsome young man in a frock coat is sitting on a mound, scratching his head and trying to write.

YOUNG MAN: I was rather lonely . . . [*He crosses it out.*]
I wandered around for a bit . . . !' [*He crosses it out again.*]
   [*Pauses and reaches for a glass and drinks from it. Sudden look of inspiration.*
   Cue rapturous symphonic music with sweeping strings.
   He jumps to his feet and, over the music, begins to declaim.]
I wandered lonely as a cloud
That floats on high o'er vales and hills . . .
   [*Camera pulls back and above to reveal him dancing – and still declaiming – among a field*
   of daffodils]
MALE VOICE-OVER: [*mature, faintly Germanic, cordial*] Only Heineken can do this. Because Heineken refreshes the *poets* other beers can't reach.
   [*Final close-up shot of Heineken can with glass of lager*]

One of a series of lager advertisements developed by Terry Lovelock, an advertising copywriter, and shown on British TV, 1974–89, continued 1991–. All are built round variations on the formula 'Heineken refreshes the parts (poets, pets, etc.) other beers can't reach'. (For sample analysis of all these 'Daffodils' passages, see 3.1.)

5.4.2   Mapping journeys

HARRY BECK, Map of London Underground, 1931 (faded original)

(See next item by Bryson for comment.)

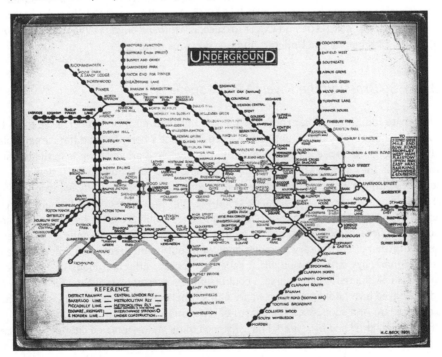

BILL BRYSON, from *Notes from a Small Island*, 1995

The London Underground Map. What a piece of perfection it is, created in 1931 by a forgotten hero named Harry Beck, an out-of-work draughtsman who realised that when you are under ground it doesn't matter where you are. Beck saw – and what an intuitive stroke this was – that as long as the stations were presented in their right sequence with their interchanges clearly delineated, he could freely distort scale, indeed abandon it altogether. He gave his map the orderly precision of an electrical wiring system, and in so doing created an entirely new, *imaginary* London that has very little to do with the disorderly geography of the city above. [. . .] The best part of Underground travel is that you never actually see the places above you. You have to imagine them. In other cities station names are unimaginative and mundane: Lexington Avenue, Potsdammerplatz, Third Street South. But in London the names sound sylvan and beckoning: Stamford Brook, Turnham Green, Bromley-by-Bow, Maida Vale, Drayton Park. That isn't a city up there, it's a Jane Austen novel. It's easy to imagine that you are shuttling about under a semi-mythic city from some golden, pre-industrial age. Swiss Cottage ceases to be a busy road junction and becomes instead a gingerbread dwelling in the midst of the great oak forest known as St John's Wood. Chalk Farm is an open space of fields where cheerful peasants in brown smocks cut and gather crops of chalk. Blackfriars is full of cowled and chanting monks, Oxford Circus has its big top, Barking is a dangerous place overrun with packs of wild dogs, Theydon Bois is a community of industrious Huguenot weavers, White City is a walled and turreted elysium built of the most dazzling ivory, and Holland Park is full of windmills.

The problem with losing yourself in these little reveries is that when you surface things are apt to be disappointing. I came up now at Tower Hill and there wasn't a tower and there wasn't a hill.

Bryson (b.1951, Iowa, USA) lived and worked in England for twenty years as a journalist, editor and writer, before moving back to the USA in 1997. As well as **travel writing,** he is the author of popular histories of LANGUAGE and CULTURE such as *Mother Tongue* (1996) and *Made in America* (1994). For Beck's map of the Underground, see previous item.

CARYL PHILLIPS, *Crossing the River*, 1993 (opening)

A desperate foolishness. The crops failed. I sold my children. I remember. I led them (two boys and a girl) along weary paths, until we reached the place where the mud flats are populated with crabs and gulls. Returned across the bar with the yawl, and prayed a while in the factory chapel. I watched as they huddled together and stared up at the fort, above which flew a foreign flag. Stood beneath the white-washed walls of the factory, waiting for the yawl to return and carry me back over the bar. In the distance stood the ship into whose keep I would soon condemn them. The man and his company were waiting to once again cross the bar. We watched a while. And then approached. *Approached by a quiet fellow.* Three children only. I jettisoned them at this point, where the tributary stumbles and swims out in all directions to meet the sea. *Bought 2 strong man-boys, and a proud girl.* I soiled my hands with cold goods in exchange for their warm flesh. A shameful intercourse. I could feel their eyes upon me. Wondering, why? I turned and journeyed back along the same weary paths. I believe my trade for this voyage has reached its conclusion. And soon after, the chorus of a common memory began to haunt me.

For two hundred and fifty years I have listened to the many-tongued chorus. And occasionally, among the restless voices, I have discovered those of my children. My Nash. My Martha. My

Travis. Their lives fractured. Sinking hopeful roots into difficult soil. For two hundred and fifty years I have longed to tell them: Children, I am your father. I love you. But understand. There are no paths in water. No signposts. There is no return. To a land trampled by the muddy boots of others. To a people encouraged to war among themselves. To a father consumed with guilt. You are beyond. Broken-off, like limbs from a tree. But not lost, for you carry within your bodies the seeds of new trees. Sinking your hopeful roots into difficult soil. And I, who spurned you, can blame only myself for my present misery. For two hundred and fifty years I have waited patiently for the wind to rise on the far bank of the river. For the drum to pound across the water. For the chorus to swell. Only then, if I listen closely, can I discover my lost children. A brief, painful communion. A desperate foolishness. The crops failed. I sold my children.

Phillips (b.1958) was born in St Kitts, brought up in Leeds, and now lives and teaches in the USA, at Yale and elsewhere. His work often explores the nature and history of post/colonialism and the consequences of global migration (e.g. *A Distant Shore*, 2003). The above passage is the Prologue to the book, which is reprised with variations in the middle and at the close (Text from *Crossing the River*, London: Vintage (1993) 2006: 1–2; also see pp. 124, 235–7.)

BILLY MARSHALL-STONEKING, 'Passage', 1990

The oldest man in the world wears shoes.
The oldest man in the world has a cowboy hat on his head.
The oldest man in the world speaks to me in English.
He rides in motor cars.
His body: fluid, capable – a perfect shock absorber.   5
One tooth knocked out in front, a red bandanna tied
around his neck, he names Names
as we bounce over the dirt track in the back
of a four-wheel drive.
'That tree is a digging stick   10
left by the giant woman who was looking for honey ants;
That rock, a dingo's nose;
There, on the mountain, is the footprint
left by Tjangara on his way to Ulamburra;
Here, the rockhole of Warnampi – very dangerous –   15
and the cave where the nyi-nyi women escaped
the anger of marapulpa – the spider.
Wati Kutjarra – the two brothers – travelled this way.
There, you can see one was tired
from too much lovemaking – the mark of his penis   20
dragging the ground;
Here, the bodies of the honey ant men
where they crawled from the sand –
no, they are not dead – they keep coming
from the ground, moving toward the water at Warumpi –   25
it has been like this for many years:
the Dreaming does not end; it is not like the whiteman's way.
What happened once happens again and again.
This is the law.

This is the power of the Song.   30
Through the singing we keep everything alive;
through the songs the spirits keep us alive.'
The oldest man in the world speaks
to the newest man in the world; my place
less exact than his.   35
We bump along together in the back of the truck
wearing shoes, belts, underwear.
We speak to each other in English
over the rumble of engine, over the roar of the wheels.
His body: a perfect shock absorber.   40

Marshall-Stoneking (b. America) now lives in Australia. For sample analysis, see POSTCOLONIALISM, Example pp. 195–8. (Text from L. Murray (ed.) *The New Oxford Book of Australian Verse*, 2nd edn, Melbourne and Oxford, Oxford University Press, 1991: 387–8.)

KATHLEEN JAMIE, 'Pathologies – A startling tour of our bodies', 2008

[The narrator is being shown the 'landscapes' of the human stomach through an electron microscope by a clinical pathologist.]

'Would you like to see more? You said you were interested in infections, I set aside a couple of infections for you . . .'

'You're very kind.'

This time the country beneath was a gorgeous sapphire blue. It had a north-facing shoreline, and a mile or so inland, so to speak, were regularly spaced ovals, turned with the narrow end towards the coast. They might have been craters, or even sports stadiums. Frank was describing it to me with his customary quiet level-headedness. He was speaking of 'columnar structures' but it took me a while to understand that he meant the ovals; they were sections cut horizontally through columns. These were acid-producing glands; we were in the lining of someone's stomach.

Between the oval structure were valleys, if you like, fanning down to the shore. Frank wanted to show me something in one of these valleys and I couldn't find it at first, it took several patient attempts – this microscope didn't have a cursor device to point at things. It was a very human moment, a collusion of landscape and language when one person tries to guide the other's gaze across a vista. And what vistas! River deltas and marshes, peninsulas and atolls. The unseen landscapes within. Looking down a microscope you might imagine you were privy to the secrets of the universe, some Gaian union between body and earth, but I dare say it's to do with our eyes. Hunter-gatherers that we are, adapted to look out over savannahs, into valleys from hillsides. Scale up the absurdly small until it looks like landscape, then we can do business.

'There!' said Frank. 'Isn't that a pastoral scene? They're grazing!'

I had it: six or seven very dark oval dots, still tiny, despite the magnification, were ranged across the blue valley, like musk oxen on tundra, seen from far above.

'This is *Helicobacter pylori* – they're bacteria. They irritate the stomach, the stomach produces too much acid, and so they cause stomach ulcers. Obvious as anything now, but they just weren't seen till 1984. It was an Australian pathologist who spotted the association between inflamed stomachs and these things. He was a bit of a crazy. No one took him seriously, no one believed stomach ulcers could be caused by bacteria. But . . . he found another crazy to work with and together they got the Nobel Prize. Probably saved thousands and thousands of lives. The thing is, you perceive what you expect, what you're accustomed to. Sometimes it needs a fresh eye, or a looser mind . . .'

'You can die of stomach ulcers?'

'Yes. You bleed.'

'Grazing' was the word. Although the landscape was bright blue – a stain called Giemsa – it was an image you might find in a Sunday night wildlife documentary. Pastoral, but wild too. So close to home, but people had walked on the moon before these things were discovered, free in the wilderness of our stomachs.

Jamie (b.1962) comes from Renfrewshire in Scotland, is a poet, travel-writer and environmentalist, and is Chair of Creative Writing at the University of Stirling. The above passage is from an essay featuring a meeting with Professor Frank Carey, consultant pathologist at Ninewells Hospital, Dundee; it is illustrated with colour photographs. (Text from *The New Nature Writing*, ed., Jason Cowley, London and New York: Granta, 2008: 44–5.)

5.4.3   Translations/Transformations

BRIAN FRIEL, from *Translations*, first performed in Derry, 1980

[Captain Lancey is a British army officer in Ireland in August 1833 who has the task of making the first detailed Ordnance Survey maps of County Donegal. In the process, the Irish place-names are being Anglicised. Owen is a young Irishman who is very 'freely' translating what Lancey says for the largely Gaelic-speaking community of Baile Beag – Anglicised as 'Bally Beg'.]

LANCEY: A map is a representation on paper – a picture – you understand picture? – a paper picture – showing, representing this country – yes? – showing your country in miniature – a scaled drawing on paper of – of – of –
(*Suddenly* DOALTY *sniggers. Then* BRIDGET. *Then* SARAH. OWEN *leaps in quickly.*)

OWEN: It might be better if you *assume* they understand you –

LANCEY: Yes?

OWEN: And I'll translate as you go along.

LANCEY: I see. Yes. Very well. Perhaps you're right. Well. What we are doing is this.
(*He looks at* OWEN. OWEN *nods reassuringly.*) His Majesty's government has ordered the first ever comprehensive survey of this entire country – a general triangulation which will embrace detailed hydrographic and topographic information and which will be executed to a scale of six inches to the English mile.

HUGH: (*Pouring a drink*) Excellent – excellent.
(LANCEY *looks at* OWEN.)

OWEN: A new map is being made of the whole country.
(LANCEY *looks to* OWEN: *Is that all?* OWEN *smiles reassuringly and indicates to proceed.*)

LANCEY: This enormous task has been embarked on so that the military authorities will be equipped with up-to-date and accurate information on every corner of this part of the Empire.

OWEN: The job is being done by soldiers because they are skilled in this work.

LANCEY: And also so that the entire basis of land valuation can be reassessed for purposes of more equitable taxation.

OWEN: This new map will take the place of the estate-agent's map so that from now
          on you will know exactly what is yours in law. [. . .]
MANUS: What sort of a translation was that, Owen?
OWEN: Did I make a mess of it?
MANUS: You weren't saying what Lancey was saying!
OWEN: 'Uncertainty in meaning is incipient poetry' – who said that?
MANUS: There was nothing uncertain about what Lancey said: it's a bloody military
          operation, Owen. And what's Yolland's function: What's 'incorrect' about the
          place-names we have here?
OWEN: Nothing at all. They're just going to be standardised.
MANUS: You mean changed into English?
OWEN: Where there's ambiguity, they'll be Anglicised.

Friel (b.1929, Omagh, Ireland) initially worked as a teacher in Derry in the North of Ireland, where
this play was first performed in 1980 by the Field Day Theatre Company formed by him and Stephen
Rae. Based on **history** and realised in **drama**, this play both demonstrates and discusses the political
nature of translation in general and of (re)naming and (re)mapping in particular (see POSTCOLONIALISM
pp. 191–2). The text is from Brian Friel, *Translations*, London, Faber & Faber, 1981: 30–2.

JO SHAPCOTT and RAINER MARIA RILKE, 'Roses' (2001, 1925)

[Here are some versions – a bouquet perhaps – of 'Roses'. They are – it is – put together from:
(i) two poems in English by Jo Shapcott published at the turn of the twenty-first century, along
with her comment explaining how they came about; (ii) two corresponding poems in French
by the Austrian poet Rainer Maria Rilke written in the first quarter of the twentieth century,
along with a strictly literal, word-for-word, line-by-line translation of them (mine for this book).
Together, in miniature, all these texts enact as well as explain some of the many ways in which
readings lead to (re-)writings and translations are kinds of transformation Feel free to add your
own 'Roses' to the bunch.]

(i)   *Rosa gallica*

          If sometimes you're surprised
          by my coolness
          it's because inside myself,
          petal against petal, I'm asleep.

          I've been completely awake while my heart
          dozed, for who knows how long,
          speaking aphids and bees to you in silence,
          speaking English through a French mouth.

                          Rosa hemisphaerica

          You see me as half-open,
          a book whose pages
          can be turned by the wind
          then read with your eyes closed;

          butterflies stream out,
          stunned to discover

they think just like you,
dab wings all over your face.

My engagement with the French Rilke took place over ten years. Looking back, I can see this is primarily a reader's book: a record of the way an author who was important to me moved into my house and, during all those imaginary discussions readers have with writers, became as close as a profound friend, or an intimate enemy, or a lover. The result was unexpected – not a collection of translations but this tender and taxing conversation.

(ii)   I
Si ta fraîcheur parfois nous étonne tant,
heureuse rose,
c'est qu'en toi-même, en dedans,
pétale contre pétale, tu te reposes.

Ensemble tout éveillé, dont le milieu
dort, pendant qu'innombrables, se touchent
les tendresses de ce coeur silencieux
qui aboutissent à l'extrême bouche.

II
Je te vois, rose, livre entrebâillé
qui contient tant de pages,
de bonheur détaillé
qu'on ne lira jamais. Livre-mage,

qui s'ouvre au vent et qui peut être lu
les yeux fermés . . . ,
dont les papillons sortent confus
d'avoir eu les mêmes idées.

I. If your freshness sometimes us astonishes so much, / happy rose, / it's that within yourself, deep inside, / petal against petal, / you yourself repose.
Together all awake, of which the middle / sleeps, while innumerable, themselves touch / the tendernesses of this silent heart / which come to an end at the extreme.
II. I see you, rose, book splayed-apart, / which contains so many pages / of happiness detailed/ that one will never read. Book-magus,
Which itself opens to the wind and can be read / the eyes closed . . . , / from which the butterflies come out confused / for having had the same ideas.

Shapcott (b. London, 1953) has twice won the National Poetry competition, is Professor of Creative Writing at Royal Holloway, University of London, and President of the Poetry Society. As the above extract from her Foreword indicates, Shapcott's versions of Rilke's French poems are not close translations but the result of a protracted 'conversation' with them. The two poems featured are the first in her series called 'The Roses'. (Texts from J. Shapcott, *Tender Taxes – Versions of Rilke's French Poems*, London: Faber and Faber, 2001: xi, 59–60.)

Rilke (1875–1926) was born an Austrian in Prague and travelled restlessly around Europe, meeting Tolstoy in Russia, acting as Rodin's secretary in Paris, and living intermittently in

Trieste, at Castle Duino, where he began composing *Duino Elegies* (pub. 1923), his most famous lyric collection in German. He met and translated the poetry of Paul Valéry later in life, and was influenced by it in his own *Poèmes Françaises*, published posthumously in 1935. The two French poems above are from that collection. (French texts from *The Complete French Poems of Rainer Maria Rilke*, ed. A. Poulin, Jr, Saint Paul: Graywolf Press: 2–3. This edition includes a freer and fuller translation by Poulin.)

W. G. SEBALD, *Austerlitz*, 2001

[The narrator recalls how memories of two places he visited in Antwerp in the 1960s – the old station waiting room and a zoo for nocturnal animals, a Nocturama – have blended in his mind.]

Over the years, images of the interior of the Nocturama have become confused in my mind with my memories of the *Salle des pas perdus*, as it is called, in Antwerp Centraal Station. If I try to conjure up a picture of that waiting-room today I immediately see the Nocturama, and if I think of the Nocturama the waiting-room springs to my mind, probably because when I left the zoo that afternoon I went straight into the station, or rather first stood in the square outside it for some time to look up at the façade of that fantastical building, which I had taken in only vaguely when I arrived in the morning. Now, however, I saw how far the station constructed under the patronage of King Leopold II exceeded its purely utilitarian function, and I marvelled at the verdigris-covered negro boy who, for a century now, has sat upon his dromedary on top of an oriel turret to the left of the station façade, a monument to the world of the animals and native peoples of the African continent, alone against the Flemish sky. When I entered the great hall of the Central Station with its dome arching sixty metres high above it, my first thought, perhaps triggered by my visit to the zoo and the sight of the dromedary, was that this magnificent although then severely dilapidated foyer ought to have cages for lions and leopards let into its marble niches, and aquaria for sharks, octopuses and crocodiles, just as some zoos, conversely, have little railway trains in which you can, so to speak, travel to the farthest corners of the earth. It was probably because of ideas like these, occurring to me almost of their own accord there in Antwerp, that the waiting-room which, I know, has now been turned into a staff canteen struck me as another Nocturama, a curious confusion which may of course have been the result of the sun's sinking behind the city rooftops just as I entered the room. The gleam of gold and silver on the huge, half-obscured mirrors on the wall facing the windows was not yet entirely extinguished before a subterranean twilight filled the waiting-room, where a few travellers sat far apart, silent and motionless. Like the creatures in the Nocturama, which included a strikingly large number of dwarf species – tiny fennec foxes, springhares, hamsters – the railway passengers seemed to me somehow miniaturized, whether by the unusual height of the ceiling or because of the gathering dusk, and it was this, I suppose, which prompted the passing thought, nonsensical in itself, that they were the last members of a diminutive race which had perished or had been expelled from its homeland, and that because they alone survived they wore the same sorrowful expression as the creatures in the zoo.

Sebald (b.1944, Bavaria; d. 2001, East Anglia) grew up and was educated in Germany. Though he settled permanently in England in the 1970s, he usually wrote about post-war Germany and the Holocaust, and was awarded many prestigious literary prizes in Germany. He founded the British Centre for Literary Translation at the University of East Anglia (1989–) and, at his death in the year the present novel was published, was Professor of European Literature there and widely tipped for the Nobel Prize for Literature. Sebald knew English well but wrote in German and did not usually translate his own work. *Austerlitz* has no paragraphing and is interspersed with black-and-white reproductions of photographs, drawings and paintings, including photographs of nocturnal animals (p. 3), station buildings (pp. 11, 309, 404–5) and maps and diagrams of a concentration camp (pp. 328–9). (Text from *Austerlitz*, trans. Anthea Bell, London: Penguin, 2002, pp. 4–6.)

5.4.4   Versions of ageing

MAY SARTON, opening of *As We Are Now*, New York, 1973

> I am not mad, only old. I make this statement to give me courage. Suffice it to say that it has taken two weeks for me to obtain this notebook and a pen. I am in a concentration camp for the old, a place where people dump their parents or relatives exactly as though it were an ash can.
>
> My brother, John, brought me here two weeks ago. Of course I knew from the beginning that living with him would never work. I had to close my own house after the heart attack (the stairs were too much for me). John is four years older than I am and married a much younger woman after Elizabeth, his first wife, died. Ginny never liked me. I make her feel inferior and I cannot help it. John is a reader and always has been. So am I. John is interested in politics. So am I.

Sarton (1912–95) was a prominent American teacher, and a writer of poems, novels and autobiographical memoirs.

SKINCARE ADVERT: 'Clarins, the problem solver', *Cosmopolitan*, February 1985

> Puffy Eyes.
> Crow's Feet.
> Help is in sight!
> Your eyes are the first place to betray your age. Don't be alarmed. Let Clarins, France's premier skin care authority, come to the rescue – with effective eye contour treatments based on natural plant extracts.
> Clarins recognizes the causes.
> Squinting. Blinking. Smiling. Crying. These are constant aggressions the delicate eye contour area endures. Even the daily application and removal of makeup take a toll. Add stress, fatigue, pollution . . . and it's no wonder your eyes reveal signs of ageing. Clearly, the need for special eye contour care is urgent!
> Clarins is the Problem-Solver.
> Clarins created light, non-oily products to effectively treat the fragile skin tissue surrounding the eyes. (Oily formulations actually cause eyes to 'puff-up'!) For 30 years, Clarins' gentle eye contour treatments have proven to be successful in the Clarins Parisian 'Institut de Beauté'. Based on natural plant extracts, these treatments are dermatologically and allergy-tested.

WILLIAM SHAKESPEARE, 'Devouring Time' (Sonnet 19), 1609

Devouring Time, blunt thou the Lion's paws,
And make the earth devour her own sweet brood;
Pluck the keen teeth from the fierce Tiger's jaws,
And burn the long-lived Phoenix in her blood;   4
Make glad and sorry seasons as thou fleet'st,
And do whate'er thou wilt, swift-footed Time,
To the wide world and all her fading sweets;
But I forbid thee one most heinous crime,   8
O, carve not with thy hours my love's fair brow,
Nor draw no lines there with thine antique pen
Him in thy course untainted do allow,
For beauty's pattern to succeeding men.   12
    Yet do thy worst, old Time; despite thy wrong,
    My love shall in my verse ever live young.

For notes on Shakespeare (1564–1616) and another Sonnet, see 5.1.2.

DENNIS SCOTT, 'Uncle Time', 1973

Uncle Time is a ole, ole man . . .
All year long 'im wash 'im foot in de sea,
long, lazy years on de wet san'
an' shake de coconut tree dem
quiet-like wid 'im sea-win' laughter,   5
scraping away de lan' . . .

Uncle Time is a spider-man, cunnin' an' cool,
Him tell yu: watch de hill an' yu se mi.
Huhn! Fe yu yiye no quick enough fe si
how 'im move like mongoose; man, yu tink 'im fool?   10
Me Uncle Time smile black as sorrow;
'im voice is sof' as bamboo leaf
but Lawd, me Uncle cruel.
When 'im play in de street
wid yu woman – watch 'im! By tomorrow   15
she dry as cane-fire, bitter as cassava;
an' when 'im teach yu son, long after
yu walk wid stranger, an' yu bread is grief.
Watch how 'im spin web roun' ya house, an' creep
inside; an' when 'im touch yu, weep . . .   20

Dennis Scott (b.1939, Jamaica) is a poet, playwright, director, actor and dancer. (Text from S. Brown, M. Morris and G. Rohlehr (eds) *Voice Print: An Anthology of Oral and Related Poetry from the Caribbean*, London, Longman, 1989: 32–3.)

5.4.5   Epitaphs and (almost) last words

EPITAPHS by Pope, Gray, Burns, *et al.*

(i)   I was as ye are nowe
and as I ye shall be

(Common late medieval epitaph)

(ii)   Here lye two poor Lovers, who had the mishap
Tho very chaste people, to die of a Clap.

(Alexander Pope (1688–1744), 'Epitaph on the Stanton-Harcourt Lovers')

(iii)   Here rests his head upon the lap of Earth
A youth to Fortune and to Fame unknown.
Fair Science frowned not on his humble birth,
And Melancholy marked him for her own.

Large was his bounty, and his soul sincere,
Heaven did a recompense as largely send:
He gave to Misery all he had, a tear,
He gained from Heaven ('twas all he wished) a friend.

No farther seek his merits to disclose,
Or draw his frailties from their dread abode
(There they alike in trembling hope repose),
The bosom of his Father and his God.

(Thomas Gray, 'The Epitaph' from 'Elegy Written in a Country Churchyard', 1751)

(iv)   Here lie Willie Michie's banes;
O Satan, when ye take him,
Gie him the schoolin' of your weans
For clever deils he'll mak them!

(Robert Burns (1759–96) *Epitaph on a Schoolmaster in Cleish
Parish*, 3. weans – infants, children. 4. deils – devils)

(v)   Here lies Lester Moore
Four slugs from a 44
No les no mor

(from a headstone in Tombstone, Arizona)

(vi)   In Memory of MARY MARIA, wife of Wm. Dodd
Who died Dec.r 12th AD 1847 aged 27
also
of their children, LOUISA, who died Dec.r 12th 1847
aged 9 months, & ALFRED who died Jan.y 3rd AD 1848
aged 2 years & 9 months
All victims to the neglect of sanitary regulation
& specially referred to in a recent lecture on
Health in this town
*And the lord said to the angel that destroyed
It is enough. Stay now thy hand* – Chronicles 1, xx 17

(from a tombstone in Bilston, Staffordshire, England)

Epitaphs (iv) and (v) are from Fritz Spiegel, *A Small Book of Grave Humour*, London, Pan, 1971. Compare: Morrison 5.4.5.

CHARLES DICKENS, opening of *Great Expectations*, first serialised in *All the Year Round*, December 1860–1

My father's family name being Pirrip and my Christian name Philip, my infant tongue could make of both names nothing longer or more explicit than Pip. So I called myself Pip, and came to be called Pip.

I give Pirrip as my father's family name on the authority of his tombstone and my sister – Mrs. Joe Gargery, who married the blacksmith. As I never saw my father or my mother, and never saw any likeness of either of them (for their days were long before the days of photographs), my first fancies regarding what they were like were unreasonably derived from their tombstones. The shape of the letters on my father's gave me an odd idea that he was a square, stout, dark man, with curly black hair. From the character and turn of the inscription, '*Also Georgiana Wife of the Above*,' I drew a childish conclusion that my mother was freckled and sickly. To five little stone lozenges, each about a foot and a half long, which were arranged in a neat row beside their grave, and were sacred to the memory of five little brothers of mine – who gave up trying to get a living exceedingly early in that universal struggle – I am indebted for a belief I religiously entertained that they had all been born on their backs with their hands in their trousers pockets, and had never taken them out in this state of existence.

Dickens (1812–70) was born in Portsmouth and lived most of his life in London. He travelled widely, including a tour of America, and was famous for his dramatic readings of his novels. *Great Expectations* has long been a popular **classic** and is one of the most widely studied and frequently adapted of his novels. See, for example, Lloyd Evans, *Master Pip* (5.2.1) and the overview of films and continuations @ 2.3.1.

CHINUA ACHEBE, *Things Fall Apart*, Ch. 13, 1958

[A death is announced in the traditional Igbo manner.]

The first cock had not crowed, and Umuofia was still swallowed up in sleep and silence when the *ekwe* began to talk, and the cannon shattered the silence. Men stirred on their bamboo beds and listened anxiously. Di-go-go-di-go-di-di-go-go floated in the message-laden night air. The faint and distant wailing of women settled like a sediment of sorrow on the earth. Now and again a full-chested lamentation rose above the wailing whenever a man came into the place of death. He raised his voice once or twice in manly sorrow and then sat down with the other men listening to the endless wailing of the women and the esoteric language of the *ekwe*. Now and again the cannon boomed. The wailing of the women would not be heard beyond the village, but the *ekwe* carried the news to all the nine villages and even beyond. It began by naming the clan: *Umuofia obodo dike*, 'the land of the brave'. *Umuofia obodo dike! Umuofia obodo dike!* It said this over and over again, and as it dwelt on it, anxiety mounted in every heart that heaved on a bamboo bed that night. Then it went nearer and named the village: *Iguedo of the yellow grinding-stone!* It was Okonkwo's village. Again and again Iguedo was called and men waited breathlessly in all the nine villages. At last the man was named and people sighed 'E-u-u, Ezeudu is dead'.

Achebe's reconstruction of Igbo life up to the time when Nigeria became a British colony (in 1914) has become a **classic** of African literature in English (it has been reprinted by Heinemann over forty times in as many years). For many people, its powerfully evocative images of an oral, organic and largely male-dominated society are held to be an accurate **representation** of pre-colonialism. Nonetheless, it must also be recognised that the novel is a **story** produced from within its own moment. Written fifty years after the events it represents, but just two before Nigeria gained independence from Britain (in 1960), and nine before the Igbo nation sought independence from the rest of Nigeria as Biafra, the narrative is also about the construction of an authentic Igbo **identity**. The title is an explicit reference to Yeats's poem *The Second Coming* (1921): 'Things fall apart; the centre cannot hold'. Achebe's **text** must therefore be read **intertextually** as well as **contextually**.

TONI MORRISON, *Beloved* (1987)

[At this point, early on in the novel, a destitute black woman woman (Sethe) is reflecting on how she bartered her body for the carving of the single word 'Beloved' on her daughter's tombstone.]

Ten minutes for seven letters. With another ten could she have gotten 'Dearly' too? She had not thought to ask him and it bothered her still that it might have been possible – that for twenty minutes, a half hour, say, she could have had the whole thing, every word she heard the preacher say at the funeral (and all there was to say, surely) engraved on her baby's headstone: 'Dearly Beloved'. But what she got, settled for, was the one word that mattered. She thought it would be enough, rutting among the headstones with the engraver, his young son looking on, the anger in his face so old; the appetite in it quite new. That should certainly be enough. Enough to answer one more preacher, one more abolitionist and a town full of disgust.

Morrison (b.1931) – novelist, university teacher and editor – makes **narratives** that may properly be regarded as **factional**: she both researches and, in Rich's phrase, 're-visions' the past. *Beloved* explores the conditions and consequences of slave infanticide through a woman who kills her own child ('Beloved') rather than see her born into the misery of slavery. This novel won the Pulitzer Prize in 1987 and its author won the Nobel Prize for Literature in 1993.

GRACE NICHOLS, 'Tropical Death', 1984

The fat black woman want
a brilliant tropical death
not a cold sojourn
in some North Europe far/forlorn

The fat black woman want   5
some heat/hibiscus at her feet
blue sea dress
to wrap her neat

The fat black woman want
some bawl   10
no quiet jerk tear wiping
a polite hearse withdrawal

The fat black woman want
all her dead rights
first night   15
third night
nine night
all the sleepless droning
red-eyed wake nights

In the heart   20
of her mother's sweetbreast
In the shade
of the sun leaf's cool bless
In the bloom
of her people's bloodrest   25

the fat black woman want
a brilliant tropical death yes

Nichols was born in Guyana in 1950 and moved to Britain in 1977. This is one of a series from her *The Fat Black Woman's Poems*, London, Virago, 1984: 19. She won the Commonwealth Poetry Prize in 1983 for her *i is a long memoried woman*.

*

Other related texts can be found on the book's website @ 5. They are organised in corresponding categories and numbered subsections.

Like all the other Parts of the book, this is only a beginning. And even then only some of many possible beginnings. Continue to add and annotate texts that you find particularly interesting for some reason: because of the language used or the way the topic is treated – or simply because you like them. Gather some of them into 'crossings', as seems appropriate . . .

TAKING IT ALL FURTHER

English and the rest of your life

PART SIX

PREVIEW

In this final part of the book we look at English in relation to the rest of life – most immediately in your case, yours. Look back here whenever you want to gauge how what you are 'doing in English' now on your programme may relate to what you are doing next, and might do afterwards when you finish formal study. Turn to it for specific practical advice, checklists and links about getting a job or further study, but also use it to help reflect and project about your life as a whole. For 'life' is here understood as extending from everything you are doing in and around English at the moment, through some of what is currently on the edges, and then stretching forward into the as-yet-unmade future. So the 'all' in 'Taking it all further', really is *all*. It embraces whatever makes life worth living (which includes but is more than just making a living) and emphasises learning in the broadest sense (which is more than formal study in the narrowest). Meanwhile, the rest of life is understood as involving everything from recreation in the routine sense of pass-time or leisure to 're-creation' in the radical sense of 'making things afresh', including oneself and one's relationship with others.

In all these areas, skills are seen as *transformable* (not merely 'transferable') and knowledge as *transformative* (not just portable information subject to 'knowledge transfer'). For the main thing you have learnt in doing English is to be critical and creative. And that means being imaginative and adaptive, not underestimating what you have done or taking it for granted. The knack is to use what you have learnt in English in fresh ways. For in the end as in the beginning – and in reality it's always somewhere between – it's your English and your life. The present material is organised as follows:

6.1 Living, learning, earning
    What now? What next? Why . . . ? What if . . . ?
6.2 English again, afresh, otherwise
    English *and* or *as* other subjects
6.3 Further study
    Postgraduate courses in and around English
6.4 Into work
    Transformable skills, transformative knowledges
    Career pathways and interesting jobs for 'English' graduates
    Towards application and interview
6.5 Play as re-creation
    Afterwords – a postlude . . .

Reading and cross-references are supplied at the end of each main section, and further activities, examples and up-to-date links can be found on the website @ 6.

6.1   LIVING, LEARNING, EARNING

> It is a commonwealth in which work is play and play is life.
>
> George Bernard Shaw, *John Bull's Other Island* (1904),
> featured at length in A.N. Whitehead's *The Aims of Education* (1953: Ch. 4)

> We're living through a certain part of history that needs us to live it and make it and write it.
> We can make that history with many others, people we will never know.
>
> Adrienne Rich, *Arts of the Possible* (2001: 167)

In moving from study to work and from education to employment, there is a tendency to see the transition simply as a matter of either/or, not this but that, now then next. To offset this tendency to think in terms of simple binaries and linear sequences, there will here be an emphasis on cycles of simultaneous processes and on triads (three-term dynamics). Hence the insistence on *living* and *learning* and *earning* as distinct from, say, 'life', 'study' and 'work'. (The former, by using the progressive '-ing' forms of the verbal nouns, suggest ongoing activities; whereas the latter, as simple nouns, suggest separate 'things'.) Such distinctions may seem purely grammatical or merely 'academic', but they turn out to be of vital practical importance as well as theoretical significance. It's the same with nouns such as 'education' and 'employment', and beguiling phrases such as 'life–work balance'; they suggest separateness rather than interdependence. Education *is* employment for some people, and life *includes* work so how can it be balanced with or against it? That is why there is here an emphasis on *studying*, *working*, *playing* as interdependent aspects of lived experience. They *are* what we *do*, and together they make for an evolving idea of 'whole living' which is very different from a 'life full of holes'. Two very different diagrammatic realisations of these issues will help set the scene – and the agenda – for the rest of this Part:

(i)   Study + Work + Play = Life

Figure 6.1 Linear, additive and static model of life made of discrete components

(ii)

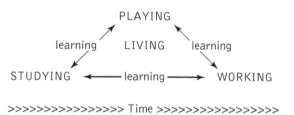

Figure 6.2   Dynamic and cyclic model of living based upon an ongoing round of learning

The obvious point about the first, 'linear' model is that it presents 'life' as though made up of a more or less fixed array of separate elements and as a kind of final product. If any 'learning' is involved it is implicit and assumed to be associated with study. In this view, summing the various pluses (+ + +) leads to a final equation (=). The obvious point about the second, 'cyclic' model is that it presents *Living* as a core process in all these activities and presents *learning* as equally essential to all of them. Studying, Working and Playing are seen as mutually interacting and reciprocally defining (hence the double-headed arrows) and as constantly changing over time (hence the >>>). Each model has its own strengths and weaknesses, and may be viewed and valued very differently. The 'linear discrete' model, depending how you see and say it, represents the conveniently compartmentalised or distressingly fragmented life; it stands for 'control' or 'alienation'. The 'cyclic flow' model, conversely, can be taken to represent the admirably integrated or awfully undifferentiated activity of living; in extreme terms – depending on your preferred way of seeing/saying – it's utopian or dystopian.

The question, practical as well as theoretical, is how do *you* prefer to see and say the dynamic of study(ing)–work(ing)–play(ing), or learning, earning, living – or however else you would care to frame and weight it. It's your language and life. Your words and world-view. My own wor(l)d-view, by heavy implication, chimes with what Shaw said and Whitehead endorsed in the first epigraph to this Part, and with what Rich said in the second. To these I would add what Oscar Wilde famously said in *The Soul of Man under Socialism* (1891): 'a map of the world that does not include Utopia is not worth even glancing at'.

What now? What next? Why . . . ? What if . . . ?

We have to keep on asking the questions *Why . . . ? What if . . . ?* They are the imagination's questions.

Adrienne Rich, *Arts of the Possible* (2001: 167)

It is important to have some idea of where you may be heading even if you don't have a specific destination, let alone a detailed map of how to get there. The question 'What now?' quickly turns into 'What next?'. That is why you are encouraged to look over this section when starting to do English in Part One. As you move into your final year of study, that next really is *next*, and whether or not you have consciously decided on a path you are certainly on one. Meanwhile, the questions may be multiplying at an alarming rate:

Go into teaching? Try for publishing, journalism or the media? Or advertising or personnel? Do further study – an MA perhaps? Or retrain for something like the Law or the Social Services or Business? Or start up your own business? Do community or charity work? Travel or go back to parents, get married, or carry on caring for your own family? Do one, some or none of these – sooner or later – depending on how you view your immediate situation and the longer-term prospects.

But what *is* your situation and how do *you* see your options? For most people the next step is never simple and straightforward (let alone thinking of the ones after that) and even if it feels automatic that might be wrong too. Nor does it ever come down to just one thing – the subject of a degree and success in it, for example. Lives are complicated and living is multiply motivated. Nonetheless, you will be making that next step with 'English' as part of your personal and educational baggage – perhaps a large part. So it will help to have an imaginative and comprehensive as well as realistic sense of what your options are.

For a personal review applying the same critical and creative techniques to yourself that you applied to a text, use the matrix @ 6.1. This adapts the 'opening moves' and 'core questions' for Initial analysis (2.1) to address your own position and possibilities in terms of *Notice–Pattern–Contrast–Feeling* and interrogate yourself with '6 *Wh- and a H?*'. Work out and play around with this from time to time to check what course you yourself are on.

READING AND LINKS The philosophy, politics and psychology of 'living as learning' developed here can be broadly identified with those of Dewey (1934), Whitehead (1953), Bruner (1986) and Epston and White (1990). At best, and always under threat, it is realised in genuine programmes of 'lifelong learning' and 'continuing education'. A good general overview, full of practical advice, for students 'Getting out of College' is Part Three of Saunders 2005. For students of English in particular, Chapters 3 and 4 of Childs 2008 and the essays by Robbins and Bowditch in Wolfreys 2011: 351–62 are helpful and realistic. There is a work-related, web-based questionnaire at the very useful *Prospects* site (referred to frequently below): www.prospects.ac.uk/cms/ShowPage/Home_page/What_jobs_would_suit_me___Prospects_ Planner. The websites of the various national subject associations for English and Writing carry discussion, guidance and updates across a wide range of topics in and out of formal education, e.g.: UK – National Association for the Teaching of English (www. nate.org.uk), National Association of Writers in Education (www.nawe.co.uk) and, still, the English Subject Centre of the Higher Education Academy (www.english.heacademy.ac.uk); US – National Council of Teachers of English (www.ncte.org); American Association of Writers & Writing Programmes (www.awpwriter.org); and the Australian Association for the Teaching of English (www.education.net.au).

6.2   ENGLISH AGAIN, AFRESH, OTHERWISE

The task, here and now, yet again, is to *re-vision* English afresh: to grasp it as not only an educational *subject* and academic *object* but also an ongoing *project* – something 'thrown forward' into the rest of life (compare 1.2.9 and 3.7). For, as has been emphasised throughout the book, English is always various kinds of 'one *and* many': language(s), literature(s), cultures(s) (see 1.1, 3.9 and @ 2.3). In fact, there are always so many and various 'ones and manies' in play, it's no wonder that each of us periodically needs to pause and take stock of where we are up to with what. The transition from 'doing English' in formal education to whatever you are doing next is obviously one such moment. It is therefore precisely at this point that you need to stand back from what you know of English and try to see it as a kind of 'whole'. Naturally this also entails acknowledging that what you know is full of 'holes'. But that's just the nature of knowledge. It's always a presence defined by an absence, and the result is a familiar yet strange kind of 'w/hole'. Either way – or rather both ways – now is a particularly good time to refresh your sense of 'English as a w/hole'.

English *and* or *as* other subjects

What follows is a diagrammatic overview of all the subjects and areas of activity that English most immediately relates to and in some measure consists of (Figure 6.3, pp. 370–1.). 'English' is therefore presented both as a subject in its own right (composed of English Language and Literature, Literary Criticism, Critical Theory, Creative Writing, etc.) and as a kind of 'inter-subject', implicated in and interfacing with many other kinds of subject (Languages, Education, Drama and Performance, Cultural and Media Studies, Publishing, etc.). But this diagram also supports thinking about English beyond formal education. For each of these 'subjects of study' has a counterpart in the worlds of work and play – employment and recreation – in the rest of life. English Language, for instance, can lead to jobs in Teaching English as a Foreign (Second, etc.) Language or for special purposes such as Literacy and clinical and forensic Linguistics (in health and law). It can also, of course, be a life-long interest that enriches conversation, thinking, writing and reading at every turn; and may lead to the learning of other languages, ancient and modern, along with related travel. Similarly with English Literature: it can lead to jobs in teaching, journalism, advertising, publishing, the media, and so forth (often supported by further subsequent training, sometimes more or less directly). But an ongoing interest in Literature can also enhance living, one's own and other people's, in all sorts of ways: from active participation in library and community literature ventures such as reading groups and literary festivals, to commitment to theatre, film and arts projects of many kinds (educational and otherwise). These include writing and publishing or producing one's own and other people's work.

So use the following diagram as a kind of multi-function 'clock' or 'compass'. Go steadily round it and at each point ask the following simple yet significant questions:

- Which of these *educational subjects* have I done within and around English? (These might include any other subjects taken on a joint or combined degree.)
- Which subjects would I still like to pursue, whether *in or out of formal education*? Or perhaps return to *study later*?
- Which of these areas of activity might I like to explore as a *job*, perhaps develop as a *career*?
- Which of these areas of activity might I like to keep going – or pick up – as an *interest* in life at large: perhaps just as a personal *hobby* but also maybe as something I could do for and with other people – a *project* even?

However precise or vague at this stage, the answers you come up with could sooner or later affect the rest of your life. And while doing this will make you acutely aware of the 'holes' in your present knowledge, these can be experienced as invitations and promises rather than threats and regrets. The rest of the subject (like the rest of life) may then be seen not so much as things undone but as things yet to do – or simply someone else's business, someone you might turn to or work with if you need. Clearly you don't have to know or do it all. No one could. But you do need to know what you know and grasp what you can do with some of it – and then just relate to the rest. That's all anyone does.

READING AND LINKS: Revealing autobiographical and institutional accounts of a variety of routes into, through, round and out of English language and literature are to be found in Knights and Thurgar-Dawson 2006 (English Literature and Writing Pedagogy); Scholes 1998, 2001 and Showalter 2003 (American, English Literature and Writing); Crystal 2009 (British, English Language); Hills 2005 (Cultural Theory); Homer *et al.* 2007 (Australian Teachers of English and Educationists). For a sample mapping of 'English in the Digital Age' see English Subject Centre, *Wordplay*, 2, 2009, and for one of 'Interdisciplinary English', see Eaglestone 2009: 137–50. Representative profiles of English student interests and employability can be found at www.english.heacademy.ac.uk/archive/projects/reports/stud_profile.doc; and a Directory of Experience and Interests of English staff/faculty at www.english.heacademy.ac.uk/find/colleagues/index.php.

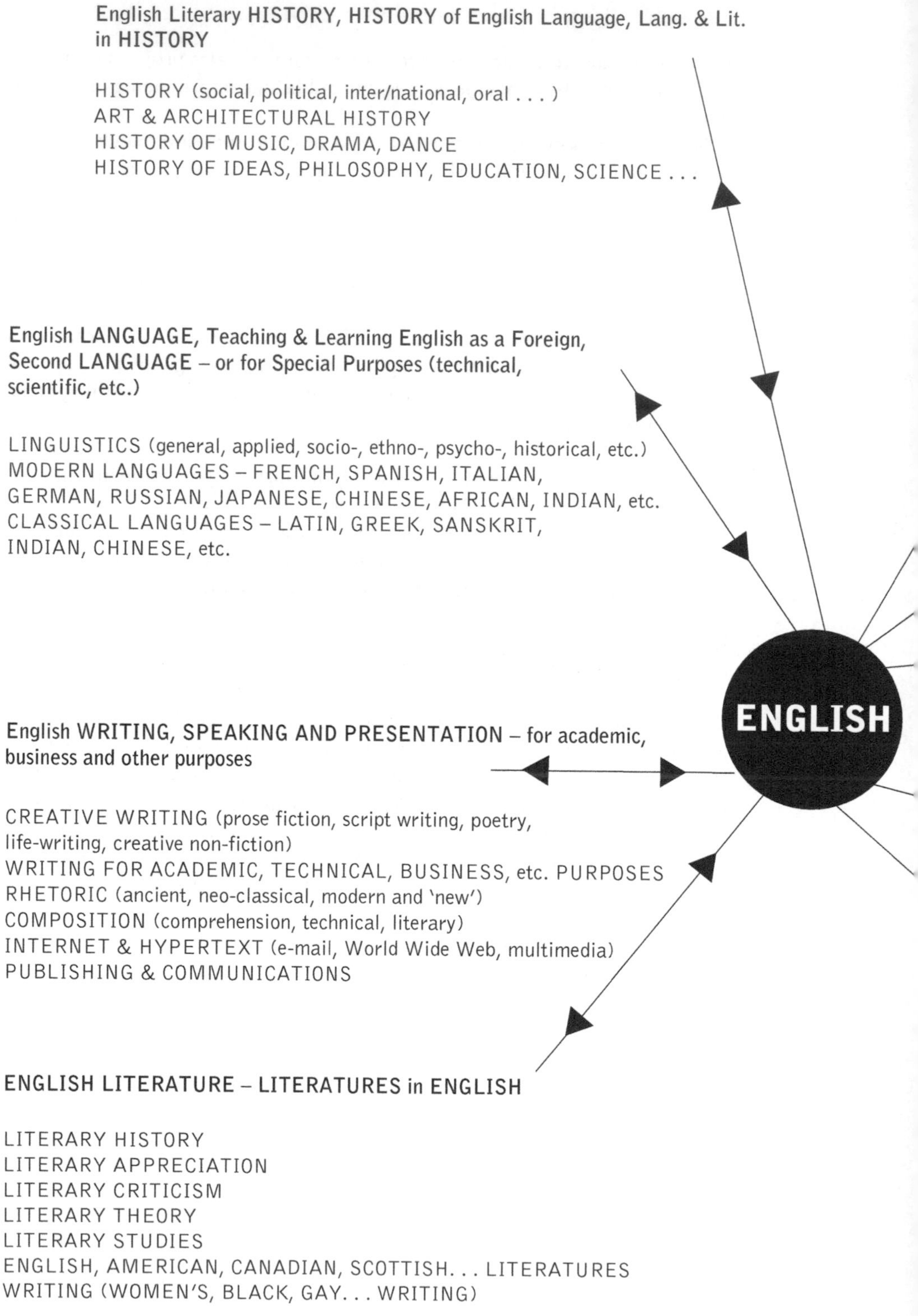

English Literary HISTORY, HISTORY of English Language, Lang. & Lit.
in HISTORY

HISTORY (social, political, inter/national, oral . . .)
ART & ARCHITECTURAL HISTORY
HISTORY OF MUSIC, DRAMA, DANCE
HISTORY OF IDEAS, PHILOSOPHY, EDUCATION, SCIENCE . . .

English LANGUAGE, Teaching & Learning English as a Foreign,
Second LANGUAGE – or for Special Purposes (technical,
scientific, etc.)

LINGUISTICS (general, applied, socio-, ethno-, psycho-, historical, etc.)
MODERN LANGUAGES – FRENCH, SPANISH, ITALIAN,
GERMAN, RUSSIAN, JAPANESE, CHINESE, AFRICAN, INDIAN, etc.
CLASSICAL LANGUAGES – LATIN, GREEK, SANSKRIT,
INDIAN, CHINESE, etc.

ENGLISH

English WRITING, SPEAKING AND PRESENTATION – for academic,
business and other purposes

CREATIVE WRITING (prose fiction, script writing, poetry,
life-writing, creative non-fiction)
WRITING FOR ACADEMIC, TECHNICAL, BUSINESS, etc. PURPOSES
RHETORIC (ancient, neo-classical, modern and 'new')
COMPOSITION (comprehension, technical, literary)
INTERNET & HYPERTEXT (e-mail, World Wide Web, multimedia)
PUBLISHING & COMMUNICATIONS

ENGLISH LITERATURE – LITERATURES in ENGLISH

LITERARY HISTORY
LITERARY APPRECIATION
LITERARY CRITICISM
LITERARY THEORY
LITERARY STUDIES
ENGLISH, AMERICAN, CANADIAN, SCOTTISH. . . LITERATURES
WRITING (WOMEN'S, BLACK, GAY. . . WRITING)

Figure 6.3 English *and* or *as* other educational subjects

EDUCATION in English, English in EDUCATION

EDUCATION (theory, methodology and practice)
HISTORY OF EDUCATION (formal and informal – including that of 'English' at elementary, primary, secondary and tertiary levels)
TEACHING, LEARNING & ASSESSMENT (individual, group; written, oral, recorded, multimedia; other, self- and peer; 'open', 'closed' and negotiated)
EDUCATIONAL METHODS & TECHNOLOGY (strategies; audio-visual; . . .)
STAFF & STUDENT SUPPORT & DEVELOPMENT (counselling, training, careers, etc.)

English TEXTS – INFORMATION in English

PUBLISHING (book, magazine, newspaper; paper, electronic; editing, design, marketing, distribution; general, specialist)
BIBLIOGRAPHY & TEXTUAL SCHOLARSHIP
LIBRARY & INFORMATION SERVICES
INFORMATION SCIENCES
COMMUNICATIONS

English STUDIES

WOMEN'S STUDIES,
GENDER STUDIES,
POSTCOLONIAL STUDIES
AREA STUDIES
ENVIRONMENTAL & ECOLOGICAL

English THEATRE AND DRAMA – PLAYS, PERFORMANCES AND RE/PRESENTATIONS partly in English

THEATRE STUDIES (textual, practical, vocational)
DRAMA & PERFORMANCE (with music and dance; on page, stage or screen; classical, contemporary; in and out of education)
VISUAL STUDIES – photography, film, video, art (fine, popular and commercial)
FILM, TV, MEDIA & MULTIMEDIA STUDIES

English (British, American, Australian, Caribbean . . .) CULTURE – CULTURES partly through English

ART, MUSIC & DANCE ('high' and 'popular')
CLASSIC & POPULAR CULTURE
HISTORY, GEOGRAPHY, SOCIOLOGY, LAW, POLITICS, HEALTH CARE, BIOLOGY, SCIENCES (theoretical and applied) . . .
CULTURAL STUDIES (British, American, Australian etc. models)
CULTURAL THEORY

6.3   FURTHER STUDY

Life beyond a degree will usually entail further study at some point, whether training for (perhaps on) the job or a period back in higher education. This may well happen several times over the course of your life. For it is unlikely you will do 'the same job' throughout your life: even if you don't change jobs, the job will change. And such is the nature of technological change and social mobility nowadays, along with increasing life expectancy and, indeed, increased expectations of life, it is best to think in terms of a life of ongoing or on-and-off learning (i.e. 'lifelong learning') rather than of learning as a once-and-for-all stage that happens towards the beginning with formal education and then just stops. In other words, as already outlined theoretically, you should be looking forward to an ongoing and variable cycle of *studying–working–playing* (6.1). So you should be thinking of your current study in relation to *further* study of one kind or another and from time to time.

You should also, again, be thinking of *learning* on a full and flexible range from practical skills and immediate know-how to intellectual insights and fuller knowledge (see 1.2; 2 and 3). The two kinds of knowing are not, of course, actually separable. In the best cases, practical know-how and abstract knowledge constantly test and prove, enrich and extend one another. But it is still convenient, at least initially, to distinguish *training* in the narrow sense from *education* in the broadest. *Training* involves learning how to do some specific procedure or application, often involving a specific technique or technology: learning how to do a report, organise a working-party, use a particular computer application or communication system. *Education* means learning about the larger picture and detailed implications, reflecting critically on the 'why' and creatively exploring alternatives in terms of 'how, who, when and where . . . else': why this – but not that or that – is being done; who will be directly – and indirectly – affected by this change, when and where else; what's the overall value – not just the immediate cost and price – of doing it this way or something else entirely. If training proposes or presupposes a given 'what' and is full of statements and instructions, education exposes 'what else' and is full of suggestions and questions about 'what if?'. The best training/education, of course, is and does both. But it is always up to the immediate trainer or trainee involved in that particular potentially educational moment (you, me, anybody) to ask as well as say what particular kind of learning is in play and at work. How far and in what directions does the 'further study' go?

For more discussion of **Training and/or/as education** and an extension of the argument to **Research inside, outside and through universities**, see **@ 6.3.**

Postgraduate courses in and around English

Postgraduate work is obviously a step 'after' undergraduate work; but it can be a natural as well as exciting one if prepared for and taken gradually. In fact, Latin *gradus*, meaning 'step', is the common core of all three 'grad' terms in that previous sentence. Choosing to do graduate work beyond a first degree is therefore best approached as a step-by-step process, not a leap in the dark. The most common form of academic study after the undergraduate *BA* (Bachelor of Arts) is the postgraduate *MA* (Master of Arts), which is usually described as 'taught' because there is a set programme of courses. Beyond that there are 'research' degrees, the most common of which is the *PhD* or *DPhil (Philosophiae Doctor* in Latin, 'Doctor of Philosophy' in English); though there are also intermediate awards such as *MPhil* (Master of Philosophy) or *MRes* (Master of Research). (For critical and creative reflection on the archaically gendered nature of these names, see 'Qualifications in need of qualification?' @ 6.3.1.)

The typical MA is taught for one year full time or two years part time. The PhD is individually supervised as a research thesis or book-length project and tends to take three years full time or up to six part time. Each of these steps is increasingly demanding and specialised, and by no means appropriate or advisable for everyone. Many people choose to step a different way in a wide-wide world. That said, there need be little mystery – and no mystique – about what actually goes on at MA and PhD levels. It may or may not be for you. So this section is mainly designed to help you decide whether or not – and then, if so, what, where, why and how far. (Postgraduate vocational for teaching qualifications and the like are mainly treated in the next section: 'Into work', 6.4.)

Planning and preparing for – or at least thinking about – postgraduate work obviously begin much earlier. In fact the first step is usually being taken while you are doing English as part of your BA. So

* Do an *under*graduate dissertation or longer project while you can! *

That is, if you are thinking about doing *post*graduate study, you should aim to do a dissertation or extended project while you are still an *under*graduate. This usually means setting it up before and for the final year of your programme. Doing such a piecc of work will enable you to see how you get on with larger scale independent study and with supervision – and whether this is really your kind of thing. It will also demonstrate to postgraduate admissions tutors and potential supervisors that you can handle it. They may even ask to see an example of your extended work, and with Creative Writing a portfolio is almost always required to support your application. (For practical advice on taking and framing an undergraduate dissertation or project, see **Longer projects**, 2.3.) Meanwhile, you can be thinking about and looking into the kinds of postgraduate study you might do. In the first instance, this is typically an *MA*.

MA programmes are usually taught by a team and assessed by essays or portfolio with opportunities for extended independent work supported by specialist supervision. The most common structure in English (as in many subjects) is (i) an introduction to advanced study and research methods; (ii) two or three specific options chosen from a range (these may change each year so check what's on when); (iii) a final dissertation or extended project on a topic of your choice with an individual supervisor. MAs are advanced and postgraduate but *not* expected to result in 'original research'. They therefore offer opportunities to push your knowledge and personal interests further and can also support professional development. MA programmes in and around English tend to be framed in a number of ways, as you would expect from the organisation and overlaps of its constituent subjects in terms of Language, Literature, Culture and Creative Writing (see 1.1, 1.3 and 6.2 above). But even when the name is broadly the same, precisely what is covered by each programme varies from place to place; so you should check out the particular emphases and options on the websites and in the literature, and follow through with visit and interview. That said, you will commonly meet generic ('umbrella') programmes with titles such as the following:

> *MA in English; MA in English Studies; MA in English Language and Literature; MA in English Language, Literature and Linguistics; MA in Teaching English as a Second Language, for Academic Purposes, etc.; MA in Applied Linguistics* (which often overlaps with the previous); *MA in English and Creative Writing; MA in Creative Writing.*

To these should be added other MAs that may contain substantial elements of 'English Language and/or Literature' along with other subjects, e.g.: *MA in Translation Studies* and *MA in*

Comparative Literature (both usually requiring another language); *MA in Literature and Film* or *MA in Literary Adaptation*; *MA in Literature and Drama*; *MA in Children's Literature*; also some *MAs in Education*. Some of these may also be worth looking at, depending where you see yourself and the subject coming from and going to, personally and professionally. For the rest, you will meet many specifically named degrees with a more or less central focus on English. Increasingly these involve links – sometimes full-scale collaborations – with colleagues from, say, History, Film, Art History, Drama and Performance Education, Creative Arts, Creative Industries, Communications, Publishing and Media. (Again, a quick reading round of the clock/compass in 'English *and* or *as* other subjects' in 6.2 will help.)

Cross-disciplinary courses across the arts and humanities are commonly framed by period, movement, genre, author, topic or approach – and often some permutation of these. This is as you would expect given the richly eclectic and flexible nature of the subjects within and around English. But you still may not think to look and investigate across the whole range. So here is a sample of the *kinds* of multi- or interdisciplinary programme on offer, running from the present backwards. New ones are naturally being configured all the time:

> *Writing for the Contemporary Media; Twenty-first-Century Texts; Modernism and Modernity; Victorian Literature and Culture; Nineteenth-Century Studies; Romanticism and Revolution; Eighteenth-Century Novel and Society; Shakespearean Texts in Performance; Renaissance Literature; Early Modern Worlds; Late Medieval Texts and Contexts; Anglo-Saxon Poetry, Prose and Culture . . .*

Meanwhile, don't forget cross-period, sometimes cross-cultural MAs on, for example: *Comedy and Satire; Tragedy; Utopian Fiction; Travel Writing; Slave Narratives; Autobiography and Life Writing; Adaptation; Media Discourse; Bibliography and Book Culture; . . .* The lists go on: hardy perennials are constantly being fertilised by fresh materials, and new theories and technologies are helping generate fresh hybrids even while demanding attention in their own right.

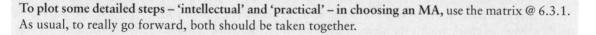

To plot some detailed steps – 'intellectual' and 'practical' – in choosing an MA, use the matrix @ 6.3.1. As usual, to really go forward, both should be taken together.

Once you have homed in on a provisional area, course or topic, it's a matter of following up with websites, printed literature, emails and phone-calls if you get more interested. The interview can be a final decider of whether it's right for all concerned (see 6.4). The relatively short time and prescribed range of an MA make it ideal for further study without making a long-term investment. For many people it is enough and just right. But some people really want and can realistically manage more. In that case – if you are advised and wise to do so – the next logical step in terms of postgraduate study is a PhD. Indeed, for supervisors as well as for some students, the MA serves as both a trial-pad and launch-platform for work beyond.

The PhD in and around English is usually an independently initiated and individually supervised piece of research leading to a thesis or project of some 80,000 to 100,000 words. Occasionally, especially in the handling of large corpora and text-editing, it is framed as a substantial and distinct research contribution to a larger and ongoing group project. Either way, like marriage – or at least like getting a dog *and* taking on a big loan – the PhD is not to be undertaken lightly. Most people who take a PhD intend to make an academic career of it or have the time and money to do it on their own terms. It should be stressed at the outset that there *are* academic jobs but they are *relatively few* and there is *fierce competition* for them. If you don't realistically intend or need such a career, you are strongly advised to do something else. Explore your interests in – and perhaps passion for – research, reading and writing another way. Do that project, research and perhaps publish on that area! But don't tie yourself into the formal and formally exacting procedures of enrolment, registration, submission and examination, and the ongoing round of having to research, draft and redraft, chapter by chapter, section by section . . . unless you feel that really is the thing for you. A research degree can give structure and may give a sense of community, institutionally and in the subject at large. But the loneliness (and sheer slog) of the long-distance researcher is real. Be aware and, if unsure, beware! Otherwise proceed with determination and delight, and eyes wide open.

The first thing you need to be aware of about a PhD is that you are expected to do 'original research' or at least make 'an independent contribution to knowledge'. So you need to think hard about whether you have actually got anything interesting and important to do and say. Supervisors are there to support and direct and perhaps stimulate and challenge you too. But the exploratory pilot or foundational planning (however you conceive it) is usually done in the course of an MA; and so it is strongly advised (some places insist on it) that you take an MA before even considering taking a PhD. So that basically is where this introduction to postgraduate study will leave you. The rest is up to you. Though if you follow the above advice, get your initial act together and approach departments and programmes and individuals accordingly, you will certainly not be on your own.

READING AND LINKS For an overview of kinds of MA course in English Language and Literature, see English Subject Centre 2008; and for essays introducing kinds of research methodology and resources (from Textual Scholarship and Biography to Literary History and Creative Writing), see Griffin 2006. Annual updates and reviews by author, genre, period and approach can be found in *The Year's Work in English Studies, Annual Bibliography of English Literature* and *Publications of the Modern Language Association*. For theoretical discussion of **Training and/as education** and **Research inside and outside universities**, and for up-to-date links on postgraduate courses, see @ 6.3.

6.4   INTO WORK

'Work', as already suggested, is best understood as part of an interdependent cycle of activities that go to make up a life: earning and learning, working and playing (see 6.1). Work may then be seen as braced alongside and being embraced by other aspects of living such as *further study*, and *re-creation*, in the strong sense of 're-creating' (re-making, refreshing) and not just the routine sense of 'recreation' as pastime, mere leisure (see 6.5). Such work in such a life is what may be called truly satisfying. But not all work is like this. In fact, for most people at least some of the time, as for the poet and librarian Philip Larkin in his poem 'Toads', work is something that 'squats' on their life ('like a toad'), fouling it up and weighing it down rather than enriching and enlightening it. In any case, naturally enough, not everyone wants a career or even a job (though most people *have* to work to earn a living); nor do most people know from the start where they want to go in life. Quite a lot of people, in fact, just want a job to see how it goes, get going and get by, earn some money and get on with the rest of life.

But however you relate to 'career pathways', 'employment', 'the world of work' or simply the need to 'get a job', it makes sense to take a good look at what you can do and what you like – and are like – and to try and match these to kinds of work there already are or that can realistically be made to happen. So whether you aim to be employed by someone else, self-employed, or otherwise employed (being a parent or carer, for example), it is a good idea to get such important preliminaries sorted out before you go any further. It is also important to weigh who is responsible, immediately and ultimately, for un- or under-employment. Your 'life' in the fullest sense may depend upon it.

At this point, it's worth turning back to questions posed earlier: **What now? What next? Why . . . ? What if . . . ?** (6.1). What kind of person with what kind of capacities and preferences are you? What trajectory do you feel and incline yourself to be on as the emphasis shifts to *work–study–play*? Notice that it's a question not only of what kind of work you want to do, but also of what kind of person in what kind of society you want to work at being, becoming. These processes intertwine.

Meanwhile . . .

> * Do some work-related study if at all possible! *

That is, ask about a *work placement* or suggest a *work-related project* as part of your programme. There is often some such opportunity later on, or at least some 'independent' or 'open' study space that can be used in this way. However you do it, the main thing is to experience and experiment with some study skills and/or subject-based knowledge beyond the subject as such. 'English Literature' as such need not be obviously at the core; but English as language and culture and communication – in practice at least – will usually be somewhere in the frame. Common projects are:

- working on local radio or newspapers or on theatre, film and arts projects;
- working in publicity and advertising or personnel departments;
- working as an assistant teacher, carer or helper in a school, hospital or community centre;
- acting as a guide at university visit days, conferences and literary festivals;
- working with a band, orchestra or theatre group on their publicity or practical arrangements;
- doing interviews or contributing to a campaign on a pressing local and/or global issue;
- setting up a website or communal wiki, or doing a creative writing workshop, or putting on a drama event with people who wouldn't normally do them; etc.

Typically, such experiences are recorded in a log or journal, written up, read round and reflected on. They may also be supported by or presented as video, website and so forth. But whatever you do, the main thing is to 'do English' so as to bring selected aspects of work experience (yours) into the critical and creative space that is education. Such things are often serious fun. And even if you find, in the event, that you *don't* want to do that kind of thing after all – that is useful too. Either way, having done a work-related project can have a decisive influence when applying for a job. It shows initiative and looks good on your CV, and is also something to talk about at interview (see 6.4). Aim to set up something while you are still studying.

Transformable skills, transformative knowledges

Here we take a detailed look at ways in which the kinds of skill and knowledge you have developed while doing English may be reframed and refocused so as to address the matter of getting a job and developing a career. Skills, it is suggested, are best approached as *transformable* rather than 'transferable': they always need adapting, never simply applying. Knowledge, meanwhile, is best grasped as *transformative*; it changes us even as we change it; it is not just an object to be moved around, no more than we are simply fixed subjects. Certainly, again, it is both more than and different from what is often currently understood by 'knowledge transference' in a merely instrumental sense. Knowledge fully grasped becomes a way of knowing, a way of seeing and being in the world – becoming more fully ourselves and open to others. Transformable skill and transformative knowledge together make for 'life skills' in the fullest and most flexible sense. They make the commonplace phrase 'you live and learn' really mean something.

The skills set out below are based on the ten essential actions in **Doing English** (1.2) and the **Critical and Creative Strategies** (2.1–3) at the beginning of the book. But here they are seen as from the end of the book (and your programme) with the emphasis on what you have already *Done in English*. Each study skill/strategy is set alongside its *Transformable* counterpart, which is the *kind* of activity you turn it into depending on what *kind* of work you do – hence *Generic*. The comments in that second column are, ideally, the kinds of thing that you will be able to say of yourself by the end of your programme. They are also the kinds of comment you hope may be said about you in references by whoever you ask to act as referees for you (on which see the next section). In reality, of course, few people are good at everything and everyone tends to be taken on for their particular strengths and what they will contribute overall. So there is a third column, here left blank, to prompt you to think about precisely *how* and *how far* – and by implication *how well* – you have actually practised the skill concerned. (This may also prompt you to think about whether you need some particular area.) It is worth taking time and trouble over this list. Turn back to it from time to time to check how you are getting on, and to see what you need further practice at or guidance in.

Table 6.1 (see over) provides a list for the kinds of knowledge (knowledges) you will have acquired having done English. As in the book at large, this is reviewed in terms of Linguistic, Literary and Cultural knowledge of English (see 1.1, 1.3). Though again it is worth emphasising that the 'know-how' involved in the skilled use of English in the previous section cannot and should not be separated off from the analytical and critical, historical and theoretical 'knowledge' of English grasped here. 'English' is what we do ourselves as well as study how others have done. (So the project of **English again, afresh, otherwise** (6.2) is worth looking at again too.)

Table 6.2 (see over) is a table of knowledges, like the previous table of skills, is presented in three columns. The first lists the *Specific subject-based knowledges* of English as an area of academic study, here expressed by noun phrases representing *what* you know about. The second lists the *Generic transformative knowledges* that each of these can be turned into, here expressed as verbal processes to emphasise their ongoing transformation into *know-how*. The third column is empty apart from the repeated questions *And you? Now . . . Next . . . ?* This is an open invitation to weigh what kinds of knowledge, actual and potential, you have in each area. No-one knows everything and equally well. But everyone can know more, differently and better. This is a 'table' that eventually you have to put together and set for yourself. It's your English, your job, and your life.

Further transformative knowledges are reviewed @ 6.4.1.

Table 6.1 A table of skills

Study skills 'Done in English': 10 actions revisited (numbers after)	TRANSFORMABLE SKILLS (Generic): what you may now be able to say of yourself, and hope others will be able to say of you in references.	How done? How well done? Which to do more of – differently, better?
Got organised, got own act together (1)	Is organised, disciplined and independent	
Turned up, took part (2)	Is reliable and punctual. Attended lectures conscientiously and participated fully in seminars. Good in discussion working with others, both leading and supporting	
Took and made notes (3)	Can gather information and develop own insights	
Read closely – read widely (4)	Has detailed powers of analysis with good contextual awareness	
Library, web, 'home'; research and referencing (5 and 6)	Can use a good range of resources, print and electronic, with skill, and bring them to bear on task in hand. Scholarly and careful research. Authoritative use of authentic materials.	
Have written essays (7)	Is highly literate and persuasive, can produce a strong and well-grounded argument that is interesting and effective. Accurate grammar and spelling, with effective layout and polished presentation	
Have given oral presentations, individual and group (8)	Speaks clearly and engagingly with a well-organised plan, good sense of audience and appropriate use of audio-visual aids (e.g. paper hand-out, transparency, power-point). (Does not just read out script with head down and no eye-contact.) Works well with others in group presentation and is able to think on feet and respond to questions.	
Revised for and took exams (9)	Can prepare for a deadline and work within time constraints: organises and reorientates prepared materials quickly and on the spot.	
Seriously enjoyed studying English (10)	Was enthusiastic, energetic and committed. Showed a genuine sense of engagement with the subject and with others studying it.	
Did analysis and interpretation (2.1–2) Handled contextual information Capable of critical and creative response	Analyses texts closely and produces convincing interpretations. Handles supporting information with relevance and purpose. Able to develop an integrated and independent response which shows critical judgement and a creative awareness of alternatives. Good at thinking both inside and outside the box – and in terms of other things than boxes.	
Wrote longer project: dissertation: critical/creative project; portfolio (2.3)	Can handle a substantial, large-scale piece of independent work: from conception and planning through research and redrafting to submission.	

Table 6.2 A table of knowledges

Specific subject-based knowledge 'Done in English' You may know about . . .	TRANSFORMATIVE KNOWLEDGE (Generic) (What it may turn into . . .) You can . . .	And you? Now . . . Next?
ENGLISH LANGUAGE – Nature and history, analysis and theory of; 'standards', varieties and variation – local, regional and global; data and corpora. Linguistic levels: phonology, graphology, morphology; vocabulary; grammar; text. Critical discourse analysis. (also see 6.2.1)	◆ Grasp change and variation in language in a variety of modes and media. ◆ Gauge appropriate style and text for particular occasions and contexts. ◆ Know when, where and how to write accurately and speak articulately with local, regional, national and global uses in mind. ◆ Be flexible and principled in dealing with complex and contentious communicative situations.	And you? Now . . . Next?
ENGLISH LITERATURE / LITERATURES IN ENGLISH – Specific periods and movements, authors and genres. Traditions, 'canons' and alternatives. Literary texts in historical contexts. Publishing and readerships. Drama, theatre and performance. Regional, national and international literatures: British (English, Irish, Scottish, Welsh . . .); American, Canadian; African, Asian, Australian, . . . Comparative literature and literature in translation. Literary criticism and theory. (also see 6.2.1)	◆ Appreciate and evaluate the aesthetic and ethical dimension of texts and performances. ◆ Understand the interplay of power and pleasure in fictional, imaginative and playful texts. ◆ Grasp the more or less universal or transcultural *and* historical or cultural-specific nature of imaginative work. ◆ Analyse specific texts in context and theorise the nature of textuality and intertextuality. ◆ Be sympathetic to and understanding of a variety of points of view while recognising the need for a critical and creative interpretation of one's own. ◆ Support and promote the essential personal, social and economic contribution of literature and other verbal arts to the creative and cultural industries. ◆ Recognise the importance of modes and models of literary and verbal recreation (including re-creation) other than the 'industrial' . . .	And you? Now . . . Next?
CULTURE, COMMUNICATION, MEDIA – Cross-cultural and multimedia nature of contemporary communication – and of earlier modes of communication differently. Specific configurations of culture and community: by age, gender, sex, class, caste, ethnicity, wealth, etc. Specific modes and media: spoken (conversation, speech, sermon, lecture, etc.); printed (hand-, steam-, photo-reprographic-); photography; telephone; radio; film; TV; broad- and narrow-cast; digital; web-based; mobile; networked, etc. Analysis, theory and practice of culture, communication and media. (also see 6.2.1)	◆ Grasp verbal language as one among many modes of expressions and media of communication, each with their own distinctive capacities and potential. ◆ Engage with words (spoken and written, electronically stored and communicated) with an understanding of the cultural constraints and technological capacities at work and in play. ◆ See culture and communication as matters of process as well as product, and personal and social as well as commercial value. ◆ Analyse actual instances of the modern media informed by a knowledge of earlier 'traditional' and current 'alternative' modes of communication. ◆ Conceive imaginative and innovative uses of the modern media informed by theory and driven by value.	And you? Now . . . Next?

Career pathways and interesting jobs for 'English' graduates

The most obvious option for students of English who want to use their subject knowledge directly is teaching. This is so obvious that for some students it is the automatic and virtually the only choice. There may well be good reasons for this. Teaching English at any level can be a satisfying and flexible as well as demanding job. But, as with further training and education in general (see 6.3), it is worth considering alternatives before a particular route. One of them may suit you better, and some of them may also draw more or less directly on your knowledge and use of English. Again, a quick spin round the clock/compass of **English *and*** or *as* **other subjects** (6.2 pp. 370–1) will remind you of the potential range.

Most of the following jobs involve capacities highly developed in English:

- Handling texts critically and creatively – close reading and resourceful writing.
- Working with other people, both colleagues and members of the public.
- Working on your own, independently, as well as interdependently as a member of a team.
- Communicating accurately and effectively in a variety of modes, notably speech and writing, along with current communications technologies.
- Being imaginative and open to change, while respecting historical tradition and cultural difference.

For convenience, these jobs are distinguished as *Using 'English' more or less directly – or indirectly.* Though obviously there are continuities and cross-overs (hence . . .).

Most of the jobs in the first column will still require further training. This may be as little as six weeks for a beginning job in English Language Teaching or as much as one and two years for some courses in Librarianship and Journalism. (A career in English Language Teaching may entail an MA in Applied Linguistics at some point.) But much of this training may be done while working, usually in some kind of basic or supporting role. Of the jobs that relate more indirectly to English (the second column), some such as Law require substantial re-training; though even then the possession of a good degree will usually mean a reduction of a year or two in the overall programme. Others such as Personnel and Administration may be entered directly at a relatively modest level if you have the right general background, aptitude and initial

Using 'English' more or less directly	*Using 'English' more or less indirectly*
Teaching English (primary, secondary, tertiary, ELT)	. . . TV and film
Librarianship	Museums and galleries
Publishing (educational, academic, technical)	Personnel and human resources administration
Journalism (newspapers, magazine, radio, TV, web)	Social and community services
Advertising and publicity	Management
Web-based media (educational, games, manuals)	Charities and campaigns
Arts administration and management (exhibitions, festivals, events)	Retail
Theatre and performance . . .	Business
	Law
	Politics
	International relations
	Translation (with another language) . . .

skills. If you have been 'doing English' in the ways set out in Part One and carried through critically and creatively as in Part Two, you will be well on the way. If you have also done a work-related project, you will be even further along. In any event, the most pressing task is to transform your subject-based skills and knowledge into what works for the job in hand. In the first instance, this is the job in mind or in prospect. Turning that into an actual job is what we address next.

Towards application and interview

This can be described as 'the job before the job': the work you have to put in to get the work you want to do. It is worth approaching as systematically and seriously as you would any large-scale project: an extended essay leading to a presentation, for example. In this case it's an application leading to an interview. To get most jobs you will need:

(i)   a 'life record' (*curriculum vitae* – CV, for short) which summarises who you are and what you have done: your qualifications, activities and experiences;

(ii) referees who know you and your work and are prepared to say something supportive and positive about you in references;

(iii) a specific cover-letter from you that focuses on that particular job and says why you think you are suitable; a short one is a good idea even if there is a special application form;

(iv) an interview to meet prospective employers in which you present yourself and make your case, and see whether you are right for the job and the job is right for you.

The whole process basically comes in two stages: the written application and the face-to-face interview. Each of these will be briefly characterised in turn, and then our old friends the questions '6 Wh- and a H-' will be used to support some joined-up thinking across the whole process.

The application is your attempt *on paper* **to get the right kind of job.** It usually consists of your covering letter addressing the particular job and a copy of your CV (which you should highlight and point for that particular job). The application draws immediately on your essay-writing skills and on your previous preparation and research. It is a kind of *essay* both as 'try-out' and 'proof' – your bid for and claim to the job (see 1.2.7). In the application you make a preliminary case based on evidence that should persuade the person reading it that you may be worth interviewing. Nobody wants to waste time with interviews so the application is basically a way of seeing whether there is any point in going further. Applications should be clear, accurate, well-presented and just long enough to do their job – which is to get you an interview, not the job itself. (Overlong applications are tiresome, scruffy ones usually go straight into the bin.)

The interview is your attempt *in person* **to get the right kind of job.** It draws on your skills in presentation (monologue) and conversation (dialogue) (see 1.2.2). It's your opportunity to demonstrate you are right for the job and to explore whether the job is right for you. A good interview is grounded in preparation as well as presentation, and – as with a seminar presentation, which it closely resembles – doing some work before will help you perform well there and then. There are just a few things you need to get right to give yourself the best chance. They all closely correspond to the kinds of thing detailed at length in terms of *before*, *during* and *after* for **oral presentation** when doing English (see 1.2.8). They may be very briefly summarised thus (with some cautionary remarks in brackets):

- Do your homework on the organisation and the job – who they are and what they want. (If you don't appear to know, you won't appear to care)
- Arrive early and get yourself composed. (Late and flustered is a disaster)
- Speak clearly and establish eye-contact. (Don't mutter or look down)
- Enthusiasm, energy and commitment go a long way. (Dullness doesn't)
- Blow your own trumpet loud and clear enough to be heard (But don't boast or deafen!)
- Be confident and specific about what you know – you have got an interview.
- Be prepared to acknowledge what you don't know – but be ready to learn.
- Have some intelligent questions to ask about the job and the organisation.
- Overall, as far as possible, treat this as another occasion for 'Serious Enjoyment'!

If your interview also involves *Giving a presentation*, go straight to that section (1.2.8). The specific audience, occasion and task will all be different from education. But everything else holds. Here you are simply 'doing English' to get a job.

For yet another use of the question '6 Wh- and a H-?' to help you sort out your application and interview strategy, turn to @ 6.4.3.

READING AND LINKS Part Three of Saunders 2005 offers good general advice on leaving college and preparing for work. Martin and Gawthrope's 'The study of English and the careers of its graduates', Knight and Yorke 2004: 69–84, continues to provide useful, more specific guidelines. Work-related Learning in English Studies is comprehensively introduced in Day 2010, including examples of kinds of project. Representative 'Benchmark statements' for English and for Creative Writing, corresponding to the transformable skill and transformative knowledge listed in 6.4.1, can be found at, respectively, www.qaa.ac.uk/academicinfrastructure/benchmark/honours/English and nawe.co.uk.benchmarks. *Occupational Profiles* for most of the career pathways listed in 6.4.2 (Publishing, Journalism, Librarianship, etc.) can be found on the *Prospects* website at: www.prospects.ac.uk/downloads/occprofiles. *The Teacher Training Agency* (www.tda.gov.uk/Recruit) is the best place to start for routes into English teaching, beginning with the section on 'Experience Teaching' and 'Life as a Teacher'. Careers Advisory Services in educational institutions should be able to help you with further personal profiling and more specific information. For further guidelines, examples and links, with updates, see @ 6.

6.5 PLAY: RECREATION AND RE-CREATION

[T]o open us to the range of possible worlds . . . to render the world less fixed, less banal, more susceptible to re-creation.

Jerome Bruner, *Actual Minds, Possible Worlds* (1986: 159)

Here we place the final emphasis on study–work–*play*. This will be done with the help of an apparently slight yet significant distinction between 'recreation' and 're-creation'. *Recreation* in the usual weak sense means leisure activity, pastime, perhaps with an emphasis upon purchase and consumption. But there is also *re-creation* in the strong sense of actively re-making and re-fashioning things, having a hand and a say in what gets transformed – not least ourselves and relationships with one another. It's like the distinction between *revision* that simply looks back and repeats and the radical *re-vision* that sees things in a new way and looks to a different future (1.2.9). Hence the subtly re-inflected *re-* in both these usages: it signals afresh, not just again. The re-creation in mind here takes time and effort, the steady accumulation of experience and expertise. It may or may not take money; at any rate money is not its essential condition and primary purpose. If re-creation is dedicated to anything it is to 'what if?': the opening up – and constant keeping open – of a 'range of possible worlds'. That, as Bruner suggests in the above epigraph and the book from which it comes, is the essential work – and play; he is very insistent on the importance of *play* – of 'actual minds' that make sense of the world. And thereby change it.

Afterwords: a postlude

This is a series of seriously playful parting gestures. They have everything to do with 'English and the rest of life' and involve using the former to throw some revealing light on the latter. Strategically, as afterwords, they are designed to close the body of the book while keeping its meanings resonating long afterwards. We start with some strings of words used by me and others in the rest of the book, and you are invited to turn them into whatever you want to make of them. The last words are wholly yours – your favourite and most precious or persistent ones. This is a 'postlude' that potentially goes on (and on . . .) after the end.

(i)　　The tenth of the ten essential actions for *Doing English* (1.2.10) was a summary exhortation:

Seriously enjoy studying English!

This still holds, with equal emphasis on all four words. In the present context it might be variously rewritten, perhaps:

> *Seriously enjoy learning life!*
> 　*Keep on enjoying using English*
> 　　*Playfully endure a life without learning*
> 　　　*English for pleasure and power – against pain and powerlessness*

How would *you* re-write it? Or what summary exhortation would you make to yourself – about English and the rest of *your* life?

(ii)　　The eleventh of the eleven *Theses on Feuerbach* by Karl Marx (referred to and rewritten in @ 3.5 Discussion) reads:

**The philosophers have only *interpreted* the world in various ways;
the point, however, is to change it.**

Marx wrote this in German in 1845 though it was not published till over forty years later when Engels included it as an Appendix in his *Ludwig Feuerbach and the End of Classical German Philosophy* (1888). Now, as I write this passage in an Afterword to the last part of the present book, I am tempted to rewrite it in yet other ways. Again playfully yet seriously, and perhaps provocatively too:

'Doing English' has *only* interpreted the world in various ways;
it has *not* changed it.

or

English interprets the world and *thereby* changes it
(But whose world and how much?)

or

English has encouraged *me* to interpret and change *my* world
(which is at least a start)

How might *you* re-write Marx's thesis (or my variations on it) on your own terms and for your own time? If you don't want to engage with any of those, then choose some other grand declaration to do with the world and change (and philosophy or English or whatever) that you care to write out or dare to sport with. Whatever you come up with – whether someone else's words, your own or, quite likely, a mixture – it can be attributed and dated accordingly. (Perhaps even acknowledge the knowledge in full academic style, as in 1.2.6.)

(iii) In the mid to late twentieth century (in my childhood) there was a very common and long-running advertising slogan for a chocolate bar (*Mars*). In advertising terms, it is a 'classic' and went like this:

A *Mars* a day helps you work, rest and play.

In the early twenty-first century and in the context of this Part of the book, I am tempted to re-cast it something like this:

A good *Poem* . . . or *Story* . . . or *Conversation* . . . or *Song* . . . a day
helps me work, rest and play.

There may be some other advertising slogan – or line from a song, or proverb, or catch-phrase – that you can do something with. Again, on your own terms and for your own time. Perhaps several, and some you share with friends . . .

The possibilities, clearly, are endless. Such 'Afterwords' might run and run, and this is a 'Postlude' that could be played again and afresh, more or less differently, for as long as anyone likes. In fact, having 'done English' and in some sense probably continuing to 'do English' throughout the rest of your life, there will be all sorts of strings of words and knotty (or nutty) phrases that you keep on coming back to simply because they keep on coming back to you. They seem to suit the occasion, or just keep popping into mind. Deeply significant, mildly irritating, or just plain persistent – they somehow stick and stay with you. (Formally, it is usually because they have some particular balance or cadence. Functionally, it is because they have the power to mean something similar yet different, at least for you and perhaps for others.) Those offered above are at once representative and singular. The line from Marx, courtesy of Engels, I find deeply significant, highly fertile and well worth recalling. The Mars bar slogan – courtesy of media repetition and childhood memories of what my friend could afford and I couldn't – I just can't forget. But there are of course umpteen other words that keep on cropping up or popping into mind – and not just the sayings of the famous and dead I did not know. There are also the many, many words of people I have known personally, now dead or still living: words of parents and children and partners, friends and relations, colleagues and students, the man who . . . the woman at . . . Obviously, I could go on and on. Equally obviously, and more immediately important, so could you.

This is where you and yours come in. For yours are the very last and most important 'Afterwords' in the book. They consist of whatever words you yourself care to write down/in/out: quotations from books, conversations from memory, notes and comments, observations of your own, probably a mixture . . . There might also be the beginnings of an alternative anthology: everything you would have liked to see in Part Five or added @ 5. Maybe another short story or poem or song, a snatch of conversation or a news report, an essay or article from a journal or website, book references and websites . . . It may even be (have been) a place to scribble a friend's telephone number, a shopping list, your own 'to do' list. Probably – but not necessarily – this will be in some shape or form of 'English'. Some of it may not be words at all. There may be diagrams or doodles, sketches or blotches. Anyway, there is a section called 'Afterwords' in the remaining pages at the very end of the book. They may not be enough, but they will be a start. And they are left empty for you to fill.

APPENDIX A
Grammatical and linguistic terms – a quick reference

This offers brief definitions and illustrations of the most common terms, along with a few fuller treatments of core topics. Items in **bold** have their own entries. *A Full Glossary of Linguistic and Grammatical Terms,* including more extensive entries on these terms as well as many others, can be found @ Appendix A.

active structures are those where the subject controls or is the cause of the action, e.g. 'The car *hit* the wall', 'Iraqi soldiers *marched* across the desert'. In **passive** structures, the subject is controlled or affected by the action, e.g. 'The wall *was hit* by the car', 'Iraqi soldiers *were marched* across the desert'. Also see **verbs**.

adjectives add extra information to nouns (hence *ad*-). Often they go before the noun and therefore *pre*-**modify** it (e.g. 'What a *beautiful clear* evening'); but they can also go afterwards and *post*-modify it, e.g. 'What an evening – beautiful and clear'.

adverbs add extra information to verbs (hence *ad*-). They are commonly formed by adding '-ly' to the adjective, e.g. 'She writes *beautifully / clearly / regularly*'. **Adverbial groups** have the same function but use more words, e.g. 'She writes *without fail, every week, from Manchester*'. These, respectively, are adverbial groups of manner, time and place. Like other *ad*- forms, they can be placed variously for emphasis, e.g. 'Every week, without fail, she writes from Manchester'.

articles are either **definite** and by implication specific ('*The* fool on *the* hill') or **indefinite** and non-specific ('*A* fool on *a* hill'). The indefinite plural is 'some' ('some fools', 'some hills').

auxiliary verbs are extra verbs that 'help' the *main* verb to do various things. They help in terms of *tense* (e.g. 'They *have* written', 'They *will* write' – time when) and *aspect* ('They *are / were* writing' – time duration) and **modality** ('They *must / might / could / ought to* write' – condition, obligation, possibility). Auxiliary verbs are themselves often supported and reinforced by corresponding **adverbs** (e.g. 'They *have* written *regularly*'; 'They *will* write *tomorrow*'; 'They *really must* write').

clauses are structural parts of **sentences**, each of which contains a **verb**. They are distinguished as *main* clauses that can stand alone and still make sense, and *dependent* or *subordinate* clauses that can not and do not. Thus in 'That fool who is living on the hill has come down at last' the main clause is 'That fool . . . has come down at last' while 'who is living on the hill' is a dependent/subordinate clause.

cohesion is everything that helps hold a text together as a 'whole', especially across sentences. This depends on **connectors** such as 'and', 'or', 'but', 'however', 'because' and 'therefore';

sustained reference to the same thing by various kinds of **noun** (e.g. 'The woman . . . Jane . . . she . . . .'); and **context-sensitive** words such as 'here / there', 'now / then', 'this / that', along with pronouns such as 'I', 'we', 'you', 'they', etc. Sheer repetition and partial **parallelism** are also important. Together, all these things support cohesive patterning in sense (**semantics**), structure (**syntax**), sound (**phonology**) and sight (**graphology**).

collocations are words that commonly occur in the company of one another: e.g. 'leaf' with 'tree', 'green' and 'autumn' as well as 'loose', 'gold' and 'turning over a new . . .'; or 'screen' with 'computer', 'film' and 'touch' as well as, say, 'Japanese silk' and ' . . . for cancer'. As these examples show, words collocate in many ways and in many **semantic** fields.

connectors are words that make explicit links between one sentence or part of a sentence and another. The most common are the *coordinators* 'and', 'but' and 'or' (which indicate addition, negation and alternation) and *conjuncts* such as 'because', 'however' and 'moreover', which signal more complex kinds of causality and **cohesion**.

connotations are the attitudes and values associated with particular words, as distinct from the basic **denotation** they may share with substantially corresponding words. 'Senior citizen', 'the elderly', 'old-age pensioner', 'old fogey' and 'wrinkly' all have very different connotations, though they all share a denotation to do with old people.

context-sensitive words (also called 'shifters' and 'deictics') are especially dependent on context to fill and fix their meanings. Personal **pronouns** ('I', 'me', 'you', 'she', 'it', 'we', 'they', etc.), the **demonstratives** 'this/these' and 'that/those', **adverbs** such as 'here', 'now', 'there' and 'then' – and whole phrases such as 'someone else' and 'the day after tomorrow' – all mean very different things depending on the persons, times and places in play. All words are sensitive to context; these are especially so.

coordination; see **connectors** and **sentences**.

deviation refers to any verbal twist or turn away from what is expected; it is always odd and sometimes humorous or shocking. 'I got up at the crack of *lunchtime*' (instead of 'dawn') and '*fcuk*' (the controversial sign for the clothing company 'French Connection United Kingdom') are both deviant in various ways. The first sports with an established **collocation** and the latter **foregrounds** (and encourages) a potential misreading. Much catchy language use, especially in poetry and advertising, has a dash of deviation.

direct speech offers a record of the words exactly as spoken and is typically signalled by quotation marks (e.g. *'My dear Mr Bennett,' said his lady to him one day*; 5.3.2). **Indirect speech** gives the gist of what was said but without direct quotation (e.g. *Mr Bennett replied that he had not*). The differences in dramatic effect and narrative perspective are always significant. In news-reporting, as in academic essay-writing, there is a corresponding difference in truth-claim. Quotations carry more authority and are expected to be both accurate and attributed.

elision is the sliding together of adjacent syllables in speech, e.g. 'she'll' for 'she will' and 'I can't' for 'I can not'. This usually means losing a vowel in the process and marking the absence with an apostrophe in writing.

ellipsis means something is deliberately missing. In casual conversation it is often the subject, e.g. 'See you tomorrow' (missing 'I shall'). In writing, significant ellipsis is conventionally marked by the insertion of three suspension dots: within square brackets for an editorial excision (e.g. the [. . .] in 5.2.2 Coetzee); and without brackets for a sense of suspense: 'But that was not all . . .'.

foregrounding applies to any verbal or perceptual feature that stands out against some internal or external *background* (see Part Four). Linguistically, this may involve **deviation**.

grammar is concerned with the structure of language. At the level of **sentence** structure, grammar is synonymous with **syntax**; at the level of **word** structure, it includes **morphology**. Grammar is one of the four big 'S's of language, 'Structure', the other three being are 'Sense' (**semantics**), 'Sound' (**phonology**), and 'Sight' (**graphology**).

graphology refers to the visual aspects of recorded language: spelling; punctuation; font styles and sizes, and all features of layout and design. It is language as 'Sight'.

lexis is a linguistically precise, if ponderous, alternative to '**word** or phrase'. It refers to what is generally known as *vocabulary* and more formally as *diction*. Talking in terms of lexis also allows us to see that, say, 'leave' and 'go out' or 'enter' and 'come in' are corresponding pairs of lexical items, even though they are of one or two words.

metaphor involves implicitly talking of one thing in terms of another, e.g. 'Then this utter fruitcake came into the room'; 'My mistress's eyes are bright suns'). When the comparison is made especially explicit (by using words such as 'like', 'as' and 'seems') we tend to talk of **simile**, e.g. 'He seems to be a complete basket case'; 'My mistress' eyes are nothing like the sun' (Shakespeare, 5.1.2). We use more or less *'dead'* metaphors much of the time ('You look *down*. What's *up*? Life been treating you *hard* . . . ?'). But these are perhaps better seen as *'dormant'* as they can quickly be prodded back into life and add colour to even quite routine statements. (That last sentence is itself a modest example, animating apparently colourless metaphors in passing.) Metaphors can be *extended* and are often freely *mixed*. A classic example is Hamlet's soliloquy 'To be or not to be . . . To take arms against a sea of troubles . . . To sleep, to dream . . .' (see 3.1).

modification, pre- and post-; see **adjectives** and **noun groups**

morphology is about the internal structure of **words** and the **grammatical** processes of word-building, e.g. making nouns plural by the addition of the *suffix* '-s' (books, trees) or by *mutation* of the stem (foot/feet, man/men); and making verbs past tense by the addition of '-ed' (walked, turned) or, again, by mutation of the stem (run/ran, write/wrote). Complex words are usually built by adding a variety of *prefixes* and *suffixes* to a *stem* (e.g. re+modern+ise, post+modern+ism) and by fastening stems together to make *compounds* (e.g. greenhouse, camera phone). It is therefore useful to distinguish *'free'* morphemes (such as 'modern' and 'green') that can stand on their own, from *'bound'* morphemes (such as 're-' and '-ise') that usually can't. Though, as 'post' and 'ism' remind us, the sheer act of featuring a bound morpheme can free it up.

nouns tend to realise experience as 'things', as distinct from **verbs** which tend to realise it as 'processes'. There are three main kinds of noun: (i) *common nouns* that refer to general types or categories of phenomena, and can be further distinguished as more or less *concrete* (table, book) or *abstract* (idea, democracy); (ii) *proper nouns* that name specific persons, places and phenomena (e.g. Tom Paine, Manchester, English); (iii) *pronouns* that 'stand for' the other nouns (hence 'pro-'), e.g. *personal* pronouns such as 'I', 'me', 'you', 'he', 'she', 'it', 'they', 'them', and *relative, interrogative* and *demonstrative* pronouns such as 'who', 'which', 'this/these' and 'that/those'. Any of these kinds of noun could fill the grammatical Subject (S.) and Object (O.) slots in the following sentence: 'S. is teaching O.' ('The lecturer / Tom / he is teaching students / Jane and Dave / them'). Also see **noun groups**.

noun groups are grammatical structures built round **nouns**. This structure is best grasped in terms of what goes before and what goes after the main noun (technically speaking, in terms of what *pre-* and *post-***modifies** the noun *head*). Thus the noun group 'A professional Eurasian woman, single and with a strong interest in music . . .' (based on the personal ad in 5.2.6) would be analysed in the first instance as follows:

/ A professional Eurasian / woman / single and with a strong interest in music /
/ pre-modification / noun head / post-modification /

This could be further analysed, at a finer level of delicacy, as: 'A professional Eurasian' (pre-modification by indefinite article + adjective + adjective), and 'single and with a strong interest in music' (post-modified by adjective + coordinator + another, subordinate noun group). And so on. As so often in language, we get structure within structure and a kind of Chinese box effect. But the basic principles of pre- and post-modification act at all levels of even the most complex noun group.

object, *direct and indirect*; see **subject**.

parallelism is any kind of repetition with variation, something done similarly yet differently, on a small or large scale. A small-scale example is Christ's claim to be 'the way, the life and the truth', which features a repeated yet varied structure of three noun groups, each consisting of the definite article and a different monosyllabic noun. Large-scale parallelism is what informs the overall structure of *King Lear*, with its main plot of a father (Lear) and un/grateful daughters and its sub-plot of father (Gloucester) and un/grateful sons. Poetry, oratory and advertising all depend for many of their basic effects on kinds of parallelism.

passive verbs; see **active** and see **verbs**.

phonology relates to the 'sound' dimension of language, as distinct from **graphology** which relates to the 'sight' dimension. To be precise, phonology deals with the sound-system of a particular language and is centrally concerned with the basic *phonemes* from which the spoken language is built. There are over forty phonemes in most varieties of spoken English (far more than the twenty-six letters of the standard written alphabet) so a special system drawn from the International Phonetic Alphabet is required to record them (see 'Alphabet of speech sounds', Appendix B). Phonology also extends to *accent* and *intonation* in speech and to *stress*, *rhythm* and *rhyme* in poetry (for which see **accent**, **speech** and **versification** in Part Four).

pragmatics deals with the practical meanings and effects of language use in context: the who, when, where and why of words as well as the what and the how. In *discourse* at large, especially *conversation*, pragmatic approaches tend to concentrate on kinds of relevance, co-operation and power and to identify the kinds of *implicature* and *inference* involved in interpreting **speech acts**. In so far as pragmatics involves kinds of 'embodied speech', 'mental mapping' and 'text world', it extends to *cognitive linguistics*.

prepositions are crucial words such as 'with', 'by', 'on', 'in', 'for', 'to' and 'from'. They hold phrases together and help point meaning, and they often go *with* or stand *in for* verbs (and so form phrasal or *multi-word* **verbs**) like those highlighted here. 'To me!' or 'By there' can thus stand in for 'Kick it to me!' or 'Put it by there'.

pronouns; see **nouns** and **context-sensitive words**.

punctuation is a system of notation developed to point up grammatical, logical and rhythmic structure in writing and print. The basic range in modern English, as represented on a standard keyboard, is: , – ( ) ; : . ? ! ' ' ' " " ". There are also more specialised marks such as / and * and abbreviations such as & and %. Punctuation is reinforced and supplemented by capitalisation at the beginning of sentences and for names, spacing between words, and extra spaces at the end of sentences. These extend to other aspects of **graphology** such as font size and design (e.g. *italic*), indentation and layout. Early manuscript punctuation is usually very slight, consisting of little more than variable placing of a point (Latin *punctum*, whence 'punctuation') and abbreviations. Long dashes (including the comma-dash, —) were widespread from the 16th to 19th centuries, and the apostrophe is becoming less stable in contemporary English. Meanwhile, the abbreviation @, previously a specialised accounting symbol meaning 'so many items @ (at a rate of) so much each', has had a new lease of life meaning 'at the website of' (as with the @s in this book).

semantics deals with the 'sense' aspects of language, what words mean. (The root is Greek *semeion*, 'sign', which also gives us *semiotics/semiology*, the study of sign-systems.) Semantics typically begins with binary categories and defines the meaning of a word in terms of, say, *animate/inanimate*, *concrete/abstract*, *human/non-human*, *female/male*, *artificial/natural*, etc. Thus 'table' (what you eat off) might be characterised as inanimate—concrete—artificial, while 'bitch' (female dog) would obviously be animate—non-human—female. But further distinctions are obviously required if you mean a 'table of statistics' (abstract not concrete) or 'to table a motion' (verb not a noun); also if 'bitch' is applied to humans (not just animals) and to people of both sexes (not just female) or, again, is used as a verb ('to bitch') and even an impersonal exclamation ('It's a bitch!'). For all these reasons, semantics as applied to actual language has to take on board the **metaphorical** aspects of meaning and to be alert to both the **grammar** and the **pragmatics** of particular utterances in context.

sentences are easier to recognise in practice than define in the abstract. Mechanically, in formal writing and print, a sentence begins with a capital letter and ends with a full stop. Grammatically speaking, a sentence usually needs at least a **subject** and main **verb** to be considered acceptable and 'complete'. For example, 'The man arrived.' is grammatically complete in this sense and would therefore be called a *major sentence*. *'The man.' and *'Arrived.', however, are not grammatically complete and would usually be considered unacceptable (hence the *). Nonetheless, it is quite possible to imagine contexts in which each of these phrases could still make perfect sense: 'The Man!' in street-talk and 'Arrived.' in a text message. These grammatically 'incomplete' but contextually acceptable structures are called *minor sentences*. In fact, in live conversation and real-time messaging, such is the interdependence and context-sensitivity of the exchanges that it is often better to talk of *utterances*, **speech acts**, and *turns* rather than of 'sentences'. Formally, meanwhile, it is useful to distinguish sentences according to their **clause** structure. 'The man arrived' is a simple, *single-clause sentence* because it has just one main verb. 'The man arrived but he is now gone' is a complex, *multi-clause sentence* because it has more than one main verb. The latter sentence is *coordinated* because it has independent clauses laid end to end and joined by a **connector** ('but'). If it said 'The man that arrived is now gone' the sentence would be *subordinated* because it includes the dependent (relative) clause 'that arrived'. Overall, then, sentences need to be grasped both formally and functionally, in terms of **pragmatics** and **semantics** as well as **grammar** and **syntax**.

speech acts are what we actually *do* with words. Most obviously, we use language to state, as *declaratives* ('I am'), to question, as *interrogatives* ('Am I?'), to command or instruct, as *imperatives/directives* ('Be aware'), and to express excitement or surprise, as *exclamatives* ('I am!'). More generally, we use words to express just about every shade of feeling and every shape of relationship that humans are capable of: from crying to bawling, and forgiving to condemning. Especially crucial are the ways in which words actually *perform* actions in the world. Such *performatives* include promising, swearing, lying, witnessing and signing; and they always require or assume some network of roles and relations to give them force. (Saying 'I do' and then signing a register at a recognised marriage ceremony is such a crucial speech act. So, in its way, is signing the formal claim and disclaimer when submitting an essay: 'I hereby certify that this is all my own work and that all sources are fully acknowledged'; see 1.2.6). But arguably all speech *acts* in so far as words affect and have effects in the rest of the world. Also see **pragmatics**.

stress in language is basically of three kinds: (i) *word stress*, in that every word of two or more syllables has one that is naturally stressed (e.g. *orch*estra, orch*es*tral, orchestr*a*tion); (ii) *utterance stress*, where speakers have the option of stressing one word or phrase rather than another, and so deliberately changing the emphasis (e.g. *What* are you doing here? What *are* you doing here? What are *you* doing here? etc.); (iii) *rhythmic stress*, overall patterning of stresses, which are relatively dispersed in casual speech and conversation, more marked in formal monologues such as lectures, political speeches and sermons, and most marked in poetry and song. Also see **versification** in Part Four.

subject, grammatically speaking, is what controls the **verb**: '*She* saw it'; '*The car* hit the wall'. The grammatical **object** is what the verb acts upon, in these cases 'it' and 'the wall'. Both of the latter are *direct* objects. In 'She gave the book to him', the direct object is 'book' and the *indirect* object is 'to him'. In 'She is a doctor', 'doctor' would be a subject *complement* as it refers to the same thing as the subject: 'doctor' is what 'she' is.

syntax is about the way phrases and **sentences**, including **noun groups** and **verb groups**, 'hold together' (it derives from Greek *syn-taxis*, 'together-touching'). It is the aspect of **grammar** that relates to **cohesion**.

verbs tend to realise experience as 'processes', as distinct from **nouns** that realise it as 'things'. Verbs are remarkably complex in form and subtle in function. But each instance can be grasped using a relatively simple array of verbal criteria, here illustrated with the verb 'to write':

tense, the basic time dimension ('when'): 'she writes' (present); 'she will write' (future); 'she wrote' (simple past); 'she has written' (past perfect); 'she had written' (past pluperfect).

aspect, the dimension of duration or frequency ('how long', 'how often'): 'she is (will be, was, has been, had been) writ*ing*' (continuous/progressive aspect); 'she did write', 'she has written' (non-continuous/perfective aspect).

modality, the dimensions of possibility, probability, obligation, concession and capacity: 'she may (might, must, ought to, can) write'; all of which can be reinforced by modal **adverbs** such as 'possibly', 'perhaps', 'certainly', 'definitely'.

active and passive, the 'doing' and 'done to' dimensions, respectively: 'She wrote the essay'; 'The essay was written (by her)' (the agency of the latter is optional). Also see **active**.

finite and non-finite, the 'specific' and 'non-specific' dimensions, respectively: 'She wrote' (specifying person and tense); 'To write or not to write' (anyone at anytime, here the *infinitive*).

transitive and intransitive, depending on whether the verbal process does or does not 'carry-through' from the **subject** to an **object**, respectively: 'She was writing an essay' and 'She was writing'; cf. 'He was reading a book' (transitive), 'He was reading' (intransitive).

It is also useful to distinguish verbs that are *dynamic* and involve actions (e.g. to go, lift, throw, run, etc.); *stative*, involving states (to be, seem, have); *perceptual* (to see, hear, feel, touch) and *communicative* (speak, listen, show, etc.). Obviously, however, some verbs belong to more than one category. 'To write', for example, is dynamic and perceptual as well as communicative.

verbal groups involve more than one **verb**. A complex verbal group might routinely (yet still remarkably) consist of various kinds of **auxiliary** verb signalling *tense* and *modality* as well as one or more *main* and *secondary* verbs accompanied by an **adverb** or two. For example:

She	has	already	missed	the train.
	auxiliary verb (past tense)	*adverb*	*main verb (past participle)*	

She	should have	tried	to come	earlier on.
	auxiliary verb (past modal)	*secondary verb*	*infinitive*	*adverb*

word classes (also called 'parts of speech') are the basic linguistic categories **noun, verb, adjective, adverb, preposition** and **article**. Together with the basic grammatical categories **subject** and **sentence** these connect to most of the terms in this 'quick reference' list.

For fuller guidance and further reference, return to the opening and turn to @ Appendix A.

APPENDIX B
An alphabet of speech sounds

The following symbols represent **standard** British English pronunciation and, for the consonants, many corresponding American words. Regional and ethnic differences abound in both countries, however, especially in vowel quality and intonation. (Also see phonetics and phonology; Carter *et al.* 2001: 41–72; Crystal 1995: 236–55 and Fromkin and Rodman 2006 – this last featuring American usage.)

CONSONANTS

Plosives (breath is held, then released quickly with an audible 'explosion')

/ p / – <u>p</u>op, u<u>pp</u>er	/ d / – <u>d</u>in, or<u>d</u>er	/ k / – <u>k</u>in, do<u>ck</u>er
/ b / – <u>b</u>in, o<u>bj</u>ect	/ t / – <u>t</u>in, brigh<u>t</u>	/ g / – good, cigar

Fricatives (breath is released gradually with audible friction)

/ f / – <u>f</u>at, <u>ph</u>ysics, e<u>ff</u>ect	/ θ / – <u>th</u>in, au<u>th</u>or	/ s / – <u>s</u>ing, per<u>s</u>on
/ v / – <u>v</u>at, e<u>v</u>er	/ ð / – <u>th</u>e, o<u>th</u>er	/ z / – <u>z</u>ing, poi<u>s</u>on
/ ʃ / – <u>sh</u>ine, <u>s</u>ugar, wi<u>sh</u>	/ h / – <u>h</u>appy, <u>h</u>inge	/ ʤ / – <u>g</u>in, <u>G</u>eorge
/ ʒ / – mea<u>s</u>ure, era<u>s</u>ure		/ ʧ / – <u>ch</u>in, wa<u>tch</u>

In addition, / h / is called an *aspirate* because it's 'breathy'; / s /, /ʃ / and / z / are called *sibilants* because they 'hiss' (as in <u>sessions</u>); and / ʤ / and / ʧ / are called *affricates* because they combine fricative and (ex)plosive properties.

Nasals are sounded in the nasal cavity: / m / – <u>m</u>at; / n / – <u>n</u>o<u>n</u>e; / ŋ / – si<u>ng</u>i<u>ng</u>
Liquids have a kind of wobble or trill: / l / – a<u>ll</u>ey, <u>l</u>itt<u>l</u>e, / r / – <u>r</u>ed, b<u>r</u>ing
Semi-vowels are in some ways like vowels: / j / – <u>y</u>et, h<u>i</u>gher / w / – <u>w</u>ill, <u>wh</u>ite

VOWELS

Short	*Long*	*Compound (diphthongs)*
/ i / – s<u>i</u>t	/ i: / – s<u>ee</u>	/ ei / – f<u>ai</u>l
/ e / – g<u>e</u>t	/ u: / – f<u>oo</u>l	/ ai / – h<u>i</u>de
/ æ / – m<u>a</u>n	/ ɔ: / – <u>awe</u>, <u>or</u>	/ ɔi / – b<u>oi</u>l
/ ɔ / – n<u>o</u>t	/ ə: / – h<u>ear</u>d	/ ɔu / – g<u>o</u>
/ u / – b<u>oo</u>k	/ a: / – b<u>ar</u>n	/ au / – h<u>ow</u>
/ ə / – <u>a</u>bout riv<u>er</u>		/ uə / – p<u>oor</u>
/ ʌ / – m<u>u</u>d		/ eə / – th<u>ere</u>
		/ iə / – h<u>ere</u>

APPENDIX C
Chronology of English by period and movement

EVENTS	LANGUAGE & LITERATURE	CULTURE COMMUNICATION & MEDIA
AD 43 Roman invasion of Celtic Britain	Celtic languages and oratures	Celtic tribal structures, myths and art forms
410 Romans leave	**Old English language** (Anglo-Saxon, Jutish and Kentish dialects): Germanic base with some traces of imperial Latin and Church Latin; highly inflected, relatively free word-order.	Germanic tribal (kin-based) society organised round house-hold, village, church and court. Heroic warrior culture with admixtures of Celtic and Roman Christianity.
432 Patrick brings Christianity to Ireland		
597 Augustine brings Christianity to England	**Anglo-Saxon orature and literature** (*c.* 450–*c.* 1100): poetry – oral-formulaic and stressed alliterative, chiefly, epic, heroic, elegiac (see 'Wulf and Eadwacer' 5.1.1) and saints' lives; prose – chiefly chronicles and sermons.	Oral and manuscript (animal skin) verbal media
449–900 Romano–Celtic Britain invaded by Germanic tribes		
1066 Norman conquest	**Middle English language** (1066–*c.* 1450): Germanic base with French and Latin superstructure; loss of inflections, fixing of word-order; onset of vowel changes. Anglo-Norman (earlier) for local administration; Paris French (later) for court and aristocracy; Latin for learning, church and international administration	Feudal (land-based) society organised round manor, castle and court, church or monastery, town and village – gradually giving way to money-based economy centred on trade and the city.
1120–80 First English 'plantations' in Wales and Ireland		Oral and manuscript culture – gradually giving way to paper and print-based culture. Religious control of learning gradually giving way to secular.
1362 English first used for opening of Parliament	**Medieval English literature:** Poetry – chiefly lyric (e.g 'Maiden in the mor lay' 5.1.1,	Pan-European notions of Christendom (braced against

EVENTS	LANGUAGE & LITERATURE	CULTURE COMMUNICATION & MEDIA
1384 Wyclif's Bible in English	romance, satire and saints' lives; versification variously alliterative and stressed (e.g. *Piers Plowman* and *Pearl* @ 5.1.1) or rhymed and syllabic (e.g. Chaucer's 'General Prologue' 5.1.1). Drama – chiefly religious Mystery Plays and some popular carnival forms (e.g. Chester *Noah* @ 5.3.2). Prose – chiefly didactic, functional, some mystical and romance.	'pagan / heathen' Muslims to the East, notably in the Crusades) and international court culture.
1415 Agincourt and Henry V's victory over the French		
1476 Caxton starts first printing press in London 1525, 1535 First printed Bibles in English: Tyndale (New Testament) and Coverdale (complete), from Cologne 1534 Break with the papacy: Church of England established 1603 Union of Crowns James I of England and VI of Scotland 1607 First permanent English settlement in America 1619 First African slaves transported to America 1642–51 English Civil War 1765 Beginning of major British influence in India	**Early Modern English** (1450–1800): Germanic base with deep layers of French and Latin, and admixtures from other European and some non-European languages (ancient Greek, Dutch, Spanish, Italian . . . Caribbean and American Indian); major vowel shift effected in speech; written form gradually standardised through printing. **Renaissance / Early Modern literature:** Drama (1580s onwards) – centred on 'public' and 'private' theatres, playhouse and court – comedies, tragedies, histories, satires (e.g. Marlowe, Shakespeare, Jonson). Poetry – principal genres: sonnet (e.g. Shakespeare 5.1.2 and Milton); lyric (e.g. Wyatt 5.1.1); neo-classical epic (e.g. Milton 5.1.3); satire and mock-heroic (e.g. Pope and Hands 5.1.3). Prose – especially the novel (e.g. Behn and Defoe 5.2.2); letters and diaries (e.g. Brews–Paston and Pepys @ 5.2.1).	Print-based culture gradually displaces, but does not replace, oral and manuscript-based culture. Brief yet decisive prominence of drama in Elizabethan and Jacobean periods, and intermittently thereafter. Rise of nation-states and sense of national identity. Christendom divides into (North European) Protestantism and (South European) Roman Catholicism, as well as the Eastern Orthodox Church. Revival of classical learning and literature and (re)editing of ancient Greek and Roman texts.

EVENTS	LANGUAGE & LITERATURE	CULTURE COMMUNICATION & MEDIA
1775–82 American War of Independence **1788** Penal colony established in Australia **1789** French Revolution begins **1801** Establishment of United Kingdom (England, Wales, Ireland and Scotland) **1840** Official colony in New Zealand **1861–65** American Civil War **1870–1910** European states divide up Africa	**Romantic & Victorian literature** (1790–1900): Poetry – chiefly lyric and adapted ballad (e.g. Blake 2.1, W. Wordsworth 5.4.1, Clare 5.3.4 and Dickinson 5.3.4); narrative and satire (e.g. Byron 5.1.3). Prose – chiefly novels of social manners, romance and realism (e.g. Austen 5.3.2 and Brontë 5.2.3 and Dickens 5.4.5); speculative or political tracts (e.g. M. Shelley @ 5.2.4) and journals and auto-biography (e.g. D. Wordsworth 5.4.1, Darwin @ 5.4.2 and Douglass @ 5.2.2). Drama – heroic, romantic and domestic, initially in verse, latterly in prose.	Belief in scientific progress blends with egalitarian models of society leading to revolutions and reforms. Industrial Revolution sharpens division between city and country and, in Britain, between industrial North and rural South; while London grows to be Cobbett's 'great Wen' (i.e. tumour). Steam-printing presses massively increase output of print material. Newspapers and novels multiply. Demand and opportunity for literacy grow. Railways, canals and steam-ships revolutionise transport communication. First practical photograph/ daguerrotype (1837) Telegraph invented (1840) Morse Code developed (1852) Typewriter invented (1860) Telephone invented (1860) Phonograph / record-player invented (1877)
1914–18 First World War **1922** Eire / Republic of Ireland formed **1931** British Commonwealth established as British Empire disintegrates **1939–45** Second World War	**Modernist & Postmodernist writings:** non-realist fiction (e.g Beckett 5.3.3) or mixed realist / non-realist (e.g. Fugard 5.3.3 and McDonagh 5.3.3), variously 'high art' or 'popular' culture. **Post/modern media productions** for radio, film and TV (e.g. Thomas 5.3.3 and Russell 5.3.1) and records and video (e.g. Queen and Flobots 5.1.5; and advertising (e.g. Heineken 5.4.1 and Clarins 5.4.4), news (e.g. 5.2.5) and chat (5.2.6).	Radio developed by Marconi (1901) First one-reel 'silent' narrative film (1903) Television invented (1926) Sound-films / 'talkies' (1928) BBC's first high-definition television broadcast in the UK (1937) NBC begins broadcasting in the USA (1939)

EVENTS	LANGUAGE & LITERATURE	CULTURE COMMUNICATION & MEDIA
1947–1980s Independence and decolonisation from India to Africa and the Caribbean to the Pacific	**Post/colonial and multicultural writings**, marking the passing of empire (e.g. Kipling 5.2.1, Achebe and Morrison 5.4.5), the resurgence of 'new' regional and national identities (e.g. Leonard 5.1.4, Kelman and Doyle 5.3.2, Fugard 5.3.3, Achebe 5.4.5, πο 5.1.5) and the possibility – or impossibility – of cross- and multicultural understanding (e.g. Rhys 5.2.3, Wei Meng 5.1.4, Scott 5.4.4 and Nichols 5.4.5; also Marshall-Stoneking and Phillips 5.4.2).	Audio-tape invented (1937)
1950– Growing dominance of USA in economic, diplomatic and military power (Korea, Vietnam, Central America); neo-colonialism		Electronic computer developed (1943)
		Transistors begin to replace valves (1948)
1950s–1975 Large-scale emigration to Britain from the Caribbean, Africa and Asia		Microprocessors developed (1978–)
		Computerised multimedia interfaces developed (1980s–)
1973 Britain joins the European Union		World Wide Web, e-mail, text-messaging and 'cyber-space' become widely available (virtual) realities for those who have resources and access . . .
1989– State Communism collapses in Eastern Europe; Yugoslavia in protracted civil war		
		Oral, manuscript and print cultures continue to be displaced but not replaced. Communications and media are ever more complex but also potentially more homogeneous – more readily 'translatable'.
1994 Formal end of apartheid in South Africa		
1999/2000– Devolved Parliament in Scotland and Assembly in Wales. Much of Africa continues in crisis; Japan and Korea dominate many world markets; China is poised for further change . . .	**'New' Englishes** recognised (African, Caribbean, Asian, Pacific) – also the promise and threat of 'World Standard English', 'Global English'.	Car transport routine; air travel increasingly common
		Cultures are increasingly global *and* local, international *and* national or regional; multi- *and* monocultural . . .
2001– Attack by Islamic extremists on World Trade Centre, New York, and Pentagon. 'War on Terrorism' declared. Invasion by USA, UK and allies of Iraq. Western intervention in Afghanistan (see 5.2.5)		Genetic 'code-cracking' and engineering accelerated. Genetically modified food, animals and medicines common – human cloning imminent.
2010/2011– World financial markets in crisis. Gulf of Mexico oil spill. Killing of Osama bin Laden. 'Arab Spring' in Middle Eastern States. Global warming accelerates.	**'Hybrid' Englishes**, screen–print–speech by permutating by region, technology and purpose. 'Global' (global/local) discourses and text types – personal, 'street' and commercial (5.2.6). Multimodal, multimedia, multicultural (5.1.5).	Communications and information networks become increasingly portable, powerful and pervasive: mobile camera phones, hand-held info-comm systems (books and multimodal), blogs, tweets and wiki-leaks . . .

APPENDIX D
Maps of Britain, the USA and the world

Figure D.1 Varieties of English and other languages in the British Isles
Drawn by R.M. Pomfret, 1997

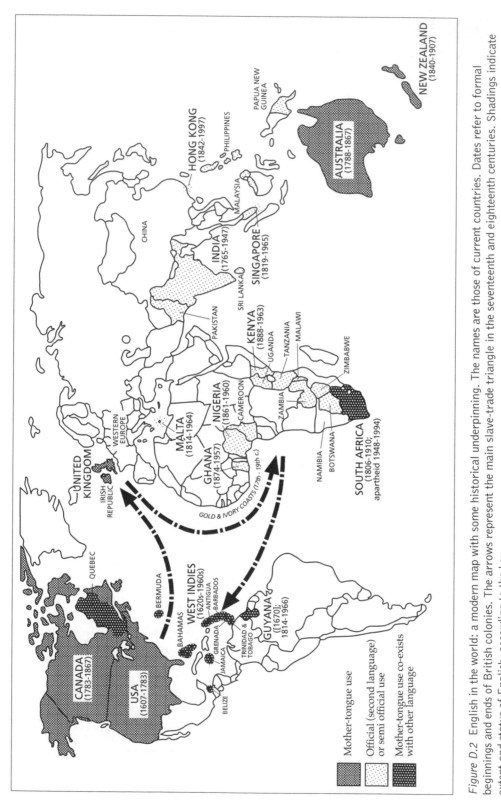

Figure D.2 English in the world: a modern map with some historical underpinning. The names are those of current countries. Dates refer to formal beginnings and ends of British colonies. The arrows represent the main slave-trade triangle in the seventeenth and eighteenth centuries. Shadings indicate extent and status of English, according to the key.

Drawn by R.M. Pomfret, 1997 (Conflated and adapted from Crystal, 1988: 8–9 and Leith, 1997: 195)

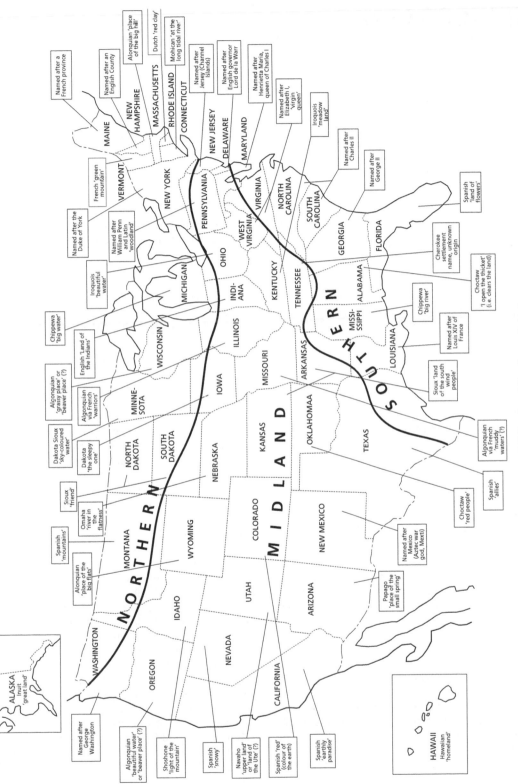

Figure D.3 The USA: origins of state names with chief Northern, Midland and Southern dialect areas
Drawn by R.M. Pomfret, 1997 (Adapted from Crystal, 1995: 94, 105 and Graddol et al., 1996: 199)

BIBLIOGRAPHY

Most of the following references are to books or parts of books. Relevant journals, as well as addresses of useful associations, can be found in the next section. Guidance on general reference books can be found in 1.2.5.

Abrams, M.H., Greenblatt, S. *et al.* (eds) (2006) *The Norton Anthology of English Literature,* 2 Vols, 8th edn, New York: W.W. Norton.

Abrams, M.H. and Harpham, G. (2009) *A Glossary of Literary Terms,* 9th edn, Boston: Wadsworth.

Agathocleous, T. and Dean A. (eds) (2002) *Teaching Literature: A Companion,* New York and Basingstoke: Palgrave.

Agamben, G. (2004) *The Opening: Man and Animal,* Stanford, CA: Stanford University Press.

Aitchison, J. (1991) *Language Change: Progress or Decay?,* Cambridge: Cambridge University Press.

Allen, G. (2000) *Intertextuality,* London: Routledge.

—— (2003) *Roland Barthes,* London: Routledge.

Alliez, E. and Goffey, A. (eds) (2011) *The Guattari Effect,* London and New York: Continuum.

Anderson, L. (2001) *Autobiography,* London: Routledge.

—— (2005) *Creative Writing: A Workbook with Readings,* London: Routledge.

Andrews, R. (ed.) (1992) *Rebirth of Rhetoric: Essays in Language, Culture and Education,* London: Routledge.

Armstrong, I. (2000) *The Radical Aesthetic,* Oxford: Blackwell.

Ashcroft, B., Griffiths, G. and Tiffin, H. (eds) (1995) *The Post-Colonial Studies Reader,* London and New York: Routledge.

—— (2000) *Post-Colonial Studies: The Key Concepts,* London: Routledge.

—— (2002) *The Empire Writes Back; Theory and Practice in Post-Colonial Literatures,* 2nd edn, London: Methuen.

Attridge, D. (1988) *Peculiar Language: Literature as Difference from the Renaissance to James Joyce,* London: Methuen.

—— (2004) *The Singularity of Literature,* London and New York: Routledge.

Attridge, D., Bennington, G. and Young, R. (eds) (1987) *Poststructuralism and the Question of History,* Cambridge: Cambridge University Press.

Attridge, D., Durant, A., Fabb, N. and MacCabe, C. (eds) (1987) *The Linguistics of Writing: Arguments between Language and Literature,* Manchester: Manchester University Press.

Auerbach, E. (1946) *Mimesis: The Representation of Reality in Western Literature,* trans. W. R. Trask, Princeton, NJ: Princeton University Press.

Avery, S., Bryan, C. and Wisker, G. (eds) (1999) *Innovations in Teaching English and Textual Studies,* London: Staff and Educational Development Association.

Badiou, A. (2001) *Ethics: An Essay in the Understanding of Evil,* trans. P. Holland, London: Verso.

Bailey, R. (1992) *Images of English: A Cultural History of the Language,* Cambridge: Cambridge University Press.

Baker, M. (ed.) (2009) *Routledge Encyclopedia of Translation Studies,* London: Routledge.

Bakhtin, M. (1968) *Rabelais and his World,* trans. H. Iswolsky, Cambridge, MA: MIT Press.

—— (1981) *The Dialogic Imagination: Four Essays,* ed. M. Holquist, trans. C. Emerson and M. Holquist, Austin: University of Texas Press.

Baldick, C. (1996) *Criticism and Literary Theory, 1890 to the Present,* London: Longman.

—— (2004) *A Concise Dictionary of Literary Terms,* 2nd edn, Oxford: Oxford University Press.

Baron, N.S. (2000) *Alphabet to Email: How Written English Evolved and Where it's Heading,* London: Routledge.

Barry, P. (2002) *Beginning Theory: An Introduction to Literature,* 2nd edn, Manchester: Manchester University Press.

—— (2003) *English in Practice: In Pursuit of English Studies,* London: Arnold.

Barthes, R. (1957) *Mythologies,* trans. A. Lavers, New York: Hill and Wang.

—— (1970) *S/Z,* trans. R. Miller, London: Cape, 1975.

—— (1977) *Image–Music–Text,* ed. and trans. S. Heath, London: Fontana.

Bartholomae, D. and Petrosky. A. (1986) *Facts, Artifacts, and Counterfacts: Theory and Method for Reading and Writing,* Portsmouth NH: Boynton Cook.

—— (eds) (2008) *Ways of Reading: An Anthology for Writers,* 8th edn, Boston and New York: Bedford/St Martin's.

Bassnett, S. (ed.) (1997) *Translating Literature,* Cambridge: D. S. Brewer for the English Association.

—— (2002) *Translation Studies,* 3rd edn, London: Routledge.

—— (ed.) (2003) *Studying British Cultures: An Introduction,* 2nd edn, London: Routledge.

Bate, J. (1991) *Romantic Ecology,* London: Routledge.

—— (2001) *The Song of the Earth,* London: Picador.

—— (2010) *English Literature: A Very Short Introduction,* Oxford: Oxford University Press.

Batsleer, J., Davies, T., O'Rourke, R. and Weedon, C. (1985) *Rewriting English: Cultural Politics of Gender and Class,* London: Methuen.

Baudrillard, J. (1995) *The Gulf War Did Not Take Place,* Bloomington IN: Indiana University Press.

—— (2002) *The Spirit of Terrorism,* trans. C. Turner, London: Verso.

Baugh, A.C. and Cable T. (2002) *A History of the English Language,* 5th edn, London: Routledge.

Belsey, C. (2002) *Critical Practice,* 2nd edn, London: Methuen.

Belsey, C. and Moore, J. (eds) (1997) *The Feminist Reader: Essays in Gender and the Politics of Literary Criticism,* 2nd edn, London: Macmillan.

Benjamin, W. (1970) *Illuminations,* ed. H. Arendt, trans. H. Zohn, London: Cape.

Bennett, A. (ed.) (1995) *Readers and Reading: A Critical Reader,* Harlow: Longman.

—— (2005) *The Author,* London and New York: Routledge.

Bennett, A. and Royle, N. (2009) *Introduction to Literature, Criticism and Theory,* 4th edn, Harlow: Prentice Hall Europe.

Bennett, T. (2002) *Formalism and Marxism,* 2nd edn, London: Methuen.

Bennett, T., Grossberg, L. and Morris, M. (eds) (2005) *New Keywords: A Revised Vocabulary of Culture and Society,* Oxford: Blackwell.

Benstock, S., Ferriss, S. and Woods, S. (2002) *A Handbook of Literary Feminisms,* New York and Oxford: Oxford University Press.

Bergson, H. (2002) *Henri Bergson: Key Writings,* eds K. Ansell Pearson and J. Mullarkey, London and New York: Continuum.

Berlin, J. (1996) *Rhetorics, Poetics, Culture: Refiguring College English Studies,* Philadelphia: National Council of Teachers of English.

Bertens, H. (2004) *Literary Theory: The Basics,* 2nd edn, London: Routledge.

Bertens, H. and Natoli, J. (eds) (2002) *Postmodernism: The Key Figures,* Oxford: Blackwell.

Bex, T. (1996) *Variety in Written English,* London: Routledge.

Bhabha, H. (ed.) (1990) *Nation and Narration,* London: Routledge.

—— (1994) *The Location of Culture,* London and New York: Routledge.

Birch, D. (1989) *Language, Literature and Critical Practice,* London: Routledge.

Bleich, D. (1978) *Subjective Criticism,* Baltimore: Johns Hopkins University Press.

Bloch, E. (1988) *The Utopian Function of Art and Literature: Selected Essays,* trans. J. Zipes and F. Mecklenburg, Cambridge, MA: Massachusetts Institute of Technology.

Bloom, C. and Day, G. (eds) (1999–2000) *Literature and Culture in Modern Britain,* 3 Vols, London: Longman.

Blyth, I. and Sellers, S. (2004) *Hélène Cixous: Live Theory,* London and New York: Continuum.

Boehmer, E. (2005) *Colonial and Postcolonial Literature,* 2nd edn, Oxford: Oxford University Press.

Booth, W. (1961) *The Rhetoric of Fiction,* Chicago: University of Chicago Press.

Bordo, S. (1993) *Unbearable Weight: Feminism, Western Culture and the Body,* California: University of California Press.

Bordwell, D. (1985) *Narration in the Fiction Film,* London: Methuen.

Bordwell, D. and Thompson, K. (2010) *Film Art: An Introduction,* 9th edn, New York: McGraw-Hill.

Bourdieu, P. (1984) *Distinction: A Social Critique of the Judgement of Taste,* trans. R. Nice, London: Routledge.

Bradford, R. (ed.) (1996) *Introducing Literary Studies,* Hemel Hempstead: Harvester Wheatsheaf.

Bragg, M. (2003) *The Adventure of English,* London: Hodder and Stoughton.

Braidotti, R. (2002) *Metamorphoses: Towards a Materialist Theory of Becoming,* Oxford and Cambridge: Polity.

Brannigan, J. (1998) *New Historicism and Cultural Materialism,* Basingstoke: Macmillan.

Branston, G. and Stafford, R. (1999) *The Media Student's Handbook,* 2nd edn, London: Routledge.

Brathwaite, E.K. (1984) *History of the Voice,* London: New Beacon Books.

Brecht, B. (1964) *Brecht on Theatre,* ed. and trans. J. Willett, London: Methuen.

Brink, A. (1998) *The Novel: Language and Narrative from Cervantes to Calvino,* Basingstoke: Macmillan.

Bristow, J. (1997) *Sexuality,* London: Routledge.

Bromley, R. (2000) *Narratives for a New Beginning: Diasporic Cultural Fictions,* Edinburgh: Edinburgh University Press.

Brook, P. (1972) *The Empty Space,* Harmondsworth: Penguin.

Brooker, P. (ed.) (1992) *Modernism/Postmodernism: A Reader,* Harlow: Longman.

Brooker, P. and Thacker, A. (eds) (2003) *Geographies of Modernism: Cultures, Spaces,* London and New York: Routledge.

Brooker, P. and Widdowson, P. (eds) (1996) *A Practical Reader in Contemporary Literary Theory,* Hemel Hempstead: Harvester Wheatsheaf.

Brooks, C. (1947) *The Well Wrought Urn: Studies in the Structure of Poetry,* New York: Harcourt, Brace.

Brumfit, C.J. and Carter, R.A. (eds) (1986) *Literature and Language Teaching,* Oxford: Oxford University Press.

Bruner, J. (1986) *Actual Minds, Possible Worlds,* Cambridge, MA: Harvard University Press.

Buell, L. (1995) *The Environmental Imagination,* Cambridge MA: Harvard University Press.

—— (2001) *Writing for an Endangered World: Literature, Culture and the Environment,* Cambridge, MA: Harvard University Press.

—— (2005) *The Future of Environmental Criticism,* Oxford: Blackwell.

Burke, L., Crowley, T. and Girvin, A. (eds) (2000) *The Routledge Language and Culture Theory Reader,* London: Routledge.

Burke, S. (1998) *The Death and Return of the Author,* 2nd edn, Edinburgh: Edinburgh University Press.

Burnley, D. (ed.) (2000) *The History of the English Language: A Source Book,* 2nd edn, Harlow: Longman.

Burton, D. (1980) *Dialogue and Discourse: The Sociology of Modern Drama Dialogue and Naturally Occurring Conversation,* London: Routledge and Kegan Paul.

Butler, J. (1993) *Bodies the Matter: On the Discursive Limits of 'Sex',* New York: Routledge.

—— (2006) *Precarious Life: The Powers of Mourning and Violence,* London: Verso.

Butler, J., Guillory, J. and Thomas, K. (eds) (2000) *What's Left of Theory? New Work on the Politics of Literary Theory,* London: Routledge for the English Institute.

Cahoone, L. (ed.) (1996) *From Modernism to Postmodernism: An Anthology,* Oxford: Blackwell.

Cameron, D. (1995) *Verbal Hygiene,* London: Routledge.

—— (ed.) (1998) *The Feminist Critique of Language,* 2nd edn, London: Routledge.

Carroll, J. and Williams, K. (2010) *Referencing and Understanding Plagiarism,* Basingstoke: Palgrave Macmillan.

Carroll, R. and Prickett, S. (eds) (1997) *The Bible: Authorized King James Version, with Apocrypha,* Oxford: Oxford University Press.

Carter, R.A. (ed.) (1982) *Language and Literature: An Introductory Reader in Stylistics,* London: Allen and Unwin.

—— (1997) *Investigating English Discourse: Language, Literacy and Culture,* London: Routledge.

—— (2004) *Language and Creativity: The Art of Common Talk,* London: Routledge.

Carter, R., Goddard, A., Reah, D., Sanger, K. and Bowring, M. (2001) *Working with Texts: A Core Introduction to Language Analysis,* 2nd edn, London: Routledge.

Carter, R. and McCarthy, M. (2006) *The Cambridge Grammar of English,* Cambridge: Cambridge University Press.

Carter, R.A. and McRae, J. (2012) *The Routledge History of Literature in English: Britain and Ireland,* 3rd edn, London: Routedge.

Carter, R.A. and Nash, W. (1990) *Seeing Through Language: A Guide to Styles of English Writing,* Oxford: Blackwell.

Carter, R. and Stockwell, P. (eds) (2008) *The Language and Literature Reader,* Abingdon: Routledge.

Cartmell, D. and Whelehan, I. (eds) (1999) *Adaptations: From Text to Screen, Screen to Text,* London and New York: Routledge.

Castle, G. (2007) *The Blackwell Guide to Literary Theory,* Oxford: Blackwell.

Castle, T. (ed.) (2003) *The Literature of Lesbianism: A Historical Anthology,* New York: Columbia University Press.

Cavanagh, D., Gillis, A., *et al.* (eds) *The Edinburgh Introduction to Studying English Literature,* Edinburgh: Edinburgh University Press.

Caws, M. A. and Prendergast, C. (eds) (1994) *World Reader,* New York: HarperCollins.

Cazeaux, C. (ed.) (2000) *The Continental Aesthetics Reader,* London: Routledge.

Célestin, R., Dalmolin, E. and de Courtviron, I. (eds) (2003) *Beyond French Feminisms,* Basingstoke: Palgrave Macmillan.

Chantler, A. and Higgins, D. (eds) (2010) *Studying English Literature,* London: Continuum.

Chatman, S. (1978) *Story and Discourse: Narrative Structure in Fiction and Film,* Ithaca, NY: Cornell University Press.

Cheshire, J, (ed.) (1992) *English around the World: Sociolinguistic Perspectives,* Cambridge: Cambridge University Press.

Chiaro, D. (1992) *The Language of Jokes,* London: Routledge.

Childs, P. (ed.) (1999) *Post-Colonial Theory and English Literature,* Edinburgh: Edinburgh University Press.

—— (2001) *Reading Fiction: Opening the Text,* Basingstoke: Palgrave.

—— (2008) *The Essential Guide to English Studies,* London: Continuum.

Coates, J. (1993) *Women, Men and Language,* Harlow: Longman.

Colebrook, C. (1999) *Ethics and Representation, from Kant to Poststructuralism,* Edinburgh: Edinburgh University Press.

—— (2002) Gilles Deleuze, London: Routledge.

Colley, L. (1992) *Britons: Forging the Nation 1707–1837,* New Haven, CT: Yale University Press.

Connor, S. (1997) *Postmodernist Culture,* 2nd edn, Oxford: Blackwell.

Cook, G. (1994) *Discourse and Literature,* Oxford: Oxford University Press.

—— (2000) *Language Play, Language Learning,* Oxford: Oxford University Press.

Corner, J. and Hawthorn, J. (eds) (1995) *Communication Studies: A Reader,* 3rd edn, London: Arnold.

Coulthard, M. (1985) *An Introduction to Discourse Analysis,* 2nd edn, London: Longman.

Coupe, L. (1997) *Myth,* London: Routledge.

—— (ed.) (2000) *The Green Studies Reader: From Romanticism to Ecocriticism,* London: Routledge.

Coyle, M., Garside, P., Kelsall, M. and Peck, J. (eds) (1990) *Encyclopedia of Literature and Criticism,* London and New York: Routledge.

Crawford, R. (2000) *Devolving English Literature,* 2nd edn, Edinburgh: Edinburgh University Press.

Critchley, S. (1999) *The Ethics of Deconstruction,* 2nd edn, Edinburgh: Edinburgh University Press.

—— (2002) *On Humour,* London and New York: Routledge.

Crowley, T. (1989) *Politics of Discourse: The Standard Language Question in British Cultural Studies,* London: Macmillan.

—— (ed.) (1991) *Proper English? Readings in Language, History and Cultural Identity,* London: Routledge.

Crump, E. and Carbone, N. (1996) *The English Student's Guide to the Internet,* New York: Houghton and Mifflin.

Crystal, D. (1996) *Re-discover Grammar,* 2nd edn, Harlow: Longman.

—— (1997) *English as a Global Language,* Cambridge: Cambridge University Press.

—— (1998) *Language Play,* London: Penguin.

—— (2003) *The Cambridge Encyclopedia of the English Language,* 2nd edn, Cambridge: Cambridge University Press.

—— (2004) *The Stories of English,* London: Penguin.

Cuddon, J. (1998) *A Dictionary of Literary Terms and Literary Theory,* 4th edn rev. C. E. Preston, Harmondsworth: Penguin/Oxford: Blackwell.

Culler, J. (1975) *Structuralist Poetics,* London: Routledge and Kegan Paul.

—— (ed.) (1988) *On Puns: The Foundation of Letters,* Oxford: Blackwell.

—— (1997) *A Very Short Introduction to Literary Theory,* Oxford and New York: Oxford University Press.

Culpeper, J. (2001) *Language and Characterisation: People in Plays and Other Texts,* Harlow: Longman.

Darwin, C. (1859) *The Origin of Species,* ed. J. Wallace, Ware: Wordsworth, 1998.

Davis, L. (1983) *Factual Fictions: The Origins of the English Novel,* New York: Columbia University Press.

Dawson, P. (2005) *Creative Writing and the New Humanities,* London: Routledge.

Deleuze, G. (1987) *Dialogues with Claire Parnet,* trans. H. Tomlinson and B. Habberjan, London: Athlone Press.

Deleuze, G. and Guattari, F. (1977) *Anti-Oedipus: Capitalism and Schizophrenia,* trans. R. Hurley *et al.,* New York: Viking Penguin.

—— (1982) *A Thousand Plateaus,* trans. B. Massumi, London: Athlone.

Dentith, S. (ed.) (1995) *Bakhtinian Thought: An Introductory Reader,* London: Routledge.

Derrida, J. (1978) *Writing and Difference,* trans. A. Bass, Chicago: University of Chicago Press.

—— (1992) *Acts of Literature,* ed. D. Attridge, New York and London: Routledge.

Derrida, J. and Malabou, C. (2004) *Counterpath: Travelling with Jacques Derrida,* Stanford CA: Stanford University Press.

Dewey, J. (1954) *Art as Experience,* New York: Capricorn.

Diedrich, M., Gates, H.L. and Pedersen, C. (eds) (1999) *Black Imagination and the Middle Passage,* Oxford: Oxford University Press.

Dixon, J. (1991) *A Schooling in 'English',* Milton Keynes: Open University Press.

Doecke, B., Howie, M. and Sawyer, W. (eds) (2006) *Only Connect: English Teaching, Schooling and*

Community, Kent Town, SA: Australian Association for the Teaching of English and Wakefield Press.

Dollimore, J. (1991) *Sexual Dissidence: Augustine to Wilde, Freud to Foucault,* Oxford: Clarendon Press.

Downing, D.B., Hurlbert, C.M., Mathieu, P.J. (eds) (2002) *Beyond English Inc.,* Portsmouth, NH: Heinemann Boynton Cook.

Doyle, B. (1989) *English and Englishness,* London: Methuen.

Duff, D. (ed.) (2000) *Modern Genre Theory: A Critical Reader,* London: Longman.

Durant, A. and Fabb, N. (1990) *Literary Studies in Action,* London: Routledge.

During, S. (ed.) (1999) *The Cultural Studies Reader,* 2nd edn, London: Routledge.

Eaglestone, R. (1997) *Ethical Criticism: Reading after Levinas,* Edinburgh: Edinburgh University Press.

—— (2009) *Doing English: A Guide for Literature Students,* 3rd edn, London: Routledge.

Eagleton, M. (2003) *A Concise Companion to Feminist Theory,* Oxford: Blackwell.

Eagleton, T. (1990) *The Ideology of the Aesthetic,* Oxford: Blackwell.

—— (2008) *Literary Theory: An Introduction,* 3rd edn, Oxford: Blackwell.

—— (2007) *How to Read a Poem,* Oxford: Blackwell.

Eagleton, T. and Milne, D. (eds) (1995) *Marxist Literary Theory: A Reader,* Oxford: Blackwell.

Easthope, A. (1983) *Poetry as Discourse,* London: Methuen.

—— (1991) *Literary into Cultural Studies,* London: Routledge.

—— (1999) *Englishness and National Culture,* London: Routledge.

Elam, K. (2002) *The Semiotics of Theatre and Drama,* 2nd edn, London: Methuen.

Elbow, P. (1981) *Writing with Power,* New York: Oxford University Press.

—— (1993) *What is English?* New York: MLA and NCTE.

Elliott, J. and Attridge, D. (eds) (2011) *Theory after 'Theory',* London: Routledge.

Ellman, M. (ed.) (1994) *Psychoanalytic Literary Criticism: A Critical Reader,* Harlow: Longman.

Erlich, V. (1981) *Russian Formalism: History-Doctrine,* 3rd edn, New Haven, CT: Yale University Press.

Esslin, M. (1961) *Theatre of the Absurd,* Harmondsworth: Penguin.

Evans, C. (1993) *English People: The Teaching and Learning of English in British Universities,* Milton Keynes: Open University Press.

—— (ed.) (1995) *Developing University English Teaching (DUET),* Lampeter: Edwin Mellen Press.

Fabb, N. and Durant, A. (2005) *How to Write Essays, Dissertations and Theses for Literary Studies,* 2nd edn, London: Longman.

Fairclough, N. (2001) *Language and Power,* 2nd edn, Harlow: Longman.

Fekete, J. (1977) *The Critical Twilight: Explorations in the Ideology of Anglo-American Literary Theory from Eliot to McLuhan,* New York: Routledge and Kegan Paul.

Fendler, S. and Wittlinger, R. (1999) *The Idea of Europe in Literature,* Basingstoke: Macmillan and University of Durham.

Fennell, B.A. (2001) *A History of English: A Sociolinguistic Approach,* Oxford: Blackwell.

Fetterley, J. (1991) *The Resisting Reader: A Feminist Approach to American Fiction,* Bloomington: Indiana University Press.

Forster, E.M. (1927) *Aspects of the Novel,* Harmondsworth: Penguin, 1962.

Foucault, M. (1986) *The Foucault Reader,* ed. P. Rabinow, Harmondsworth: Penguin.

—— (1998) *Aesthetics: Method and Epistemology,* ed. J. Faubion, London: Penguin.

Fowler, R. (ed.) (1981) *Literature as Social Discourse,* London: Batsford.

—— (1991) *Language in the News: Discourse and Ideology in the Press,* London: Routledge.

—— (1996) *Linguistic Criticism,* 2nd edn, Oxford: Oxford University Press.

Freeborn, D., French, P. and Langford, D. (1999) *Varieties of English,* 3rd edn, London: Macmillan.

Fromkin, V., Rodman, R. and Hyams, N. (2006) *An Introduction to Language,* 9th edn, New York: Harcourt Brace Jovanovich.

Gallagher, C. and Greenblatt, S. (2001) *Practicing New Historicism,* Chicago: Chicago University Press.

Garrard, G. (2004) *Ecocriticism,* London: Routledge.

Garvin, P. (ed.) (1964) *A Prague School Reader on Esthetics, Literary Structure and Style,* Washington: Georgetown University Press.

Gates, H.L. (2004) *The Third World of Theory,* Oxford: Oxford University Press.

Gates, Jnr, H.L. (ed.) (1986) *The Classic Slave Narratives,* New York: Mentor.

—— (1995) *Loose Canons: Notes on the Culture Wars,* Oxford: Oxford University Press.

Gates, H.L. and McKay, N.Y. (eds) (2003) *The Norton Anthology of African American Literature,* 2nd edn, New York: W.W. Norton.

Gavins, J. and Steen, G. (eds) (2003) *Cognitive Poetics in Practice,* London: Routledge.

Genosko, G. (2009) *Félix Guattari: A Critical Introduction,* London: Continuum.

Geok-Lin Lim and Spencer, N. (eds) (1993) *One World of Literature,* Boston: Houghton Mifflin.

Gikandi, S. (1996) *Maps of Englishness: Writing Identity in the Culture of Postcolonialism,* New York: Columbia University Press.

Gilbert, S.M. and Gubar, S. (2000) *The Madwoman in the Attic: The Woman Writer and the Nineteenth-Century Literary Imagination,* 2nd edn, New Haven and London: Yale University Press.

Giles, J. and Middleton, T. (eds) (1995) *Writing Englishness 1900–1950: An Introductory Sourcebook on National Identity,* London: Routledge.

Gilroy, P. (1993) *The Black Atlantic: Modernity and Double Consciousness,* London: Verso.

—— (2001) *Nations, Cultures and the Allures of Race,* London: Penguin.

Glover, D. and Kaplan, C. (2000) *Genders,* London: Routledge.

Goatly, A. (2011) *Critical Reading and Writing: An Introductory Coursebook,* 2nd edn, London: Routledge.

Goddard, A. (2012) *Doing English Language,* London and New York: Routledge.

Goodman, S and Graddol, D. (eds) (1996) *Redesigning English: New Texts, New Identities,* London: Open University and Routledge.

Goodman, S. and O'Halloran, K. (eds) (2006) *The Art of English: Literary Creativity,* Basingstoke: Palgrave Macmillan.

Goring, P., Hawthorn, J. and Domnhall, M. (2001) *Studying Literature,* London: Arnold.

Graddol, D. (1997) *The Future of English?* London: The British Council.

Graddol, D., Leith, D. and Swann, J. (eds) (1996) *English: History, Diversity and Change,* London and New York: Routledge and the Open University.

Graff, G. (1987) *Professing Literature: An Institutional History,* Chicago: University of Chicago Press.

Green, A. (2009) *Starting an English Literature Degree,* Basingstoke: Palgrave Macmillan.

Green, K. and LeBihan, J. (1996) *Critical Theory and Practice: A Coursebook,* London: Routledge.

Greenbaum, S. and Quirk, R. (1990) *A Student's Grammar of the English Language,* London: Longman.

Greenblatt, S. and Gunn, G. (eds) (1992) *Redrawing the Boundaries: The Transformation of English and American Studies,* New York: Modern Language Association.

Grice, H.P. (1975) 'Logic and Conversation', in P. Cole and J. Morgan (eds) *Syntax and Semantics 3: Speech Acts,* New York: Academic Press.

Griffin, G. (ed.) (2005) *Research Methods for English Studies,* Edinburgh: Edinburgh University Press.

Grossberg, L., Nelson, C. and Treichler, P. (eds) (1992) *Cultural Studies,* New York: Routledge.

Guattari, F. (1996) *The Guattari Reader,* ed. G. Genosko, Oxford: Blackwell.

—— (2001) *The Three Ecologies,* trans. I. Pindar and P. Sutton, London: Continuum.

Gubar, S. and Kamholtz, J. (eds) (1993) *English Inside and Out: The Place of Literary Criticism,* New York: Routledge.

Guy, J. and Small, I. (1993) *Politics and Value in English Studies,* Cambridge: Cambridge University Press.

Hall, D. (2003) *Queer Theories,* Basingstoke: Palgrave Macmillan.

Hall, S. (1996) *Critical Dialogues in Cultural Studies,* London: Routledge.

Halliday, M.A.K. and Hasan, R. (1989) *Language, Context and Text: Aspects of Language in a Social-Semiotic Perspective,* Oxford: Oxford University Press.

Halliday, M.A.K. and Matthiessen, C. (2004) *An Introduction to Functional Grammar,* 3rd edn, London: Arnold.

Haraway, D. (1997) *Modest_Witness @ Second_ Millennium. FemaleMan©_ Meets-Oncomouse ™,* London: Routledge.

—— (2004) *The Haraway Reader,* London: Routledge.

Hardt, M. and Negri, A. (2004) *Multitude: War and Democracy in the Age of Empire,* London: Penguin.

Harland, R. (1984) *Superstructuralism: The Philosophy of Structuralism and Poststructuralism,* London: Methuen.

Harmer, J. (2001) *The Practice of English Language Teaching,* 3rd edn, Harlow: Longman.

Harper, G. (ed.) (2006) *Teaching Creative Writing,* London and New York: Continuum.

—— (2010) *On Creative Writing,* Bristol and Buffalo: Multilingual Matters.

Haslett, M. (2000) *Marxist Literary and Cultural Theories,* Basingstoke: Macmillan.

Hawisher, G.E. and Selfe, C.L. (eds) (2001) *Global Literacies and the World-Wide Web,* London and New York: Routledge.

Hawkes, T. (1972) *Metaphor,* London: Methuen.

—— (2003) *Structuralism and Semiotics,* 2nd edn, London: Methuen.

Hawthorn, J. (2000) *A Glossary of Contemporary Literary Theory,* 3rd edn, London: Arnold.

Head, D. (ed.) (2006) *The Cambridge Guide to Literature in English,* 3rd edn, Cambridge: Cambridge University Press.

Herman, V. (1995) *Dramatic Discourse: Dialogue as Interaction in Plays,* London: Routledge.

Higgins, J. (1999) *Raymond Williams: Literature, Marxism and Cultural Materialism*, London: Routledge.

Hills, M. (2005) *How to Do Things with Cultural Theory*, London: Hodder Arnold.

Hirschkop, K. and Shepherd, D. (eds) (2001) *Bakhtin and Cultural Theory*, 2nd edn, Manchester: Manchester University Press.

Hobsbawm, P. (1996) *Metre, Rhythm and Verse*, London: Routledge.

Hodge, R. (1990) *Literature as Social Discourse: Textual Strategies in English and History*, Oxford: Polity.

Hodge, R. and Kress, G. (1993) *Language as Ideology*, 2nd edn, London: Routledge.

Hoey, M. (2001) *Textual Interaction: An Introduction to Written Discourse Analysis*, London: Routledge.

Holland, N. (1990) *Holland's Guide to Psychoanalytic Psychology and Literature-and-Psychology*, New York: Oxford University Press.

Holquist, M. (2002) *Dialogism: Bakhtin and his World*, 2nd edn, London: Routledge.

Holub, R. (1984) *Reception Theory: A Critical Introduction*, London: Methuen.

hooks, bell (1994) *Teaching to Transgress*, London and New York: Routledge.

Hopkins, C. (2009) *Thinking About Texts: An Introduction to English Studies*, 2nd edn, Basingstoke: Palgrave.

Howatt, A.P.R. (1984) *A History of English Language Teaching*, Oxford: Oxford University Press.

Hughes, G. (2000) *A History of Words in English*, Oxford: Blackwell.

Humm, M. (1994) *A Reader's Guide to Contemporary Feminist Literary Criticism*, Hemel Hempstead: Harvester Wheatsheaf.

Hurford, J.R. (1994) *Grammar: A Student's Guide*, Cambridge: Cambridge University Press.

Hutcheon, L. (1989) *The Politics of Postmodernism*, London: Routledge.

—— (2006) *The Theory of Adaptation*, London and New York: Routledge.

Iser, W. (1978) *The Act of Reading: A Theory of Aesthetic Response*, Baltimore: Johns Hopkins University Press.

Jacobs, R. (2001) *A Beginner's Guide to Critical Reading: An Anthology of Literary Texts*, London: Routledge.

Jameson, F. (1972) *The Prison-House of Language: A Critical Account of Structuralism and Russian Formalism*, Princeton, NJ: Princeton University Press.

—— (1981) *The Political Unconscious: Narrative as a Socially Symbolic Act*, London: Methuen.

Jauss, H.R. (1982) *Towards an Aesthetics of Reception*, trans. T. Bahti, Brighton: Harvester Press.

Jaworski, A. and Coupland, N. (eds) (1999) *The Discourse Reader*, London: Routledge.

Jefferson, A. and Robey, D. (eds) (1986) *Modern Literary Theory: A Comparative Introduction*, London: Batsford.

Jenkins, J. (2009) *World Englishes: A Resource Book for Students*, 2nd edn, Abingdon: Routledge.

Jenkins, K. (2003) *Refiguring History: New Thoughts on an Old Discipline*, London: Routledge.

Joghin, J. and Malpas, S. (eds) (2003) *The New Aesthetics*, Manchester: Manchester University Press.

Kachru, B. (1986) *The Alchemy of English: the Spread, Models and Functions of Non-Native Englishes*, Oxford: Pergamon.

—— (ed.) (1992) *The Other Tongue: English across Cultures*, Urbana and Chicago: University of Illinois Press.

Kachru, B., Kachru, Y. and Nelson, C. (eds) (2009) *The Handbook of World Englishes*, Oxford: Blackwell.

Kaplan, C. (1996) *Questions of Travel: Postmodern Discourse of Displacement*, Durham, NC: Duke University Press.

Kearney, R. (1994) *The Wake of Imagination*, London: Routledge.

—— (1998) *Poetics of Imagining: Modern to Postmodern*, Edinburgh: Edinburgh University Press.

—— (2002) *On Stories*, London and New York: Routledge.

Kearney, R. and Rasmussen, D. (eds) (2001) *Continental Aesthetics: Romanticism to Postmodernism*, Oxford: Blackwell.

Kennedy, G. (1998) *An Introduction to Corpus Linguistics*, Harlow: Longman.

Kerridge, R. and Sammells, N. (eds) (1998) *Writing the Environment: Ecocriticism and Literature*, London: Zed Books.

Knights, B. (ed.) (2007) *Masculinities in Texts and Teaching*, Basingstoke: Palgrave.

Knights, B. and Thurgar-Dawson, C. (2006) *Active Reading: Transformative Writing in Literary Studies*, London: Continuum.

Kress, G. (1995) *Writing the Future: English and the Making of a Culture of Innovation*, Sheffield: National Association for the Teaching of English.

Kristeva, J. (1986) *The Kristeva Reader*, ed. T. Moi, Oxford: Blackwell.

Labov, W. (1972) *Language in the Inner City*, Philadelphia: University of Pennsylvania Press.

Lacan, J. (2006) *Écrits: The First Complete Edition in English*, trans. B. Fink, New York: Norton.

Lakoff, G. and Johnson, M. (1980) *Metaphors We Live By*, Chicago: University of Chicago Press.

Leavis, F.R. (1936) *Revaluation,* Harmondsworth: Penguin, 1972.

—— (1948) *The Great Tradition,* Harmondsworth: Penguin, 1972.

Lechte, J. and Zournazi, M. (eds) (2003) *The Kristeva Critical Reader,* Edinburgh: Edinburgh University Press.

Leech, G.N. (1969) *A Linguistic Guide to English Poetry,* London: Longman.

Leech, G.N. and Short, M. (1981) *Style in Fiction: A Linguistic Introduction to English Fictional Prose,* Harlow: Longman.

Lefevere, A. (1992) *Translation, Rewriting and the Manipulation of Literary Fame,* London: Routledge.

Leitch, V.B. *et al.* (eds) (2010) *The Norton Anthology of Theory and Criticism,* 2nd edn, New York: W.W. Norton.

Leith, D. (1997) *A Social History of English,* 2nd edn, London: Routledge.

Lentricchia, F. (1980) *After the New Criticism,* London: Athlone Press.

Lentricchia, F. and McLaughlin, T. (1995) *Critical Terms for Literary Study,* 2nd edn, Chicago: University of Chicago Press.

Lister, M., Dovey, J., Giddings, S., Grant, I. and Kelly, K. (2009) *New Media: A Critical Introduction,* London and New York: Routledge.

Lodge, D. (ed.) (1972) *20th Century Literary Criticism,* Harlow: Longman.

—— (1992) *The Art of Fiction,* Harmondsworth: Penguin.

Lodge, D. and Wood, N. (eds) (2008) *Modern Criticism and Theory: A Reader,* 3rd edn, Harlow: Longman.

Loomba, A. (1998) *Colonialism/Postcolonialism,* London: Routledge.

Lucas, John (1990) *England and Englishness: Ideas of Nationhood in English Poetry 1688–1900,* London: Hogarth.

Lukacs, G. (1962) *The Historical Novel,* trans. H. and S. Mitchell, London: Merlin.

Lyotard, J.-F. (1986) *The Postmodern Condition: A Report on Knowledge,* trans. G. Bennington, Manchester: Manchester University Press.

McArthur, T. (1992) *The Oxford Companion to the English Language,* Oxford: Oxford University Press.

—— (1998) *The English Languages,* Cambridge: Cambridge University Press.

McCaw, N. (2008) *How to Read Texts: A Student Guide to Critical Approaches and Skills,* London: Continuum.

McCrum, R., Cran, W. and MacNeil, R. (1992) *The Story of English,* 2nd edn, London: Faber & Faber and BBC Books.

Macey, D. (2000) *The Penguin Dictionary of Critical Theory,* London: Penguin.

McFarlane, B. (1996) *Novel to Film. An Introduction to the Theory of Adaptation,* Oxford: Oxford University Press.

McGann, J.J. (1988) *The Beauty of Inflections,* Oxford: Oxford University Press.

—— (2001) *Radiant Textuality: Literary Studies After the World Wide Web,* London and New York: Palgrave/St Martin's.

—— (2007) *The Point is to Change It: Poetry and Criticism in the Continuing Present,* Tuscaloosa: University of Alabama Press.

McHale, B. (1992) *Constructing Postmodernism,* London: Routledge.

Macherey, P. (1978) *A Theory of Literary Production,* trans. G. Wall, London: Routledge and Kegan Paul.

McIntyre, D. and Busse, B. (eds) (2010) *Language and Style: In Honour of Mick Short,* Basingstoke: Palgrave Macmillan.

McQuillan, M. (ed.) (2000) *The Narrative Reader,* London: Routledge.

McQuillan, M., Purves, R., Macdonald, G. and Thomson, S. (eds) (1999) *Post-Theory: New Directions in Criticism,* Edinburgh: Edinburgh University Press.

McRae, J. (1991) *Literature with a Small 'l',* Basingstoke: Macmillan.

McRae, J. and Vethamani, M.E. (1999) *Now Read On: A Course in Multicultural Reading,* London: Routledge.

Makaryk, I.R. (ed.) (1993) *Encyclopedia of Contemporary Literary Theory: Approaches, Scholars, Terms,* Toronto; University of Toronto Press.

Malpas, S. (ed.) (2001) *Postmodern Debates,* Basingstoke: Palgrave.

Marcus, L. (1994) *Auto/biographical Discourses,* Manchester: Manchester University Press.

Marshall, B. (1992) *Teaching Postmodernism: Fiction and Theory,* London: Routledge.

May, S. (2007) *Doing Creative Writing,* London and New York: Routledge.

Maybin, J. and Mercer, N. (eds) (1996) *Using English: From Conversation to Canon,* London and New York: Routledge and the Open University.

Maybin, J. and Swann, J. (2006) (eds) *The Art of English: Everyday Creativity,* Basingstoke: Palgrave Macmillan.

—— (2010) *The Routledge Companion to English Language Studies,* London and New York: Routledge.

Medvedev, P. and Bakhtin, M. (1978) *The Formal Method in Literary Scholarship: An Introduction to Sociological Poetics,* trans. A. Wehrle, Baltimore: Johns Hopkins University Press.

Mercer, N. and Swann, J. (eds) (1996) *Learning English: Development and Diversity,* London and New York: Routledge and the Open University.

Metz, C. (1974) *Film Language: A Semiotics of the Cinema,* trans. M. Taylor, New York: Oxford University Press, Chs. 2 and 8.

Midgley, M. (2005) *The Essential Mary Midgley,* ed. D. Midgley, London: Routledge.

Miller, J.H. (1987) *The Ethics of Reading,* New York: Columbia University Press.

Mills, S. (1995) *Feminist Stylistics,* London: Routledge.

—— (2004) *Discourse,* London: Routledge.

Milne, D. (ed.) (2003) *Modern Critical Thought: An Anthology of Theorists Writing on Theorists,* Oxford: Blackwell.

Milner, A. (1996) *Literature, Culture and Society,* London: University College London Press.

—— (2002) *Remaking Cultural Studies: The Promise of Cultural Materialism,* London: Sage.

Milroy, J. and Milroy, L. (1999) *Authority in Language: Investigating Standard English,* 3rd edn, London: Routledge.

Moi, T. (2002) *Sexual/Textual Politics,* 2nd edn, London: Methuen.

Monk, N., Neelands, J., Heron, J., and Rutter, C.C. (2011) *Open-space Learning: A Study in Trans-disciplinary Pedagogy,* London: Bloomsbury Academic.

Montgomery, M. (1996) *An Introduction to Language and Society,* 2nd edn, London: Routledge.

Montgomery, M., Durant, A., Fabb, N., Furniss, T. and Mills, S. (2012) *Ways of Reading: Advanced Reading Skills for Students of English Literature,* 4th edn, London: Routledge.

Moore, B. (ed.) (2001) *Who's Centric Now? The Present State of Post-Colonial Englishes,* Oxford: Oxford University Press.

Moore-Gilbert, B., Stanton, G. and Maley, W. (eds) (1997) *Postcolonial Criticism: A Critical Reader,* London: Longman.

Morley, D. (2007) *The Cambridge Introduction to Creative Writing,* Cambridge: Cambridge University Press.

Morris P. (ed.) (1994) *The Bakhtin Reader,* London: Arnold.

Mukarovsky, J. (1936) *Aesthetic Function: Norm and Value as Social Facts,* trans. M. Suino, Ann Arbor: University of Michigan Press.

Mulhern, F. (2000) *Culture/Metaculture,* London: Routledge.

Mullany, L. and Stockwell, P. (2010) *Introducing English Language: A Resource Book for Students,* Abingdon: Routledge.

Murphy, P.D. (1995) *Literature, Nature and Other Eco-Feminist Critiques,* New York: State University of New York Press.

Nash, W. (1982) *The Language of Humour: Style and Technique in Comic Discourse,* Harlow: Longman.

—— (1992) *An Uncommon Tongue: the Uses and Resources of English,* London: Routledge.

Nash, W. and Stacey, D. (1997) *Creating Texts: An Introduction to the Study of Composition,* London and New York: Longman.

Newman, J., Cusick, E. and La Tourette, A. (eds) (2004) *The Writer's Workbook,* 2nd edn, London: Arnold.

Norris, C. (1991) *Deconstruction: Theory and Practice,* 2nd edn, London: Methuen.

—— (2007) *Fiction, Philosophy and Literary Theory,* London and New York: Continuum.

O'Donnell, W. and Todd, L. (1992) *Variety in Contemporary English,* London: Routledge.

OED (*Oxford English Dictionary*) (1928, 2nd edn 1989) ed. R. Burchfield, J. Simpson *et al.,* Oxford: Oxford University Press.

Onega, S. and Landa, J. (eds) (1996) *Narratology: An Introduction,* Harlow: Longman.

O'Sullivan, T., Hartley, J., Saunders, D., Montgomery, M. and Fiske, J. (1994) *Key Concepts in Communication and Cultural Studies,* 2nd edn, London: Routledge.

Palmer, D.J. (1965) *The Rise of English Studies,* Oxford: Oxford University Press.

Palmer, F. (1992) *Literature and Moral Understanding,* Oxford: Oxford University Press.

Parkin-Gounelas, R. (2001) *Literature and Psychoanalysis: Intertextual Readings,* Basingstoke: Palgrave.

Parrinder, P. (1991) *Authors and Authority: English and American Criticism, 1750–1900,* 2nd edn, Basingstoke: Macmillan.

Parry, B. (2004) *Postcolonial Studies: A Materialist Critique,* London: Routledge.

Pavis, P. (1991), *Theatre at the Crossroads of Culture,* trans. L. Kruger, London: Routledge.

Payne, M. (ed.) (1996) *A Dictionary of Critical and Cultural Theory,* Oxford: Blackwell.

Peel, R., Patterson, A. and Gerlach, J. (2001) *Questions of English: Aesthetics, Democracy and the Formation of the Subject,* London: Routledge.

Pennycook, A. (1994) *The Cultural Politics of English as an International Language,* London and New York: Longman.

—— (1998) *English and the Discourses of Colonialism,* London: Routledge.

—— (2007) *Global Englishes and Transcultural Flows,* London: Routledge.

Pepper, D. (1993) *Ecosocialism: From Deep Ecology to Social Justice,* London: Routledge.

Plasa, C. and Ring, B. (eds) (1994) *The Discourse of Slavery: Aphra Behn to Toni Morrison*, London: Routledge.

Platt, J., Weber, H. and Ho, M.L. (1984) *The New Englishes*, London: Routledge and Kegan Paul.

Pope, R. (1995) *Textual Intervention: Critical and Creative Strategies for Literary Studies*, London and New York: Routledge.

—— (2005) *Creativity: Theory, History, Practice*, London and New York: Routledge.

Pratt, M.L. (1992) *Imperial Eyes: Travel Writing and Transculturation*, London and New York: Routledge.

Preminger, A. and Brogan, T. (1993) *The New Princeton Encyclopedia of Poetry and Poetics*, Princeton, NJ: Princeton University Press.

Prince, G. (1987) *A Dictionary of Narratology*, Lincoln: University of Nebraska Press.

Procter, J. (ed.) (2000) *Writing Black Britain: An Interdisciplinary Anthology*, Manchester: Manchester University Press.

Propp, V. (1928) *Morphology of the Folktale*, Austin: University of Texas Press, 1975.

Punter, D. (2000) *Postcolonial Imaginings: Fictions of a New World Order*, Edinburgh: Edinburgh University Press.

Purdie, S. (1993) *Comedy: The Mastery of Discourse*, Hemel Hempstead: Harvester Wheatsheaf.

Quayson, A. (ed) (2011) *The Cambridge History of Postcolonial Literature*, 2 vols, Cambridge: Cambridge University Press.

Quirk, R. and Widdowson, H.G. (eds) (1985) *English in the World: Teaching and Learning the Language and Literatures*, Cambridge: Cambridge University Press and the British Council.

Rampton, B. (2005) *Crossing: Language and Ethnicity among Adolescents*, 2nd edn, Harlow: Longman.

Rancière, J. (2004) *The Politics of Aesthetics: The Distribution of the Sensible*, trans. G. Rockhill, London: Continuum.

—— (2009) *The Aesthetic Unconscious*, trans. D. Keates and J. Swenson: Cambridge: Polity.

Rand, M. (2003) *Psychoanalysis and Literature*, Basingstoke: Palgrave Macmillan.

Redfern, W. (1984) *Puns*, Oxford: Blackwell.

Regan, S. (ed.) (1992) *The Politics of Pleasure: Aesthetics and Cultural Theory*, Buckingham and Philadelphia: Open University Press.

Reid, I. (1992) *Narrative Exchanges*, London: Routledge.

Rice, P. and Waugh, P. (eds) (2001) *Modern Literary Theory: A Reader*, 4th edn, London: Arnold.

Rich, A. (2001) *Arts of the Possible*, New York: Norton.

Richards, I.A. (1924) *The Principles of Literary Criticism*, London: Routledge and Kegan Paul, 1967.

—— (1929) *Practical Criticism: A Study of Literary Judgement*, London: Routledge and Kegan Paul.

Ricks, C. and Michaels, L. (eds) (1990) *The State of the Language in the 1990s*, London and New York: Faber.

Rimmon-Kenan, S. (2002) *Narrative Fiction: Contemporary Poetics*, 2nd edn, London: Methuen.

Rivkin, J. and Ryan, M. (eds) (2004) *Literary Theory: An Anthology*, 2nd edn, Malden, MA and Oxford: Blackwell.

Robbins, R. (2000) *Literary Feminisms*, Basingstoke: Macmillan.

Robson, M. and Stockwell, P. (2005) *Language in Theory: A Resource Book for Students*, London: Routledge.

Royle, N. (ed.) (2000) *Deconstructions: A User's Guide*, Basingstoke: Palgrave Macmillan.

Rudnytsky, P. (ed.) (1993) *Transitional Objects and Potential Spaces: Literary Uses of D.W. Winnicott*, New York: Columbia University Press.

Rushdy, A. (1999) *Neo-Slave Narratives*, Oxford: Oxford University Press.

Ryan, K. (ed.) (1996) *New Historicism and Cultural Materialism*, London: Arnold.

Rylance, R. and Simons, J. (eds) (2001) *Literature in Context*, Basingstoke: Palgrave.

Said, E. (1978) *Orientalism*, New York: Random House.

—— (1993) *Culture and Imperialism*, London: Chatto and Windus.

Samuel, R. (ed.) (1989) *Patriotism: The Making and Unmaking of British National Identity* (3 vols), London: Routledge.

Sanders, A. (1997) *The Short Oxford History of English Literature*, 2nd edn, Oxford: Oxford University Press.

Sanders, J. (2006) *Adaptation and Appropriation*, London: Routledge.

Saunders, D. (ed.) (2005) *The Complete Student's Handbook*, London: Unwin/Arnold.

Schiffrin, D., Tannen, D. and Hamilton, H. (eds) (2001) *The Handbook of Discourse Analysis*, Boston and Malden, MA and Oxford: Blackwell.

Scholes, R. (1985) *Textual Power: Literary Theory and the Teaching of English*, Binghampton: Yale University Press.

—— (1998) *The Rise and Fall of English Studies: Reconstructing English as a Discipline*, New Haven, CT: Yale University Press.

—— (2002) *The Crafty Reader*, New Haven, CT: Yale University Press.

Scholes, R., Comley, N. and Ulmer, G. (2002) *Text Book: An Introduction to Literary Language*, 3rd edn, New York: St Martin's Press.

Schwarz, B. (ed.) (1996) *The Expansion of England: Race, Ethnicity and Cultural History*, London: Routledge.

Sedgwick, E.K. (1990) *Epistemology of the Closet*, Berkeley, CA: University of California Press.

Sefton-Green, J., Thomson, P., Jones, K. and Bresler, L. (eds) (2011) *The Routledge International Handbook of Creative Learning*, London: Routledge.

Selden, R. (ed.) (1989) *The Theory of Criticism,* Harlow: Longman.

Selden, R., Widdowson, P. and Brooker, P. (2005) *A Reader's Guide to Contemporary Literary Theory*, 5th edn, London: Pearson Longman.

Shepherd, V. (1993) *Playing the Language-Game,* Milton Keynes: Open University Press.

Short, M. (1996) *Exploring the Language of Poems, Prose and Plays,* Harlow: Longman.

Showalter, E. (1977) *A Literature of Their Own,* London: Virago, 1979.

—— (2002) *Teaching Literature*, Malden, MA and Oxford: Blackwell.

Sim, S. (ed.) (2001) *The Routledge Companion to Postmodernism*, London: Routledge.

Simpson, P. (1993) *Language, Ideology and Point of View,* London: Routledge.

—— (1997) *Language through Literature: An Introduction,* London: Routledge.

Sinfield, A (1992) *Faultlines: Cultural Materialism and the Politics of Dissident Reading,* Oxford: Oxford University Press.

—— (1994) *Cultural Politics – Queer Reading,* London.

Singer, A. and Dunn, A. (eds) (2000) *Literary Aesthetics: A Reader,* Oxford: Blackwell.

Skinner, J. (1998) *The Stepmother Tongue: An Introduction to New Anglophone Fiction,* Basinsgstoke: Palgrave.

Smith, J.J. (1996) *An Historical Study of English: Function, Form and Change,* London: Routledge.

Sollors, W. (2008) *Ethnic Modernism*, Cambridge, MA: Harvard University Press.

Spivak, G.C. (1996) *The Spivak Reader*, ed. D. Landry and G. MacLean, London: Routledge.

—— (1999) *A Critique of Postcolonial Reason,* Cambridge, MA: Harvard University Press.

Stam, R. (2005) *Literature through Film: Realism, Magic and the Art of Adaptation,* Oxford: Blackwell.

Stockwell, P. (2002) *Cognitive Poetics: An Introduction,* London: Routledge.

Stott, R. and Avery, S. (eds) (2001) *Writing with Style,* Harlow: Longman.

Stott, R. and Chapman, P. (eds) (2001) *Grammar and Writing,* Harlow: Longman.

Stott, R., Snaith, A. and Rylance, R. (eds) (2001) *Making your Case: A Practical Guide to Essay Writing,* Harlow: Longman.

Stott, R., Young, T. and Bryan, C. (eds) (2001) *Speaking your Mind: Oral Presentation and Seminar Skills,* Harlow: Longman.

Stubbs, M. (1983) *Discourse Analysis: The Sociological Analysis of Natural Language,* Oxford: Blackwell.

Sturrock. J. (2002) *Structuralism*, 2nd edn, Oxford: Blackwell.

Sullivan, N. (2003) *A Critical Introduction to Queer Theory*, Edinburgh: Edinburgh University Press.

Swann, J., Pope, R. and Carter, R. (eds) (2011) *Creativity in Language and Literature: The State of the Art,* Basingstoke: Palgrave Macmillan.

Talib, I.S. (2002) *The Language of Postcolonial Literatures,* London: Routledge.

Tannen, D. (ed.) (1982) *Spoken and Written Language: Exploring Orality and Literacy,* Norwood, NJ: Ablex.

—— (1992) *You Just Don't Understand: Women and Men in Conversation,* London: Virago.

Thieme, J. (ed.) (1996) *The Arnold Anthology of Postcolonial Literatures in English,* London: Arnold.

Todd, L. (1984) *Modern Englishes: Pidgins and Creoles,* London: Blackwell and Deutsch.

Toolan, M.J. (2001) *Narrative: A Critical Linguistic Introduction,* 2nd edn, London: Routledge.

Trask, R.L. (1999) *Language: The Basics,* London: Routledge.

Traugott, E.C. and Pratt, M.L. (1980) *Linguistics for Students of Literature,* New York: Harcourt Brace Jovanovich.

Trudgill, P. (1990) *The Dialects of England,* Oxford: Blackwell.

Trudgill, P. and Hannah J. (1994) *International English: A Guide to the Varieties of Standard English,* 3rd edn, London: Arnold.

Tuhiwai Smith, L. (1999) *Decolonising Methodologies: Research and Indigenous Peoples*, London and Dunedin: Zed Books and Otago University Press.

Turner, G. (1993) *Film as Social Practice,* London: Routledge.

Veeser, H.A. (ed.) (1989) *The New Historicism,* New York: Routledge.

Venuti, L. (ed.) (2000) *The Translation Studies Reader,* London: Routledge.

Voloshinov, V.N. (1973) *Marxism and the Philosophy of Language,* trans. L. Matejka and I. Titunik, New York: Seminar Press.

Vygotsky. L.S. (1934) *Thought and Language,* trans. E. Hanfmann and G. Vakar, Cambridge MA: MIT Press, 1962.

Walder, D. (1998) *Post-colonial Literature in English,* Oxford: Blackwell.

—— (ed.) (2003) *Literature in the Modern World: Critical Essays and Documents,* 2nd edn, Oxford: Oxford University Press and Open University Press.

Wales, K. (2011) *A Dictionary of Stylistics,* 3rd edn, London: Longman.

Wall, C. (ed.) (1989) *Changing Our Own Words: Essays on Cultural Theory and Writing by Black Women*, London: Routledge.

Wandor, M. (2008) *The Author Is Not Dead, Merely Somewhere Else: Creative Writing Reconceived*, Basingstoke: Palgrave Macmillan.

Waugh, P. (1984) *Metafiction: The Theory and Practice of Self-Conscious Fiction*, London: Methuen.

Weedon, C. (1996) *Feminist Practice and Post-structuralist Theory*, 2nd edn, Oxford: Blackwell.

Wellek, R. and Warren, A. (1963) *The Theory of Literature*, 3rd edn, Harmondsworth: Penguin.

Wheale, N. (ed.) (1995) *The Postmodern Arts: An Introductory Reader*, London: Routledge.

Whitehead, S. J. (2002) *Men and Masculinities*, Cambridge: Polity.

Whitla, W. (2010) *The English Handbook: A Guide to Literary Studies*, Malden and Oxford: Wiley-Blackwell.

Widdowson, H.G. (1992) *Practical Stylistics and the Teaching of Literature*, Oxford: Oxford University Press.

Widdowson, P. (ed.) (1982) *Re-reading English*, London: Methuen.

—— (1999) *Literature*, London: Routledge.

—— (2004) *The Palgrave Guide to English Literature and its Contexts, 1500–2000*, Basinstoke: Palgrave Macmillan.

William, R. (1979) *Politics and Letters: Interviews with New Left Review*, London: Verso.

Williams, P. and Chrisman, L. (eds) (1993) *Colonial Discourse and Postcolonial Theory: A Reader*, Hemel Hempstead: Harvester Wheatsheaf.

Williams, R. (1958) *Culture and Society, 1780–1950*, Harmondsworth: Penguin.

—— (1966) *Modern Tragedy*, London: Chatto and Windus.

—— (1977) *Marxism and Literature*, Oxford: Oxford University Press.

—— (1983) *Keywords: A Vocabulary of Culture and Society*, 2nd edn, London: Flamingo.

Winchester, S. (2003) *The Meaning of Everything: The Story of the Oxford English Dictionary*, Oxford: Oxford University Press.

Winnicott, D.W. (1974) *Playing and Reality*, Harmondsworth: Penguin.

Wolfreys, J. (ed.) (2001) *Introducing Literary Theories: A Guide and Glossary*, Edinburgh: Edinburgh University Press.

—— (2002) *Introducing Twenty-First Century Criticism*, Edinburgh: Edinburgh University Press.

—— (ed.) (2010) *The English Literature Companion*, Basingstoke: Palgrave Macmillan.

Womack, K. and Todd, F. (2002) *Formalist Criticism and Reader Response Theory*, Basingstoke: Palgrave Macmillan.

Wright, E. (1997) *Psychoanalytic Criticism: A Reappraisal*, Oxford and Cambridge: Polity.

Wynne-Davis, M. (ed.) (1989) *Bloomsbury Guide to English Literature*, London: Bloomsbury.

Young, R. (ed.) (1981) *Untying the Text: A Post-structuralist Reader*, London: Routledge and Kegan Paul.

—— (2001) *Postcolonialism: An Historical Introduction*, Oxford: Blackwell.

—— (2004) *White Mythologies: Writing History and the West*, 2nd edn, London: Routledge.

Young, T. (2008) *Studying English Literature: A Practical Guide*, Cambridge: Cambridge University Press.

Yule, G. (2010) *The Study of Language*, 4th edn, Cambridge: Cambridge University Press.

Žižek, S. (2002) *Welcome to the Desert of the Real!*, London: Verso.

—— *The Žižek Reader*, ed. E. Wright and E. Wright, Oxford: Blackwell.

RELEVANT JOURNALS AND ASSOCIATIONS

All these national and international associations have websites as well as journals:

College English (US National Council of Teachers of English).

English in Australia (Australian Association for the Teaching of English).

English (The English Association, UK).

English and Media Magazine (UK National Association for the Teaching of English).

European Journal of English Studies (European Society for the Study of English).

Wordplay (English Subject Centre, UK Higher Education Academy).

These are some major journals, arranged by topic:

Language: *English Today* (Cambridge University Press).

Literature: *Critical Quarterly* (Blackwell).

Language and Literature: *Changing English*; *Language and Literature* (Poetics and Linguistics Association, International).

Creative Writing: *New Writing: The International Journal for the Theory and Practice of Creative Writing* (Routledge).

Critical Theory: *Textual Practice* (Routledge); *Paragraph* (Edinburgh University Press).

Life-Writing: *Auto/Biography* (Arnold).

Postcolonial: *Interventions* (Routledge); *Wasafiri* (University of London).

Translation: *Translation and Literature* (Edinburgh University Press).

Journals that supply annual reviews of the field and updated bibliographies, mostly sponsored by research associations, are:

Annual Bibliography of English Language and Literature (Modern Humanities Research Association).

Modern Language Association (MLA) International Bibliography of Books and Articles on the Modern Languages and Literatures (Modern Language Association of America).

The Review of English Studies (Oxford University Press).

The Year's Work in English Studies and *The Year's Work in Critical and Cultural Theory* (The English Association, UK).

For recurrently useful websites and text archives, see **Library, web, 'home'** (1.2.5).

INDEX

This includes all significant references to terms, topics, persons and places. Highlighting is similar to that used throughout the book. Items in SMALL CAPITALS (e.g. LITERATURE, FEMINISM, POSTMODERNISM) refer to the larger categories in Parts One and Three. Words in **bold** (e.g. **author**, **canon**, **discourse**, **standards**) refer to key terms in Part Four. Page numbers highlighted in **bold** indicate the main reference and best place to start, or the presence of the 'text' itself. Substantial further items on the companion website are referenced by @ and section number (e.g. STYLISTICS @ 3.10; **addresser** @ 4).